W9-DDW-628

Understanding and Preventing

Violence

Volume 3
Social Influences

Albert J. Reiss, Jr., and Jeffrey A. Roth, eds.

Panel on the Understanding and Control
  of Violent Behavior
Committee on Law and Justice
Commission on Behavioral and Social Sciences
  and Education
National Research Council

NATIONAL ACADEMY PRESS
Washington, D.C. 1994

NATIONAL ACADEMY PRESS   2101 Constitution Avenue, N.W.   Washington, D.C.   20418

The panel study on understanding and preventing violence was supported by grants from the National Science Foundation, the Centers for Disease Control and Prevention of the U.S. Department of Health and Human Services, and the National Institute of Justice of the U.S. Department of Justice.   Additional funding to support publication of the commissioned papers was provided by the John D. and Catherine T. MacArthur Foundation, the National Institute of Mental Health of the U.S. Department of Health and Human Services, and the National Institute of Justice.

Library of Congress Cataloging-in-Publication Data
(Revised for vol. 3)

Understanding and preventing violence.

"Panel on the Understanding and Control of Violent
Behavior, Committee on Law and Justice, Commission on
Behavioral and Social Sciences and Education, National
Research Council."
    Includes bibliographical references and indexes.
    Contents: v. [1]. [without special title]
—v. 3. Social influences.
    1. Violence—United States. 2. Violence—United
States—Prevention. 3. Violent crimes—United States.
I. Reiss, Albert J. II. Roth, Jeffrey A., 1945-
III. National Research Council (U.S.). Panel on the
Understanding and Control of Violent Behavior.

HN90.V5U53 1993 V. 3 303.6   92-32137
ISBN 0-309-04594-0 (v. 1)
ISBN 0-309-05080-4 (v. 3)

First Printing, May 1994
Second Printing, November 1994

PANEL ON THE UNDERSTANDING AND CONTROL OF VIOLENT BEHAVIOR

Contents

Foreword

In cities, suburban areas, and even small towns, Americans are fearful and concerned that violence has permeated the fabric of their communities and degraded the quality of their lives. This anxiety is not unfounded. In recent years, murders have killed about 23,000 people annually, while upward of 3,000,000 nonfatal but serious violent victimizations have occurred each year. These incidents are sources of chronic fear and public concern over the seeming inability of public authorities to prevent them.

Because of this concern, three federal agencies requested the National Research Council to carry out a comprehensive review of research applicable to the understanding and control of violence. Within the general topic of violence, the three sponsors expressed somewhat different sets of priorities. The National Science Foundation's Law and Social Science Program sought a review of current knowledge of the causes of violent behavior and recommendations about priorities in funding future basic research. The other two sponsors were more concerned with the application of that knowledge to the prevention and control of violence. The National Institute of Justice sought advice on how to prevent and control violent crimes, using the combined resources of criminal justice and other agencies. The National Center for Injury Prevention and Control of the Centers for Disease Control and Prevention sought assistance in setting priorities in efforts to prevent injuries and deaths from violent events.

In response, the Commission on Behavioral and Social Sciences and Education, through its Committee on Law and Justice, established the Panel on the Understanding and Control of Violent Behavior and took primary responsibility for shaping the specific mandate and composition of the panel. Two features of its mandate carried particular weight. First, to draw implications from past research and to chart its future course, the perspectives and models of biological, psychological, and social science research on violence should be integrated. Second, as a matter of science policy, the panel's work should orient the future allocation of research and evaluation resources toward the development and refinement of promising strategies for reducing violence and its consequences.

Early on, the panel recognized that the extraordinary breadth of its mandate demanded the mobilization of expertise beyond that of its own members and staff. Therefore, in addition to preparing a number of internal review memoranda, it commissioned a number of reviews and analyses by experts in certain specialized topics. Although the commissioned papers reflect the views of their authors and not necessarily those of the panel, all were valuable resources for the panel. From the entire set, the panel selected 15 for publication in supplementary volumes because it found them particularly useful. The panel is grateful to all the authors and to the discussants who prepared comments for the panel's Symposium on Understanding and Preventing Violence.

This volume contains four commissioned reviews of social influences on violent events and violent behavior. Robert Sampson and Janet Lauritsen review social research on how the risks of violent criminal offending and victimization are influenced by characteristics of communities, specific situations, and individuals. Jeffrey Fagan and Angela Browne survey research literature on violence among spouses and intimates. Candace Kruttschnitt reviews research exploring the persistent differences in violence levels between men and women. Panel member Klaus Miczek and his colleagues review research on animal and human subjects on the roles of psychoactive substances in violent events. The panel members believe that, like themselves, others will find these reviews to be extremely helpful resources.

Understanding
and Preventing
Violence

Volume 3
Social Influences

Violent Victimization and Offending: Individual-, Situational-, and Community-Level Risk Factors

Robert J. Sampson and Janet L. Lauritsen

INTRODUCTION

The purpose of this paper is to (1) summarize current knowledge on individual-, situational-, and community-level sources of criminal violence; (2) identify key problems of causal interpretation in existing research; and (3) suggest new directions for future research and policy. Although violence has not been an understudied phenomenon in American criminology, a synthesis of the causes and consequences of criminal violence across multiple levels of analysis has not been undertaken. Indeed, most of the more than 2,000 studies of violence published since 1945 (Bridges and Weis, 1989:14) have been descriptive and focused either on individual-level correlates of violent offending or, to a much lesser extent, on community-level correlates of violence rates. As a consequence, extant reviews tend to emphasize individual-level factors (especially age, race, and sex) or particular classifications such as family violence (e.g., Ohlin and Tonry, 1989) and criminal career violence (e.g., Weiner, 1989). By contrast, our goal in this review is to show how a multilevel perspective on both victimization and offending may substantially increase the understanding

Robert J. Sampson is at the Department of Sociology, University of Chicago. Janet L. Lauritsen is at the Department of Criminology and Criminal Justice, University of Missouri, St. Louis.

and control of violence. Because there appears to be little consensus in the social science literature on how multilevel factors should be defined, we describe in more detail our conceptualization of these terms.

Our use of the terms "individual," "situational," and "community" corresponds closely to Short's (1985) definition of the "individual," "micro-," and "macro-" levels of analysis (see also Short, 1990:11). The *individual level* of explanation typically inquires as to characteristics of individuals that explain behavior. In our discussion of individual-level risk factors for violence, we specifically focus on the ascribed and achieved characteristics of individuals that are statistically associated with violent victimization and offending. For example, we examine how the risks of violent victimization and offending are distributed across characteristics such as age, sex, race, marital status, lifestyle, and socioeconomic status. Our intention, though, is not only to provide a descriptive summary of statistical findings, but to suggest how, and in what ways, individual characteristics are causally related to the risk of violent victimization and offending.

By *situational-level* risk factors, we are referring to those factors, broadly defined, that influence the initiation or outcome of a violent event. This conceptualization corresponds to Short's (1990:11) definition of the microlevel, where attention is focused on the unfolding of events and the interaction of parties involved in events. Situational-level analyses usually treat the violent incident, or event, as the unit of analysis. Included in our review is a discussion of such factors as the presence and type of weapon, the presence of drugs or alcohol, the role of bystanders or third parties during violent events, and victim resistance and retaliation. However, we expand the traditional conceptualization of situational-level analyses to include a discussion of the victim-offender overlap and how victim-offender relationships are related to violence. These factors are included because we believe that the simultaneous consideration of victims, offenders, and their past and present interactions provides a more complete context for studying the initiation and outcomes of violent events.

The macrosocial or *community level* of explanation asks what it is about community structures and cultures that produces differential rates of crime (Byrne and Sampson, 1986; Bursik, 1988; Short, 1990:11). For example, what characteristics of communities are associated with high rates of violence? Are communities safe or unsafe because of the persons who reside in them or because of community properties themselves? Can changes in community structure affect violent crime rates? As implied by these questions, the goal of macrolevel research is not to explain individual involvement in criminal behavior but to isolate characteristics of communities, cities, or societies that lead to high rates of criminality. Examples of macrolevel risk factors include residential mobility, population density, heterogeneity, and income inequality. These and other factors are assessed for both intraurban (e.g., local community, neighborhood) and interurban (e.g., city, metropolitan area) units of analysis, although for substantive reasons discussed below we place more weight on between-community variations in rates of criminal violence.

CRITERIA

Conclusions about the correlates of violence are naturally linked to the universe of studies under consideration. Because our review is highly focused we applied systematic criteria for inclusion of research. Although exceptions arise, the studies analyzed in this paper were selected based on the following criteria:

(1) Studies in which serious interpersonal violence (e.g., assault, homicide, robbery, and rape) is measured directly are our primary focus. Issues surrounding the measurement of violence are discussed as needed; however, we should note that our intention herein is to avoid studies that present overall measures (e.g., total scales, index crimes) in which violence is confounded with property or other crime types (e.g., drug use, status offenses). Also, many delinquency studies focus on such events as schoolyard theft ("robbery") and minor fighting. Except where important for historical or theoretical reasons, these studies are generally not considered.

(2) Analyses of objective social characteristics of individuals, situations, and community context are emphasized, as opposed to those studies focusing on internal psychological states, perceptions, or biological/ constitutional conditions.[1] Because individual-level social characteristics have received disproportionate attention in the past, we tend to highlight the theoretical and policy implications of community-level factors. As we make clear, however, the study of community-level processes is not possible without a thorough understanding of individual- and situational-level correlates.

(3) We emphasize studies that present empirical data, especially those that have representative (e.g., national-level) or large

enough samples to draw reasonable conclusions. However, this does *not* rule out the selective use of important ethnographic work that bears directly on issues of concern.

(4) We focus on American studies or those written in the English language, particularly those published in refereed journals. Moreover, we emphasize urban-based research from the past 20 years that has formed the bulk of multivariate studies of violence.

(5) In general, we attempt to assess the substantive and (where appropriate) causal importance of key factors. Consequently, we focus on the magnitude of effects as opposed to mere statistical significance.

Although not strict criteria for inclusion, we also make a special effort to highlight (a) micro-macro linkages (i.e., the simultaneous consideration of both individual- and community-level risk factors in violence) and (b) the connection between violent victimization and violent offending. We believe that much previous research on violence is problematic because of the causal confounding and alternative causal interpretations that can arise in designs relying on a single level of analysis. Furthermore, we contend that the victim-offender overlap can provide fundamental insights into the etiology of violence; hence we pay close attention to studies that allow assessment of the causal role that offending may play in increasing victimization risk, and vice versa. Too often in the past these issues have been treated separately as if they were unrelated (see Reiss, 1986a; Sampson and Wooldredge, 1987; Sampson and Lauritsen, 1990). In contrast, by highlighting micro- (individual/ situational) and macro- (community) linkages in the study of violence, in addition to victim-offender relationships, we believe that our understanding of the social structural and contextual sources of violence is improved. To our knowledge the literature on violence has not been critically assessed from this perspective before, especially in a framework that points to future research designs needed to address remaining etiological questions.

Before turning to a road map outlining our review, two issues deserve further clarification. Given the vast literature and multiple measures of both violence and community factors, we do not present in tabular form the magnitudes of effect for all studies and factors—preliminary efforts found this to be unworkable. As noted above, the Bridges and Weis (1989) review located more than 2,000 studies of violence—a universe larger than that relevant to other comprehensive reviews (e.g., see Visher and Roth, 1986). Perhaps more of a problem, we discovered an almost unlimited supply of incomparable measures and incomparable techniques, especially in community-level studies. For example, a concept as seemingly straightforward as "poverty" has been measured in at least 20 different ways, ranging from dichotomous groupings of communities through census-based percentage measures to factor-analytic scores. Complicating matters further, researchers have employed many different analytical techniques and styles of data presentation. This issue is discussed more below, but we emphasize at the outset that the nature of past research makes it difficult to present summary figures representing magnitudes of effect that are comparable across studies.

Second, there is a plethora of theories of violence that have been advanced in the criminological literature. Some of these, such as the subculture of violence theory (Wolfgang and Ferracuti, 1967), are well known and have been explicated quite well in other sources. A seemingly reasonable strategy, then, especially in a review devoted to empirical risk factors in violence, is simply to ignore theory and concentrate on the findings. However, findings alone do not speak for themselves and are generally devoid of meaning when stripped of substantive content. More to the point, empirical research designs are valid only to the extent that the substantive model under consideration is valid and properly specified. Our compromise is therefore to couch, no matter how briefly, the correlates of violence in substantive perspective. We refer readers to appropriate sources on theoretical issues for more detail, particularly individual-level theories that are more widely known. Thus, theories per se are not reviewed, but key substantive themes are emphasized in an effort to shed light on the importance of empirical findings, especially multivariate, community-level, or contextual studies.

This review is divided into seven major sections. First, the literature on factors underlying an individual's risk of violent victimization is assessed. This section includes a review not only of demographic correlates (e.g., age, race, and sex) emphasized in previous research, but of lifestyle and routine activity factors as well. In a similar fashion, the second section reviews the individual-level correlates of violent offending. In the third section, an overview is presented of situational-level risk factors in violence, along with analyses that consider victim-offender relationships and the concept of a victim-offender overlap. The fourth and fifth sections assess community-level determinants of violent crime and metropolitan (i.e., city-level) sources of violence, respectively. In the sixth section, some key problems and pitfalls in attributing causal interpretations to findings from past research are examined. Finally, the last section identifies promising directions for future research designs and public policy initiatives.

INDIVIDUAL-LEVEL RISK FACTORS IN VIOLENT VICTIMIZATION

Our focus in this section is on factors related to the risk of violent victimization among individuals. Here, we address the following questions: What are the overall risks of violent victimization to individuals? How are these risks distributed across individual characteristics such as age, sex, race, marital status, and socioeconomic status? Are these differences stable over recent time periods? How are individual-level differences in risk explained by theories of victimization? Finally, how might some of the limitations of extant victimization research be minimized? We begin with a brief overview of the general aspects of violent victimization.

Victimization research over the past 20 years has produced several consistent findings. One of the primary findings is that the annual risk of becoming a victim of a crime of personal violence (i.e., homicide, rape, robbery, or assault) is relatively low (Gottfredson, 1986; U.S. Department of Justice, 1989). For example, the combined risk of suffering a violent victimization by either rape, robbery, or assault in 1987 was estimated at approximately 1 in 33.[2] The risk of suffering a victimization from a personal crime of violence is considerably less than that of suffering a theft victimization—in 1987, the rate of reported theft victimization (approximately 1 in 14) was more than twice the rate of reported violent victimization (U.S. Department of Justice, 1989). Although this risk may seem low on an annual basis, the lifetime risk of violence for any particular crime is much higher. For example, the annual risk of becoming a victim of homicide is about 1 in 10,000, but the lifetime risk of being murdered is approximately 1 in 369 for white females, 1 in 131 for white males, 1 in 104 for black females, and as high as 1 in 21 for black males (U.S. Department of Justice, 1985; see also Fingerhut and Kleinman, 1990).

As suggested by the differences in lifetime homicide risks, the second major finding in individual-level analyses is that the distribution of violent victimization is not random. Rather, the risk of experiencing personal violence varies considerably across demographic and social groups (Hindelang, 1976; Hindelang et al., 1978; Cohen et al., 1981a,b; Gottfredson and Hindelang, 1981; Skogan, 1981; Sparks, 1982; Gottfredson, 1986; Miethe et al., 1987; U.S. Department of Justice, 1988a). The pattern of systematic differences found across different demographic and socioeconomic subgroups has been fairly consistent across analyses utilizing either the Uniform Crime Report (UCR) data or the National Crime Survey (NCS) data in the United States (e.g., see Gottfredson, 1986). Patterns of association similar to those found in the United States have also been found in analyses using data from other countries such as England (Hough and Mayhew, 1983), the Netherlands (van Dijk and Steinmetz, 1983), and Australia (Braithwaite and Biles, 1984). To describe these patterns of violent victimization, we present, as briefly as possible, bivariate and then multivariate findings of research examining individual-level risk factors associated with victimization by homicide, assault, robbery, and rape. Particular attention is paid to the magnitude and consistency of findings in multivariate research, as well as their theoretical importance. Limitations of these analyses and their consequences for our understanding of violent victimization are discussed.

BIVARIATE FINDINGS

It should be mentioned at the outset that the vast majority of knowledge about the risk of violent victimization has been obtained through analyses of National Crime Survey data. The NCS is an ongoing survey conducted by the Bureau of Justice Statistics, designed to measure the extent of personal and household victimization in the United States. Interviews are conducted at six-month intervals with all persons 12 years of age or older living in a household. By using NCS data, it is possible to estimate the extent of victimizations that are not reported in official police data (due to nonreporting of incidents, arrest bias, etc.) and to calculate prevalence measures of violent victimization for specific individual subgroups (see Reiss, 1981; Langan and Innes, 1990). Therefore, the NCS constitutes the best available data source on the risk of victimization for persons living in the United States.[3]

Age

Age is one of the most important predictors of an individual's risk of violent victimization (Hindelang et al., 1978). The NCS data for 1987 indicate that the risk of personal violent victimization is highest for persons under 25 years of age (U.S. Department of Justice, 1989). After age 25, the risk of such victimization gradually declines such that by age 65, the risk of suffering a violent victimization is approximately one-tenth that of persons under 25 years of age. This bivariate age-victimization relationship—a relatively high level of victimization in youth and young adulthood followed by a gradual decline in risk—is observed for the crimes of homicide, rape, and assault (and, therefore, violent victimization in general). Differences in the risk of robbery victimization across age groups are not as great as those found for other violent crimes (Hindelang et al., 1978; Cohen et al., 1981b).

In addition to contributing to the overall risk of violent victimization, age appears to be related to the nature of crime-specific victimizations. In an analysis of NCS victimization narratives for juvenile victims (age 12-17) of personal crime, Garofalo et al. (1987) found that assaults reported by juveniles were overwhelmingly minor in nature—that is, they were often the result of an inability to resolve common disputes and rarely led to serious injury on the part of the victim. For robbery as well, the relative nature of the event was reported to be less serious among juvenile victims than among adults. Although a large proportion of all victimization reported in the NCS is relatively minor in nature (Skogan, 1981; Sparks, 1982), juvenile victimization appears to be least serious overall in terms of both injury levels and monetary loss. Therefore, although juveniles appear to be at high risk for violent personal victimization, the victimizations they do suffer are more likely to have minor consequences compared to those of adults.[4]

Sex[5]

For all crimes of personal violence—with the obvious exception of rape—males are at greater risk for victimization than females (U.S. Department of Justice, 1989). The annual rate of homicide victimizations for males is nearly three times greater than the annual rate for females (U.S. Department of Justice, 1986). The lifetime risk of becoming a victim of homicide is estimated to be between three and four times greater for males (1 in 84) than females (1 in 282) (U.S. Department of Justice, 1985). For the crimes of robbery and assault, males are approximately 1.5-2 times more likely to become victims. On the other hand, women are overwhelmingly the victims of rape. NCS data estimate the risk of attempted or completed rape for females to be approximately 1 in 770 annually (U.S. Department of Justice, 1989). Furthermore, these relationships between sex and the risk of violent victimization have remained fairly constant over the last decade. Smith (1987), for example, reports that the proportion of female victims of robberies and assaults has remained stable, whereas the proportion of female homicide victims has increased slightly over the past 10 years.

As was true for the relationship between age and overall risk of violence, the nature of victimization for males and females differs. First, for assault and robbery victimizations, men are more likely than women to report injury (U.S. Department of Justice, 1989).[6] Second, according to victim reports, offenders attacking males are more likely to be armed: between 1973 and 1982, approximately 41 percent of male and 29 percent of female victims of violent crime were attacked by offenders with weapons (U.S. Department of Justice, 1988a). Rape is an obvious exception to this pattern. Excluding homicide, rape is the crime with the highest level of injury (Hindelang et al., 1978) and is perpetuated largely against females.

Race

Both NCS and UCR data confirm that blacks are disproportionately the victims of homicide, rape, and robbery (U.S. Department of Justice, 1988a). Blacks are approximately five times more likely than whites to become victims of homicide (U.S. Department of Justice, 1986) and approximately three to four times more likely to report victimization by rape and robbery (U.S. Department of Justice, 1989). Higher rates of black victimization by homicide (compared to whites) have been found throughout the last century (Wolfgang, 1958; Block, 1975), and recent trends indicate a continuation of this differential (Shin et al., 1977; Farley, 1980; Hawkins, 1985). As noted earlier, the lifetime risk of homicide victimization is approximately three times greater for black women than for white women, and approximately four times greater for black men than for white men (U.S. Department of Justice, 1985).

Assault victimization rates for blacks and whites do not differ significantly in magnitude, although the majority of assault victimizations reported by blacks are incidents of aggravated assault, whereas among whites, simple assaults comprise the majority (U.S. Department of Justice, 1989). The lack of race differences in assaults overall may be the result of differences in reporting. For example, it has been suggested that blacks underreport less serious forms of assault and/or that whites overreport minor assaults (Skogan, 1981; Gottfredson, 1986).

Two- and three-way associations for age, sex, and race suggest that the relationships among these factors are, generally speaking, additive. Thus, for certain subgroups the relative risk of violent victimization is quite high. In particular, young, black males are approximately 22 times more likely than older, white females to become the victims of violent crime (U.S. Department of Justice, 1989). Within these three-way associations, age continues to have the largest independent effect followed by sex and race.

Marital Status

Although somewhat less studied than age, race, and sex, marital status has also been found to be substantially related to the risk of violent victimization (Hindelang et al., 1978; Cohen et al., 1981b; Miethe et al., 1987; U.S. Department of Justice, 1989). Overall, NCS estimates suggest that unmarried persons are nearly four times more likely to become the victims of robbery, rape, or assault than are those currently married (U.S. Department of Justice, 1989). The exception to this pattern is for widowed persons who have the lowest risk of violent victimization. Never-married persons have the highest risk of victimization, followed closely by divorced and separated persons (U.S. Department of Justice, 1989). At the extreme ends of the scale, those never married are approximately 11 times more likely than widowed persons,[7] and more than 3 times more likely than currently married persons, to become the victims of assault. On the other hand, the differences by marital status for robbery and rape are not as pronounced (U.S. Department of Justice, 1989). Finally, when sex and marital status are considered simultaneously, marital status is more strongly related to victimization risk among females than among males (U.S. Department of Justice, 1989).

Socioeconomic Status

Not surprisingly, family income is inversely related to the risk of personal victimization (Hindelang, 1976; Hindelang et al., 1978; Cohen et al., 1981a,b; Miethe et al. 1987; U.S. Department of Justice, 1989). However, the overall magnitude of the effect of family income is not as large as the magnitudes for the indi-

vidual-level characteristics previously discussed (namely, age, race, sex, and marital status). For violence in general, the risk of victimization is approximately twice as great for persons whose family income is reported to be less than $7,500 compared to those whose family income is higher than $50,000 (U.S. Department of Justice, 1989). Specific crimes of violence also have varying relationships to family income. For example, there is little relationship between rape and family income, although women whose families earn less than $7,500 are again most likely to become victims. The risk of rape among women in the remaining income categories is approximately equal. Income is somewhat more strongly related to the risk of assault, with those at the lowest end of the income distribution reporting twice the risk of victimization as those at the highest end. Of all violent crimes, income is most strongly related to the risk of robbery—poorer persons report a robbery rate about three times higher than persons at the upper ends of the income distribution (U.S. Department of Justice, 1989).

The relationship between education and violent victimization is less consistent than the relationship between family income and personal victimization (U.S. Department of Justice, 1989). In fact, persons with the least amount of education report the lowest level of violent victimization. Excluding this category of education, and with slight fluctuations, the general relationship between education and victimization is negative but small in magnitude. It has been suggested that the ability to accurately recall victimizations may be affected by one's level of education. For example, highly educated respondents in the NCS appear to be more "productive" when recalling victimization events (Skogan, 1981). The relationship between socioeconomic status (either income or education) and rape victimization is also small in magnitude and is more uniformly distributed across women in different income and education groups (U.S. Department of Justice, 1989).

Finally, of the common indicators of an individual's socioeconomic status, unemployment is most strongly related to the risk of violent victimization (U.S. Department of Justice, 1989). Those who are unemployed are at the greatest risk of robbery, assault, and rape, followed by persons in school, the employed, those unable to work, those keeping house, and the retired.[8] Overall, the unemployed are more than twice as likely as the employed to suffer a violent victimization (U.S. Department of Justice, 1989).

It is thus clear that the risk of suffering a violent victimization is differentially distributed across social and demographic groups. Extant data suggest that age has the largest bivariate relationship with the risk of homicide, assault, robbery, and rape. Sex and race are also related to violent victimization, as is marital status, although these effects are slightly smaller in magnitude. Two-way relationships among most forms of violent victimization and each of the indicators of socioeconomic status are generally negative in direction, but even smaller in magnitude. Although each of the individual-level characteristics discussed above appears related to victimization, it is possible that these associations are spurious. To assess this possibility, we direct our attention to the research literature that has considered some or all of these individual-level factors simultaneously.

MULTIVARIATE FINDINGS

Despite the rather large body of research on the individual-level risk of victimization, there have been relatively few multivariate analyses that directly examine the risk of violent victimization in the United States. This is due in part to the relative rarity of violent crime: because of its infrequency, it is difficult to test reliably for the independent effects of many of the above-mentioned correlates. Nevertheless, some major studies have examined the interrelationships among demographic and socioeconomic (as well as other) characteristics and violent victimization in the United States (e.g., Hindelang et al., 1978; Cohen et al., 1981a,b; Miethe et al., 1987). More specifically, Hindelang et al. (1978) analyzed the 1972 NCS (eight-city survey) data in order to examine the independent effects of social and demographic factors on whether or not a person reported a personal victimization (defined as assault, robbery, rape, and personal larceny with contact). Cohen et al. (1981a) examined robbery victimization using 1973 to 1977 NCS data combined, and Cohen et al. (1981b) analyzed similar factors for their effects on the risk of assault victimization using 1974 and 1977 NCS data combined. Miethe et al. (1987) also examined a set of demographic and socioeconomic factors for their effects on violent victimization[9] using the 1975 NCS (13-city survey) data.

Although the dependent variables and statistical techniques differed across studies, the general patterns and relative magnitudes of effects found in each of the analyses are compatible. Hindelang et al. (1978) for example, found that the most important predictors of personal victimization were age, marital status, sex, and employment status: young, single, unemployed males had the highest risk of personal victimization.[10]   Cohen et al.

(1981a) found that age, employment status, race, and income had significant and independent effects on robbery victimization.[11] Namely, younger persons, the unemployed, blacks, and poorer persons had the highest risk of being robbed. Cohen et al. (1981b) also found that age, marital status, and employment status had the greatest independent effects on the probability of assault. Finally, Miethe et al.'s (1987) findings agree: age, sex, and marital status are the predominant demographic risk factors predicting violent victimization. Miethe et al. (1987) also found a relatively small but significant negative effect for income. Only in the case of robbery victimization was race found to be a significant predictor (Cohen et al., 1981a). The lack of an independent race effect on assault is not surprising when one considers the negligible bivariate effect found in the NCS data.[12]

Direct comparisons of the magnitude of effects found in prior analyses of violent victimization are not possible given the variety of statistical controls and analytical techniques. However, in the analyses noted above, partial effects were most often no more than twice the risk of the reference group—a magnitude that is determined in part by the measurement level of the independent factors. Miethe et al. (1987), for example, found that males were approximately twice as likely as females to suffer a violent victimization, independent of race, income, marital status, and age. However, certain combinations of these risk factors produce much higher risks of victimization for some subgroups. In particular, Cohen et al. (1981a) estimated that young, poor, unemployed black males living alone had a risk of robbery victimization nearly 10 times greater than the national average.

THEORETICAL INTERPRETATIONS

These individual-level correlates of victimization have formed the basis of "lifestyle" (Hindelang, 1976; Hindelang et al., 1978; Garofalo, 1987) or "routine activity" (Cohen and Felson, 1979; Cohen et al., 1981b) theories of victimization risk.[13] The essential proposition of "lifestyle-routine activity" theories is that the convergence in time and space of suitable targets and the absence of capable guardians may lead to increases in crime, independent of the structural and cultural conditions that may motivate individuals to engage in crime (e.g., poverty, unemployment, subcultural values). Derived from this general proposition, the "principle of homogamy" in lifestyle theory states that persons are more likely to be victimized when they disproportionately associate with, or come in contact with, members of demographic groups that contain a disproportionate share of offenders (Hindelang et al., 1978:256-257). Young single males, for example, are more likely to pursue social activities outside the household than are older, married, or female persons, and hence are more likely to place themselves in situations where victimization exposure is increased.[14] Moreover, younger persons may suffer a higher risk of violent victimization than older persons because the former are more likely to associate with other youth who are themselves disproportionately involved in violence (Hindelang et al., 1978).

The limitations of lifestyle-routine activity theory and research have been discussed at length elsewhere (see, for example, Gottfredson, 1984; Maxfield, 1987; Garofalo, 1987; Miethe et al., 1987; Sampson and Wooldredge, 1987). The most common criticism of empirical research has been the inadequate measurement of explanatory variables; demographic and social characteristics of individuals are used primarily as proxies or indirect indicators for lifestyle activities that persons engage in routinely. Social and demographic characteristics are argued to have effects on the risk of victimization because they determine, to a large extent, "systematic differences in role-structured behavior" via differences in expectations, constraints, opportunities, and preferences for activities (Cohen et al., 1981a:648). The principal critique of much of the multivariate literature is thus that direct measures of lifestyle activities are not included in the models containing social and demographic characteristics (Hindelang et al., 1978; Cohen et al., 1981a,b; Gottfredson, 1986; Miethe et al., 1987; Garofalo, 1987). Consequently, the effects of routine activities or specific behaviors have not been distinctly separated from the ascribed and achieved characteristics of victims. Exactly what types of behaviors put individuals at higher risk for violence has not yet received thorough attention.

Exceptions to the lack of direct indicators of lifestyle include measures of activities such as employment status that specifically ascertain what people do during a relatively large portion of their day. The extent of nighttime activities away from the home is also considered to be a direct measure of lifestyle in that activities away from home and activities typically occurring at night are assumed to be more likely to involve either decreased guardianship or increased contact with offenders. These factors—nighttime and daytime activities away from the home—were considered by Miethe et al. (1987) in their analysis of violent victimization.[15] They found that although extent of nighttime activity significantly and positively influenced risk of violent victimization, the effect was smaller in magnitude than most of the other demographic variables considered. Furthermore, the inclusion of these activity measures did not significantly attenuate the magnitude of the effects of sex, income, marital status, and age. Major daytime activity as measured was found to have no significant independent effect on risk of violent victimization. In light of these findings, Miethe et al. (1987:188) conclude that there is "little support for the mediational role of routine activity/lifestyle variables on the demographic correlates of violent victimization." By contrast, there were much larger effects of lifestyle on theft victimization.

These findings are intriguing but not definitive. First, nighttime activity was measured as a dichotomy and consequently may underestimate victimization risk for persons who engage in night activities most often. Second, as measured, this variable was not able to capture the nature of away-from-home activities, nor whether particular activities were engaged in alone or with strangers, friends, or family. Third, the measurement of the major activity variable was constructed on the basis of predictability of behaviors. In other words, persons in school were included in the same category as the employed because they presumably depart and return to their homes at predictable times during the day—an element of routine activities assumed to be of interest to motivated offenders. However, as analyzed, the comparison group for major activity included homemakers, retirees, those unable to work, and the unemployed. Thus, included in one category were those with high risks (the unemployed) and low risks (homemakers and retirees). Measurement problems, then, may have been responsible for the lack of effect of major daytime activity on the risk of violent victimization.

More direct tests of lifestyle-routine activity hypotheses have been conducted with data from countries other than the United States (Corrado et al., 1980; van Dijk and Steinmetz, 1983; Hough and Mayhew, 1983; Braithwaite and Biles, 1984; Gottfredson, 1984; Sampson, 1987b; Sampson and Lauritsen, 1990; Kennedy and Forde, 1990; Miethe and Meier, 1990). Similar examinations have not been conducted for the general U.S. population, primarily because the major source of victimization data—the NCS—does not include measures of routine activities detailed enough for adequate assessment of lifestyle-routine activity hypotheses (but see Lynch, 1987, for an exception with regard to victimization at work). Indeed, the lack of direct measures coupled with the rarity of personal violence has made lifestyle-routine activity hypotheses of violence extremely difficult to test with U.S. data.

On the other hand, direct measures of routine activities derived from foreign data sets—especially the number of nights per week out alone, type of activity typically engaged in at night, mode of transportation used, extent of drinking, and self-reported offending behaviors—have been significantly linked to the risk of personal victimization. Corrado et al. (1980), for instance, found a similar demographic pattern in Canadian data compared to that in the United States. However, the inclusion of a crude measure of out-of-home activities (divided at the median) had a significant effect on the risk of violent victimization (robbery, assault, and sexual assault): persons who spent more time away from home were approximately three times more likely to be victimized than persons who centered their time at home. The inclusion of this variable did not attenuate the effects of sex and age but did decrease the magnitude of the effect of marital status. Smith (1982) similarly finds that those out-of-home activities that increase contact with strangers are most victimogenic. Similarly, Hough and Mayhew (1983), van Dijk and Steinmetz (1983), and Gottfredson (1984) found that frequency and type of nighttime activities are related to the risk of violence. In particular, Gottfredson (1984) reports that the use of public transportation and nighttime activities such as drinking or going out to pubs increase personal victimization in Great Britain whereas activities such as attending church are associated with lower risk. Also, using data from Great Britain, Hough and Mayhew (1983) found that the frequency of nighttime activity combined with the extent of drinking was important for determining the level of risk among persons under 30 years of age. Finally, Kennedy and Forde (1990), using Canadian data, examined the relative effects of a variety of routine activities on assault and robbery victimization. They report that certain types of activities—especially how often one goes to bars or takes walks at night—are directly related to the risks of violent victimization. Furthermore, these effects persisted despite statistical controls for traditional demographic factors (age, sex, family income) and neighborhood characteristics (e.g., percent single person households and percent low income families).

In sum, recent analyses strongly suggest that details concerning the type and extent of daytime and nighttime activities are necessary for adequately assessing lifestyle-routine activity models of violent victimization. Previous analyses using the NCS data have been limited because of the unavailability of measures such as the type of nighttime activities engaged in, the use of public transportation, drinking, and other self-reported deviance such as offending (see more below). It is thus possible that the patterns regarding direct effects of lifestyle are unique to countries such as Great Britain, where cultural and structural conditions (e.g., racial composition) are quite different. Consequently, we can only speak generally about individual-level lifestyle factors associated with the risk of violent victimization for the U.S. population as a whole, and we are unable to specify precisely why it is that traditional social and demographic factors (including age, sex, race, and employment status) are related to differences in the risk of violent victimization. Clearly, future research on violence needs to focus more specifically on the development of individual-level measures necessary to test lifestyle-routine activity hypotheses using U.S. data.

INDIVIDUAL-LEVEL RISK FACTORS IN VIOLENT OFFENDING

Having reviewed the individual-level factors underlying the risk of violent victimization, we now turn our attention to the issue of violent *offending*. This section is similar in scope to the previous section in that we review basic individual-level correlates. For example, we focus on questions such as: How are the individual-level factors of age, sex, race, socioeconomic status, and family structure related to the likelihood of committing violent crimes? Are these patterns consistent across sources of data? Have they remained stable over time? Also, what are the current limitations of individual-level analyses of violent offending?

Prior research on individual-level correlates of offending has discussed in great detail the methodological issues that may limit the generalizability of findings (e.g., Hindelang, 1978; Hindelang et al., 1979; Hindelang, 1981; Blumstein et al., 1986); therefore, we will mention only a few of these limitations here. One of the primary concerns is the source of data on offending—whether or not the findings are based on official, self-report, or victimization data. Findings based on official data (e.g., UCR arrest data or imprisonment data) are limited to the extent that apprehended offenders differ in some way from nonapprehended offenders, whereas findings based on self-report surveys may be limited either by the respondents' intentional or unintentional errors in reporting or by sampling restrictions (e.g., an almost exclusive focus on juveniles or males). A third source of data—the NCS—also provides information on the *perceived* age, race, and sex of offenders; however, it should be reiterated that victims have been found to underreport certain types of incidents, especially those involving victimizations by family members and acquaintances (Law Enforcement Assistance Administration, 1972). These potential sources of error should be kept in mind as we review the correlates of violent offending.

DEMOGRAPHIC FACTORS

Age

Age is one of the major individual-level correlates of violent offending (Hindelang, 1981; Hirschi and Gottfredson, 1983; Greenberg, 1985; Farrington, 1986; Steffensmeier et al., 1989). In general, arrests for violent crime peak around age 18 and decline gradually thereafter (U.S. Department of Justice, 1988a). More than two-thirds of those arrested for violent crimes are age 30 or younger (U.S. Department of Justice, 1988a). The relationship between age and violent crime is less peaked than that for age and property crime in that a larger proportion of violent crimes are committed by persons over age 20 (Hindelang et al., 1981; Farrington, 1986; Jamieson and Flanagan, 1989:489; Steffensmeier et al., 1989). In other words, the age-specific rate of violent offending declines more gradually, and after a later peak, than the age-specific rate of property offending (see U.S. Department of Justice, 1988a; Steffensmeier et al., 1989). Victim reports of offender characteristics in NCS data support the age patterns found in UCR data: victims estimate that the majority of (lone) violent offenders are less than 30 years of age (Jamieson and Flanagan, 1989:308).

Steffensmeier et al. (1989) also report that there are differences in age distributions within types of violent crime. Analyzing 1980 UCR data, they report that the mean age of offenders arrested for robbery (17 years) is lower than the mean age of homicide (19 years) or assault (21 years) arrestees. Personal offenses against family members peak even later, at about 24 years old (Steffensmeier et al., 1989:815). Furthermore, the age distribution for robbery is much more peaked than the normal distribution whereas age distributions for other violent offenses are flatter than normal. These analyses suggest that robbery offending declines more rapidly with age than does assault or homicide offending, especially when these crimes are committed against family mem-

bers. The NCS victim reports support these findings; the estimated age distribution for lone robbery offenders is more peaked
than the estimated age distributions for assault and rape offending
(U.S. Department of Justice, 1989).

Sex

Even though sex is one of the strongest demographic correlates of violent offending, analyses of violence have concentrated
almost exclusively on male offending (Harris, 1977; Simon and
Baxter, 1989). Consequently, detailed accounts of male-female
differences in violent offending are rare (see Kruttschnitt, in this
volume). When sex differences are examined, males are far more
likely than females to be arrested for all crimes of violence including homicide, rape, robbery, and assault (Simon, 1975; Hindelang,
1979; Hindelang et al., 1979; Smith and Visher, 1980; Hindelang,
1981; Hill and Harris, 1981; Simon and Baxter, 1989; Bridges and
Weis, 1989). Females constitute, on average, only 11 percent of
arrestees for all of these crimes (U.S. Department of Justice, 1988a);
however, the proportion of female offenders arrested for the crime
of rape (1%) is estimated to be far lower. The NCS data closely
parallel findings from UCR arrest data in that approximately 14
percent of (lone) violent offenders were reported by their victims
to be female (U.S. Department of Justice, 1989).

Hill and Harris (1981) compared sex-specific arrest rates for
violent crimes using 1953 and 1977 UCR arrest data. They found
that in 1953, males were approximately five times more likely
than females to be arrested for murder. The ratios for manslaughter (12 to 1), robbery (23 to 1), and aggravated assault (5 to 1)
indicate that females were much less involved in violent offending than were males in the early 1950s (1981:661). Robbery offending in particular, along with rape offending, appears to be the
most disproportionately male crime. By 1977 these sex ratios had
changed to 6 to 1 for murder, 9 to 1 for manslaughter, 13 to 1 for
robbery, and 4 to 1 for aggravated assault. Therefore, although
sex-specific *rates* for all crimes increased over this period, the
1977 *ratios* suggest that the proportion of violent crimes committed by females increased more quickly over these two decades for
the crimes of manslaughter, robbery, and aggravated assault. Only
for the crime of murder has there been a greater acceleration in
the male crime rate than in the female crime rate (Hill and Harris, 1981:661).

Smith and Visher (1980) conducted a meta-analysis of studies gating the sex-crime relationship to examine the extent to which statistical associations varied according to study characteristics. They found that, overall, the relationship between sex and crime is greater when violent and officially recorded crimes are examined (versus property offenses and self-reports) and is greater among whites than nonwhites. They also found that the magnitude of the sex-crime association has decreased slightly over time, supporting the findings reported by Hill and Harris (1981). Simon and Baxter (1989) reach a similar conclusion in their analysis of cross-cultural data on female homicide offending rates: women continue to play a minor role in violent offending around the world.

Race

Race is another individual-level factor found to be substantially related to violent offending (Hindelang, 1978; Elliott and Ageton, 1980; Ageton, 1983, Bridges and Weis, 1989; U.S. Department of Justice, 1989). Although whites are arrested for the majority of all violent crimes (approximately 52%), blacks are significantly overrepresented in arrest data: blacks comprise 47 percent of violent crime arrestees yet constitute 12 percent of the U.S. population (U.S. Department of Justice, 1988a). For persons under 18 years of age, the ratio of black to white arrest rates for violent offenses is approximately 9 to 1 (Hindelang et al., 1979). The NCS victim reports support the finding of disproportionate black involvement in violent crime, but these data suggest that the race and violent crime association may not be quite as strong. Victims report that in lone-offender violent crime incidents, blacks constituted about 25 percent of the offenders. This percentage varies by crime type; black representation was higher in rape and robbery incidents, whereas white representation was higher in assaults (U.S. Department of Justice, 1988a).

Hindelang (1978) has investigated the extent to which black over-representation in official data is due to differential involvement in violent crime or to differential selection into the criminal justice system via arrests by police. In comparing the distribution of arrestees by race from the 1974 UCR to the distribution of perceived race of offenders derived from the 1974 NCS, he found some evidence for the differential selection hypothesis with respect to assault and rape. Overall, though, NCS victim reports suggest that most of the race difference found in arrest rates for violence is due to greater black involvement in personal crimes, especially robbery. For example, in 1974 both the NCS and the UCR estimate the proportion of black offenders committing robbery to be 62 percent. We compared similar data for personal violent crimes using 1987 NCS and 1987 UCR data and found much the same pattern as reported earlier by Hindelang (1978). However, we found a somewhat larger discrepancy between the two estimates of racial involvement (U.S. Department of Justice, 1988b:182-184, 1989:Table 41). For instance, the NCS estimate of the extent of black involvement in robbery in 1987 is 51 percent, whereas the UCR data show that 63 percent of robbery arrestees were black. These differences between UCR and NCS data do not necessarily indicate a change in the underlying relationship between race and violence, particularly if race is related to group versus lone offending and this changed over time. In the 1987 data there was also a higher proportion of reported "other" racial group involvement in violent crime than in 1974.

Age-Sex-Race

Each of the above ascribed characteristics of individuals combines to produce substantial variation in age-race-sex-specific offending rates. In particular, Hindelang (1981) has examined rape, robbery, and assault offending rates (estimated from 1973 through 1977 NCS data) for demographic subgroups. The subgroup with the highest rate of offending for each of these crimes was 18- to 20-year-old black males. Black males of all ages had rates of offending that were higher than those estimated for white males. Overall, offending rates were approximately three, five, and fourteen times greater among black males compared to white males for the crimes of assault, rape, and robbery, respectively. Female rates of violent offending were substantially lower than male rates with one exception—white males ages 12 to 17 had offending rates for robbery and assault that were roughly comparable to those of black females of the same age. Between ages 18 and 20, white males' violent offending rates increase (as do rates for black males), but black and white female rates decline. Apparently, females are most likely to engage in violent offending before age 17, whereas male involvement peaks somewhat later (between 18 and 20 years of age). Race differences among females for assault offending are roughly the same magnitude as those among males, whereas female race differences for robbery are less pronounced than male race differences in part because of lower level of involvement in robbery offending (Hindelang, 1981:Table 1). Laub and McDermott (1985) report that between 1973 and 1981 there was a decline in race differences among female juvenile offenders for assault crimes and that this decline could be attributed to a decrease in black female offending.

The limitations of these findings are discussed at length by Hindelang (1981), including the concern that race-age-sex estimates are based solely on NCS victim reports of lone offender crimes and that the NCS data produce incidence rates instead of prevalence rates. This problem of incidence rates versus prevalence rates is important to the extent that each age-race-sex subgroup contains different proportions of repeat offenders. The UCR data share a similar limitation in that arrest incidents (and not offenders) are used as the unit of analysis. The potential inaccuracy of victims' reports of an offender's age, race, and perhaps sex in the NCS data is also a concern but is not considered a serious limitation. Hindelang (1981), for example, compared NCS rape victims' reports of their offender's age and race to police reports of the offender's demographic characteristics and found substantial agreement. Victims' reports of race agreed with police reports in more than 96 percent of the cases. Similarly, the accuracy of age estimates was very good (89% or higher) and was highest for offenders less than 20 (96%) and more than 45 years of age (96%). Of course, these findings are not definitive because arrests are often made on the basis of victims' descriptions of offenders.

Bridges and Weis (1989) conducted a meta-analysis of correlations reported in studies examining sex, race, and violent crime. They found that variation in the magnitudes of these relationships across studies was related to differences in the level of the data used (e.g., individuals, households, cities, etc.) and whether the analysis was based on offenders as opposed to victims. In the case of sex, male-female differences were greater in violent offending than in violent victimization. For race effects, analyses of offender data produced greater race-violence coefficients than did analyses of victimization. The presence of statistical controls diminished the effect of race on violence but had no effect on the overall magnitude of the sex-violence relationship. Consequently, their results suggest that the relationship between sex and violent offending is strong and stable, whereas the association between race and violent crime is particularly sensitive to the level of analysis and the presence or absence of statistical controls.

SOCIOECONOMIC AND FAMILY FACTORS

Social Class

The association between social class and violent offending continues to be one of the most contested relationships in the literature (e.g., see Tittle et al., 1978; Hindelang et al., 1979; Elliott and Ageton, 1980; Thornberry and Farnworth, 1982; Elliott and Huizinga, 1983; Ageton, 1983; Brownfield, 1986; and Bridges and Weis, 1989). Hindelang et al. (1979) and others have noted the methodological problems in this area: "Unlike sex and race, social class data are not available for either UCR arrestees or for offenders in victimization surveys. Thus, if understanding the relationship of social class to serious offending is our aim, data limitations are much more severe for social class than for sex or race" (1979:1002). The reliance, then, on self-report data has led to questions concerning the validity of such data for examining violent crime. Still, Hindelang et al. (1979) have argued that the self-report method is capable of dealing with serious offending behavior and, further, that no evidence of differential self-report validity has been found by social class.

Bridges and Weis (1989), in their meta-analysis, also examined variation in the social class-violent crime association. They report, as did Hindelang et al. (1979), that much of the discrepancy in findings across studies of violent offending is due to the level of analysis and to the presence or absence of statistical controls. As was true for race, they found that the magnitude of association between social class and violent offending decreased when individual-level data were used and when statistical controls for correlates of violence were included. The type of data used (i.e., official versus self-report) also had a marginal effect on the relationship; findings that used official data show a stronger negative effect than findings based on other sources.

With the exception of Thornberry and Farnworth (1982) and the vast research in the area of family violence (e.g., see, Gelles, 1985; Straus and Gelles, 1986; Gelles and Straus, 1988; Ohlin and Tonry, 1989), most of the recent literature directly examining social class and violence has been based on samples of adolescents. For example, Elliott and Ageton (1980) used self-report data from a nationally representative sample of 1,716 adolescents in the National Youth Survey and found that social class (based on a comparison of middle-, working-, and lower-class youth) was negatively related to the mean frequency of predatory crimes against persons (a scale including robbery and aggravated, simple, or sexual assault). This relationship was due in part to the differences across social classes in high-frequency offending. The authors also found an interaction between race and class, which suggests that lower-class black youth were particularly likely to report higher levels of involvement in these personal violence offenses.

Elliott and Huizinga (1983) report more extensive data from the National Youth Survey on the relationship between social class and offense-specific prevalence and incidence scales of violence for both males and females. In analyzing several waves of this longitudinal data base, their results suggest that class differences are more apparent when incidence measures as opposed to prevalence measures are used. They also find class differences in the frequency of minor and felony assault by males such that lower-class youth are more likely to commit offenses than middle-class youth. Few differences were found between middle- and working-class or working- and lower-class males. Among females there were comparable class differences in levels of felony assault but no differences in minor assault levels. A more extensive analysis of female offending behavior using the National Youth Survey found class effects for aggravated assault offending in the first two waves of data and for involvement in gang fighting in four out of five waves of data (Ageton, 1983). In these instances, lower-class females, like males, were more likely to report involvement in assaults against persons.

The above research emphasizes the importance of the measurement of violent offending; findings using incidence measures may differ from findings using prevalence measures. Additionally, the measurement of "social class" is a concern (Thornberry and Farnworth, 1982; Brownfield, 1986). Although there appears to be differential involvement in serious violent offending by social class, these findings depend to some extent on the conceptualization and operationalization of the social class measure. Brownfield (1986) finds that the strength of the class-violence relationship among individuals varies depending on whether a neo-Marxist conception of class categories is used, versus a more gradational measure of socioeconomic status that combines occupation and education measures. A small relationship was found in two studies of youth using the gradational measure, but none was found using the alternative measure (Brownfield, 1986).

Additional limitations of the class-violence literature are discussed by Thornberry and Farnworth (1982), who argue that although the overall relationship between class and juvenile violence is weak, the relationship among adults may be stronger. In fact, they found in a reanalysis of Wolfgang's (1958) Philadelphia cohort data that for white adults the father's occupational status was negatively related to violent behavior, whereas for black adults the respondent's own education level was negatively related to arrests for violence. The causal implications of these findings are not yet clear—it is possible that there is a reciprocal relationship between the social class of an adult and levels of criminality. Among juveniles this is less problematic, but it is an issue that has not yet been adequately resolved.

Family Structure and Process

There are at least three ways in which family factors have been examined in the literature on violent offending. The first pertains to the marital status of offenders. Studies of prison inmates have found that most offenders are not married (78 percent) and that white inmates are disproportionately divorced or separated. Black inmates, on the other hand, are just as likely not to be married as blacks in the general population (U.S. Department of Justice, 1988a). These findings, of course, are quite limited. We do not know whether an offender's marital status is a consequence of his or her offending behavior, and data representing the prison population may not be representative of the overall population of violent offenders. Consequently, the meaning of these findings is unclear.

Second, and more importantly, family structure and intervening "family processes" (e.g., Laub and Sampson, 1988) have been correlated with aggression and other serious criminal behaviors among children and adolescents. The relationship between juvenile delinquency and these family factors has been reviewed extensively elsewhere (see Loeber and Stouthamer-Loeber, 1986), but we find that studies focusing exclusively on family factors and violent behavior are rare. This is, perhaps, to be expected given that we are focusing our discussion on those serious violent behaviors not typically engaged in by youth. Nonetheless, extant research suggests that children living in "broken" homes are slightly more likely to engage in aggressive behaviors than children living in two-parent homes (Farrington and West, 1971; Wilkinson, 1980; McCord, 1982). However, the magnitude of this relationship is weak, and these results are not unanimous across adolescent subgroups or types of aggressive behaviors. Rankin (1983) also reports a small effect of family structure on fighting (children in single-parent homes are more likely to report fighting), but no differences in other assaultive behaviors.

Research on family functioning or intervening family processes typically examines factors such as parental neglect, punishment styles, punitiveness, marital conflict, parental attitudes toward deviance, and parental criminality for their effects on children's offending behaviors. Parental neglect in the form of either lack of supervision or lack of other involvement has been found to be positively related to aggressive behaviors in children (Bandura and Walters, 1959; McCord et al., 1961; Farrington, 1978; Loeber and Stouthamer-Loeber, 1986). Punishment styles of parents are also related to aggressiveness and serious criminality: yelling, threatening, and hitting children is associated with increased aggressive behaviors among children (Bandura and Walters, 1959; McCord et al., 1961; Farrington, 1978; McCord, 1982; Wells and Rankin, 1988). Factors such as marital discord and conflict have similarly shown positive, but small, associations with aggression and serious criminality (Bandura and Walters, 1959; Farrington and West, 1971). Finally, parental criminality also tends to show a positive correlation with aggression among children (Glueck and Glueck, 1950; Hutchings and Mednick, 1975; Farrington, 1978) as does parental aggressiveness (Bandura and Walters, 1959) and paternal alcoholism (McCord, 1982).

Loeber and Stouthamer-Loeber (1986:121) summarize in tabular form the overall relationships between these family factors and juvenile delinquency. In general, family functioning or process variables such as those discussed above were more consistently associated with delinquency than were family structure variables. Recent multivariate analyses focusing exclusively on violent behavior (assault, robbery) also suggest that the quality of family life may be more important than family structure. For example, Van Voorhis et al. (1988) found that family structure had no independent effect on violent behavior (fighting and assault combined), whereas overall home quality was negatively and significantly related to violence. Although there are many methodological limitations in the family-aggressive behavior literature (see Loeber and Stouthamer-Loeber, 1986, for an extensive discussion), these findings suggest that family functioning may be a more important factor than family structure and that more explicit attention should be paid to the effects of family functioning on juvenile aggression and its relationship to later violent offending as an adult (see also Farrington, 1978).

A third, related, way in which family factors have been studied with respect to violence has been in the "cycle of violence" or "violence breeds violence" literature (see Kruttschnitt et al., 1986, 1987; Widom, 1989a,b). These recent and extensive reviews suggest that the research on intergenerational transmission of violence is inconclusive and plagued with methodological problems. Although there is agreement concerning the correlation between suffering abuse as a child and perpetrating abuse as adults, the magnitude of the relationship is quite small and many violent offenders report no history of child abuse (Widom, 1989a). It is also the case that most abused children do not go on to commit abusive or violent acts as adults (Kruttschnitt et al., 1987; Widom, 1989a). Consequently, recent analyses have sought to discover the factors that break the "cycle of violence."

Kruttschnitt et al. (1987) report that children who suffer from emotional neglect (in addition to physical abuse) and who have no emotional support system inside or outside the home are more likely to be abusive as adults. Widom (1989a) found that age at the time of abuse, sex, temperament, and intelligence were protective factors from future involvement in violence. However, Widom argues for caution when interpreting these results: to say that certain factors appear to protect children from perpetuating future violence does not imply that the effects of child abuse are eliminated. The effects may be manifested in other ways, including depression, anxiety, or even suicide, and these links have not been adequately assessed (Widom, 1989a).

ADDITIONAL FINDINGS

A variety of other factors have been studied in conjunction with violent behavior among juveniles including analyses of school achievement and attachment (Andrew, 1979; Liska and Reed, 1985; Friedman and Rosenbaum, 1988), associations with delinquent peers (Friedman and Rosenbaum, 1988), and prior involvement in crime (Blumstein et al., 1988; Farrington et al., 1988). Perhaps surprisingly, analyses of school and peer factors and their relationship to violence have not been as extensive as investigations of relationships discussed earlier (e.g., age, sex, social class). Nevertheless, small and relatively consistent effects have been reported. Friedman and Rosenbaum (1988) found that time spent doing homework was inversely related to juvenile assault and robbery offending, and that time spent with delinquent peers was positively related to juvenile violence (this is also consistent with Elliott et al.'s, 1985, analysis of "index" offending). Liska and Reed (1985) considered the reciprocal effects that parental attachment, school attachment, and violence might have on each other. They found that for white males, parental attachment decreased violent behavior and that violent delinquency led to future decreases in both school and parental attachment. They argue that for white males at least, "parents, not the school, are the major institutional sources of delinquency control" (1985:558) and that their findings imply that factors associated with school attachment and achievement may be *consequences* of violence and not causal factors.

Finally, it should be noted that by distinguishing prevalence of offending from incidence (or frequency) of offending, "criminal career" research (see Blumstein et al., 1986) suggests that certain individuals are disproportionately involved in violent offending. However, research by Blumstein et al. (1988) and Farrington et al. (1988) suggests that offenders do not typically "specialize" in violent crimes such as homicide, assault, and robbery, and that "escalation" in terms of the seriousness of offending over periods of time is not common. A possible exception to the lack of specialization holds for persons who have prior involvement in robbery (Farrington et al., 1988). Overall, "the more impulsive, violent crimes of homicide, rape, and weapons violations were among the least specialized" (Blumstein et al., 1988:342).[16] Consequently, although violent offenders often have prior records of extensive involvement in crime, the prediction of violence from these records is very difficult (Piper, 1985).

SUMMARY

Of all the individual-level correlates discussed above, ascribed demographic characteristics appear to have the strongest associations with violent offending. Sex and age are clearly and consistently associated with all forms of violent behavior, whereas race and social class have smaller and less consistent relationships to violent offending. Family structure and functioning are associated with juvenile violence and aggression, but multivariate analyses suggest that family functioning or process variables such as parental neglect and punishment styles (i.e., quality of family life) are more important than family structure characteristics (i.e., one versus two parents). Physical abuse as a child also appears to be related to future violent behavior, but the reasons for this association are not yet clearly understood. Other correlates of violence such as school attachment and achievement are even smaller in magnitude, and causal analyses (e.g., Liska and Reed, 1985) suggest that school factors may not be as important as family factors or other social and demographic characteristics. Finally, although violent offenders typically have prior criminal records, the prediction of future violence from these records has been extremely difficult.

As noted throughout the above discussion, much of the extant literature in each of the areas relating social factors to violent offending suffers from methodological or causal interpretation limitations. These limitations include sampling (e.g., a focus on males or juveniles only, unrepresentative samples), the domain of the dependent variable (studies of specific violent crimes are surprisingly rare), analytical techniques (multivariate statistical controls are also rare), issues of causal direction (temporal ordering and reciprocal effects are typically ignored), the general failure to distinguish participation in violent offending from frequency of violent offending (Blumstein et al., 1986), and the paucity of studies examining the intervening mechanisms and social processes that might explain the effects of demographic factors such as age, race, and sex.[17]

An equally important limitation of prior individual-level analyses of both violent offending and victimization is that they generally have not considered the possible effects that situational- or community-level factors might have on an individual's experiences with violence. It is possible that individual-level correlates of victimization and offending are the same because of the structural or situational contexts in which particular demographic subgroups typically find themselves. Situational-level variables or community-level factors may thus be responsible for a small or large portion of the individual-level risk for violent victimization and offending.

Additionally, individual-level research has for the most part treated victims of violence and violent offenders as though they were mutually exclusive groups (Reiss, 1981; Jensen and Brownfield, 1986). The remainder of the paper therefore considers the additional and perhaps crucial role of victim-offender relationships and the structural context—both situational and community—in which violence occurs. Our contention is that a consideration of these other levels of analysis may help to better explicate the sources of both violent victimization and offending.

SITUATIONAL-LEVEL RISK FACTORS
AND VICTIM-OFFENDER RELATIONSHIPS

Situational or microlevel (Short, 1990:11) inquiry has traditionally focused on circumstances surrounding the violent event
itself. Although the analysis of "events" may at first seem
unproblematic, designating "situational-level" factors is neither
easy nor obvious. As Block (1981:743-744) has observed:

> The criminal event can be thought of as one instance surrounded
> by a microenvironment of social relationships, physical struc-
> tures, and weapons of potential use, a macroenvironment of neigh-
> borhood and community, a history of social relationships, and
> ideas of violence and danger, self-defense, social class, and segre-
> gation. The two actors, victim and offender, interact with and
> are affected by these structures, but they retain individuality;
> their behavior can never be fully predicted.

The complex nature of situations, combined with a lack of definitional consensus over situational-level factors, leads us to broadly
define situational-level risk factors as those factors, outside the
individual (Monahan and Klassen, 1982:293), that influence the
initiation, unfolding, or outcome of a violent event.[18] Based on
this conceptualization and past treatments of violent events, we
therefore focus on such factors as the presence and type of weapon,
the presence of drugs or alcohol, the role of bystanders, and victim resistance and retaliation. We also include a discussion of
the victim-offender overlap as well as a review of how victim-
offender relationships are related to violence. We believe that the
simultaneous consideration of victim-offender dynamics, including past histories and present behaviors and relationships, provides a more complete framework for studying the contextual aspects of violent events.

VICTIM-OFFENDER OVERLAP

Our review in the previous two sections clearly reveals that
prior research on the risk of violent victimization and offending
has concentrated on demographic and socioeconomic characteristics of the individual. The common message running throughout
this prior work is that victims and offenders share a similar demographic profile: both violent offenders and victims of violent
crime tend to be young, male, and black and to live in urban areas
(see also Hindelang, 1976, 1981; Hindelang et al., 1978; Gottfredson,
1986). Some research even suggests that victims and offenders
are one and the same (Wolfgang, 1958; Singer, 1981). By consider-

ing in detail the concept of victim-offender overlap, we hope to answer the question of how, and in what ways, violent offending increases an offender's risk of victimization.

The traditional explanation of the link between victims and offenders is the subculture of violence theory. Formulated originally by Wolfgang and Ferracuti (1967), the subcultural theory proposes that in certain areas and for certain subgroups of the population, there is a subcultural value system that supports the use of violence and other behaviors (e.g., sexual machismo) not emphasized in the dominant culture. In an application of subcultural theory to the victim-offender dyad, Singer (1981) argues that the existence of a subcultural normative system increases the likelihood that an individual will alternate between the role of offender and victim. In particular, victims of crime may become offenders because of norms that justify retaliation (Singer, 1981; Fagan et al., 1987). Conversely, offenders may become victims because they hold values that support the initiation of violence to resolve disputes. For example, subculturally induced aggressive behaviors (e.g., starting fights) are thought to result in an increased risk of victimization (i.e., "victim precipitation"). Subculture of violence theories therefore suggest that offending behavior may affect the risk of victimization *and* that victimization experiences may affect the probability of offending.

Although rarely studied, the logic of the lifestyle-routine activity theory (Hindelang et al., 1978; Cohen and Felson, 1979; Cohen et al., 1981b; Garofalo, 1987) also suggests that criminal and deviant lifestyles may directly increase victimization because of the nature of the offending behavior itself. As Jensen and Brownfield (1986:87) have argued in a recent paper, offense activity can be considered a characteristic of lifestyles or a type of routine activity that increases the risk of victimization because of the vulnerability or culpability of people involved in those activities. Membership in a gang, for example, involves close proximity to fellow offenders and criminal events (e.g., gang fights) in which rival offender groups are present. It is also well established that most delinquency is committed in groups (Zimring, 1981); assaults, in particular, often take place in contexts where retaliation probability is high (e.g., bars, social clubs, parties). Moreover, assaultive behavior by definition requires more than one person, meaning that the victimization potential of fighting is at a maximum.

Sparks (1982) has further suggested that offenders make ideal targets because they may be victimized with relative impunity.

That is, offenders are likely to be viewed by other potential offenders as particularly vulnerable because "offender" victims are probably less willing to call the police than "nonoffender" victims. In addition to not reporting an offense for fear of implicating themselves in criminal behavior, offender victims may also feel that the police are likely to disbelieve or discount their victimization experience. Persons whose lifestyles include violence thus face a heightened risk of victimization as a direct result of their predatory offending and association with other offenders.

Even deviant lifestyles (e.g., extensive drinking, drug use, "partying") that do not involve actual violence may place persons at risk of victimization. As Jensen and Brownfield (1986) note, many activities that involve the "recreational and social pursuit of fun" increase victimization risk. For example, according to lifestyle theory, persons who drink extensively or go "cruising" for social activity, especially at night, are at higher risk for assault because such behavior often occurs at bars, parties, and other places where victimization risk is heightened. This idea is consistent with Sherman et al.'s (1989) finding that relatively few "hot spots" produce a large proportion of predatory crime. Indeed, Sherman et al. (1989:39) found that all robberies and rapes in Minneapolis during 1986 occurred at less than 3 percent of "places," particularly bars, parks, adult bookstores, and convenience stores.

Drinking to excess also lowers guardianship potential and thus may increase victimization risk not just for assault, but for other personal crimes such as robbery. The notion of victimization with impunity (Sparks, 1982) applies to general deviance as well. Nonviolent offense activity such as drug dealing and group-oriented drug consumption has especially high victimization potential. For instance, dealers and users are ripe for exploitation by predatory offenders who, with good reason, have little fear of victim-initiated police intervention.

Despite its potential importance to theoretical explanations of violence, there is surprisingly little empirical research that bears directly on the offending-victimization link. As Jensen and Brownfield (1986:98) concluded, "A major individual level variable, offense activity, has been ignored in recent elaborations of a formal opportunity or routine activity theory of personal victimization." An important reason for this is that most criminological studies examine either offending *or* victimization—few data sets are designed to examine victim-offender interrelationships. Those few studies that have explored the "victimogenic" potential of offending are quite revealing. For instance, Gottfredson (1984) reports a positive association between suffering a personal victimization (assault, robbery, theft from person) and self-reported offending in the British Crime Survey. This relationship holds for those who have engaged in assault or other personal violence and for those who reported engaging in other minor delinquencies. Hough and Mayhew (1983) found a similar offender-victim link using the same data. Studies in the United States have also established an empirical association between being the victim of an assault and reports of assaulting others (e.g., Singer, 1981; Sparks et al., 1977).

Taken together, these studies suggest the important role of violent and deviant lifestyles in fully understanding personal victimization risk. However, most research has been bivariate in nature and has not considered the potential confounding effects of demographic factors (e.g., age, sex, marital status) and conventional lifestyle variables (e.g., nights out of the home). It is thus unclear whether offending has an impact on the risk of violent victimization that is not accounted for by sociodemographic factors. Also, if the principle of homogamy is correct, then demographic predictors should continue to have direct effects on victimization that are independent of a victim's propensity for criminal offending.

In an intriguing exploration of these issues, Jensen and Brownfield (1986) report positive associations between routine activities such as "cruising," going to parties and bars, and violent victimization among a sample of high school youth. They found a similar positive relationship between ever having been in trouble with the police and victimization. Interestingly, they report that none of their conventional lifestyle measures were independently related to victimization when "delinquent lifestyle" indicators were controlled. Because their demographic indicators show little direct effect on victimization, and because they find a moderate to strong relationship between offending and victimization, Jensen and Brownfield argue that the factors that explain the links between background characteristics and victimization may be the same factors that explain the links between these characteristics and offending.

Building on this idea, Sampson and Lauritsen (1990) examined the independent effect of violent offending behavior and deviant lifestyles (e.g., drinking, drug use) on the risk of personal victimization. Data used for these analyses were derived from the 1982 and 1984 British Crime Surveys. Multivariate analyses showed that offense activity—whether violent or minor deviance—was directly related to the risk of assault. The inclusion of lifestyle measures (including nights out, extent of drinking, and self-reported violence) did attenuate the magnitudes of the effects of sex and marital status, but the independent effect of age remained consistently strong. Furthermore, the effects of self-reported involvement in deviance or violence maintained for both the 1982 and the 1984 models of assault risk, even when neighborhood levels of violence were controlled for.[19]

Similar effects of offending lifestyles on the risk of violent victimization have been shown in longitudinal, multivariate analyses using the National Youth Survey (Lauritsen et al., 1991). Adolescents and young adults who reported engaging in offense activities (including assault, theft, and vandalism) were found to be approximately two to three times more likely to report assault and robbery victimization than youth who reported no offense involvement. Moreover, increased involvement in offending "lifestyles"—either through increases in time spent with delinquent peers or through one's own offending—had large positive effects on robbery and assault victimization, controlling for race, age, sex, family structure, family income, neighborhood characteristics, and prior propensity toward victimization. Evidence was also found for reciprocal effects, whereby increases in victimization predicted changes in offense involvement. However, an offending lifestyle continued to have a direct effect on victimization even when reciprocal effects were controlled. Therefore, national data sets from two different countries strongly suggest that violent offending and violent victimization are intimately connected and that this relationship cannot be explained away by traditional demographic and social correlates of crime.

VICTIM-OFFENDER RELATIONSHIPS

As emphasized in the seminal research by Wolfgang (1958) suggesting that homicide victimization was more likely to result from disputes among family members and acquaintances than strangers, consideration of the nature of the relationship between victim and offender in violent incidents has been extensive in criminological literature. As Loftin et al. (1987) argue, the victim-offender relationship is an important variable in studies of personal violence because it places the event within the context of social structures (1987:259), and like the victim-offender overlap, an analysis of victim-offender relationships helps illustrate the situational context of a particular event. We thus briefly overview victim-offender relationships and their associations with violent crime (because of space limitations we urge readers to consult original sources and other reviews).

Loftin et al. (1987) demonstrate that the measurement of victim-offender relationships is neither easy nor consistent across studies. They found that conceptualization of the victim-offender relationship varied considerably across studies due to the lack of standardization or to definitions that were multidimensional, overlapping, or vague. Even though official data are considered the best available on homicide incidents (Hindelang, 1974; O'Brien, 1985), the "unknown" relationship category in the Federal Bureau of Investigation homicide data is large enough to suggest that stranger homicides may be underestimated (Riedel, 1987). On the other hand, it is also suspected that assault incidents among friends and family are underreported in victimization studies. Furthermore, series victimizations—which are more likely to occur among family members and friends—are excluded from most NCS tabulations and analyses. Caution is clearly required when interpreting the associations between victim-offender relationships and violence.

The NCS data suggest that robbery is the violent crime most likely to involve strangers—victims are approximately four times more likely to be robbed by strangers than by nonstrangers.[20] However, for rape and assault, differences in incidence rates between stranger and nonstranger crimes are much smaller. Victim reports suggest that one's chances of being raped or assaulted by a nonstranger are approximately equal to one's chances of being victimized by a stranger (U.S. Department of Justice, 1989). Because it is suspected that victims generally underreport victimizations by nonstrangers, it seems reasonable to suggest that rape and assault are, more often than not, crimes occurring among nonstrangers.

The majority of homicides also appear to be committed by nonstrangers—either relatives, friends, or acquaintances of the victim. For example, Williams and Flewelling (1988) found that approximately two-thirds of homicides occurring in cities with populations greater than 100,000 were among nonstrangers. Because stranger homicide is even more rare in nonurban areas, the national percentage of homicides committed by nonstrangers is probably somewhat higher. As might be expected, nonstranger homicides are likely to be the result of interpersonal disputes, such as arguments over property and money, lovers' triangles, and brawls involving alcohol or drugs. Stranger homicides, on the other hand, are more likely to be the result of circumstances involving the commission of other felonies such as robbery (Williams and Flewelling, 1988).

Other studies have examined the extent to which violent crimes are interracial or intraracial in composition (Sampson, 1984; Block, 1985; Wilbanks, 1985; Zahn and Sagi, 1987; Silverman and Kennedy, 1987; Messner and South, 1986; Cook, 1987; O'Brien, 1987; South and Felson, 1990). These analyses agree that the majority of violent crimes are disproportionately intraracial: for example, whites tend to assault other whites and blacks tend to assault other blacks more so than expected based on chance encounters (Sampson, 1984; O'Brien, 1987). Racial crossover is especially rare in nonfelony homicide (Cook, 1987). Given that most nonstranger homicides are also assault homicides, and that the routine activities and residences of blacks and whites are in large part segregated, these findings are not surprising. For example, Block (1985) argues that for assault homicides, the relationship between victim and offender is likely to be one of residential proximity. Felony homicides (e.g., robbery-murders) are more likely than nonfelony homicides to be interracial because they typically involve strangers (Block, 1985; Cook, 1987; Zahn and Sagi, 1987). In felony homicides as in robberies, black offenders are more likely to victimize whites than white offenders are to victimize blacks (Wilbanks, 1985). Again, however, this is exactly what we would expect given racial distributions in the United States—variations in the relative sizes of the black and white populations explain the patterning of interracial violence (Sampson, 1984; O'Brien, 1987; Messner and South, 1986; South and Felson, 1990).

The intersexual composition of violent encounters has also been examined (Wolfgang, 1958; Pokorny, 1965; Silverman and Kennedy, 1987; O'Brien, 1988). In the case of homicide, both male and female offenders are likely to choose males as their victims (Wolfgang, 1958; Pokorny, 1965; O'Brien, 1988). As social distance increases, violent crimes in general are more likely to involve both male offenders and male victims. Assault is the violent crime most likely to be intrasexual in nature (O'Brien, 1988), whereas rape is almost exclusively intersexual. It may seem obvious that violent crime is more likely to be intersexual than interracial in nature; racial segregation in the United States is far more extensive than segregation by sex (O'Brien, 1988).

One final point concerning intersexual differences in violent events should be made. When women are involved in intersexual violent crimes as victims, the consequences are likely to be much more serious than when women are victimized by women. Men, on the other hand, tend to suffer less serious consequences when they are victimized in intersexual violent crimes. For more extensive discussions of the etiology and consequences of intersexual violence, readers are referred to the literature reviewing family violence (e.g., Gelles, 1985; Gelles and Straus, 1988; Ohlin and Tonry, 1989).

OTHER SITUATIONAL FACTORS

In this subsection we briefly focus on other factors traditionally considered in situational-level analyses, including the presence of alcohol and drugs, the presence and type of weapon, the role of third parties or bystanders, and victim resistance. The fact that certain factors may be considered either "individual" or "situational" (e.g., alcohol/drug use, violent offending) suggests that further development of situational concepts is needed to clarify these distinctions.

Alcohol and Drug Use

As discussed earlier, the use of alcohol and drugs is related to the risk of violent victimization. There is also evidence that excessive drinking and illegal drug use may place persons at increased risk for violent offending and consequently may be viewed as having an effect on the initiation or outcome of an event. The literature on offending is perhaps more problematic than victimization research because both excessive drinking and propensity to violence may be different aspects of an underlying construct of antisocial behavior. In this case, drinking is not a causal factor in offending, although it may be a facilitating one. Not surprisingly, then, the literature on violence and alcohol use is complex and ambiguous (see especially Collins, 1989) and much beyond the scope of the present review. Nevertheless, it does seem fair to conclude, as does Collins (1989), that very few causal connections have been established. As Collins (1989:63) argues, "Although the weight of the empirical evidence for a relationship between drinking and interpersonal violence is impressive, it probably overstates the importance of drinking as a causal factor in the occurrence of interpersonal violence."

The drug use literature is also complex and beyond the scope of our review (see Tonry and Wilson, 1990). However, it is clear that drug use is related to violent offending (Goldstein, 1989). At least three substantive reasons have been offered to explain the drug-violence connection. The first is a psychopharmacological link in that ingestion of some drugs (e.g., pentachlorophenol, PCP) may have biochemical effects that lead persons to become aggressive and violent. Second, the "economic-compulsive" model suggests that drug users engage in violence (e.g., robbery) to support their drug habits. The third factor relates to the intrinsically violent world of dealing in illicit markets. In other words, violence is systemic to the distribution networks of drug dealing (Goldstein, 1989). Whatever the causal linkage, it is clear that both drug use and excessive alcohol use are correlated with violence.[21]

Presence and Type of Weapon

The role that weapon use plays in either the initiation or the outcome of violent events has been discussed most extensively in the literature on robbery and gun availability (Cook, 1979, 1982, 1987; Block and Block, 1980; Pierce and Bowers, 1981). In robbery incidents, the presence of a gun has been found to be associated with a lower risk of injury, most likely a result of the fact that victims are less likely to resist an offender armed with a gun (Cook, 1987). However, when injury does occur in armed robberies, the extent of injury to the victim is likely to be far more serious (Cook, 1987). Similarly, the proportion of victims reporting some injury in robbery incidents increases as the deadliness of the weapon declines (Cook, 1987).

However, it is unclear whether the presence of a weapon during a robbery incident is more important than the offender's intention to harm. Current research is divided on this issue, primarily because the question of whether or not homicide is the actualization of an individual's intent to kill, or the result of a weapon being present under the right circumstances, is difficult to test (see Fisher, 1976; Cook, 1983). Data necessary for fully testing these assumptions are simply not available. Consequently, we are unable to say if the presence of a particular type of weapon has an independent influence on the outcome of a violent encounter exclusive of an offender's intention to harm.

Victim Resistance

In a related manner, situational analyses have studied the role that victim resistance plays in the outcome of violent events. As is true of situational-level analyses in general, there exist numerous unresolved problems, such as the type of victim behaviors that constitute "resistance." One of the broadest definitions of victim resistance is discussed by Skogan (1981). He argues that perhaps all activities persons undertake to reduce their chances of victimization, such as risk avoidance (e.g., reducing contact with offenders by moving out of high-crime neighborhoods or staying at home) and risk management (e.g., reducing one's chances of victimization given one's spatial contact with offenders), can be considered victim resistance. In other words, at one level of abstraction nearly all activities that persons initiate to decrease the likelihood of victimization (even such as installing alarms and purchasing or carrying firearms) are instances of resistance.

Nevertheless, it has typically been the case that analyses of victim resistance within given violent events focus on whether the victim engaged in "forceful resistance" behaviors (such as fighting) or "nonforceful resistance" behaviors (such as talking to offenders or trying to run away). Block and Skogan (1986) studied these aspects of victims' behaviors during incidents of stranger violence using data from the NCS. Forceful resistance was found to decrease the success of robberies but was related to higher risks of attack and injury (without reductions in success) in cases of rape. Nonforceful resistance also reduced the success of robberies but was unrelated to attack or injury risks in rape incidents. Thus, variations in these findings by crime type make generalizations about the consequences of victim resistance during violent incidents highly problematic. Block and Skogan (1986) discuss several of the limitations of their research, especially the fact that with the data it was impossible to determine whether the victim was even able to resist, given the circumstances of the event, and that the sequencing of events (resistance and outcome) was indeterminable. Ideally, two types of data are needed for adequate assessment of the role of victim resistance: (1) panel data on individuals that temporally distinguish risk management and avoidance techniques from victimization experiences (Skogan, 1981), and (2) detailed event descriptions that also allow temporal distinctions to be made between resistance behaviors and various indicators of outcome (Block and Skogan, 1986).

Felson and Steadman (1983) described the systematic patterns of violent encounters by analyzing 159 reports of homicide and assault incidents among incarcerated offenders. Although traditional limitations of self-report data are of concern here, the authors also point out that the degree of "resistance" or aggression by victims is probably underestimated because cases in which victims were thought to have initially provoked the incident by their own attack would not be included in the sample (i.e., self-defense assaults). Nonetheless, in these assault cases, victim resistance in the form of retaliation was associated with increased aggression on the part of the offender and increased likelihood of death for the victim. Similarly, a victim's use of weapons was also associated with a higher risk of death for the victim. Felson and Steadman point out that in assault cases, the role of victims' behaviors is more complex than the concept of "victim precipitation" (Wolfgang, 1958) suggests.

Presence of Third Parties

The role of third parties in the initiation or outcome of violent events has received only limited attention in the literature.[22] In Felson and Steadman's (1983) analysis, third parties' behaviors were characterized as antagonistic in the majority of violent events. They found that when third parties did attempt to mediate disputes underlying assaults, their efforts typically had no effect on the likelihood that the event would result in a homicide. The lack of research attention to the effects of third parties (including bystanders or witnesses) raises questions concerning the role of "capable guardians" in routine activity explanations of violence. Clearly, this concept means more than the simple presence of a third person—these persons must be willing and able to be guardians. The role of capable guardians becomes even more difficult to ascertain, given that the willingness to become a capable guardian is probably not distributed randomly across situational contexts. For example, assault incidents occurring in bars may be aggravated by the presence of persons who are intoxicated, or they may be aggravated for reasons having to do with the fact that people are not randomly drawn into bars, especially bars located in well-known "hot spots" of predatory crime (cf. Sherman et al., 1989). Consequently, our knowledge about the role of third parties in violent encounters is very limited; in some instances their presence might diffuse the intensity of encounters (e.g., by trying to break up a fight or by calling the police), whereas in other cases they may increase the severity of the outcome (by encouraging escalating actions, providing weapons, and becoming physically involved). Undoubtedly, more research is required to provide even basic descriptions of the role of third parties across situational contexts before their relative effects on violent encounters can be assessed.

Situational and Ecological Context

A final key question concerns the role of ecological proximity to crime and social disorder in predicting victimization risk. A recent study by Fagan et al. (1987:588) suggests that the correlation between victimization and offending may be spurious—a function of the areas in which victims and offenders live. Their basic argument is that the link between victimization and offending may be confounded "by the convergence of correlates of criminal events and offenders in urban areas." For example, living in low-income urban areas where the offender pool is large may increase victimization risk, regardless of one's individual propensity to engage in crime. Although they did not examine the independent effect of offending on victimization, Fagan et al. (1987) found that violent victimization was significantly related to drinking problems, peer delinquency, and neighborhood family violence. This study is important in that it suggests the need to simultaneously account for the social ecology of criminal behavior. In particular, it suggests that controlling for ecological proximity to violence may reduce the individual-level relationship between offending and victimization.

The related "principle of homogamy" in lifestyle theory states that persons are more likely to be victimized when they disproportionately associate with or come in contact with offenders. Although this principle has typically been conceived in individual-level terms, it has clear relevance at the community level. As Garofalo (1987) posits in a recent revision of lifestyle theory, the structural constraint of residential proximity to crime has a direct effect on victimization that is unmediated by individual lifestyle. Specifically, Garofalo (1987) argues that constraints of the economic system and especially housing markets dictate in large part where people live. Although individual lifestyles may thus predict variations in victimization within a given environment, the base level of risk that they face is "heightened by sheer proximity to—and hence exposure to—potential offenders" (Garofalo, 1987:38).

It follows that multilevel models including both demographic and lifestyle measures along with ecological and/or situational measures of the extent of crime can provide further insights into the risk factors for violent victimization. Research by Sampson and Lauritsen (1990) utilizing British Crime Survey data found support for this notion. When an ecological measure of neighborhood violence was included in their models of individual-level personal victimization, area violence rate was positively associated with risk. This effect was significant and independent of traditional demographic factors, lifestyle and routine activities measures, and self-reported involvement in deviance and offending. It should be noted, though, that the latter effects were not diminished by controls for proximity to violence.

In addition, Sampson (1987b) has shown that the risk of violent victimization by strangers is significantly and positively related to neighborhood levels of family disruption, percent of single-person households, and residential mobility, when age, marital status, sex, and neighborhood socioeconomic status and unemployment rates are controlled. Thus, regardless of key individual-level factors emphasized in past research, the data suggest that community (and presumably situational) contexts of anonymity and its correlates (e.g., prevalence of single-person households, mobility) directly increase the risk of stranger violence (see also Kennedy and Forde, 1990).

SUMMARY

The data necessary for assessing independent situational-level causes of violent encounters not only are unavailable but would be difficult to conceptualize given the opportunity. Most situational-level data contain only incident-based cases of violence and hence constitute conditional risks; that is, existing samples do not include encounters that were successful in the avoidance of violence. Consequently, situations with similar characteristics but different outcomes (i.e., violence and nonviolence) are difficult to compare. In other words, unconditional situational data including "nonincidents" are not collected often, nor is there a substantive literature that might guide such an endeavor. Thus, we are prevented from examining how variations across situations are causally related to the probability that violent events will occur.

Moreover, our review of situational-level factors demonstrates that victimization and offending are tightly connected and need to be examined in a more unified perspective that takes account of the structural properties of social environments (see also Reiss, 1986a). Accordingly, we now turn to an explicit focus on the community structure of both violent offending and victimization. We discuss later the features of research designs that might be able to address some of the problems discussed throughout this section.

COMMUNITY-LEVEL SOURCES OF VIOLENCE

The purpose of this section is to review empirical research on the community-level correlates of criminal violence. A subsequent section reviews research conducted at the metropolitan (e.g., city, county, standard metropolitan statistical area [SMSA]) level. As noted in the introduction, the goal of macrolevel research is not to explain individual involvement in criminal behavior but to isolate characteristics of communities, cities, or societies that lead to high rates of criminality (Short, 1985; Byrne and Sampson, 1986). Within this framework we generally place more weight on, and therefore begin with, studies that examine neighborhoods or other intraurban units of analysis. Cities and metropolitan areas are large, highly aggregated, and heterogeneous units with politically defined and hence artificial ecological boundaries. Although intraurban units of analysis (e.g., census tracts, wards, block groups) are imperfect proxies for the concept of local community, they generally possess more ecological integrity (e.g., natural boundaries, social homogeneity) than cities or SMSAs and are more closely linked to the causal processes assumed to underlie the etiology of crime (see also Taylor et al., 1984; Bursik, 1988).

Contemporary research on communities and crime owes an intellectual debt to the work of nineteenth century European ecologists and social statisticians. Yet as Levin and Lindesmith (1937:801) have correctly observed, social scientists often "attribute greater originality to contemporary studies and less value to the old than is actually warranted by the facts in the case." Although space limitations preclude detailed review, the facts suggest that consideration of community-level sources of violence should begin with recognition of the original contributions of nineteenth century researchers such as Guerry, Quetelet, Rawson, and Mayhew (for a review see Morris, 1958; Levin and Lindesmith, 1937). Their ecological, or community-level, perspective on crime united three major concerns that contrast with the individual-level emphasis prevalent in modern criminology (Morris, 1958:42):

(1) a primary interest in crime as a social or collective phenomenon, of which individual behavior is a component, rather than in motivation of crime in the individual,

(2) the quantification and statistical analysis of data relating to crime and criminals to illustrate variations in time and place, and

(3) a stress on the role of objective social-structural factors

such as poverty and density of population in determining and perpetuating crime.

THE SHAW AND MCKAY MODEL

A community-level orientation to criminological research later came to fruition in the United States with the twentieth century work of Shaw and McKay (1942, 1969). Indeed, although their focus was primarily on delinquency, the research of Shaw and McKay forms the infrastructure for modern American studies of the ecology of violence. As Bursik (1988) and others (e.g., see Short, 1969; Morris, 1970) have argued, few works in criminology have had more influence than *Juvenile Delinquency and Urban Areas* (Shaw and McKay, 1942). In this classic work, Shaw and McKay argue that three structural factors—low economic status, ethnic heterogeneity, and residential mobility—led to the disruption of local community social organization, which in turn accounted for variations in rates of crime and delinquency (see also Shaw et al., 1929; Kornhauser, 1978; Sampson and Groves, 1989).

The origins of this thesis can be traced to Clifford Shaw's early work in Chicago (see Shaw et al., 1929), where he was one of the first American researchers to demonstrate the marked variations in delinquency rates within a major city. Shaw and his later associate McKay (1931) showed that the highest delinquency offender rates in Chicago (based on referrals to the Cook County Juvenile Court) were located in deteriorated zones in transition next to the central business and industrial district. Rates of delinquency were found to decrease as distance from the center of the city increased; the exceptions were areas also characterized by industry and commerce. These findings led Shaw and McKay to conclude that delinquent behavior was closely related to the growth processes of the city as outlined by Park and Burgess (e.g., Park et al., 1925). It should be noted that the relationship between community factors and delinquency was substantial. For example, Shaw and McKay (1969) reported a correlation of .89 between delinquency rates in Chicago's community areas and a proxy measure of poverty—the percentage of families on relief. The correlation between population change and delinquency was .69, and the correlation of heterogeneity (percentage foreign born and Negro heads of families) was .60 (Shaw and McKay, 1969:144-153).

Shaw and McKay (1942) also demonstrated that high rates of delinquency persisted in certain areas over many years, regardless of population turnover. More than any other, this finding led them to reject individualistic explanations of delinquency and focus instead on the processes by which delinquent and criminal patterns of behavior were transmitted across generations in areas of social disorganization and weak social controls (1942:320). Shaw and McKay then located the causes of crime in the structural context of local communities and changes taking place in the wider urban ecology. From this viewpoint the "ecological fallacy"—inferring individual-level relations based on aggregate data—is not at issue because the unit of causal explanation and analysis is the community itself.

Most of the ecological research initially spawned by Shaw and McKay was concerned with economic status and its relationship to delinquency rates. For example, Lander (1954), Bordua (1958), and Chilton (1964) each attempted to replicate the basic Shaw and McKay model. These studies are not reviewed here because they focused on delinquency rates dominated by relatively minor offenses (e.g., larceny, vandalism) and hence are of indirect relevance to our focus on violence. Suffice it to note, however, that although discrepancies arose in multivariate analyses, this body of research essentially confirmed Shaw and McKay's emphasis on economic status as a correlate of delinquency. As Gordon (1967:943) summarized the works of Lander, Bordua, and Chilton, "There should no longer be any question about the ecological relations between . . . SES [socioeconomic status] and official delinquency rates."

Despite the major focus on nondifferentiated delinquency rates in ecological research, three studies in the mid-twentieth century did underscore the role of community-level socioeconomic status in delineating patterns of violence. Bullock (1955) studied the ecological distribution of homicide occurrence rates among the census tracts of Houston between 1945 and 1949. Like Shaw and McKay, but focusing on more serious crime, Bullock demonstrated that homicides were disproportionately concentrated in areas characterized by physical deterioration of dwelling units, unemployment, low economic status, and low median education. For example, Bullock (1955:569) reported that homicide rates were correlated −.60 and .64 with percent educated and percent unemployed, respectively. Schmid (1960) correlated offense-specific crime variables, including robbery, with numerous social structural variables for census tracts in Seattle. Schmid (1960:531) found that the median income of an area had a significant inverse relationship to both street robbery (−.53) and business robbery (−.32). Bensing and Schroeder (1960) empirically documented that homicides were disproportionately concentrated in a small number of areas in Cleveland. They described the high-rate areas as those with the "lowest socioeconomic status, most undesirable neighborhood conditions, greatest financial dependency, the most acute problems of space and crowded housing conditions, the least stability of the population, the greatest social maladjustment and family and individual adjustment problems, and the poorest health" (Bensing and Schroeder, 1960:184). Their description of Cleveland homicide areas reads like Shaw and McKay's account of delinquency areas in Chicago some 30 years earlier.

RECENT COMMUNITY-LEVEL STUDIES OF VIOLENCE

After a hiatus in the 1960s, the past two decades have witnessed a sharp increase in research focused on variations in urban crime rates (e.g., see the reviews in Byrne and Sampson, 1986; Bursik, 1988). Like Shaw and McKay, the general thesis of this social-ecological branch of research is that characteristics of ecological units have social effects on crime that are not solely attributable to the characteristics of individuals. However, this recent upsurge in research has departed from the Shaw and McKay model in at least four important respects. First, recent research has been concerned primarily not with delinquency rates but with variations in criminal violence—especially homicide. Second, the vast majority of recent research has been conducted not at the local community level but at much higher levels of aggregation such as the city, county, or SMSA. Third, the list of variables considered has been expanded much beyond poverty, racial composition, and mobility to include such factors as inequality, density, housing structure, family disruption, region, and opportunities for crime.

Fourth, there has been much more concern in recent years with the limitations of official data. Note that all of the studies discussed thus far, including Shaw and McKay, utilized officially based crime rates. The general criticisms of official data are well known and need not be repeated here. Suffice it to say that the major issue with respect to community research concerns the extent to which official crime rates reflect ecological biases in official reaction to illegal behavior (Hagan et al., 1978; Smith, 1986; Sampson, 1986c). In particular, conflict theorists argue that lower-status communities may have higher delinquency rates in part because police concentration is greater there compared to higher-status areas. The type of community in which police-citizen encounters occur may also influence the actions taken by police (Hagan et al., 1978; Sampson, 1986c). In support of this idea, Smith (1986) demonstrated that the probability of arrest across communities declines substantially with increasing socioeconomic status—independent of crime type and other correlates of arrest decisions. The reliance on official data thus raises the question of whether Shaw and McKay's findings, and the host of census-based studies following them, are in part artifactual.

The official data problem has been addressed in two basic ways. The most common has been to limit the domain of inquiry to serious crimes such as homicide and robbery where police biases are thought to be minimal. A wide-ranging body of research shows that, for serious crimes, police bias and underreporting are very small and/or unrelated to individual-level and community variables of interest (for a detailed review see Gove et al., 1985). Second, in the last 20 years self-report and victimization data have been brought to bear on the validity of official statistics (see Hindelang et al., 1981). Although self-report studies have generally been either national in scope (e.g., Elliott and Ageton, 1980) or specific to one locale (e.g., Hindelang et al., 1981), between-community estimates of crime rates based on self-reports have been utilized in a few studies. More common has been the use of victimization surveys to provide an alternative window from which to view the ecological correlates of violent crimes such as assault and robbery. For example, the National Crime Survey has been utilized to estimate both city- and neighborhood-level correlates of violent victimization.

Parenthetically, it should be noted that the use of both offenses officially reported to the police and victimizations reported to survey interviewers seems to imply a focus on crime *occurrence* rates rather than *offender* rates as employed by Shaw and McKay (1942). A crucial point, however, is that for serious personal offenses such as homicide and aggravated assault, offenders tend to commit offenses relatively close to their homes (Bensing and Schroeder, 1960; Pittman and Handy, 1964; Pokorny, 1965; Pyle et al., 1974; Brantingham and Brantingham, 1984). For all intents and purposes, then, victimization occurrence rates and official offense or arrest rates, particularly at the city level, are tapping the same general dimension with respect to violence. In fact, as we shall see, a general convergence of community-level findings between official police statistics and victimization data has been achieved.

Poverty and Deprivation

Not surprisingly, a large proportion of recent neighborhood-based studies of violence have emphasized dimensions of poverty and economic inequality. Unlike Shaw and McKay, however, the majority of these have employed multivariate methods that seek to estimate the effects of economic structure *independent* of other factors such as population composition. For example, Block (1979) examined officially recorded homicides, aggravated assaults, and robberies that occurred in the mid-1970s in 76 community areas of Chicago. The most important predictor of variations in violent crime across Chicago areas, controlling for other factors, was "proximity," defined by Block (1979:48) as the ratio of families earning more than three times the poverty level to those earning 75 percent or less. He argued that although this can be viewed as an income disparity measure, "it can be more properly thought of as an indicator of spatial proximity of middle class and poor" (Block, 1979:48). He also showed that homicide rates were significantly and substantially correlated not only with proximity (.75), but also with percent in poverty (.64), percent black (.69), and percent female-headed families (.63). Correlations identical in sign and virtually in magnitude were also present for robbery and aggravated assault. The significant predictors of variations in violent crime rates across community areas in Chicago uncovered by Block (1979) were thus quite similar to the delinquency correlates found by Shaw and McKay some 50 years earlier in the same city.

Two studies of violent personal crimes in Houston published in the 1970s mirrored the findings of Bullock in that city in the 1940s. Specifically, both Beasley and Antunes (1974) and Mladenka and Hill found (1976) substantial correlations between violent crime and poverty indicators across 20 police districts. For Beasley and Antunes, the correlation was −.78 for median income, whereas in Mladenka and Hill the correlation between poverty and violence was .93. Both studies also reported large and significant correlations between violent crime and the factors of density (.68 and .70) and percent black (.74 and .81). Again, the general similarity to Shaw and McKay is apparent: violent crime rates were disproportionately concentrated in high-density poverty areas characterized by a large proportion of minorities.

The 1980s produced several studies of homicide that applied multivariate techniques to assess the independent effects of local community structure. Another Chicago-based study examined community-level variations in gang homicide rates as measured by the Gang Crime Unit of the Chicago Police Department (Curry and Spergel, 1988). The main focus was on "poverty," which was measured via a principal components factor scoring of percent population below the poverty level, unemployment rate, and mortgage investment (1988:393). When percent black, percent Hispanic, and poverty were simultaneously entered into a multiple regression equation, poverty had significant positive effects on gang homicide rates for 1978-1981 and 1982-1985. In particular, their data showed that the standardized coefficient reflecting the direct effect of poverty on 1978-1981 gang homicide rates was .42, with controlling for percent black and percent Hispanic. Poverty also had the largest effect on *change* in homicide rates from 1978-1981 to 1982-1985. Curry and Spergel concluded that gang homicide rates are directly related to poverty (1988:395).

Messner and Tardiff (1986) analyzed homicide rates across 26 neighborhoods in Manhattan in 1981. They also found a strong positive relationship between poverty and homicide ($r = .55$, $p < .01$), but the multivariate results were somewhat ambiguous. Poverty correlated so highly with percent black (.72) that the former had a significant effect on homicide only when percent black was not in the model. In addition, the Gini index of inequality had an insignificant effect on homicide, whereas the most consistent and strongest correlate of homicide in Manhattan was the divorce rate. Messner and Tardiff (1986:312) concluded that it is not relative deprivation generated by inequality that is conducive to violence, but absolute level of poverty in conjunction with pervasive levels of marital dissolution.

Studies utilizing victimization rates have also questioned the strength of the effects of poverty and relative inequalities in income on violence once other factors are controlled. In a series of studies, Sampson (1983, 1985a, 1986a) utilized Bureau of the Census neighborhood characteristics data in conjunction with victimization survey data from the NCS. Each household record in the NCS sample contained information on the social-demographic characteristics of the neighborhood in which the household was sampled. Results derived from analysis of variance showed that, overall, poverty and inequality exhibited weak or insignificant effects on violence (aggravated assault, simple assault, rape, and robbery) compared to other neighborhood characteristics such as density of housing (percent units in structures of five or more units), residential mobility (percent of persons 5 years of age and older living in a different house than they did five years earlier), and family structure (percent female headed families and percent divorced/ separated). For example, income inequality had insignificant effects on violent victimization in urban areas once racial composition and divorce rates were controlled (Sampson, 1985a, 1986a). The exception was the consistent positive effect of neighborhood unemployment rates on violent victimization, especially for residents of central cities (Sampson, 1986a:36).

A similar pattern was found in another victimization study where Smith and Jarjoura (1988) analyzed data collected from interviews with random samples of 11,419 individuals residing in 57 neighborhoods in Rochester (New York), Tampa-St. Petersburg (Florida), and St. Louis. Interviews were conducted with approximately 200 persons in each neighborhood, and Smith and Jarjoura aggregated data on victimizations and social characteristics to produce a data file consisting of 57 neighborhoods. The major dependent variable was rate of violent crime—robberies and assaults per 1,000 residents. The independent variables included percentage low income, residential mobility, racial heterogeneity, population density, percentage aged 12-20, percent single-parent households, percentage nonwhite, and percent living alone. In an evaluation of Shaw and McKay's (1942) basic model, Smith and Jarjoura (1988) discovered a significant interaction between mobility and low income in explaining violence. Specifically, mobility was positively associated with violent crime rates in poorer neighborhoods but not in more affluent areas. The main effects of mobility and income were not significant when the interaction term was in the model. Smith and Jarjoura (1988) concluded that communities characterized by rapid population turnover and high levels of poverty have significantly higher violent crime rates than either mobile areas that are more affluent or poor areas that are stable.

The role of poverty and economic status in understanding violence at the community level is thus not altogether clear. On the one hand, it is significantly associated in almost all studies of violence. On the other hand, differences emerge in the conclusions drawn regarding the independent role that poverty plays in explaining violence. The data in several of the studies suggest that the effect of poverty is either weak or conditional on community contexts of mobility and change. This latter point is crucial, and we thus turn to the second major factor highlighted by Shaw and McKay that may help to shed light on the meaning of poverty in an ecological context.

Mobility and Community Change

One of the fundamental claims made by Shaw and McKay (1942) was that population change and turnover had negative consequences for the social control of delinquency. In particular, a high rate of mobility, especially in an area of decreasing population, was inferred to foster institutional disruption and weakened community controls (Kornhauser, 1978). The existing research on mobility has not been as extensive as that on economic status, but it has been revealing. For example, Block's (1979:50) study of Chicago's community areas revealed consistent negative correlations between percent neighborhood stability and the violent crimes of homicide, robbery, and aggravated assault (−.47, −.50, and −.40, respectively; all $p < .05$). Neighborhood stability also had significant negative effects on homicide even after proximity was controlled (1979:53).

As introduced above, Smith and Jarjoura (1988) found a significant positive effect of neighborhood mobility (percentage of households occupied by persons who lived there less than three years) on rates of violence only in low-income neighborhoods. In fact, this interaction of mobility and poverty was the largest determinant of violence. Although neither mobility nor income had significant main effects, the ratio of coefficient to standard error for the mobility-income interaction was 3.44; by contrast, the other predictors of violence all had ratios less than 3 (Smith and Jarjoura, 1988:41). In community contexts of poverty at least, mobility appeared to have important consequences for violence. Notably, the mobility-income interaction did not emerge for property crime, because mobility had a direct positive effect on burglary rates (Smith and Jarjoura, 1988:44).

Although no consistent interactions were uncovered, victimization data from the National Crime Survey show that residential mobility has significant positive effects on rates of violent victimization (Sampson, 1985a:29-30). After controlling for other neighborhood-level correlates of victimization, parameter estimates from analysis of variance models revealed that violent victimization rates for residents of high-mobility neighborhoods were double those of residents in low-mobility areas (Sampson 1985a:30; 1986a:44).

There are, however, conceptual and methodological problems that plague mobility research. As Kornhauser (1978:107) has noted, mobility indices such as Shaw and McKay's (1942) were ill designed to measure mobility; instead they were chosen to support the contention that delinquency was linked to the disturbances in social organization engendered by city growth. Perhaps more crucially, an essential feature of the ecological model is a focus on neighborhood *change* over time and its consequences for crime (Bursik, 1988). Thus, although mobility rates of an area have been linked to delinquency rates in cross-sectional designs, until recently few studies in the Shaw and McKay tradition have actually investigated processes of neighborhood change in a longitudinal perspective (but see Bursik and Webb, 1982; Heitgerd and Bursik, 1987, with regard to delinquency rates).

Recognizing this gap, Taylor and Covington (1988) have recently published an important study of neighborhood changes in ecology and violence. Their research investigated changes in community structure and the violent crimes of murder and aggravated assault for 277 Baltimore city neighborhoods in the period 1970-1980. The two dimensions of ecological change examined were economic status and family status. Their thesis was that neighborhoods experiencing declines in relative economic status and stability should also experience increases in relative violence (Taylor and Covington, 1988:561). In support of this notion, their findings showed that increasing entrenchment of the urban "underclass" in the form of increasing poverty and minority concentration was linked to increases in violence. In other words, in the city's lower-income neighborhoods that changed for the worse in terms of an increasing concentration of the ghetto poor, violence rose sharply. Gentrifying neighborhoods that were experiencing rapid change in terms of unexpected increases in owner-occupied housing, one-unit structures, and changes in family status also experienced large increases in violence (see also McDonald, 1986; Covington and Taylor, 1989). Taylor and Covington interpret this to mean that processes of change lead to increasing violence. As they summarized the pattern of change in Baltimore in the 1970s (Taylor and Covington, 1988:583):

> [T]he two most major changes experienced by urban neighborhoods were the further solidification of underclass neighborhoods and the appearance of gentrifying neighborhoods. . . . In Baltimore, both of these changes were associated with unexpected increases in relative violence levels. The patterning of ecological change parameters with violence changes suggested that in underclass neighborhoods the violence was related to increased relative deprivation, and that in gentrifying neighborhoods the violence was linked to increasing social disorganization.

Thus, changes in both relative economic status and relative stability (in terms of housing, family) were linked to unexpected increases in violence.

In short, extant research suggests that rates of mobility and neighborhood change are related to community violence. However, what seems most salient about change is its linkage to the downward spiral of a neighborhood becoming increasingly poor (see also Schuerman and Kobrin, 1986; Wilson, 1987; Rose and McClain, 1990). The notion of an interaction between underclass entrenchment and residential change is discussed later in more detail, as are problems with causal interpretations of this phenomenon.

Heterogeneity and Racial Composition

Racial and ethnic heterogeneity has always been accorded a central role in Shaw and McKay's research (e.g., see Kornhauser, 1978), even though in their writings Shaw and McKay (1942:153) referred mostly to population composition. This is not surprising because their data showed that delinquency rates were higher in predominantly black/foreign-born areas than in areas of maximum heterogeneity. For example, Shaw and McKay's (1942:155) data indicate that the delinquency rate in areas with more than 70 percent black/foreign born (8.2) was more than double the rate (3.9) in areas of maximum heterogeneity (e.g., 50-59% black/foreign born).

Similarly, most research on violence has examined racial composition—usually percent black—rather than racial heterogeneity per se. The general and consistent finding has been that percentage black is positively and strongly related to rates of violence. For example, Block (1979) showed that homicide rates were significantly and substantially related to percent black ($r = .69$), as did Beasley and Antunes (1974), Mladenka and Hill (1976), Messner and Tardiff (1986), Sampson (1985a), Roncek (1981), and Smith and Jarjoura (1988). The dispute arises over the strength of the direct effect of racial composition on violence. Some report that the percent black effect remains strong even after controlling for other factors (e.g., Beasley and Antunes, 1974; Roncek, 1981), whereas others find a sharply attenuated effect of race once other factors are controlled (e.g., Block, 1979; Curry and Spergel, 1988; Sampson, 1985a; Messner and Tardiff, 1986).

An exception to the reliance on composition measures is Smith and Jarjoura (1988), who explored a probability-based measure of racial heterogeneity—the probability that two randomly selected individuals from a neighborhood will be members of different racial groups. This measure of heterogeneity was significantly correlated (r = .43) with violent crime rates (1988:39) and percent nonwhite (r = .59), but despite significant effects on violent crime independent of mobility and poverty in multivariate regressions, racial heterogeneity was rendered insignificant once family structure (percent single-parent families) was controlled.

Thus, although there is little question that percent black and heterogeneity are strong and pervasive correlates of violent crime rates, there is reason to doubt whether racial composition or heterogeneity has unique explanatory power. Additionally, the theoretical status of racial composition at the community level is questionable. As reviewed earlier, race is a salient individual-level predictor of both violent offending and victimization, especially for robbery and murder. To the extent that community-level variations between racial composition and violent crime merely reflect the aggregation of individual-level effects, the value of community-level research is called into question. The general problem of cross-level misspecification is discussed in more detail in a later section dealing with problems of interpretation.

Housing and Population Density

Although infrequently studied, recent research by Roncek and colleagues (Roncek, 1981; Roncek et al., 1981; Roncek and Faggiani, 1986) has highlighted the potential role that the physical structure and density of housing may play in understanding patterns of violent crime. Roncek (1981) found that the percentage of units in multiunit housing structures was a consistent and rather strong predictor of block-level variations in violent crime in Cleveland and San Diego. Land area in acres, population size, and the percent of primary- individual households also had significant and substantively important effects on violence, despite age and race composition. As Roncek (1981:88) summarizes, "The most dangerous city blocks are relatively large in population and area with high concentrations of primary individuals and apartment housing." This general pattern was confirmed in other model specifications, where Roncek also found that proximity to public housing projects and public high schools had significant positive effects on violence (Roncek et al., 1981; Roncek and Faggiani, 1986). In a similar vein, Schuerman and Kobrin (1986:97) found that increases in multiplex dwellings and renter-occupied housing were major predictors of increases in crime rates in Los Angeles neighborhoods.

Roncek (1981:88) argues that such findings are consistent with linking features of residential areas to crime through the concept of anonymity: primary-individual households and high proportions of multiunit structures are posited to increase levels of anonymity. For example, as the number of households sharing common living space increases, residents are less able to recognize their neighbors, to be concerned for them, or to engage in guardianship behaviors (Roncek, 1981:88). This notion is derived in part from the defensible space notion that characteristics of the built environment influence the spatial distribution of crime (for a review of this literature, see Taylor and Gottfredson, 1986).

Similar arguments were supported in studies of violent victimization using neighborhood characteristics data in conjunction with the NCS. Sampson (1983:282-283) reported a strong positive influence of the percentage of housing units in structures of five or more units on rates of robbery and assault victimization—regardless of individual risk factors such as age, race, and sex. For example, the ratios of robbery victimization rates for those living in high-density neighborhoods versus those living in low-density neighborhoods were 2.6, 3.6, 3.6, 3.8, 3.5, 3.4, 3.2, and 3.4 for white male adults, white male juveniles, white female juveniles, white female adults, black male adults, black male juveniles, black female juveniles, and black female adults, respectively. Thus it can be seen that rates of victimization are two to three times higher in high-density neighborhoods *regardless* of compositional factors such as age, race, and sex. Moreover, the effect of density was independent of other key neighborhood characteristics (see Sampson, 1985a).

Finally, several studies report a significant and large association between population density and violent crime. The average correlation across neighborhoods between population density and violent crime rates is .68 in the studies of Beasley and Antunes (1974), Mladenka and Hill (1976), and Smith and Jarjoura (1988). In the latter multivariate study, density also had one of the strongest effects on violent crime, despite controlling for a host of social and economic variables. Characteristics of the physical environment related to housing and population density thus appear to increase the level of violent crime regardless of compositional factors.[23]

Family Structure

Although largely ignored in early ecological research, several recent studies have turned to examination of the community-level consequences of family structure. One reason is that high levels of family "disruption" (e.g., divorce rates, female-headed families with children) may facilitate crime by decreasing community networks of informal social control. Examples of informal social control include neighbors' taking note of or questioning strangers, watching over each others' property, assuming responsibility for supervision of general youth activities (e.g., teenage peer groups), and intervening in local disturbances (e.g., see Taylor et al., 1984; Sampson, 1986a; Sampson and Groves, 1989). Note that this conceptualization does *not* necessarily require that it is the children of divorced or separated parents that are engaging in crime. Rather, the idea is that family disruption can have community-wide contextual properties. For instance, youth in stable family areas, regardless of their own family situation, probably have more controls placed on their leisure time activities, particularly with peer groups (Anderson, 1990:91). A well-documented fact in prior research is that delinquency is a group phenomenon (Zimring, 1981); hence neighborhood family structure is likely to be important in determining the extent to which neighborhood youth are provided the opportunities to form a peer-control system free of the supervision or knowledge of adults (Reiss, 1986a).

Felson and Cohen (1980; see also Cohen and Felson, 1979) also note the potential influence of family structure not just on the control of offenders, but on the control of criminal targets and opportunities. They argue that traditional theories of crime emphasize the criminal motivation of offenders without considering adequately the circumstances in which criminal acts occur. Notably, predatory crime requires the convergence in time and space of offenders, suitable targets, and the absence of effective guardianship. The spatial and temporal structure of family activity patterns plays an important role in determining the rate at which motivated offenders encounter criminal opportunities. Compared to married couples, for example, single and divorced persons may be especially vulnerable to personal crimes of violence (e.g., rape, robbery) as a result of decreased guardianship both at home and in public. In support of this idea, Felson and Cohen (1980) demonstrated that primary-individual households had a significant and positive effect on crime trends in the United States in the period 1950-1972, independent of factors presumed to reflect the supply of motivated offenders (e.g., unemployment, youthful age).

The salience of family structure has been supported at the neighborhood level with respect to violence. Studies reporting a large and positive relationship between measures of family disruption (usually percent female-headed families or divorce rate) and rates of violence include Block (1979), Messner and Tardiff (1986), Sampson (1985a, 1986a), Roncek (1981), Smith and Jarjoura (1988), and Schuerman and Kobrin (1986). What is especially striking is the strength of family disruption in predicting violence in multivariate models. For example, Sampson (1985a, 1986a) found that rates of violent victimization were two to three times higher among residents of neighborhoods with high levels of family disruption compared to low levels, regardless of alternative predictors such as percent black and poverty. In fact, the percentage of female-headed families helped to explain in large part the relationship between percent black and crime. Namely, percent black and percent female-headed families were positively and significantly related; however, when percent female-headed families was controlled, percent black was not significantly related to violent victimization (1985a:27).

Similarly, Messner and Tardiff (1986) found that when percent divorced and percent poverty were controlled, the relationship between percent black and homicide rates was insignificant. Smith and Jarjoura (1988) report that family structure, especially percent single-parent families, helps account for the association between race and violent crime at the community level; racial composition was not significantly related to violent crime in multivariate models once percent single-parent families had been included.

Therefore, it seems that recent emphases on family structure are based on consistent empirical support. Perhaps more to the point, this correlate does not appear to be the result of other factors we typically associate with violence such as poverty, race, and density. Rather, the effect of family disruption is usually independent and large. We now explicate the potential intervening constructs that may help to explain *why* family disruption and other community structural factors are related to violence.

Community Social Disorganization

A theoretical focus on community social organization, or the lack thereof, provides a useful integrating strategy for understanding the mediating social processes that underlie community-level effects on violence. In general, community social organization may be conceptualized as the ability of a community structure to realize the common values of its residents and maintain effective social controls (Kornhauser 1978:120; Bursik, 1988; Sampson, 1988). The *structural* dimensions of community social organization can be measured in terms of the prevalence and interdependence of social networks in a community—both informal (e.g., density of friendship ties and acquaintanceship) and formal (e.g., organizational participation)—and in the span of collective supervision that the community directs toward local problems (Shaw and McKay, 1942; Kornhauser, 1978; Sampson and Groves, 1989). This approach is grounded in what can be termed the systemic model (Sampson, 1988), in which the local community is viewed as a complex system of friendship and kinship networks, and formal and informal associational ties rooted in family life and ongoing socialization processes. Social organization and social disorganization are thus seen as different ends of the same continuum with respect to systemic networks of community social control. As Bursik (1988) notes, when formulated in this way, social disorganization is clearly separable not only from the processes that may lead to it (e.g, poverty, mobility), but also from the degree of criminal behavior that may be a result.

A major dimension of social disorganization relevant to violence is the ability of a community to supervise and control *teenage peer-groups*—especially gangs (Sampson and Groves, 1989). It is well documented that delinquency is primarily a group phenomenon (Shaw and McKay, 1942; Thrasher, 1963; Short and Strodtbeck, 1965; Zimring, 1981; Reiss, 1986b) and hence that the capacity of the community to control group-level dynamics is a key theoretical mechanism linking community characteristics with crime. Indeed, a central fact underlying Shaw and McKay's research was that the majority of gangs developed from the unsupervised, spontaneous play group (Thrasher, 1963:25). Shaw and McKay (1969) thus argued that residents of cohesive communities were better able to control the teenage behaviors that set the context for group-related violence (see also Thrasher, 1963:26-27; Short, 1963:xxiv; Short and Strodtbeck, 1965; Anderson, 1990). Examples of such controls include supervision of leisure-time youth activities, intervention in street-corner congregation (Maccoby et al., 1958; Thrasher, 1963:339; Shaw and McKay, 1969:176-185), and challenging youth "who seem to be up to no good" (Taylor et al., 1984:326; Skogan, 1986:217). Socially disorganized communities with extensive street-corner peer groups are also expected to have higher rates of adult violence, especially among younger adults who still have ties to youth gangs (Thrasher, 1963).

A second dimension of community social organization involves *local friendship networks* and *the density of acquaintanceship*. Systemic theory holds that locality-based social networks constitute the core social fabric of human-ecological communities (Sampson, 1988). When residents form local social ties, their capacity for community social control is increased because they are better able to recognize strangers and are more apt to engage in guardianship behavior against victimization (Taylor et al., 1984:307; Skogan 1986:216). Also, the greater the density of friendship networks among persons in a community, the greater is the constraint on deviant behavior within the purview of the social network (Krohn, 1986:84).

A third component of social organization is the rate of *local participation in formal and voluntary organizations.* Community organizations reflect the structural embodiment of local community solidarity (Hunter, 1974:191), and with this in mind, Kornhauser (1978:79) argues that institutional instability and the isolation of community institutions are key factors underlying the structural dimension of social disorganization. Her argument, in short, is that when links between community institutions are weak the capacity of a community to defend its local interests is weakened. Shaw and McKay (1969:184-185), and more recently Taylor et al. (1984) and Simcha-Fagan and Schwartz (1986:688), have also argued that a weak community organizational base serves to attenuate local social control functions regarding youth.

It is difficult to study social disorganization directly, but at least two recent studies provide empirical support for the theory in terms of its structural dimensions. First, Taylor et al. (1984) examined variations in violent crime (mugging, assault, murder, rape, shooting, and yoking) across 63 street blocks in Baltimore in 1978. Based on interviews with 687 household respondents, Taylor et al. (1984:316) constructed block-level measures of what they termed social ties and near-home responsibilities. The former measured the proportion of respondents who belonged to an organization to which co-residents also belonged, whereas the latter measure tapped the extent to which respondents felt responsible for what happened in the area surrounding their home. Both of these dimensions of informal social control were significantly related to community-level variations in violence. Specifically, social organizational ties and near-home social control had standardized effects on violence rates of −.20 and −.24, respectively (Taylor, 1984:320). Taylor et al. (1984:317) also showed that blocks with higher neighborhood identification (and presumably greater social cohesion), as indicated by the proportion of residents who were able to provide a neighborhood name, had significantly lower rates of violence. These results support the social disorganization hypothesis that levels of organizational participation and informal social control (especially of local activities by neighborhood youth) inhibit community-level rates of violence (see also Taylor et al., 1984:326).

Second, Sampson and Groves (1989) analyzed the British Crime Survey (BCS), a nationwide survey of England and Wales conducted in 1982 and 1984. Sampling procedures resulted in the proportionate selection of 60 addresses within each of more than 200 ecological areas in Great Britain. The sample drawn from each geographical unit was representative of a relatively small, homogeneous locality that reasonably approximated the concept of "local community." Survey-generated responses were aggregated in each of the 238 areas, and structural variables were constructed (e.g., means, percentages). Sampson and Groves (1989:789) report that the prevalence of unsupervised peer groups in a community had the largest overall effect on rates of victimization by mugging/street robbery and stranger violence in Great Britain (betas = .35 and .19, respectively) in 1982. Local friendship networks had a significant and substantial negative effect (beta = −.19) on robbery, whereas rates of organizational participation had significant inverse effects on both robbery and stranger violence (Sampson and Groves, 1989:789). Moreover, the largest overall effect on personal violence *offending* rates came from unsupervised peer groups (Sampson and Groves, 1989:793). Unsupervised peer groups also had large and substantial positive effects on robbery and assault in the 1984 BCS, whereas local friendship networks again had significant inverse effects (Sampson and Groves, 1989:798).

These empirical results suggest that communities characterized by sparse friendship networks, unsupervised teenage peer groups, and low organizational participation had disproportionately high rates of violence. Furthermore, variations in these structural dimensions of community social disorganization were shown by Sampson and Groves (1989) to mediate in large part the effects of community socioeconomic status, residential mobility, ethnic heterogeneity, and family disruption in the manner predicted by social disorganization theory. Mobility had significant inverse effects on friendship networks; family disruption was a significant predictor of unsupervised peer groups; and socioeconomic status had positive effects on organizational participation. When combined with the results of research on gang delinquency that point to the salience of informal and formal institutional community structures in controlling the formation of gangs (Short and Strodtbeck, 1956; Thrasher, 1963; Hagedorn, 1988), the empirical data suggest that the structural elements of social disorganization have relevance for explaining macrolevel variations in violence rates (see also Bursik, 1988).

Community Cultures and Ethnography

Theoretically, at least, social disorganization theory also focuses on how the ecological segregation of communities gives rise to what Kornhauser (1978:75) terms *cultural* disorganization—the attenuation of societal cultural values. In particular, poverty, mobility, heterogeneity, and other structural features of urban communities are hypothesized to impede communication and obstruct the quest for common values, thereby fostering cultural diversity with respect to nondelinquent values (Kornhauser, 1978:75). A consequence of the cultural fragmentation engendered by structural features such as urbanization and heterogeneity (see also Fischer, 1975) is the formation and transmission of deviant and violent subcultures. Accordingly, a major component of Shaw and McKay's theory was that heterogeneous, low-income, urban communities spawned the formation of delinquent organizations (e.g., gangs) with their own subcultures and norms perpetuated through cultural transmission.[24]

The ethnographic study of community cultures and value systems in relation to social disorganization has not received nearly the same attention as quantitative studies that examine variations in crime rates. This is unfortunate because community ethnographies and gang studies provide important insights into culturally patterned, group responses to structurally imposed conditions. It is beyond the scope of this paper to attempt an assessment of community ethnography, much less come to some conclusion regarding the validity of cultural theories of violence. However, a brief discussion of community ethnographies is useful in underscoring the need for an integrated research approach to macrolevel sources of violence.

In general, ethnographic studies suggest that the ecological basis for the formation of local street-corner groups and gangs is especially pronounced in urban, lower-income, heterogeneous neighborhoods (Thrasher, 1963; Spergel, 1964; Short and Strodtbeck, 1965; Suttles, 1968; Keiser, 1970; Rieder, 1985; Horowitz, 1987; Hagedorn, 1988). A related thread running through many ethnographic studies is the idea that structurally disorganized communities are conducive to the emergence of cultural value systems and attitudes that seem to legitimate, or provide a basis of tolerance for, violence. For example, Suttles's (1968) account of the social order of a Chicago slum neighborhood characterized by poverty and heterogeneity supports Thrasher's (1963) emphasis on age, sex, ethnicity, and territory as markers for the ordered segmentation of slum culture. Namely, Suttles found that single-sex, age-graded primary groups of the same ethnicity and territory emerged in response to threats of conflict and community-wide disorder and mistrust. Although the community subcultures that Suttles (1968) discovered were provincial, tentative, and incomplete (Kornhauser, 1978:18), they nonetheless undermined societal values against delinquency and violence.

Similarly, Anderson's (1978) ethnography of a bar in Chicago's South Side black ghetto shows how collective or group processes construct a segmented social order. Within the extended primary group that gathered at "Jelly's" bar, mainstream values such as a "visible means of support" and "decency" were indeed primary values, but there coexisted residual values associated with deviant subcultures (e.g., hoodlums) such as "toughness," "getting big money," "going for bad," and "having fun" (1978:129-130, 152-158). In Anderson's (1978:210) analysis, lower-class residents do not so much "stretch" mainstream values as "create their own particular standards of social conduct along variant lines open to them." In this context the use of violence is not valued as a primary goal, but is still expected and tolerated as a fact of life (Anderson, 1978:134; see also Horowitz, 1987). In the case of certain primary groups such as hoodlums, violence is seen as one of the few ways to gain respect or affirmation of self (Anderson, 1978:158). Much like Rainwater (1970), Suttles (1968), and Horowitz (1987), Anderson's ethnographic research suggests that in certain community contexts the wider cultural values are simply not relevant—they become "unviable."

To be sure, there is great dispute whether subcultural values are in fact genuine or are in essence fake values that are used to rationalize behavior. Liebow's (1967) study of a black slum in Washington questions the authenticity of a community culture that is in opposition to the wider culture. Rather than assuming an historical continuity in values, Liebow (1967) argues that lower-class values were recreated as persons time and again experienced the same structural conditions. Relying on Liebow's research, Kornhauser (1978:20) further critiques cultural theories by asserting,

> The "culture" thus constructed is not an authentic subculture, nor are its "values" objects of genuine commitment. It is a

pseudoculture. Its function is ideological: to rationalize failure. It neither commands allegiance nor guides behavior; rather, it follows behavior.

In her viewpoint, violence is therefore not valued but is instead a situational response to the structurally imposed conditions of social disorganization.

Whether or not community subcultures are authentic or merely "shadow cultures" (Liebow, 1967) cannot be resolved here. However, that seems less important than acknowledging that community contexts seem to shape what can be termed cognitive landscapes or ecologically structured norms (e.g., normative ecologies) regarding appropriate standards and expectations of conduct (cf. Liebow, 1967; Suttles, 1968; Rainwater, 1970; Anderson, 1978, 1990; Horowitz, 1987; Rieder, 1985). That is, in certain structurally disorganized communities it appears that a system of values emerges in which violence is less than fervently condemned and hence expected as part of everyday life. These ecologically structured social perceptions and tolerances in turn appear to influence the probability of violent encounters (Horowitz, 1987). In this regard we believe that Kornhauser's attack on subcultural theories misses the point. By attempting to assess whether subcultural values are authentic in some deep, quasi-religious sense, Kornhauser (1978:1-20) loses sight of the processes by which cognitive landscapes rooted in normative ecologies can influence rates of violence. Indeed, the idea that dominant values become existentially irrelevant in certain community contexts is a powerful one, albeit an idea that has not had the research exploitation it deserves. We return later to a discussion of community ethnographies and how they might be more profitably linked to structurally oriented studies of variation in crime rates.

SUMMARY

To recapitulate, studies of violence have both confirmed and substantially extended the basic Shaw and McKay model of community structure and delinquency. Almost without exception, studies of violence find a positive and usually large correlation between some measure of area poverty and violence—especially homicide. However, the strength of poverty in explaining violence once other community factors are controlled has been called into question. Many of the studies reviewed find weak direct effects of poverty or conditional effects. In particular, it appears that poverty is most important in the context of community *change*.

A similar phenomenon emerges for racial composition and heterogeneity: although violence rates are usually higher in neighborhoods with a high percentage of blacks or minorities, the direct effect of race is often quite weak. The more consistent and sturdy structural correlates of violence seem to be residential mobility or change—especially when linked to increasing poverty and social dislocation—and the factors of family disruption and housing/population density.

Additionally, there is evidence that intervening dimensions of community structural disorganization, such as unsupervised peer groups, attenuated local friendship networks, and low organizational participation, have positive effects on violence. Also based on community ethnographies, there is some evidence to suggest that structurally disorganized communities with weak social controls give rise to the formation of delinquent gangs and cultural norms that increase the probability of violent encounters. There are clearly many weaknesses in the community-level literature that need explication, especially regarding interpretations of causality and the authenticity of cultural attitudes promoting violence. Before discussing these, however, we turn to a brief summary of findings based on interurban units of analysis.

METROPOLITAN-LEVEL STUDIES

Probably because of the greater ease of data availability, recent literature on violence in relation to characteristics of metropolitan-level or interurban units of analysis such as cities and standard metropolitan statistical areas is much more extensive than research at the local community level. A recurrent theme in this body of research has been the potential criminogenic effects of income inequality, especially between the races, on violence. Inequality is thought to generate subjective feelings of relative deprivation and latent hostility, leading to criminal acts of violence born of frustration (e.g., see Messner, 1982; Blau and Blau, 1982; Balkwell, 1990). Another dominant concern has been regional effects on the homicide rate. The fact that southern states exhibit homicide rates higher than other regions has led to speculation that there exists a value system that supports and reinforces violent behavior (Gastil, 1971). This perspective, widely known as the "subculture of violence" thesis, has also been applied to the explanation of disproportionately high rates of black violence in American cities (Wolfgang and Ferracuti, 1967; Curtis, 1975).

TABLE 1 Recent Macro Level (city, SMSA, state) Studies of Homicide

Author(s)	Unit of Analysis	Data Year
Gastil (1971)	States, SMSAs	1960
Bailey (1984)	Cities	1960, 1970
Loftin and Hill (1974)	States	1960
Jackson (1984)	Cities	1970
Loftin and Parker (1985)	Cities	1970
Messner (1983b)	Cities	1970
Sampson (1985b)	Cities	1970
Sampson (1986b)	Cities	1980
Williams and Flewelling (1988)	Cities	1980
Blau and Blau (1982)	SMSAs	1970
Blau and Golden (1986)	SMSAs	1970
Crutchfield et al. (1982)	SMSAs	1970
DeFronzo (1983)	SMSAs	1970
Messner (1982)	SMSAs	1970
Messner (1983a)	SMSAs	1970
Rosenfeld (1986)	SMSAs	1970
Simpson (1985)	SMSAs	1970
Williams (1984)	SMSAs	1970
Huff-Corzine et al. (1986)	States	1970
Parker and Smith (1979)	States	1970
Smith and Parker (1980)	States	1970

SOURCE: Data from Land et al. (1990).

To illustrate these trends, Table 1 is a list of 21 major studies identified by Land et al. (1990) that examine variations in homicide rates across macrolevel units of cities, SMSAs, and in a few cases, states.[25] The following variables are represented in this body of research: population size, population density, percent of the population that is black, percent youth (e.g, percent age 15-29), percent male divorce rate, percent of children not living with both parents, median family income, percent families living in poverty, the Gini index of income inequality, the unemployment rate, and a dichotomous variable indicating those cities or metropolitan areas located in the South. Despite the wide variety of measures, the majority of studies in Table 1 were clearly focused on economic deprivation and inequality.

Detailed inspection of these studies reveals a host of differences that render a summary of findings difficult if not impossible. For one, the model specifications, techniques of analysis, time periods of study, and units of analysis differ widely across studies—much more than is the case at the community level (see also Byrne and Sampson, 1986). Comparison of multivariate standardized regression coefficients across studies is especially ill-advised because of widely discrepant model specifications and variances. Perhaps then it is not surprising that the findings themselves are highly inconsistent. As Land et al. (1990:931) concluded after their detailed review, "Virtually no structural covariate exhibits estimated effects that are statistically significant and of invariant algebraic sign across all studies." For example, poverty has both positive (Bailey, 1984) and negative (Messner, 1982) significant coefficients in different specifications, and is insignificant in many other models (Blau and Blau, 1982; Crutchfield et al., 1982; Simpson, 1985). The Gini index of income inequality also shows considerable inconsistency, sometimes directly related (Simpson, 1985) and sometimes not related (Williams, 1984) to rates of homicide. The only apparent exception to this pattern is percent divorced, which has rather consistent positive associations with homicide in the minority of studies in which it was measured (e.g., Blau and Blau, 1982; Williams, 1984). Percent black also shows a fairly consistent pattern of positive covariation with homicide (Messner, 1982, 1983b; Blau and Blau, 1982; Bailey, 1984; Simpson, 1985; Sampson, 1986b).

In short, the dozens of macrolevel studies conducted over the past 20 years or so are not easily interpretable in terms of the independent influences of urban social structure on violence. What can account for these highly variable findings? In addition to differing time periods and units of analysis (e.g., states, SMSAs, cities), Land et al. (1990) maintain that the single greatest threat to comparability across studies is the presence of high levels of association among explanatory variables. Typically referred to as multicollinearity, redundancy among predictor variables threatens the statistical inferences that can be drawn from the numerous studies based on multiple regression. Specifically, collinearity among explanatory variables can result in large confidence intervals and instability of coefficients across model specifications (Hanushek and Jackson, 1977:86-96). Gordon (1967) warned many years ago that overlap among predictor variables leads to the "partialling fallacy"—the allocation of all explained variance to that regressor among a highly interrelated set of regressors that possesses the higher correlation with the dependent variable(s), even though there may be no theoretical or substantive basis for doing so (Land et al., 1990). The simple fact is that variables such as percent black, poverty, unemployment, median income, and inequality are usually highly intercorrelated. The assessment of independent effects results in highly unstable regression models, making comparison of magnitudes of effect extremely difficult and problematic.

To address this problem, Land et al. (1990) have conducted what may be the most comprehensive analysis to date of homicide rate variation at the metropolitan and state level. They first identified what they termed a "baseline regression model" that incorporated the major predictor variables used by the 21 studies in Table 1. The predictor variables, labeled "structural covariates," were population size, population per square mile, percent black population, percent of the population age 15 to 29, percent divorced males, percent of children not living with both parents, median family income, percent of families living below the official poverty level, the Gini index of income concentration, percent unemployed, and a dichotomous variable indicating southern location. These 11 variables were measured at the city, SMSA, and state levels of analysis for 1960, 1970, and 1980. The cities examined for 1980 number almost 1,000 (904); the SMSAs, 259.

Using multivariate regression models similar to prior research, Land et al. (1990) report, as expected, substantial variability and fluctuation in regression coefficients across time periods and units of analysis. However, when the authors analyzed the dimensionality of the structural covariates through principal components analysis, two clusters of variables were found to consistently "hang together" over time and space. The first factor was termed a *population structure component* and consisted of population size and population density. The second factor was labeled *resource deprivation/ affluence* and included three income variables—median income, percent of families below the poverty line, and the Gini index of income inequality—in addition to percent black and percent of children not living with both parents. Although these variables seem to tap somewhat different concepts, Land et al. (1990) found they could not be separated empirically. In particular, there was no empirical justification for treating deprivation measures (i.e., poverty) and inequality as separate independent variables.[26] As Land et al. (1990:944) argue, cities, SMSAs, and states with high (low) levels of absolute deprivation also tend to have high (low) levels of inequality. Percent black was also substantially collinear with economic indicators. On the other hand, four variables—*percent divorced males, percent age 15 to 29, unemployment rate*, and *South*—varied independently.

Based on these results, Land et al. (1990) entered the two components of resource deprivation/affluence and population struc-

TABLE 2 Standardized Regression Coefficients of Structural Covariates of Homicide Rates for U.S. Cities, SMSAs, and States in 1960, 1970, and 1980

	1960			1970			1980		
	City	SMSA	State	City	SMSA	State	City	SMSA	State
Population structure	11^a	.04	$.15^a$	$.20^a$	$.25^a$	$.19^a$	$.19^a$	$.18^a$	$.27^a$
Resource deprivation	$.56^a$	$.45^a$	$.60^a$	$.58^a$	$.57^a$	$.77^a$	$.53^a$	$.54^a$	$.80^a$
Percent divorced	$.10^a$	$.24^a$	$.36^a$	$.18^a$	$.28^a$	$.32^a$	$.12^a$	$.26^a$	$.58^a$
Percent ages 15-29	−.06	−.01	$.32^a$	.00	.01	$.24^a$	$−.11^a$	-.03	$.17^a$
Unemployment rate	$−.11^a$	$−.12^a$	-.01	$−.09^a$	$−.23^a$	-.01	.18	$−.09^a$	−.09
Southern region	$.20^a$	$.36^a$	$.24^a$	$.13^a$	$.14^a$	.00	$.16^a$	$.14^a$	-.08

^{a}Significant at $p \leq .05$, one-tailed.

SOURCE: Data from Land et al. (1990:948-949).

ture along with the four single variables in an attempt to examine the invariance of homicide determinants across time and space. Table 2 summarizes the major findings; entries are standardized regression coefficients for cities, SMSAs, and states for the three time periods covered by recent research—1960, 1970, and 1980. The results are quite consistent and substantively interpretable. As Land et al. (1990:947) summarize, "Three structural indexes/ covariates—population structure, resource deprivation/affluence, and percent of the male population divorced—now exhibit statistically significant relationships to the homicide rate in the theoretically expected direction across all time periods and levels of analysis." For example, Table 2 shows that resource deprivation has a consistent and large positive effect on homicide, independent of all other factors. This suggests that, all else being equal, cities with a large poor population in conjunction with a high percentage of black residents and single-parent families with children, have disproportionately high homicide rates. Further, homicide rates are larger in cities/states/regions with large populations and high male divorce rates. In terms of magnitude, resource deprivation has the largest effect, generally followed by male divorce rate and population structure. Other variables show more inconsistencies, although there is a tendency for homicide to be higher in the South, and in areas with a high percentage of youth and low employment.

The large effect of resource deprivation/affluence on homicide is substantively consistent with Wilson's (1987) recent conceptualization of *concentration effects*. He argues that the social transformation of the inner city has resulted in a disproportionate concentration of the most disadvantaged segments of the urban black population—especially poor, black, female-headed families with children. Factors leading to the increased segregation of poor blacks include opposition from organized community groups to public housing projects in stable neighborhoods and political decisions to neglect rehabilitation of single-family residential units (Massey, 1990; Sampson, 1990). Urban minorities have also been especially vulnerable to structural economic changes related to the deindustrialization of central cities (e.g., shift from goods-producing to service-producing industries, increasing polarization of the labor market into low-wage and high-wage sectors, "high-tech" innovations, and relocation of manufacturing out of the inner city). This social milieu differs significantly from the environment that existed in inner cities in previous decades (Wilson 1987:58; Rose and McClain, 1990). In particular, the exodus of middle- and upper-income black families from the inner city removes an important social buffer that could deflect the full impact of prolonged joblessness and industrial transformation (see also Hagedorn, 1988). Wilson's (1987:56) thesis is based on the assumption that the basic institutions of an area (e.g., churches, schools, stores, recreational facilities) would remain viable if much of the base of their support came from more economically stable families in inner-city neighborhoods (i.e, those with vertical social class integration).

Wilson's (1987) concept of social isolation in areas of concentrated poverty may help explain the Land et al. (1990) findings and also those of Taylor and Covington (1988) noted earlier, who found that increasing entrenchment of the urban minority underclass was associated with large increases in violence. Land et al.'s (1990) results also go beyond Wilson by suggesting that the clustering of economic and social indicators appears not only in 1980 and in neighborhoods of large cities, but also for the two previous decennial periods and at the level of macrosocial units as a whole. In other words, those cities (as well as SMSAs and states) that had low incomes, high poverty levels, and great economic inequality in 1960, 1970, and 1980 also had large concentrations of blacks and children living in poverty (Land et al., 1990:944). Moreover, Land et al. present evidence in support of Wilson's argument that concentration effects grew more severe from 1970 to 1980 in large cities—"the numerical values of the component loadings of percent poverty, percent black, and percent of children under 18 not living with both parents are larger in 1980 than 1970" (Land et al., 1990:945). Therefore, not only are various indicators of urban disadvantaged populations highly related, they are increasing in concentration (Massey and Eggers, 1990).

Metropolitan-level results for robbery and rape parallel in large part Land et al.'s (1990) findings for homicide. The first and most obvious point is that the overlap among explanatory variables is the same whether robbery, assault, rape, or homicide is analyzed. As might be expected, then, a similar pattern appears whereby percent black and different measures of deprivation/ poverty are positively related to each other and to both robbery (Danziger, 1976; Crutchfield et al., 1982; Blau and Blau, 1982; Carroll and Jackson, 1983; Blau and Golden, 1986; Byrne, 1986; Rosenfeld, 1986; Sampson, 1986b) and rape (Blau and Blau, 1982; Peterson and Bailey, 1988; for further review, see Brantingham and Brantingham, 1984:289-294). Moreover, both Flango and Sherbenou (1976) and Harries (1976) analyzed the multidimensionality of independent variables and extracted factors similar to Land et al. (1990). Namely, Flango and Sherbenou (1976:337) found that percent black, percent female-headed families, and low median income covaried together, whereas Harries (1976) discovered that percent black and percent female headed households loaded on a single factor. These "deprivation" indices were in turn significantly related to city-level variations in violence.

Perhaps more clear cut is the factor of divorce: several studies have found a strong direct effect of divorce on rates of robbery (e.g., Blau and Blau, 1982; Blau and Golden, 1986; Sampson, 1986b), assault (Blau and Golden, 1986), and rape (Blau and Golden, 1986; Petersen and Bailey, 1988). Again, this parallels the Land et al. (1990) finding of a consistent direct effect of the male divorce rate on homicide that is unaccounted for by socioeconomic factors and racial composition. In fact, the effect of divorce on robbery and rape is generally greater than that of socioeconomic factors and racial composition in studies where the former has been distinctly measured (e.g., Blau and Golden, 1986; Sampson, 1986b; Petersen and Bailey, 1988). For example, in the most recent study to focus explicitly on city-level variations in rape rates, Petersen and Bailey (1988) found that the divorce rate had the largest effect on rape (beta = .45), followed by percent black (.29), overall inequality (.25), church membership (–.19), and black/white inequality (.12).

Other than what Land et al. (1990) refer to as resource deprivation/ affluence and the divorce rate, macrolevel research has shown a rather consistent direct effect on robbery of either population size/density or housing density (Flango and Sherbenou, 1976; Danziger, 1976; Harries, 1976; Carroll and Jackson, 1983; Byrne, 1986; Sampson, 1987a). The density/size findings replicate the population structure conclusion drawn by Land et al. (1990).[27] In a study of variations in violent crime across 65 SMSAs in 1970, Crutchfield et al. (1982) also demonstrated that independent of traditional socioeconomic and demographic controls, population mobility had significant and rather substantial effects on rape, assault, and murder for a sample of SMSAs, a finding supportive of the community-level research reviewed earlier. Finally, Baron and Straus (1987) found that state-level rape rates were directly related to an index dominated by mobility and family disruption.

RACIAL DISAGGREGATION

The Land et al. (1990) approach is important because it provides a summary index of the effects of poverty and relative deprivation on homicide. However, the resource deprivation index still confounds racial composition, and consequently does not allow examination of poverty and family structure independent of race. This result presents a problem because the large structural differences among black and white communities in terms of family structure and poverty (see Wilson, 1987) may account for the compositional effect of percent black in aggregate analyses. Racial differences are so strong that even the "worst" urban contexts in which whites reside with respect to poverty and family disruption are considerably better off than the average (i.e., mean level) context of black communities (Sampson, 1987a:354). For example, regardless of whether a black juvenile is raised in an intact or a "broken" home, or a rich or poor home, he/she will not grow up in a community context similar to whites with regard to family structure and poverty.

One way to examine these contextual issues is through racial disaggregation of both the crime rate and the explanatory variables of theoretical interest (e.g., poverty, family structure), thereby deconfounding race at the aggregate level. This approach was used in research by Sampson (1987a) that examined racially disaggregated rates of homicide and robbery by juveniles and adults in more than 150 U.S. cities in 1980. Racially disaggregated rates of violent offending were estimated from race, age, and sex-specific arrest data corrected for city-level differences in enforcement patterns (Sampson, 1987a:358-360). Substantively, the model focused on the exogenous factors of black male joblessness and economic deprivation, and their effects on violent crime as mediated by black family disruption. The rationale stemmed largely from Wilson's (1987) argument that the labor market marginality of black males and accompanying economic deprivation have had profound negative implications for the black community, especially black women with children. From this viewpoint, a major structural determinant of black family disruption is black male joblessness and persistent poverty in the black community. Family disruption was hypothesized to subsequently increase violence because of weakened informal social control (Sampson, 1987a:352-353).

Overall, the results supported the main hypothesis and showed that the scarcity of employed black males relative to black women was directly related to the prevalence of families headed by females in black communities. In turn, black family disruption was substantially related to rates of black murder and robbery, especially by juveniles. These effects were independent of income, region, race and age composition, density, city size, and welfare benefits. The consistent finding that family disruption had stronger effects on juvenile violence than on adult violence, in conjunction with the inconsistent findings of previous research on individual-level delinquency and broken homes (Wilkinson, 1980), tends to support the idea that the effects of family structure are related to macrolevel patterns of social control and guardianship, especially regarding youth and their peers (Felson and Cohen 1980; Sampson 1986b; Sampson and Groves, 1989). Moreover, the results suggested a partial solution as to why unemployment and economic deprivation have had weak or inconsistent effects on violence rates in past research: although joblessness or even poverty may not have direct effects on crime, they do have significant effects on family disruption, which in turn is a strong predictor of variations in urban black violence.[28]

The results also revealed that despite a tremendous difference in mean levels of family disruption among black and white communities, the percentage of white families headed by a female had a large positive effect on white juvenile and white adult violence. In fact, the predictors of white robbery were shown to be in large part identical in sign and magnitude to those for blacks. Therefore, Sampson (1987a) concluded that the effect of family disruption on black crime was independent of commonly cited alternative explanations (e.g., poverty, region, urbanization, age composition) and could not be attributed to unique cultural factors within the black community.

OPPORTUNITY STRUCTURES

In addition to the sociodemographic and economic variables reviewed above, a few recent studies have focused on macrolevel variations in opportunity structures and how they affect violence. We discuss here two of the more salient opportunity structures—aggregate patterns of leisure activity and gun availability. In an innovative study of the former, Messner and Blau (1987) report a significant positive association between violence rates and routine activities as conceptualized by Cohen and Felson (1979). To determine the prevalence of leisure activity that takes place at home they constructed a measure of aggregate level of television viewing for 124 SMSAs in 1980. The level of nonhousehold leisure activities was operationalized by the supply of sports and entertainment establishments. These establishments include commercial cinemas and drive-ins, entertainment producers, and profit-making professional and semiprofessional sports establishments that "summarize the availability and the opportunities for a wide range of activities that take place outside of the household" (Messner and Blau, 1987:1039).

Controlling for region, percent black, percent poor, and the age, race, and sex composition of SMSAs, Messner and Blau (1987:1043) found consistent significant effects of aggregate routine activity patterns on violence. The nonhousehold activity index had positive effects on homicide, rape, robbery, and assault, whereas the television viewing index had significant negative effects on rape, robbery, and assault. These effects were lower in magnitude than poverty and racial composition, but the television viewing index had a rather substantial relationship with robbery (third largest effect) and assault (second largest effect). Messner and Blau's (1987) conclusion was that nonhousehold activities place members of the population at a relatively high risk for personal victimization, independent of the supply of motivated offenders. Contrariwise, an increase in leisure activities at home reduces violent victimization. These findings support the basic contention of the routine activity model (Cohen and Felson, 1979). A potential problem with these results is that high levels of violence may lead people to change their activity patterns. The issue of reciprocal effects is discussed more below.

Another factor that has caused great concern in policy debates is the effect of gun ownership on violence. We cannot do justice to this debate, but we can briefly highlight research that specifically focuses on the question of whether gun availability affects patterns of violence across cities. Perhaps the most definitive test can be found in Cook's (1979) analysis of the relationship between gun availability and robbery rates in the 50 largest American cities in 1975. Guns were found to be present in a high proportion of robberies (45 percent) and robberies perpetrated with guns were much more likely to result in the death of the victim than robberies without guns. However, Cook's results showed that an increase in the density of guns in a city—defined as the fraction of households in a city that owns guns—had no effect on the overall robbery rate (1979:743). This finding suggests that gun availability may increase the lethality or seriousness of robberies (by increasing robbery-murder) but that it does not necessarily increase the robbery *rate*. Similar results were obtained by Bordua (1986) in a study of county-level variations in firearms ownership and violent crime in Illinois. Once county-level factors such as poverty and urbanization were controlled, Bordua found no consistent relationship between firearms ownership and rates of homicide or other violent crimes.

The evidence to date points to the overall conclusion that metropolitan differences in gun ownership are probably not a major factor in the etiology of violence. As Bordua (1986:188) concluded, the most plausible interpretation "is that variation in firearms ownership has no independent causal effect on violent crime at all." The issue is complex and unresolved, however, for there may be counterbalancing effects that account for these null findings. For example, Cook (1979) notes that an increase in gun availability may actually decrease the robbery rate because potential robbery victims are more likely to be armed in cities where gun ownership is widespread. Pierce and Bowers (1981) argue that restriction of guns could actually lead to more violence because potential offenders may feel less restrained if fewer guns are being carried into assault-prone situations. If true, gun density could have both positive and negative effects on the violent crime rate.

Although current research has not effectively disentangled these possibilities, it is nonetheless clear that the simple assumption that more guns necessarily means more violence is not borne out by the evidence.

PROBLEMS OF INTERPRETATION

This paper has synthesized current knowledge on individual, situational, and macrolevel risk factors in understanding violence. Unfortunately, it is evident that numerous problems plague this sort of research, especially inferences as to the causal status of community characteristics. Among other limitations, the use of varying and sometimes highly aggregated units of analysis, potentially biased sources of information on violence, widely varying analytical techniques, and high correlations among independent variables all lead to considerable ambiguity in the attempt to forge general conclusions. However, rather than dwell on these methodological limitations of macrolevel research, many of which have been explicated above or in other sources (e.g., Land et al., 1990), this section considers more fundamental and as yet unresolved problems relating to (1) reciprocal effects of violence on community structure and routine activities, (2) the failure to examine macrolevel processes of theoretical interest, and (3) cross-level misspecification and selection effects. We believe that these three issues are most central to an inability to make definitive conclusions about the independent causal effects of individual- and community-level sources of criminal violence. We then conclude with a discussion of research strategies that may help alleviate these pitfalls.

FEEDBACK EFFECTS

A typical assumption of most community-level research is that crime is an endogenous variable—something to be explained by a variety of social and demographic variables such as poverty and mobility. The problem with this approach is that crime and its consequences (e.g., fear) may themselves have important effects on community structure, thereby confounding easy interpretation of the relationships among community social phenomena and crime. As Bursik (1986:63-64) has stated, "There may not be a simple, unidirectional causal structure in which crime and delinquency rates are only the outcome of ecological processes. Rather, within the context of ongoing urban dynamics, the level of delinquency in an area may also directly or indirectly cause changes in the composition of an area."

Skogan (1986) has recently provided an insightful overview of some of the "feedback" processes that may further increase levels of crime. These include (1) physical and psychological withdrawal from community life, (2) weakening of the informal social control processes that inhibit crime, (3) a decline in the organizational life and mobilization capacity of the neighborhood, (4) deteriorating business conditions, (5) the importation and domestic production of delinquency and deviance, and (6) further dramatic changes in the composition of the population. For example, to the extent that people shun their neighbors and local facilities out of fear of violence, fewer opportunities exist for friendship networks and neighborhood organizations to take hold (see also Taylor and Gottfredson, 1986:404). As Skogan (1986:217) reminds us, "Fear does not stimulate participation in collective efforts to act against crime; rather, it often has the effect of undermining commitment to an area and interest in participation." Relatedly, predatory street violence is often accompanied by commercial decline and business relocation out of inner-city areas where there is a perceived risk of violence against the customer population. Therefore, violence itself may lead to a weakening of local friendship bonds, informal social control, and the mobilization capacity of communities. Because these are defining elements of social disorganization, serious questions are raised concerning the direction of causal effects between community structure and violence.

The research noted earlier on firearms ownership illustrates a similar point with respect to self-protection and responses to violence. Even if a positive relationship were definitively established between firearms (e.g., gun density) and crime, the nature of the causal interpretation is far from straightforward. As Bordua (1986) notes, those most vulnerable to violent crimes such as rape (e.g., women) may purchase weapons out of a perceived need for self-defense. In fact, the finding that female gun ownership is related positively to the murder rate is attributed by Bordua (1986) to females' purchase of weapons in high-crime areas for defensive purposes. Kleck (1984) further argues that gun robbery and robbery-murder may induce commercial establishments to take self-protective measures with regard to firearms. These studies suggest that the relationship between gun density and crime is complex because of potential reciprocal effects of violence (Cook, 1979:753).

It follows that the whole area of self-protective responses to violence is problematic in that many community-level opportunity variables may be directly influenced by the violence rate (Cook, 1986). Private security, minimizing cash at convenience stores, and alteration of lifestyles (e.g., reduction in going out at night) are but a few plausible responses to violence in the community (see also Sherman et al., 1989). Again, however, community-level variations in what may be responses to violence are often simply used as causal predictors of violence. For example, the Messner and Blau (1987) study reviewed above used aggregate levels of at-home routine activities to explain violence rates. As with gun ownership, however, responses to violence (e.g., staying at home) in part determine a community's structure of opportunities and level of routine activities, which may in turn feed back into the violence rate in an ongoing reciprocal fashion. On the flip side, consider Cook's (1986) observation that a reduction in the commercial robbery rate may be followed by a reduction in incentives for self-protection (e.g, guards, minimizing cash), thereby increasing the attractiveness of stores as robbery targets. Similarly, once residents of a community feel that streets are safe they are more apt to utilize public facilities and hence generate new opportunity structures for crime.

Perhaps the most salient consequence of violent crime is sheer demographic collapse—extreme population loss and/or selective out-migration from the neighborhood. As Skogan (1986:223) has argued, the massive suburbanization of the United States following World War II may be the most consequential effect of crime on American society. Although sparse, there is evidence to support this view. Bursik (1986) showed that delinquency rates greatly accelerated processes of neighborhood decline in Chicago from 1950 to 1970. At the national level, Sampson and Wooldredge (1986) found that rates of violence were inversely related to population change from 1970 to 1980 in the nation's 55 largest cities. Such a "hollowing out" of many city centers may lead to further deterioration and decline, which, through feedback processes, can increase violence and disorder (see also Reiss, 1986a:8; Wallace and Wallace, 1990). As noted earlier, Wilson (1987) has argued that the crime-influenced exodus of middle- and working-class blacks from many ghetto neighborhoods may have removed an important "social buffer."

In short, predatory crimes of violence such as robbery are fearful to the majority of citizens and can quickly symbolize the decline of communities. Moreover, the activities of potential victims and offenders interact in ways that mutually structure the opportunities for violence in a dynamic process (Cook, 1986; Reiss,

1986a). It should not be surprising then to consider that violence rates are not simply the outcome of ecological processes but are also important components of that process and can have important effects on the dynamics of urban change (Bursik, 1986). What is particularly problematic from the present perspective is that many of the community-level characteristics thought to cause violence (e.g., mobility, population loss, increasing concentration of the underclass, gun ownership, routine activities, weak friendship networks, attenuation of local social control and community organizations) may themselves be affected by feedback processes from violent crimes such as robbery. These feedback processes are very complex, and no one has successfully estimated their relative magnitudes (Skogan, 1986). To make matters more complicated, some research suggests that crime does not necessarily lead to neighborhood decline; in fact, some neighborhoods prosper despite high crime (Taub et al., 1984; McDonald, 1986). We should thus recognize that simple interpretation of the link between urban social structure and violence is not possible.

MEDIATING COMMUNITY PROCESSES

Even if the above problems were resolved, serious measurement deficiencies prevent macrolevel researchers from doing much more than speculating. For the most part, researchers have simply inferred the existence of intervening community processes, even though the correlation of violence with ecological characteristics is consistent with many different theoretical perspectives. For example, the typical aggregate-level study, as reviewed above, shows us that factors such as percent black, poverty, and family disruption are predictive of violence rates. Although useful as a preliminary test, this strategy does not really go beyond the steps taken by Shaw and McKay more than 40 years ago. As Kornhauser (1978) argues, most criminological theories take as their point of departure the same independent variables—especially stratification factors such as socioeconomic status. However, the variables that *intervene* between community structure and violence are at issue, and to adequately test competing theories it is necessary to establish the relationship to violence of the interpretive variables each theory implies (cf. Kornhauser, 1978:82).

The lack of direct tests of community-level theories does not stem from a lack of theoretical insight but rather a lack of relevant data. As Heitgerd and Bursik (1987) conclude, traditional ecological studies are not well suited to an examination of the formal and informal networks hypothesized to link community social structure and crime. Such an examination requires extensive and prohibitive data collection within each of the communities in the analysis (Heitgerd and Bursik, 1987:785). Similarly, Reiss (1986a:26-27) notes that because governments collect very little information on the collective properties of administrative units for which they routinely report information, "little causal information is available for those same units."

The crux of the problem is that previous macrolevel research has relied primarily on *census data* that rarely provide measures for the variables hypothesized to mediate the relationship between community structure and violence. Ethnographic research (e.g., Suttles, 1968; Hagedorn, 1988) is an exception to this pattern in that it provides rich descriptive accounts of community processes central to theoretical concerns. Yet as Reiss (1986a:27) argues, ethnographies provide limited tests of theories by focusing on a single community or, at most, on a cluster of neighborhoods in which community properties do not display sufficient variation. Also, although some studies have examined quantitative dimensions of informal social control (e.g., Maccoby et al., 1958; Kapsis, 1976; Simcha-Fagan and Schwartz, 1986), they have been limited to a few select communities, which precludes comprehensive multivariate analysis. Consequently, empirical examination of *between-community* differences in social disorganization and other community-level processes has been rarely undertaken. In point of fact, with the exception of data from Baltimore (Taylor et al., 1984) and Great Britain (Sampson and Groves, 1989), there have been few if any direct tests of the effects of social disorganization and community social control on rates of violence.

Another related problem is that culture is commonly ignored in macrolevel research even though a key element of macrolevel explanation focuses on how community cultures and value systems produce differential rates of crime (cf. Short, 1990:11-12; Luckenbill and Doyle, 1989). "Structural determinants" of crime are emphasized in large part because virtually all census-derived measures may be classified as structural. An abundance of convenient structural measures does not make culture irrelevant, however. In fact, many of the concepts suggested by criminological theory such as "hostility," "alienation," and "southern values" (e.g., see Blau and Blau, 1982) are related in some way to culture or to its fragmentation in modern urban life. Even when culture is addressed in ecological research, it is haphazard. For example, it is commonplace to use region and percent black as indicators of "subculture" even though one cannot adequately test the subculture of violence thesis with census data.

A major flaw in prior research on violence, then, is simply that key concepts have rarely if ever been adequately measured. As a consequence the transmission processes through which neighborhood effects operate—whether contagion, socialization, institutional, or social comparison processes—are largely unknown (see also Mayer and Jencks, 1989). Note that the lack of measurement of social interactions and mediating processes is also directly linked to the definition and conceptualization of communities themselves. Essentially, criminological research is dominated by analysis of statistical neighborhoods defined by administrative concerns (e.g., census tracts) that may or may not correspond to social patterns of interaction and cohesion. However, as Tienda (1989:6) has argued, "Social dimensions of the definition of neighborhoods are crucial because they derive from interaction patterns, which ultimately are the primary mechanisms through which neighborhood effects can be transmitted." It is therefore doubly problematic that most efforts to establish the existence of community influences on violence are based on the ecological or structural characteristics of places to the neglect of social interaction and social networks within spatial domains.

CROSS-LEVEL MISSPECIFICATION

Perhaps the major conceptual and methodological problem underlying macrolevel research is the mistaken assumption that the unit of analysis automatically determines the level of causal explanation. We reviewed a host of studies that correlated census data with crime rates for some aggregate units (e.g, communities, cities, SMSAs) and thereby claimed to be macrosocial investigations. The ecological fallacy is irrelevant, it is usually argued, because an interest in individuals is disavowed. The problem with this strategy is that an apparent ecological or structural effect may in fact arise from individual-level causal processes. For example, an observed macrolevel result such as the correlation of median income or percent black with violence rates may simply represent the aggregate of relationships occurring at lower levels of social structure and not a manifestation of processes taking place at the level of the community as a whole. Indeed, the section on individual-level risk factors demonstrated the potential power of compositional confounding with regard to factors such as race and social class. Even though rates of crime may not be used to make inferences about individuals, individuals commit the crimes that constitute the rates.

Consider further the basic facts on delinquency. Research has consistently demonstrated the early onset of many forms of delinquency and its long-term stability (Robins, 1966; West and Farrington, 1977; Sampson and Laub, 1990). These general differences among individuals that are stable over time have profound implications for an ecological study of crime. For example, longitudinal research suggests that delinquent tendencies are fairly well established at early ages—even at age 8 or so, and certainly by the early teens (Glueck and Glueck, 1950). Antisocial children tend to fight, steal, become truant, drop out of school, drift in and out of unemployment, live in lower-class areas, and go on to commit adult crime. The causal nature of the relationship between achieved adult characteristics (e.g, employment status) and adult crime is thus fraught with methodological difficulties. In fact, in *Deviant Children Grown Up*, Robins (1966) offered the provocative hypothesis that antisocial behavior predicts class status more efficiently than class status predicts antisocial behavior.

If area differences in rates of violence are the result of the characteristics of individuals selectively located in those communities (Kornhauser, 1978:114), what then do we make of the findings derived from macrolevel criminology? For example, is the relationship between the concentration of poverty and crime rates caused by an aggregation of individual-level effects of social class, or by a genuine community-level effect; or is it simply a differential selection of individuals into communities based on prior (e.g., antisocial) behavior? Perhaps it is simply that common third factors cause individuals both to commit violence and to perform poorly in the occupational sphere. Moreover, if violent and antisocial tendencies are formed at early (preteen) ages, what plausible roles can community labor markets and economic stratification play in understanding violence?

The fallacy of assuming macrostructural effects on the basis of the unit of analysis is pervasive even when an aggregate measure does not have an immediately evident counterpart on the microlevel (e.g., inequality, density). Simply put, macrolevel research is not immune to questions concerning the level at which causal relations operate. The level at which a causal relation occurs is a complex issue that is not solved simply by the nature of the way in which variables are measured or the unit for which they are measured, because psychological and sociological causal factors may underlie relations observed at *both* the individual and the aggregate levels. In particular, the concrete actions of individuals feed back to shape the collective environment (Tienda, 1989). Thus the unit of analysis does not necessarily define the level of causal explanation, and the information contained in aggregate data is not necessarily generated by macrosociological processes.

On critical examination, ecological research often seems overly simplistic and unable to tackle hard questions, especially regarding selection effects. As Tienda (1989:23) has argued, "If systematic selection processes are the primary mechanism bringing together individuals with similar socioeconomic characteristics and behavioral dispositions within defined spatial areas, then neighborhood effects may represent little more than an aggregation of the selection process." To demonstrate that community factors accentuate the manifestations and ramifications of individual behavior, the feedback mechanisms between individual behavior and the social context must be modeled (Tienda, 1989:18). The preponderance of cross-sectional community-level studies in criminology greatly compounds the problem because communities change and so do individuals.

Problematic though they may be, however, community-level inferences are not the only issue at stake in cross-level misspecification. On the other side is the "individualistic fallacy"—the often-invoked assumption that individual-level causal relations necessarily generate individual-level correlations. The fact of the matter is that research conducted at the individual level rarely questions whether obtained results might be spurious and confounded with community-level processes. A good example can be seen in the case of race, one of the most important individual-level correlates of violence as shown earlier. Wilson's (1987) thesis of social isolation and concentration effects suggests a possible contextual explanation for the race-violence link among individuals. Consider that although approximately 70 percent of all poor whites lived in nonpoverty areas in the five largest U.S. central cities in 1980, only 15 percent of poor blacks did. Moreover, whereas only 7 percent of poor whites lived in extreme poverty areas, almost 40 percent of poor blacks lived in such areas (Wilson, 1987:58).

The consequences of these differential ecological distributions by race raise the substantively plausible hypothesis that individual-level correlations by race (and also class) may be systematically confounded with important differences in community contexts. As Wilson (1987:58-60) argues,

> Simple comparisons between poor whites and poor blacks would
> be confounded with the fact that poor whites reside in areas

which are ecologically and economically very different from poor blacks. Any observed relationships involving race would reflect, to some unknown degree, the relatively superior ecological niche many poor whites occupy with respect to jobs, marriage opportunities, and exposure to conventional role models.

Regardless of a black's individual-level family or economic situation, the average community of residence differs dramatically from that of a similarly situated white (see also Sampson, 1987a; Stark, 1987). Therefore, the relationship between race and violence may be accounted for largely by community context (e.g., segregation, concentration of family disruption and joblessness, social isolation, sparse social networks). We simply do not know, and cannot know, given the typical individual-level research design.

In short, the confluence of selective aggregation into communities, cross-level misspecification (e.g., compositional effects, individualistic fallacy), multicollinearity and nonexperimental designs, a static conceptualization of community structure, the early onset of many forms of violence, and crude measurement of community characteristics suggest that multilevel research is still in its infancy. Although space limitations preclude detail, we therefore conclude with some positive research strategies that may help to resolve these outstanding issues and provide policy inputs.

FUTURE RESEARCH DIRECTIONS AND POLICY IMPLICATIONS

Needed Research

The major implication of our review is the need for criminological research and policy on violence to integrate more effectively the individual, situational, and community levels of analysis. One general approach to this need is *contextual analysis*, in which information on communities is combined with individual-level data to explain violence. Contextual analysis permits examination not only of the main effects of community structure on individual behavior but also of the interaction between community and individual characteristics. Recent advances in multilevel hierarchical modeling are especially appealing because they allow the parameterization of the way in which individual-level relationships vary across social contexts such as schools and communities (Raudenbush and Bryck, 1986). These approaches eliminate the tendency in criminological research to ignore either the micro- or the macrolevel, based on disciplinary biases and data availability. As revealed throughout this paper, most prior research on violence involves study of either individual effects *or* community-level effects—almost no research has examined both (see also Reiss, 1986a; Gottfredson and Taylor, 1986). Most individual-level research is thus inadequate because it neglects variation in community characteristics, whereas community-level research fails to take account of individual difference constructs. Also, both the individual and the macrolevels have tended to ignore the microsituational context (Short, 1985) of violent events. Accordingly, linking the individual, situational, and community levels through contextual specification appears to be a crucial agenda in future studies of violence.

To meet these goals requires major new initiatives in research design and conceptualization. Perhaps the most pressing issue is the importance of studying neighborhood and individual *change* as a means to distinguish contextual from selection effects. In particular, understanding mechanisms that produce alternative neighborhood trajectories is essential to avoid confounding selection effects with neighborhood effects in the study of ecologically concentrated violence (cf. Tienda, 1989:18). Controlling for background characteristics is *not* enough, because contextual analysis per se does not deal with selection processes. As Tienda (1989) argues, multilevel models that simply combine person and place characteristics without regard to the potential endogeneity of neighborhood characteristics are methodologically flawed. Therefore, longitudinal designs that follow not only changes in the structure, composition, and organization of communities but also the individuals who reside there are needed to establish the unique contribution of individuals and communities to crime and delinquency (Reiss, 1986a:29).

A longitudinal, contextual approach to violence research is also consistent with the life-course perspective. Elder (1985:17) has defined the life course as pathways through the age-differentiated life span, where age differentiation "is manifested in expectations and options that impinge on decision processes and the course of events that give shape to life stages, transitions, and turning points." The life-course framework seems especially fruitful in organizing research on individual-level continuity and change over the life span in relation to community context. For example, how do early childhood characteristics (e.g., antisocial behavior) lead to adult behavioral outcomes and sorting processes related to area of residence? How do life transitions (e.g., unemployment, divorce) and situational-level factors (e.g., victim-offender relationship, presence of third parties) *interact* with community context? Does effective family social control and transmission of nonviolent values depend on levels of community social disorganization? Do the effects of community differ across stages of the life cycle? How do violent offending and victimization interact over the life cycle? These and many other questions are ideally suited to a concern with multilevel influences on the trajectories of individual and community change.

Even if we are interested only in macrolevel processes, the longitudinal study of communities is essential for making causal inferences regarding the effects of communities on violence rates. As noted earlier, there are substantive reasons to expect that violence has feedback effects on major dimensions of community structure. Moreover, communities appear to have "careers" in crime (Reiss, 1986a; Schuerman and Kobrin, 1986), and several key hypotheses concerning the link between communities and rates of violence were explicitly formulated in terms of change (e.g., increasing concentration of the underclass, effect of residential turnover on disruption of social networks). To disentangle community social processes and the potential reciprocal effects of violence requires longitudinal designs in which temporal ordering can be established and change processes explicitly modeled.[29]

Another major research need is for direct examination of the social processes and interactions through which both individual and community effects are transmitted. As for the individual level, research on both victimization and offending has established little more than that sociodemographic factors (e.g., age, race, sex, employment) are important correlates of violence. This is unsatisfactory, not just to policy makers, but to social science theories of violence causation. Although beyond the scope of this paper, we need much more concentrated efforts to measure the mediating social processes underlying victimization (e.g., routine activities, lifestyles) and offending (e.g., peer networks, cultural values, school climate). In particular, research directly addressing the social basis for the race-violence link in contemporary urban America seems especially important. Street (1989:29) has argued that without the willingness to confront and analyze the reality of race, "we cannot make headway in dealing with crime in this country." To the extent that past trends in research designs simply continue, we will indeed not make headway in uncovering the social processes that foster urban violence—the leading cause of death among young black males (Fingerhut and Kleinman, 1990:3292).

Community-level measurement needs are probably even greater than those at the individual level. We documented earlier how criminological research has largely failed to directly examine community processes of theoretical relevance. To address this requires a new, though perhaps costly, measurement strategy: survey instruments designed to measure community concepts and administered with community sampling frames in mind. For example, survey measures could be constructed to capture community-level patterns of informal social control, friendship networks, subcultural values, rates of organizational participation, and much more. Some preliminary attempts have been made (e.g., Taylor et al., 1984; Simcha-Fagan and Schwartz, 1986; Sampson and Groves, 1989), but we need surveys designed to test community-based theories on units of analysis defined by the research question, not by governmental agencies. There is nothing inherently deficient about a measurement strategy designed at the macrolevel. The problem is that the measurement task is difficult and requires the outlay of large research funds.

A different approach is ethnographic analysis, because we can learn much about community structure and violence from ethnographic studies that we cannot learn from multivariate analyses of census data and survey measures. Given the importance of community cultures and value systems in criminological theories of violence, it is disturbing that modern criminology has reified multivariate methodology as the engine of scientific progress. We believe that a more balanced perspective calls for quantitative research to be supplemented with community ethnography. Hagedorn's (1988) *People and Folks: Gangs, Crime and the Underclass in a Rustbelt City* and Sullivan's (1989) *Getting Paid: Economy, Culture, and Youth Crime in the Inner City* are but two recent examples of how rich and provocative community ethnographic/ qualitative research can be (see also Katz, 1988).

PUBLIC POLICY

Last, but certainly not least, a multilevel approach guided by a substantive focus on community-level processes has constructive implications for public policy. The reason is that many of the hypothesized community-level sources of violence noted throughout this paper (e.g., residential instability, concentration of poverty and family disruption, high-density public housing projects, attenuation of social networks) are determined, both directly and indirectly, by the policy decisions of public officials. Take, for example, municipal code enforcement and local governmental policies toward neighborhood deterioration. In *Making the Second Ghetto: Race and Housing in Chicago, 1940-1960*, Hirsch (1983) documents in great detail how lax enforcement of city housing codes played a major role in accelerating the deterioration of inner-city Chicago neighborhoods. More recently, Daley and Meislen (1988) have argued that inadequate city policies with regard to code enforcement and repair of city properties contributed to the systematic decline of New York City's housing stock and, consequently, of entire neighborhoods. When considered in conjunction with the practices of redlining and disinvestment by banks or "block-busting" by real estate agents (Skogan, 1986), local policies toward code enforcement—which on the surface seem far removed from crime—have in all likelihood contributed to crime through neighborhood deterioration, forced migration, and instability.

The provision of city municipal services in terms of public health and fire safety—decisions presumably made with little if any thought to crime and violence—also appears to have been salient in the social disintegration of poor communities. As Wallace and Wallace (1990:427) argue, based on an analysis of the "planned shrinkage" of New York City fire and health services in recent decades, "The consequences of withdrawing municipal services from poor neighborhoods, the resulting outbreaks of contagious urban decay and forced migration which shred essential social networks and cause social disintegration, have become a highly significant contributor to decline in public health among the poor." The loss of social integration and networks from planned shrinkage of services may increase behavioral patterns of violence that can themselves become "convoluted with processes of urban decay likely to further disrupt social networks and cause further social disintegration" (Wallace and Wallace, 1990:427). This pattern of destabilizing feedback noted earlier and also by Skogan (1986) appears central to understanding the role of governmental policies in fostering the downward spiral of high-crime areas.

Decisions by government on public housing paint a similar picture. Bursik (1989) has shown that the planned construction of new public housing projects in Chicago in the 1970s was associated with increased rates of population turnover, which in turn were related to increases in crime—independent of racial composition. More generally, Skogan (1986:206) notes how urban renewal and forced migration contributed to the wholesale uprooting of many urban communities, especially the extent to which freeway networks driven through the hearts of many cities in the

1950s destroyed viable, low-income communities. Indeed, the instability forced upon low-income minority neighborhoods by governmental urban renewal decisions was profound. In Atlanta, one in six residents was dislocated through urban renewal, the great majority of whom were poor (Logan and Molotch, 1987:114). Nationwide, fully 20 percent of all central-city housing units occupied by blacks were lost in the period 1960-1970. As Logan and Molotch (1987:114) observe, this displacement does not even include that brought about by more routine market forces (evictions, rent increases, commercial development).

Perhaps most disturbing, Wilson (1987:20-62) documents the negative consequences of policy decisions to concentrate minorities and the poor in public housing. Opposition from organized community groups to the building of public housing in their neighborhoods, de facto federal policy to tolerate extensive segregation of blacks in urban housing markets, and the decision by local governments to neglect the rehabilitation of existing residential units (many of them single-family homes) have led to massive, segregated housing projects that have become ghettos for the minorities and disadvantaged (see also Massey, 1990; Sampson, 1990). The social transformation of the inner city, triggered in large part by governmental policy, has thus led to the disproportionate concentration of the most disadvantaged segments of the urban black population in a few areas. The result is that even given the same objective socioeconomic status, blacks and whites face vastly different environments in which to live, work, and raise their children (Massey and Kanaiaupuni, 1990:18). When linked to the probable effects of concentrated urban poverty and family disruption on community social organization, as reviewed above, governmental housing policies clearly become relevant to crime control policy. Moreover, to the extent that segregation and concentrated poverty represent structural constraints embodied in public policy, concerns raised earlier about self-selection confounding the interpretation of community-level effects on violence are considerably diminished. As Massey and Kanaiaupuni (1990:20) have argued, public housing represents a federally funded, physically permanent institution for the isolation of black families by race and class, and must therefore be considered an important structural constraint on ecological area of residence.

In short, government matters, and the political economy of place (Logan and Molotch, 1987) must be explicitly incorporated into theories and policies of community-level social organization. The reason is that what seem to be "noncrime" policies (e.g., where or if to build a housing project, enforcement of municipal codes, reduction in essential municipal services, rehabilitation of existing residential units, disbursement of the disadvantaged) can have important indirect effects on violence. As detailed above, many community characteristics implicated in violence, such as residential instability, concentration of poor, female-headed families with children, multiunit housing projects, and disrupted social networks, appear to stem rather directly from planned governmental policies at local, state, and federal levels. This conceptualization diverges from the natural market assumptions of the earlier social ecologists (e.g., Park et al., 1925) by considering the role of political decisions in shaping community structure.

On the positive side, the implication of this community-level perspective is that there are in fact policy options that may help reverse the tide of community social disintegration. Among others, these might include *resident management of public housing* (to increase stability), *tenant buy-outs* (to increase home ownership and commitment to locale), *rehabilitation of existing low-income housing* (to preserve area stability, especially single-family homes), *disbursement of public housing* (versus concentration), and *strict code enforcement* (to fight deterioration). Moreover, there are recent examples that such policies are viable and, in fact, have stabilizing effects on communities and hence potential for crime reduction (e.g., see the programs described in Reiss, 1989; Sampson, 1990; more generally, see Logan and Molotch, 1987).

CONCLUSION

For these and other reasons discussed throughout this paper, the prospects appear promising for merging a community-level approach to violence with more traditional concerns regarding individual and situational factors. The unique value of a multilevel perspective is that it leads away from a simple "kinds of people" analysis to a focus on how social characteristics of collectivities foster violence. Based on the theoretical conceptualization and empirical literature reviewed earlier, we thus conclude that community-level factors such as (but not limited to)[30] the *ecological concentration of the urban underclass, residential mobility and population turnover, family disruption, housing* and *population density, criminal opportunity structures* (e.g., levels of nonhousehold leisure activities, gun density), and dimensions of local *social or-*

ganization (e.g., informal social ties, density of acquaintanceship, supervision of street-corner peer groups, organizational density and strength) represent fruitful areas of future inquiry, especially because they are affected by public policies regarding housing and municipal services. Moreover, our review suggests that individual-level characteristics (e.g., age, race, sex, poverty, divorce) and situational context (e.g., victim-offender relationship) in all likelihood *interact* with these community characteristics (see also Gottfredson and Taylor, 1986) to explain both victimization by violence and criminal careers in violent offending. Implementation of multi-level, longitudinal research designs that capture the inextricable link between violent victimization and violent offending will not be cheap but appears essential nonetheless.

ACKNOWLEDGMENT

We are grateful to Steve Gottfredson, Lloyd Street, Leonard Eron, and members of the Panel on the Understanding and Control of Violent Behavior for very helpful comments on an earlier version of this paper.

NOTES

1   Because of space limitations we are also unable to consider in any detail the role of social learning factors in the etiology of violence. For a theoretical overview of social learning theory and behaviorism, especially with regard to aggression, see Bandura and Walters (1959) and Eron (1987).

2   Data presented in reports of the National Crime Survey are usually reported as rates per 1,000 (or 10,000) persons in the population at risk. To provide a comparative indicator of an individual's risk of violent victimization, we have converted published rates into a "1 in X" chance of victimization (see Reiss, 1981).

3   The NCS household surveys discussed herein were not specifically designed to capture victimizations against commercial establishments (e.g., robberies of convenience stores and gas stations). This distinction suggests caution in the comparison of NCS robbery victimizations with UCR arrest data on robberies that include commercial targets.

4   Conclusions from NCS data do not apply to homicides. Recent evidence suggests that the homicide rate for juveniles is rising faster than for adults. In fact, some cities report as much

as a 100 percent increase in violence among juveniles in the period 1985-1990 alone (Recktenwald and Myers, 1991). A recent report by the Centers for Disease Control also shows that the firearm death rate among U.S. black males more than doubled from 1984 to 1988 (Fingerhut et al., 1991).

5   Our use of the term "sex," as opposed to "gender," is merely descriptive and not intended to suggest that male-female differences in offense involvement or victimization are the simple result of biological factors. For a detailed review of this literature, see Kruttschnitt in this volume.

6   Of course, women are much more likely to be the victims of "purse snatching" than men. However, purse snatching without the use of force is personal larceny, not robbery or assault (cf. Feeney and Weir, 1975).

7   Age, of course, is part of the reason for the magnitude of this relationship. However, see section below on multivariate relationships.

8   Again, it is likely that part of this association is due to the relationship between age and victimization risk.

9   Victims of violent crime were defined as those persons who reported an assault, robbery, or personal larceny with contact.

10   Gender was not considered in this analysis because of a limited number of reported robberies against females.

11   Gender was also not considered in this analysis, apparently for theoretical reasons.

12   Education was not evaluated as an independent predictor in any of the above-mentioned analyses. However, given the weak bivariate relationship found in the NCS it is unlikely that this measure would have contributed independently and significantly to the risk of violent victimization.

13   Space limitations preclude a detailed review of the lifestyle and routine activity approach. For comprehensive reviews the reader is referred to the original sources (Hindelang et al., 1978:Chap. 11; Cohen and Felson, 1979; Cohen et al., 1981b) and to Gottfredson (1986), Garofalo (1987), and Maxfield (1987). In this paper we assume theoretical compatibility between the lifestyle and routine activity approaches (see especially Maxfield, 1987; Garofalo, 1987).

14   Lifestyle-routine activity theories tend to assume that one's home is safer than areas outside the home and that the risk of violence from family members is lower than the risk of violence from nonfamily members. This assumption has recently come

into question by research showing that for certain subgroups (e.g., women, children), this may not be the case (see generally Ohlin and Tonry, 1989).

15 The dichotomous measure of major daytime activity compared those employed and persons attending school to all others. Night activity was dichotomized to reflect persons who go out (on average) less than once per week versus those who go out one or more times a week.

16 Most studies (see Wolfgang et al., 1987, for an exception) have analyzed either juvenile or adult samples. Different findings with respect to specialization and escalation of offending might be found if we followed the same individuals over both the juvenile and the adult phases of offending careers.

17 These methodological problems are not discussed further because they have been addressed elsewhere (for recent overviews, see Blumstein et al., 1986; Weiner, 1989; Bridges and Weis, 1989). Nonetheless, they should not be overlooked; overcoming even a few of these limitations could substantially increase our understanding of violent offending.

18 The conceptual confusion over situational factors has been discussed at length by Monahan and Klassen (1982). An empirical example of the problem can be seen in Denno's (1986) analysis of victim, offender, and situational characteristics of violent crime. At one point, she defines situational factors to include family income and the sociodemographic characteristics of the participants (1986:1143). At another, she considers "offender" variables to be individual-level factors "measured independently of the offense event"—a definition that would seem to subsume the demographic characteristics (e.g, age, race, sex) of the participants earlier attributed to a situation. Like Monahan and Klassen (1982) we do not consider attributes of individuals (e.g., race, sex, income) to be situational factors.

19 Fagan et al. (1987) have argued that the individual-level relationships between victimization and offending may be spurious and due to the areas in which both victims and offenders live.

20 Interpretations of "nonstranger" (including acquaintances, friends, and family members) versus "stranger" differences are also complicated by the fact that the nonstranger category contains a wide variety of social relationships. For example, the definition of an acquaintance may include asymmetrical relationships in which the offender is familiar with the victim but not vice versa or is someone familiar to the victim by sight only.

21 For more extensive reviews of this literature, see Collins

(1989), Goldstein (1989), and especially the articles in Tonry and Wilson (1990).

22 The effect of third parties on the initiation of a violent event would be extremely difficult to determine empirically, given that the presence of additional persons is likely to be correlated with other contextual factors not included in the model.

23 Although not typically thought of as a property of local communities, urbanization is strongly related to violent crime, independent of compositional factors (Laub, 1983; Sampson and Groves, 1989). See Fischer (1975) and Laub (1983) for theoretical discussions of the link between urbanization and crime. Unfortunately, very few studies have examined between-community variations in violent crime in nonurbanized areas.

24 Of course, criminology is rich in cultural explanations of crime, especially regarding lower-class culture and the subculture of violence (for a review see Kornhauser, 1978; Short, 1990). In terms of violence, the most prominent explanation continues to be the subculture of violence theory (Wolfgang and Ferracuti, 1967). The basic tenet of subcultural theory is that "overt use of force or violence . . . is generally viewed as a reflection of basic values that stand apart from the dominant, central, or parent culture" (1967:385). However, neither the theory of lower-class culture nor the subculture of violence refers explicitly to community-level causal processes.

25 We focus on the Land et al. (1990) study because it brings together in one paper the key metropolitan-level studies of violence conducted in recent years. Indeed, all of the studies in Table 1 have appeared since 1960 and have formed the basis for much recent discussion on the macrolevel sources of criminal violence (see also the review by Byrne and Sampson, 1986; Messner and Sampson, 1991). Space limitations preclude a discussion of each study—readers are urged to consult the originals for more details. For an excellent review of earlier research on metropolitan differences in violence, see Brantingham and Brantingham (1984:281-294). The latter also provide a discussion of regional-level studies of violence and metropolitan-level studies focused on crimes other than homicide.

26 In a recent paper appearing after the Land et al. (1990) study, Balkwell (1990) shows that ethnic income inequality had a positive net effect on homicide rates across 150 SMSAs in 1980 even after controlling for poverty, race, and geographic region.

27 Very few studies have examined macrolevel variations in violent crime among rural areas and suburbs. However, evidence

does exist that the correlates of suburban violence are quite similar to those in urban areas. For example, Stahura and Sloan (1988) found that the major predictor of violent crime rates across U.S. suburbs was a factor almost identical to the resource deprivation/ affluence factor identified by Land et al. (1990). Specifically, the factor most related to violent crime in the suburbs was comprised mainly of percent poor and percent black (Stahura and Sloan, 1988:1111).

28 In further analyses of these data, Messner and Sampson (1991) disaggregated the measure of employed black males per 100 black females into its constituent components—the sex ratio (males per female) and the unemployment rate. Results showed that both components had significant negative effects on black family disruption, which again had positive effects on black violence rates. Interestingly, however, even though the sex ratio had the largest effect on family disruption—and by implication a negative indirect effect on violence—the sex ratio had a positive direct effect on violence. Therefore, family disruption appears to operate as a suppressor variable in explaining the counterbalancing effects of sex ratio on violence. That is, only when family disruption is controlled does the expected positive effect of sex ratio composition (males per female) on violence emerge. Furthermore, the indirect effect of the relative availability of employed black males on violence (Sampson, 1987a) appears to stem mostly from the simple demographic factor of imbalanced sex ratios.

29 "Case-control" methodology (see Schlesselmann, 1982; Loftin and McDowall, 1988) may be an especially attractive device for studying both individual- and community-level violence in longitudinal perspective. Although case-control methodology is usually retrospective, communities and individuals could be matched on key confounding characteristics (e.g., demographic background) and then followed up and examined in terms of salient intervening processes (e.g., subcultural values, disruption of social networks) thought to account for variation in violence. Not only is case-control methodology useful for controlling key theoretical factors through matching, but it provides an efficient and cost-effective way to counteract the low base rate of violence (Loftin and McDowall, 1988).

30   Because of space limitations, we did not focus on community-level dimensions of formal social control by the police and courts. These and other community-level variations (e.g., drug distribution networks, medical and trauma services) should not be overlooked in future work. Moreover, we did not examine the structural sources of violence by agents of official social con-

trol (e.g., police homicide, brutality, coercion). See Smith (1986) and Jacobs and Britt (1979), respectively, for empirical analyses of the community-level determinants of police use of coercion and deadly force.

REFERENCES

Ageton, S.
1983   The dynamics of female delinquency, 1976-1980. *Criminology* 21:555-584.

Anderson, E.
1978   *A Place on the Corner.* Chicago: University of Chicago Press.
1990   *Streetwise: Race, Class, and Change in an Urban Community.* Chicago: University of Chicago Press.

Andrew, J.
1979   Violence and poor reading. *Criminology* 17:361-365.

Bailey, W.C.
1984   Poverty, inequality, and city homicide rates: Some not so unexpected findings. *Criminology* 22:531-550.

Balkwell, J.
1990   Ethnic inequality and the rate of homicide. *Social Forces* 69:53-70.

Bandura, A., and R. Walters
1959   *Adolescent Aggression.* New York: Ronald Press.

Baron, L., and M. Straus
1987   Four theories of rape: A macrosociological analysis. *Social Problems* 34:467-489.

Beasley, R.W., and G. Antunes
1974   The etiology of urban crime: An ecological analysis. *Criminology* 11:439-461.

Bensing, R.C., and O. Schroeder
1960   *Homicide in an Urban Community.* Springfield, Ill.: Charles C. Thomas.

Blau, J., and P.M. Blau
1982   The cost of inequality: Metropolitan structure and violent crime. *American Sociological Review* 47:114-129.

Blau, P.M., and R. Golden
1986   Metropolitan structure and criminal violence. *Sociological Quarterly* 27:15-26.

Block, C.R.
1985   Race/ethnicity and patterns of Chicago homicide, 1965 to 1981. *Crime and Delinquency* 31:104-116.

Block, R.
1975   Homicide in Chicago: A nine year study (1965-1973). *Journal of Criminal Law and Criminology* 66:496-510.

1979   Community, environment, and violent crime. *Criminology* 17:46-57.

1981   Victim-offender dynamics in violent crime. *Journal of Criminal Law and Criminology* 72:743-761.

Block, R., and C. Block
1980   Decisions and data: The transformation of robbery incidents into official robbery statistics. *Journal of Criminal Law and Criminology* 71:622-636.

Block, R., and W. Skogan
1986   Resistance and nonfatal outcomes in stranger-to-stranger predatory crime. *Violence and Victims* 1:241-253.

Blumstein, A., J. Cohen, J. Roth, and C. Visher, eds.
1986   *Criminal Careers and "Career Criminals."*   Washington, D.C.: National Academy Press.

Blumstein, A., J. Cohen, S. Das, and S. Moitra
1988   Specialization and seriousness during adult criminal careers. *Journal of Quantitative Criminology* 4:303-346.

Bordua, D.
1958   Juvenile delinquency and "anomie": An attempt at replication. *Social Problems* 6:230-238.

1986   Firearms ownership and violent crime. Pp. 156-188 in J. Byrne and R.J. Sampson, eds., *The Social Ecology of Crime.*   New York: Springer-Verlag.

Braithwaite, J., and D. Biles
1984   Victims and offenders: The Australian experience. Pp. 3-10 in R. Block, ed., *Victimization and Fear of Crime: World Perspectives.* Washington, D.C.: U.S. Government Printing Office.

Brantingham, P., and P. Brantingham
1984   *Patterns in Crime.* New York: Macmillan.

Bridges, G., and J. Weis
1989   Measuring violent behavior: Effects of study design on reported correlates of violence. Pp. 14-34 in N. Weiner and M. Wolfgang, eds., *Violent Crime, Violent Criminals.* Beverly Hills, Calif.: Sage Publications.

Brownfield, D.
1986   Social class and violent behavior. *Criminology* 24:421-438.

Bullock, H.A.
1955   Urban homicide in theory and fact. *Journal of Criminal Law, Criminology, and Police Science* 45:565-575.

Bursik, R.J., Jr.
1986   Delinquency rates as sources of ecological change. Pp. 63-76 in J. Byrne and R.J. Sampson, eds., *The Social Ecology of Crime.* New York: Springer-Verlag.

1988   Social disorganization and theories of crime and delinquency: Problems and prospects. *Criminology* 26:519-552.

1989   Political decision-making and ecological models of delinquency: Conflict and consensus. Pp. 105-117 in S. Messner, M. Krohn, and A. Liska, eds., *Theoretical Integration in the Study of Deviance and Crime.* Albany: State University of New York at Albany Press.

Bursik, R.J., Jr., and J. Webb
1982 Community change and patterns of delinquency. *American Journal of Sociology* 88:24-42.

Byrne, J.
1986 Cities, citizens, and crime: The ecological/nonecological debate reconsidered. Pp. 77-101 in J. Byrne and R.J. Sampson, eds., *The Social Ecology of Crime.* New York: Springer-Verlag.

Byrne, J., and R.J. Sampson
1986 Key issues in the social ecology of crime. Pp. 1-22 in J. Byrne and R.J. Sampson, eds., *The Social Ecology of Crime.* New York: Springer-Verlag.

Carroll, L., and P. Jackson
1983 Inequality, opportunity, and crime rates in central cities. *Criminology* 21:178-194.

Chilton, R.
1964 Continuity in delinquency area research: A comparison of studies for Baltimore, Detroit, and Indianapolis. *American Sociological Review* 29:71-83.

Cohen, L., and M. Felson
1979 Social change and crime rate trends: A routine activities approach. *American Sociological Review* 44:588-607.

Cohen, L., D. Cantor, and J. Kluegel
1981a Robbery victimization in the United States. *Social Science Quarterly* 66:644-657.

Cohen, L., J. Kluegel, and K. Land
1981b Social inequality and predatory criminal victimization: An exposition and test of a formal theory. *American Sociological Review* 46:505-524.

Collins, J.
1989 Alcohol and interpersonal violence: Less than meets the eye. Pp. 49-67 in N. Weiner and M. Wolfgang, eds., *Pathways to Criminal Violence.* Newbury Park, Calif.: Sage Publications.

Cook, P.
1979 The effect of gun availability on robbery and robbery murder: A cross-section study of fifty cities. Pp. 743-781 in R. Haveman and B. Zellner, eds., *Policy Studies Review Annual,* Vol. 3. Beverly Hills, Calif.: Sage Publications.

1982 The role of firearms in violent crimes. Pp. 236-291 in M. Wolfgang and N. Weiner, eds., *Criminal Violence.* Beverly Hills, Calif.: Sage Publications.

1983 *Robbery in the United States: An Analysis of Recent Trends and Patterns.* Washington, D.C.: National Institute of Justice.

1986 The demand and supply of criminal opportunities. Pp. 1-28 in

M. Tonry and N. Morris, eds., *Crime and Justice: An Annual Review*, Vol. 8. Chicago: University of Chicago Press.

1987 Robbery violence. *Journal of Criminal Law and Criminology* 78:357-376.

Corrado, R., R. Roesch, W. Glackman, J. Evans, and G. Leger
1980 Lifestyles and personal victimization: A test of the model with Canadian survey data. *Journal of Crime and Justice* 3:129-139.

Covington, J., and R. Taylor
1989 Gentrification and crime: Robbery and larceny changes in appreciating Baltimore neighborhoods during the 1970s. *Urban Affairs Quarterly* 25:142-172.

Crutchfield, R., M. Geerken, and W. Gove
1982 Crime rate and social integration: The impact of metropolitan mobility. *Criminology* 20:467-478.

Curry G.D., and I. Spergel
1988 Gang homicide, delinquency, and community. *Criminology* 26:381-406.

Curtis, L.
1975 *Violence, Race, and Culture.* Lexington, Mass.: Heath.

Daley, S., and R. Meislin
1988 New York City, the landlord: A decade of housing decay. *New York Times* February 8.

Danziger, S.
1976 Explaining urban crime rates. *Criminology* 14:291-295.

De Fronzo, J.
1983 Economic assistance to impoverished Americans. *Criminology* 21:119-136.

Denno, D.
1986 Victim, offender, and situational characteristics of violent crime. *Journal of Criminal Law and Criminology* 77:1142-1158.

Elder, G.
1985 Perspectives on the life course. Pp. 23-49 in G. Elder, ed., *Life Course Dynamics.* Ithaca, N.Y.: Cornell University Press.

Elliott, D., and S. Ageton
1980 Reconciling race and class differences in self-reported and official estimates of delinquency. *American Sociological Review* 45:95-110.

Elliott, D., and D. Huizinga
1983 Social class and delinquent behavior in a national youth panel: 1976-1980. *Criminology* 21:149-177.

Elliott, D., D. Huizinga, and S. Ageton
1985 *Explaining Delinquency and Drug Use.* Beverly Hills, Calif.: Sage Publications.

Eron, L.
1987 The development of aggressive behavior from the perspective of a developing behaviorism. *American Psychologist* 42:435-442.

Fagan, J., E. Piper, and Y. Cheng
  1987 Contributions of victimization to delinquency in inner cities. *Journal of Criminal Law and Criminology* 78:586-613.
Farley, R.
  1980 Homicide trends in the United States. *Demography* 17:177-188.
Farrington, D.
  1978 The family background of aggressive youths. Pp. 73-92 in L. Hersov, M. Berger, and D. Schaffer, eds., *Aggression and Antisocial Behavior in Childhood and Adolescence.* Oxford: Pergamon.
  1986 Age and crime. Pp. 189-250 in M. Tonry and N. Morris, eds., *Crime and Justice: An Annual Review of Research*, Vol 7. Chicago: University of Chicago Press.
Farrington, D., and D. West
  1971 A comparison between early delinquents and youth aggressiveness. *British Journal of Criminology* 11:341-358.
Farrington, D., H. Snyder, and T. Finnegan
  1988 Specialization in juvenile court careers. *Criminology* 26:461-488.
Feeney, F., and A. Weir
  1975 The prevention and control of robbery. *Criminology* 20:102-105.
Felson, M., and L. Cohen
  1980 Human ecology and crime: A routine activity approach. *Human Ecology* 8:389-406.
Felson, R., and H. Steadman
  1983 Situational factors in disputes leading to criminal violence. *Criminology* 21:59-74.
Fingerhut, L., and J. Kleinman
  1990 International and interstate comparisons of homicide among young males. *Journal of the American Medical Association* 263:3292-3295.
Fingerhut, L., J. Kleinman, E. Godfrey, and H. Rosenberg
  1991 Firearm mortality among children, youth, and young adults 1-34 years of age, trends and current status: United States, 1978-88. *Monthly Vital Statistics Report* 39(11):1-16.
Fischer, C.
  1975 Toward a subcultural theory of urbanism. *American Journal of Sociology* 80:1319-141.
Fisher, J.
  1976 Homicide in Detroit. *Criminology* 14:387-400.
Flango, E., and E. Sherbenou
  1976 Poverty, urbanization, and crime. *Criminology* 14:331-346.
Friedman, J., and D. Rosenbaum
  1988 Social control theory: The salience of components by age, gender, and type of crime. *Journal of Quantitative Criminology* 4:363-382.

Garofalo, J.
1987 Reassessing the lifestyle model of criminal victimization. Pp. 23-42 in M. Gottfredson and T. Hirschi, eds., *Positive Criminology*. Newbury Park, Calif.: Sage Publications.

Garofalo, J., L. Siegel, and J. Laub
1987 School-related victimizations among adolescents: An analysis of National Crime Survey narratives. *Journal of Quantitative Criminology* 3:321-338.

Gastil, R.
1971 Homicide and a regional culture of violence. *American Sociological Review* 36:412-27.

Gelles, R.
1985 Family violence. *Annual Review of Sociology* 11:347-367.

Gelles, R., and M. Straus
1988 *Intimate Violence*. New York: Simon and Schuster.

Glueck, S., and E. Glueck
1950 *Unraveling Juvenile Delinquency*. New York: Commonwealth Fund.

Goldstein, P.
1989 Drugs and violent crime. Pp. 16-48 in N. Weiner and M. Wolfgang, eds., *Pathways to Criminal Violence*. Newbury Park, Calif.: Sage Publications.

Gordon, R.
1967 Issues in the ecological study of delinquency. *American Sociological Review* 32:927-944.

Gottfredson, M.
1984 *Victims of Crime: The Dimensions of Risk*. Home Office Research Study No. 81. London: Her Majesty's Stationery Office.
1986 Substantive contributions of victimization surveys. In M. Tonry and N. Morris, eds., *Crime and Justice: An Annual Review of Research*, Vol. 7. Chicago: University of Chicago Press.

Gottfredson, M., and M. Hindelang
1981 Sociological aspects of criminal victimization. *Annual Review of Sociology* 7:107-128.

Gottfredson, S., and R. Taylor
1986 Person-environment interactions in the prediction of recidivism. Pp. 133-155 in J. Byrne and R.J. Sampson, eds., *The Social Ecology of Crime*. New York: Springer-Verlag.

Gove, W., M. Hughes, and M. Geerken
1985 Are Uniform Crime Reports a valid indicator of the index crimes? An affirmative answer with minor qualifications. *Criminology* 23:451-502.

Greenberg, D.
1985 Age, crime, and social explanation. *American Journal of Sociology* 91:1-21.

Hagan, J., A.R. Gillis, and J. Chan
   1978   Explaining official delinquency: A spatial study of class, con-
          flict, and control. *Sociological Quarterly* 19:386-398.
Hagedorn, J.
   1988   *People and Folks: Gangs, Crime and the Underclass in a Rustbelt
          City.* Chicago: Lake View Press.
Hanushek, E., and J. Jackson
   1977   *Statistical Methods for Social Scientists.* New York: Academic
          Press.
Harries, K.
   1976   Cities and crime: A geographic model. *Criminology* 14:369-
          386.
Harris, A.R.
   1977   Sex and theories of deviance: Toward a functional theory of
          deviant type-scripts. *American Sociological Review* 42:3-16.
Hawkins, D.
   1985   Black homicide: The adequacy of existing research for devising
          prevention strategies. *Crime and Delinquency* 31:83-103.
Heitgerd, J.L., and R.J. Bursik, Jr.
   1987   Extracommunity dynamics and the ecology of delinquency.
          American Journal of Sociology 92:775-787.
Hill, G., and A. Harris
   1981   Changes in the gender patterning of crime, 1953-1977: Oppor-
          tunity vs. identity. *Social Science Quarterly* 62:658-671.
Hindelang, M.
   1974   The Uniform Crime Reports revisited. *Journal of Criminal Jus-
          tice* 2:1-17.
   1976   *Criminal Victimization in Eight American Cities.* Cambridge,
          Mass.: Ballinger.
   1978   Race and involvement in common-law personal crimes. *Ameri-
          can Sociological Review* 43:93-109.
   1979   Sex differences in criminal activity. *Social Problems* 27:143-
          156.
   1981   Variations in sex-race-age-specific incidence rates of offending.
          American Sociological Review 46:461-474.
Hindelang, M., M. Gottfredson, and J. Garofalo
   1978   *Victims of Personal Crime: An Empirical Foundation for a
          Theory of Personal Victimization.* Cambridge, Mass.: Ballinger.
Hindelang, M., T. Hirschi, and J. Weis
   1979   Correlates of delinquency: The illusion of discrepancy between
          self-report and official measures. *American Sociological Re-
          view* 44:995-1014.
   1981   *Measuring Delinquency.* Beverly Hills, Calif.: Sage Publica-
          tions.
Hirsch, A.
   1983   *Making the Second Ghetto: Race and Housing in Chicago 1940-
          1960.* Chicago: University of Chicago Press.

Hirschi, T., and M. Gottfredson
    1983   Age and the explanation of crime. *American Journal of Sociology* 89:552-584.
Horowitz, R.
    1987   Community tolerance of gang violence. *Social Problems* 34:437-450.
Hough, M., and P. Mayhew
    1983   *The British Crime Survey: First Report.* Home Office Research Study No. 76. London: Her Majesty's Stationery Office.
Huff-Corzine, L., J. Corzine, and D. Moore
    1986   Southern exposure: Deciphering the South's influence on homicide rates. *Social Forces* 64:906-24.
Hunter, A.
    1974   *Symbolic Communities.* Chicago: University of Chicago Press.
Hutchings, B., and S. Mednick
    1975   Registered criminality in the adoptive and biological parents of registered male adoptives. In R. Fieve, D. Rosenthal, H. Brill, eds., *Genetic Research in Psychiatry.* Baltimore: Johns Hopkins University Press.
Jackson, P.
    1984   Opportunity and crime: A function of city size. *Social Science Research* 68:172-193.
Jacobs, D., and D. Britt
    1979   Inequality and police use of deadly force: An empirical assessment of a conflict hypothesis. *Social Problems* 26:403-411.
Jamieson, K., and T. Flanagan
    1989   *Sourcebook of Criminal Justice Statistics-1988.* Washington, D.C.: U.S. Department of Justice.
Jensen, G., and D. Brownfield
    1986   Gender, lifestyles, and victimization: Beyond routine activity theory. *Violence and Victims* 1:85-99.
Kapsis, R.
    1976   Continuities in delinquency and riot patterns in black residential areas. *Social Problems* 23:567-580.
Katz, J.
    1988   *Seductions of Crime: The Sensual and Moral Attractions of Doing Evil.* New York: Basic.
Keiser, R.L.
    1970   *The Vice Lords: Warriors of the Streets* (fieldwork edition). New York: Holt, Rinehart and Winston.
Kennedy, L., and D. Forde
    1990   Routine activities and crime: An analysis of victimization in Canada. *Criminology* 28:137-152.
Kleck, G.
    1984   The relationship between gun ownership levels and rates of violence in the United States. Pp. 99-135 in D. Kates, ed., *Firearms and Violence: Issues of Public Policy.* New York: Ballinger.

Kornhauser, R.
1978 *Social Sources of Delinquency.* Chicago: University of Chicago Press.
Krohn, M.
1986 The web of conformity: A network approach to the explanation of delinquent behavior. *Social Problems* 33:81-93.
Kruttschnitt, C., L. Heath, and D. Ward
1986 Family violence, television viewing habits, and other adolescent experiences related to violent criminal behavior. *Criminology* 24:235-268.
Kruttschnitt, C., D. Ward, and M.A. Scheble
1987 Abuse-resistant youth: Some factors that may inhibit violent criminal behavior. *Social Forces* 66:501-519.
Land, K., P. McCall, and L. Cohen
1990 Structural covariates of homicide rates: Are there any invariances across time and space? *American Journal of Sociology* 95:922-963.
Lander, B.
1954 *Toward an Understanding of Juvenile Delinquency.* New York: Columbia University Press.
Langan, P., and C. Innes
1990 The risk of violent crime. In N. Weiner, M. Zahn, and R. Sagi, eds., *Violence: Patterns, Causes, Public Policy.* New York: Harcourt Brace Jovanovich.
Laub, J.
1983 Urbanism, race, and crime. *Journal of Research in Crime and Delinquency* 20:183-198.
Laub, J., and M.J. McDermott
1985 An analysis of serious crime by young black women. *Criminology* 23:81-98.
Laub, J., and R.J. Sampson
1988 Unraveling families and delinquency: A reanalysis of the Gluecks' data. *Criminology* 26:355-380.
Lauritsen, J., R. Sampson, and J. Laub
1991 The link between offending and victimization among adolescents. *Criminology* 29:265-292.
Law Enforcement Assistance Administration
1972 *San Jose Methods Test of Crime Victims.* Statistics Technical Report TT No. 1. Washington, D.C.: Law Enforcement Assistance Administration.
Levin, Y., and A. Lindesmith
1937 English ecology and criminology of the past century. *Journal of Criminal Law and Criminology* 27:801-816.
Liebow, E.
1967 *Tally's Corner.* Boston: Little, Brown.

Liska, A., and M. Reed
  1985 Ties to conventional institutions and delinquency: Estimating reciprocal effects. *American Sociological Review* 50:547-560.
Loeber, R., and M. Stouthamer-Loeber
  1986 Family factors as correlates and predictors of juvenile conduct problems and delinquency. Pp. 29-150 in M. Tonry and N. Morris, eds., *Crime and Justice: An Annual Review of Research*, Vol. 7. Chicago: University of Chicago Press.
Loftin, C., and R. Hill
  1974 Regional subculture and homicide: A examination of the Gastil-Hackney thesis. *American Sociological Review* 39:714-724.
Loftin, C., and E. MacKenzie
  1990 Building national estimates of violent victimization. Commissioned paper for the National Academy of Sciences Symposium on "The Understanding and Control of Violent Behavior," Destin, Fl., April.
Loftin, C., and D. McDowall
  1988 The analysis of case-control studies in criminology. *Journal of Quantitative Criminology* 4:85-98.
Loftin, C., and R. Parker
  1985 An errors-in-variable model of the effect of poverty on urban homicide rates. *Criminology* 23:269-287.
Loftin, C., K. Kindley, S. Norris, and B. Wiersema
  1987 An attribute approach to relationships between offenders and victims in homicide. *Journal of Criminal Law and Criminology* 78:259-271.
Logan, J., and H. Molotch
  1987 *Urban Fortunes: The Political Economy of Place.* Berkeley: University of California Press.
Luckenbill, D., and D. Doyle
  1989 Structural position and violence: Developing a cultural explanation. *Criminology* 27:419-436.
Lynch, J.
  1987 Routine activities and victimization at work. *Journal of Quantitative Criminology* 2:283-300.
Maccoby, E., J. Johnson, and R. Church
  1958 Community integration and the social control of juvenile delinquency. *Journal of Social Issues* 14:38-51.
Massey, D.
  1990 American apartheid: Segregation and the making of the underclass. *American Journal of Sociology* 96:329-357.
Massey, D., and M. Eggers
  1990 The ecology of inequality: Minorities and the concentration of poverty, 1970-1980. *American Journal of Sociology* 95:1153-1188.

Massey, D., and S. Kanaiaupuni
1990 Public Housing and the Concentration of Poverty. Working paper, Population Research Center, University of Chicago.
Maxfield, M.
1987 Lifestyle and routine activity theories of crime: Empirical studies of victimization, delinquency, and offender decision-making. *Journal of Quantitative Criminology* 3:275-282.
Mayer, S., and C. Jencks
1989 Growing up in poor neighborhoods: How much does it matter? *Science* 243(March):1441-1445.
McCord, J.
1982 A longitudinal view of the relationship between paternal absence and crime. Pp. 113-128 in J. Gunn and D. Farrington, eds., *Abnormal Offenders, Delinquency and the Criminal Justice System*. London: Wiley.
McCord, W., J. McCord, and A. Howard
1961 Familial correlates of aggression in non-delinquent male children. *Journal of Abnormal Social Psychology* 62:79-93.
McDonald, S.
1986 Does gentrification affect crime rates? Pp. 163-202 in A.J. Reiss, Jr., and M. Tonry, eds., *Communities and Crime*. Chicago: University of Chicago Press.
Messner, S.
1982 Poverty, inequality, and the urban homicide rate. *Criminology* 20:103-114.
1983a Regional and racial effects on the urban homicide rate: The subculture of violence revisited. *American Journal of Sociology* 88:997-1007.
1983b Regional differences in the economic correlates of the urban homicide rate: Some evidence on the importance of cultural context. *Criminology* 21:477-488.
Messner, S., and J. Blau
1987 Routine leisure activities and rates of crime: A macro-level analysis. *Social Forces* 65:1035-1052.
Messner, S., and R. J. Sampson
1991 The sex ratio, family disruption, and rates of violent crime: The paradox of demographic structure. *Social Forces* 69:693-714.
Messner, S., and S. South
1986 Economic deprivation, opportunity structure, and robbery victimization: Intra- and interracial patterns. *Social Forces* 64:975-991.
Messner, S., and K. Tardiff
1986 Economic inequality and levels of homicide: An analysis of urban neighborhoods. *Criminology* 24:297-318.

Miethe, T., and R. Meier
1990 Opportunity, choice, and criminal victimization. *Journal of Research in Crime and Delinquency* 27:243-266.
Miethe, T., M. Stafford, and J. Long
1987 Social differentiation in criminal victimization: A test of routine activities/lifestyle theories. *American Sociological Review* 52:184-194.
Mladenka, K., and K. Hill
1976 A reexamination of the etiology of urban crime. *Criminology* 13:491-506.
Monahan, J., and D. Klassen
1982 Situational approaches to understanding and predicting individual violent behaviors. Pp. 292-319 in M. Wolfgang and N. Weiner, eds., *Criminal Violence*. Beverly Hills, Calif.: Sage Publications.
Morris, T.
1958 *The Criminal Area*. London: Routledge and Kegan Paul.
1970 Book review of *Juvenile Delinquency and Urban Areas*, 2nd ed. *British Journal of Criminology* 10:194-196.
O'Brien, R.
1985 *Crime and Victimization Data*. Beverly Hills, Calif.: Sage Publications.
1987 The interracial nature of violent crimes: A re-examination. *American Journal of Sociology* 92:817-835.
1988 Exploring the intersexual nature of violent crimes. *Criminology* 26:151-170.
Ohlin, L., and M. Tonry, eds.
1989 *Family Violence*. Chicago: University of Chicago Press.
Park, R.E., E. Burgess, and R. McKenzie
1925 *The City*. Chicago: University of Chicago Press.
Parker, R.N., and M.D. Smith
1979 Deterrence, poverty, and type of homicide. *American Journal of Sociology* 85:614-624.
Peterson, R., and C. Bailey
1988 Forcible rape, poverty, and economic inequality in U.S. metropolitan communities. *Journal of Quantitative Criminology* 4:99-120.
Pierce, G., and W. Bowers
1981 The Bartley-Fox gun law's short-term impact on crime in Boston. *Annals of the American Academy of Political and Social Science* 455:120-137.
Piper, E.
1985 Violent recidivism and chronicity in the 1958 Philadelphia cohort. *Journal of Quantitative Criminology* 1:319-344.
Pittman, D., and W. Handy
1964 Patterns in criminal aggravated assault. *Journal of Criminal Law, Criminology, and Police Science* 55:462-470.

Pokorny, A.
   1965   Human violence: A comparison of homicide, aggravated as-
          sault, suicide and attempted suicide. *Journal of Criminal Law,*
          Criminology, and Police Science 56:488-497.
Pyle, G., E. Hanten, P. Williams, A. Pearson, J. Doyle, and K. Kwofie
   1974   *The Spatial Dynamics of Crime.* Chicago: Department of Geo-
          graphic Research, University of Chicago.
Rainwater, L.
   1970   *Behind Ghetto Walls: Black Families in a Federal Slum.* Chi-
          cago: Aldine.
Rankin, J.
   1983   The family context of delinquency. *Social Problems* 30:466-
          479.
Raudenbush, S., and A. Bryck
   1986   A hierarchical model for studying school effects. *Sociology of*
          Education 59:1-17.
Recktenwald, W., and L. Myers
   1991   849 killings put 1990 in a sad record book. *Chicago Tribune*
          1,7.
Reiss, A.J., Jr.
   1981   Towards a revitalization of theory and research on victimiza-
          tion by crime. *Journal of Criminal Law and Criminology* 72:704-
          713.
   1986a Why are communities important in understanding crime? Pp.
          1-33 in A.J. Reiss, Jr., and M. Tonry, eds., *Communities and*
          Crime. Chicago: University of Chicago Press.
   1986b Co-offender influences on criminal careers. Pp. 121-160 in A.
          Blumstein, J. Cohen, J. Roth, and C. Visher, eds., *Criminal Ca-*
          reers and "Career Criminals." Washington, D.C.: National
          Academy Press.
Reiss, A.J., Jr., ed.
   1989   *Proceedings of the Workshop on Communities and Crime Con-*
          trol. Committee on Research on Law Enforcement and the Ad-
          ministration of Justice, National Research Council. Washing-
          ton, D.C.: National Criminal Justice Reference Service.
Riedel, M.
   1987   Stranger violence: Perspectives, issues, and problems. *Journal*
          of Criminal Law and Criminology 78:223-258.
Rieder, J.
   1985   *Canarsie: The Jews and Italians of Brooklyn Against Liberal-*
          ism. Cambridge, Mass.: Harvard University Press.
Robins, L.
   1966   *Deviant Children Grown Up.* Baltimore: Williams and Wilkins.
Roncek, D.
   1981   Dangerous places: Crime and residential environment. *Social*
          Forces 60:74-96.

Roncek, D., and D. Faggiani
  1986 High schools and crime: A replication. *Sociological Quarterly* 26:491-505.
Roncek, D., R. Bell, and J. Francik
  1981 Housing projects and crime: Testing a proximity hypothesis. *Social Problems* 29:151-166.
Rose, H., and P. McClain
  1990 *Race, Place and Risk: Black Homicide in Urban America.* Albany: State University of New York Press.
Rosenfeld, R.
  1986 Urban crime rates: Effects of inequality, welfare, dependency, region, and race. In J. Byrne and R. Sampson, eds., *The Social Ecology of Crime.* New York: Springer-Verlag.
Sampson, R.J.
  1983 Structural density and criminal victimization. *Criminology* 21:276-293.
  1984 Group size, heterogeneity, and intergroup conflict. *Social Forces* 62:618-639.
  1985a Neighborhood and crime: The structural determinants of personal victimization. *Journal of Research in Crime and Delinquency* 22:7-40.
  1985b Race and criminal violence: A demographically disaggregated analysis of urban homicide. *Crime and Delinquency* 31:47-82.
  1986a Neighborhood family structure and the risk of criminal victimization. Pp. 25-46 in J. Byrne and R. Sampson, eds., *The Social Ecology of Crime.* New York: Springer-Verlag.
  1986b Crime in cities: The effects of formal and informal social control. Pp. 271-311 in A.J. Reiss, Jr., and M. Tonry, eds., *Communities and Crime.* Chicago: University of Chicago Press.
  1986c Effects of socioeconomic context on official reaction to juvenile delinquency. *American Sociological Review* 51:876-885.
  1987a Urban black violence: The effect of male joblessness and family disruption. *American Journal of Sociology* 93:348-382.
  1987b Personal violence by strangers: An extension and test of the opportunity model of predatory victimization. *Journal of Criminal Law and Criminology* 78:327-356.
  1988 Community attachment in mass society: A multilevel systemic model. *American Sociological Review* 53:766-769.
  1990 The impact of housing policies on community social disorganization and crime. *Bulletin of the New York Academy of Medicine* 66:526-533.
Sampson, R.J., and W.B. Groves
  1989 Community structure and crime: Testing social-disorganization theory. *American Journal of Sociology* 94:774-802.
Sampson, R.J., and J.H. Laub
  1990 Crime and deviance over the life course: The salience of adult social bonds. *American Sociological Review* 55:609-627.

Sampson, R.J., and J. Lauritsen
    1990 Deviant lifestyles, proximity to crime, and the offender-victim link in personal violence. *Journal of Research in Crime and Delinquency* 27:110-139.
Sampson, R.J., and J. Wooldredge
    1986 Evidence that high crime rates encourage migration away from central cities. *Sociology and Social Research* 70:310-314.
    1987 Linking the micro- and macro-level dimensions of lifestyle-routine activity and opportunity models of predatory victimization. *Journal of Quantitative Criminology* 3:371-393.
Schlesselmann, J.
    1982 *Case-Control Studies.* New York: Oxford University Press.
Schmid, C.
    1960 Urban crime areas, part I. *American Sociological Review* 25:527-542.
Schuerman, L., and S. Kobrin
    1986 Community careers in crime. Pp. 67-100 in A.J. Reiss, Jr., and M. Tonry, eds., *Communities and Crime.* Chicago: University of Chicago Press.
Shaw, C., and H. McKay
    1931 Social factors in juvenile delinquency. Vol. 2 of *Report of the Causes of Crime.* National Commission of Law Observance and Enforcement. Washington, D.C.: U.S. Government Printing Office.
    1942 *Juvenile Delinquency and Urban Areas.* Chicago: University of Chicago Press.
    1969 *Juvenile Delinquency and Urban Areas* (rev. ed.). Chicago: University of Chicago Press.
Shaw, C., F. Zorbaugh, H. McKay, and L. Cottrell
    1929 *Delinquency Areas.* Chicago: University of Chicago Press.
Sherman, L., P. Gartin, and M. Buerger
    1989 Hot spots of predatory crime: Routine activities and the criminology of place. *Criminology* 27:27-56.
Shin, Y., D. Jedlicka, and E. Lee
    1977 Homicide among blacks. *Phylon* 38:398-407.
Short, J.F., Jr.
    1963 Introduction to the abridged edition. Pp. xv-liii in F. Thrasher, *The Gang: A Study of 1,313 Gangs in Chicago.* Chicago: University of Chicago Press.
    1969 Introduction to the revised edition. Pp. xxv-liv in C. Shaw and H. McKay, eds., *Juvenile Delinquency and Urban Areas.* Chicago: University of Chicago Press.
    1985 The level of explanation problem in criminology. Pp. 51-74 in R. F. Meier, ed., *Theoretical Methods in Criminology.* Beverly Hills, Calif.: Sage Publications.

1990   *Delinquency and Society*. Englewood Cliffs, N.J.:   Prentice-Hall.

Short, J.F., and F. Strodtbeck
1965   *Group Process and Gang Delinquency*. Chicago: University of Chicago Press.

Silverman, R., and L. Kennedy
1987   Relational distance and homicide: The role of the stranger. *Journal of Criminal Law and Criminology* 78:272-308.

Simcha-Fagan, O., and J. Schwartz
1986   Neighborhood and delinquency: An assessment of contextual effects. *Criminology* 24:667-704.

Simon, R.
1975   *Women and Crime*. Lexington, Mass.: D.C. Heath.

Simon, R., and S. Baxter
1989   Gender and violent crime. Pp. 171-197 in N. Weiner and M. Wolfgang, eds., *Violent Crime, Violent Criminals*. Beverly Hills, Calif.: Sage Publications.

Simpson, M.
1985   Violent crime, income inequality, and regional culture: Another look. *Sociological Focus* 18:199-208.

Singer, S.
1981   Homogeneous victim-offender populations: A review and some research implications. *Journal of Criminal Law and Criminology* 72:779-788.

Skogan, W.
1981   Assessing the behavioral context of victimization. *Journal of Criminal Law and Criminology* 72:727-742.
1986   Fear of crime and neighborhood change. Pp. 203-229 in A.J. Reiss, Jr., and M. Tonry, eds., *Communities and Crime*. Chicago: University of Chicago Press.

Smith, D.R.
1986   The neighborhood context of police behavior. Pp. 313-341 in A.J. Reiss, Jr., and M. Tonry, eds., *Communities and Crime*. Chicago: University of Chicago Press.

Smith, D.R., and G.R. Jarjoura
1988   Social structure and criminal victimization. *Journal of Research in Crime and Delinquency* 25:27-52.

Smith, D.R., and C. Visher
1980   Sex and involvement in deviance/crime: A quantitative review of the empirical literature. *American Sociological Review* 45:691-701.

Smith, M.
1987   Changes in the victimization of women: Is there a new female victim? *Journal of Research in Crime and Delinquency* 24:291-301.

Smith, M.D., and R.N. Parker
  1980 Type of homicide and variation in regional rates. *Social Forces* 59:137-147.
Smith, S.
  1982 Victimization in the inner city: A British case study. *British Journal of Criminology* 22:386-402.
South, S., and R. Felson
  1990 The racial patterning of rape. *Social Forces* 69:71-94.
Sparks, R.
  1982 *Research on Victims of Crime.* Washington, D.C.: U.S. Government Printing Office.
Sparks, R., H. Glenn, and D. Dodd
  1977 *Surveying Victims.* London: Wiley.
Spergel, I.
  1964 *Racketville, Slumtown, Haulburg.* Chicago: University of Chicago Press.
Stahura, J., and J. Sloan, III
  1988 Urban stratification of places, routine activities and suburban crime rates. *Social Forces* 66:1102-1118.
Stark, R.
  1987 Deviant places: A theory of the ecology of crime. *Criminology* 25:893-909.
Steffensmeier, D., E.A. Allan, M. Harer, and C. Streifel
  1989 Age and the distribution of crime. *American Journal of Sociology* 94:803-831.
Straus, M., and R. Gelles
  1986 Societal change and change in family violence from 1975 to 1985 as revealed by two national surveys. *Journal of Marriage and the Family* 48:465-479.
Street, L.
  1989 Why focus on communities? Pp. 27-34 in A.J. Reiss, Jr., ed., *Proceedings of the Workshop on Communities and Crime Control.* Committee on Research on Law Enforcement and the Administration of Justice, National Research Council. Washington, D.C.: National Criminal Justice Reference Service.
Sullivan, M.
  1989 *Getting Paid: Economy, Culture, and Youth Crime in the Inner City.* Ithaca, N.Y.: Cornell University Press.
Suttles, G.
  1968 *The Social Order of the Slum.* Chicago: University of Chicago Press.
Taub, R., D.G. Taylor, and J. Dunham
  1984 *Paths of Neighborhood Change: Race and Crime in Urban America.* Chicago: University of Chicago Press.
Taylor, R., and J. Covington
  1988 Neighborhood changes in ecology and violence. *Criminology* 26:553-590.

Taylor, R., and S. Gottfredson
   1986   Environmental design, crime, and prevention: An examination of community dynamics. Pp. 387-416 in A.J. Reiss, Jr., and M. Tonry, eds., *Communities and Crime.* Chicago: University of Chicago Press.
Taylor, R., S. Gottfredson, and S. Brower
   1984   Block crime and fear: Defensible space, local social ties, and territorial functioning. *Journal of Research in Crime and Delinquency* 21:303-331.
Thornberry, T., and M. Farnworth
   1982   Social correlates of criminal involvement: Further evidence on the relationship between social status and criminal behavior. *American Sociological Review* 47:505-517.
Thrasher, F.
   1963   *The Gang: A Study of 1,313 Gangs in Chicago* (rev. ed.). Chicago: University of Chicago Press.
Tienda, M.
   1989   Poor People and Poor Places: Deciphering Neighborhood Effects on Behavioral Outcomes. Paper presented at the annual meeting of the American Sociological Association, San Francisco, August 9-13.
Tittle, C., W. Villemez, and D. Smith
   1978   The myth of social class and criminality: An empirical assessment of the empirical evidence. *American Sociological Review* 43:643-656.
Tonry, M., and J.Q. Wilson, eds.
   1990   *Drugs and Crime.* Chicago: University of Chicago Press.
U.S. Department of Justice
   1985   *The Risk of Violent Crime.* Washington, D.C.: U.S. Department of Justice.
   1986   *Crime in the United States, 1985.* Washington, D.C.: U.S. Department of Justice.
   1988a *Report to the Nation on Crime and Justice,* 2nd ed. Washington, D.C.: U.S. Department of Justice.
   1988b *Crime in the United States, 1987.* Washington, D.C.: U.S. Department of Justice.
   1989   *Criminal Victimization in the United States, 1987.* A National Crime Survey Report, June. Washington, D.C.: U.S. Department of Justice.
van Dijk, J., and C. Steinmetz
   1983   Victimization surveys: Beyond measuring the volume of crime. *Victimology* 8:291-301.
Van Voorhis, P., F. Cullen, R. Mathers, and C.C. Garner
   1988   The impact of family structure and quality on delinquency: A comparative assessment of structural and functional factors. *Criminology* 26:235-261.

Visher, C., and J. Roth
1986 Participation in criminal careers. Pp. 211-191 in A. Blumstein, J. Cohen, J. Roth, and C. Visher, eds., *Criminal Careers and "Career Criminals."* Washington, D.C.: National Academy Press.

Wallace, R., and D. Wallace
1990 Origins of public health collapse in New York City: The dynamics of planned shrinkage, contagious urban decay and social disintegration. *Bulletin of the New York Academy of Medicine* 66:391-434.

Weiner, N.
1989 Violent criminal careers and "violent career criminals." Pp. 35-138 in N. Weiner and M. Wolfgang, eds., *Violent Crime, Violent Criminals.* Beverly Hills, Calif.: Sage Publications.

Wells, L., and J. Rankin
1988 Direct parental controls and delinquency. *Criminology* 26:263-285.

West, D., and D. Farrington
1977 *The Delinquent Way of Life.* London: Heinemann.

Widom, C.S.
1989a The intergenerational transmission of violence. Pp. 137-201 in N. Weiner and M. Wolfgang, eds., *Pathways to Criminal Violence.* Beverly Hills, Calif.: Sage Publications.
1989b Child abuse, neglect, and violent criminal behavior. *Criminology* 27:251-272.

Wilbanks, W.
1985 Is violent crime intraracial? *Crime and Delinquency* 31:117-128.

Wilkinson, K.
1980 The broken home and delinquent behavior. Pp. 21-42 in T. Hirschi and M. Gottfredson, eds., *Understanding Crime.* Beverly Hills, Calif.: Sage Publications.

Williams, K.
1984 Economic sources of homicide: Reestimating the effects of poverty and inequality. *American Sociological Review* 49:283-289.

Williams, K., and R. Flewelling
1988 The social production of criminal homicide: A comparative study of disaggregated rates in American cities. *American Sociological Review* 53:421-431.

Wilson, W.J.
1987 *The Truly Disadvantaged: The Inner City, the Underclass, and Public Policy.* Chicago: University of Chicago Press.

Wolfgang, M.
1958 *Patterns in Criminal Homicide.* New York: John Wiley & Sons.

Wolfgang, M., and F. Ferracuti
1967 *The Subculture of Violence.* London: Tavistock.

Wolfgang, M., T. Thornberry, and R. Figlio
    1987 *From Boy to Man, From Delinquency to Crime.* Chicago: University of Chicago Press.
Zahn, M., and P. Sagi
    1987 Stranger homicides in nine American cities. *Journal of Criminal Law and Criminology* 78:377-396.
Zimring, F.
    1981 Kids, groups, and crime: Some implications of a well known secret. *Journal of Criminal Law and Criminology* 72:867-885

Violence Between Spouses and Intimates: Physical Aggression Between Women and Men in Intimate Relationships

Jeffrey Fagan and Angela Browne

INTRODUCTION

In the 1960s, Americans began to ask important questions about violence. The National Commission on the Causes and Prevention of Violence, known as the Kerner Commission, concluded in 1969 that the United States was the world's leader in rates of homicide, assault, rape, and robbery. To most people, crime in general and violent crime in particular became major sources of discontent (Gurr, 1989; Weiner and Wolfgang, 1985). However, this early concern with criminal victimization focused primarily on violent incidents outside the home. Like the commission, most Americans believed that the risk of personal attack or injury lay in individuals beyond one's circle of intimates. Violence in the family—if recognized at all—was rarely considered criminal unless a death occurred. The average family, it was assumed, afforded at least some measure of nurturance and protection to its members. Twenty years later, we are now aware of the extent of violence between family members in our society and the seriousness of that violence in terms of physical and non-physical injury.

Jeffrey Fagan is at the School of Criminal Justice, Rutgers University. Angela Browne is at the University of Massachusetts Medical Center.

In the past two decades, there has been an upsurge of inquiry into violence between intimates. The growth of social services in the 1960s, designed primarily to wrestle with extramarital social problems such as stranger crime or substance abuse, not only focused public policy on the economic behavior of families (Gilbert, 1983), but also opened up the family as a social institution amenable to public scrutiny. Accordingly, family social interactions became increasingly subject to social interventions and legal sanctions (Wexler, 1982). Until public policy focused attention on the private realm of family life, few people considered the home to be other than "a compassionate, egalitarian, peaceful affair in which violence played no part" (Wardell et al., 1983).

Three major trends in this era raised doubts about this tranquil view of American family life. First, the "discovery" of child abuse through medical and sociological research in the mid-1960s focused public attention on family violence (e.g., Caffey, 1946; Silverman, 1953; Kempe et al., 1962; see also Gil, 1970). Child abuse victims had a visceral and emotional public appeal. Several national organizations came into being to promote services and financial support for child victims, and to work for statutory changes and improved protections. A nationwide reporting system was implemented during the 1970s, and laws mandated formal reports to designated agencies by parents, teachers, and police officers who became aware of child abuse or neglect.

Second, political activism by feminist organizations at that time helped make visible the use of physical force as a means of intimidation or coercion within the family and elevated it to prominence as a social concern (U.S. Commission on Civil Rights, 1978; Schechter, 1982). Much of this awareness was engendered by the modern women's movement which, in the 1960s, began to examine violence against women around the issue of rape. Such discussion revealed the prevalence of women experiencing sexual assaults by intimate male partners, rather than strangers, and provided a forum for the identification of the physical assault of wives as a problem of previously unrecognized national proportions.

Concern over the harm to women (specifically, serious injuries and fatalities), and also to the children for whom they cared, intensified as the public became aware of the confluence of family violence and other violent behaviors outside the family. Violence in the home, previously informally condoned because it was "private," was now defined in a social context as deviant and placed in the public domain, marking a "moral passage" in American

social history (Gusfield, 1967). As incidence and prevalence estimates became established, family violence became an issue of
focus for researchers, medical and mental health treatment pro-
viders, and policy makers.

Third, the emphasis on victimization in criminal justice research and practice in the 1970s identified family violence as an
important and complex phenomenon confronting the police and
courts (Parnas, 1967; Bard and Zacker, 1971; Wilson, 1977). During the 1970s, sweeping legal and police policy changes were in-
stituted in response to public concern and social science investigations. Victim support was an important component of political
activism that sought to reorient legal institutions toward fulfill-
ing the entitlement of the rights of victims. Feminist groups
decried the secondary victimization of "special victims," including victims of rape and wife abuse.

Research on marital violence in the United States has now
spanned nearly three decades. National surveys estimate that an
act of physical violence is committed by a family member in
nearly half of all homes during an average 12-month period in the
United States (see, e.g., Straus et al., 1980; Gelles and Straus,
1988). Minimum estimates from these surveys indicate that acts
of physical aggression between spouses occur in one of six homes
each year. Injuries and lethal injuries from partner violence fall
disproportionately on women. A minimum of two million women
are severely assaulted annually by their male partners (Straus and
Gelles, 1986), and more than half the women murdered in the
United States are killed by male partners or ex-partners (Browne
and Williams, 1989; Zahn, 1989). Rosenberg et al. (1984) estimated that more than 20,000 hospitalizations occur each year due
to acts of violence in the home. These estimates have remained
remarkably consistent over time, even in the face of increased
awareness and intervention.

Yet, despite the growing evidence that criminal violence frequently occurs between family members as well as between acquaintances and strangers, criminologists today continue to study
these patterns separately. There have been few efforts to integrate the empirical literature on aggression within families with
other perspectives on violence. Knowledge utilization in the policy
development process also has selectively incorporated the independent bodies of empirical research and theoretical traditions.
Family violence continues to be defined and studied by criminologists as a separate crime type, rather than as a specific variety of
violence or aggression (cf. Williams and Flewelling, 1988), and is

more often treated as a "specialization" similar to white-collar crime or substance use. In turn, criminal justice policy toward wife assault has reflected research paradigms and theories of criminal or violent behavior toward strangers, rather than either an integrated perspective or a perspective incorporating the unique contributions of family violence research.

Marital Violence Defined

In this paper, the discussion of research and policy on violence between intimate adult partners includes physical assault, sexual assault, and homicide, committed, threatened, or attempted by spouses, ex-spouses, common-law spouses, or cohabitants toward their partners. We also note other harmful behaviors that occur as part of the natural history of marital violence: psychological abuse, economic deprivation, threats to others in the family, and threats as a method of coercion. These behaviors co-occur with physical assault, and although we do not focus on them specifically, they are part of the "ecology of aggression" that characterizes marital violence. They may also constitute antecedents of physical aggression, part of the maintenance of a pattern of marital violence, or displacements of aggression when assaults desist.

Definitions in the study of violence between intimates have varied extensively. Bandura (1973) defined aggression as behavior that results in personal injury or property destruction. Bandura's definition is consistent with the definition of family violence offered by Gelles and Straus (1979) as "an act carried out with the intention of, or perceived intention of, physically hurting another person." Gelles and Straus distinguished violence from aggression, which includes any malevolent action, regardless of whether physical harm is involved. However, they excluded verbal aggression, marital rape, and sexual assaults from their definition of family violence.

Collins (1988), focusing exclusively on violent behaviors, defines violence as an actual or attempted physical attack and terms this "expressive interpersonal violence." Such broad conceptual definitions require careful attention to the operational definitions and attendant measures in the studies reviewed. For example, although Straus and Gelles define violence as actions undertaken with the intent or perceived intent to harm, their measure assesses neither intent nor perceptions.

In this paper, we are concerned with aggression between adults in families or intimate cohabitating relationships that reflects the intent to harm or to create a painful condition. These behaviors include attempted or completed physical assaults, homicides, and sexual assaults. We are also concerned with property destruction that is intended to harm the partner and with the threat of force. The extensive literature on victimization of spouses or partners— along with its broader implications for the understanding and control of violent behavior—warrants focusing this essay specifically on aggression between intimately related adults. Also, the differences in jurisprudential issues regarding children and elderly dependents, and the variations in administrative response systems, require a broader and more complex analysis. Accordingly, the terms wife assault, marital violence, and spouse abuse are sometimes used interchangeably to describe the phenomenon of assaults and abuse by partners or spouses in current or former intimate relationships in which they are or were cohabiting.

Organization of This Paper

In this paper, we examine empirical and theoretical knowledge on violence between adult partners. The first section traces the evolution of theory, research, and policy on partner violence. The historical, cultural, social, and legal foundations of current efforts are reviewed. In the following section, a social epidemiology of assaults between partners is established, including estimates of participation and frequency rates, characteristics of victims and assailants, and an assessment of "risk markers" for marital violence. Patterns of spousal homicide and their relationship to other forms of partner and stranger violence are also discussed. This section includes a critical review that assesses the limitations and strengths of empirical research and theory. Specifically, we examine the validity and reliability of current indices and the overall strength and limitations of current knowledge. We discuss the unique context of families that complicates sampling and measurement decisions, as well as the critical interdependence of definition, measurement, and interpretation.

Then the broader implications of empirical knowledge for explanation and theory are assessed. We examine several explanatory frameworks suggested by the epidemiology and risk factors evident in marital violence and integrate them within a broader conceptual framework. The examination concludes with discussions linking research on marital violence to the larger study of violent behavior.

After that, current policies and interventions are examined, including empirical evidence of their effectiveness and their validity in terms of current knowledge. Both social and legal interventions are discussed, as is the interaction among policy, theory, definition, and knowledge of family violence. This includes an analysis of the social processes of problem definition and the sociology of knowledge about violence between adult intimates. The influence of these processes on what we know and do about marital violence is analyzed.

Finally a research agenda is set forth for the advancement of theory, methods, and empirical knowledge of partner violence, and research to integrate the perspectives is specifically (but not exclusively) recommended. We conclude with a discussion that integrates knowledge of assaults between intimate partners with other forms of violence within families and violence outside the context of families.

EVOLUTION OF KNOWLEDGE AND POLICY ON MARITAL VIOLENCE

The new social knowledge of violence between adult partners developed during an era in which social intervention in family life had gained widespread support and created a context for defining marital violence as an urgent social problem. The ensuing social and political processes shaped both the knowledge of marital violence and policy responses. The nature of the problem and its etiological roots were subjected to varying interpretations and definitions. As would be expected, definitions, research traditions, and policy development all varied according to the interests and perspectives of the definers. Thus, the perspectives that were influential in the development of knowledge and policy responses to marital violence reflect differing assumptions regarding its definition and etiology, as well as concerns with the "ownership" of marital violence as a social problem.

CROSS-CULTURAL PERSPECTIVES

Marital violence is intrinsic to many cultures. Levinson (1988) using cross-cultural data on family violence from the Human Relations Area Files (HRAF) data base (Lagace, 1979) identified eight varieties of marital violence in 330 societies.[1] Levinson (1988, 1989) estimated the prevalence of wife beating[2] in a representative sample of 90 societies from the 330 cultural groups in the

HRAF data base. Wife beating occurred in 84.5 percent of the 90 cultures. It occurred "at least occasionally" in all or nearly all households in 18.8 percent of the societies, and in a majority (but not all) in 29.9 percent. Husband beating was reported in 6.7 percent of all societies; it was rare or unheard of in 73.1 percent and occurred in a minority of households in 20.2 percent. Other studies (cited in Levinson, 1989) report comparable data: Wife beating occurs in 71 to 92 percent of the societies studied.

Motivations for wife beating in these societies included sexual jealousy or infidelity (45.5%), insubordination or disobedience by the wife (25.5%), and the wife's failure to meet "household responsibilities" (23.3%). Societal responses to wife beating varied extensively. In 91.2 percent of the societies, intervention by outsiders occurred. These interventions included help or intercession by kin or neighbors (17.6%), shelter for the wife (14.7%), legal intervention (17.6%), marital violence as grounds for divorce (11.8%), and supernatural sanctions (e.g., casting a spell)—in an unspecified proportion. In 29.4 percent of the societies, interventions are limited to beatings that exceed societal norms for the "physical discipline" of wives. Interventions were reportedly unavailable in 8.8 percent of the societies. The study gave no indication of the legal status of wife or husband assaults in the societies studied.

Such comparative studies are complicated by several methodological and design issues. Family configurations and kinship networks vary extensively across societies, and the meaning of family and the nature of marital bonds are obviously culture specific. Consensus on a universal definition of family violence is no more evident in cross-cultural research than in contemporary research in the United States (Korbin, 1977). Variations in injury, motivation, and context are consistent with variations in the social organization of these societies, the meanings attached to marital violence, and the unique family configurations (e.g., Gartner, 1990). Other sources of design variability include measurement inconsistencies, sampling problems in defining the boundaries of cultures and stratifying them, and uneven attention to the variables that are thought to cause cross-cultural variation. Anthropological studies also tend to avoid explicit comparisons of two or more cultures, limiting tests of the factors that actually influence cultural variations (Levinson, 1988). However, coding and validation procedures in the HRAF data base may have offset some of these limitations.

HISTORICAL LEGACIES OF PUBLIC POLICY ON MARITAL VIOLENCE

Cultural and legal supports for marital violence toward wives have existed in Western civilization for more than 3,000 years. In ancient Rome, physical domination of wives by husbands was acknowledged in the "law of marriage," formalized by Romulus in 753 B.C. (Pagelow, 1984). Davidson (1978) quotes Friar Cherubino of Siena in the late 1400s as recommending in his Rules of Marriage that husbands respond to an offense by a wife by first scolding, bullying, and terrifying. If that did not produce the desired results, they were then instructed to "take up a stick and beat her soundly . . . ". Blackstone's (1765) commentary on English common law accorded legal rather than moral authority to men's domination in family matters. In a system in which wives occupied the same status as children, Blackstone noted that the civil law "gave the husband the same, or a larger, authority over his wife: allowing him for some misdemeanors, to beat his wife severely with scourges and cudgels . . . for others only moderate chastisement."

After the colonization of North America, the social and legal history of reform efforts for marital violence shows cyclical patterns dating to the Puritan era in Massachusetts in the 1640s (Pleck, 1987). Throughout American history, interest in criminal sanctions against marital violence has coincided with both heightened concern about state responsibility to enforce public morality and increased fear of crime (Pleck, 1989). According to Stark and Flitcraft (1983:330), "Virtually every 20 years . . . the popular press has joined women's groups and charitable organizations to denounce wife beating, child abuse, and related forms of family violence in the strongest terms."

Reform Movements Toward Women and Children From the Puritans Through the Nineteenth Century

The first American law prohibiting beating female spouses was enacted in the Puritan era in 1641 in the Massachusetts Bay Colony. This law was modified two years later to include violence against husbands. Pleck (1989:24) notes that laws against wife and child beating were intended primarily to serve as a "symbolic affirmation" of biblical principles, and that the Puritans upheld and justified the use of "legitimate" physical force by parents, masters, or husbands. Men were allowed to punish their children and wives physically, whereas wives or children were never allowed to punish their husbands or parents. Respect for family privacy and the husband's authority sharply limited the number of arrests under these sanctions. By 1663, enforcement under these laws had virtually ceased. The next law against wife beating (and evidently the last one for 200 years) was passed in 1672 in the Plymouth Colony. However, only 12 cases of spouse assault against wives were prosecuted in the Plymouth Colony court from 1633 to 1802 (Pleck, 1987).[3]

No further laws against wife assault or other forms of family violence were enacted until a Tennessee law was passed in 1850, followed by a Georgia law seven years later and by an Alabama Supreme Court ruling in 1871. Rather, during this time court rulings continued to define the limitations of legal intervention for spouse assault. A Mississippi court ruling in 1824 said that a husband, in cases of "great emergency," had the right to discipline his wife physically so long as it was done in a moderate manner, "without being subjected to vexatious prosecution (*Bradley* v. *State*, 1 Miss. 157). The "rule of thumb" (1866) permitted a man to beat his wife "with a stick as large as his finger but not larger than his thumb," a reform that was deemed "compassionate" by limiting the weapons a man could use against his spouse (*State* v. *Rhodes*, 61 Phil. L. [N.C.] 453; cited by Browne, 1987).[4] However, in a subsequent ruling in the same case, the court declined to "interfere with family government in trifling cases" (*State* v. *Rhodes*, 61 N.C. 453, 353, 1868; cited in Pleck, 1989).

The era beginning in the 1870s and continuing through the turn of the century was again a period of activism to stop wife beating and other forms of family violence. It was fueled by growing sympathy with victims of domestic abuse and was coupled with the child protection movement, itself a function of middle-class outrage over the conditions of the urban poor, primarily immigrants who labored in increasingly industrialized cities (Platt, 1969). Dobash and Dobash (1979) describe two short-lived periods of public concern and social action against wife beating. Mill's (1869) famous essay, "The Subjection of Women" decried the battering of wives and resulted in a report to the British parliament in 1874. In the same decade, both British and American legislatures took some limited actions to protect women. Americans revoked a few laws of chastisement, while the British offered "meager protection against cruelty and allowed divorce on this ground" (Mill, 1869:5).

In 1871, Alabama became the first state to rescind a husband's legal right to beat his wife, noting that the "wife is entitled to the same protection of the law that the husband can invoke for himself . . . " (*Fulgham* v. *State*, 46 Ala. 146-147). A North Carolina court followed suit in 1874 but qualified its ruling by advising that if no permanent injury was inflicted or "dangerous" violence shown, it was best to "draw the curtain, shut out the public gaze, and leave the parties to forget and forgive" (*State* v. *Oliver*, 70 N.C. 60, 61-62). Although Pleck (1987) contends that these were atypical legal opinions, the lack of prosecution of cases of wife assault, and the public priorities on family privacy and patriarchal authority, suggest that such legal opinions accurately reflected the attitudes of the times, even if not cited in subsequent cases.

Fear of crime and perceived threat to the moral order were prime motivators of fueling public concern during this period. The crime rate escalated rapidly after the Civil War, both within and outside the home. Laws against wife beating at this time often called for stiff punishment: statutes authorized flogging at the whipping post in three states, an expression of the regard for domestic violence as a serious crime with strong accountability for violators (Pleck, 1989). However, only a few perpetrators were ever flogged for wife abuse, and those who were flogged were disproportionately African American. During this period, family stability and Victorian morality were guiding ethics, and Pleck (1989) reports that more attention was given to the protection of victims and to stabilizing the family unit that to the punishment of offenders. Reconciliation was the goal of intervention, and divorce from an abusive mate was not encouraged.

By the 1890s, Pleck (1989) reports that concern with wife and child abuse began to fade. Society turned to social casework, rather than law enforcement, as the preferred intervention, and cases that were identified were attributed increasingly to economic hardship, family problems, or psychiatric disturbance (Gordon, 1988). General interest in family violence declined until the 1960s.

EMERGENCE OF MARITAL VIOLENCE AS A POLICY ISSUE

The rediscovery of wife abuse in this century was due in large part to the work of feminist activists and clinical researchers who documented and publicized the issue (Martin, 1976; Roy, 1977; Hilberman and Munson, 1978; Walker, 1979). Victims of spouse assault, overwhelmingly women, presented themselves to feminist grassroots organizations via rape hot lines started by these groups, as well as victim assistance agencies or rape crisis centers (Schechter, 1982). These grassroots organizations quickly defined a wide range of services needed by marital violence victims: shelter, transportation, counseling, legal assistance, and child care (Schwendinger and Schwendinger, 1983). They also defined the limitations of existing legal remedies to sanction offenders or offer protection to victims.

Recognition by feminists of the problems and limitations of justice system responses spurred the development of other services for women victims of marital violence as well. Building on the models developed for rape victims, feminist organizations opened crisis intervention and victim assistance programs for women victims of marital violence, started shelters for victims and their children, and formed specialized legal assistance programs for both civil and criminal actions (Schechter, 1982). Through state and national political organizations, they mobilized to reform legislation regarding laws of protection, to eliminate requirements for divorce filing to obtain an order of protection, and to simplify the prosecution of marital rape.

Their early influence was critical in defining wife battering as a multifaceted public policy issue whose solutions spanned the organizational boundaries of specific social or legal institutions.

As marital violence became a public issue, the criminal justice system was obliged to respond in new ways. Traditionally, marital violence was perceived as an ever-present and perhaps intractable problem, creating dangerous situations for the police and difficult-to-resolve cases for the courts (Parnas, 1967; Fields, 1978). Early writings on police responses to family violence were critical, citing their refusal to get involved in family disputes (Fields, 1978), their avoidance of arrest and other criminal sanctions (Field and Field, 1973; Martin, 1976; Roy, 1977; Dobash and Dobash, 1979), and their inappropriate use of nonlegal remedies such as mediation (Eisenberg and Micklow, 1977). Police viewed family disturbance calls as dangerous to responding officers (Parnas, 1967; Bard, 1970; cf. Garner and Clemmer, 1986), and otherwise viewed family disturbances as problematic and intractable interpersonal conflicts that were inappropriate for police attention (Wilson, 1977).

Prior to the early 1970s, many police departments actually had "hands-off" policies (Elliott, 1989). Police training manuals clearly specified that, in responding to domestic disputes, arrest was to be avoided whenever possible (International Association of Chiefs of Police, IACP, 1967).[5] When arrests were made, they often were classified as misdemeanors, which typed them as less serious from the outset (Goolkasian, 1986). A wife usually could not obtain a restraining order against a violent husband unless she were willing to file for divorce at the same time (Fleming, 1979; U.S. Commission on Civil Rights, 1978, 1982). Orders of protection were typically not available on an emergency basis and often carried no provisions for enforcement or penalties for violation. In some states, a single assault was not considered sufficient grounds for a divorce action, and until the mid-1970s, women who eventually killed their mates to protect themselves or their children from harm or death found the traditional plea of self-defense unavailable.

The new social knowledge of family violence led to recognition that domestic disputes were a major problem facing law enforcement and that specific solutions needed to be framed within a legal context (Langan and Innes, 1986; Dutton, 1988a). Political activity by feminists exerted pressure on the criminal justice system to fulfill its mandate to treat violence toward women as a serious crime (Martin, 1976; Fields, 1978). In addition to changes in protection orders, law reform efforts also focused on statutory changes to permit or mandate arrests without corroboration in wife assault cases (Browne and Williams, 1989).

By 1980, 47 states had passed some type of domestic violence legislation (Kalmuss and Straus, 1983; Lerman and Livingston, 1983). The emphasis of this legislation was on enforcing victims' rights, increasing their legal options, and protecting victims and those near them from further assault. Substantive criminal law was also challenged to recognize a history of abuse and threat as part of a legal defense in marital homicides by women in cases in which the male was not actively threatening or abusing his wife at the time of the incident (Schneider, 1980; Schneider and Jordan, 1981; Sonkin, 1987).

Within the criminal justice system and among its stakeholders, there were several movements that created favorable conditions for developing responses to marital violence. Police training in crisis intervention implicitly acknowledged the responsibility to respond effectively to violent situations.[6] Victim-witness services proliferated in the early 1970s and were magnets within the criminal justice system for victims of marital violence, who quickly became a major portion of the caseloads of victim advocates' programs. Victimization as a social movement reflected the concerns of several constituencies with divergent interests. Groups opposed to what they perceived as lenient sentencing of offenders saw the victims' "movement" as a force to balance the rights of the accused against the rights of the victims. Victims of child abuse and wife assault were sympathetic victims. As special constituencies, their needs for protection from both offenders and shabby treatment by criminal justice agencies were seen by victims' rights advocates as staking legitimate claims to their share of the "finite rights" in criminal law.

The responses of criminal justice systems varied. In Philadelphia, a women's group started a voluntary program of legal counseling in the District Attorney's office to inform victims of their options. Class action lawsuits in New York (*Bruno* v. *McGuire*), California (*Scott* v. *Hart*), and Connecticut (*Thurman* v. *City of Torrington*) set the groundwork for later legislation that strengthened legal options and mandated police reactions to marital violence. Special prosecutors for marital violence, supported by federal grants, were appointed in locations such as Santa Barbara, California, and White Plains, New York.

DISAGGREGATION OF RESPONSES TO MARITAL VIOLENCE

Although the feminist community's interest in domestic violence and the victims' services trends coincided in time, there still remained distinctions between the way the problem of and solutions to marital violence were viewed in the respective quarters. The separate origins of the responses to marital violence—feminist grassroots organizations on the one hand and criminal justice system auspices on the other—led to different approaches to stopping violence. These differences were reflected in the service emphases of programs sponsored in these divergent milieus, their interpretation of the role of criminal law, and ultimately, the types of organizations involved in social interventions. Fagan et al. (1984) identified three types of approaches: feminist, social control, and legalistic.

Feminist Approaches

Feminist approaches focused their attention on the woman victim. Little attention was paid to the family unit as a whole, apart from children who were at risk for injury. In fact, many marital violence projects generally believed there was a conflict of interest in serving both the victim and a "family" unit that included her victimizer. Feminism was an explicit part of the conceptualization of these efforts, and informed the types of interventions and the approaches to working with victims. The emphasis was on protecting women from further harm, on providing options and means for them to take concrete steps to end the abuse, and on an empowerment model of service delivery to victims.

In addition to political and legal activism, feminist approaches most often were expressed in shelters or crisis intervention programs. These originated in grassroots organizations and later in private (usually nonprofit) organizations. Shelters and crisis intervention programs reflected concerns with victim protection. They also held fundamentally different views about the resolution of marital violence (Fagan et al., 1984) and defined wife abuse more broadly, consistent with their central concern about the harm to women and their intimate understanding of the progression of marital violence from nonphysical aggression to attacks resulting in severe physical injury. Shelter clients typically included both mothers and children, and their needs were complex.

Issues such as the relationship between wife abuse and sex roles in the family or sex inequalities in society remain part of the fundamental assumptions underlying a feminist service approach and are incorporated explicitly into the services offered. The feminist perspective sees the social institutions of marriage and the family as special contexts that may "promote, maintain, and even support men's use of physical force against women" (Bograd, 1988:12). In the feminist approach, the critical task is working to ensure freedom from violence for women; the critical question is why men use physical force against their partners and what function this serves society in a given historical context (Yllo, 1988).

Social Control Approaches

In contrast, social control approaches generally emphasized the family unit. The family was viewed as the client, and the victim was incorporated into this perspective as a cocontributor to the problem. The theoretical position of programs with this approach is often a family systems model: all family members are seen as part of a "system" of violence, with roles in maintaining that violence. Solutions are believed to require "treating" all members, and the treatment approach is typically based on the supposition that early intervention will be able to head off severe violence before criminal justice sanctions are necessary. Social control interventions—in sharp contrast to empowerment models—are predicated on the notion that the authority of the legal system will exercise control over the "disputants" and coerce or influence family members to stop the violence. These approaches gravitated toward social service agencies, either with formal ties to the courts (e.g., diversion or mediation programs) or with access to legal interventions (e.g., protective service or mental health agencies).

In this model, decisions to invoke legal or quasi-legal sanctions are more likely to occur when violence has reached a severe level that is drastically affecting the family system (Frieze and Browne, 1989). By focusing on family integrity and maintenance, this approach often does not address the risks posed by a persistent pattern of violence in the relationship for some period of time *prior* to help seeking by a family member, or weigh risks from a lengthy pattern of violence toward intimates and strangers that an assaultive spouse may have brought with him to the relationship (Fagan et al., 1983; Shields et al., 1988). Thus social control approaches may underestimate the severity of risk to victims from their insistence on working with the family as a coresponsible unit, exacerbating patterns of rationalization and threats already present in the situation.

Legalistic Approaches

Legalistic approaches most often were sponsored by and affiliated with criminal justice agencies. These approaches focused on the victim and the assailant in the context of laws that were being broken, and were rooted in assumptions of specific deterrence (Sherman and Berk, 1984; Berk and Newton, 1985; Langan and Innes, 1986; Williams and Hawkins, 1989a). Deterrence approaches emphasized the application of legal sanctions through arrest and prosecution of assailants, or invoking the threat of legal sanction through civil remedies that carried criminal penalties if violated. Mandatory arrest policies in several states (Goolkasian, 1986) reflect this approach to marital violence. Innovations included special prosecutors to enhance prosecution services and make them more accessible to victims of marital violence. A small number of these programs linked extralegal services (e.g., shelter, counseling, civil legal representation) to the special prosecution units (Fagan et al., 1984).

Differences in approaches, values, and presuppositions in these perspectives began the process of disaggregation of interventions for marital violence and laid the foundation for separate but sometimes parallel response systems. Each approach was informed and conditioned by different assumptions about, and definitions of, marital violence and victimization, and relied on different research traditions and bodies of knowledge to foster its approach. Each type developed within divergent institutional bases consistent with their definition of the problem, their approach to working with victims, their philosophy of organizational administration, and their theory about why violence occurs and how it stops (Fagan et al., 1984).

CONTROVERSIES IN DEFINITION, MEASUREMENT, AND EXPLANATION

Once marital violence rose to the status of a "social problem," several definitions emerged that varied according to the interests and perspectives of the definer. These definitions varied on several dimensions: the victim-offender relationship, the type of abusive or violent behavior, the nature of harm or injury to the victim, and the motivation or situational context of violent events. Explanatory models of marital violence also varied, particularly in the level of explanation or the locus of etiological factors.

Early definitions were rooted in the experiences and activities of public and private agencies that saw the *victims* of family violence. Fundamental differences between community-based and public agencies in clientele, philosophical bases of service delivery, advocacy orientation for their clients, and professional styles contributed to the separate understanding and knowledge of aggression in families.

Following the publication of Kempe et al.'s (1962) "The Battered Child Syndrome," child welfare agencies saw battered children in increasing numbers, as hospital staff and social workers identified and reported children as suspected victims of child abuse. Workers viewed family violence primarily as a problem affecting children (and later, adolescents) and broadened the definition to include sexual and emotional abuse, as well as physical neglect.

The emergence of grassroots programs for rape victims in the 1960s and, soon after, the development of shelter services for women began to identify significant numbers of adult victims of family violence who also fit the definition of "battered." Victim assistance and police crisis intervention programs further identified a wide range of family victims, from children to the elderly. Government activity in family violence in the 1970s not only legitimated wife and child assaults as social problems, but also subtly redefined them as valid areas of state intervention.

Partly because of the early influences of the medical community (child abuse) and the criminal justice system (wife abuse), disagreements arose over the importance of physical *injury* in the definition of marital violence. The importance of emotional mal-treatment, and harassment, and persistent denigration or the ac-crual of harm from isolated and relatively inconsequential acts that nevertheless occurred in regular episodes became the subject of debate, because little or no physical injury resulted. Although important to the well-being of victims, definitions that included these dimensions were considered to have little relevance to the codified behaviors of concern to the criminal court. Instead, criminal justice policy and research relied on definitions that stressed codi-fied behavior to inform legal policy or response.

Some researchers followed suit. Straus (1990b) explicitly fo-cused on these dimensions of spouse assault precisely because of their presumed fit with legal statutes on assault (Straus, 1989; Browne, 1993). Although their use was not incorporated into standard assessments of partner assault, dimensions of harm have been well integrated into other criminological research measures (e.g., Sellin and Wolfgang, 1964). Some wife abuse researchers, concerned with the measurement of harm and the explanation of behavior, employed definitions of physical and nonphysical injury (e.g., psychological harm) and their corresponding measures (Walker, 1979; Dobash and Dobash, 1979; Tolman, 1989), and contended that wife assault could not be understood without more complex measures of the actions perpetrated and their impact on the vic-tims.

The *context* of marital violence also was the focus of disagree-ment in definition and research methods. Like nonphysical inju-ries, it was considered irrelevant to legal decision making or to epidemiological measurement. Nevertheless, because of the com-plex family dynamics in marital violence and its recurrent pattern in families, aggression within families is difficult to understand in isolation from the context in which it occurs (Dobash and Dobash, 1983; Browne, 1987). Context-dependent methods have been used in a variety of other research arenas (e.g., Moore, 1978, with youth gangs; Waldorf, 1973, with opiate users; Adler, 1985, with cocaine sellers).

The uneven application of these methods in spouse abuse be-came a source of controversy and confusion about the parameters of marital violence. The Conflict Tactics Scales (CTS; Straus, 1978, 1990a) became the most consistent instrument for assessing the types of violence that occur between couples and their fre-quency. It typifies approaches that separate the context from the assaultive acts, as well as the injuries sustained, and has become the baseline for providing epidemiological estimates and comparisons across samples (see discussion in following section). The controversy surrounding the CTS symbolized the debate over how to conceptualize, define, measure, and explain violence between spouses.

For example, prevalence rates of violence by males and females were similar (Steinmetz, 1977; Straus, 1989), yet the frequency of both general and serious violence was higher for men (Gelles and Straus, 1990) whereas the prevalence rate of injury was substantially higher for women (Stets and Straus, 1990). Estimates of violence also changed when the "seriousness" of an act was arbitrarily determined apart from situational factors such as the relative strength or size of the participants, the repetition of assaultive acts during an incident, the threats and menace that accompanied physical actions, or the injuries incurred (Straus, 1978; Straus et al., 1980; Browne, 1993; Saunders, 1988).

Accordingly, conclusions about the severity of marital violence or its explanations were fundamentally different for researchers using context-specific approaches (e.g., Frieze et al., 1980; Berk et al., 1983) versus cross-sectional surveys (Straus et al., 1980). However, these differences also reflected the confounding of samples, methods, and measures among the researchers who were criticizing each other. Even so, context was rarely viewed as a separate dimension of marital violence, often for reasons as simple as the difficulty of measuring it (e.g., Straus, 1990a).

In sum, divergent views and definitions of marital violence, as well as the disparate programs and services that followed, fostered the separation of research paradigms according to the milieus in which they were applied. Marital violence was alternately explained as a result of family dysfunction or interaction patterns, individual pathology, situational factors that influenced marital dynamics, social pathology, or the behavioral product of ideological supports or cultural beliefs in the patriarchical social and economic organization of society. Research on marital violence conducted in one paradigm had limited utility in another social arena. The study of marital violence remained separate from the study of violence toward strangers, and criminologists made few attempts to integrate the emerging knowledge of violence in the home with other research or policy on violence. The policies that followed each definition and explanation, and the balkanization of the literature, were the natural outcomes of these developments.

SOCIAL EPIDEMIOLOGY OF MARITAL VIOLENCE

Empirical reports of violence between adults in families first appeared in the social science literature in the 1960s (e.g., Parnas, 1967; Pitman and Handy, 1964). Within 10 years, numerous studies of wife beating and spouse abuse had been published (O'Brien, 1971; Sprey, 1971; Straus, 1973; Gelles, 1974; Martin, 1976; Roy, 1977; Hilberman and Munson, 1978; Gaquin, 1977-1978, among others). In many cases, these studies relied on small samples of battered women or violent couples who defined themselves as experiencing family violence before being included in the research. In 1977, the first epidemiological estimates of family violence from a general population sample were published (Straus, 1978). In the 1980s, research on abusive men appeared (Sonkin and Durphy, 1985; Gondolf, 1985b; Dutton and Browning, 1987, 1988). Today, hundreds of studies have been published on violence between spouses and intimates.

However, this burgeoning literature on violence between partners is inconsistent. It reflects the definitional controversies and methodological concerns that have shaped and influenced empirical research (Fagan, 1988). Meta-analyses show that design artifacts (samples, measures, definitions, and aggregation of data) may explain the broad variation in estimates of the extent, severity, and correlates of family violence (Weis, 1989; Bridges and Weis, 1989), as well as in theoretical interpretations. In this section, we review basic knowledge on violence between spouses and intimates. The epidemiology of marital violence is examined, and estimates are compared for the research paradigms that have most influenced theory and knowledge. Next, we review the characteristics of victims, assailants, and couples involved in violence. The validity of contemporary knowledge is reviewed, and sources of error and bias are examined. The section concludes with an analysis of risk factors that characterize marital violence.

PARTICIPATION AND FREQUENCY OF MARITAL VIOLENCE

The two primary sources of epidemiological data on marital violence—the National Family Violence Surveys and the National Crime Survey—are based on nationwide probability samples of households. In each method, brief interviews with respondents are completed. Beyond that, there are fundamental differences in their methodologies that heavily influence their results. Nevertheless, these two efforts have provided baseline knowledge about national trends in family violence for nearly two decades. Our discussion of the distribution of marital violence examines primarily dimensions of participation (the prevalence rate). Yet research on criminal careers has shown that the correlates differ for the various dimensions of criminality: participation, frequency, and seriousness (Blumstein et al., 1985). Accordingly, we also examine these other dimensions of marital violence to better understand its distribution and complexity.

Surveys of Violence in the Home: National and Local Studies

National estimates of the incidence and prevalence of marital violence have been derived from self-reports of assaultive behavior. Data are obtained through telephone surveys or interviews with general probability samples of couples. Researchers typically report the percentage of respondents who have exhibited assaultive behaviors or at least one item on a scale of specific behaviors. This is termed the participation rate per 1,000 respondents. Rarely do family violence researchers calculate offending rates (cf. Williams and Hawkins, 1989b), despite their obvious importance in differentiating offender types (e.g., see Blumstein et al., 1985, 1986). Local studies have used variations of these techniques, modifying sampling or data collection procedures to reflect specific hypotheses about the distribution of marital violence and appropriate methods for eliciting sensitive information.

The first general population study of family violence in the United States was the 1975 National Family Violence Survey (NFVS), based on interviews with a probability sample of 2,143 intact couples in households. Straus (1978) and Straus et al. (1980) reported that 16 percent of all marital couples experienced physical aggression during the year before the survey; 28 percent had experienced physical aggression at some point in their relationship. Among those reporting at least one act of violence in the past year, more than one in three involved acts such as punching, kicking, hitting with an object, beating up, and assaults with a gun or knife. These items formed the "severe violence" scale[7] (or what Straus initially termed "wife beating"). Straus and his colleagues reported that 3.8 percent of female respondents and 4.6 percent of males were victims of at least one of these acts of "severe violence." (Unfortunately, only one spouse per couple was included in each sampled family, so comparisons of violence were based on aggregate rates of unrelated males and females.) Questions on rape or other forms of sexual aggressive acts were not included in the 1975 study but were included in the 1985 survey.

The NFVS used the Conflict Tactics Scales (Straus, 1978, 1979)—items that operationalized tactics used by couples to settle conflicts into specific acts. Rational, verbal, and physically aggressive acts were included in the scale. Aggressive acts included eight items, ranging in severity from throwing objects to using a gun or knife. An additional item on "choking" was included in the 1985 survey and two later waves with the 1985 panel. Threats of violence were considered nonviolent acts (Straus and Gelles, 1990). Respondents reported whether and how often they had engaged in each of the CTS behaviors during the past year. They also reported whether each behavior had ever happened during their lifetime. Straus et al. (1980) reported "violence participation" rates for both members of the couple.

In the years following the first publication of data based on the CTS scales, more than 40 other researchers have used modified versions of the CTS to estimate physical aggression between couples (Straus and Gelles, 1990). The samples, the conditions for administering the CTS items, and the procedures for aggregating scale scores varied widely in these studies. For example, some researchers have used the CTS indices to measure abuse by including threats of violence, others have confined their analyses to physical attacks, and others have expanded the scale to include marital rape. Together with sample differences, these measurement decisions no doubt explain much of the extraordinary variation in the rates of marital violence that are evident in these studies. Table 1 shows participation rates per 1,000 persons for studies that have used the CTS, with samples classified as general population probability samples, local probability samples, or nonprobability samples of victims or assailants. Only studies with reports of marital violence in the past year were included.

National Probability Samples Among the national probability samples, participation rates for overall violence (number of persons per 1,000 population) are consistent for the 1975 and 1985 National Family Violence Surveys (Straus et al., 1980; Straus and Gelles, 1990). Straus and colleagues report a decrease in male participation in wife assault from 121 to 110 per 1,000 males from the 1975 to the 1985 surveys, and a slight increase in female participation in husband assault from 110 to 120 per 1,000 females. Recall that the 1975 surveys were based on in-person interviews with married or intact couples, whereas the 1985 surveys were conducted via telephone with one adult member of the

TABLE 1 Past Year Prevalence Rates of Violence Among Intimates (per 1,000 population)[a]

Study	Sample (N)	Any Violence by Husband or Male Partner	Any Violence by Wife or Female Partner
1. National Probability Samples			
Straus and Gelles (1990)	6,002	116	124
Straus et al. (1980)	2,143 couples	121	116
Straus and Gelles (1986)	3,520 couples	110	120
Elliott et al. (1985)	1,725 (ages 18-24)	368	471
2. Local or Statewide Probability Samples			
Schulman (1979)	1,793 Kentucky women	100	—
Russell (1982)	644 San Francisco women[b]	260	—
Kennedy and Dutton (1987)	708	112	—
Nisonoff and Bitman (1979)	297 household sample	160	110
M.D. Smith (1986)[c]	315	206	—
M.D. Smith (1987)	604 Toronto women	144	—
3. Nonprobability Local Samples			
Rouse (1984)	120 men	108	—
Makepeace (1983)[d]	244 dating couples, college students	137	93
Brutz and Ingoldsby (1984)	288 Quakers	146	152
Dutton (1986a)	75 batterers	183	—
Makepeace (1981)[c]	2338 students and dating couples	206	120
Meredith et al. (1986)	304	220	180
O'Leary and Arias (1988)	393 dating couples	340	420
Szinovacz (1983)	103	260	300
Clarke (1987)	318 women	274	102
Lockhart (1987)	307 blacks and whites	355	—
Barling et al. (1987)[d]	187	740	730
Frieze et al. (1980)	137 Pennsylvania women ever married and comparison group	340	270
Levinger (1966)	600 divorce filings	370	—
Mason and Blankenship (1987)	155 Michigan undergraduates	18	22

[a]Rates are for acts occurring during the previous 12 months.
[b]Currently or ever married at time of interview.
[c]Rates only for lifetime prevalence.
[d]Study did not report whether rates are for the previous year or lifetime.

SOURCES: Straus and Gelles (1990); Frieze and Browne (1989); Ellis (1989).

household randomly selected and nonintact couples (recently divorced or separated) included.

When CTS measures are used in face-to-face interviews with a younger sample, the prevalence rates increase substantially. Elliott et al. (1985) reported rates among a national probability sample of 1,725 young adults (ages 18-24) in 1983 that were more than three times higher than the rates obtained by Straus and colleagues in any of the iterations of the NFVS. These data were obtained from the National Youth Survey (NYS), a panel study of a national probability sample of youths in which data are obtained through in-person interviews. In the sixth wave, conducted in 1983, Elliott et al. (1985) found higher rates for violence by women than by men, for both general and serious violence, whereas Straus and colleagues found few differences by gender for either type of violence.

Yet when the 1985 NFVS rates are calculated for the 18-24 age group, the results still show important differences in prevalence estimates for the NFVS and NYS data sets. Table 2 compares male and female participation rates in spouse assault using the CTS items for three samples: the NYS sample, the 1975 NFVS sample, and the 18- to 24-year-old respondents from the 1985 NFVS. The NYS analyses included a third index, severe violence, comprised of the three most serious items from the CTS scales: used a gun or knife, beat up, and hit with an object.

Table 2 illustrates the influence of study design and methods on prevalence estimates. Prevalence rates were higher for respondents ages 18 to 24 in the 1985 NFVS than for the total NFVS samples (1975 and 1985). This is consistent with the high participation rates in stranger violence for general populations in this age range (Gottfredson and Hirschi, 1990; Greenberg, 1985). In fact, Straus et al. (1980) report the highest violence rates for families in which the respondent is under 30 years old, nearly three times the rate of those between 31 and 50 years of age. Accordingly, the higher rate for the age 18 to 24 NFVS sets suggests that age-related patterns of marital violence are consistent with patterns of stranger violence.

However, participation rates for the 18- to 24-year age group in the NFVS are substantially lower than for the 18-24 NYS data set. The NYS data show higher rates overall than the NFVS data for respondents ages 18-24 for both wife-to-husband and husband-to-wife violence, for both male and female respondents, and for all three levels of violence. Patterns of gender differences in the two data sets vary by type and severity of violence. For general

TABLE 2 Prevalence of Marital Violence by Sex of Respondent

Study	Violence Level					
	General		Serious		Severe	
	Male	Female	Male	Female	Male	Female
1975 National Family Violence Study[a]						
Straus et al. (1980)						
Husband-to-wife	12.8	11.3	3.5	4.1	na	na
Wife-to-husband	11.2	11.7	5.1	4.3	na	na
National Youth Survey[b]						
Elliott et al. (1985)						
Husband-to-wife	37.5	36.1	7.4	11.4	2.3	6.7
Wife-to-husband	42.9	51.2	22.0	22.7	2.3	1.2
1985 National Family Violence Study[c]						
Husband-to-wife	10.8	12.3	1.4	5.0	0.7	2.1
Wife-to-husband	12.6	12.4	5.0	4.6	1.9	0.8
1985 National Family Violence Study, 24 years of age and younger (N = 397)						
Husband-to-wife	22.6	29.8	1.3	13.8	0.5	4.8
Wife-to-husband	26.6	36.4	8.0	16.6	1.1	2.9

NOTE: na indicates data not available.

[a]The data were collected through 2,143 face-to-face interviews and include only married and cohabiting couples of any age.
[b]The data were collected through one interview from a six-year panel design of youths aged 18-24.
[c]The data were collected through 5,360 telephone interviews. Thereis also an added item on the 1985 CTS, "choked him/her/you," inserted after "beat him/her/you up." This item was included in the severe violence type. In addition, the 1985 sampling frame also included recently separated or divorced individuals and single parents.

violence, females in the NYS and 18-24 1985 NFVS data sets report higher rates of wife-to-husband violence than do males. For serious violence, women in the 18-24 1985 NFVS sample report higher rates of serious violence for both male and female perpetrators. For the NYS data, gender differences are evident only for female reports of husband-to-wife serious violence and wife-to-husband general violence. The most consistent pattern across the data sets is the higher rate of serious husband-to-wife violence by males reported by female partners.

These inconsistencies across data sets for the 18- to 24-year-old groups point to several methodological influences on the variations in base rates and patterns of gender differences. The NYS was a panel design, and the rates were obtained in the sixth interview. Respondents were more likely to be acclimated to the interview format and to offer more open responses. Both NFVS interviews involved the first contact with the research. The NYS is a private face-to-face interview, compared to the telephone interview in the 1985 NFVS. The NFVS respondents had no prior contact with the research, and the interview conditions for respondents were not controlled. Although the effects of telephone versus in-person interviews on response bias or base rates have been questioned for general social or opinion surveys (Groves and Kahn, 1979), these effects remain unknown for the more complex domain of marital dynamics. Moreover, the data sets vary on the inclusionary criteria for "couple": the 1975 NFVS was limited to intact couples; the 1985 NFVS included both intact and recently separated or divorced couples.

Finally, although both studies used the CTS items, differences in the context of the interviews and social desirability may have influenced the reports. The NYS tapped a wide range of deviant behaviors, whereas the NFVS was a study of family dynamics. These differences may have contributed to the lower base rates reported in both iterations of the NFVS interviews, and after controlling for age in the NFVS, compared to the NYS results. Further analyses and experimentation with methodological strategies are needed to unravel the sources of these disparities, but the implications of study design for prevalence estimates are evident from this comparison.

State and Local Probability Samples Table 1 also shows wide variation in prevalence estimates of marital violence among local probability samples. Prevalence estimates of marital violence vary from 100 to 260 per 1,000 respondents for husbands or male partners. The rates again reflect differences in study design and methodology. For example, a 1979 telephone survey with 1,793 women in Kentucky (Schulman, 1979) found that 21 percent of the respondents had been physically attacked at least once and that 4.1 percent were victims of severe violence, consistent with the Straus et al. (1980) reports. Similar results were obtained by Kennedy and Dutton (1989) for a Canadian sample of males and females. However, Russell's (1982) interviews with a random sample of San Francisco women who reported that they were or had been married yielded past year prevalence estimates more than two times higher than Schulman's estimates. Yet the lifetime prevalence estimates (26%) were comparable to both the Schulman (1979) and the Straus et al. (1980) estimates. Again, especially for past year prevalence estimates, face-to-face interviews seem to result in higher prevalence estimates than telephone interviews.

Other design artifacts also influence prevalence estimates, especially marital status of respondents. In the Kentucky survey, two-thirds of the women who had been recently divorced or separated from their partners reported physical violence in their former relationships, compared to fewer than one in three married women (Schulman, 1979). A review by Ellis (1989) of research on marital violence by males found that aggression among married couples was lower than among unmarried cohabitating couples. Ellis also found consistent evidence of more severely violent acts toward separated women by their estranged partners than in other marital or cohabitational statuses. A Long Island sample of 297 residents again showed that violence rates among those previously married (and separated at the time of interview) were higher than for those currently married (Nisonoff and Bitman, 1979).

Thus, the exclusion of noncohabiting couples in the 1975 NFVS may have underestimated the rates of physical aggression toward women. Other segments of the population at risk for marital violence are often not represented in national and local surveys: for example, those who do not speak English fluently (Chin, 1994); the very poor and all individuals who are homeless; and persons hospitalized, institutionalized, or incarcerated at the time a survey is conducted.

Nonprobability Local Samples Researchers have attempted to estimate prevalence rates among specific samples using convenience, purposive, or other nonrandom sampling methods. Table 1 shows that the estimates generally are higher among these samples for reports of violence by male partners. Reports of marital violence by victims in intervention programs are predictably higher, as are reports of severe violence. For example, weapon use was reported by 25.7 percent of 2,792 victims in family violence intervention programs (Fagan et al., 1984), compared to less than 3 percent in the Straus et al. (1980) survey. Downs et al. (1989) found that 41 percent of a Buffalo, New York, sample (N = 45) of battered women in shelters or support groups had been threatened with a gun or a knife in the past year. Fagan et al. (1984) reported that the severity of violence was greater for women in shelters than in any other type of legal or social intervention.

Washburn and Frieze (1981) compared three groups of self-selected women in the Pittsburgh area who had experienced physical assault at the hands of their spouses: (1) women who had sought help from area shelters, (2) women who had filed legal action to have the husband removed from the home for abuse, and (3) women who responded to posted notices in business establishments about the research project (as cited in Frieze and Browne, 1989). Women filing legal action were less seriously abused than women from the shelter but more seriously abused than the nonintervention group. Researchers attempting to find a group of nonabused women to compare with a sample of physically abused wives in Pittsburgh found that 34 percent of a control comparison group (matched by residential block) also reported being attacked by a partner in the past year (Frieze et al., 1980).

Estimates of Severe Violence Among both probability and convenience samples, base rates of severe violence are lower than the rates of general violence, but differences across studies again reflect research design characteristics. Straus and Gelles (1990) report that rates of severe violence varied across several studies, from 8 to 102 per 1,000 men and from 25 to 59 per 1,000 women. Participation in severe violence by males was far higher in the Kentucky telephone survey of women than comparable reports in the NFVS data: 87 per 1,000 respondents (Schulman, 1979).

Prevalence estimates decrease when both males and females report on male-to-female violence: 34 per 1,000 women in the Straus et al. (1980) study and 23 per 1,000 women in a Canadian sample (Kennedy and Dutton, 1987) were victims of severe violence, compared to the rates obtained by Russell (1982), Schulman (1979), and Frieze et al. (1980). This trend suggests that although males and females may agree on the prevalence of marital violence, they rate its severity differently. Reports by women of rates of severe violence by males in dating, cohabitating, or engaged couples were also far higher than in studies with probability samples of only intact or married couples (Makepeace, 1983; Clarke, 1987; Billingham and Sack, 1987; Roscoe and Benaske, 1985; Pirog-Good and Stets, 1989).

Incidence Estimates: Frequency of Offending Few studies using the CTS items report the mean number of aggressive acts between adults in the home within a time period. This index could be calculated from the CTS scales: CTS items in the 1985 survey included past year frequency measures as well as prevalence rates. The items are constructed as categorical scales rather than specific numbers. Calculations of the specific incidence of marital violence would require estimation and substitution of midpoint frequencies for each category.[8] However, these results are rarely reported. Although information is lost when high-end estimates are truncated, validity threats (for the small percentage whose behaviors lie at the extremes of the distribution) are outweighed by the elimination of skewness in estimates of the number of acts.

Table 3 shows participation and offending rates calculated for 6,002 respondents in the 1985 NFVS data set. Only rates of male-to-female violence are shown: male reports of offending and female reports of victimization. We focus on violence toward female partners in this table because of women's higher risks of injury (Stets and Straus, 1990) and also to provide comparisons with the empirical literature on marital violence that has emphasized the victimization of women. Each cell shows the percentage of respondents *within* each demographic group participating in the behavior, the number (in parentheses), and the past year offending rates for the active offenders (Lambda) for respondents reporting at least one event. To illustrate, 17.1 percent of African American males reported at least one incident of marital violence in the past year, and they averaged 4.3 incidents in that time. The offending rates were calculated by using midpoint substitutions for the categorical items in the 1985 NFVS (Gelles and Straus, 1988). Chi-square tests were conducted for prevalence rates, and *F*-tests for offending rates.

Table 3 shows that females reported victimization rates for general violence that are comparable to male reports of offending (10.4 versus 10.7%). However, females report male offending rates (7.3 assaults per year) more than twice as high as those that males report (3.1). Rates are disaggregated by relationship history and sociodemographic characteristics of the respondent's household.

Unfortunately, reliable data on employment patterns of both partners were not available for these analyses.

Race For male reports, participation rates are highest for African American males. There were no significant differences in participation rates for female reports. Offending rates did not differ significantly by race. However, rates overall were higher for female [$p(F) < .01$] than for male reports.

Age As in Table 2, younger respondents indicated significantly higher participation rates. More than one in five reported that at least one incident of marital violence had occurred in the past year. Offending rates were significantly higher for female reports, again $p(F) < .001$.

Income There were no significant differences for participation rates, but there were significant differences by both sex of respondents and income level for offending rates. Rates overall were higher for female reports and for incomes of less than $20,000 annually.

Urbanism There were no significant differences for male reports of general violence, but women in central cities were significantly more likely to report male violence. Once again, there were significant differences in male offending rates as reported by females [$p(F) < .001$].

Marital Status Intact couples were significantly more likely to experience marital violence, according to male and female reports. Nearly one in three women of married couples (31.9%) reported victimization within the past year, a rate almost twice the 17.7 percent reported by males. The same patterns of sex differences were reported here too: females reported higher offending rates by males than male reports of their own offending rates [$p(F) < .001$].

Length of Relationship Participation rates were highest among couples who had been together the shortest time. Patterns were similar and statistically significant for both male and female reports. The greater risk for short relationships may reflect the early termination of these relationships and the survival of nonviolent relationships for longer periods. Once again, females re-

TABLE 3 Participation and Offending Rates for Interpersonal Violence Toward Female Partners in the Past Year (male self-reports of offending, female reports of victimization) ($N = 6,002$) [a,b]

	General Violence		p(F)			Serious Violence		p(F)		
	Male	Female	Group	Sex	Group by Sex	Male	Female	Group	Sex	Group by Sex
Total sample	10.4 (255)	10.7 (368)				1.3 (32)	4.3 (148)			
	3.1	7.3				4.5	6.1			
Race			ns	*c*	ns			ns	ns	ns
African American	17.1 (24)	10.7 (30)				4.2 (6)	5.2 (14)			
	4.3	8.6				3.8	7.9			
Hispanic	14.1 (12)	14.4 (27)				3.9 (3)	6.9 (13)			
	3.9	10.1				1.8	8.8			
White	9.7 (195)	10.6 (290)				1.1 (21)	4.8 (110)			
	3.9	6.8				5.4	5.6			
Other	12.4 (22)	9.3 (17)			1.0	0.9 (2)	4.2 (7)			
	7.9					6.8				
	2.7									
Chi square	9.74[d]	3.09				14.13[e]	4.13			
Gamma	(.19)	(.04)				(.36)	(.14)			
Respondents age			ns	*f*	ns			ns	ns	ns
18-25	20.2 (43)	20.6 (81)				1.1 (2)	9.5 (37)			
	2.5	6.7				1.8	4.5			
26-35	16.9 (122)	14.2 (152)				2.9 (21)	5.5 (59)			
	3.5	6.7				4.1	5.3			

36-50	7.2 (57) 3.2	8.8 (98) 7.2		0.9 (7) 7.4	3.1 (35) 7.0	ns
Over 50	4.5 (32) 2.3	4.4 (38) 11.0		0.2 (2) 1.0	1.9 (17) 10.9	
Chi square	91.85g	95.82g		23.16g	45.54g	ns
Gamma	(-.45)	(-.40)		(-.52)	(-.40)	

Family income (thousands of dollars)

0.0-9.9	10.3 (19) 4.2	12.0 (51) 9.7		2.2 (4) 2.7	6.6 (28) 5.6	ns
10.0-19.9	13.9 (65) 3.2	8.3 (60) 11.0		1.9 (9) 1.4	4.4 (32) 8.8	
20.0-29.9	11.2 (62) 2.5	12.3 (97) 6.4		1.9 (5) 2.5	5.0 (39) 4.1	ns
30.0-39.9	9.4 (46) 4.1	10.9 (58) 4.8		1.6 (8) 7.2	3.8 (20) 4.8	
40.0-49.9	7.8 (21) 2.4	12.6 (39) 4.3		1.2 (3) 2.8	3.4 (10) 2.4	ns
50.9 and over	8.7 (34) 1.7	10.7 (46) 3.2		0.3 (1) 2.2	2.5 (11) 4.2	
Chi square	10.20	7.75		6.97	10.26	
Gamma	(-.12)	(.03)		(-.24)	(-.27)	

Household location

Central city	10.6 (67) 2.9	14.1 (132) 6.3		1.1 (7) 2.8	6.0 (56) 5.4	ns
Suburb of central city	10.8 (132) 3.2	10.4 (171) 7.8		1.5 (18) 6.4	4.1 (68) 6.3	

f ns f ns

continued

TABLE 3 (Continued)

	General Violence					Serious Violence				
			p(F)					p(F)		
	Male	Female	Group	Sex	Group by Sex	Male	Female	Group	Sex	Group by Sex
City of 2,500 outside of urban area	9.3 (56)	7.4 (56)				1.2 (7)	2.8 (24)	ns		
	3.1	7.9				1.6	7.3			
Chi square	1.03	21.63g				.42	11.76e			
Gamma	(-104)	(-.21)				(.02)	(-.24)			
Marital status			ns	f	ns			ns	ns	ns
Never married	12.1 (6)	4.3 (6)				0.0 (0)	0.0 (0)			
	1.9	10.1				0.0	0.0			
Couple	17.7 (20)	31.9 (40)				2.7 (3)	18.3 (23)			
	2.7	7.0				3.8	4.2			
Married	10.1 (220)	11.1 (314)				1.2 (26	4.3 (122)			
	3.2	7.2				5.0	6.3			
Divorced/separated	7.8 (9)	2.2 (8)				2.3 (3)	0.6 (2)			
	2.9	8.8				1.6	14.6			
Chi square	7.90h	92.778				2.9	77.87g			
Gamma	(-.22)	(-.44)				(-.03)	(-.50)			

								ns	ns

Years with present partner		ns		f		ns			
0-3	17.2 (72)		23.8 (108)		2.5 (11)		10.2 (46)		
	2.8		5.6		3.1		4.4		
4-10	15.2 (85)		18.5 (124)		2.0 (11)		8.1 (54)		
	3.6		8.6		2.1		6.5		
11-20	10.2 (58)		9.2 (65)		0.9 (5)		3.4 (24)		
	3.4		6.0		16.0		5.2		
More than 20	3.4 (26)		5.1 (57)		0.3 (2)		1.9 (21)		
	1.9		8.6		1.3		9.3		
Chi square	74.40g		143.30g		14.50^e		66.43g		
Gamma	(-.42)		(-.42)		(-.51)		(-.48)		

Educational disparity		ns		ns		ns		ns	ns
<Wife	10.7 (51)		14.5 (96)		1.5 (7)		7.7 (51)		
	3.6		8.9		3.6		5.3		
Equal	10.0 (117)		13.1 (202)		1.1 (12)		4.8 (74)		
	3.3		7.3		7.9		1.8		
<Husband	11.7 (85)		8.4 (66)		1.8 (13)		2.4 (18)		
	2.7		4.8		1.8		6.4		
Chi square	1.36		14.74g		1.68		22.38g		
Gamma	(.04)		(-.06)		(.10)		(-.31)		

Parent-to-child violence		f		ns		f		ns	ns
General violence									
Yes	17.2 (112)		14.1 (156)		1.3 (9)		6.3 (68)		
	2.9		8.4		2.2		6.1		
No	7.8 (143)		8.8 (214)		1.3 (24)		3.4 (81)		
	3.3		6.4		5.4		6.1		
Chi square	46.08g		22.36g		0.00		14.91g		
Gamma	(.42)		(.26)		(.00)		(.31)		

continued

TABLE 3 (Continued)

	General Violence		p(F)			Serious Violence		p(F)		
	Male	Female	Group	Sex	Group by Sex	Male	Female	Group	Sex	Group by Sex
Serious violence			ns	c	f			ns	ns	ns
Yes	26.6 (31)	22.4 (44)				4.6 (5)	12.1 (24)			
	3.7	13.3				2.4	9.4			
No	9.5 (225)	9.8 (325)				1.1 (27)	3.8 (125)			
	3.0	6.5				4.9	5.5			
Chi square	35.28g	30.88g				10.12e	31.83g			
Gamma	(.55)	(.45)				(.61)	(.55)			
Woman was pregnant during abuse			ns	f	ns			ns	ns	ns
Yes	14.5 (14)	16.4 (16)				2.4 (30)	8.1 (139)			
	2.8	6.3				2.1	3.6			
Chi square	1.63	3.03				.77	3.20			
Gamma	(.18)	(.24)				(.29)	(.32)			

[a]For males, each cell shows the participation rate, the number of males in the category participating, and the annual offending rate for males with at least one violent act. For females, each cell shows the prevalence of victimization, the number of women victimized in the category, and the incidents of victimization of those women victimized at least once.

[b]ns .05.

[c]$p(F)$ = .01.

[d]$p(X^2)$ = .05.

[e]$p(X^2)$ = .01.

[f]$p(F)$ = .001.

[g]$p(X^2)$ = .001.

[h]$p(F)$ = .05.

ported higher offending rates than did males, regardless of the length of the relationship [$p(F)$ < .001].

Educational Disparity We computed participation and offending rates based on respondent reports of their educational level relative to their partner. The first row includes couples where the male partner's educational attainment was greater than the female's. The second row includes couples in which both partners had equal educational attainment, and the third row shows couples for which the female partner had a higher educational attainment. There were no significant differences in participation rates reported by males, but females reported significantly higher participation in marital violence by men in couples where the male had higher educational attainment or where the partners had equal education. Where the female had higher educational attainment, there were lower participation rates. Offending rates were higher for female reports of victimization, but there were no differences by educational disparity in offending rates.

Comorbidity With Other Family Violence We also computed participation and offending rates for two comorbidity factors: violence during pregnancy and parent-to-child violence. For those involved in abuse during pregnancy, there were no significant differences in participation rates for either male or female reports of marital violence, but offending rates once again were higher for female reports of male offending rates.

Male self-reports of their own comorbidity of marital violence with any parent-to-child violence (17.4%) were greater than female reports about males (14.3%). That is, for both males and females, the probability of marital violence was significantly greater for couples in which there was also parent-to-child violence. These estimates include couples where either parent is involved in parent-to-child violence. Females reported higher offending rates of marital violence by males than males did of their own behavior [$p(F)$ < .001].

For serious parent-to-child violence, we found similar patterns, but at higher base rates. That is, among males in couples involved in severe parent-to-child violence, 26.9 percent also were involved in marital violence, a rate higher than the 22.5 percent reported by females about males. However, females once again reported higher offending rates by males than males did about themselves. Moreover, there were significant group differences: offending rates for marital violence were higher for those involved in parent-to-child violence $[p(F) < .01]$. The significant interaction effect $[p(F) < .05]$ suggests that female reports of male offending rates in couples with severe parent-to-child violence were higher than male self-reported rates, regardless of participation in severe parent-to-child violence. In other words, where comorbidity was reported by females, female reports of male offending rates for marital violence by males was greatest.

Severe Marital Violence There were fewer distinct patterns found for participation in serious marital violence and no significant differences in offending rates by sex or demographic group. Participation rates were slightly (and significantly) higher for African American males. Although males and females reported significant differences by age group, the patterns differed: females reported the highest participation for younger males (ages 18-25), but males between ages 26 and 35 reported higher participation rates. Once again, female reports of base rates of participation were higher for all age groups. There were no differences by family income.

There were significant differences by marital status for female reports but not males: serious violence by males (as reported by females) was most prevalent among married couples. Serious violence also was more prevalent among couples in shorter marriages, and significant differences were reported by males and females. Female reports showed higher base rates. According to females, serious marital violence was more prevalent in central-city households and least prevalent in rural areas. Males reported no significant difference by area size. Participation rates in serious violence were lowest (according to females) in couples where the woman had higher educational attainment. Males reported no differences and lower base rates.

There were no significant differences in the prevalence of serious marital violence in couples where the female partner was pregnant. For any parent-to-child violence, participation rates by males in marital violence were significantly higher according to female reports, but not for male self-reports. In couples where there was severe parent-to-child violence, both males and females reported significantly higher participation in marital violence. However, females reported higher participation rates by men in severe marital violence (12.2%) than did men (4.6%).

Summary By using parameters of criminal careers, Table 3 shows that females are no more likely than males to report marital violence perpetrated by males, but they are more likely to rate it as more severe and more frequent. That is, females consistently reported higher offending rates than did males for general violence, but there were few differences in the perceptions of participation rates. The use of offending rates illustrates differences in marital violence that are not evident when only participation rates are reported, particularly within sociodemographic groups. For severe violence, female reports of male participation were consistently higher. Although females also reported higher offending rates by males for severe marital violence than did men, these differences were not significant, owing to the very small cell populations. The results also show the importance of comorbidity as a cue for identifying risk factors and epidemiological surveillance of violence risks.

Continuity, Discontinuity, and Desistance in Marital Violence
There is some evidence that careers in marital violence follow patterns similar to careers in stranger violence or property crime, with discernible patterns of initiation, escalation, continuity (or persistence) and then desistance. For example, marital homicide seems to follow an age distribution similar to robbery (Mercy and Saltzman, 1989), peaking between 18 and 24 years of age. Straus et al. (1980) also found similar age peaks, with participation rates nearly three times greater among persons between 18 and 25 years of age than older persons. There also is evidence that marital violence escalates in frequency and severity over time (Walker, 1984; Pagelow, 1984; Fagan et al., 1984), evidence gathered primarily from samples of female victims of marital violence. Bowker (1983, 1986a), Fagan (1989), and Feld and Straus (1989) found evidence of desistance from wife assault.

Whether there is a continuity of marital violence over multiyear periods may vary by research design and samples. Feld and Straus (1989) used panel data from the 1985 NFVS and a second wave in 1986 to determine whether marital violence is stable across a two-year period. They found that among 380 male and female respondents, patterns of desistance and continuity varied by severity of violence in the first year. More than half (53%) continued their participation in severe violence, 10 percent reduced the severity of their violence to minor, and 33 percent reported no violence during the second year. Minor assaults in year 1 by either spouse were associated with more serious assaults over year 2, suggesting patterns of escalation.

Recidivism studies also illustrate the discontinuity, either lasting or temporary, that may result from interventions. Sherman and Berk (1984) found a six-month desistance rate after police intervention of 81.2 percent from official records (new complaints) and 71.1 percent from victim reports. Dunford et al. (1990, 82.6%) and Hirschel et al. (1991, 76.5%) found similar desistance rates in experiments involving police intervention. Using victim reports, Fagan et al. (1984) reported a six-month desistance rate of 72 percent for women who had sought help from several types of intervention, and 90 percent among those whose cases proceeded to criminal prosecution. When injury was used as the recidivism criterion, the six-month desistance rate was 94 percent.

There are several limitations to these analyses. The brevity of the study periods (six months to two years) may not capture the developmental patterns of marital violence that seem to unfold over far longer periods (Fagan, 1989) and may overestimate desistance. For example, in desistance studies (e.g., Bowker, 1983), marital violence was continuous or escalating over periods lasting 3 to 15 years. Also, males who are serial assailants, who move to commit assaults in one marriage after another, are not captured in either the household surveys or the criminal justice experiments. These men in particular are likely to minimize or deny their marital violence in interviews.

Nevertheless, the criminal justice experiments and the Feld and Straus (1989) contribution show the varied career trajectories of escalation, continuity, and desistance that are evident in marital violence. Marital violence may be episodic, with lengthy intervals of nonviolence interrupted by shorter periods of intensive violence (Walker, 1984; Browne, 1987). Similar to desistance from other patterned behaviors, desistance during short periods may simply be a lull in a recurring cyclical pattern or false desistance. Fagan (1989) suggests that at least two years of nonviolent partnership is necessary to use the term desistance. Advances in knowledge of battering careers will come from research to identify the correlates of marital violence that persists, escalates, or desists over lengthier time periods.

Victimization Surveys

Data on violence between couples also has been collected through the National Crime Survey (NCS) and less often through surveys of personal victimization within the family. The National Crime Survey reports extensive information about personal victimization, based on interviews with a probability sample of households who are interviewed in consecutive six-month periods. A period of six months is thought to improve the accuracy of recall of victimization incidents. Indications of victim-offender relationship, including specific questions about spouses, cohabitating partners, and ex-spouses, as well as "familiar acquaintances," also provide estimates based on the social distance of victim and offender. The inclusion of frequency measures allows calculation of both offending and victimization rates.

The NCS does not use the CTS measures that are ubiquitous in studies of marital violence. NCS items are designed to correspond with Uniform Crime Report (UCR) categories that law enforcement agencies use to compile official crime statistics, rather than to specific acts of violence or conflict resolution within families. Accordingly, comparisons of victimization and offending rates are limited to aggregate indices of violence and do not address severity or specific acts. The aggregation procedures for family violence in the NCS also differ from specific family violence surveys, with estimates of the distribution of violent acts receiving more emphasis than the prevalence of specific types of behaviors within marriages or couple relationships. Moreover, specific analyses of violence within marriages or between ex-spouses or current or formerly cohabitating partners are not routinely reported.

Three specific studies of family violence have been reported from the NCS data. Gaquin (1977-1978) analyzed 1973-1976 NCS data on victims of spouse abuse,[9] reporting both the occurrence of spouse abuse and the rates of victimizations of individuals. For occurrences, spouses or ex-spouses committed 3.9 assaults per 1,000 women over the three years, whereas 0.3 assault per 1,000 males was committed by women spouses or ex-spouses. Spouse abuse accounted for 14.8 percent of all assaults against women. Moreover, the risk of assault was far greater for separated and divorced women than for married women. Among separated women, for example, 11.5 percent were victims of assault; more than half of these assaults (54.6%) were spouse abuse incidents. Among divorced women, 7.6 percent were victims of assault, and 27.9 percent of the assaults were spouse abuse incidents. However, these estimates counted occurrences, not individuals. Nevertheless, similar trends emerge after adjustments to reflect the rates of persons victimized. Among separated women, 27.1 per 1,000 respondents were victims of spouse abuse, with an average of 2.4 incidents per individual each year. Among divorced women, only 10 per 1,000 were victimized at a rate of 2.1 incidents.

Lentzner and DeBerry (1980) analyzed "intimate violence" using NCS data, also from 1973-1976. "Intimates" included both related individuals (spouses and ex-spouses) and others who were well-known to each other (e.g., friends, neighbors, classmates, co-workers). Strangers, near-strangers (someone known by sight only), or casual acquaintances were included in the "nonintimate" category. Nearly one-third of all incidents of violence were committed by intimates over the four-year interval; two-fifths resulted in injuries, and 13 percent were serious enough to require hospitalization or medical care. Lentzner and DeBerry also found that women in estranged couples (divorced or separated) were at far greater risk for intimate violence than widowed, never-married, or currently married women.

Langan and Innes (1986) reported prevalence rates and calculated an individual's risk of being victimized for certain crime types using NCS data from 1978 to 1982. They included rape, robbery, and assault as violent crimes. Violent victimizations of women by family members averaged 420,000 over the five years, for a prevalence rate of 4.2 victims per 1,000 women. Langan and Innes (1986) estimated that 2.1 million men were victims of domestic violence at least once during an average 12-month period, consistent with the 1980 NFVS estimates. They also noted that, compared with victims of stranger violence, victims of domestic violence were at far greater risk of recurring victimization. Of those assaulted at least once by an adult domestic partner, 32 percent were victimized again within six months of the initial report. Among victims of stranger violence, victimization recurred among 13 percent of those reporting at least one incident in the previous six months.[10] The expected frequency of victimizations for this group was 1.62.

Langan and Innes (1986) also analyzed 1982 data and compared all forms of violence as well as specific types of assault for victimizations by family members of males and females. Violent victimization rates for females were lower than males (2.31 per 1,000, compared to 4.07), but the incidence (frequency) of victimization was similar (1.11 and 1.07 incidents per victim). Analyses from later years of NCS data on assaults by intimates provide similar estimates of violence against women. Wiersema and Loftin (1994) report a prevalence rate of 2.3 incidents per 1,000 women in 1987. Similar to Langan and Innes (1986), their definition specified rape, robbery, and assaults by spouses, ex-spouses, boyfriends, or ex-boyfriends. Table 4 shows annual rates of violent victimizations, focusing on assault and based on compilations of assault data from NCS annual reports from 1983 to 1987. For assaults

TABLE 4 Percent Distribution of Crimes of Violence Involving Nonstranger Victimizations by Victim-Offender Relationship[a]

		Victim-Offender Relationship			
		Percent Victimized	Spouse	Ex-Spouse	Well-Known, Not Related
1987	Assault	19.5	6.6	3.9	79.0
	Aggravated	18.3	5.0	3.9	80.6
	Simple	20.0	7.1	3.9	78.5
1986	Assault	19.8	7.8	3.7	69.4
	Aggravated	20.3	6.0	2.4[b]	69.7
	Simple	19.6	8.5	4.2	69.3
1985	Assault	23.1	8.3	6.0	40.0
	Aggravated	21.0	7.7	2.3[b]	40.3
	Simple	24.0	8.6	7.5	41.2
1984	Assault	23.2	9.2	4.7	43.8
	Aggravated	24.3	10.6	4.3	44.8
	Simple	22.8	8.5	4.9	43.4
1983	Assault	18.9	8.1	3.5	44.8
	Aggravated	17.9	8.4	2.7[b]	44.2
	Simple	19.2	7.9	3.8	45.1

[a]Single-offender victimizations only.
[b]Estimate based on 10 or fewer sample cases.

SOURCE: Criminal Victimization in the United States, 1983-1987 Reports.

against females (over age 14), Table 4 illustrates the greater risk to separated and divorced women from assaults by nonstrangers over an 11-year period from 1977 to 1987. The overall victimization rate of females peaked at 19.2 per 1,000 population in 1982 and reached its lowest levels for the two most recent years reported. Nearly three in four single-offender victimizations of separated or divorced women were committed by nonstrangers, compared to less than half the assaults against married or widowed women.[11] This disparity was greatest for the two most recent years, when the overall rate of victimization of females was at its lowest point. Unfortunately, these estimates are limited by NCS procedures that do not report annual gender-specific victimizations by spouses, boyfriends, or girlfriends. Nevertheless, the greater risk to divorced/separated females of victimization by a nonstranger again is evident.

Accordingly, prevalence rates from the National Crime Survey have been consistent over nearly 15 years and several types of analyses. Fluctuations reflect variations in the definitions used in annual reports, as well as definitions and aggregation procedures used in special analyses of marital violence. Moreover, changes in item construction in later years of the study to include nonmarital cohabitants created new designations that complicated assessments of long-term trends. Nevertheless, the NCS data consistently show the extent to which women face risks of violent victimization in the home from nonstrangers, whereas men are at greater risk of violence from strangers. In particular, the critical period of separation of married women from spouses seems to pose the highest risk of violent victimization.

Official Records

Prior to the first victimization or household surveys, research on family violence relied on official data drawn from the criminal justice, mental health, social work, and clinical records of both public and private agencies (Weis, 1989). These sources of official data remain unreconciled and marked by discrepancies, due to their focus on different aspects of the problem. Unlike child abuse, there are few central repositories or mandatory reporting laws that govern the aggregation of data on marital violence. Although criminal justice data focus on offenders, nearly all other sources of official data focus on victims. Moreover, there is little cross-reporting of incidents of marital violence across official agencies.

Medical facilities, safe houses and shelters, and psychotherapists also may provide information on victims of family violence but are limited in estimating its extent, frequency, or severity. These data are narrow in focus, usually contain little information on violent events, and are limited by the decision of individuals to seek help or treatment (Frieze and Browne, 1989).

For severe marital violence against females, both police calls and emergency rooms provide some indicators of its incidence. Stark et al. (1979) found that few cases of marital violence treated in an emergency room were reported to police. Nevertheless, they estimated that 22.5 percent of all injuries presented by women to an urban hospital emergency ward were caused by a male partner's assault.[12] A later study by Stark et al. (1981) estimated that more than 1.5 million women in the United States seek medical assistance annually for injuries sustained in an assault by a male partner. The same study found very low treatment rates for male victims of female violence.

Although their limitations are well known, criminal justice records may be the most critical source among these, due to the regularity with which they are collected and reported, their wide availability, and the legal proscriptions on reporting categories and practices. However, they also produce biased samples of offenders and offenses, and are especially prone to selective underreporting of assaults and rapes (Skogan, 1981). The few direct comparisons of self-report and official data reveal that official underreporting is most serious for respondents who are the most frequent assailants (see Elliott and Huizinga, 1984, regarding adolescents; Petersilia, 1980, for adults). Moreover, NCS data are unequivocal on the severe underreporting of marital violence to criminal justice agencies (Gaquin, 1977-1978; Lentzner and DeBerry, 1980; Langan and Innes, 1986).

In general, criminal justice records are limited in providing accurate estimates of the *epidemiology* of marital violence (cf. Saltzman et al., 1990). They focus on crime events, rather than individuals, and are problematic for developing incidence estimates (cf. Sherman et al., 1989). Limitations include the willingness of victims to report marital violence to the police, and variations in local arrest policies and documentation procedures. For example, Sherman et al. (1990) reported that arrests for marital violence in Milwaukee exceeded 5,000 per year during 1986-1989, but that fewer than 1,000 arrests for marital violence were made in Washington, D.C., a city of comparable size, during the same period.

Nevertheless, police records have provided important information about the *distribution* of marital violence and assessments of the effectiveness of criminal justice responses. Levens and Dutton (1980), in a study of calls for service to the Vancouver (British Columbia) police switchboard, determined that 17.5 percent of all calls for police service were for "family disturbances" and 13.5 percent were for husband-wife disputes. Sherman and Berk (1984), Dunford et al. (1989), and Sherman et al. (1990) have conducted experiments on the specific deterrent effects of arrest in cases of marital violence that provide estimates of its prevalence. Berk and Newton (1985) studied the effects of police responses to 262 incidents of marital violence in Santa Barbara, California, sampled from police records of domestic disturbances. To determine the spatial dimensions of marital violence, Sherman et al. (1989) examined the distribution of calls to police in Minneapolis for domestic distrubances according to their concentration in specific social areas.

Estimates of the prevalence of marital violence were made from police records in Atlanta, Georgia, by Saltzman et al. (1990), using incident reports to identify fatal and nonfatal intimate and family assaults. In addition to married couples, they included as "intimate" those couples who were emotionally intimate at the time of the incident or in the time before it. These were defined as relationships among relatives and in-laws, married and unmarried partnerships, or terminated partnerships. They relied on police classifications of victim-offender relationships that appeared in incident descriptions.

Extrapolating to the Atlanta population, the prevalence of family and intimate assault victimization was 4.9 per 1,000 males and 11.6 per 1,000 females. Rates of fatal assaults were comparable for men and women, but therefore were higher for women as a percentage of all assaults. Rates for married and cohabiting couples were not reported. By linking these reports to police records, Saltzman et al. (1990) concluded that family and intimate assaults occur within a context of repeated violence both by and toward the same individuals. Their efforts represent an important step in realizing the potential of official records for epidemiological surveillance of marital violence. The sensitivity of prevalence estimates to definitions of "family," "intimate," or "marital" is also evident in this effort.

Official records evidently have improved with the social activism that resulted in the "criminalization" of family violence. Mandatory arrest laws in states such as Washington and local policies elsewhere (e.g., Milwaukee) will create new criminal justice data bases on domestic violence that correspond more closely to the populations whose violent behavior is reported to the police. Easing access to restraining orders in states such as Massachusetts and Pennsylvania can be expected to have similar effects. New Jersey also has mandated data collection on reports of domestic violence to police, even if those reports do not result in arrest.

HOMICIDES OF SPOUSES AND INTIMATES

Homicide rates in the United States vastly exceed rates for other countries. Gartner (1990) reported that U.S. homicide rates for victims over 14 years of age during 1950-1980 were 14.92 per 100,000 males and 4.18 per 100,000 females. These rates were nearly three times higher than the next highest country (4.89 for males in Finland and 1.51 for females in Canada). Many studies have shown that homicides in the United States are frequently committed by family members, often in marital relationships (Wolfgang, 1958; Zimring et al., 1983; Browne and Flewelling, 1986; Daly and Wilson, 1987, 1988; Reidel et al., 1985; Williams and Flewelling, 1988; Mercy and Saltzman, 1989; Jurik and Winn, 1990).

For example, Reidel et al. (1985), using UCR Supplemental Homicide Reports (SHRs) from eight cities, showed that 18.7 percent of all homicides from 1978 occurred within families. Straus (1986) calculated that nearly half of the intrafamily homicides (48%) were spouse murders. Of these "family" homicides, 39.7 percent were committed by women, but there was extensive intercity variation (from 50.0 to 27.9%). Using SHRs, Mercy and Saltzman (1989) identified 16,595 homicides among legal or common-law spouses between 1976 and 1985, or 8.8 percent of all homicides nationally over the 10-year period. Using presentence investigations for 158 homicide defendants, Jurik and Winn (1990) found that 52 percent of female perpetrators killed partners or ex-partners, compared to 10 percent of males.

Williams and Flewelling (1988) disaggregated homicides in 168 cities in 1980-1984 by victim-offender relationship and the nature of the precipitating event. Two-thirds of the homicides involved either family members or acquaintances and were attributed to interpersonal conflicts. Using the same data, Carmody and Williams (1987) showed that 52 percent of women victims were killed by spouses, former spouses, cohabitating partners, or noncohabitating boyfriends. Browne and Williams (1989) showed that the homicide rate for female partners is 56 percent of the rate of male spouses. Yet their involvement is disproportionately in marital homicide: outside the family, women were responsible for only 14 percent of all murders, compared to 38 percent in the home.

Women also are disproportionately the victims of marital homicide. Using SHRs, both Straus (1986) and Browne and Williams (1989) found that more wives were killed by husbands than husbands killed by wives: a ratio of two to one similar to the Reidel et al. (1985) study. Mercy and Saltzman (1989) reported that women were 1.3 times more likely to be killed by a spouse than were men.

Using aggregate data from SHRs, Browne and Williams (1989) found more than a 25 percent decrease in female-perpetrated partner homicides from 1976 through 1984. (These data were for all individuals age 15 and over, and included marital, ex-marital, and common-law partners, as well as boyfriends and girlfriends.) This decline began in 1979, at about the time that domestic violence legislation and extralegal resources for abused women were coming into place. States having more domestic violence legislation and other resources targeted for *abused* women (e.g., shelters, crisis lines, and specialized legal assistance) tended to have lower rates of female-perpetrated partner homicide overall, and Browne and Williams (1989) speculated that the presence of such resources was associated with the decline in homicides from 1979 through 1984. The strongest correlation was with the presence of shelters and other extralegal resources for escape and support. Although SHRs do not provide information about couples' histories prior to the lethal incidents, this finding is compatible with studies that show a substantial proportion of homicides by women against their male partners occurring in response to the male partner's aggression, or what Zimring et al. (1983) call the "female use of lethal counterforce" (e.g., see Wolfgang, 1958, 1967; Chimbos, 1978; Totman, 1978; Wilbanks, 1983).

Findings on partner homicides perpetrated by males were much less clear. Although there was a weak negative association between the presence of extralegal resources (such as shelters) and male-perpetrated partner homicide, no association was found between domestic violence legislation and rates of female homicide victimization. Apparently, for homicidal assaults, the increase in legal and extralegal resources—designed in part to increase the salience of legal sanctions and to deter marital, and particularly severe, assaults—was effective only in reducing the use of "last-resort" options by women.

Homicide and Ethnicity

Until recently, the focus of most studies on lethal violence has been restricted to formal or common-law marriages (Silverman and Mukhergee, 1987; Mercy and Saltzman, 1989; Straus, 1986). In part, this may be because studies of nonfatal violence or aggression between unmarried couples have only recently been undertaken, and many of these studies fail to disaggregate their data into victim/offender or gender-based categories (Sugarman and Hotaling, 1989; see Miller and Simpson, 1991, for an exception). Studies of "dating violence" are limited almost exclusively to students in high school or college, leaving unknown the incidence or severity of intimate assaults for individuals who are not attending school or who are past school age and dating or living with intimate partners. Although recent analyses report a slight decrease in lethal violence for married couples, generalizations of these trends to other forms of intimate relationships may be incorrect or misleading.

In further analyses, again using aggregated data from the SHR, Browne and Williams (1993) analyzed trends in partner homicide from 1976 through 1987 both by gender and *type* of intimate relationship (i.e., married versus unmarried couples). *Unmarried* was used to refer to individuals who were dating or living with their partners but who had not resided together long enough to meet general criteria for common-law marriages as determined by the police at the time of the homicide incident. *Marital* was used to indicate formally married, common-law, and ex-married partners. These three categories were combined for two reasons: First, common-law and ex-married partner homicides account for a relatively small percentage of lethal violence between intimate partners during this period—11 percent and 4 percent, respectively. Second, initial analyses revealed that trends for common-law homicides were similar to those for formal marriages, and that rates for homicides involving ex-partners showed no consistent trend. Using these categorizations, analyses of trends in lethal victimization by intimate partners for 1976 through 1987 revealed quite different patterns for married and unmarried couples: there was a slight decrease in lethal violence for married couples, but an increase in such violence between women and men in unmarried relationships.

Again, analyses of the data by gender confirmed the *differential* risks for women in partner relationships, regardless of relationship type. For married couples, although the rate of lethal victimization declined for both women and men during the 12-year period, the drop in the rate at which husbands were killed by their wives was greater than the rate at which wives were killed by their husbands. For unmarried couples, although the lethal victimization rate for men in nonmarital relationships varied unsystematically during this period, the rate of unmarried women being killed by their partners increased significantly. This increase occurred, moreover, in the face of intensified social control attempts (e.g., sanctions and shelter) during the same years.

One possible explanation for this divergence in trends is that the general decrease in the rates of marital homicide—as well as the *absence* of a decrease in the lethal victimization rates for unmarried women—is related to the targeting of societal interventions primarily toward women and men in formal or marriage-like relationships (Browne and Williams, 1993). For example, in many states, domestic violence legislation focuses primarily on addressing problems of safety and access for those who are married or in common-law relationships. Few if any services (except on a few high school or college campuses) are structured for individuals in dating or living-together relationships in which assault occurs. Thus it is possible that the failure of social control attempts to also emphasize the dangers for unmarried couples may leave out those relationship types with potentially the highest risk for lethal violence against women.

In addition to gender differences, the social epidemiology of marital homicide reveals distinct patterns of risk by ethnicity. Block (1987) analyzed 12,872 domestic homicides in Chicago from 1965-1981, and found substantially fewer marital homicides in Chicago for 1965-1981 among Latinos than among African Americans and whites. She also found that the rates per 100,000 population changed over time for each of four racial/ethnic groups. These estimates were further complicated by changes in the census definition of ethnicity in the 1980 iteration. Nevertheless, she did find that marital homicides as a percentage of domestic homicides were relatively constant across racial groups, ranging from 72 to 80 percent. However, the percentage of marital homicides committed by males varied from 33.6 percent for non-Latino African Americans to 53.2 percent for non-Latino whites.

From police incident reports, Saltzman et al. (1990) found that the risk of fatal assaults was three times greater for nonwhites than for whites in Atlanta. Kuhl's (1989) analysis of spousal homicides in California from 1974-1986 also revealed that non-Latino women more often were victims of spousal homicide outside Los Angeles, but that African American males were victims most often in that county. Jurik and Winn (1990), using logit models to examine gender differences, however, found that race was not a significant predictor of gender differences in homicide.

Partner Homicides as Situated Events

Several studies (Gelles, 1974; Chimbos, 1978; Totman, 1978; Luckenbill, 1977; Steadman, 1982; Browne, 1987) found that spousal homicides occur most often inside the home and take place in a series of stages that often follow other types of assaultive incidents. Zahn (1989) characterizes spousal homicide as an escalating series of events beginning with personal criticisms or defiance of behavioral edicts. Katz (1988) suggests that marital homicide is a last-resort effort of spouses to maintain control or to rectify a subjectively perceived violation of some personal moral belief. Jurik and Winn (1990:239) found that women were more likely than men to kill in the home within a context of economic dependence, past attacks, and victim-initiated physical conflicts. Local studies, primarily with samples of women incarcerated for homicide, suggest that a substantial portion of homicides by women against their male partners are in response to the partners' physical aggression and threat (see Browne, 1987, for a review of these studies).

Although more men kill their spouses or partners than are killed by women, Browne (1987) found that abused women kill in response to different provocations than do abusive men. Browne studied women charged in the death or serious injury of violent mates. These women had often endured years of severe assault and threat. Most had unsuccessfully searched for alternative solutions, killing only when they felt hopelessly trapped in a desperate situation from which they could see no practical avenue of escape. Almost all had sought police intervention, although during the period in which these women were living with their partners—from the mid-1960s to the late 1970s—legal and extralegal resources targeted for abused wives either were not available or were just beginning to be put in place. Many of the women had attempted to leave the relationship but in retaliation were even more seriously threatened or attacked. A few had been separated or divorced from their partners for up to two years yet were still experiencing life-threatening violence and harassment before the final incident.

Typically, the killing of the abuser was unplanned and occurred during the period of threat before an assault, in the midst of a violent episode, or during a failed escape attempt by the woman. In some cases, women who had endured abuse for years killed only when the partners' violence and threat turned toward their children. Most of the women in the homicide group had no prior history of violent or even illegal behavior, yet their attempts to survive with an increasingly assaultive and threatening mate— and their inability to find resources that would effectively mitigate the danger—eventually led to their own acts of violence (see Totman, 1978, for similar findings).

Estimates of marital homicides remain problematic due to different methods of aggregation in different jurisdictions, the difficulty of classifying the marital or cohabitational status of the victim and offender, and equally difficult classifications of homicides as assault or robbery homicides. Samples reflect diversity similar to the studies in Table 1 and, as noted, the SHR form contains no information about prior histories of assault between the couples. As measurement improves in these dimensions, estimates of the locations and risk factors for marital homicide are likely to improve and contribute substantively to policy interventions.

MARITAL RAPE

Marital rape is a dimension of family violence often excluded from the marital violence research of the 1970s. Although items on the 1985 NFVS (Gelles and Straus, 1988) asked whether sexual assaults have occurred,[13] the question was asked only of women married or "partnered" at the time of the interview. Our analyses of the 1985 NFVS show that among the 2,942 currently married or partnered women, 1.3 percent reported an attempt to force them to have sex with their partner in the past year. Less than one percent (0.8%) completed the attempt. More than half (53%) reported only one attempt, and about one in five (19%) reported more than two attempts. Also, similar to other research (Fagan et al., 1984; Browne, 1987), nearly all (93%) the women who experienced repeated attempts to force sex in the past year also endured multiple incidents of other forms of marital violence.

Researchers studying marital rape typically avoid the term "rape" and instead usually ask respondents if they were ever sexually assaulted by their spouse or partner (Fagan et al., 1984) or if they were "forced to have sex" with their partner (Walker, 1984). Some studies ask about "unwanted sexual experiences" (Russell, 1982), or having sex in response to force or to the threat of force or violence (Finkelhor and Yllo, 1983). Pagelow (1984) asked women if they had submitted to sexual demands to prevent beatings or other reprisals. Such diversity in item construction obviously suggests caution in comparing studies or drawing conclusions.

Empirical research has shown consistently that marital rape is an integral part of patterns of marital "violence" (Russell, 1982; Frieze, 1983; Fagan et al., 1984; Walker, 1984) and may be an antecedent to marital homicide (Browne, 1987). Marital rape has been reported in relationships in which no other forms of physical abuse has occurred (e.g., Russell, 1982; Finkelhor and Yllo, 1983). However, it seems to be most frequently reported as a form of domination in relationships in which other violent behaviors co-occur (Russell, 1982; Frieze, 1983).

In Russell's (1982) study of women in San Francisco, among women who had ever been married 14 percent said they had been raped by a husband or ex-husband. Finkelhor and Yllo (1983, 1985) found that 10 percent of the women cohabitating with a spouse or intimate male in a representative sample of 323 women in Boston reported at least one sexual assault, and 50 percent reported they had been raped at least 20 times, by their spouses. Fagan et al. (1984) reported that 6.3 percent of women seeking services from domestic violence intervention programs said they sought help because of a sexual assault, and 23 percent reported having been sexually assaulted at some point in the relationship.

Marital rape is highly correlated with other forms of marital assault. In Bowker's (1983) volunteer sample of (N = 146) women victims of marital violence, 23 percent reported both sexual and nonsexual physical assaults. Other studies report slightly higher rates. Sexual assaults were reported by one-third of the women victims of marital violence studied by Prescott and Lesko (1977; cited in Frieze and Browne, 1989 and Frieze, 1983); 37 percent of the women (N = 325) studied by Pagelow (1984); 46 percent of the women interviewed by Shields and Hannecke (1983); and 51 percent of the women in Walker's (1984) study of 435 self-identified victims of marital violence. Accordingly, rates appear to be slightly lower in representative samples than in volunteer samples of women victims of marital violence or women in shelters or intervention programs. (Although, as noted, "representative" samples tend to exclude some groups in which the prevalence of intimate aggression is thought to be quite high.)

Fagan and Wexler (1985) examined sexual assault as part of marital violence based on self-reports from 2,792 women in 23 family violence intervention programs. The authors used Guttman scaling procedures to construct indices from the CTS items, modifying the scales in two ways. A CTS abuse scale added verbal abuse (threats, insults, harassment) and sexual assault to the CTS assault items. A CTS violence scale added only sexual assault, but excluded verbal abuse. For the CTS violence measure, sexual assault scaled as the most serious of the CTS items (coefficient of scalability = .639; coefficient of reproducibility = .890). Moreover, explained variance of marital violence using ordinary least squares regression models was significantly higher for the modified CTS violence measure (including sexual assault) than for measures in which it was excluded. The results provided empirical support for the inclusion of marital rape as a dimension of severe marital violence, and perhaps the most severe nonfatal type of marital assault.

Browne (1987) also found that sexual assault occurred as part of the most violent physical attacks. Bowker (1983), Shields and Hannecke (1983), and Browne (1987) reported that nonsexual physical assaults were more severe among women who experience both sexual and nonsexual assaults than among those who are spared sexual assault.

The exclusion of marital rape from research on marital violence is difficult to understand empirically or to justify conceptually. Straus (1990a) agrees that marital rape is "harmful" but cautions that subsuming it within a definition of family violence or abuse would create conceptual confusion and inhibit theory development. He argues that definitions of violence should include specific acts that are consistent with legal usage, and that reflect normative standards of conduct and humane values.

Normative *ambiguity* regarding sexual assault in marriage may stem from the changing legal status of marital rape. Until the mid-1970s in the United States, rape of one's wife was not a criminal offense. By 1980, only three states had completely eliminated the marital rape exemption from their laws, and five others had modified it (Frieze and Browne, 1989). National trends, in fact, moved in quite the opposite direction. By 1982, 13 other states had extended their exemptions to include cohabitating couples as well as those legally married (Mettger, 1982). Marriage laws also traditionally have viewed marriage as giving implied consent by the wife to grant sexual relations to her husband and granting to husbands the right to use force to obtain compliance. In many states, this implied consent may extend to a couple when separated, unless specifically prohibited through a legal separation order.

The convergence of extreme forms of nonsexual marital violence and sexual assault suggests that they share etiological factors and are manifestations of a particularly dangerous pattern of marital violence. There is substantial evidence to concur with the conclusion of Frieze (1983:552) that marital rape is "one of the most serious forms of battering." For some couples, marital rape is an antecedent to homicide. In considering marital violence as a problem that society wants to remedy, and in the implicit focus on harm and risk markers for patterns of severe violence and lethal assault, this is a neglected aspect—both empirically and legally—that must be integrated into the study of and response to violence occurring between adult partners for our knowledge to be complete or our remedies effective.

GENDER DIFFERENCES IN MARITAL VIOLENCE:
OFFENDING AND VICTIMIZATION

Although there may be circumstances in which men and women share equal proclivities for aggressive behavior, Maccoby and Jacklin (1974:274) concluded that "there is a sex-linked differential readiness to respond in aggressive ways to the relevant experiences." Eron and Huesmann (1989:65) concluded that male aggression is more prevalent and serious, more stable over time, and attributable to different socialization experiences in our society. Outside the home, it is widely accepted that men are more likely to commit robberies or assaults (Weiner and Wolfgang, 1985) and homicides (Zahn, 1989) than women (see Kruttschnitt, in this volume). Simon and Baxter (1989) reported that the increased participation in crime by women in the United States following World War II has been limited to property crimes, not crimes of violence.

However, there is a lively and contentious debate on gender differences between men and women in physical assaults between spouses or partners. Depending on the data source and the dimension of marital violence, gender differences may point to greater injury risk for women or, conversely, higher "violence" rates for women. The two perspectives are not easily reconciled, and the disparity goes to the heart of definitional and philosophical debates in the study of family violence. Moreover, perceptions of the relative violence rates for men and women may reflect different parameters of criminal careers that are used to weigh the evidence.

Both victimization data and intervention reports suggest that more women are victimized than men (Browne, 1993). NCS data suggest that women are victimized more often by male spouses or ex-spouses than strangers, and also by the broader group of "intimates" (Gaquin, 1977-1978; Lentzner and DeBerry, 1980; Langan and Innes, 1986). NCS data also show that injuries sustained by women from marital violence were more frequent, more serious, and more often required medical care (Langan and Innes, 1986). Stets and Straus (1990) showed that more women than men are injured from marital assault in the home and are also injured more often. Homicide data shows that more women than men are victims of marital homicide. From the earliest origins of family violence intervention programs, women victims sought services and protection more often than men (Fagan et al., 1984). However, these programs often directed their outreach to women, were staffed by women, oriented their services toward women, and in residential programs, could only accommodate women.

However, self-reports reveal a different and more complex pattern. Gender-specific participation rates for marital violence are about 10 percent in both the 1975 NFVS data (Straus et al., 1980) and the 1985 resurvey (Straus and Gelles, 1986). The participation rates of reported wife-to-husband assaults[14] were slightly higher than husband-to-wife assault rates when data were aggregated over the two surveys, but the prevalence of severe assaults was slightly higher for males.[15] Statistical significance was not reported. The rates were computed based on combined male and female reports and then recomputed from the reports of only women in the 1985 sample. Adjusting the rates for assaults that produced injuries showed marked gender differences; however, males inflicted injury-assaults at a rate of 3.5 per 1,000, compared to 0.6 per 1,000 for women (Straus, 1989). These reports correspond more closely to the NCS rates reported by Gaquin (1977-1978), Langan and Innes (1986), and others.

Offending rates for males are also much higher. Straus (1989) reports that assault and severe assault frequencies (lambdas) for male spouses or partners are 21 percent greater than the rates for women. The offending rate (lambda) for males committing at least one assault in the 1985 NFVS was more than 7.21 assaults in the previous year and for females, 5.95 assaults (Straus, 1989).[16] For *severe* assault, the rates were 6.1 for men and 4.28 for women, a 42 percent difference. These disparities are even higher among younger respondents (ages 18-25), the group with the highest participation rates (see Table 3). Unfortunately, the limited research on offending rates precludes theory tests that distinguish parameters of "battering careers" for offenders, despite empirical evidence of different predictors of participation versus frequency rates (Blumstein et al., 1985, 1986).

Although the *prevalence of injury* is reported in the NCS and the NFVS, the *frequency of injury* is rarely reported (Fagan and Wexler, 1985). Stets and Straus (1990) report only whether either partner was hurt badly enough to "need to see a doctor." No specific list of injuries was provided, confounding the measure of injury with economic and geographical variables, as well as the willingness to disclose injuries from family violence publicly. Thus, the psychometric properties of the measure of injury are uncertain. Yet the severity and frequency of specific acts of violence have been found to correlate with the severity of injury in other studies (Fagan and Wexler, 1985; Frieze et al., 1980) and in turn bear on the question of gender differences.

Moreover, sampling decisions that exclude other than intact

couples or include only women using interventions can skew estimates of gender-specific offending rates. For example, women in shelters report far higher offending rates by male partners (Straus, 1990b). Separated/divorced women reported higher victimization rates in the NCS than did married women (Lentzner and DeBerry, 1980). Okun (1986) studied 300 women in a Michigan shelter and found a rate of 68.7 assaults per year. Fagan et al. (1984) found that more than half of the women (*N* = 270) in a variety of intervention programs reported "frequent" (more than once a month) severe abuse (physical and sexual assaults, weapon use, weapon threats) in the past year. Other validity threats to these data are discussed below.

Methodological Problems in Interpreting Gender Differences and Mutuality

The question of "mutual combat" (Berk et al., 1983) goes to the heart of the debate on gender differences in marital violence. Stets and Straus (1990), using 1985 NFVS data, show that for 49 percent of the 825 respondents who experienced one or more assaults during the past year, both parties engaged in assaultive behaviors. Similar rates were obtained in the 1975 NFVS. Despite the comparable rates of assaultive behaviors between men and women in the two NFVS data sets, it is misleading to characterize marital violence as mutual violence. Unlike the Berk et al. (1983) study, the sequencing of events in the NFVS does not address mutuality in the same incident. Events may have occurred far apart in time, yet be aggregated for the same reporting year. Mutuality is also difficult to assess because of gender differences in self-reports of assaultive behaviors. Underreporting of the incidence and severity of marital violence by men has been well-established (Szinovacz, 1983; Edelson and Brygger, 1986; O'Leary and Arias, 1988), and raises questions about the "mutuality" of assaults—especially severe assaults, in which women are more likely to be injured. Correcting this bias would in fact increase the rate of mutuality. Other data suggest that men and women rate the severity of violence differently, even when they agree that it occurred (see Table 3).

Although published research from the NFVS data has emphasized the "equality" of violence participation rates for women and men, Straus et al. (1980) list five reasons to interpret issues of gender equality in marital violence cautiously: (1) the perpetration of "severely" violent acts is greater for men than women; (2)

violence by husbands does more damage due to their greater size and physical strength; (3) the offending rate (Lambda) for men is higher than for women—that is, the number of times that men hit women is greater; (4) men often hit women when they are pregnant, posing dangers of miscarriage and infertility; and (5) women remain in marriages and thus at risk for injury more often than men, primarily due to their economic circumstances (Gelles, 1974).

In addition, methodological problems in both the NCS and the NFVS limit comparisons of gender differences or conclusions. Perhaps most important is the infrequent reporting of offending rates (lambdas) for both data sources. Rarely are marital violence events analyzed in which multiple acts occur, perhaps by both parties, in a complex interaction. For example, one battering event may involve several specific acts, yet either these acts are given even weight or only the most serious act is reported. The order of individual acts is almost never obtained in national surveys; that is, over the course of a reporting period, we cannot state who hit whom first.[17] Even when questions are posed about who initiated conflict, these items are not specific to the use or threat of violence. Also, in the NFVS, assessments of agreement in the CTS are precluded because only one marital partner participates. Thus, assessments of male- and female-perpetrated assaults are based on aggregated data from different households.

In the NCS, data are limited to reporting the number of "serial victimizations." Problems of interpretation and validity concerns also limit conclusions about gender differences based on NCS data. NCS questions are posed in the context of a "crime" survey, raising difficulties for respondents who may define spouse assaults as a "family" matter. Items about spouse assault are framed as an act by a former spouse who "has no right to that" (Langan and Innes, 1986), introducing subjectivity into respondents' classifications of events and possible confusion among respondents about the appropriateness of certain behaviors by role of the perpetrator (e.g., husband or father) and the legal context of a specific event. Similarly, NFVS surveys pose their items in the context of "family conflict," thus ruling out reports of assaults that may be interpreted in some other way.

Moreover, to extrapolate from estimates of assault occurrences to classifications of individuals as violent (as is done in the interpretation of NFVS results) skips over important conceptual and definitional concerns about the interpretation of "assault" by respondents, decisions on aggregation and reporting of data on discrete behaviors, and what behaviors constitute violence. Certainly, the comparative assault, severe assault, and injury assault rates reported by Straus and his colleagues suggest that men more often commit assaultive acts than women. Yet by classifying respondents as "violent" or "assaultive" on the basis of participation rates on CTS or NCS items, a framework of interpretation is imposed that suggests no gender differences (see Browne, 1993; Dobash et al., 1992).

Until there are (1) a more complete understanding of differential validity by gender of self-reports of marital violence, (2) calculations of offending rates as well as participation rates across a variety of sampling and measurement conditions, and (3) careful attention to definitional parameters of assaultiveness and violence, conclusions about the absence of gender differences are unwarranted. The weight of current empirical evidence on frequency, injury, victimization, and homicide suggests that such conclusions are premature and incomplete.

Social Locations of Marital Violence and Homicide

The social structural correlates of marital violence vary according to the data source and design features of various studies, as well as the type of violence. Research using official records or samples of families that present themselves for services suggests that marital violence occurs more often among poor minority families in which neither spouse has attained more than a high school education (Fagan et al., 1984; Saltzman et al., 1990). Self-report studies (Straus et al., 1980) and voluntary samples (Bowker, 1983; Walker, 1984; Shields et al., 1988) typically have found a weaker but still inverse relationship between social class and marital violence. Bridges and Weis (1989) attribute these disparities to differences in study designs and basic methods of measurement that are typical of various data sources.

Nonlethal Marital Violence

Comparisons of social structural correlates of marital violence from either the NCS or the NFVS have been limited to participation rates. Table 3 briefly shows social structural correlates of male-to-female marital violence for both participation and offending rates. Moreover, the data suggest region-specific models, variation by male or female participation in violence, and ethnicity by region interactions.

Household Surveys Straus et al. (1980) report that violence did not vary by region but was correlated with urbanism. However, the rates of marital violence were higher both in cities and in rural areas and lowest in suburbs. They reported higher participation rates for both male and female racial minorities, male high school graduates (with no college education) and female high school dropouts, younger couples with the lowest incomes, and those with "blue-collar" occupations or unemployed men.

Table 3, using 1985 NFVS data, showed higher participation rates in general violence for younger couples in central-city areas with incomes below $20,000 who were under 25 years of age.

Information on Latinos in these surveys is limited; no information was provided in the 1975 NFVS. Straus and Smith (1990) provided more detailed comparisons of Hispanics and whites from the 1985 NFVS data. However, these comparisons did not differentiate between white and nonwhite Hispanics, or Hispanics from varying countries and cultures. Overall, marital violence was more prevalent among Hispanics for both assault and severe assault, particularly in the Northeast and South, in cities, among both blue- and white-collar families, and in poor families.

Ethnic-specific rates of all forms of family violence were constructed for Mexican Americans by Sorenson and Telles (1991). They compared family violence among whites and Mexican Americans using global measures of "family violence" from Epidemiological Catchment Area surveys. The items combined several CTS items into one.

Victimization Surveys NCS data suggest similar patterns. Nearly two in three (65.6 percent) victims of assault by spouses or ex-spouses had incomes of less than $10,000 in 1978 (Lentzner and DeBerry, 1980). NCS data for 1985-1987 show that income and victim-offender relationships are inversely associated for violent victimizations. In higher-income families, violent victimizations more often involved strangers; in lower income families, nonstrangers were assailants in more than half of the reported victimizations for assault and robbery. However, there is little evidence of consistent patterns of victimization in the NCS by other social structural factors. Whites and African Americans reported comparable victimization rates for assaults by spouses and ex-spouses (Lentzner and DeBerry, 1980; Langan and Innes, 1986), in contrast to the NFVS data presented in Table 3 and by Straus et al. (1980).

Participants in Intervention Programs Among participants in intervention programs, similar correlates emerge. Fagan et al. (1983) analyzed reports about male spouses from 270 women participants in social and legal intervention programs. OLS regressions showed that the race of the assailant (nonwhite) predicted his concurrent involvement in both stranger and marital violence, but was a weak predictor of either the severity or the frequency of marital violence. However, low educational attainment of assailants was a strong predictor of both their marital and their stranger dimensions of violence. Fagan et al. also found interactions between situational (e.g., respondents' alcohol use, childhood violence experiences of victim and assailant) and social structural correlates for each dimension of violence.

The obvious sampling biases here suggest caution, but the findings illustrate the concentration of social correlates of violence with the most violent couples. Nevertheless, we know little about middle- and upper-class couples that experience extreme forms of violence but avoid participation in the public sector. They also are undersampled in national surveys and likely use their higher social status to resolve or escape violence (Bowker, 1983, 1986b).

Spatial Distribution of Marital Violence Research on the social locations of domestic violence also suggest that there may be spatial or ecological concentrations. Research in Kansas City (Meyer and Lorimor, 1977) showed that 5.2 percent of police calls for disturbances were dispatched to addresses with five to eight calls in the same year. Sherman et al. (1989) analyzed data on locations of repeat calls for service for "domestic disturbances," a broad category that includes loud stereos, family fights, neighbor disputes, and family violence. Nearly 25,000 domestic disturbances in Minneapolis in 1986 (from December 1985 to December 1986) were recorded in 8.6 percent of all locations; 9.1 percent of the addresses with at least one domestic disturbance call accounted for 35.9 percent of all domestic calls. Sherman et al. (1989) reported results of a Boston study (Pierce et al., 1988) in which 9 percent of apartments reporting any calls for "family trouble" over a five-year period accounted for about 28 percent of all such calls.

The criminogenic influence of place on domestic disturbances remains ambiguous, however. Many of the areas in which calls were concentrated involved high-rise buildings with multiple addresses. In these settings, close proximity between neighbors may result in greater reporting of disturbances. Sherman et al. (1989)

also posit that these areas or buildings may be receptors for the types of people most likely to experience, or to call police about, domestic problems. Without knowing either specific addresses or the nature of the calls, the correlation of domestic disturbance with place remains speculative. Weisburd et al. (1989) argued that situation-specific models of crime commission would lead naturally to identification of "hot spots" of specific crime types such as violent offenses. Instead, they found strong correlations between domestic disturbances and other crime types that occurred in residences, such as residential burglaries and robberies of persons. In general, these were areas that manifested signs of the incivilities that suggest growing social disorganization, but there was no evidence of crime-specific patterns regarding violence within or outside the home.

Evidently, there are weak correlations between social area and the occurrence of violent crimes among nonstrangers or in domestic situations. Rather than signifying causal relationships, the concentration suggests that ecological factors may be facilitators or supportive of marital violence. The correlations may also represent reciprocal processes; for example, men who are assaultive and threatening with their families may also exhibit problematic behaviors at work and experience job or income loss.

The evidence of effects of place (social location) also are equivocal. Although places themselves may be criminogenic, it is unclear whether they directly contribute to marital violence, simply host individuals who are more likely to engage in it (i.e., concentration effects), or indirectly facilitate crime through weak social controls. The unique context of the home itself in our societal structure seems to contribute to the disproportionate occurrence of victimization of spouses or partners. These correlations suggest the presence of other ecological factors in socially disorganized areas that place certain couples at greater risk than others.

Marital Homicides

Historically, there has been regional variation in homicide rates (Zahn, 1989). As noted, Browne and Williams (1989) found variations by state in female-perpetrated partner homicides that were negatively correlated with legal resources and social spending for interventions for abused women. Indicators of urbanism[18] and the male homicide rate predicted the female homicide rate, suggesting an urban concentration of female-perpetrated partner homicides. However, Browne and Williams (1989) did not examine the availability of resources by race. Other researchers (Schechter, 1982) have noted that resources for women at risk often are unavailable or inaccessible to minority women.

Analyses of intrafamily homicides by Williams and Flewelling (1988) revealed strong correlations between ecological variables and marital homicides resulting from family conflict. Homicides resulting from family conflict were highly correlated with two indicators of poverty: percent black (.605) and percent poor (.560), exceeded only by the correlations for acquaintance homicide. However, in multivariate relationships, the contributions to explained variance for these variables were consistent across models for other homicide types. Evidently, resource deprivation and social disintegration (measured by the divorce rate) have a pervasive impact on city-to-city variations in all forms of criminal homicide.

Several studies of marital homicides using local and national data (Block, 1987; Zimring et al., 1983; Kuhl, 1989; Saltzman et al., 1990; Mercy and Saltzman, 1989) identified disproportionate involvement of racial minorities. For example, Kuhl found gender-region-race interactions in California that resulted in higher marital violence rates for African American males in Los Angeles and Hispanic women in other areas of the state.

Using 1976-1985 SHR data, Mercy and Saltzman (1989) found that African Americans accounted for 45.4 percent of all spouse homicide victims, and their rate was 8.4 times higher than the white rate. White *wives* had twice the risk of spousal homicide, but African American women had homicide victimization rates moderately lower than the rate for African American males. Age adjustment did not change these rates overall or for whites; however, the risk of spouse homicide decreased for African Americans after age 24 (Mercy and Saltzman, 1989:595). Overall, racial differences declined with age. The prevalence of spouse homicides was 7.7 times higher in interracial couples (2.9% of all homicides) than intraracial marriages. This discussion should not deflect the greater importance of socioeconomic factors than race in explaining domestic homicide (Centerwall, 1984) or the fact that family or nonstranger homicide rates are more sensitive to socioeconomic factors than are stranger homicide rates (Parker and Smith, 1979; Smith and Parker, 1980).

Research on domestic homicides in Kansas City in the 1970s (Breedlove et al., 1977) showed that police had responded to at least five prior calls for service at about 50 percent of the addresses where domestic homicides occurred in the two years preceding the homicide. Sherman et al. (1990) contend, however, that residential mobility among both domestic and stranger homicide victims and perpetrators mitigates any linkage between addresses and individuals. They found weak predictions of domestic homicides from recurring prior calls for service linked to individuals among domestic homicides in Milwaukee. Homicide victims evidently reside in the types of buildings that have high prevalence and frequency of police calls for recurring domestic disturbances. These studies suggest that a safer conclusion would attribute residential patterns and ecological processes to places rather than individuals in establishing social locations of domestic homicides.

Accordingly, there is some evidence that marital homicide is an urban phenomenon, more often located in social areas that typify the problems of urban areas: poverty, residential mobility, weak family structures, and concentrations of minority populations. Although the data suggest an ecological concentration of marital homicide, more specific studies are needed that tie homicides to specific locales; that measure their social area characteristics; and that are disaggregated by the race, social status, and abuse histories of the participants.

EPIDEMIOLOGY OF INJURIES

The relative risks and severity of injuries sustained in marital violence vary according to data sources. NCS data provide the only consistent basis for comparing marital and other violence, and consistently reaffirm the greater risks of injury to people in the home. Lentzner and DeBerry (1980) reported that more than 75 percent of the victims of violence (assault, rape, and robbery) involving "related intimates" suffered injuries, compared to 54 percent of victims of nonstranger violence. More than 80 percent of all assaults against spouses and ex-spouses resulted in injuries, and spouses and ex-spouses had the highest rates of internal injuries or unconsciousness (7.0 percent) and broken bones (6.9%).

Similar trends persisted in NCS data on assault through the 1980s, although NCS data do not consistently use the "intimate" designation. Victimization data show that 36 percent of victims of nonstranger assault sustained physical injury in the 1987 survey, compared to 22 percent of victims of stranger assaults. Unfortunately, the NCS data do not permit injury breakdowns by victim-offender relationship and victim gender.

Stets and Straus (1990) used three measures of "injury" to compare injury risk for males and females from the National Family Violence Surveys (1975 and 1985). First, respondents were asked

whether they had been hurt badly enough as a result of any assault in the past year to require medical attention (need to or
actually see a doctor). Second, assaulted respondents were asked
whether they took time off from work because of violent incidents. Third, they were asked how many days they spent in bed
due to illness. The latter was collapsed into a dichotomous measure. Few victims reported "needing" to see a doctor: 3 percent
of women victims and 0.4 percent of male victims.

These rates increased after controlling for the severity of assault: among victims of severe assault, 7.3 percent of the women
needed medical attention, compared to 1.0 percent of the males (p
< .05). Similar findings were reported for time off from work. For
days in bed, women were more likely to report being bedridden
for one or more days, but differences were not significant for severe violence. Reports using NCS data, in contrast, showed that
19.0 percent of the spouse or ex-spouse victims of assault sought
medical care and 13 percent were treated in a hospital (Lentzner
and DeBerry, 1980).

The injury rates based on these measures should be considered underestimates. As noted earlier, no direct measure of injury
was employed in the 1975 or 1985 NFVS protocols. Responses to
the question of needing to see a doctor would be confounded with
individual respondents' thresholds of severity of physical injuries
or pain to motivate them to seek formal medical care. Further,
women victims of marital violence often refrain from actually
seeing a doctor, even when injured quite severely, due to shame,
threats by the abuser against seeking outside help, and fear that
seeking medical attention would identify them as the victims of
marital violence (Walker, 1984; Browne, 1987; Stark and Flitcraft,
1983).

To measure nonphysical or psychological injuries, Stets and
Straus (1990) used self-reports of psychosomatic symptoms, depression and stress. More women victims than men reported all
three forms of nonphysical injury, and the gender differences intensified with the severity of violence. Even with these limited
measures of injury, and the absence of specific types of injuries or
standardized measures of depression or stress, the negative consequences of marital violence were greater for women. However,
the cross-sectional data complicate any causal inferences from
these results.

Although comparisons are confounded by design differences
between the NCS and the NFVS, injury rates in the NFVS appear
lower than in the NCS data, despite the higher rates of marital

violence in the former. Stets and Straus (1990:158) dismiss gender differences as being "not particularly strong or large," although their measures did not differentiate among types of injury and required subjective judgments of unproven psychometric validity. Neither data source reported the *frequency* of injuries, and only the NCS considered specific types of injury. Accordingly, injury as a dimension of marital violence is difficult to evaluate in the NFVS, and participation-incidence confounding may exist in the NCS analysis of injury.

Studies that measured both the frequency and the severity of injury show the strong association between behavior and injury, and between the frequency of behavior and the frequency and severity of injury. Among women who sought help from family violence intervention programs (N = 270), 56 percent reported being the victim of abuse[19] at least once a month (Fagan and Wexler, 1985). Bruises, lacerations, broken bones, or more serious injuries were reported by 66 percent of the victims, and 59 percent reported being injured "occasionally" or "frequently." About one in three women who had children were victims of marital violence during pregnancy, and 4 percent of the women overall reported miscarriages due to marital violence.

Table 5 shows the zero-order correlations between the specific types of violence from the CTS and injury scales. As mentioned earlier, the CTS (violence) scale was created by using Guttman scaling methods and was modified from the Straus (1979) CTS scale to include sexual assault. Nearly all the specific behavioral items were significantly correlated with the severity of injury and the frequency of violence. The acts of nonphysical violence (verbal threats) are correlated only with the injury variables. However, the Pearson correlation coefficients are lower than would be expected if injuries and violent acts were dimensions of one phenomenon.

Evidently, injury and violent behaviors represent dimensions of marital violence that overlap only partially, yet add considerably to its measurement by including the dimension of harm. In turn, the epidemiology of marital violence may be vulnerable to criterion-dependent biases. When applied to tests of theory, varying measurement strategies also yield differential explanations and validity of theoretical models (see Table 6 below) or evaluations of the effects of interventions (see Table 7 below). Accordingly, using one dimension or the other exclusively is likely to yield an incomplete understanding of the etiology of marital violence. Estimates based solely on behavioral counts merely identify indi-

TABLE 5 Zero-Order Correlation Coefficients for Marital Violence Measures ($N = 2{,}792$)

Violence Measure	Verbal Threats or Abuse	Push, Slap, or Scratch	Threaten Punch, Choke, or Kick	With Object or Weapon	Hit With Object or Weapon	Sexual Assault
CTS (violence)	.62[a]	.53[a]	.41[a]	.57[a]	.52[a]	.53[a]
Frequency of abuse	.08	.14[b]	.13[b]	.15[c]	.16[c]	.16[c]
Most serious injury	.17[c]	.28[a]	.31[a]	.06	.13[c]	.09
Abuse during pregnancy	.14[c]	.17[c]	.13[b]	.05	.12[b]	-.009
Duration of abuse	.02	-.01	.07	.07	.05	-.008
Frenquency of injury	.12	.07	.26[a]	.00	-.04	-.05

[a] $p = .001$.
[b] $p = .01$.
[c] $p = .05$.

SOURCE: Fagan and Wexler (1985).

viduals that engage in assaultive acts; the injury and harm from these acts, as well as their meaning, should also be addressed to fully explain the behaviors (see Carmody and Williams, 1987; Browne, 1993; Fagan and Wexler, 1985).

VALIDITY AND RELIABILITY OF EPIDEMIOLOGICAL RESEARCH

Several factors that may affect the validity of estimates of marital violence have already been discussed in the context of gender differences: data sources, samples, measurement strategies, interviewing procedures, methods of aggregating and analyzing data, and definition-classification links. The extensive validation procedures for the NCS support its utility as a general crime survey, but validity threats remain that are specific to the measurement of marital violence. In this section, we review other validity and reliability issues in epidemiological research on marital violence, and also identify some of the validation efforts for the NFVS and other studies.

Official Records

Official records have the obvious limitations of serving the data collection needs of the agencies that gather them and the variability that characterizes definitions of behaviors as well as procedures for recording and reporting. Accordingly, law enforcement data will collapse a wide variety of acts into categories such as "domestic disturbance," or even "spouse assault," under new legislation that calls for mandatory arrest or criminal penalties for violations of court orders. Mental health agencies collect information appropriate for diagnosis, treatment planning, monitoring services provided, and decision making. Medical records also chart diagnoses and treatments.

Victimization Surveys

The NCS survey, as a measure of criminal victimization, partially addresses the specific varieties of marital violence. Behaviors are measured in items that correspond to *penal* code categories, but these may overlook conceptually important distinctions in the severity of *marital* violence. The NCS is usually administered in the presence of both adults in an intact household (interviewers are instructed to interview separately when possible, but joint interviews generally occur). In this context, the intimate relationship between offender and victim poses obvious validity threats that are less salient for stranger victimizations. When faced with an ongoing relationship between victim and offender, victims may be likely to minimize the severity of marital violence or underreport its occurrence (Gelles, 1978). The disparity between NCS and NFVS estimates of marital assault rates may in part reflect these differences in interview formats.

Self-Report Studies

Because marital violence by definition occurs most often in private settings, self-reports must play a central role in empirical research. Research on measures of sensitive topics, including violent behaviors, shows the self-report method to be quite reliable (Straus, 1979; Hindelang et al., 1981; Bridges and Weis, 1989). Unlike official records, self-reports also have a greater potential for modification and improvement than official records (Bridges and Weis, 1989; Weis, 1989). The CTS measures used in the NFVS represent the most widely cited metric of epidemiological data on family violence. The CTS has been used in a variety of sampling and procedural conditions. Accordingly, the extensive research on its validity and reliability describes the state of self-report research in marital violence and its inherent problems.

Reliability Estimates Several studies have confirmed the general factor structure of the Conflict Tactics Scales under a variety of sampling and measurement conditions. Three factors have been identified in several studies that replicate those derived by Straus (1979): verbal reasoning, verbal aggression, and physical aggression. For example, Jorgensen (1977) found three factors that he labeled "high-," "medium-," and "low-"intensity factors that parallel the three factors identified by Straus (1979). Hornung et al. (1981) assessed the reliability of the CTS for the study of 1,793 women in Kentucky (Schulman, 1979) and found four factors: reasoning, psychological abuse, physical aggression, and "life-threatening violence." Barling et al. (1987) also identified a fourth factor for psychological aggression. Straus (1990b) reconciles the differences between his 1979 factor analyses and these studies by citing variations in sampling and data collection procedures, as well as modifications of certain CTS items.

Straus (1990b) summarized data from six studies that reported Alpha reliability coefficients for these three scales of the CTS, including three that measured marital violence. For physical aggression, Barling et al. (1987) reported an Alpha coefficient of .88 for husband-to-wife violence; Mitchell and Hodson (1983) reported an Alpha coefficient of .69 for reports by battered women; and Winkler and Doherty (1983) reported an Alpha coefficient of .83 for couples.

Validity Estimates Validation research generally has lagged behind other research efforts in marital violence, with greater interest and attention to epidemiological estimates and tests of etiological theory. Despite the common use of official records in self-report studies of stranger crime (e.g., Hindelang et al., 1981; Elliott and Huizinga, 1984), few studies on marital violence have used either known group differences or external criteria for validation.[20]

Validity strategies have ranged from parental confirmation of college students' reports of violence in the home (Bulcroft and Straus, 1975), to using reports from a couple to assess agreements on how often and seriously marital violence occurred (Szinovacz, 1983; Browning and Dutton, 1986). However, neither adolescents (Fagan and Wexler, 1987b; Kruttschnitt and Dornfield, 1992) nor parents (Marsh et al., 1983) may be reliable informants about violence in their families. Straus (1979, 1990b) is equivocal about the concurrent validity of the CTS measures, citing evidence that establishes neither their validity nor their invalidity. For example, the highest correlation of parent and student reports in Bulcroft and Straus (1975) was .64, whereas other correlations varied extensively. Weis (1989) suggests that validity is inflated due to same-method effects.

Other studies that estimated concurrent validity show similarly varied results. We have already mentioned the limitations of the NVFS due to reliance on reports from one member of each couple. Yet Szinovacz (1983) found differential validity by respondent characteristics for both spouse assault and child abuse. She found only 40 percent agreement for violence by female spouses in 103 couples, and 27 percent agreement on the male partner's violence, but substantial agreement on the nonoccurrence of violence. Browning and Dutton (1986) reported correlations between men's and women's reports of the husband's violence of .65. Edelson and Brygger (1986) found that female partners of 29 males in treatment reported significantly higher rates of violence than the males for 4 of 13 specific acts. They cautioned that inappropriate treatment decisions might result, endangering female partners of male assailants in treatment.

O'Leary and Arias (1988) studied 369 couples recruited through newspaper advertisements and radio announcements to assess violence before marriage as an antecedent of later discord and aggression. Overall, agreement rates for violence by either husband and wife were high (68-72%), but agreement on violence by the husband was only moderate (39-40%). Jouriles and O'Leary (1985) reported nearly identical results with samples ($N = 65$) of couples in marital therapy and matched samples ($N = 37$) from a nearby community. All these studies examined the validity of prevalence rates from various samples; no studies were found that analyzed concurrent validity on the frequency of violence.

There has been little research on response effects or task effects in family violence research, two other important sources of error. Weis (1989) suggests that marital violence is especially prone to response errors for several reasons: marital violence is highly emotional and often traumatic, it is very salient because of its low frequency but harmful consequences, and it is serial or chronic in that the same behaviors often occur over a long period of time. Response errors also may result from the weak social desirability of violence toward loved ones (Gelles, 1978; Loftus, 1980; Resick and Reese, 1986; cf. Straus, 1990b) and the presence of alcohol in a large percentage of cases (Fagan et al., 1983; Miller et al., 1988). Unfortunately, randomized response techniques (Fox and Tracy, 1986) have been underutilized in research on marital violence. Other sources of error and threats to validity in applications of the CTS include the telephone method of administration in the 1985 survey (i.e., task-related errors), the setting, the anonymity of respondents, the recall period, and respondent characteristics that may affect responses.

Construct validity for the CTS seems to be high because it produces findings consistent with both theoretical and empirical propositions (Straus, 1990b). This includes research on risk factors for violence that are evident in both general population and treatment or clinical samples, marital dynamics of violent and nonviolent couples (Szinovacz, 1983), personality factors associated with both stranger and family violence, and lack of social desirability (Resick and Reese, 1986).

However, the construct validity of the CTS is far weaker when harm and consequence measures are used as criteria (Fagan and Wexler, 1985) or when other measures of violence in marriage are included in the scales, such as marital rape. Straus (1990b) suggests that these strategies confound physical aggression with other domains of marital conflict. Yet this controversy raises the fundamental question of operational definitions of marital violence. Whether marital violence is defined unidimensionally (Straus, 1979, 1990b) or multidimensionally (Hudson and McIntosh, 1981; Alford, 1982; Fagan and Wexler, 1985; Bridges and Weis, 1989) is not simply a matter of preference. These divergent measurement strategies reflect approaches to measurement of a complex phenomenon that occurs in specific contexts and situations. Such factors mediate and shape the very behaviors implied by the term "family" violence. Although criminological research has recognized the multidimensionality of violence and the sensitivity of theory tests to measurement, the hegemony of CTS measures has limited the development of validation criteria in research on marital violence and, in turn, the advance of theory and explanation.

Finally, the wide range of participation rates for Tables 1 and 2 raises questions about the external validity of the findings of the research using self-reports and suggests, as noted earlier, that method-dependent biases (Widom, 1990) may contribute to disparate findings. Sampling decisions in both victimization and self-report methods have excluded vulnerable populations that have reported high rates of victimization or offending in other studies. Specific exclusions have included separated and divorced people and those without telephones.

Some critics (e.g., Pelton, 1979) suggest that valid and reliable self-reports of intrafamilial violence are unattainable. Response effects that emanate from interview formats and item construction are persistent validity threats in both victimization and self-report research on assaults between partners (Weis, 1989). In the context of the family, response effects are especially acute for assaultive behaviors that are frequent, emotionally traumatic, and acted out between people who are intimates and have ongoing relationships that themselves are modified by the violence between them (Gelles, 1978). Weis (1989) poses a research agenda to address these concerns that requires a step back before we take steps forward. The unique methodological issues in research on marital violence suggest the need for greater attention to the psychometric properties of measures and their validity in various study designs and samples. This specifically requires multimethod efforts and multi-indicator research to settle empirically the dimensionality of marital violence and to assess the validity of competing definitions and their measures.

CHARACTERISTICS OF PERPETRATORS, VICTIMS, AND COUPLES

There has been much research on the prevalence of assaults within marriage, the damage it does, its female victims, and the dynamics of relationships in which violence occurs. There also is much knowledge about marital violence that results in self-defensive homicide by abused women, and about the characteristics of victims who seek help from shelters or other resources for women who are threatened or abused by their partners. Less is known about the characteristics of *men* who engage in marital violence, or about those men who kill current or ex-wives or girlfriends. Interview studies with women victims have supplied most of the current knowledge, although research with samples of assaultive spouses has grown in recent years. In this section, we summarize knowledge on the characteristics of assaultive partners and couples in which one or both partners are assaultive, and we evaluate the status of current research.

Men Who Engage in Marital Violence

Until recently, research on marital violence has relied on victim reports, mostly from women, for information on the nature of violent events and the characteristics of victims and assailants (see Frieze and Browne, 1989, for a review of this literature). The few studies of violent men have been limited to small samples of repeatedly assaultive participants in treatment programs (Sonkin, 1987; Maiuro et al., 1986), voluntary or self-selected samples (Shields et al., 1988; Rosenbaum and O'Leary, 1981), or assailants identified by the criminal justice system who also frequently are violent (Dutton and Strachan, 1987; Hamberger and Hastings, 1988; Edelson and Brygger, 1986). Accordingly, variations in definitions, researcher effects, sampling strategies, program criteria, and measurement techniques introduce validity threats into the emerging literature on assaultive partners.

For example, clinicians working with abusive or violent men and couples note that men vastly underreport their violent behaviors, minimize the harm it does or its severity, or even deny the behavior (Szinovacz, 1983; Ganley and Harris, 1978; O'Leary and Arias, 1988). Even when confirming their participation in assaultive behaviors, assaultive partners may claim more involvement by the victim (provocation, mutuality) than is justified by either witness or police reports (Sonkin and Durphy, 1985) or may excuse violent behavior as the result of alcohol (Kantor and Straus, 1987). The elements of coercion and social control in criminal justice settings may also affect the validity of self-reports and the assessment of behavioral variables in research with assaultive males. Thus, Dutton (1988a) concludes that differing profiles of wife assaulters may reflect the variations in research strategies more than substantive differences in typologies. With these limitations in mind, this section reviews empirical knowledge on the characteristics of male partners and violent relationships.

Personality Characteristics and Concurrent Behaviors   A brief review of profiles of assaultive men reveals a bewildering array of findings. In general, wife abusers have been reported to have the following characteristics: low self-esteem (Ganley and Harris, 1978; Pagelow, 1984; Neidig et al., 1986); extreme jealousy (Davidson, 1978; Rounsaville, 1978; Bowker, 1983); need for control (Elbow, 1977; Fleming, 1979; Browning and Dutton, 1986) but lacking in assertiveness (Rosenbaum and O'Leary, 1981; Telch and Lindquist, 1984); suicidal personality (Browne, 1987); abusiveness toward children (Washburn and Frieze, 1981; Straus, 1983); involvement in alcohol and drug abuse (Walker, 1984; Coleman and Straus, 1983; Kantor and Straus, 1987, 1989; Miller et al., 1988); wide variations in moods (Fleming, 1979; Walker, 1979); hostility or anger (Novaco, 1976; Maiuro et al., 1986); distortion of cognitive perceptions of social cues (Novaco, 1976; Bandura, 1973); strong sex-role stereotypes (Gondolf, 1988; Saunders, 1987); and lack of verbal skills (Novaco, 1976; Browning and Dutton, 1986; Maiuro et al., 1986; Rosenbaum and O'Leary, 1981).

Conditioning and social learning processes also may contribute to the development and habituation of assaultive behavior. Dutton and Strachan (1987) characterized assaultive men as needing to exert power in marital relationships but lacking the verbal resources to do so, which leads to chronic frustration that increases the risk for aggression. Violence may be gratifying and therefore self-reinforcing as a response to marital conflict (Novaco, 1976, cited in Dutton, 1988b). Moreover, once aggressive habits are developed, any form of arousal (even self-generated arousal) can be construed as anger provoking and, in turn, can trigger an incident involving aggression (Bandura, 1973). In this view, assaultive men may be inclined to respond to a variety of stimuli by initiating anger and then aggression toward spouses or partners as a source of gratification (Dutton, 1988a). This in turn may explain the habituation of assault within marriage. However, the interaction of gratification processes and other personality factors is unknown.

Efforts to develop typologies of assaultive men have tried to reconcile the complex literature on personality factors (see Dutton, 1988a, for a comprehensive review). One of the sources of discrepancy in these findings may be their aggregation of several types of assaultive men into homogeneous categories of assailants. However, as in homicide research, disaggregation of distinct assailant types may result in unique configurations of personality and background characteristics for each type.

Efforts to construct typologies of assaultive men divide them on personality factors (Elbow, 1977; Hamberger and Hastings, 1986a,b; Caesar, 1988), their involvement in violence toward strangers and intimates (Fagan et al., 1983; Shields et al., 1988; Hotaling and Straus, 1989); combinations of assaultive and other behaviors such as alcohol use (Gondolf, 1988); or sex-role stereotyping (Saunders, 1987). However, these efforts have confounded dependent and explanatory variables in typology development. The procedures for typology construction also may contribute to different configurations or typologies. Typologies have been based on cluster analysis (Saunders, 1987), a priori categories (Shields et al., 1988), and principal components techniques (Hamberger and Hastings, 1986a).

Profiles or typologies typically identify more and less assaultive males who vary on the frequency and severity of their behaviors. Typologies also have detected categories in which severe violence and other behaviors (e.g., excessive alcohol use), developmental histories (e.g., childhood exposure to parental violence), or personality factors (sex-role stereotyping) conjoin. For example, Saunders (1987) found one type of severely assaultive male who was abused in his family of origin and also abuses alcohol.

This is a promising strategy for reconciling the complex array of personality factors and behavioral variables evident among assaultive males. Yet much of the research is limited to self-selected samples of wife assaulters (Saunders, 1987) or to reports from victims about their assailants (Gondolf, 1988). Realization of the potential of these strategies for explaining violence awaits further research with samples of both assaultive and nonassaultive men, as well as validation efforts using alternate measures and research designs.

In an effort to sort out the extensive and conflicting evidence on personality and behavioral characteristics that typify assaultive men, Hotaling and Sugarman (1986) reviewed more than 400 empirical studies of husband-to-wife violence. Their review focused on 52 studies that employed case-comparison designs assessing 97 specific variables. Hotaling and Sugarman (1986) identified three "risk markers" that showed consistently strong associations with male violence toward women in case-control or experimental studies: sexual aggression toward wives, experiencing or witnessing violence during childhood, and perpetrating violence toward their own (and/or their partners') children. Alcohol usage also was consistently associated with assaultive behavior by male partners in seven of nine studies reviewed.

Variables that comprise measures of socioeconomic status also were associated with assaultive partners, but the associations obtained in studies with small clinical samples were not replicated with larger general population samples (Straus et al., 1980; Schulman, 1979). Other studies reported curvilinear relationships between either educational or occupational status and assaultive behaviors. Another factor also consistently associated with marital violence (but in a small number of studies) was involvement in violence toward strangers. Sexual aggression toward spouses has been discussed earlier in the section on marital rape. Below, we briefly review research on violence toward both intimates and strangers, childhood exposure to violence, concurrent violence toward children, and alcohol usage among assaultive males.

Alcohol Consumption and Marital Violence A Gallup poll, cited by Coleman and Straus (1983), found that almost one in four respondents believed alcohol to be the cause of family violence. Historical analyses by Pleck (1987) trace popular beliefs about alcohol use and marital violence to the colonial era. Winick (1983) described how popular culture portrays the effects of drinking and drug use on wife assaults: in Tennessee Williams' *A Streetcar Named Desire*, a drunken Stanley Kowalski strikes his pregnant wife Stella and later strikes his sister-in-law Blanche DuBois (herself a former alcoholic) on the night that Stella delivers their first baby. Similar episodes occurred in Edward Albee's *Who's Afraid of Virginia Woolf*, when George and Martha drink through the night and become increasingly abusive to each other, although only verbally.[21] In *The Brothers Karamazov*, Dostoevski hints (but does not directly imply) that alcohol may have led Dmitri to kill his father. In the 1980s, the musical satirist Kinky Friedman penned the darkly humorous song "I'd Kill My Mother for Another Line of Cocaine." Kantor and Straus (1987) point out that these images not only link substance abuse and family violence, but also depict causal relationships and portray these behaviors as an underclass phenomenon.

Empirical evidence on the contributions of intoxication to aggression in families shows a persistent correlation, especially for severe assaults and injuries, but only for alcohol.[22] Several studies mentioned earlier show that the strong correlation is evident in a variety of sampling and measurement conditions. Kantor and Straus (1987) reviewed 15 empirical studies on alcohol and spouse assault, and found a wide range of reports of the presence of alcohol among couples experiencing violence—from 6 to 85 percent. As would be expected, reports on the incidence of alcohol use among assaultive spouses in clinical samples[23] were higher than in general population studies or police samples. Using victim reports about assaultive partners, both Gondolf (1988) and Fagan et al. (1983) found that the severity of wife abuse was positively associated with alcohol use by the assailant. Saunders (1987) reported similar results with samples of assaultive men in treatment. Shields et al. (1988) found that men violent only toward their spouses less often used drugs or sought help for drug problems than men violent outside the home, and that alcohol use did not discriminate among different types of assailants.

Two studies examined the incidence of alcohol use in a nationally representative population of families. Coleman and Straus (1983) analyzed data from the first NFVS, which asked about the frequency of intoxication from alcohol but not whether drinking preceded or co-occurred with spouse assault. The frequency of alcohol consumption and assaults between cohabitants were positively associated. Past year rates of assaults were nearly 15 times greater for husbands who were drunk "often" compared to "never" during that time. However, for the most frequent alcohol users (i.e., those who were "almost always" drunk), assault rates were half those of the often drunk respondents.[24] The authors conclude that the heaviest drinkers are "anesthetized" both emotionally and physiologically, but although rates of alcohol use were high among assaultive spouses, they were no higher than among the general population.

Kantor and Straus (1987) analyzed data from the 1985 NFVS to examine the "drunken-bum" theory of wife assault by males. Unlike the first version, the second survey asked if there was drinking at the time of a violent incident. In 76 percent of the households where assaults occurred, alcohol was not used immediately prior to the incident. However, after controlling for respondents' usual drinking patterns, there was a positive association between the percentage who were assaultive and drinking immediately prior to assaults. Among "binge" drinkers, nearly half (48.4%) were drinking prior to an assault, compared to fewer than one in five

(19.4%) for "infrequent" drinkers. Analyzing their data by social class and occupational status, Kantor and Straus (1987) found that the relationships of violence to (1) approval of violence, (2) general drinking patterns, and (3) drinking antecedent to violence were strongest for blue-collar workers. However, the authors caution that more than 80 percent of all respondents in the highest-frequency drinking categories did not assault their female partners at all in the year prior to the survey, and nearly two-thirds of blue-collar workers were nonviolent during the study year.

Establishing a precise relationship between intoxication and marital violence is made difficult by variation in measures of spouse assault, alcohol or drug use (frequency, severity of intoxication, and impairment), and sampling and research designs. There also has been little research on ethnic-specific relationships between alcohol and marital violence, despite important distinctions in alcohol and violence patterns among various Hispanic ethnicities (Glick and Moore, 1990). The causal order of marital violence and alcohol use may be difficult to establish or may even reverse in order, depending on specific incidents (Kantor and Straus, 1987).

Experimental research shows that the intoxication-aggression association is mediated by expectancies about the effects of the substance (Taylor, 1983; Fagan, 1990), which in turn reflect cultural norms and beliefs about alcohol. (However, most of the experimental evidence is based on studies with college students and has not been tested with married or cohabiting couples or in the complex context of the home.) Both the Kantor and Straus (1987) and the Coleman and Straus (1983) studies also suggest that expectancies develop through social learning processes: for example, reactions to alcohol and behaviors while intoxicated are observed in the family context (witnessing family violence and the instrumental use of physical aggression).

There are several alternative interpretations of the alcohol-assault relationship in marital violence. Personality factors may interact with intoxicants to contribute to marital violence. Alcohol may modulate psychopathology (Hamberger and Hastings, 1988); that is, it may produce aggression, depression (the "maudlin" drunk), excessive gaiety and exaggerated behavior, or simply a flattened affect. Star (1980) characterized persons violent toward family members as needing power and control, and likens violent male spouses to alcohol users in such characteristics as extreme jealousy, external blame, sexual dysfunction, and bizarre mood shifts. Speiker (1983) found that both assaultive partners and their victims tended to blame alcohol for the violence, and that men used it as an excuse for their violence.

Intoxication and marital violence also may be spuriously associated or explained by some third factor. For stranger violence, there is consistent evidence that the association with intoxicants is spurious and mediated by the context in which intoxication occurs and the social set of individuals in that scene (Fagan, 1990). Shields et al. (1988) found that intoxication preceding assault (from drugs other than alcohol) occurred more often among "generally" and "stranger-only" men than among "family-only" assaultive husbands, and that alcohol did not discriminate among their three types. They interpret both violence and drug use as part of an "overall deviant lifestyle." Alcohol use may be a response to an anger or aggression stimulus that simultaneously provokes assaultive behaviors. For example, needs for power and control have been associated with both marital violence and alcohol use.

Alcohol also may alter cognitions, and thus vary perceptions and interpretations of cues that occur during interactions from neutral to threatening (Taylor, 1983; Frieze and Browne, 1989). Coleman and Straus (1983) draw on deviance disavowal theories to explain behaviors among people who do not view themselves (or their behaviors) as deviant but need some excuse (such as alcohol) for their unacceptable behavior (see also Gelles, 1974). By "explaining" violence toward spouses as the result of intoxication, their social standing and self-image are preserved. The behavior is deviant, but not the individual (see Scott and Lyman, 1968, for a discussion of how people give accounts of their deviant acts).

Intoxication also may provide a "time out" for such deviance to occur. This is similar to the processes described by MacAndrew and Edgerton in their (1969) cross-cultural studies, when the norms for conventional and appropriate behavior can be set aside temporarily. However, this process is seen as the result of some external factor (e.g., intoxicants), rather than as a conscious decision to behave outside acceptable boundaries (see, for example, Critchlow-Leigh, 1986). Coleman and Straus (1983) suggest that these processes actually could promote the behavior by offering an advance excuse for the acts.

Other theories also would apply if we accept the claims of Star (1980) and Speiker (1983) that male violence in the family is an expression of power and control. Power motivation theory (McClelland and Davis, 1972; McClelland, 1975) suggests that drinking and violence may be a means of asserting power and control in the family. However, other studies of family violence (Dobash and Dobash, 1979; Bowker, 1983) conclude that the maintenance of masculine power and control is a motivation for all domestic violence, independent of external factors and without explicit disavowal of their acts.

The findings regarding alcohol and the Bowker (1983) and Dobash and Dobash (1979) studies agree that socioeconomic status also is important and interacts with intoxication to increase the severity of violence.[25] However, the intoxication-family aggression relationship is present even when there is disapproval of violence. Also, the relationship is not confined to working-class men; it is evident among middle-class men who threaten or assault their wives. For middle-class men, processes of deviance disavowal and "time out" may permit the assault of spouses. For working-class men, expectancy of behaviors during intoxication, reinforced by both social learning experiences and societal approval for the use of force within families to assert and to maintain supremacy, may contribute to violence during intoxication. Kantor and Straus (1989) suggest that both processes operate among working-class men. Bowker (1983) found that the men most violent toward spouses were working-class men who were most deeply embedded in "male subcultures," as measured by time spent in bars with male comrades. Thus, the interaction of personality, social network, situation or setting, and cultural norms provides a powerful influence on individual behaviors in the family while intoxicated.

Concurrent Violence Toward Children Family violence researchers have looked most closely at the co-occurrence of wife and child abuse. For example, Washburn and Frieze (1981) found that males who abused their wives were more likely to be abusive toward their children than were nonviolent men. Walker (1979) and Browne (1987) found that extreme violence toward women was associated with violence toward children. Telch and Lindquist (1984) discriminated between maritally violent and nonviolent couples based on the male partner's violence toward children. Similarly, a 1978 evaluation of child abuse programs found that 38 percent of the children in the programs came from families in which the wife was also abused (American Humane Association, 1980). Victims in family violence intervention programs reported that about one male in four physically punished one or more children "too harshly" (Fagan et al., 1984).

However, at least some of the reported child abuse or neglect in maritally violent families may come from the female victim of spouse assault. Gil (1970) found that in families with physically abused children, fathers were more often the abuser, whereas mothers were more likely to be reported as neglecting the child. Reports from battered women's shelters (Fagan et al., 1984) and NCS data (Lentzner and DeBerry, 1980) indicate that some child and adolescent abuse may be the unintended result of parental violence. For instance, the adolescent who attempts to intervene in the parental fight may receive blows intended for the mother.

We reported earlier in Table 3 that 17.4 percent of the men who reported any violence toward the child in the family also reported that they were violent toward their spouse (and female reports of male violence were higher than men's self-reports). Hotaling and Straus (1989) reported both child and spouse assault in 21.6 percent of the 1975 NFVS and 18.4 percent of the 1985 survey. In families for which both spouse and child assault were reported in the 1985 survey, participation rates for husbands in both aggression and severe violence toward strangers were significantly higher than in families for which only one (or no) form of family violence was reported. For example, 6.6 percent of the husbands who assaulted both children and wives also were involved in severe violence toward strangers (involving injury), compared to 0.9 percent of husbands who assaulted only wives but not children (p = .000).

Straus (1983) also reported a strong association between frequent child abuse and severe marital violence in the 1975 NFVS. Of parents reporting no marital violence, 7 to 10 percent frequently abused their children. For those engaged in marital violence, Straus distinguished between "ordinary violence" (or simple assault) and severe violence. More than *half* of the males who were severely violent toward female partners (about 5% of all male partners) abused their children three or more times during the year prior to the survey. For males involved in "ordinary" violence, less than 15 percent were involved in frequent child abuse. Straus also showed that mothers who were victims of frequent abuse victimized their children more often and more seriously. Although neither cell percentages nor statistics were reported, the sample size and large between-group differences suggest that the results were significant.

Evidently, the risk of generalized violence within the home increases with the frequency and severity of assaults toward any single target of aggression. Nevertheless, the cognitive processes of victim selection are not well understood, and there is insufficient evidence to determine whether personality factors or socialization experiences influence the identity and number of individuals victimized by a violent parent or spouse. Controlled studies using samples of high-risk groups (similar to Shields et al., 1988) may be necessary to take the first steps in understanding victim selection and the generalization of violence in the home.

Childhood Exposure to Violence Exposure to violence as a child—either as a witness of parental violence or as a victim of child abuse—is an important precursor of adult violence toward children or toward spouses (Gelles, 1974; Pagelow, 1984; Fagan et al., 1983; Straus, 1983; Hotaling and Sugarman, 1986; Browne, 1987; Caesar, 1988; Rosenbaum and O'Leary, 1981). Most studies have cited the importance of childhood exposure to violence in later domestic violence (see Browne, 1987:23-35). The strength of the link to subsequent involvement in marital violence has been revealed in a variety of reports. In general, both national and special population studies indicate the following:

• Boys and girls are more at risk to abuse their own children as adults if they were abused themselves as children or adolescents.
• Both boys and girls, but particularly boys, are at increased risk to abuse an intimate partner in later adult relationships if they were abused as children or adolescents.
• Boys are at greatly increased risk to abuse female partners in adult relationships if they *witnessed* abuse between parental figures in their childhood homes.
• Girls are at somewhat increased risk to be abused by a male partner in adulthood if they witnessed abuse in their childhood homes.
• Children who have both *experienced* child (or adolescent) abuse and *witnessed* abuse between parental figures demonstrate a sharply increased risk of being involved in an abusive relationship as adults, compared to individuals without these dual experiences (e.g., Straus et al., 1980; Kalmuss, 1984; Hotaling and Sugarman, 1986).

In a review of case-control studies, Hotaling and Sugarman (1986) found childhood exposure to violence for males to be a particularly strong risk factor for marital violence as an adult. They differentiated between witnessing violence as a child, a strong risk factor, and being a victim of violence by a parent or caregiver. Nevertheless, Hotaling and Sugarman (1986:111) concluded that "the use and past exposure to violent behavior is common in the lives of batterers." Other studies have shown that from 37 to 47 percent of male assailants had witnessed parental violence, and about a third had been beaten or frequently suffered harsh discipline as children (e.g., Fagan et al., 1983).

In a study of the backgrounds of 270 men involved in marital violence (men who assaulted their partners) compared to "generally" violent men, childhood exposure to violence was the strongest predictor (explaining 26% of the variance) of involvement in both intra- and extrafamilial violence (Fagan et al., 1983). This study also found that the same variables were strong predictors of the severity of injury to the spouse, especially among those involved in "generally" violent behavior.

Pagelow (1984) provides specific examples of the social psychological processes that comprise intergenerational transmission: the internalization of violence through modeling, reinforcement, opportunities for practice, and teaching of its functional value. Miller and Challas (1981) offer a more complex view. They found that childhood violence experiences were mediated by other factors, including poverty and educational attainment. Rather than becoming violent adults, child abuse victims may instead lead adult lives marked by poor socialization, financial dependency, and emotional instability. Such detailed analyses may explain the differential contributions of intermittent versus contingent childhood victimization toward later violence.

Although empirical evidence underscores the importance of early childhood socialization to violence, intergenerational theories have not adequately specified the structures, processes, and contingencies that shape the "transfer" of violence from one generation to the next. Moreover, social learning processes may be mitigated by other socialization processes (Widom, 1988). Intergenerational theory suggests that abusive parents serve as role models for their children, who learn that such family behavior is normative, is an acceptable mode for dealing with anger and conflict (Straus, 1979), and—most important—has a functional value in establishing and maintaining dominance and control in the marital relationship.

Lacking in these theories, however, are constructs that describe the natural or social processes whereby values are transmitted or behaviors modeled. For example, learning may occur through an accumulation of small transactions or in major events, and can be reinforced by either social rewards or some other form of gratification. Accordingly, Bowker (1983) suggests that the maintenance of power in the relationship may have elements of gratification that are powerful reinforcers.

Marital Violence and Stranger Violence A few studies have attempted to explore the involvement of wife batterers in other violent behaviors. Gayford (1975) found that 50 percent of a sample of wife abusers reportedly had spent time in prison, and 33 percent of these prison terms were for violent offenses toward strangers (although Gayford's sample was highly skewed toward extreme behaviors). Flynn (1977), in a study of abused women, found that at least one-third of the assailants had previous records of other types of criminal assaults, and Walker (1979) estimated that 20 percent of the husbands of the women she interviewed were violent with other individuals besides their wives. White and Straus (1981) reported that men who are violent toward their wives were arrested or convicted for a "serious" crime (a property or violence crime toward a stranger) at almost twice the rate—and "severely" violent husbands at almost four times the rate—of nonviolent spouses.

Only recently has there been any systematic study on the intersection of these behaviors. Using newspaper advertisements and chain referral methods (Biernacki and Waldorf, 1981), Shields et al. (1988) recruited men from the St. Louis area who had committed assaults against their female partners or toward strangers. Through interviews, they examined socialization patterns and other characteristics of three types of violent men: those violent only toward spouses, those violent only toward persons outside the family, and the overlapping "generally" violent men. Their results suggest that "generally" violent men and men violent only toward non-family members are virtually indistinguishable in terms of background characteristics, but that wife abusers were in fact quite different in terms of social structural variables (e.g., socioeconomic status), educational attainment, attitudes, and prior conviction rates. However, these patterns were far from static: nearly 45 percent of the "generally" violent men began their adult violence careers victimizing only *non*-family members.

Fagan et al. (1983), based on reports from 270 women in family violence intervention programs, found that 46 percent of spouse abusers had been arrested previously for other violence. These men were also the most frequently and severely violent in the home. The most violent spousal assailants were also those who were violent toward strangers, whereas those less violent at home usually were not violent toward strangers. The longer the duration and more severe the abuse at home, the more likely were these men to also assault strangers. This finding is consistent with Frieze et al. (1980), whose severely battering husbands were more likely to have been involved in fights outside the home than were "mildly" violent (or nonviolent) husbands.

Bandura (1973) cautions that different types of violence may have different determinants. Consistent with this, some researchers have argued that family violence in general—and spousal violence in particular—are special and distinct types of violence and should not be viewed as a subset of violent behavior (Dobash and Dobash, 1979; Wardell et al., 1983). The few studies of generally violent men show, however, that they are more similar to stranger assailants than to those violent only within their families (Shields and Hannecke, 1983).

In sum, adult violence in general, and particularly the more severe forms of marital violence by men, may be strongly linked to childhood exposure to violence and to early socialization experiences. Thus, it seems that for at least some individuals, "violence begets violence" and may well be passed through generations. This suggests that our knowledge of adult violence by males toward both strangers and family members may be enhanced by knowledge of violence socialization in early childhood, as well as by evidence of adult violence toward intimates. What remain unknown are exactly how such socialization occurs—how it is perceived, learned, and reinforced, both in childhood and during other crucial developmental stages—and the mediating variables and cognitive processes that influence the substance of what is learned. Missing also from this framework is the specific trigger that allows the lessons of early childhood to be activated.

Women Victims of Marital Violence

For many years, empirical research on marital violence focused predominantly on women, most of whom were victims who had sought services. The types of services sought by victims are associated with their social and economic circumstances, as well as with the severity of assaults and injuries they sustained (Frieze and Browne, 1989; Fagan et al., 1984). Moreover, help-seeking behaviors further influence the characteristics of victims in different settings. Accordingly, knowledge of victim' backgrounds was confined for some time to higher-risk groups of women whose resources limited them to public services. For example, Washburn and Frieze (1980), in a study in southwestern Pennsylvania, reported systematic differences among groups of women in shelters, women who filed for legal assistance, and women who responded to a research solicitation. Shelter clients more often were separated from their partners, were African American, and were unemployed. They were younger, had lower incomes and were less educated, and more often had small children. They had the fewest resources and were most in need of financial support. Other women in the study commented that they preferred to seek temporary shelter with relatives or to use credit cards to pay for a motel.

Women who had filed for legal assistance comprised an intermediate group. They were separated, worked full time, had higher educational and family income levels than women in shelters, and had older children. Their racial composition was consistent with the area makeup. They experienced similar levels of violence to the women in shelters, but more often were violent toward their male partners. They less often expressed powerlessness, and they felt that they were doing something to change the situation. The third group, respondents to solicitations, most often were still married to their assailants and generally had higher socioeconomic status. Their victimizations had not occurred recently, and they had experienced the least serious violence among the three groups.

Fagan et al. (1984), in a sample of nearly 2,800 victims in 23 intervention programs across the country, reported similar differences in victim characteristics according to the type of program service and setting. Consistent with Washburn and Frieze (1980), shelter victims were younger, poorer, and less educated, and more often had small children than participants in legal or other social interventions. Women in shelters had experienced more frequent and serious abuse, although women in other groups had longer histories of marital violence. Shelter residents more often reported abuse during pregnancy, miscarriages due to abuse, and sexual assaults by their spouses. Also, they had more often witnessed violence between their parents as children.

The NFVS, NCS, and other general population studies indicated the diverse socioeconomic backgrounds of victims. Although these studies indicated that younger women from lower social class backgrounds more often were victims of both simple and severe marital violence, the association with social class and income was weaker but still positive.

Other than their abuse histories and socioeconomic status, there do not appear to be consistent patterns that differentiate women victims from nonvictims. Hotaling and Sugarman's (1986) review of 52 case-control studies found that only *one* of 42 potential risk markers for women—witnessing parental violence as a child or adolescent—was consistently associated with being a victim of marital violence. This was also the one factor that characterized both assaultive spouses and their victims. Neither personality nor behavioral characteristics were evident as risk markers for women in the Hotaling and Sugarman review. For example, the weight of empirical evidence suggests that alcohol use does not distinguish women victims from other women.[26] Many of the symptoms that victims exhibit evidently are sequelae of marital violence rather than antecedents or concurrent factors (Walker, 1984; Margolin, 1988).

Patterns of Homicide Between Intimates

There is little information on the characteristics and dynamics of couples in which marital homicides occur. Wolfgang (1967) reported that 60 percent of the men who were killed by spouses "precipitated" their own deaths through physical violence toward their spouses, compared to 5 percent of the women perpetrators. Wilbanks (1983) reported similar findings: Men killed by their spouses were more likely to have been violent toward those spouses than were the victims of male offenders. Other studies show that marital homicide is often the culmination of a lengthy history of violence and threats (Browne, 1987; Chimbos, 1978; Gillespie, 1988). Jurik and Winn (1990) found that 86 percent of the women perpetrators of homicide reported physical conflicts with their male partner-victims, and 44 percent of the homicides resulted directly from conflict with their partners (defined as domestic disputes, marital violence, or conflicts over property). However, among male perpetrators, 27 percent reported prior physical conflict with their victims, and only 8 percent reported partner conflict.

Chimbos (1978) found that nearly all the female perpetrators had been beaten by their partners. Women victims of marital violence accounted for 40 percent of all women convicted of murder or manslaughter in an Illinois women's correctional center (Lindsey, 1978). In a study of women incarcerated in California for killing their partners, Totman (1978) stated that 93 percent reported being physically abused and 67 percent said that the homicide was in defense of themselves or a child. Lindsey and other researchers also reported that these women had frequently called the police for help prior to the fatal incident (Frieze and Browne, 1989).

Recent studies have examined the characteristics of abusive relationships in which women commit partner homicides. Browne

(1986, 1987) compared 42 cases of women charged with the death or serious injury of their mates (based on in-depth, face-to-face pretrial interviews, as well reviews of available evidence) with 205 cases in which women were in abusive relationships but did not take severely viôlent action. Several factors distinguished the homicide group from the abuse-only group: Men in the homicide group were more likely to abuse alcohol—many were intoxicated daily or nearly every day by the end of the relationship (80 versus 40%); they were more likely to use street drugs (primarily co-caine) (29 versus 8%); and they were more likely to have made threats to kill the woman and others (89 versus 59%). Physical attacks on women in the homicide group were more frequent, and more severe in terms of the infliction of injuries. Women in the homicide group also were more likely to have been sexually abused—and sexually abused frequently—by their partners than women in the nonhomicide group (respectively, 75 versus 59%) had been sexually assaulted by their mates at least once). All of these differences were statistically significant.

In addition, men in the homicide group were significantly more likely to abuse their own or their partners' children (71 versus 51%). They also were the most violent toward strangers and more often had witnessed violence between parental figures (according to the womens' reports). Most (92%) of the men in the homicide group had arrest histories ranging from drunk driving to murder, compared to almost none of the women. In the majority of cases resulting in homicide, the severity of the man's violence and threats toward family members escalated over time, although the frequency of violent assaults showed varying patterns. As previously noted, almost all of the women in the homicide group had sought intervention from the criminal justice system, obviously without success, before the fatal event (see also Lindsey, 1978; Saltzman et al., 1990; and Sherman and Berk, 1984, as cited in Browne and Williams, 1989).

Just as homicide is the extreme violent act, early studies suggest that relationships in which marital homicide occurs might be the most violent of all relationships before homicide occurs. (As mentioned earlier, however, little detail is known about abuse histories in relationships in which men kill their female partners, due in part to the paucity of research on this topic and in part to the difficulty of obtaining reports from male abusers that accurately reflect frequency, severity, or actions.) These cases also represent the greatest disparity between the need for help and the ineffectiveness of protective interventions. Later, we discuss the social psychological processes that explain how a nonviolent woman can commit a homicide under these circumstances.

From the accumulation of knowledge on marital violence, patterns are evident in the characteristics of individuals and couples who engage in, or are victimized by, assaultive behaviors. These characteristics comprise a set of epidemiological risk factors to assess the probability of the occurrence of partner assault (see Last, 1983, for a discussion of the concept of "risk marker"). The probability of assaultive behavior within a couple is associated with any of these factors individually, and the probability increases as a function of the number of factors present.[27] Obviously, the presence of risk factors within a family should not be construed as a causal relationship. It is difficult to explain, for example, how age "causes" spouse assault. In the following material, risk factors that are associated with the occurrence of marital violence are discussed. The presence of combinations of these factors, in turn, suggests explanatory frameworks for understanding their contributions to marital violence. These frameworks are discussed later in this paper.

Risk Factors Shared by Both Partners

The presence of risk factors shared by both partners suggests a strong probability of the occurrence of partner assault within that family. Three factors are evident as risks for both males and females: witnessing family violence as a child or adolescent, age, and problematic alcohol use. Although Hotaling and Sugarman (1986) found weak evidence of alcohol use as a risk of victimization of women in their review of case-control studies, recent evidence (Kantor and Straus, 1987; Miller et al., 1988) more consistently suggests a greater use of alcohol among women victims compared to nonvictims. Moreover, Miller et al. (1988) also found associations of both victimization and problematic alcohol use with women's childhood exposure to marital violence.

Age is correlated with marital violence for men, but only weakly for women. Age also is a consistent risk marker for men's involvement in stranger violence (see Sampson and Lauritsen, in this volume) and nonviolent crime (Gottfredson and Hirschi, 1986). Correspondingly, consistent evidence in probability samples and community surveys shows the greater risk of victimization among younger women. The evidence on witnessing violence for both men and women (Goodwin and Guze, 1984) is discussed earlier, as are patterns of alcohol use among assaultive males.

Risk Factors for Wife Assaults by Males

Empirical evidence indicates that males who are most frequently and severely assaultive toward female partners also are assaultive toward others in the family and toward strangers. Accordingly, risk factors for frequent and severe wife assault include assaults against female partners during their pregnancy, sexual violence toward women partners, physical (and/or sexual) victimization of their own or their partners' children, and assaults on strangers. The convergence of violent behaviors among the most seriously assaultive males strongly suggests a generalized pattern of violence with indiscriminate processes of victim selection, although intimate victims are likely to experience the most frequent—and possibly the most severe—assaults.

Family income and socioeconomic status are risk markers for assaults by men, but not for victimization of women. They may also be mediating influences through which attitudes supportive of marital violence can be reinforced (Bowker, 1983; Smith, 1990). However, as in the study of social class and violence generally (Brownfield, 1986), measurement and sampling problems suggest caution in weighing these factors. Nevertheless, the evidence on educational attainment and occupational status (but not unemployment per se) is consistent with the findings on family income level.

Personality characteristics overall do not appear to be risk factors for partner assault by males, with the exception of verbal skills and assertiveness. Assertiveness deficits were found in several studies (e.g., Rosenbaum and O'Leary, 1981; Telch and Lindquist, 1984; Dutton and Browning, 1988).

Attitudes toward traditional sex roles did not appear to be consistent risk factors in case-control studies (Hotaling and Sugarman, 1986), but sex-role orientation may contribute to spouse assault by males as cultural or ecological factors (Yllo, 1983, 1988; Dutton, 1988b), rather than as situational factors or microsocial interactional processes. For example, concentrated attitudes regarding male dominance, objectification of women as chattel, and warrior-like virility have been validated as a scale of hypermasculinity by Sullivan and Mosher (1990). In experimental studies with college men using guided imagery, Mosher and Tomkins (1988) found that hypermasculinity contributed to attitudes supportive of marital rape among a voluntary sample of 146 college men.

In telephone interviews with a probability sample of 604 Toronto women, Smith (1990) found that male partners who (in the view of their female partners) expressed attitudes and beliefs supportive of patriarchy (defined as power of males over women in the home regarding money, social interactions, and sex) were significantly more likely to engage in marital violence in the past year. They also expressed approval for the use of violence against wives in response to arguments, defiance of their will, or insults. Smith goes on to describe "patriarchical wife beaters" as low-income spouses, less educated, and in relatively low-status jobs.

Viewing sex-role orientation as a proximal influence may mask the actual contributions of pervasive attitudinal factors toward wife assault. Moreover, most research on sex roles has focused on the presence of these attitudes, rather than on their strength. Yet other research (Saunders et al., 1987) shows that the strength of sex-role expectations is associated with attitudes supportive of the assault of female partners. Accordingly, traditional sex-role orientation appears to be a risk factor, although it appears to be more appropriately conceived as a distal influence mediated through other individual or situational factors. Thus, as we discuss further, male assailants whose sex-role orientation is strongest may use it as a cultural defense, a neutralization technique (Sykes and Matza, 1957), or as an account (Scott and Lyman, 1968) or excuse for wife assault.

Risk Factors for Victimization Among Women

Fewer risk markers are evident for victimization of women. Witnessing violence as children or adolescents and problematic alcohol use are consistent risk factors. However, there is little evidence to confirm the temporal order of drinking and victimization, leaving open the question of drinking as a reciprocal process or response to assaults. Pregnancy and either separation or divorce also place women at greater risk during victimization by spouses or partners. Unlike the evidence for males, social structural variables are weakly associated with victimization of women, with the exception of age. Evidence of victims' traditional sex-role orientation is weak and inconclusive. Hotaling and Sugarman (1986) report no other research that has uncovered personality variables or predispositions that are valid risk factors for women's victimization (e.g., passivity, aggressivity, hostility, dominance) or that can discriminate victims from women not victimized.

Risk Factors for Assaults in Couple Relationships

Risk factors for wife assault within couples generally describe either demographic characteristics or relationship dynamics. Family social status (income, specifically) is a consistent risk marker, as are the recency of separation or divorce and the recency of the start of the relationship. Couples that are socially isolated and have status differentials due to educational or occupational incompatibility are at greater risk. Marital power, a complex concept involving decision-making power, access to resources, and status variables, evidently is a factor, but Hotaling and Sugarman (1986) caution that this attribute interacts with other variables (e.g., absolute resources of the family, tactics used to assert power) in the occurrence of spousal assault. However, these variables are consistently risk factors for victims of severe violence (Walker, 1984; Browne, 1987).

Theoretical Implication of Risk Factors

These risk factors suggest several important trends with implications for the explanation of wife assault and its connections to other forms of violence. First, the results suggest that, for women victims, only variables relating to their socioeconomic and marital status place them at greater risk. There is little evidence regarding personality variables that place women at risk for victimization, and there seem to be no factors suggesting that women contribute to their own victimization. Second, the consistent evidence for both men and women that witnessing violence as a child contributes to either assault or victimization supports social learning explanations. Witnessing violence evidently conveys functional value to spouse assault that differs for men and women, or may even establish it as a normative behavior that does not require a response. Similar research on the intergenerational nature of alcohol use also suggests that these factors may converge across generations.

Third, the generalized and multiple violence of seriously assaultive male partners suggests that explanations of violent behavior within families and toward strangers may be reconciled. Although there appear to be unique processes and factors that make women partners more frequent targets of violence, the co-occurrence of multiple forms of violence also suggests that victim selection is a meditating process in need of further theoretical attention. Related to this is the fourth implication: risk factors for stranger violence overlap extensively with risk factors for wife assault. As wife assault becomes more serious, both the behaviors and the risk factors become nearly isomorphic. There is consistent evidence that severe violence toward both female partners and strangers is part of a generalized pattern of violence with shared risk factors. In turn, stranger and wife assaults seem to be dimensions of violence careers.

Fifth, the convergence of risk factors that implicate social class and social status for assaultive males suggests that there are social structural correlates of wife assault similar to stranger assaults. What is unknown is whether the assault of female partners is concentrated in areas marked by social disorganization, poverty, and other ecological risk factors of stranger violence. The correlation among men of social class and social structural variables with participation in both wife assault and stranger violence suggests that for some wife assaults, there are risk factors that reflect social area effects and social disorganization. These include the salience of formal and informal social controls, the anonymity of urban areas with high residential mobility, limited economic mobility, and patterns of family disintegration. Ecological studies of marital homicide show the association of these factors; their correlation with partner assaults is suggested but unproven.

Finally, cultural factors, such as orientation toward traditional sex roles and partriarchical beliefs,[28] seem to interact with situational and personality variables that are risk factors for assaults by males. These factors may also be ecological risk factors for aggregate rates of spouse assault (Yllo, 1983, 1988) or homicide (Browne and Williams, 1989). Viewing them as ecological factors suggests influences that are mediated by social interactions, social structural variables, and specific situations in the occurrence of marital violence. An ecological approach is discussed in the next section.

Risk factors, of course, are not causal factors. They reflect the convergence of epidemiological factors, co-occurring behaviors, consequences of partner assault, and status variables. Few studies on wife assault have examined risk factors while controlling for the severity of marital violence (Fagan et al., 1984). Alternate methods, such as multiple group designs to introduce these controls, also are not common in the literature on marital violence. Whether the configuration of risk factors differs by level of violence—and their mutability as relationships evolve and violence progresses—also are not clear. This does not diminish the significance of risk factors for developing conceptual frameworks and explanations of marital violence.

EXPLANATORY FRAMEWORKS

There is a basic difference between the causes of crime and its occurrence (Clarke and Cornish, 1985). The explanatory theories that address initial involvement in a behavior may address neither its continuance nor its desistance. Farrington (1979) has suggested that the different stages of a criminal career may require different explanations, whereas Blumstein et al. (1985) proposed that the predictors of noninvolvement in crime may differ from the predictors of early desistance and persistent crime. Strategies to typify assaultive spouses or couples experiencing violence also reveal that each group may reflect unique etiological factors (Dutton, 1988a). Explanations of physical aggression between adult partners range from cultural embeddedness to more individually based theories. In this section, we review some of the more prominent explanatory constructs and offer suggestions for an integration of theories to encompass individual and environmental influences.

PATRIARCHY, SOCIAL NETWORKS, AND SOCIAL EMBEDMENT

Early theories on marital violence, particularly those describing violence by husbands toward wives, viewed this aggression as an outworking of a culture that engendered and maintained the domination of men over women in every aspect of social life (e.g., Martin, 1976; Dobash and Dobash, 1979; Walker, 1979). Dobash and Dobash (1979) describe partriarchical influence as culturally normative (Yllo, 1988), whereas Straus (1976) refers to the marriage license as a "hitting license." These theorists contend that the beliefs that support marital violence simply express more general cultural norms and values that uphold a hierarchical, patriarchal social organization. Such norms have been linked with wife assault in empirical studies in the United Kingdom (Dobash and Dobash, 1979), Canada (Smith, 1990), and the United States (Bowker, 1984; Yllo and Straus, 1984).

To explain the contributions of patriarchy to marital violence, economic inequalities and cultural portrayals of women are cited as manifestations of male orientation and hegemony (Dobash and Dobash, 1979; Pagelow, 1984). Straus (1976) identified nine specific manifestations of a male-dominant structure that support wife assault[29] and concluded that the relative weakness of criminal penalties in wife assault cases (until the 1980s) reflects cultural norms that have resulted in the institution of marriage carrying with it an (implied or explicit) immunity to prosecution for abuse by the male partner. Economic inequalities place a lesser value on women's labor or social contributions and reinforce the dominant role played by men in most labor markets. Fewer women occupy elective office than men, and popular culture offers fewer portrayals of women in egalitarian social positions in cinema, television, or print media. These cultural and economic indicators reflect women's lower social status, in turn reinforcing male attitudes of superiority and the legitimation of domination. Smith (1990) showed empirically that the strength of these attitudes explained marital violence by men (reported by women) in a representative sample of Toronto women.

Less clear, however, are the *origins* of cultural norms that emphasize male domination or the *processes* that translate such cultural norms into specific socialization processes that contribute to or attenuate a propensity for assaultive behavior. Subcultural explanations of marital violence emphasize the translation of broader cultural norms into microsocial interactions within specific networks. Bowker (1984) concluded that the better integrated the assaultive husband was in male subcultures, the more severe was his violence in the home.[30] He located gratification from wife assault in the realm of patriarchal imperatives: the cultural transmission of values that demand male domination, and the reinforcement of those values through socialization as children in male-dominated families and later social embedment in violence-supporting social relationships in a violence-tolerant culture. The importance of reinforcing societal values, modeled in early childhood and refined in adult years, indicates that both environmental (or normative) supports for domination of women as a group and situational interactions at a social or subcultural level contribute to male violence toward women. Bowker (1984:135) contends that:

> the myriad peer-relationships that support the patriarchal dominance of the family and the use of violence to enforce it may constitute a subculture of violence. The more fully a husband is immersed in this subculture, the more likely he is to batter his wife.

An expansion of these theories is needed to account for individuals raised in families not headed by a male figure. However, the reinforcement of values of male domination and power is likely to occur through myriad independent social networks that tacitly condone violence toward women or at least fail to sanction it negatively. Embedment in these networks poses a high risk of severe violence in the home. In addition, engulfment within a network of social relationships often minimizes attachments to people in other social networks (Eckland-Olsen, 1982), limiting exposure to other cultural or belief orientations. With social embedment comes the gratification of social acceptance and social identity, often built up over a lifetime of socialization. Alternatively, abandoning the assaultive behavior and losing control in the home may risk social disapproval. The more deeply embedded he is in the social context, the more dependent the assailant may become on that social world for approval and for a positive interpretation of his behavior. Conversely, desistance from marital violence has been shown to be associated with changes in the micronetworks that comprise the social worlds of assailants (Fagan, 1989; Bowker, 1983, 1986a).

POWER, CONTROL, AND DOMINATION

Although power motivation theories were first developed by McClelland and colleagues (McClelland et al., 1972; McClelland and Davis, 1972; McClelland, 1975) regarding drinking behaviors, they follow naturally from patriarchal theories as explanations of assaults by males against their female partners. The basic premise unifying the more recent integration of these theories is that assault is used to assert or maintain power within the relationship, particularly the power to gain victories in confrontations. Straus (1978) and Browne (1987) argue that one episode of violence can permanently alter the balance of marital power toward a strongly husband-dominant pattern. However, the empirical evidence about marital power is inconclusive (Hotaling and Sugarman, 1986), because the conceptualization and measurement of power and adherence to traditional sex-role expectations vary extensively.[31]

Other studies emphasize the importance of power *balances* in a partner relationship. Using a three-group design, Dutton and Strachan (1987) assessed assaultive male spouses, "maritally conflicted" male spouses, and "satisfactorily married" males on their power motives, and successfully classified more than 90 percent of the subjects. In a similar effort, Coleman and Straus (1986), using 1975 NFVS data, found that marital violence was lowest in "egalitarian" couples that shared domestic chores and decisions.

However, both male and female aggression was highest in couples in which females were dominant (i.e., had the greatest influence in decision making and control over resources). Thus, in couples in which the female partner has greater access to resources and/or decision-making power, female aggression may be either a response to male aggression or an aggressive reaction to confrontations over power.

Power motives and adherence to patriarchical ideology converge in research on patriarchy and marital violence. The translation of partriarchical ideology into specific attitudes or perceptions of marital power is evident in empirical work by Straus (1976:note 29), Yllo and Straus (1984), and Smith (1990). (Others, such as Dobash and Dobash, 1979, view patriarchy as a system of economic and cultural control that preserves the dominance and power of males over women.) For example, Smith's items measuring patriarchical attitudes include (1) men's control over whether women work outside the home, (2) men's control over women's social activities, (3) the importance of showing that the male is head of the house, and (4) a man's right to have sex with his wife/partner, even when she does not want to.

If males are socialized to expect dominance or power within the relationship, aggression may be initiated from frustration over an inability to control their female partners. For example, Smith's items for approval of violence against wives confound marital power with violence. He includes in this scale items on violence to exert one's wishes, violence in response to insults, violence to enforce behavioral codes (e.g., prohibitions against a wife's drinking), violence to retaliate for infidelity, and violence in response to a woman's physical aggression.

Issues of intimacy and the threat of dependency also may trigger violence in partner relationships. According to Browning and Dutton (1986), males experience anger most readily in circumstances in which they perceive an impending loss of control over either intimacy or distance. For example, using vignettes, Browning and Dutton found that men reported anger at women's attempts at autonomy in the relationship, as well as attempts by women partners to intensify levels of intimacy and commitment. Unsatisfied power needs may produce physiological arousal that is interpreted as anger and, especially for males with limited verbal skills, may be expressed through physical aggression. Similarly, increased demands for intimacy may be fear producing, and trigger verbal or physical assaults as a mechanism to increase distance and restore the "balance of power" to the male's control.

Threats to hegemony or control may also result from the male's emotional dependence on, or intimacy with, the victim (Browne, 1987). Browne suggests that many men have been conditioned to fear emotions they interpret as weakness. Thus, when they experience these emotions, they may look for alternate explanations and put the blame on others (e.g., their women partners) for "making" them feel uncomfortable or simply for making them feel too much. In a comparative study, women in severely abusive relationships reported being attacked *because* the man cared. Just the perception that another person was so vital to his daily existence and happiness became something to defend against: The man's need for the woman seemed to him a power in her hands, and he would lash out to balance the equation (Browne, 1987). (See also Dutton and Browning's, 1987, 1988, discussions of power struggles and intimacy anxieties as causative factors in wife assault.) For boys raised in an abusive environment, later feelings of dependency or vulnerability may be unbearable. The arousal engendered by emotions of love and desire becomes more anxiety provoking than pleasant. Thus, in addition to proactive desires for dominance and control, the neutralization of dependence and the reassertion of emotional distance may also be powerful reinforcers of marital violence.

Finally, the gratification that men experience from marital hegemony and male domination may also reinforce aggressive behaviors. Gratification from marital violence may come from achieving/maintaining the instrumental motive of dominance, from the expressive release of anger and aggression in response to perceived power deficits, from attainment of the positive social status that domination affords, or even from the "hearts-and-flowers" aftermath of many battering incidents (e.g., see Walker, 1979).

Evidence of the cessation of marital violence following restoration of the balance of marital power further suggests the importance of power equality in the prevention of violence (Bowker, 1983, 1986a). Bowker suggested that the involvement of external sources of social control (legal and social, as well as kinship networks) was a successful strategy in equalizing power relationships as an antecedent to the cessation of wife assault. In support of this theory, an association between egalitarian decision making and nonviolence was reported by Coleman and Straus (1986) using the 1985 NFVS data. In discussing criminal justice sanctions, Dunford et al. (1989) suggest that the significance of police involvement—although not necessarily by arrest—is the reallocation of marital power to victims to control offenders' behaviors through the threat of legal sanction (in this case, outstanding warrants for their arrest).

In the extreme case of partner homicide, Browne and Williams (1989) found that simply the *presence* of resources such as domestic violence legislation, shelters, and other services for abused women was associated with a sharp decline in rates of all female-perpetrated partner homicides. Although it is known that only a minority of abused women go to shelters or become involved in legal action against their mates, Browne and Williams theorized that such resources may have symbolic as well as tangible significance, because the existence of legal and extralegal sanctions both provides a social statement that supports victims' perceptions of the seriousness of such violence and may engender a sense of empowerment and alternatives. Thus, empowerment is one explanation for the deterrent effect of legal sanctions.

EARLY CHILDHOOD SOCIALIZATION: WITNESSING AND OBSERVING VIOLENCE

As noted earlier, an individual-level explanation of marital violence is that such behavior has been modeled for both victims and assailants (Pagelow, 1984; Hotaling and Sugarman, 1986; Browne, 1987). In particular, social learning analyses view aggressive habits as developing from the learning experiences of individuals and focus on the original milieus in which such habits are acquired (e.g., by observation in the family of origin), the instigators or aversive stimuli in the current environment that trigger aggression, and the maintenance of aggressive habits through the immediate consequences that reward or punish such aggression (Dutton, 1988b). Thus, sex-role socialization may interact with observation of instrumental violence in the family of origin to shape perceptions of aversive circumstances (such as female independence) and acceptable or socially desirable responses. Further, the salience of social and legal controls in later years may determine whether circumstances reinforce or extinguish these socially learned responses.

Lessons of a Violent Home

Children growing up in violent homes learn much about the instrumental value of violence. Bandura (1973) showed that children in a laboratory setting remember and then imitate aggressive actions that are modeled for them. He also found that boys imitated these behaviors more spontaneously than girls, even when not directly encouraged to do so. Acts performed by an adult male were more likely to be imitated than those performed by women, especially among male children. Children's imitation was equally strong when the male was someone they knew well but did not like, as when the child had a nurturing relationship with the male (see Pagelow, 1984).

The context of these lessons is the cultural perpetuation of a dominant role for males, which facilitates the adoption of force or threat as a model for interpersonal interactions (Herzberger, 1983). Thus, boys are encouraged as children to control their own circumstances, to express anger directly, and to not back down or compromise. When faced with a loss of control in adult (marital) relationships or frustration in their efforts to remain dominant, men raised in a violent home are more likely to respond with violence.

Men raised in violent homes also more quickly and acutely perceive threats or loss of control. Like women victims, men who grow up in violent homes experience feelings of helplessness, fear, and loss of control over their own safety, even when they themselves are not victims. As children, they may come to hate the abuser, yet still learn that the most violent person in the household also seems to be the most powerful and the least vulnerable to attack or humiliation by others (Browne, 1987). Thus, when these men perceive a threat of emotional pain or loss of control in an adult relationship, they may follow early models by resorting to violence themselves, in an attempt to avoid the potential for further victimization and pain.

Within this theoretical framework, violent behaviors learned during early childhood socialization are either strengthened or inhibited during later developmental stages by the family's connection to the broader culture and its sociocultural reinforcers (e.g., perceptions of neighborhood attitudes and behavioral norms toward violence and sex roles) (Dutton, 1985), or by the perceived deterrent effects of sanctions (Bowker, 1983; Sherman and Berk, 1984). As in social learning during adolescent years, such ecological factors may well serve to inhibit violence toward either nonfamily members, spouses, or perhaps both.

CAREERS IN VIOLENCE

Career criminal research has identified distinct phases through which behavioral patterns develop, escalate, are maintained, and eventually desist. Earlier, we discuss empirical research on these career phases in marital violence. Blumstein et al. (1985) contends that different variables are needed to explain behaviors in each of these phases. Fagan (1989) specifically addressed the variables that influence the maintenance and desistance of marital violence by males. Moreover, there seem to be important differences between assailants who victimize only spouses and those who are "generally violent." However, few studies have examined the course of battering "careers," or changes in victimization patterns within and outside the family. Yet career perspectives have obvious importance regarding the conceptualization of marital violence as a phenomenon nested within a broader explanation of violence, requiring separate or integrated theory.

Ironically, the independent bodies of empirical and theoretical literatures on marital and stranger violence are in substantial agreement on many empirical and theoretical issues. For example, both disciplines are concerned with the family origins of violence and the early childhood socialization processes that shape later violent behavior (Dodge et al., 1990; Widom, 1989; Rivera and Widom, 1990). Yet few researchers have either studied the two phenomena as one, or even contrasted the extant knowledge of family abusers or stranger assailants. There has been no research on the comparative validity of theories of aggression for family versus stranger assaults, and there are few epidemiological studies to empirically measure the coincidence of family and stranger assault. However, the rare studies spanning the two behaviors suggest that there may be a critical, if overlooked, relationship between familial and extrafamilial violence.

Victim Selection and Violence Careers

Anecdotal data from victims and shelter workers suggest that men who are violent with their female partners will seek out other victims if cut off from a battering relationship. Not unlike other career violent offenders (Katz, 1988), they are likely to move on to other relationships and resume violence, albeit with another victim. Desistance for one victim may be initiation for another. Shields et al. (1988) examined the intersection of family and stranger violence, as well as shifts over time in victim relationships among a sample of self-selected male assailants. The design compared men who were assaultive toward intimate partners with a comparison group of men who were not violent at home. Respondents were classified as (1) domestic violence only;

(2) stranger violence only—or those violent only toward persons outside the family; and (3) generally violent men, who fell into both categories.

Victimization patterns of domestic (only) assailants were far from static, however: nearly 45 percent of the generally violent men began their adult violence careers victimizing only strangers. In other words, their circle of victims widened over time to include family members. There were no indications that generally violent men narrowed their circle of victims over time to include one group or the other, an important finding on desistance; the number of victims actually grew over time. However, it was uncertain whether the total number of violent incidents remained the same or whether some violence was displaced from one group of victims to the other. What did not occur was displacement of violence within the home to stranger victims. Although violence careers are mutable over time, men who are domestically violent only tend to remain within that pattern.

Shields et al. found that "generally violent" and "stranger violence only" males were virtually indistinguishable in terms of background characteristics such as age or length of the relationship. Yet the "domestic violence only" men differed from the others in several ways. They were from higher social status groups and had higher educational attainment, although this may well be an artifact of the self-selected sample. These men also more often had drug and alcohol problems, had extramarital affairs, and were exposed to violence as children. They less often had evidence of psychopathology, but manifested other personality traits often associated with battering: jealousy, low self-esteem, and depression. They also had fewer contacts with the law and were less embedded in violent subcultures than the generally violent men.

Based on reports from 270 women in interventions about their partners, Fagan et al. (1983) found that 46 percent of spouse abusers had been previously arrested for other violence. Men arrested for stranger violence also were the most frequently and severely violent in the home. Men who were less violent at home usually were not violent toward strangers. The longer and more severe the abuse at home, the more likely were these men to also assault strangers. This finding is consistent with Washburn and Frieze (1981), whose severely battering husbands were more likely to have been involved in fights outside the home than were mildly violent (or nonviolent) husbands.

Thus, there may be different types of violence careers. However, Bandura (1973) cautions that different types of violence may have different determinants. Consistent with this, researchers who espouse explanatory constructs such as patriarchy argue that family violence in general, and wife abuse in particular, are special and distinct types of violence and should not be viewed as a subset of violent behavior (Dobash and Dobash, 1979; Wardell et al., 1983). The few studies of "generally" violent men show, however, that they are more similar to stranger assailants than to those who are violent only within their families (Shields and Hannecke, 1983).

Integrating Theories of Marital and Stranger Violence

There is consistent evidence that violence toward both strangers and intimates is learned early on in the home (Pagelow, 1984; White and Straus, 1981; Walker, 1979, 1984; Fagan et al., 1983; Fagan and Wexler, 1987a; Dodge et al., 1990; cf. Widom, 1988). A corollary view suggests that violent behaviors result from a developmental sequence, beginning with weak parental supervision and family conflict in early childhood, leading to a pattern of successively weakening social and psychological bonds (Loeber and Stouthamer-Loeber, 1986; Patterson and Dishion, 1985). These approaches have much appeal in light of the robust findings on violence in the childhood backgrounds of violent individuals.

What may set apart stranger from marital violence—or explain its overlap for a subset of offenders—are the concepts of culturally sanctioned sexual inequalities and traditional sex-role socialization. By integrating these perspectives into a general learning model, it may be possible to understand and explain the various manifestations of violent behavior and patterns of victim selection. Therefore, where sex-role socialization during early childhood is most traditional, concurrently with socialization to violence, one would expect to find both extrafamilial and familial violence. In the presence of one of these primary socialization influences but not the other, we would expect to find men who confine their violence to either familial or extrafamilial domains.

Support for this notion derives from several theoretical and empirical perspectives. Subcultural theories (e.g., Wolfgang and Ferracuti, 1967) and social learning theories (e.g., Bandura, 1973, 1979) address the learned aspects of violent behavior. Akers et al. (1979) show that social learning processes explain a wide range of behaviors from crime to substance abuse. Hotaling and Sugarman (1986) described the empirical evidence on early childhood socialization and later violence in the home, whereas Bowker (1983) showed how social supports for violence in the home are sustained and reinforced in later adult life. Where violence is learned, sanctioned, and reinforced through cultural or behavioral norms in the immediate community, violence will more likely be chronic and/or more serious.

Yet many males and females avoid violence in adult life, *despite* childhood victimization or other socialization to violence as children or adults (Widom, 1989). Estimates of the prevalence of adult violence among abused male children suggest that the majority avoid later violence as adults (Miller and Challas, 1981; Rivera and Widom, 1990). Accordingly, immunities toward family violence are also of etiological interest. For those who do not demonstrate later involvement with violence, either internal or external controls (or both) develop. Megargee (1983) described how such inhibitors may restrain violent behaviors, even in the presence of strong motivation or habituation toward violence. Where motivation is high, but so too are restraints on violence, violence may be unlikely.

Distinctions among "generally" violent males, those violent only toward family members, and those violent only toward nonfamily members suggest that there are processes specific to victim selection in the development of violent behaviors. Social learning processes describe how socialization occurs where both the utility and the behavioral norms that express male dominance, as well as the functional value of violence, are passed down (Bandura, 1979). Social supports for violence toward women or children may contribute to male sex-role socialization during childhood (Dobash and Dobash, 1979; Russell, 1982) and help explain in part the selection of family members as victims. When childhood and adolescent socialization includes the threat and/or use of male violence toward family members, there may exist a propensity to commit violent acts against family members during later adult years. It seems that victim selection also may be socially learned, as are violent behavior and its functional value and significance with both strangers and family members.

NEUTRALIZATION OF VIOLENT BEHAVIOR

When deviant behaviors occur that violate either self-standards or social norms, a variety of mechanisms may be mobilized to explain the behavior or neutralize self-punishment. The rationalization or externalization of blame has been used to explain other forms of deviance and criminality. Sykes and Matza (1957) suggested that the denial of responsibility was one of several "techniques of neutralization" that individuals use to justify criminal behavior. The perception of being the victim rather than the perpetrator is a common technique used by delinquents to neutralize culpability for their conduct. As discussed earlier, beliefs about the effects of specific intoxicants also have fostered the "excuse function" of substances. The "relaxed standards of accountability" under the influence of certain substances are sometimes used to explain the occurrence of certain behaviors during intoxication (Collins, 1988). It is likely, then, that the "excuse" function of marital violence has cultural determinants.

Such processes appear to be evident among male perpetrators of marital violence. Shields and Hannecke (1983) found that 68 percent of male spouse assailants externalized the cause of their behavior by attributing it to the wife's behavior or to alcohol. "Excuses" for spouse assaults were offered by 21 percent of the men ($N = 75$) studied by Dutton (1985). Although the remainder accepted *responsibility* for their actions, their *justifications* typically blamed the victim for these actions or discounted the behaviors as due to uncontrollable arousal or subgroup norms. Moreover, those who attributed their behavior to their wives were more likely to minimize the *severity* of their actions. Similar reports from men in treatment for spouse assault (Ganley, 1981; Sonkin et al., 1985) describe both the minimization of spouse assault and victim blaming or, alternatively, accepting responsibility but redefining the behavior as consistent with cultural norms.

This notion of disavowal of deviance by assaultive males essentially relocates blame for behavior from the individual to an attribute or behavior of the adversary or to an imperative in the immediate context. When all else fails, disavowal leads to claiming conformity with cultural norms. This not only serves to excuse misbehavior but also reassures others that the behaviors themselves do not challenge the legitimacy of the violated norms. Thus, wife assaulters do not challenge the sanctity of marriage or societal laws against assault.

The cognitive restructuring of events that is necessary to neutralize self-punishment for disapproved behavior involves four types of mechanisms: (1) cognitive restructuring of the behavior itself through euphemistic labeling of the violence, palliative comparison, or moral justification; (2) cognitive restructuring of the behavior-effect relationship through diffusion or displacement of responsibility; (3) cognitive restructuring of the effects of violence by minimizing or ignoring them; and (4) cognitive restructuring of the victim through dehumanizing or victim blame (Bandura, 1979). These processes also neutralize perceptions of social controls that proscribe behavior, leading to what Dutton (1982) referred to as "deindividuated violence," in which control over behaviors shifts from external cues to internal stimuli.

The plausibility of the disavowal framework depends on the acceptance of these accounts of behavior by society. Whether assailants can legitimate their behaviors in frameworks that are culturally salient depends on social norms. Disavowals or accounts help avoid the assignment of an identity to individuals that is consistent with their deviant behavior (e.g., Scott and Lyman, 1968). Collins (1983) suggests that there is a synergistic relationship between cultural acceptance of such accounts and the relocation of blame to external sources that are widely thought to "cause" or at least to excuse such behaviors. When cultural evaluations accept that marital conflict can cause aggressive or violent behaviors, then these accounts are more often honored by society, and the use of such excuses is greater.

Social Judgment Theory and Commission of Homicides by Abused Women

Most of the explanatory frameworks discussed thus far have focused on the perpetration of partner violence by males, in part because male violence is more frequent and severe, and in part because case-control studies have failed to find factors that differentiate women victims of marital violence from nonvictims. One form of violence by women—that of partner homicide in abusive relationships—has generated theory building and research, however. Although women comprise the majority of *victims* in marital homicides, it is the woman who *kills* her spouse or partner that gets public and legal attention. As discussed, many women who kill their spouses have been the victims of extreme forms of marital violence. Yet the majority of victims of severe marital violence do not kill their assailants. The factors and processes that explain such a drastic difference in the outcome of an extremely violent relationship have important theoretical implications.

Browne's (1987) comparative study of abused women who were charged with marital homicides described some of the psychosocial processes that transform marital violence into a fatal confrontation, the progression of assaults to uncontrolled rage on the part of the abusive mate, and victim and societal responses that reinforce the assailant's ability to perpetrate such severe actions—and thus become the antecedents to a lethal event. Women in the homicide group killed to avert what they believed to be their own imminent death or severe harm to their children. As people involved in neither violent nor property crimes, they would be predicted to be nonviolent in nearly all social contexts. Further, there were no systematic differences in the backgrounds of these women from women in the comparison group that would constitute risk markers for their later involvement in a homicide. The women differed only in their attempts or threats to commit suicide; arguably a response to the extremity of the danger with which they lived.

Men in the two groups, however, differed in the severity of their violence both within the family and outside it, their involvement with substances, their threats to kill their partners or others, and their use of sexual violence toward their spouses. It was the extremity of the men's behaviors that distinguished the lethal cases. The male homicide victims seemed to have replaced any empathy with the need for absolute control, eliminating an important block to their continued escalation of violent aggression.

Women's difficulty in leaving these relationships is a combination of several factors: their continuing bond to the males based on a "caretaker" doctrine consistent with their own sex-role socialization, the intensification of violence and the threat of violent reprisals against them or the children if they leave the abuser, shock reactions of victims to abuse, and practical problems in actually separating (see Browne, 1987:ch. 5 and 7). The bond may also be explained, in part, by the interaction of powerful reinforcers of extreme maltreatment alternating with more positive behaviors, to produce a traumatically based bond between victim and assailant (Dutton and Painter, 1981). Given threats against leaving, as well as threats within the relationship, the constant fear of violence regardless of the action taken leaves no choices that do not carry a high risk of danger.

Browne (1986, 1987) utilizes social judgment theory as one way to understand the drastic shift that these women made from victim to perpetrator. For example, Sherif and Hovland's (1961) model of social judgment involves the concept of a continuum on which incoming stimuli are ordered. The "latitude of acceptance" is that range of possibilities with which an individual is willing to agree or to which an individual can adapt. Latitudes are defined by end points, or anchors, that determine the extremes of the scale. Internal anchors are those originating within the individual, whereas external anchors are provided by outside factors or social consensus. Past learning experiences also affect how acceptable or unacceptable a person will find a particular stimulus. In the absence of external factors, an individual's internal anchors play a major role in how he or she will evaluate events. According to social judgment theory, if stimuli continue to fall at the end of the continuum or even slightly above the end point, this will produce a shift of the range toward that anchor—or assimilation. However, if a stimulus is too far beyond the others, a contrast effect will ensue, and the stimulus will be perceived as being even more extreme than it really is.

If one views the escalation of violent acts by the abuser as ordered along a continuum, the "latitude of acceptance" for a battered woman would be that range of activities to which she could adapt. This latitude would be affected by four dimensions frequently discussed in the literature on family violence: (1) the degree to which the woman had been socialized to adjust to or accept a (marital) partner's behavior; (2) prior experiences with similar stimuli—such as witnessing violence in her childhood home; (3) the degree to which external stimuli were present or absent and supported or disconfirmed the appropriateness of the events she was experiencing; and (4) the degree to which she perceived herself as trapped within the violent situation, without alternatives for escape or remediation. Because society's standards on violence against wives are ambiguous, and because abused women often become relatively isolated from others and hesitant about discussing their victimization with others, over time most abused women become primarily dependent on internal anchors to form judgments relative to the violence they are experiencing.

As abusive acts continue to fall near the extreme ends of the continuum, social judgment theory would predict that a battered woman's latitude of acceptance would shift to assimilate them. As demonstrated by findings on other victims of trauma, human beings in extreme environments are able to alter their behavior quite dramatically if it seems necessary to survive. Thus, when the behaviors of the abuser are extreme, a woman may adapt far beyond normal limits in order to coexist. A certain level of abuse and threat becomes the status quo. Survival is the salient criterion: The latitude of acceptance is what the victim believes she can live through.

However, according to social judgment theory, a "contrast" phenomenon should come into effect if an act occurs that falls significantly outside the "normal" range. In recounting events preceding the lethal incidents, women in the homicide group often noted that there was a sudden change in the pattern of violence, which suggested to them that their death was imminent. Otherwise, an act would suddenly be beyond the range of what the woman was willing to assimilate. Frequently, this involved the physical abuse of a child or the discovery that the abuser had forced sexual activity with an adolescent daughter.

Contrast theory would predict that once. the woman defined an event as significantly *outside* the latitude of what she could accept, she would then perceive that act as being more extreme than it actually was. However, given the tendency of abused women to employ denial to survive and to understate the levels of violence in their relationships, it is probable that women in the homicide group were at last simply making an assessment more in keeping with the way in which an outside observer would evaluate the level of violence. At this point, denial and minimalization gave way to sudden, often spontaneous, action, moving the victim from a concentration on internal coping strategies to the extreme agency of homicide (Browne, 1987).

Whether theory developed in extreme cases is valid elsewhere on the distribution of marital violence is uncertain. For example, there have been no similar applications of social judgment theory to other women victims of abuse and no research on whether social judgments inevitably alter perceptions of acceptable alternatives. However, Bowker (1983, 1986b) offers evidence from women who ended violence in their relationships that social judgments are not altered when there is the intercession of social and legal institutions (e.g., the presence of strong external anchors) to balance marital power. Thus it appears that the interaction between social or institutional responses and marital dynamics contributes to social judgments about acceptable behaviors by assailants and behavioral choices of victims.

Integrated Explanation of Marital Violence

Evidence from the perspectives presented suggests that cognitive and emotional factors are interpreted through social psychological processes and cultural beliefs to explain the occurrence of marital violence. Social networks and their subcultural milieus determine the social construction of behavior patterns and shape the cognitive and emotional processes that transform arousal into marital aggression. Victimization also influences cognitive processes: Dodge et al. (1990:1682) showed in longitudinal research that

> harmed children are likely to develop biased and deficient patterns of processing social information, including a failure to attend to relevant cues, a bias to attribute hostile intentions to others, and a lack of competent behavioral strategies to solve interpersonal problems. These patterns in turn were found to predict the development of aggressive behavior [and lead] . . . a child to conceptualize the world in . . . ways that perpetuate the cycle of violence.

These cognitive processes in turn are further influenced by cultural and situational factors that determine the norms, beliefs, and sanctions regarding behaviors following arousal during marital conflict or stress.

Three major independent variables increase the probability of violence during microsocial interactions: (1) psychological proclivity for the exercise of physical violence toward the spouse (e.g., personality factors); (2) beliefs that instrumental goals will be achieved through the use of physical force; and (3) arousal that provides the motivation for the (male's) assaultive behavior against the spouse or partner. Each of these factors in turn influences cognitive processes that interpret both the situation and the appropriate behavioral response.

Cultural Factors

Stark and McEvoy (1970) found that about 25 percent of males in a national survey would approve of a male slapping his wife under certain circumstances. Smith (1990) showed the association between such beliefs and marital violence by the male in a couple. Such cultural beliefs are expressed through the individual who believes, as he perceives social norms, that violence within families is an acceptable or normative response to marital conflict. Culture therefore has both direct effects, through expectancy of appropriate behaviors when angry or aroused, and indirect effects, through its influence on mediating cognitive processes that define complex emotions such as anger. Moreover, these cultural beliefs are more likely to produce "accounts" that allow an abuser to shift blame to the victim, to alcohol, or to some other external factor and therefore neutralize any self-punishment or social sanctions for the aggression.

Cultural factors, including beliefs about permitted behaviors in specific milieus, and the cultural meaning of marital violence (ceremonies, spiritual or religious uses, social interaction) shape the context in which behavioral norms are interpreted. These settings and social contexts also influence the choice of behaviors, and convey the rules and norms proscribing behaviors, the cognitive interpretation of the situation, and therefore the probability of marital violence while in that situation.

Personality Factors

A propensity toward marital violence reflects explanations regarding the use of physical force to resolve perceived conflicts. This concept resembles Megargee's (1983) concept of "habit strength" in his "algebra of aggression," but it also includes basic intrinsic motivations for violence. It is also similar to the "set" in Zinberg's (1984) explanation of behavior following intoxication as the result of interactions among set (personality), substance, and setting.

An example of an individual personality factor is the propensity to use violence to resolve interpersonal conflicts, or the habit strength of violence that has been socially reinforced through past experiences in childhood and during later stages of social and personality development. Violence may be considered the "appropriate" response to anger or the behavior that an individual has learned best achieves his goals. Accordingly, the reinforcement of experiences learned from childhood exposure (either in the home or nearby in other closely observed relationships) provides a set of behaviors that are invoked in response to conditions that raise fear, anger, vulnerability, or other strong emotions.

Specific Motivation

Arousal is a transitional state marked by emotional instability. Many of the socioeconomic markers of marital violence may also signify frustration from failure to achieve socially defined expectations of (male) success. This can contribute to a chronic state of frustration and arousal that assailants may label as anger (Browne and Dutton, 1990). These markers also can signify stresses that trigger fear, anxiety, self-derogation, or other states of emotional discomfort. Arousal may come from threats of loss of control in the relationship, feelings of rejection or abandonment, threats from intimacy or emotional dependence on the spouse or partner, or threats to social status from outside the relationship. Browne (1987) argues that even emotional states engendered in positive intimate relationships—such as desire or longing—may be reinterpreted by assaultive males as frustration or displeasure; this effect is again mediated by whether intimate relationships in childhood were anxiety provoking or nurturing.

The response to arousal determines the occurrence of spouse assault. A complex calculus will determine whether the male partner becomes violent under conditions of arousal: earlier lessons about "what works" to quell anxiety or release anger (Sonkin and Durphy, 1985), what he perceives as potential consequences (Bowker, 1983; Carmody and Williams, 1987), what he has seen others do in similar situations (Bandura, 1973; Dutton, 1988a), and his control over his rage or fear (Browne, 1987; Katz, 1988). Other factors also may influence whether an attack occurs, especially whether past attacks have been gratifying (i.e., resulted in the reduction of arousal, anger, or anxiety or in the restoration of control) and the gains have outweighed any aversive consequences.

Summary

Rather than being a linear process, marital violence is more likely a reciprocal process in which individual, situational, and cultural factors have multiple and recursive interactions leading to aggressive or nonaggressive behaviors. That is, situational variables and interactions with family members are likely to affect variations in the behaviors that follow arousal. These relationships then will alter the individual's selection of contexts or situations in which assaults may occur, his social construction or cognitive interpretation of these contexts, and the probability of aggressive behaviors. The influence of larger political, economic, and social-organizational influences—on culture and proximal social controls of violence in general, and wife assaults in particular—must also be acknowledged.

The interaction among personality, social context, and arousal seems critical to understanding marital violence. Individuals form perceptions of their environments and internalize the expected responses to social situations through the development of personality, which itself is a socially determined process. Both psychological and social experiences with intimates, shaped by the arousal produced by marital dynamics or experiences outside the marital relationship, socialize partners not only to the responses to anger but also to the expected social behaviors that accompany that state. Zinberg (1984) suggests that individuals select explanatory constructs from a range of cognitive and emotional perceptions available to them and that responses follow the available explanations of the situation. The boundaries of those responses are determined by three factors: (1) perceptions of the expected environment, (2) personality variables such as relative ego autonomy, and (3) responses to the specific marital context.

These three factors are influenced strongly by social learning processes that carry forward the lessons of childhood and adolescence. Social learning processes teach male spouses about the expected behaviors in marriage (or intimate relationships) and also influence personality factors by raising apprehensions about danger or moral ambiguity. The delicate interplay of these factors responds to the social cues of the setting in which couples interact. From these cues, marital violence by male spouses may follow logically from the controls that are internally activated and the social controls present in the setting.

At the social and cultural levels, weak social organization or social ambivalence about violence against wives and children may permit or promote violence within families at the group or neighborhood level. Individuals may initially have diverse experiences with behaviors in various settings but ultimately are likely to gravitate toward social contexts that offer a match between personal proclivities (base rates of aggression, beliefs in the legitimacy of violence, use of accounts based on cultural interpretations of marital assaults) and what is both socially expected and permitted in that scene. However, such personal proclivities may also include a desire for acceptance in nonviolent social worlds, and selective processes of affiliation may ensue, depending on the type of social gratification sought.

CRIMINAL JUSTICE POLICY

Significant changes have taken place in criminal justice policy toward marital violence over the past 20 years. These developments were preceded by criticisms of the police, and the criminal justice system more generally, for failing to respond effectively to spouse assault. Specifically, critics claimed that sanctions for violence against family members were rare or weak, that criminal justice agencies often did not regard or process cases of marital violence with the seriousness accorded to stranger violence, that victims of marital violence were not afforded the protection given to victims of stranger violence via punishment and control of offenders, and that low sanction severity actually contributed to or reinforced the underlying causes of marital violence (Elliott, 1989). Moreover, several theoretical perspectives implicate weak societal responses as facilitating the progression of marital violence.

The social and political processes described earlier in this paper gave rise to significant reforms and experiments in criminal justice processing of cases of marital violence. This section reviews the major developments in this era, noting the contributions of marital violence research in each area. The section also analyzes social and organizational processes in the criminal justice system that influence utilization of research on marital violence.

POLICE INTERVENTIONS

Early criticisms of police handling of cases involving assaults on wives, coupled with litigation and growing awareness of the seriousness of marital violence, have led to significant changes in policy and practice in many jurisdictions (Goolkasian, 1986). As we discuss later in this section, these efforts were focused more on sanction and control of offenders than on victim protection. In general, such efforts were designed to make the police response to marital violence more aggressive and to increase the likelihood that sanctions would be forthcoming for incidents of spouse assault. Specifically, policy changes were intended to increase the probability of arrest in reported cases of misdemeanor wife assault.

In a review of criminal justice responses to marital violence, Elliott (1989) concludes that one-third of all domestic disturbance calls involve some form of domestic violence, with the majority of these involving assaults between "intimate" cohabitants or former cohabitants. Based on observational studies of police intervention in domestic disturbances, Dutton (1987, 1988b) found that arrest occurs in only 21.2 percent of wife assault cases in which prima facie evidence exists for arrest.[32] Elliott (1989) estimated that the probability of arrest varied from 12 to 50 percent, but found mixed support for the claim that arrest is less likely to occur for family than stranger violence.

Both research and litigation have led to mandatory arrest policies in some jurisdictions for incidents in which there is probable cause of wife assault.[33] Class action law suits in Oakland, California (*Scott* v. *Hart*), and New York City (*Bruno* v. *McGuire*) established a legal basis for mandatory arrest policies. A civil suit in Torrington, Connecticut (*Thurman* v. *The City of Torrington*) extended Fourteenth Amendment rights to women in domestic relationships. The court ruled that the police department's failure to enforce restraining orders constituted a policy that provides less protection for victims of both marital and parent-to-child violence. The policy created a de facto administrative classification that discriminates against women who are victims of domestic violence, and the municipality was liable for damages. In *Hynson* v. *City of Chester Legal Department*, the court ruled that police officers lose their limited immunity if they were aware that failure to enforce protections in domestic relationships was a violation of Fourteenth Amendment rights.

The premise is that strict and swift application of criminal sanctions in wife assault cases will better protect victims and reduce the likelihood of repeat violence. The empirical basis for these policies derives both from accumulated evidence of the ineffectiveness of nonarrest or informal police dispositions of family violence calls (Martin, 1976; Bowker, 1983; Morash, 1986) and from experimental evidence of the deterrent effects of arrest compared to nonarrest dispositions (Sherman and Berk, 1984; Tauchen et al., 1986; Jaffe et al., 1986).

The Minneapolis Domestic Violence experiment has been the most influential study in the development of policies to increase the likelihood of arrest in misdemeanor wife assault cases. It was designed as a test of the specific deterrent effects of arrest on the recurrence of wife assault and was intended to provide a critical test of the effectiveness of legal sanctions compared to nonlegal, informal police responses. Sherman and Berk (1984) used an experimental design in two Minneapolis police precincts to randomly assign violent family disputes to one of three police responses: arrest, separation of victim and assailant, and advice/mediation. The study was limited to situations in which the assailant was present when the police arrived. During the six-month follow-up, biweekly interviews with victims and reviews of official reports of family violence were collected. Despite the repeated measures on subsequent violence, dichotomous measures of recidivism were used. Neither the severity, the incidence, nor the time to recurrence was reported.

Sherman and Berk (1984) concluded that arrest was more effective in reducing subsequent violence in misdemeanor wife assault cases than other police responses. Those arrested had the lowest recidivism rate based on official (10%) and victim (19%) reports. There was no evidence of differential effects across conditions based on offender characteristics, although within-group differences were found. This led to their recommendation that "police adopt arrest as the favored response to domestic assault on the basis [in the original] of its deterrence power" (as cited in Dunford et al., 1989:1). A subsequent reanalysis by Tauchen et al. (1986) offered more qualified support for the deterrent effects of arrest. Findings from the Minneapolis experiment, together with results of nonexperimental studies comparing arrest with other police dispositions of spouse assault cases (Berk and Newton, 1985), provided evidence that influenced police policy and legislation nationwide (Sherman and Cohn, 1989). Thus, for several years, the Minneapolis study provided critical, determining evidence in criminal justice policy development for wife assault.

However, several reviews (Binder and Meeker, 1988; Fagan, 1989; Elliott, 1989; Lempert, 1989) have cited internal and external validity problems in the Minneapolis experiment that, together with contradictory results from replications in Omaha (Dunford et al., 1989, 1990) and Charlotte, North Carolina (Hirschel and Hutchinson, 1992; Hirschel et al., 1991, 1992), raise serious questions about the deterrent effects of arrest on repeat spouse assault. In both the Omaha and the Charlotte replications, there were no significant differences in recidivism for any type of police response (advice, warning, citation, arrest) for several measures of recidivism. Moreover, the incidence of recidivism in Charlotte was *highest* for the arrest group [$p(F)$ = .03], which directly contradicted the results in Minneapolis.

Results of additional replication experiments are available for experiments in Colorado Springs (Berk et al., 1992), Dade County (Pate and Hamilton, 1992), and Milwaukee (Sherman et al., 1991). Only Dade County reported results similar to the original Minneapolis experiment: a reduction in the prevalence of recidivism for arrested suspects in both official records and interviews. Even here, the reduction reported in official records was not statistically significant. In the Charlotte, Colorado Springs, Milwaukee, and Omaha experiments, analysis of official records showed that arrest was associated with higher rates of reoffending; but results based on interview data showed that arrest was associated with lower rates of reoffending. Except for the Colorado Springs experiment, none of the results approached traditional levels of statistical significance.

Reviewing the five replications, together with the original Minneapolis experiment, Sherman (1992) reported that three experiments found that rates of spouse assault escalated among male arrestees who were unemployed or unmarried. The results suggest that arrest has variable effects on different types of people and also people in different types of neighborhoods. Sherman (1992) claims that escalation of spouse assault following arrest was evident in neighborhoods in Milwaukee and Omaha where there were concentrations of poverty and social disorganization, but escalation was not evident in economically stable areas where employment was lower and poverty less acute.

How could replication results diverge so sharply from the original finding? Is arrest an effective deterrent only in one location due to its unique circumstances, or was the experiment flawed and were the results simply a Type II error? Several limitations in the design of the Minneapolis experiment suggest that it was a seriously flawed effort. First, the follow-up period was relatively short (six months), given the episodic and cyclical patterns of family violence observed by Walker (1979, 1984) and Frieze et al. (1980). Second, self-reports from abusers were not obtained, which left out the possibility of a "hidden" violence period toward strangers, the original victim, or other victims in the home. Third, no distinctions were made in the level and nature of violence, leaving open questions of the relative harm (e.g., injury, intimidation) that may have accrued from battering incidents.

Fourth, the biweekly interview process may have depressed recidivism rates through research effects, response effects, or task-specific biases. Awareness by offenders of victim interviews may have deterred or simply postponed recidivism during the study period. The validity of victim' reports may have been compromised because assailants often were residing with them during the follow-up period. Victim attrition also was evident but not analyzed. Fifth, not all precincts in Minneapolis participated in the experiment. Finally, other forms of wife abuse, such as persistent denigration or economic reprisal, were not investigated. These forms of abuse, noted in several studies on wife battery (e.g., Frieze et al., 1980; Walker, 1979, 1984; Russell, 1982), are emotionally harmful even if not posing threats to physical safety and often are antecedents of physical violence (Walker, 1979, 1984).

Perhaps the most significant omission from the Minneapolis experiment was the exclusion of other than ". . . simple [misdemeanor] domestic assaults. . . . Cases of life-threatening or severe injury, usually labelled as a felony . . . were excluded from the design . . ." (Sherman and Berk, 1984:263). Thus, selection biases of participating officers' processes may have been evident in the exclusion of individual cases from the randomization procedure, based on the arresting officers' judgment about the severity of violence or the risk to the victim of nonarrest. Offenders who had left the scene also were excluded from the experiment. Accordingly, incomplete randomization introduced serious sampling biases and validity threats (Berk et al., 1988).

The exclusion of offenders who absconded also limits police response for potentially serious cases. Assailants' violence histories are critical to the analysis of desistance via deterrence (Fagan, 1989). Research on criminal careers shows that persistent offenders differ from the "innocents" or desisters in previous studies (Blumstein et al., 1985). Male spouses with histories of severe violence at home more often are violent toward strangers, have more often been arrested for violent offenses, and more often injure both domestic and stranger victims (Fagan et al., 1983; Shields et al., 1988). Male partners with longer histories of police contacts also more often drop out of spouse abuse treatment programs (Hamberger and Hastings, 1989).

Sanctions (including arrest with an uncertain outcome) may affect these persistent offenders far less than first- or one-time offenders, or husbands who are violent only within the home. Accordingly, the effect size in the Minneapolis experiment may be confounded with sample artifacts. Although Sherman and Berk (1984) report that most of the men in the sample had repeatedly assaulted their partners prior to the experimental incident, within-group differences are not reported. Berk (personal communication, 1986) states that assailants with lengthier histories of either wife assault or stranger violence had higher recidivism rates than others, regardless of experimental conditions.

The Omaha, Charlotte, and other replications followed experimental designs similar to the Minneapolis study, adding refinements that addressed many of its limitations. For example, all police calls for domestic violence during the 4:00 to 12:00 p.m. shift in the city of Omaha were randomly assigned to three treatment groups: (1) those in which the perpetrator would be arrested, (2) those in which the perpetrator would be separated from the victim, and (3) those in which police would "mediate" the dispute. Cases were sampled around the clock in Charlotte, where the use of a police-issued citation also presented a unique intervention option. Randomized treatment was conducted only for cases in which both perpetrator and victim were present at the scene when the police arrived. However, data on those cases in which the perpetrator was not present were collected and analyzed separately in Omaha.

Both studies employed official and self-report measures to judge the effectiveness of the treatments in deterring reassault and threats over a six-month period. Official recidivism measures included new arrests and complaints for any crimes committed by the suspect against the victim, found in official police records. Victims were interviewed for self-reports of (1) fear of violence, (2) pushing or hitting, and (3) physical injury. Victims were interviewed at the end of the first week (or shortly thereafter) following the incident that resulted in police contact and again six months later.

Neither study found that arrest was an effective deterrent. In Omaha, for example, "arresting suspects had no more effect in deterring future arrests or complaints than did separating or counseling them"; similarly, victim reports showed "no significant differences between the treatment groups" (Dunford et al., 1989:34). Moreover, analyses controlling for prior arrests, ethnicity, and other variables showed no significant differences between police responses in terms of reassault and threat. Results from the other replications were inconsistent as well.

Dunford et al. (1989) argue that a policy that encourages arrest when probable cause exists may have greater promise for reducing subsequent assaults. They contend, similar to Ford (1983), that victims can then use the criminal justice process to negotiate their own security with suspects/spouses. Thus, according victims, the option for arrest becomes an empowerment strategy.

Reciprocity Between Formal and Informal Sanctions

Williams and Hawkins (1989a) expand the deterrence framework for arrests for wife assault to include both direct and indirect costs as *perceived* ramifications of arrest specific to the assailant's social context. For example, Williams and Hawkins (1989a) analyzed responses from telephone interviews with 494 males in a nationwide probability sample. Respondents were asked to imagine what would happen if they were arrested for an attack on their wives. All respondents had reported one or more assaults on a spouse or female partner during 1987. Respondents believed that arrest would have deleterious consequences for their personal lives were it to occur, including disrupted social relationships and humiliation before family and friends. However, responding to hypothetical scenarios, they viewed the loss of a job or a jail remand highly unlikely as a consequence of assaults.

Carmody and Williams (1987) also analyzed responses about the perceived certainty and severity of sanctions for wife assault based on the 1985 NFVS data. Responses from men who reported using physical force against their wives (N = 174) were compared with nonassaultive men (N = 1,452). Four hypothetical "sanctions" were measured: arrest, social condemnation, separation or divorce from the partner, and retaliatory force by the partner. Men viewed retaliatory force by the partner as the *least* likely consequence of wife assault. The perceived severity of this reaction was quite low as well. The perceived certainty of arrest was also quite low, although the perceived severity score suggested that men viewed this sanction as very serious if it did occur. Male respondents did consider the possibility of a loss of respect from friends and relatives as both likely and severe. However, although the loss of the partner as a result of wife assault was considered a severe outcome, it was perceived as very unlikely.

Assaultive and nonassaultive men did not differ significantly in their perceptions of the certainty (not very likely) and severity (very severe) of arrest or of their partners separating from them or getting a divorce. However, assaultive men did perceive it as more likely that their partners would respond with physical aggression than did nonassaultive men. Conversely, nonassaultive men perceived the certainty and severity of social condemnation as significantly greater than did assaultive men. Finally, although the distributions were similar for one-time and repeat offenders, the perceived severity of arrest was significantly lower for men who had assaulted their partners more than once (Carmody and Williams, 1987).

Associations of perceived sanctions with assailants' social area and social class were not reported. However, arrest probabilities are mediated by social ecological variables (D.A. Smith, 1986). Thus, whether the deterrent effects of arrest interact with the social area in which it occurs is unknown but potentially important, given the apparent concentration of serious wife assault in poor and working-class neighborhoods. Disaggregation by social area of the findings on perceived and actual deterrent effects will resolve some of these questions.

Evidently, both the perceived and the actual deterrent effects of arrest seem to diminish for assailants familiar with the "going rates" of punishment for wife assault in the criminal justice system. These rates may be even lower for areas in which stranger violence or other crime problems are assigned a high priority. The deterrent effects of sanctions may depend not simply on police decisions to arrest, but also on the cumulative effects of sanctions at subsequent stages of criminal justice processing.

Williams and Hawkins (1986, 1989b) conceived informal controls as internalized social psychological controls that facilitate conformity or generate greater fear of law violation. Where specific deterrent effects are based on the internalization of the perceived costs of law violation (that is, punishment costs), informal social controls suggest costs associated with the act itself (Williams and Hawkins, 1992). Williams and Hawkins (1986, 1989b) specify three types of costs that create informal controls: attachment costs (e.g., the loss of valued relationships), stigma (e.g., social opprobrium, embarrassment), and commitment costs (e.g., loss of job or economic opportunity) (see also, Carmody and Williams, 1987; Miller and Simpson, 1991). Thus, Williams and Hawkins (1986, 1989b) are consistent with other deterrence theorists in suggesting a reciprocal and complementary relationship between formal and informal controls for spouse assault. They state, for example, that ". . . persons (may) anticipate that others will disapprove of their arrest for committing a certain act, and they (may) refrain from that activity because they fear the stigma of being caught" (1986:562-563). Thus, for all these types of costs, extralegal punishment may be contingent on legal sanction.

Arrest of spouse assailants may result in deterrence processes that operate through *both* legal sanctions (Sherman and Berk, 1984; Dutton et al., 1991) and informal social controls (loss of self-esteem, disrupted social ties, job loss, and shame) (Berk and Newton, 1985; Dunford et al., 1989; Sherman et al., 1992). These effects were observed in paradigms using both hypothetical scenarios (Williams and Hawkins, 1986, 1989b) and actual arrests (Dutton et al., 1991). Offenders who desist from further violence following arrest may be responding not only to the potential legal costs, but also to the implications of arrest for relationships with peers, employers, spouses, and neighbors. But where social costs are low, the deterrent effects of legal sanctions may be weak. Sherman et al. (1991), for example, found that living in what they termed "ghetto poverty" neutralized the attachment and commitment costs associated to legal sanctions for spouse assault for unmarried and unemployed males. Thus, the deterrent effects of legal sanctions for spouse assault depend on raising both *social costs* and *punishment* costs. Raising social costs in turn requires that there are meaningful threats from possible job loss, social stigmatization, and relationship loss associated with spouse assault.

PROSECUTION OF MARITAL VIOLENCE

Major developments in the prosecution of family violence cases have centered on increasing the percentage of cases formally prosecuted and on improving the quality and aggressiveness of that prosecution. Prosecutors receive family violence cases in two ways. In many jurisdictions, police refer nearly all arrests to the prosecutor for screening, evaluation, and formal charging. In others, police screen many cases prior to formal charging by prosecutors. In these cases, as well as those in which the police have declined to arrest, victims can sign complaints directly with prosecutors. Regardless of how the case is obtained, prosecutors then decide to decline or accept the charges and to pursue a conviction in the courts on the original or modified charges.

Historically, like the police, prosecutors were accused of disinterest in family violence cases (Ellis, 1984). Specific criticisms suggested that they failed to file charges (i.e., dismissed charges) or to aggressively pursue convictions and sanctions against the offenders (Martin, 1976; Field and Field, 1973; Fields, 1978; Lerman, 1986). Stanko (1982) described the reliance of prosecutors on gender stereotypes to determine victim credibility and the precedence of goals of successful prosecution over the needs of victims. Factors influencing prosecutorial discretion included the questionable wisdom of intervening in family affairs, the motivation and potential "culpability" of the victim, and the perceived reluctance of victims to complete the court process.

Research on factors that influence prosecution of marital violence cases reflects the absence of specific decision-making criteria and the generalization of prosecutorial discretion for stranger and family violence cases. Schmidt and Steury (1989) analyzed screening decisions of 38 prosecutors in 408 domestic violence cases in Milwaukee. Logit analyses showed that the severity of injury and the defendant's prior arrest record influenced screening and filing decisions more than the evidentiary strength of the case. In fact, prosecutors were not reluctant to charge even in weak cases. Defendants who failed to attend charging conferences and who had drug or alcohol involvement were especially likely to be prosecuted.

Elliott (1989) suggests that a high dismissal rate by prosecutors in wife assault cases offers police further disincentives to make an arrest or to carefully investigate and gather evidence for a successful prosecution. Others (Fagan et al., 1984; Ford, 1983) suggest that prosecutors often find an unreceptive judicial audience for wife assault cases, especially in sentencing deliberations. With serious sanctions not forthcoming, prosecutors have little incentive to aggressively pursue a wife assault case through conviction and sentencing. Though there was consistent evidence that the majority of wife assault cases were dismissed, both Schmidt and Steury (1989) and Elliott (1989) found little evidence that different factors were involved in the decision to prosecute family violence cases compared to stranger violence crimes. Differences were attributed in part to the quality of evidence, but primarily to differences in victim/witness cooperation—a complex issue in the prosecution of family violence cases.

Innovations in Prosecution of Marital Violence

The major developments in prosecutorial responses to wife assault have evolved from two primary sources: research on victim-witness programs in the 1970s and special prosecution programs (e.g., Forst and Hernon, 1985) more often aimed at improving the efficiency and effectiveness of the prosecution function. Successful experiments with special prosecution programs for targeted offender types (e.g., organized crime, career criminals) provided incentives for organizational innovations to address marital violence.

The special concerns of abused women in the criminal courts coincided with these innovations, although the impetus for reform may have derived from other interests. Victim-witness programs established the special circumstances that "vulnerable" victims faced in the prosecution process: intimidation and fear of reprisal, a possibly lengthy adjudication process, and interruption of basic social supports such as cash or housing. They provided counsel for victims, advocacy to expedite hearings and notification of appearances whenever possible, linkages to critical social services (e.g., shelter, counseling, social service advocacy), and advocacy for protective legal interventions (e.g., restraining orders). These programs also fostered significant legislative changes regarding evidence to simplify proceedings and to minimize the emotional difficulty of confronting a hostile court setting: for example, elimination of the requirement that divorce or dissolution proceedings be initiated prior to issuing a protective (restraining) order, use of depositions or videotaped testimony in lieu of court hearings, and relaxing of corroboration requirements in misdemeanor cases.

Special prosecution programs created an atmosphere within prosecutors' offices in which family violence cases had high status, providing incentives for vigorous prosecution without competing with other units for scarce investigative or trial resources. They also simplified procedures; in some programs, prosecutors could sign complaints and serve as plaintiffs. Some programs also did not allow victims to withdraw complaints or request dismissal once charges had been filed, thus increasing the likelihood of a complaint resulting in a conviction while decreasing the negative reaction from judges for consuming court calendars and resources.

In effect, these programs established policies of mandatory prosecution or pretrial diversion (with the option for prosecution retained) of all wife assault cases referred by police. Although larger jurisdictions have adopted these concepts, there remain many locales in which marital violence cases compete for the attention of prosecutors. Research on marital violence, which has identified the high likelihood of repeat violence in domestic assaults as well as the special needs of victims, rarely has influenced rural or even suburban counties to improve the prosecution of these cases.

Although research on marital violence has provided significant, influential information to inform these innovations, its contributions have been limited to establishing the range of supportive services that were critical to sustaining successful prosecutions. What has not occurred—despite strong empirical evidence of the chronic, escalating nature of family violence and its overlap in many cases with stranger crimes (Fagan and Wexler, 1987a)—is a reordering of priorities regarding prosecution of family violence cases. With few exceptions, wife assault cases continue to be evaluated and prosecuted with little difference from other violence cases (Schmidt and Steury, 1989). The organizational, fiscal, and procedural accommodations necessary within prosecutors' offices to effectively pursue sanctions in family violence cases still are not commonplace.

SANCTION AND CONTROL OF WIFE ASSAULTERS: TREATMENT INTERVENTIONS

Court-mandated treatment of wife assault is essential to the criminal justice system objective of reducing recidivism (Dutton, 1988b). Treatment options support this goal in four ways. First, treatment provides a dispositional option for judges in imposing sanctions. It is an "intermediate" sanction and form of social control that is harsher than probation but less drastic than incarceration. Whether or not incarceration is an appropriate sanction in a particular case, judges often are reluctant to invoke such "last-resort" sanctions for marital violence when the victim has not been injured severely (Dutton, 1988a; Goolkasian, 1986). They may fear the consequences to victims of the removal of economic support, and they may still (inappropriately) view marital violence cases as less serious than stranger violence and thus less serious in the allocation of scarce jail space. The availability of a dispositional option makes these cases more salient for judges and, in turn, for prosecutors and police.

Second, treatment has been seen as a means to protect women who chose not to dissolve their relationship, but whose violent partners would not seek treatment voluntarily. Third, treatment placements provide a form of control that strengthens the traditional probation sanction. Monthly, superficial contacts with probation officers for misdemeanor offenses are replaced by weekly or biweekly therapeutic interventions in a structured milieu. Failure to abide by probation conditions mandating treatment participation can result in court action and possibly an escalation in sanction severity. Fourth, treatment has specific clinical value for recidivism reduction. Treatment interventions often are specifically designed to reinforce the substantive meaning of the arrest sanction (Ganley, 1981). The format challenges assailants' beliefs that their arrest and conviction were unjust or that their use of violence was justified. The specific learning components of contemporary treatment models (Sonkin et al., 1985; Saunders, 1988) enable offenders both to learn alternative responses for conflict management or anger control and to internalize the negative consequences of violent behavior.

Treatment alternatives and options have a long-standing place in the criminal justice system (Gendreau and Ross, 1979). Dispositions with treatment components are common for drug offenders, drunk driving, (diagnosed) mental illness, and other offenders whose actions are presumed to be the result of some underlying behavioral problem or social skills deficit. Also common are options for diversion prior to prosecution, in which the outcome of treatment interventions influences the disposition of the case. Treatment groups for offenders convicted of wife assault began in the 1970s. Today, the prevailing approach involves treatment as part of a court sanction following conviction, usually in conjunction with probation supervision. Important distinctions exist among family systems, anger management-assertiveness, and feminist treatment models (Dutton, 1988a). Treatment groups focusing on anger management operate by challenging the violent male's rationalization system that neutralizes self-punishment and helps attribute the cause of violence to the spouse or some other external factor. For many programs, a primary objective is to directly undermine such cognitive, habit-sustaining mechanisms in assaultive males (Browne and Dutton, 1990).

For example, to the extent that an assailant believes that his wife's (or partner's) injuries were minimal or that she was to blame for the conflict, the more likely he is to view his subsequent arrest as unjust. Treatment models confront these beliefs, as well as general attitudes about women (sex-role orientation) and beliefs about power in dyadic relationships (Eddy and Myers, 1984; Dutton, 1988a). Treatment also focuses on anger detection, control, and management to influence cognitive and behavioral abilities.

These programs have been widely accepted as an option for criminal justice processing, in part because they reflect explanations of wife assault that do not challenge basic assumptions within criminal justice agencies about the causes of crime. The philosophical base of offender treatment for marital violence—stressing individual responsibility and behavioral control—is compatible with contemporary intervention models in the criminal justice system. This, in turn, creates a political context in which treatment can be linked to probation sanctions. Court-ordered treatment, under probationary conditions, in effect is the social control component of the legal sanction. However, evidence of its effectiveness is inconclusive due to weak evaluation designs. Recent evaluations (Saunders and Hanusa, 1984; Dutton, 1987; Edelson et al., 1987) reported that 64 to 84 percent of treatment participants were not violent after treatment, although measurements, follow-up times, and definitions varied.

Feminist therapy calls for a more basic resocialization of men and, in lieu of anger management, a redirection of their view of women and sex roles and of their instrumental use of violence to retain power and domination (Gondolf, 1985a). The social and cultural supports that reinforce the maintenance of power are critical to this model (Gondolf, 1985b; Bowker, 1983; Fagan, 1989). Although there is much evidence to support them, critical perspectives on violence (Walker, 1984; Gondolf, 1985b; Browne, 1987) have been less influential in guiding the development of sentencing options and treatment interventions for marital violence than models based on anger management and behavior modification. Sanction and control continue today to express perspectives that regard violence as an act of individual deviance.

Improving the efficacy of mandated treatment interventions depends on the resolution of critical issues. First, retention rates of assailants in counseling programs vary according to the personality characteristics and behavioral problems of participants (Hamberger and Hastings, 1988). Models tailored to specific types of assaultive males are necessary. Second, ineffective treatment compromises victim safety. Accordingly, procedures are needed to audit the effect of interventions for assailants on the safety of victims. Third, treatment experiments with credible sanctions for control conditions (that address safety issues, for example) are required to strengthen the empirical evidence on treatment effectiveness. Moreover, current programs reach only a small fraction of assaultive males (Saunders and Azar, 1989). Research is needed both on the long-term effectiveness of current approaches and on mechanisms to make such programs available to a larger number of assaulters.

CONTRIBUTIONS OF RESEARCH ON MARITAL VIOLENCE TO CRIMINAL JUSTICE POLICY

How has research on marital violence influenced criminal justice policy? The competing explanations of marital violence differ not only in their locus (from individual pathology to social structure and cultural beliefs), but also in their implications for policy and intervention. Explanations of marital violence suggest policies that range from individual offender control to resocialization or macrosocial changes in behavioral and attitudinal norms, and ultimately in the redistribution of social and economic power between women and men.

These competing explanations have drawn empirical support through quite divergent research paradigms. In this section, we briefly trace the paradigms of social science and social control that follow from the various explanations of marital violence, and examine their impact on knowledge and policy.

Paradigms of Social Science

The policy emphasis on deterrence through arrest and prosecution places greater premium on *individual* explanations of marital violence than on other models. Accordingly, research on marital violence that identifies the causes and remedies within individual assailants has had the strongest currency for criminal justice policy development. Research on offenders has greater utility in a system geared toward offender sanction and control. However, research that examines the validity of ecological theories or ideological explanations has been valued less in a jurisprudential setting in which the occurrence of codified behaviors is the critical issue. For researchers studying marital violence, the measurement of situation and context—critical for theory development and testing—adds much to explanations of the motivational component of violence. Yet these variables have not been fully integrated in policies on arrest or prosecution, possibly limiting their effects.[34]

These distinctions are symbolic of deeper divisions in research traditions and paradigms. The virtual separation of family and stranger violence research (other than for homicide) reflects important differences in theory, definition, measurement, and research paradigms (Fagan and Wexler, 1987a). There have been numerous criticisms of social scientific efforts to explain marital violence (e.g., see Dobash and Dobash, 1979; Wardell et al., 1983), particularly the use of methods derived from the natural sciences and the attempt to develop a "science of man" (Becker, 1963). Such studies have difficulty acknowledging the context and meaning of specific acts. Yet theorists studying drug use (Zinberg, 1984), delinquency, and violence by gang members (Klein and Maxson, 1989), and even drug-related violence (Goldstein, 1989) have identified the importance of context in sorting out the motivation of specific acts. Further, in research on marital violence, there has been disagreement on the importance of nonphysical harm and injury, despite their usefulness in understanding the phenomenon, as well as on explicit measures of physical aggression such as the Conflict Tactics Scales (Straus, 1979, 1990a).

Fagan and Wexler (1985), for example, found that the explanatory power of risk factors in OLS models of marital violence varied according to the definition of aggression or violence used. Table 6 shows the results of OLS regression analyses predicting six different measures of marital violence for each of three sets of

TABLE 6 Summary of OLS Regression Models of Marital Violence Measures by Victim, Assailant, and Situation Variables (N = 270) (percent variance explained, F-value)

Violence or Abuse Measure	Victim Characteristics	Assailant Characteristics	Situational Factors
CTS violence	4.2 (1.43)	37.0 (15.83)[a]	6.3 (1.54)
CTS aggression	2.8 (0.93)	37.6 (16.26)[a]	2.7 (0.63)
Most serious injury	1.4 (0.56)	12.1 (3.71)[b]	9.3 (2.36)[c]
Frequency of abuse	4.7 (1.53)	7.6 (2.11)	13.2 (3.46)[b]
Duration of abuse	16.3 (6.31)[a]	28.1 (10.35)[a]	53.2 (26.14)[a]
Frequency of injury	4.7 (1.61)	10.7 (3.25)[b]	26.4 (8.26)[a]

[a]$p(F)$ = .001.
[b]$p(F)$ = .01.
[c]$p(F)$ = .05.

explanatory variables derived from risk markers for victims, assailants, and couples (see Hotaling and Sugarman, 1986). The CTS violence measure was a scale derived from the CTS assault items (Straus, 1983) and modified to include sexual assault. The CTS abuse scale added verbal abuse (threats, insults, harassment) and sexual assault to the CTS violence items.[35] The data are based on self-reports of abuse histories from victims who participated in legal and social interventions (N = 270). Explained variance of marital violence for each of the three predictor sets varied according to the measure of marital violence. The results show the *risk of underestimation of the severity of marital violence when only one behavioral dimension of that violence is considered.* Moreover, evaluations of the comparative effectiveness of interventions also may vary according to the measure of violence or accrued harm.

With the same data set, the efficacy of legal and social interventions was compared by using several measures of marital "violence" following legal or social interventions: the CTS aggression and CTS violence scales, calls to police, the severity of injuries sustained, and the occurrence of specific acts of harassment (such as threats to children or the victim, or economic reprisals). Results are shown in Table 7. (Data were based on self-reports by victims for each variable during a four-month period following participation in legal, social, or other family violence interventions.)

Results show that the *efficacy* of interventions varied according to the measure used. Mean scale scores for recipients of each service are shown, and significant differences with nonrecipients are indicated in the table. Analysis of variance (ANOVA) results for each intervention differed according to the measure of marital violence or abuse. For example, abuse and violence toward recipients of restraining orders were greater than for recipients of other services, but restraining order recipients called the police fewer times. The severity of injury varied little among recipients of vastly different services, but measures of aggression and violence varied extensively. Participants in mediation programs experienced less harassment but higher rates of aggression and violence than recipients of other services. Moreover, covariates for prior calls to police were significant for each measure. The implications of discrepant definitions and measures of spouse abuse for policy and program development are apparent.

Certainly, the social and legal meanings of aggression and violence differ, and theory on marital violence should encompass

TABLE 7 Analysis of Variance of Postintervention Aggression by Type of Intervention[a]

Intervention	CTS Aggression	CTS Violence	Severity of Injury	Calls to Police[b]	Harassment
Legal services	0.83	0.49	1.07	0.28	0.84
Legal advocacy	−.83	0.49	1.07	0.29	0.87
Sherter services	0.90	0.47	1.08	0.32[c]	0.93[d]
Information and referral	0.79[c]	0.45[d]	1.07[d]	0.25	0.75
Nonlegal advocacy	0.79	0.43	1.09	0.29	0.86[d]
Mediation	1.06	0.53	1.12	0.24	0.35
Counseling	0.87	0.49	1.08	0.25	0.71
Restraining order	1.18[d]	0.71[d]	1.10	0.27	0.65
Covariates					
Calls to police	e	e	e	e	e
Prior injury	d	ns	ns	ns	ns

NOTE: ns indicates data is not significant.

[a]Mean scale scores.
[b]Categorical scale for postintervention calls to police.
[c]$p(F) = .05$.
[d]$p(F) = .10$.
[e]$p(F) = .001$.

SOURCE: Fagan et al. (1984).

both dimensions. The social meaning of aggression is critical to theory that places these acts in the larger context of violence toward wives. However, these distinctions may have little bearing on criminal justice policy because the nonphysical dimensions of aggression—with the exception of threat—are less relevant (or perhaps not at all relevant) to codified law and, accordingly, to the criminal justice process. Yet, in the evaluation of legal policy, distinctions between physical injury and nonphysical harm (e.g., economic retaliation or psychological abuse) can lead to very different conclusions about behavioral change and the impact of law reform.

Family violence research has been concerned with explaining the occurrence of aggression in families, not just assaults. It has focused on identifying explanations of a broad range of aggressive acts (threats, physical abuse, harassment) to design interventions that will reduce the likelihood of their recurrence for the victim and, by extension, by the assailant. In-depth research on marital violence has extensively applied a context-specific approach to discern the intention and meaning of aggressive acts as part of theory construction and validation, and has used measures that include both physical and nonphysical injury to test theory (Dobash and Dobash, 1983). Samples have generally been clinical or purposive samples of victims or former victims (Frieze and Browne, 1989). Theories derived from this research have examined the ecological and societal contributions to aggression, factors again extraneous to the logic of the criminal justice process.

Criminological research, in contrast, relies on studies of offenders more than on victimization research for policy development. Research utilization in criminal justice has emphasized studies with several discernible characteristics: offenders as subjects, not respondents; experiments or quasiexperiments, rather than descriptive studies with clinical samples; violence measures that operationalize codified law or behaviors and that also deemphasize nonphysical aggression, injury, or harm; independent variables that operationalize official responses to marital violence or the flow of cases through the system and test explicit formulations of deterrence theory; and—most important—policy applications that directly contribute to strategies to sanction and control offenders as a means of reducing marital violence. Exceptions to this are the theories and empirical knowledge that have informed the design of treatment programs for males who assault their women partners.

Given this emphasis, important information from other studies or paradigms has not been used to inform criminal justice policy. We know, for example, that men who assault female partners often assault strangers as well; that the severity of spousal assault is well correlated with stranger assaults (Fagan et al., 1983); that domestic assailants may move on from one abusive relationship to another (Elliott, 1989); and that abusive male partners may generalize their violence from intimates to strangers (Shields et al., 1988). Yet there is little evidence that prosecutors use such information to target men who assault spouses (frequently, severely, or in conjunction with other assaults) for high-priority prosecution. Similar research suggests that prior calls to police for domestic violence are a risk factor for serious injury (Fagan and Wexler, 1987a). Yet few law enforcement agencies report routine checks for prior domestic disturbances as a criterion or guideline for specific response decisions. Threats in the context of a long-standing violent relationship should be regarded differently from threats to strangers (Walker, 1984), but again these rarely inform police response decisions.

The selectivity of the criminal justice system in utilizing research on marital violence reflects policies that determine their function in marital violence cases. A narrow view—emphasizing offender detection and punishment—suggests that the current state of affairs does not merit significant change. For example, Zimring (1989) suggests that a specific jurisprudence of family violence is unnecessary, but even in this view the effectiveness of criminal justice policies may benefit from knowledge gained in research on marital violence. The reverse condition also seems to be important: Knowledge of the general violence patterns of a male who assaults his spouse should signify the risks of further violence in that couple. If criminal justice policies expand to include victim protection and the use of criminal sanctions to avert violence, the contributions of research on marital violence to improving the effectiveness of policy are obvious.

IMPACTS ON POLICY THROUGH LEGAL PRECEDENT: APPLICATION OF THE SELF-DEFENSE PLEA TO BATTERED WOMEN

Marital homicide cases illustrate the complexity of introducing research on marital violence into the adjudication process. The development of defense strategies for abused women who kill their assailants (Fiora-Gormally, 1978; Thyfault, 1984; Thyfault et al., 1987) has provided a unique opportunity to influence criminal justice policy. Unlike the processes that influenced other criminal justice or legislative reforms, the introduction of research on marital violence into courtroom deliberations—and, ultimately, into case law—is the result of tactical maneuvers by defense attorneys to establish the context of extreme violence and to show how the conditions of violence can shape the perceptions, social judgments, and responses of victims to their assailants. The result is a slow but perceptible accumulation of case law that is built on research on marital violence and reflects the foundations of its unique research paradigms (Thyfault, 1984).

In general, *self-defense* is defined as the justifiable use of a reasonable amount of force against an adversary, when one reasonably believes that one is in immediate danger of unlawful bodily harm and that the use of such force is necessary to avoid this harm (LaFave and Scott, 1972). This perception, and the decision on how much force is needed to prevent further assault, need only be *reasonable*, even if it turns out later to be erroneous. Whether the use of force (or the amount of force used) against an assailant is justified on the grounds of self-defense depends in large part on the perceptions of the defender and whether those perceptions can be shown to be reasonable in light of the circumstances of the case. Components of the self-defense plea, including imminent danger, equal force, accuracy of perceptions, and (in some states) efforts to retreat, require evidence derived from analyses of the history and context of violence in the relationship.

The key to the use of the self-defense plea for abused women lies in the definition of what perceptions are reasonable for a female victim of physical or sexual assault (Schneider, 1980; Schneider and Jordan, 1981). Evidence on the basis of these perceptions in abused women derives directly from the studies of victims of severe wife assault, the context of violence and its influence on the victims' perceptions and judgments, and the circumstances surrounding the history of the assaultive relationship. A history of physical abuse alone does not justify the killing of an abuser (i.e., being a "battered woman" is not a defense for homicide). Having been physically assaulted or threatened by the abuser in the past is pertinent to such cases only as it contributes to the defendant's state of mind at the time the killing occurred, in that it formed a reasonable basis for the woman's perception of (herself or a child) being in imminent danger of severe bodily harm or death at the hands of her partner.

Thus, Browne (1987) interprets the application of the self-defense plea to battered women cases as requiring more than simply a history of physical abuse. Also necessary is a knowledge of the history of the circumstances surrounding both prior violence and the specific fatal incident. These are critical for establishing the woman's perceptions at the time of the homicide—particularly in evaluating the imminent danger to herself based on the escalating history of previous violence and the absence of any means to stop it. Browne notes that the use of this defense is not intended to establish new law, but rather that it uses family violence research to inform "existing statutes to account for differences in the experiences of women and men . . . so that the same standard can be applied to all victims" (Browne, 1987:175).

SOCIAL ORGANIZATION OF THE COURTS AND MARITAL VIOLENCE

In many jurisdictions the "criminalization" of marital violence resulted in a sudden, rapid increase in the number of wife assault defendants arrested and referred to lower or superior courts

(Goolkasian, 1986). In effect, an entire new class of defendants entered the criminal justice system, whose offenses and (at times) offender characteristics were quite different from former case types. If the utilization of research on marital violence has been selective, one explanation may lie in the unique nature of marital violence cases in the criminal court and the conflicts generated by this new class of defendants in the social organization of the court and the established norms within it. Organizational perspectives that stress the structural context of legal decision making suggest that holistic (Emerson, 1983) and working group processes of decision making (Eisenstein and Jacob, 1977) will determine case outcomes, leaving little room for the more objective contributions of research. Family violence research generally has not addressed the social organizational issues that influence policy changes in the criminal justice system.

If sanctions are the product of structural factors in the courts (Hagan and Bumiller, 1983), then the effects of organizational characteristics should prove significant. The going rate for an offense is *the sanction that officials expect an offender to receive for specific offenses* and is thought to be influenced by organizational factors independent of case-specific variables (Casper and Brereton, 1984). Emerson (1983) defines the "stream of cases" facing officials as influencing legal decisions in several respects. Cases are evaluated for prosecution and sentencing relative to other cases, as well as on their merits. Thus, the relative seriousness of cases changes at different stages of processing, so that a case may appear to be more serious at arrest than at sentencing, when other cases have been winnowed out.

Accordingly, a felony assault against a wife may seem quite serious to the arresting officer faced with less serious domestic incidents, but less serious at sentencing in contrast to stranger cases involving offenders with prior criminal records. This process may be especially sensitive to the differential processes of accumulating a prior record for domestic versus other assaults. In sorting cases for prosecution—or prioritizing cases for last-resort sanctions—criminal justice officials may look for guidance to a "going rate." The relatively brief history of wife assault cases in criminal courts and the shifting priorities for prosecution in many urban areas have not allowed such a rate to develop among the closed social network of court actors involved in prosecution and adjudication policy.

The ability to invoke last-resort solutions, such as imprisonment, is a critical organizational function. Jacob (1983) observed that prosecutors in criminal court possess more information than other courtroom personnel and have a disproportionate influence over the disposition of cases. By introducing a new class of cases into an established "stream," prosecutors may alter the group dynamics developed over a lengthy period and in response to a shared experience base. Moreover, prosecutors have the "upper hand" traditionally, and their actions disproportionately influence the legal culture and routines of the criminal court (Jacob, 1983). The formalization of marital violence cases by prosecutors may introduce changes in the standard operating procedures and victim characteristics for personnel routinely involved in stranger violence cases. Further, a new set of legal actors (e.g., special prosecutors, victim advocates) has been introduced into the court system, specific to these cases.

Thus, the calculus of sanction severity may be influenced by changes in the legal actors, the formality and nature of their roles, the balance of knowledge of case specifics, and the absence of a going rate for punishment. In other words, the types of consensus usually present among criminal court actors may not be present when a new class of cases is introduced. In fact, dissent might result among legal officials concerning the going rate for marital violence, based not only on the absence of a knowledge base but also on their own attitudes toward marital violence and its severity.

These processes have been observed in the introduction of juvenile offenders into criminal courts (Hassenfeld and Cheung, 1985) and more generally in studies of organizational change in criminal courts (Mather, 1979). Although not a concern easily remedied by research on marital violence, this is an area in which understanding of the dynamics of organizational change can be influential. Fagan et al. (1984) found that changes in policy and procedure occurred and *endured* for marital violence cases when the political incentives and fiscal resources were provided to accommodate new procedures. For example, rather than displacing organizational functions or people, systems were expanded to accommodate the new class of cases and the people to process them. Judges remained reluctant to incarcerate marital violence cases other than the most seriously injurious ones. Thus, the creation of dispositional options was especially important in maintaining the calculus of when last-resort sanctions such as incarceration were invoked.

Paradigms of Social Control

The problem definition of marital violence reflected in criminal justice policies is one of individual pathology, and the appropriate remedy has been a strategy of deterrence and offender control (Gelles and Cornell, 1985). Earlier, the compatibility of offender treatment with this core philosophy was seen as a facilitator to research utilization of the growing knowledge about males who assault their female partners. For example, early treatment models were based on social learning principles (Dutton, 1988b; Sonkin et al., 1985)—an outlook especially compatible with individual deviance explanations of marital violence. The creation of treatment programs for wife assaulters provided the types of social and organizational accommodation described above to sustain change throughout the systems of social and legal control.

Offender control that protects victims, however, may be more difficult to implement and may lead to conflicts in paradigms of control. Specifically, conflicts may arise when risk factors suggest incarceration, but the going rate or prevailing offender control policies do not dictate incarceration. That is, *victim* protection policies may suggest that offender controls be activated that might otherwise not be used in an *offender*-focused policy.

For example, in an overcrowded local jail, a policy might be developed to ease overcrowding in which arrestees for marital violence can be released on low bail or their own recognizance. They may appear to be less of a danger than other violent offenders or alleged drug dealers, whose crimes threaten "public safety" and not the relatively "private" matter of family conflict. Exemptions from these release policies certainly are warranted in some (if not all) marital violence cases. Yet this places victim protection considerations in marital violence cases—and attendant offender control strategies—in direct conflict with other crime control strategies and broader criminal justice policy issues. Research on marital violence is *unequivocal* about the danger to victims posed by the balance of policy toward offender-based decision making; the chronic, escalating nature of marital violence poses special danger when retaliation for an arrest becomes a potential trigger for a violent or lethal episode (Browne, 1987). Yet the clash of control paradigms is apparent when considerations of public danger (from "street" criminals) and private safety of battered women compete for priority as factors in decision making and resource assignment.

Research on the differential effects of criminal justice sanctions also suggests that legal sanctions and social control of offenders are more effective for less serious cases (Fagan et al., 1984), but that victim protection models (e.g., removal of victims to a shelter, mandatory overnight incarceration of offenders) are more appropriate for more serious cases. Such disaggregation and prioritization of marital violence cases has not been evident in criminal justice policy development. Although some prioritization of cases for prosecution may occur, the winnowing process following arrest (Dutton, 1988b) suggests that police responses should consider the severity of violence and the consequences of an arrest in terms of both subsequent offender control decisions *and* victim protection considerations.

Knowledge about patterns of wife assault indicates that victim protection should also be a basic element in an offender control strategy for more serious cases, based on the potential harm unleashed (via retaliation) for victims in serious cases where arrests have occurred but offender control is uncertain. Although threats of victim retaliation occur in some stranger cases, they are not sufficiently frequent to merit a policy response. Moreover, such threats may not be considered legally salient enough to invoke a criminal justice response. (Yet when such threats occur in politically salient cases such as organized crime or high-level drug dealing, protection from reprisals is usually afforded to witnesses.) However, there is a potential interaction between offender control and victim protection in nearly all marital violence cases, especially when the victim and assailant share the custody of children or when prior threats have occurred. If invoking victim protection is associated with offender control strategies, a disincentive may be created for intervention. This conflict in control paradigms is rooted in the larger issues of measurement and definition, system capacity, organizational dynamics among system agencies, and the social and organizational "currency" of marital violence cases.

IMPLICATIONS FOR THEORY AND RESEARCH

Several complementary directions for research are evident from the foregoing review: the integration of stranger and marital violence behaviors to expand the concepts of criminal and marital violence careers; the patterns and processes of desistance from marital and other forms of intrafamily violence; the covariation of perceptions and salience of deterrence with social area characteristics; the cognitive and developmental effects of witnessing marital violence during childhood and adolescence; the relationship among variables such as intoxication, arousal, fear of intimacy, and aggression; and the interventions that empower victims and in turn strengthen the effects of those interventions. Methodological development is needed to validate and reconcile current measures of behavior and consequences. As new empirical evidence develops, triangulation of knowledge from separate research endeavors should be integrated to refine theory and explanatory models.

The literature cited in this paper also illustrates the methodological *dilemmas* of research on marital violence. Retrospective studies and the preponderance of victim reports as data sources highlight the limitations of theory and research on offender behavior. Victims may be too intimidated to report ongoing violence or unaware of aggression displaced onto new victims when the assailant leaves home. New efforts are needed to focus on assailants as research subjects—both to validate previous research and to answer new questions on career patterns of partner assault. Research on assailants also will help sort out the influences, perceptions, and decision-making processes of offenders in the intervals surrounding incidents of marital assault.

DO WE NEED A SPECIAL THEORY OF MARITAL VIOLENCE?

Is a special theory needed for marital violence and for violence that occurs within families? For decades, theorists have disagreed on whether specific forms of deviant behaviors are unitary or isomorphic phenomena. Similar debates within both criminology and family violence research have failed to resolve whether family violence is a special case of violence (Gelles and Straus, 1979). The continuing balkanization of marital violence research has added to the disagreement on the generality of violence in family settings. How can a broader theoretical base be developed?

If family violence is part of a generalized pattern of violent behaviors, can we then expect its career parameters and phases to parallel other types of violence patterns? The unique circumstances of, and situational influences in, family life form a special context that facilitates violence toward (particularly female) spouses. Gelles and Straus (1979) suggest that certain characteristics intrinsic to family life create the context and dynamics for violence, whereas partriarchical views (Dobash and Dobash, 1979; Yllo, 1988) suggest that cultural imperatives create motivations for violence unique to a "marital" setting.

Yet a general theory of violence has much appeal in light of the robust findings on violence in the childhood backgrounds of many familial and extrafamilial offenders. We reviewed consistent evidence that violence toward both strangers and intimates is learned early on in the home and reinforced through social interactions in later developmental phases. Social learning theorists suggest several processes, from modeling to reinforcement (Bandura, 1973; Pagelow, 1984). What may set apart stranger from intimate violence, or explain its overlap for a subset of offenders, are the concepts of culturally sanctioned sexual inequalities and traditional sex-role socialization.[36]

For example, Bowker (1983) showed how social supports for violence in the home are sustained and reinforced in later adult life. Where violence is learned, sanctioned, and reinforced through cultural or behavioral norms in the immediate community, it will more likely be chronic and/or more serious. By integrating these perspectives into a general learning model, it may be possible to understand and explain the various manifestations of violent behavior and the patterns of victim selection.

Many males avoid violence in adult life, despite strong socialization to violence as children or adults. Most abused male children avoid later violence as adults (e.g., see Miller and Challas, 1981) but may go on to live unproductive and unhappy lives marked by financial difficulties and behavioral problems such as high divorce rates and problematic alcohol use. Accordingly, the immunities toward family violence are also of etiological relevance. For those who do not grow up to become violent adults, either internal or external controls (or both) develop. Megargee (1983) described the way such inhibitors may restrain violent behaviors, even in the presence of strong motivation or habituation toward violence. Where motivation is high but so too are restraints on violence, violence is not likely to occur.

Distinctions among "generally" violent males, those violent toward family members only, and those violent toward nonfamily members only, suggest that cognitive processes shape victim selection in the development of aggression toward others. The internalization of social norms for violence toward women or children may contribute to male sex-role socialization during childhood (Dobash and Dobash, 1979; Russell, 1982), and help explain in part the selection of family members as victims. When childhood and adolescent socialization includes the threat or use of male violence toward family members, there may exist a propensity to commit violent acts against family members during adult years.

We have moved closer to understanding the relationship between different forms of family violence and their overlap with stranger violence. Despite the separation of theory and research in different forms of family and stranger violence, common etiological factors and correlates are evident. The implications of this paper regarding the status of men in families, the cultural supports for socialization of sex roles, and the ecological supports for family and stranger violence, suggest common ground for further theoretical work on the triggering of violent episodes. However, we still know relatively little about why patterns of victimization vary. Understanding the cognitive processes that shape victim selection are critical to resolving the question of factors that influence the generality of violence.

RESEARCH ON DESISTANCE FROM FAMILY VIOLENCE

Desistance research is an important part of the study of criminal careers, but a neglected one in the literature on violence and aggression in families. Fagan (1989) proposed a model for desistance from marital violence that identifies social psychological processes of decision making and extrication from social supports for marital violence. Questions of central importance to desistance research focus on the role and perception of sanctions, compared to personal circumstances, and the way in which formal and informal sanctions are interpreted.

The important role of peer supports for maintaining desistance suggests research to describe how patriarchal norms *originate*, and are operationalized, communicated, and reinforced. It is still unclear how patriarchy is translated to legitimate the use of violence to maintain dominance in the family. The recent evidence on social approval among adolescents for sexual aggression toward women (date rape) suggests that patriarchal beliefs develop well before adulthood and marriage (e.g., see Margolin et al., 1989). For these questions, ethnographic research in naturalistic settings may be especially valuable in understanding how peer norms are enforced and how they influence the development of violence careers and interactional styles in intimate relationships. Also, research on the ability of many men to avoid the predictable consequences of patriarchal influences will point out the sociolegal and moral restraints that help avert wife assault (Morash, 1986).

Desistance research also should focus on carefully specified issues of definition: conceptualization of desistance as a total cessation, a decreasing frequency or severity, or increasing intervals between "relapses", of violence. Selection of a period for desistance that is too long risks problems in recall, but selecting too short a period risks enumerating "false desistance." Desistance research with assailants in both domestic-only and general violence categories can reveal shifts in victimization patterns and factors that influence choices regarding victims.

SPECIFIC DETERRENCE

The discrepancy between the results of the Minneapolis experiment and the replication experiments calls for further experimentation. Differences in the samples and social areas from which cases were drawn, the substantive interventions of police in the experiments, and design and measurement artifacts may all explain the contradictory findings. Together with important research on the meaning and interpretation of arrest (Carmody and Williams, 1987; Williams and Hawkins, 1989a), the perception and salience of deterrent interventions seems to covary with assailant background characteristics and the social area in which the couple resides.

Longer follow-up and more sensitive measures will provide more information on the interpretation and salience of legal sanctions. Measurement and design also may produce artifactual results—for example, the use of dichotomous recidivism variables or emphasis on behavior to the exclusion of consequences—that hides both good and bad results. Concurrent extralegal sanctions, such as shelter and social disclosure, should be included in deterrence research. Strategies such as social disclosure and shelter involvement with victims also should be integrated as covariates into tests of the *combined effects* of legal and social sanctions. Sensible policy would recognize the variety of types of wife assaulters and incorporate these covariates in explaining the effects of sanctions. For example, police may alter their response in cases from informal to formal knowing that threats, property damage, or other nonphysical but chronic aggression has occurred as a prelude to a violent episode.

VIOLENCE CAREERS

The integration of stranger and intimate violence in career criminal research is a critical gap. Epidemiological data show not only that there are distinct types of "battering careers" but also that careers in marital and stranger violence converge as violence in either domain becomes more frequent and serious. As noted,

Blumstein et al. (1985) have identified specific career types—from "innocents" who have little to no criminal activity, to "desisters" who quit after a very short interval of criminal involvement, to "persisters" who often are high-rate offenders involved in serious crime. They concluded that each type is explained by unique etiological factors, and that the social and personal processes that sustain longer patterns also vary for desisters and persisters.

The concept of different battering careers in men who assault female partners is worthy of empirical study and can accommodate etiological questions as well as the development of career parameters. Unified theoretical perspectives on family and stranger violence can be tested to determine if a "special" theory of family violence is warranted. Career studies should examine the mutability of these patterns over time, changes in the ratio of inter- and intrafamily violent acts (both frequency and severity), and the risk markers or developmental sequences that may explain these shifts. The confluence of risk factors for both stranger and marital violence also suggests that paradigms from ecological research and explanations be integrated with research on violence toward intimate female partners.

Career research requires both general population samples and representative samples of known and self-identified offenders. Sampling at the extreme of the distribution of violent behaviors is necessary to ensure sufficient representation of high-rate and serious assailants. Research on the processes of initiation, escalation, and desistance requires more intensive study with smaller samples, using ethnographic methods to sample on the dependent variable. This complementary strategy can explore processes more effectively with populations generally unknown to official sources, whose behaviors otherwise remain hidden.

Retrospective study is the characteristic limitation of such career research, but recent developments, primarily in research on narcotics use and crime (Speckart and Anglin, 1986; Anglin and Speckart, 1988), offer techniques to minimize recall problems. Using key life events to establish temporal anchors, Anglin and Speckart (1988) traced the addiction careers of treated and untreated heroin users in California. Many of their subjects were over 50 years of age and were recalling with accuracy events of more than 30 years ago. These methods can be translated to the study of intrafamily violence to construct violence histories that have evolved over many years and through a variety of influences. Victimization patterns and displacement, other shifts in the frequency or severity of violence (lulls, episodes, relapses after lengthy desistance periods), and contributing situational factors (e.g., peer group embedment, legal or social sanctions, life events such as the birth of a child) can be temporally anchored over a multidecade period to establish "natural" violence careers and the factors that affect their course. How these patterns vary by social area and the social status of offenders are other important questions

ANALYSIS OF ORGANIZATIONAL CHANGE AND RESEARCH UTILIZATION

Study of the implementation and organizational accommodation of reform is a potentially fruitful avenue for research. Fagan et al. (1984) analyzed the ways in which services for victims were implemented, changed over time, and became institutionalized. They also examined the conditions that influenced the process of institutionalization and accommodation. Specific factors included the ability to establish "domain" or an area of acknowledged expertise, leadership, institutional sponsorship, personal and organizational incentives, ideology, and resources.

This type of research can address the social, organizational, and political dynamics of change in criminal justice policy and factors that influence its implementation and effectiveness. Despite inroads toward strengthening criminal justice responses, police and prosecutors still are likely to resist the loss of discretion, absent broader systemic changes that increase the salience of sanctions and the options for intervention. Careful research to illustrate the circumstances of organizational accommodation in a complex social system will contribute to the integration of marital violence cases in the criminal justice system.

Further study also is needed about the conditions under which marital violence or other criminological research has informed criminal justice policy toward spouse assault. Identifying the conditions under which research has been rejected or accepted, both organizationally and in terms of the research itself, can launch a body of knowledge on research utilization. Other studies are required on the extent to which policy changes have been influenced by research.

TREATMENT RESEARCH

Experiments on treatment effectiveness are critical. Development of outlets for judges to sanction offenders will effectively increase the salience of marital violence cases in the criminal justice system. Effective treatment also will provide greater safety for victims, although safety procedures should be an important element of all program designs for interventions. The development of types of treatment for specific types of assailants will also advance theory as well as effective programs.

Experimental research should include multiple group designs with multiple measures and sufficient follow-up periods to determine the supports that help avoid the decay of treatment. Implementation of experimental interventions should also receive close attention, to avoid the confounding of program failure with theory failure. Continuous measures of the independent variable are needed to discern further the reasons for the effects of treatment.

DEVELOPMENTAL EFFECTS OF WITNESSING MARITAL VIOLENCE

Research is needed to explain what is learned—and how that learning occurs—when children and adolescents observe marital violence in their homes of origin and in homes nearby. What types of stimulation or arousal occur when children observe parental conflict? How does reinforcement occur during later developmental stages? How is it linked to participation in other aggressive behaviors? What factors mediate or *offset* potential negative outcomes?

Experimental research in laboratory settings using vignettes and simulations should include children and adolescents of different age cohorts to examine learning processes and age-specific sensitivities to learning. Experiments should also test methods to extinguish learning or arousal as an intervention for children or adolescents who may be at risk from exposure to or witnessing marital violence. Interventions should be tested both for children in homes where marital violence occurs and for children who live in social areas with high rates of child abuse or spouse assaults.

INTERVENTIONS THAT EMPOWER VICTIMS

The complex strategies to end violence that were identified by Bowker (1983, 1986a,b) suggest that combinations of legal and social interventions, both formal and informal, can be used by victims to help bring about the cessation of marital violence. The efficacy of arrest or other sanctions depends in part on the specific means that victims want to use to end violence and bring about other changes that they may desire. Further research with victims is needed to identify the attributes of formal legal or social interventions that are effective in ending violence, by having victims participate in the substance and process of offender control. Similar research on informal sanctions also is necessary to determine what strategies empower victims to bring resources to bear within the relationship.

Specific strategies for empowerment should focus on neutralizing violence by raising its costs and altering the balance of marital power. Legal and social interventions should also be evaluated for their contributions to victim support and empowerment.

CONTINUING CONTROVERSY OVER GENDER DIFFERENCES

After little attention in the literature for more than a decade, gender differences in marital violence again have become a topic of debate (Straus, 1989; cf. Browne, 1993). The stakes are high in this controversy, because the interpretation of marital violence and the formulation of policies depend on the construction of definitions and measures of physical conflicts between spouses. The higher rates of severe assault by male spouses, the greater percentage of women injured by and requiring medical treatment for injuries inflicted by spouses or ex-spouses, and the twice higher rate of killings of female than male spouses, demonstrate important gender differences in assaults between intimate partners. Clearly, the victims of severe outcomes of partner assaults are women.

Evidence of the "mutuality" of violence overlooks the harm of marital violence that accrues differentially to women. The paradigm of behavioral counts brushes aside the disproportionate rate of injury and fatality among women victims, as well as their greater difficulty in restraining their assailants and in escaping. Further, there are validity problems in obtaining marital agreement about the origins of violent incidents and the frequency or level of force used. Claims that marital violence is mutual, or that women are as "violent" or assaultive as men in marriage, rely heavily on reports of participation rates—a misleading indicator of violent behavior when examined apart from offending rates.

The debate on gender differences has important implications for prevention and intervention. Browne and Williams (1989) showed that resource availability for woman victims of marital violence was associated with a reduction in the rate of female-perpetrated homicides. Yet, the implication of the "mutuality" assumption is that such interventions may be less effective than generalized violence prevention activities that target both men and women. Although these may make important contributions to reducing marital violence, they belie the greater risks to women of fatalities at the hands of their spouses (Browne and Williams, 1989).

CONCLUSIONS

The perspectives in this paper represent an effort to locate and explain marital violence in two larger theoretical contexts: interpersonal violence and the unique domain of family relations. The implications of the knowledge gained in the quarter century of empirical research on marital violence also can inform theory, research, and policy in other areas. Yet family violence continues to be viewed as an idiosyncratic crime, much like white-collar crime, and remains outside the mainstream of criminological theory and research (Fagan and Wexler, 1987a). The result is a focus on unique causes and solutions of specific crime types, that overlooks the common origins of different behaviors and the importance of situational influences on crime events and later stages of criminal careers. Advances in theory and practice to control marital violence may depend on integrative research that draws from a broader spectrum of empirical knowledge.

What We Still Need to Know

As research on marital violence advances, the questions that shape these efforts have become more focused on specific issues. The theoretical integration of explanations of marital violence with other forms of family violence will require testing assumptions about the processes and specific factors that distinguish these behaviors.

The triggers for arousal leading to assaults on wives, and the cognitive restructuring (of cues or interactions) that shapes aggressive responses to arousal, are important areas for theory and research. These are the transactional processes that explain the motivational component of an assault by a male spouse. In turn, the processes that translate cultural beliefs into social contexts and subcultural influences are critical to understanding how marital violence may be ecologically nested. Finally, the learning rules that shape intergenerational processes are little understood, as are the conditions under which early childhood witnessing is mitigated for nonviolent individuals in later life.

The latter presents important avenues for research and theory. Among couples or individuals with high concentrations of risk factors, important information can be gained from understanding the factors that mitigate marital violence. What kinship networks, marital dynamics, cultural supports and sanctions, relationship dynamics, and social controls influence these individuals? How are cultural dynamics mitigated in the distribution of marital power? What is the salience of legal controls and deterrents? Case-control studies can begin to answer many of these questions.

There also appear to be differences in the perception of sanctions and the interpretation of their meaning. The inconsistency between the experiments on arrest and their replications, and the implications of the Omaha study for coordination of arrest with later stages of criminal justice processing, suggest further research on how the meaning of arrest is conveyed to offenders. Are these sanctions perceived differently in different social areas and by different types of individuals?

With the early focus on the deterrent effects of arrest in misdemeanor cases of wife assault, much of the research on the criminal justice system's response to marital violence has focused on and been designed to test the effects of different police responses during domestic disturbance calls. As noted, in such research the focus in on the *offenders*, with women victims used as reporters of both current violence and recidivism.

However, another aspect of the justice system's response to violence in marital relationships—the existence of legislation designed to further protect and compensate victims of domestic violence—has received almost no attention by social science researchers. Such legislation would include ex parte and "permanent" (typically six months to one year) orders for the abuser to desist from abuse and/or vacate the home, orders for the transfer of custody of minor children to the victim, orders that the abuser provide monetary compensation to the victim for injuries and other losses, and stipulations that violations of such orders by the abuser constitute a criminal offense (e.g., see Browne, 1993).

In this area, it is particularly critical that the research be primarily victim focused: Although state domestic violence statutes vary somewhat in their terms, all require some degree of initiation on the part of the victim in empowering the justice system to act. Conversely, although judges and other justice system officials can express concern or disagreement, most statutes stipulate that victims' requests that orders be rescinded must be honored by the courts.

Browne (1986, 1987) point out that although such legislation is the *primary* legal response in most states to the problem of domestic violence, little systematic research has been done either on abused women's use of these legal options (once police contact has been made) or on the effectiveness of these options in producing the protection they are meant to provide. For example, little is known empirically about (1) the frequency with which women who have been informed of these options by police initiate actions under these provisions or chose not to pursue them; (2) the exogenous (e.g., relationship and social) circumstances associated with victims' decisions to initiate or not initiate action; (3) which criminal justice responses appear to facilitate or to impede victims' use of legal provisions for protection; (4) what factors influence women to follow through with these protections or ask that they be rescinded, once the orders have been obtained; or (5) the outcomes of their decisions as they relate to an increase or decrease in reassault or threat by the partner. Thus it is important to understand both victim circumstances—in terms of threat, relationship history, other support systems, and other exogenous variables—and the interaction between victims and the criminal justice system if we are to understand the patterns of use of domestic violence legislation or its effectiveness.

Research shows that interventions focused on victims can empower them to use legal sanctions and informal social resources to assist them in stopping violence (Bowker, 1983). How the use of these strategies is promoted by efforts to broaden their reach (through legislation, services to protect women victims as they pursue options, etc.), and in turn their effectiveness, should also guide plans for victim services. The safety of women whose spouses are in treatment has become a central issue in the design of interventions. Evaluation research and experimentation for women victims pursuing legal options, as well as those with assailants in treatment, should begin to address seriously this aspect of program or system impact.

Finally, larger questions demand an integration of the study of family violence with the more general literature on violence in society. Can we realistically expect marital violence to decrease when rates of stranger violence continue at high levels? What ecological effects ensue from these high rates of violence that reciprocally alter informal social controls (e.g., family disintegration) and divert resources toward punishment and control (Skogan, 1989)? What are the effects on marital violence of marriages falling under increasing economic strain, a factor closely related to arousal states that may trigger assaults? The nesting of marital violence within larger ecological forces that influence violence rates in general suggests that efforts to reduce and control family violence are intertwined with macrosocial efforts to reduce violence throughout society.

ACKNOWLEDGMENTS

The authors are grateful to Christopher Maxwell for assistance in data analysis, and to Joan McCord and Delbert Elliott for their thoughtful comments on the manuscript.

NOTES

1   These included killing young brides, forced suicides by new wives, wife beating, husband beating, husband-wife brawling, forced suicide of wives, wife raiding, and marital rape.

2   Wife beating was defined as the physical assault of a wife by her husband and includes slapping, shoving, hitting, pushing, hitting with an object, burning, cutting, or shooting. Its prevalence in a society was measured on an ordinal scale from rare (occurs not at all or in a small percentage of households) to common (occurs in all or nearly all households). The severity of wife beating was also measured on an ordinal scale from painful (beating results in pain but no debilitating injury) to mutilation or death (permanent physical injuries such as loss of digits or limbs, or death).

3   Another study found that 57 wives and 128 husbands were prosecuted for both verbal and physical abuse in the six New England colonies between 1630 and 1699. The women were typically charged with "nagging," rather than with physical assaults (Koehler, 1980, cited in Pleck, 1987).

4   According to Pleck (1989), Judge Buller in England first asserted the rule in 1783. He was ridiculed by the press, and a cartoonist lampooned him as "Judge Thumb." Pleck found no court rulings that explicitly endorsed the "rule of thumb."

5   IACP (1967:3) training materials stated that ". . . in dealing with family disputes, the power of arrest should be exercised as a last resort" (cited in Elliott, 1989).

6   Ironically, it was dissatisfaction with the "crisis intervention" and "conflict management" roles adopted by police that led to legislation in Pennsylvania and Massachusetts enabling women victims of marital violence to obtain protective orders that brought marital violence into the criminal jurisdiction. Mandatory arrest statutes and policies followed these developments.

7   Severe violence included kicking, biting, hitting with the fist, hitting or trying to hit with an object, beating up, threatening with a gun or knife, and using a gun or knife.

8   See Elliott and Huizinga (1983) for a discussion of the validity issues in this procedure.

9   Spouse abuse was defined as an assault without theft in which the offender was the victim's spouse or ex-spouse. No distinction was made between spouse or ex-spouse in that iteration of the NCS. Cohabitating adults also were excluded in the definition. Although the survey made no distinction between current and former spouses, the offender did not have a right to be in the victim's home in 26 percent of the spouse abuse victimizations. Gaquin assumed that these assaults were inflicted by ex-spouses.

10   The construction of NCS items does not permit precise calculations of the interval between victimizations. Respondents are asked to indicate whether they had been victimized in the previous six months. Accordingly, the range of elapsed time between incidents may be from six months to one year, depending on when in the recall periods the incidents actually occurred.

11   The percentage of nonstranger victimizations of females who were never married was greater than for married females but less than for divorced or separated females. However, the age range may explain disparities between never-married women and others. Never-married women were more likely to include females less than 20 years of age and involved in dating relationships with males who were at the peak age for assault victimizations.

12   Another 10 percent were difficult to classify, but the authors suggested that they had some of the indicators of marital assaults.

13   The items ask whether, in the past year, the husband or partner ever tried to, or forced the respondent to, have sexual relations by using physical force, such as holding the respondent down, or hitting or threatening to hit the respondent. Other items ask how many times this happened in the past year and if it happened before the reporting year.

14   Assaults included the following: threw objects at the other person; pushed, grabbed, or shoved; slapped; kicked, bit, or hit with a fist; hit or tried to hit with something; beat up the other; choked; threatened with a gun or knife; used a gun or knife. Any one of these acts constituted an assault. The sample included married and cohabitating couples. Marital violence in separated and divorced couples was not measured because of their exclusion from the sample.

15   As mentioned earlier, severe violence included kicking, biting, hitting with the fist, hitting or trying to hit with an object, beating up, threatening with a gun or knife, using a gun or knife.

16   These rates were calculated only for couples in which a female committed at least one assault. Elsewhere, Straus (1990a) reports an offending rate for males of "over six assaults per year," presumably in all couples where at least one assault occurred. No comparable rate is provided for women.

17   In the 1985 NFVS, the question of who struck the first blow is limited to the most recent event.

18   Percent urban population, percent African American, population mobility.

19   Abuse included six items: threats of violence, push/slap/ shove·(minor violence), punch/kick/bite, threaten with weapon, use a weapon, and sexual assault.

20   An exception is Sherman and Berk (1984), who collected data on both official and self-reports of violence following police intervention in Minneapolis. Dunford et al. (1989) also collected both official and self-report data but did not report a correlation.

21   Martha then went on to have sexual relations with their young dinner guest, a male assistant professor, illustrating the image of alcohol as a disinhibitor of sexual behaviors as well as aggression.

22   Hotaling and Sugarman (1986) found that abuse of other substances was not a significant risk factor that was positively correlated with spouse assault. Rather, they found an equal number of studies that indicated either positive or negative associations of spouse abuse with other substances. Accordingly, alcohol but not the use of other substances appears to be a significant correlate of wife assault.

23   Based on reports from spouse abuse victims (in shelters) or assailants in treatment programs.

24   The survey did not inquire about the co-occurrence of intoxication and spouse abuse—whether violence occurred while either of the partners was intoxicated. Fagan et al. (1983) asked victims whether drug or alcohol use accompanied violence. There was a modest, positive association for alcohol use, but a weak, negative association for drug use during violent episodes.

25   This does not deny the distribution of family violence across social classes. See Straus et al. (1980) and Straus and Gelles (1986).

26   Only one study seems to show otherwise: Miller et al. (1988), comparing alcoholic women in treatment (N = 45) with women in a random sample of households (N = 40) and controlling for age, found that alcoholic women more often were victims of marital violence. However, alcohol use and witnessing marital

violence were correlated with each other as well as with spouse assault, suggesting a spurious relationship. Kantor and Straus (1987), using NFVS data, also found an association between alcohol use and victimization, but the Miller study suggests that there is a "third factor" in the relationship.

27 Whether the function is linear or nonlinear has not been empirically assessed for spouse assaults, but there have been efforts to assess risk factors for child abuse and neglect (Starr, 1988). Similar efforts have been applied to adolescent substance use (Bry et al., 1982). This approach has rarely been used in criminological research.

28 See Straus (1976) and Yllo (1983) for specific variables for patriarchy. Gender inequalities (wage differentials, labor market segmentation, political representation) and media portrayals of women are most often cited as indices of patriarchy.

29 Use of force as defense of male authority, normative attitudes supporting violence toward wives, compulsive masculinity, economic constraints and discrimination, burdens of child care (and failure to provide relief of these burdens), myth of the intrinsic weakness of the single-parent household, preeminence of the caretaker/wife role for women, women's negative self-image, male orientation of the justice system.

30 Bowker analyzed reports from 1,000 victims on the relation between social embedment in male subculture and the severity of husband's violence toward wives. Embedment was measured by the frequency of assailant contacts with males only and the number of visits to bars without his wife. For both measures, social embedment in male subcultures was significantly associated with the frequency and severity of spouse assault (Bowker, 1986a,b).

31 Power is defined alternately in terms of dominance, decision making, and relative levels of resources (Frieze and McHugh, 1981); the stronger taking advantage of the weaker (Finkelhor, 1983); coercion through the threat of physical violence (Straus et al., 1980); or demographic characteristics that reflect aggregate social status of ethnic or racial groups (Berk et al., 1983).

32 Dutton (1987) compares this to the finding of Hood and Sparks (1970) that police made arrests in 20 percent of the cases where they attended and decided that a crime had been committed.

33 Most jurisdictions authorize arrest whenever there is probable cause that a felony assault has occurred. The degree of injury or the presence of a weapon generally qualifies a felony charge. For

misdemeanors, there are restrictions on arrest in assault cases including corroboration or "in-presence" requirements (Lerman, 1986). Thus, victims must initiate a complaint or warrant to effect an arrest. The intent of mandatory arrest statutes is to eliminate these restrictions on misdemeanor wife assault, the most common charge category for domestic assaults, and to allow officers to make misdemeanor arrests on the basis of either the victim's hearsay or their own probable cause determination. In California, these conditions were established by providing concurrent status as both felony and misdemeanor for domestic assault. Other states (e.g., Washington) have mandated arrest in all domestic assaults based on probable cause or victim complaint.

34 For example, the decision to prosecute an assailant charged with his nth assault should take into account the recurring nature of these events and the risk that chronic assaults pose for an escalation of violence and injury.

35 For the abuse and violence scales, Guttman scaling procedures were used to create continuous variables. The coefficient of scalability was .639 for violence and .591 for abuse. The coefficient of reproducibility was .916 for violence and .891 for abuse, both well within the conventional thresholds for acceptance of scale properties (Edwards, 1957). As noted earlier, both procedures placed sexual assault atop the hierarchies of abuse and violence.

36 Socialization processes also may reinforce status hierarchies based on males' economic roles in the family as well as their superior physical strength. The link among power differentials or status hierarchies, male socialization processes, and violence in the family is beyond the scope of this paper. Straus (1976) has examined these links in greater detail, showing how wife assault by males is determined in part by their acceptance of violence, which in turn is a normative process.

REFERENCES

Adler, P.A.
  1985 *Wheeling and Dealing.* New York: Columbia University
Akers, R.L, M. Krohn, L. Lanza-Kaduce, and M. Radosevich
  1979 Social learning and deviant behavior: A specific test of a general theory. *American Sociological Review* 44:635-655.
Alford, R.D.
  1982 Intimacy and disputing styles within kin and nonkin relationships. *Journal of Family Issues* 3:361-374.

American Humane Association
  1980 *National Analysis of Official Child Abuse and Neglect Reporting (1978)*. Washington, D.C.: U.S. Department of Health and Human Services.
Anglin, M.D., and G. Speckart
  1988 Narcotics use and crime: A multisample, multimethod analysis. *Criminology* 26(2):197-234.
Bandura, A.
  1973 *Aggression: A Social Learning Analysis*. Englewood Cliffs, N.J.: Prentice Hall.
  1979 The social learning perspective: Mechanisms of aggression. In H. Toch, ed., *Psychology of Crime and Criminal Justice*. New York: Holt, Rinehart and Winston.
Bard, M.
  1970 *Training police as Specialists in Family Crisis Intervention*. National Institute of Law Enforcement and Criminal Justice. Washington, D.C.: U.S. Department of Justice.
Bard, M., and J. Zacker
  1971 The prevention of family violence: Dilemmas of community intervention. *Journal of Marriage and the Family* 33:677-682.
Barling, J., K.D. O'Leary, E.N. Jouriles, D. Vivian, and K.E. MacEwen
  1987 Factor similarity of the Conflict Tactics Scales across samples, spouses, and sites: Issues and implications. *Journal of Family Violence* 2:37-55.
Becker, H.
  1963 *Outsiders: Studies in the Sociology of Deviance*. New York: Free Press.
Berk, R.A., and P.J. Newton
  1985 Does arrest really deter wife battery? An effort to replicate the findings of the Minneapolis Spouse Abuse Experiment. *American Sociological Review* 50(2):253-262.
Berk, R.A., S.F. Berk, D.R. Loseke, and D. Rauman
  1983 The myth of mutuality in battering. In D. Finkelhor, R. Gelles, G. Hotaling, and M. Straus, eds., *The Dark Side of Families*. Beverly Hills, Calif.: Sage Publications.
Berk, R.A., G. Smyth, and L.W. Sherman
  1988 When random assignment fails: Some lessons from the Minneapolis spouse abuse experiment. *Journal of Quantitative Criminology* 4(3):209-223.
Berk, R., A. Campbell, R. Klap, and B. Western
  1992 The deterrent effect of arrest in incidents of domestic violence: A Bayesian analysis of four field experiments. *American Sociological Review* 57:698-708.
Biernacki, P.A., and D. Waldorf
  1981 Snowball sampling: Problems and techniques of chain referral sampling. *Sociological Methods and Research* 10(2):141-163.

Billingham, R.E., and A.R. Sack
  1987 Conflict resolution tactics and the level of emotional commit-
        ment among unmarrieds. *Human Relations* 40: 59-74.
Binder, A., and J.W. Meeker
  1988 Experiments as reforms. *Journal of Criminal Justice* 16(4):347-
        358.
Blackstone, W.
  1765 *Commentaries on the Laws of England, Book 4.* Philadelphia,
        Pa.: R. Welsh & Co. (reprinted in 1897).
Block, C.R.
  1987 Lethal Violence at Home: Racial/Ethnic Differences in Domes-
        tic Homicide in Chicago, 1965 to 1981. Paper presented at the
        annual meeting of the American Society of Criminology, Chi-
        cago, November.
Blumstein, A., D.P. Farrington, and S. Moritra
  1985 Delinquency careers: Innocents, desisters, and persisters. In
        M. Tonry and N. Morris, eds., *Crime and Justice: An Annual
        Review of Research*, Vol. 6. Chicago: University of Chicago
        Press.
Blumstein, A., J. Cohen, J.A. Roth, and C.A. Visher, eds.
  1986 *Criminal Careers and "Career Criminals."* Washington, D.C.:
        National Academy Press.
Bograd, M.
  1988 Feminist perspectives on wife abuse: An introduction. In. M.
        Bograd and K. Yllo, eds., *Feminist Perspectives on Wife Abuse.*
        Beverly Hills, Calif.: Sage Publications.
Bowker, L.
  1983 *Beating Wife-Beating.* Lexington, Mass.: D.C. Health.
  1984 Coping with wife abuse: Personal and social networks. In A.R.
        Roberts, ed., *Battered Women and Their Families.* New York:
        Springer.
  1986a The meaning of wife beating. *Currents* 2:39-43.
  1986b Empowering Women: The Only Way to End Domestic Vio-
        lence. Paper presented at the third national conference of the
        National Coalition Against Domestic Violence, St. Louis, Mo.,
        July.
Breedlove, R.K., J.W. Kennish, D.M. Sanker, and R.K. Sawtell
  1977 Domestic violence and the police: Kansas City. Pp. 22-33 in
        *Domestic Violence and the Police: Studies in Detroit and Kan-
        sas City.* Washington, D.C.: Police Foundation.
Bridges, G., and J.G. Weis
  1989 Measuring violent behavior: Effects of study design on reported
        correlates of violence. In N.A. Weiner and M.E. Wolfgang, eds.,
        Violent Crime, Violent Criminals. Newbury Park, Calif.: Sage
        Publications.
Browne, A.
  1986 Assault and homicide at home: When battered women kill. In

M.J. Saks and L. Saxe, eds., *Advances in Applied Social Psychology*, Vol. 3. Hillsdale, N.J.: Lawrence Erlbaum Associates.

1987　*When Battered Women Kill*. New York: Macmillan/Free Press.

1993　Violence against women by male partners: Prevalence, incidence, and policy implications. *American Psychologist* 48:1077-1087.

Browne, A., and D.G. Dutton

1990　Risks and alternatives for abused women: What do we currently know? In R. Roesch, D.G. Dutton, and V.F. Sacco, eds., *Family Violence: Perspectives in Research and Practice*. Vancouver: Simon Fraser University.

Browne, A., and R. Flewelling

1986　Women as Victims or Perpetrators of Homicide. Paper presented at the annual meeting of the American Society of Criminology, Atlanta, Ga., November.

Browne, A., and K.R. Williams

1989　Exploring the effects of resource availability and the likelihood of female-perpetrated homicides. *Law & Society Review* 23(1):75-94.

1993　Gender, intimacy, and lethal violence: Trends from 1976 through 1987. *Gender and Society* 7:78-98.

Brownfield, D.

1986　Social class and violent behavior. *Criminology* 24:421-438.

Browning, J.J., and D.G. Dutton

1986　Assessment of wife assault with the conflict tactics scale: Using couple data to quantify the differential reporting effect. *Journal of Marriage and the Family* 48:375-379.

Brutz, J.L., and B.B. Ingoldsby

1984　Conflict resolution in Quaker families. *Journal of Marriage and the Family* 46:21-26.

Bry, B.H., P. McKeon, and R.J. Pandina

1982　Extent of drug use as a function of number of risk factors. *Journal of Abnormal Psychology* 91:273-79.

Bulcroft, R.A., and M.A. Straus

1975　Validity of Husband, Wife, and Child Reports of Conjugal Violence and Power. Unpublished paper, Family Research Laboratory, University of New Hampshire, Durham.

Caesar, P.L.

1988　Exposure to violence in families of origin among wife abusers and maritally nonviolent men. *Violence and Victims* 3(1):49-64.

Caffey, J.

1946　Multiple fractures in the long bones of infants suffering from chronic subdural hematoma. *American Journal of Roentgenology, Radium Therapy, and Nuclear Medicine* 56:163-173.

Carmody, D.C., and K.R. Williams

1987　Wife assault and perceptions of sanctions. *Violence and Victims* 2(1):25-38.

Casper, J.D., and D. Brereton
1984 Evaluating criminal justice reforms. *Law & Society Review* 18:122-144.

Centerwall, B.S.
1984 Race, socioeconomic status and domestic homicide, Atlanta 1971-72. *American Journal of Public Health* 74:813-815.

Chimbos, P.D.
1978 Marital Violence: A Study of Interspousal Homicide. Unpublished manuscript, R. & E. Research Associates, San Francisco.

Chin, K.
1994 Out-of-town brides: International marriage and wife abuse among Chinese immigrants. *Journal of Comparative Family Studies* 25:53-70.

Clarke, C.
1987 Domestic Violence: A Community Survey. Unpublished manuscript, Department of Psychology, University of Illinois, Champaign.

Clarke, R.V., and D.B. Cornish
1985 Modeling offenders decisions: A framework for research and policy. In M. Tonry and N. Morris, eds., *Crime and Justice: An Annual Review of Research*, Vol. 6. Chicago: University of Chicago Press.

Coleman, D.H., and M.A. Straus
1983 Alcohol abuse and family violence. Pp. 104-124 in E. Gottheil, K.A. Druley, T.E. Skoloda, and H.M. Waxman, eds., *Alcohol, Drug Abuse and Aggression*. Springfield, Ill.: Charles C. Thomas.
1986 Marital power, conflict, and violence in a nationally representative sample of American couples. *Violence and Victims* 1(2):141-157.

Collins, J.J., Jr.
1983 Alcohol use and expressive interpersonal violence: A proposed explanatory model. Pp. 5-25 in E. Gottheil, K.A. Druley, T.E. Skoloda, and H.M. Waxman, eds., *Alcohol, Drug Abuse and Aggression*. Springfield, Ill.: Charles C. Thomas.
1988 Suggested explanatory frameworks to clarify the alcohol use/violence relationship. *Contemporary Drug Problems* 15:107-121.

Critchlow-Leigh, B.
1986 The powers of John Barleycorn: Beliefs about the effects of alcohol on social behavior. *American Psychologist* 41:751-764

Daly, M., and M. Wilson
1987 Evolutionary social psychology and family homicide. *Science* 242:519-524.
1988 *Homicide.* New York: Aldine de Gruyter.

Davidson, T.
1978 *Conjugal Crime.* New York: Hawthorne Books.

Dobash, R.E., and R.P. Dobash
1979 *Violence Against Wives: A Case Against the Patriarchy.* New York: Free Press.
1983 The context-specific approach. Pp. 261-276 in D. Finkelhor, R.J. Gelles, G.T. Hotaling, and M.A. Straus, eds., *The Dark Side of Families: Current Family Violence Research.* Beverly Hills, Calif.: Sage Publications.
Dobash, R.P., R.E. Dobash, M. Wilson, and M. Daly
1992 The myth of sexual symmetry in marital violence. *Social Problems* 39:71-91.
Dodge, K.A., J.E. Bates, and G.S. Petit
1990 Mechanisms in the cycle of violence. *Science* 250(December):1678-1683.
Downs, W.R., D. Werner, and B.A. Miller
1989 Differential Patterns of Partner-to-Woman Violence: A Comparison of Samples of Community, Alcohol-Abusing, and Battered Women. Paper presented at the annual meeting of the American Society of Criminology, Reno, Nev., November.
Dunford, F.W., D. Huizinga, and D.S. Elliott
1989 The Omaha Domestic Violence Policy Experiment. Final Report, National Institute of Justice, U.S. Department of Justice, Washington, D.C.
1990 The role of arrest in domestic assault: The Omaha Police Experiment. *Criminology* 28(2):183-206.
Dutton, D.G.
1982 Severe wife battering as deindividuated violence. *Victimology: An International Journal* 7(1-4):13-23.
1985 An ecologically nested theory of male violence toward intimates. *International Journal of Womens Studies* 8(4):404-413.
1986a The outcome of court-mandated treatment for wife assault: A quasi-experimental evaluation. *Violence and Victims* 1(3):163-175.
1986b Wife assaulter's explanations for assault: The neutralization of self-punishment. *Canadian Journal of Behavioural Science* 18(4):381-390.
1987 The criminal justice response to wife assault. *Law and Human Behavior* 11(3):189-206.
1988a Profiling of wife assaulters: Preliminary evidence for a trimodal analysis. *Violence and Victims* 3(1):5-30.
1988b *The Domestic Assault of Women: Psychological and Criminal Justice Perspectives.* Boston: Allyn and Bacon.
Dutton, D.G., and J.J. Browning
1987 Power struggles and intimacy anxieties as causative factors of violence in intimate relationships. In G. Russell, eds., *Violence in Intimate Relationships.* New York: Spectrum.
1988 Concern for power, fear of intimacy and aversive stimuli for wife abuse. Pp. 163-175 in G.T. Hotaling, D. Finkelhor, J.T. Kirkpatrick, and M. Straus, eds., *Family Abuse and Its Conse-*

quences: New Directions for Research. Beverly Hills, Calif.: Sage Publications.

Dutton, D.G., and S.L. Painter
1981 Traumatic bonding: The development of emotional attachments in battered women and other relationships of intermittent abuse. *Victimology: An International Journal* 6:139-155.

Dutton, D.G., and C.E. Strachan
1987 Motivational needs for power and dominance as differentiating variables of assaultive and non-assaultive male populations. *Violence and Victims* 2(3):145-156.

Dutton, D.G., S.G. Hart, L.W. Kennedy, and K.R. Williams
1991 Arrest and the reduction of repeat wife assault. In E. Buzawa and C. Buzawa, eds., *Domestic Violence: The Changing Criminal Justice Response.* Westport, Conn.: Greenwood.

Eckland-Olsen, S.
1982 Deviance, social control, and social networks. *Research in Law, Deviance, and Social Control* 4:271-299.

Eddy, M.J., and T. Myers
1984 *Helping Men Who Batter: A Profile of Programs in the United States.* Austin: Texas Council on Family Violence.

Edelson, J.L., and M.P. Brygger
1986 Gender differences in reporting of battering incidences. *Family Relations* 35:377-382.

Edelson, J.L., M. Syers, and M.P. Brygger
1987 Comparative Effectiveness of Group Treatment for Men Who Batter. Paper presented at the third national conference on Family Violence Research, University of New Hampshire, Durham.

Edwards, A.
1957 *Techniques of Attitude Scale Construction.* New York: Appleton, Century and Crofts.

Eisenberg, S.W., and P.L. Micklow
1977 The assaulted wife: "Catch 22" revisited. *Women's Rights Law Reporter* Spring-Summer:3-4.

Eisenstein, and H. Jacob
1977 *Felony Justice: An Organizational Analysis of Criminal Courts.* Boston: Little, Brown and Company.

Elbow, M.
1977 Theoretical consideration of violent marriages. *Social Casework* 58:515-526.

Elliott, D.S.
1989 Criminal justice procedures in family violence crimes. In L. Ohlin and M. Tonry, eds., *Family Violence,* Vol. 11: *Crime and Justice, An Annual Review of Research.* Chicago: University of Chicago Press.

Elliott, D.S., and D. Huizinga
1983 Social class and delinquent behavior in a national youth panel. *Criminology* 21:149-77.

1984   The Relationship Between Delinquent Behavior and ADM Prob-
        lems. Report No. 26, The National Youth Survey, Behavioral
        Research Institute, University of Colorado, Boulder.
Elliott, D.S., D. Huizinga, and B. Morse
1985   The Dynamics of Delinquent Behavior: A National Survey Progress
        Report. Institute of Behavioral Sciences, University of Colo-
        rado, Boulder.
Ellis, D.
1989   Male abuse of a married or cohabitating female partner: Appli-
        cation of sociological theory to research findings. *Violence and
        Victims* 4(4):235-256.
Ellis, J.E.
1984   Prosecutorial discretion to charge in cases of spouse assault: A
        dialogue. *Journal of Criminal Law and Criminology* 75:56-102.
Emerson, R.
1983   Holistic effects in social control decision making. *Law & Soci-
        ety Review* 17:425-455.
Eron, L.D., and L.R. Huesmann
1989   The genesis of gender differences in aggression. In M.A. Luszcz
        and T. Nettelbeck, eds., *Psychological Development: Perspec-
        tives Across the Life Span*. The Netherlands: Elsevier Science
        Publishers.
Fagan, J.A.
1988   Contributions of family violence research to criminal justice
        policy on wife assault: Paradigms of science and social control.
        Violence and Victims 3(3):159-186.
1989   Cessation of family violence: Deterrence and dissuasion. In L.
        Ohlin and M. Tonry, eds., *Family Violence*, Vol. 11: *Crime and
        Justice: An Annual Review of Research*. Chicago: University
        of Chicago Press.
1990   Intoxication and aggression. In J.Q. Wilson and M. Tonry, eds.,
        Drugs and Crime, Vol. 13: *Crime and Justice: An Annual
        Review of Research*. Chicago: University of Chicago Press.
Fagan, J., and S. Wexler
1985   Complex Behaviors and Simple Measures: Understanding Vio-
        lence and Aggression in Families. Paper presented at the an-
        nual meeting of the American Society of Criminology, San Di-
        ego, Calif., November.
1987a   Crime in the home and crime in the streets: The relation be-
        tween family violence and stranger crime. *Violence and Vic-
        tims* 2(1):5-21.
1987b   Family origins of violent delinquents. *Criminology* 25(3):643-
        669.
Fagan, J., D. Stewart, and K. Hansen
1983   Violent men or violent husbands? Background factors and situ-
        ational correlates of domestic and extra-domestic violence. In

D. Finkelhor, R. Gelles, G. Hotaling, and M. Straus, eds., *The Dark Side of Families.* Beverly Hills, Calif.: Sage Publications.

Fagan, J., E. Friedman, S. Wexler, and V. Lewis
1984 *The National Family Violence Evaluation: Final Report*, Vol. I: *Analytic Findings.* San Francisco: URSA Institute.

Farrington, D.P.
1979 Longitudinal research on crime and delinquency. In N. Morris and M. Tonry, eds., *Crime and Justice: An Annual Review of Research*, Vol. 1. Chicago: University of Chicago Press.

Feld, S.L., and M.A. Straus
1989 Escalation and desistance of wife assault in marriage. *Criminology* 27(1):141-161.

Field, M.H., and H.F. Field
1973 Marital violence and the criminal process: Neither justice nor peace. *Social Service Review* 47:221-240.

Fields, M.
1978 Wife beating: Government intervention policies and practice. In *Battered Women: Issues of Public Policy.* Washington, D.C.: U.S. Commission on Civil Rights.

Finkelhor, D.
1983 Common features of family abuse. In D. Finkelhor, R.J. Gelles, G.T. Hotaling, and M.A. Straus, eds., *The Dark Side of Families: Current Family Violence Research.* Beverly Hills, Calif.: Sage Publications.

Finkelhor, D., and K. Yllo
1983 Rape in marriage: A sociological view. In D. Finkelhor, R.J. Gelles, G.T. Hotaling, and M.A. Straus, eds., *The Dark Side of Families.* Beverly Hills, Calif.: Sage Publications.
1985 *License to Rape. Sexual Abuse of Wives.* New York: Holt, Rhinehart & Winston.

Fiora-Gormally, N.
1978 Battered wives who kill: Double standard out of court, single standard in? *Law and Human Behavior* 2(2):133-165.

Fleming, J.B.
1979 *Stopping Wife Abuse.* Garden City, N.Y.: Anchor Press/Doubleday.

Flynn, J.D.
1977 Recent findings related to wife abuse. *Social Case Work* 58:17-18.

Ford, D.A.
1983 Wife battery and criminal justice: A study of victim decision making. *Family Relations* 32:463-475.

Forst, B.E., and J.C. Hernon
1985 The Criminal Justice Response to Victim Harm. Research in Brief, National Institute of Justice, U.S. Department of Justice, Washington D.C.

Fox, J.A., and P.A. Tracy
   1986 *Randomized Response: A Method for Sensitive Surveys.* Sage
         Series on Quantitative Applications in the Social Sciences, No.
         58. Beverly Hills, Calif.: Sage Publications.
Frieze, I.H.
   1983 Investigating the causes and consequences of marital rape. *Signs*
         8:532-553.
Frieze, I.H., and A. Browne
   1989 Violence in marriage. In L. Ohlin and M. Tonry, eds., *Family
         Violence,* Vol. 11: *Crime and Justice: An Annual Review of
         Research.* Chicago: University of Chicago Press.
Frieze, I.H., and M.C. McHugh
   1981 Violence in Relation to Power in Marriage. Paper presented at
         the annual Research Conference of the Association for Women
         in Psychology, Santa Monica, Calif., March.
Frieze, I.H., J. Knoble, G. Zomnir, and C. Washburn
   1980 Types of Battered Women. Paper presented at the meeting of
         the Association of Women in Psychology, Santa Monica, Calif.,
         March.
Ganley, A.L.
   1981 Participants Manual: Court-Mandated Therapy for Men Who
         Batter: A Three Day Workshop for Professionals. Center for
         Womens Policy Studies, Washington, D.C.
Ganley, A.L., and L. Harris
   1978 Domestic Violence: Issues in Designing and Implementing Pro-
         grams for Male Batterers. Paper presented at the annual meet-
         ing of the American Psychological Association, Toronto, Au-
         gust.
Gaquin, D.A.
   1977- Spouse abuse: Data from the National Crime Survey. *Victimology:
   1978   An International Journal* 2(3-4):632-642.
Garner, J., and E. Clemmer
   1986 Danger to Police in Domestic Disturbances: A New Look. Re-
         search in Brief, National Institute of Justice, U.S. Department
         of Justice, Washington, D.C.
Gartner, R.
   1990 The victims of homicide: A temporal and cross-national com-
         parison. *American Sociological Review* 55(1):92-106.
Gayford, J.J.
   1975 Wife battering: A preliminary study of 100 cases. *British Medi-
         cal Journal* 1(January):194-197.
Gelles, R.J.
   1974 *The Violent Home: A Study of Physical Aggression Between
         Husbands and Wives.* Beverly Hills, Calif.: Sage Publications.
   1978 Methods for studying sensitive family topics. *American Jour-
         nal of Orthopsychiatry* 48(July):408-424.

Gelles, R.J., and C.P. Cornell
  1985 *Intimate Violence in Families.* Beverly Hills, Calif.: Sage Publications.
Gelles, R.J., and H. Mederer
  1985 Comparison or Control: Intervention in Cases of Wife Abuse. Paper presented at the annual meeting of the National Council on Family Relations, Dallas, Texas, November.
Gelles, R.J., and M.A. Straus
  1979 Determinants of violence in the family: Toward a theoretical integration. In W. Burr, R. Hill, F.I. Nye, and I.L. Triss, eds., *Contemporary Theories About the Family.* New York: Free Press.
  1988 *Intimate Violence.* New York: Simon and Schuster.
  1990 The medical and psychological costs of family violence. In M.A. Straus and R.J. Gelles, eds., *Physical Violence in American Families: Risk Factors and Adaptations to Violence in 8,145 Families.* New Brunswick, N.J.: Transaction Publishers.
Gendreau, P., and R.R. Ross
  1979 Effective correctional treatment: Bibliography for cynics. *Crime and Delinquency* 25:463-489.
Gil, D.
  1970 *Violence Against Children: Physical Child Abuse in the United States.* Cambridge, Mass.: Harvard University Press.
Gilbert, N.
  1983 *Capitalism and the Welfare State: Dilemmas of Social Benevolence.* New Haven, Conn.: Yale University Press.
Gillespie, C.K.
  1988 *Justifiable Homicide.* Columbus: Ohio State University Press.
Glick, R., and J. Moore, eds.
  1990 *Drugs in Hispanic Communities.* New Brunswick, N.J.: Rutgers University Press.
Goldstein, P.J.
  1989 Drugs and violent crime. Pp. 16-48 in N.A. Weiner and M.E. Wolfgang, eds., *Pathways to Criminal Violence.* Newbury Park, Calif.: Sage Publications.
Gondolf, E.W.
  1985a Anger and oppression in men who batter: Empiricist and feminist perspectives and their implications for research. *Victimology: An International Journal* 10(1):311-324.
  1985b Fight for control: A clinical assessment of men who batter. *Social Casework: The Journal of Contemporary Social Work* 66(1):48-54.
  1988 Who are those guys? Toward a behavioral typology of batterers. *Violence and Victims* 3:187-204.
Goodwin, D.W., and S.B. Guze
  1984 *Psychiatric Diagnosis*, 3rd ed. New York: Oxford University Press.

Goolkasian, G.A.
1986 Confronting Domestic Violence: The Role of Criminal Court Judges. Research in Brief, National Institute of Justice, U.S. Department of Justice, Washington, D.C.

Gordon, L.
1988 *Heroes of Their Own Lives: The Politics and History of Family Violence.* New York: Viking Press.

Gottfredson, M., and T. Hirschi
1986 The true value of lambda would appear to be zero. *Criminology* 24:213-34.
1990 *A General Theory of Crime.* Palo Alto, Calif.: Stanford University Press.

Greenberg, D.F.
1985 Age, crime and social explanation. *American Journal of Sociology* 91:1-21.

Groves, R.M., and Kahn, R.L.
1979 *Surveys by Telephone: A National Comparison with Personal Interviews.* New York: Academic Press.

Gurr, T.R.
1989 Historical trends in violent crime: Europe and the United States. Pp. 21-54 in T.R. Gurr, ed., *Violence in America*, Vol. I: *The History of Crime.* Newbury Park, Calif.: Sage Publications.

Gusfield, J.
1967 On legislating morals: The symbolic process of designating deviance. *California Law Review* 58(January):54-73.

Hagan, J., and K. Bumiller
1983 Making sense of sentencing: A review and critique of sentencing research. In A. Blumstein, J. Cohen, S.E. Martin, and M.H. Tonry, eds., *Research on Sentencing: The Search for Reform,* Vol 2. Washington D.C.: National Academy Press.

Hamberger, K.L., and J.E. Hastings
1986a Characteristics of spouse abusers: Predictors of treatment acceptance. *Journal of Interpersonal Violence* 1(3):363-373.
1986b Personality correlates of men who abuse their partners: A cross-validational study. *Journal of Family Violence* 1:323-341.
1988 Characteristics of male spouse abusers consistent with personality disorders. *Hospital and Community Psychiatry* 39:763-770.
1989 Counseling male spouse abusers: Characteristics of treatment completers and dropouts. *Violence and Victims* 4(4):275-286.

Hassenfeld, Y., and P. Cheung
1985 The juvenile court as a people-processing organization: A political economy perspective. *American Journal of Sociology* 90:801-825.

Herzberger, S.
1983 Social cognition and the transmission of abuse. In D. Finkelhor, R. Gelles, G. Hotaling, and M. Straus, eds., *The Dark Side of Families.* Beverly Hills, Calif.: Sage Publications.

Hilberman, E., and K. Munson
  1978 Sixty battered women. *Victimology* 2(3/4):460-471.
Hindelang, M., T. Hirschi, and J.G. Weis
  1981 *Measuring Delinquency.* Beverly Hills, Calif.: Sage Publications.
Hirschel, J.D., and I.W. Hutchison, III
  1992 Female spouse abuse and the police response: The Charlotte, North Carolina Experiment. *Journal of Criminal Law and Criminology* 83:73-119.
Hirschel, J.D., I.W. Hutchinson, III., C.W. Dean, J.J. Kelley, and C. Pesackis
  1991 Charlotte Spouse Assault Replication Project: Final Report. National Institute of Justice, U.S. Department of Justice, Washington, D.C.
Hirschel, J.D., I.W. Hutchison, III, and C.W. Dean
  1992 The failure of arrest to deter spouse abuse. *Journal of Research in Crime and Delinquency* 29:7-33.
Hood, R.G., and R. Sparks
  1970 *Key Issues in Criminology.* New York: McGraw Hill.
Hornung, C., B. McCullough, and T. Sugimoto
  1981 Status relationships in marriage: Risk factors in spouse abuse. *Journal of Marriage and the Family* 43:679-692.
Hotaling, G.T., and D.B. Sugarman
  1986 An analysis of risk markers in husband to wife violence: The current state of knowledge. *Violence and Victims* 1(2):101-124.
Hotaling, G.T., and M.A. Straus
  1989 Intrafamily violence, and crime and violence outside the family. In L. Ohlin and M. Tonry, eds., *Family Violence*: Vol. 11: *Crime and Justice: An Annual Review of Research.* Chicago: University of Chicago Press.
Hudson, W.W., and S.R. McIntosh
  1981 The assessment of spouse abuse: Two quantifiable dimensions. *Journal of Marriage and the Family* 43:873-885.
International Association of Chiefs of Police
  1967 Training Key 16: Handling Domestic Disturbance Calls. International Association of Chiefs of Police, Gaithersburg, Md.
Jacob, H.
  1983 Courts as organizations. In L. Mather and K. Boyum, eds., *Empirical Theories About the Courts.* New York: Longman.
Jaffe, P., D.A. Wolfe, A. Telford, and G. Austin
  1986 The impact of police charges in incidents of wife abuse. *Journal of Family Violence* 1:37-49.
Jorgensen, S.R.
  1977 Societal class heterogamy, status striving, and perception of marital conflict: A partial replication and revision of Pearlin's contingency hypothesis. *Journal of Marriage and the Family* 39:653-689.

Jouriles, E.N., and K.D. O'Leary
  1985 Interspousal reliability of reports of marital violence. *Journal of Consulting and Clinical Psychology* 53:419-21.
Jurik, N. and R. Winn
  1990 Gender and homicide: A comparison of men and women who kill. *Violence and Victims* 5(4):227-242.
Kalmuss, D.
  1984 The intergenerational transmission of marital aggression. *Journal of Marriage and the Family* 46:11-19.
Kalmuss, D.S., and M.A. Straus
  1983 Feminist, political, and economic determinants of wife abuse services. In D. Finkelhor, R. Gelles, G. Hotaling, and M. Straus, eds., *The Dark Side of Families*. Beverly Hills, Calif.: Sage Publications.
Kantor, G.K., and M.A. Straus
  1987 The "drunken bum" theory of wife beating. *Social Problems* 34:213-321.
  1989 Substance abuse as a precipitant of wife abuse victimizations. *American Journal of Drug and Alcohol Abuse* 15:173-193.
Katz, J.
  1988 *Seduction of Crime: Moral and Sensual Attractions in Doing Evil*. New York: Basic Books.
Kempe, C.H., F.N. Silverman, B.F. Steele, W. Droegemueller, and H. Silver
  1962 The battered child syndrome. *Journal of the American Medical Association* 181:107-112.
Kennedy, L.W., and D.G. Dutton
  1987 Edmonton Area Series Report No. 53: The Incidence of Wife Assault in Alberta. Population Research Laboratory, University of Alberta, Edmonton.
  1989 The incidence of wife assault in Alberta. *Canadian Journal of Behavioural Science* 21(1):40-54.
Klein, M.W., and C.S. Maxson
  1989 Street gang violence. In N.A. Weiner and M.E. Wolfgang, eds., *Violent Crime, Violent Criminals*. Newbury Park, Calif.: Sage Publications.
Korbin, J.E.
  1977 Anthropological contributions to the study of child abuse. *Child Abuse and Neglect* 1:7-24.
Kruttschnitt, C., and M. Dornfield
  1992 Will they tell? Assessing preadolescents' reports of family violence. *Journal of Research in Crime and Delinquency* 29:136-47.
Kuhl, A.
  1989 Patterns of Victimization in Spousal Homicide in California, 1974-1986. Unpublished manuscript, Office of the Attorney, Sacramento, Calif.

LaFave, W.R., and A.W. Scott, Jr.
1972 *Handbook on Criminal Law.* St. Paul, Minn.: West Publishing.
Lagace, R.O.
1979 The Human Relations Area File (HRAF) probability sample. *Behavior Science Research* 14:211-229.
Lagan, P.A., and C.A. Innes
1986 *Preventing Domestic Violence Against Women.* Bureau of Justice Statistics. Washington, D.C.: U.S. Department of Justice.
Last, J.M.
1983 *A Dictionary of Epidemiology.* New York: Oxford University Press.
Lempert, R.
1989 Humility is a virtue: On the publication of policy relevant research. *Law & Society Review* 23(1):145-161.
Lentzner, H.R., and M.M. DeBerry
1980 *Intimate Victims: A Study of Violence Among Friends and Relatives.* Bureau of Justice Statistics. Washington, D.C.: U.S. Department of Justice.
Lerman, L.G.
1986 Prosecution of wife beaters: Institutional obstacles and innovations. In M. Lystad, ed., *Violence in the Home: Interdisciplinary Perspectives.* New York: Brunner-Mazel.
Lerman, L.G., and F. Livingston
1983 State legislation on domestic violence. *Response* 6:1-27.
Levinger, G.
1966 Sources of marital dissatisfaction among applicants for divorced. *American Journal of Orthopsychiatry* 36:804-806.
Levens, B.R., and D.G. Dutton
1980 *The Social Service Role of the Police.* Ottawa: Solicitor General of Canada.
Levinson, D.
1988 Family violence in cross-cultural perspective. In V.B. van Hasselt, R.L. Morrison, A.S. Bellack, and M. Hersen, eds., *Handbook of Family Violence.* New York: Plenum.
1989 *Family Violence in Cross-Cultural Perspective.* Newbury Park, Calif.: Sage Publications.
Lindsey, K.
1978 When battered women strike back. *Viva* 58/59:66-74.
Lockhart, L.L.
1987 A reexamination of the effects of race and social class on the incidence of marital violence: A search for reliable differences. *Journal of Marriage and the Family* 49:603-610.
Loeber, R., and M. Stouthamer-Loeber
1986 Models and meta-analysis of the relationship between family variables and juvenile conduct problems and delinquency. In N. Morris and M. Tonry, eds., *Crime and Justice: An Annual*

Review of Research, Vol. 7. Chicago: University of Chicago Press.

Loftus, E.
1980 *Memory*. Reading, Mass.: Addison-Wesley.

Luckenbill, D.F.
1977 Criminal homicide as a situated transaction. *Social Problems* 25:176-186.

MacAndrew, C., and R. Edgerton
1969 *Drunken Comportment: A Social Explanation*. Chicago: Aldine.

Maccoby, E.E., and C.N. Jacklin
1974 *The Psychology of Sex Differences*. Palo Alto, Calif.: Stanford University Press.

Maiuro, R.D., T.S. Cahn, and P.P. Vitaliano
1986 Assertiveness deficits and hostility in domestically violent men. *Violence and Victims* 1(4):279-290.

Makepeace, J.M.
1981 Courtship violence among college students. *Family Relations* 30:97-102.
1983 Life events stress and courtship violence. *Family Relations* 32:101-109.

Margolin, G.
1988 Interpersonal and intrapersonal factors associated with marital violence. In G.T. Hotaling, D. Finkelhor, J.T. Kirkpatrick, and M.A. Straus, eds., *Family Abuse and its Consequences: New Directions for Research*. Newbury Park, Calif.: Sage Publications.

Margolin, L., P.B. Moran, and M. Miller
1989 Social approval for violations of sexual consent in marriage and dating. *Violence and Victims* 4(1):45-56.

Marsh, E.J., C. Johnston, and K. Kovitz
1983 A comparison of the mother-child interactions of physically abused and nonabused children during play and task situations. *Journal of Clinical Child Psychology* 12:332-46.

Martin, D.
1976 *Battered Wives*. New York: Kangaroo Paperbacks.

Mason, A., and V. Blankenship
1987 Power and affiliation, motivation, stress and abuse in intimate relationships. *Journal of Personality and Social Psychology* 52:203-210.

Mather, L.
1979 *Plea Bargaining or Trial? The Process of Criminal Case Disposition*. Lexington, Mass.: Lexington Books.

McClelland, D.C.
1975 *Power: The Inner Experience*. New York: Irvington Publishers.

McClelland, D.C., and W.N. Davis
1972 The influence of unrestrained power concerns on drinking in

working class men. In D.C. McClelland, W.N. Davis, R. Kalin, and E. Wanner, eds., *The Drinking Man*. New York: Free Press.

McClelland, D.C., W.N. Davis, R. Kalin, and E. Wanner
1972 *The Drinking Man*. New York: Free Press.

Megargee, E.I.
1983 Psychological determinants and correlates of criminal violence. In M.E. Wolfgang and N.A. Weiner, eds., *Criminal Violence*. Beverly Hills, Calif.: Sage Publications.

Mercy, J.A., and L.E. Saltzman
1989 Fatal violence among spouses in the United States, 1976-85. *American Journal of Public Health* 79:595-599.

Meredith, W.H., D.A. Abbott, and S.L. Adams
1986 Family violence: Its relation to marital and parental satisfactions and family strengths. *Journal of Family Violence* 1:299-305.

Mettger, Z.
1982 A case of rape: Forced sex in marriage. *Response* 5(2):1-2, 13-16.

Meyer, J.K., and T.D. Lorimor
1977 Police Intervention Data and Domestic Violence: Exploratory Development and Validation of Prediction Models. Unpublished manuscript, Kansas City Police Department, Kansas City, Mo.

Mill, J.S.
1869 On the subjection of women. In A. Rossi, ed. (1970) *Essays on Sex Equality*. Chicago: University of Chicago Press.

Miller, B.A., W.R. Downs, and D.M. Gondoli
1988 Spousal violence among alcoholic women as compared to a random household sample of women. *Journal of Studies on Alcoholism* 50:533-540.

Miller, D., and G. Challas
1981 Abused Children as Parents. Paper presented at the national conference on Family Violence Research, University of New Hampshire, Durham, July.

Miller, S., and S. Simpson
1991 Courtship violence and social control: Does gender matter? *Law & Society Review* 25:335-367.

Mitchell, R.E., and C.A. Hodson
1983 Battered Women: The Relationship of Stress, Support, and Coping to Adjustment. Paper presented at the annual meeting of the American Psychological Association, Washington D.C., August.

Moore, J.
1978 *Homeboys*. Philadelphia: Temple University Press.

Morash, M.
1986 Wife battering. *Criminal Justice Abstracts* 18(2):252-271.

Mosher, D.L., and S.S. Tomkins
 1988   Scripting the macho man: Hypermasculine socialization and enculturation. *Journal of Sex Research* 25: 60-84.
Neidig, P., D. Friedman, and B. Collins
 1986   Attitudinal characteristics of males who have engaged in spouse abuse. *Journal of Family Violence* 1:223-233.
Nisonoff, L., and I. Bitman
 1979   Spouse abuse: Incidence and relationship to selected demographic variables. *Victimology* 4:131-139.
Novaco, R.
 1976   The functions and regulation of the arousal of anger. *American Journal of Psychiatry* 133(1):1124-1128.
O'Brien, J.E.
 1971   Violence in divorce-prone families. *Journal of Marriage and the Family* 33:962-698.
Okun, L.
 1986   *Women Abuse: Facts Replacing Myths.* Albany, N.Y.:   State University of New York Press.
O'Leary, K.D., and I. Arias
 1988   Assessing agreement of reports of spouse abuse. In G.T. Hotaling, D. Finkelhor, J.T. Kirkpatrick, and M.A. Straus, eds., *Family Abuse and its Consequences: New Directors for Research.* Newbury Park, Calif.:   Sage Publications.
Pagelow, M.D.
 1984   *Family Violence.* New York: Praeger
Parker, R.N., and M.D. Smith
 1979   Deterrence, poverty and type of homicide. *American Journal of Sociology* 85:614-624.
Parnas, R.J.
 1967   Police response to domestic violence. *Wisconsin Law Review* 31:914-60.
Pate, A., and E.E. Hamilton
 1992   Formal and informal deterrents to domestic violence: The Dade County spouse assault experiment. *American Sociological Review* 57:691-697.
Patterson, G.R., and T.J. Dishion
 1985   Contributions of families and peers to delinquency. *Criminology* 23:63-80.
Pelton, L.G.
 1979   Interpreting family violence data. *American Journal of Orthopsychiatry* 49:194-210.
Petersilia, J.
 1980   Career criminal research: A review of recent evidence. In N. Morris and M. Tonry, eds., *Crime and Justice: An Annual Review of Research*, Vol. 2. Chicago: University of Chicago Press.
Pierce, G.L., S. Spaar, and L.R. Briggs
 1988   The Character of Police Work: Strategic and Tactical Implica-

tions. Center for Applied Social Research, Northeastern University, Boston.

Pirog-Good, M.A., and J.E. Stets, eds.,
1989 *Violence in Dating Relationships: Emerging Social Issues.* New York: Praeger.

Pitman, D.J., and W. Handy
1964 Patterns in criminal aggravated assault. *Journal of Criminal Law and Criminology* 55: 462-67.

Platt, A.M.
1969 *The Child Savers.* Chicago: University of Chicago Press.

Pleck, E.
1987 *Domestic Tyranny: The Making of American Social Policy Against Family Violence From Colonial Times to the Present.* New York: Oxford University Press.
1989 Criminal approaches to family violence, 1640-1980. In L. Ohlin and M. Tonry, eds., *Family Violence*, Vol. 11: *Crime and Justice: An Annual Review of Research.* Chicago: University of Chicago Press.

Prescott, S., and C. Lesko
1977 Battered women: A social psychological perspective. In *Battered Women: A Psychosociological Study of Domestic Violence.* New York: Van Nostrand Rheinhold.

Reidel, M., M.A. Zahn, and L. Mock
1985 *The Nature and Patterns of American Homicides.* Washington, D.C.: U.S. Government Printing Office.

Resick, P.A., and D. Reese
1986 Perception of family social climate and physical aggression in the home. *Journal of Family Violence* 1:71-83.

Rivera, B., and C.S. Widom
1990 Childhood victimization and violent offending. *Violence and Victims* 5(1):19-36.

Roscoe, B., and N. Benaske
1985 Courtship violence experienced by abused wives: Similarities in patterns of abuse. *Family Relations* 34:419-424.

Rosenbaum, A., and R.D. O'Leary
1981 Marital violence: Characteristics of abusive couples. *Journal of Consulting and Clinical Psychology* 49(1):63-76.

Rosenberg, M.L., R.J. Gelles, P.C. Holinger, E. Stark, M.A. Zahn, J.M. Conn, N.N. Fajman, and T.A. Karlson
1984 Violence, Homicide, Assault, and Suicide. Unpublished manuscript, Centers for Disease Control, Atlanta.

Rounsaville, B.J.
1978 Theories in marital violence: Evidence from a study of battered women. *Victimology* 3(1-2):11-31.

Rouse, L.P.
1984 Conflict Tactics Used by Men in Marital Disputes. Paper pre-

sented at the second national conference for Family Violence Researchers, University of New Hampshire, Durham, July.

Roy, M.
1977   *Battered Women: A Psychosocial Study of Domestic Violence.* New York: Van Nostrand.

Russell, D.E.H.
1982   *Rape in Marriage.* New York: Macmillan

Saltzman, L.E., J.A. Mercy, M.L. Rosenberg, W.R. Elsea, G. Napper, R.K. Sikes, R. Waxweiler, and the Collaborative Working Group for the Study of Family and Institute Assaults in Atlanta
1990   Magnitude and patterns of family and intimate assaults in Atlanta, Georgia, 1984. *Violence and Victims* 5(1):3-18.

Saunders, D.G.
1987   A Typology of Men Who Batter: Three Types Derived from Cluster Analysis. Paper presented at the third national conference on Family Violence Research, University of New Hampshire, Durham, July.
1988   Other "truths" about domestic violence: A reply to McNeely and Robinson-Simpson. *Social Work* 179-184.

Saunders, D.G., and S.T. Azar
1989   Treatment programs for family violence. In L. Ohlin and M. Tonry, eds., *Family Violence*, Vol. 11: *Crime and Justice: An Annual Review of Research.* Chicago: University of Chicago Press.

Saunders, D.G., and D.R. Hanusa
1984   Cognitive-Behavioral Treatment of Abusive Husbands: The Short-Term Effects of Group Therapy. Paper presented at the second national conference on Family Violence Research, University of New Hampshire, Durham, August.

Saunders, D.G., A.B. Lynch, M. Grayson, and D. Linz
1987   The inventory of beliefs about wife beating: The construction and initial validation of a measure of beliefs and attitudes. *Violence and Victims* 2(1):39-58.

Schecter, S.
1982   *Women and Male Violence.* Boston: South End Press.

Schmidt, J., and E.H. Steury
1989   Prosecutorial discretion in filing charges in domestic violence cases. *Criminology* 27(3):487-510.

Schneider, E.M.
1980   Equal rights to trail for women: Sex bias in the law on self-defense. *Harvard Civil Rights-Civil Liberties Law Review* 15:623-647.

Schneider, E.M., and S.B. Jordan
1981   Representation of women who defend themselves in response to physical or sexual assault. In E. Bochnak, ed., *Women's Self Defense Cases: Theory and Practice.* Charlottesville, Va.: The Michie Company Law Publishers.

Schulman, M.
   1979   A Survey of Spousal Violence Against Women in Kentucky. Unpublished manuscript, Law Enforcement Administration, U.S. Department of Justice, Washington, D.C.
Schwendinger, J.R., and H. Schwendinger
   1983   *Rape and Inequality.* Beverly Hills, Calif.: Sage Publications.
Scott, M.B., and S.M. Lyman
   1968   Accounts. *American Sociological Review* 33(1):46-62.
Sellin, T., and M.E. Wolfgang
   1964   *The Measurement of Delinquency.* New York: Wiley & Sons.
Sherif, M., and C. Hovland
   1961   *Social Judgement.* New Haven, Conn.: Yale University Press.
Sherman, L.W.
   1992   *Policing Domestic Violence: Experiments and Directions.* New York: Free Press.
Sherman, L.W., and R.A. Berk
   1984   The specific deterrent effects of arrest for domestic assault. *American Sociological Review* 49:261-272.
Sherman, L.W., and E.G. Cohn
   1989   The impact of research on legal policy: The Minneapolis violence experiment. *Law & Society Review* 23(1):117-144.
Sherman, L.W., P.R. Gartin, and M.E. Buerger
   1989   Hot spots of predatory crime: Routine activities and the criminology of place. *Criminology* 27(1):27-55.
Sherman, L.W., J.D. Schmidt, D. Rogan, and C. De Riso
   1990   Predicting domestic homicide: Prior police contact and gun threats. In M. Steinman, ed., *Redefining Crime: Responses to Women Battering.* Cincinnati, Ohio: Anderson Publishing.
Sherman, L.W., J.D. Schmidt, D.P Rogan, P. Gartin, E.G. Cohen, D.J. Collins, and A.R. Bacich
   1991   From initial deterrence to long-term escalation: Short custody arrest for poverty ghetto domestic violence. *Criminology* 29:821-850.
Sherman, L.W., D.A. Smith, J.D. Schmidt, and D.P. Rogan
   1992   Crime, punishment, and stake in conformity: Legal and informal control of domestic violence. *American Sociological Review* 57:680-690.
Shields, N., and C.R. Hanneke
   1983   Battered wives' reactions to marital rape. Pp. 132-147 in D. Finkelhor, R.J. Gelles, G.T. Hotaling, and M.A. Straus, eds., *The Dark Side of Families: Current Family Violence Research.* Beverly Hills, Calif.: Sage Publications.
Shields, N., G.J. McCall, and C.R. Hanneke
   1988   Patterns of family and non-family violence: Violent husbands and violent men. *Violence and Victims* 3:83-98.

Silverman, F.N.
1953   The roentgen manifestations of unrecognized skeletal trauma in infants. *American Journal of Roentgenology* 69:413-426.

Silverman, R.A., and S.K. Mukhergee
1987   Intimate homicide: An analysis of violent social relationships. *Behavioral Sciences and the Law* 5:37-47.

Simon, R.J., and S. Baxter
1989   Gender and violent crime. In N.A. Weiner and M.E. Wolfgang, eds., *Violent Crime, Violent Criminals*. Newbury Park, Calif.: Sage Publications.

Skogan, W.G.
1981   *Issues in the Measurement of Victimization*. Washington, D.C.: U.S. Government Printing Office.
1989   Social change and the future of violent crime. Pp. 235-250 in T.R. Gurr, ed., *Violence in America*, Vol. I: *The History of Crime*. Newbury Park, Calif.: Sage Publications.

Smith, D.A.
1986   The neighborhood context of police behavior. In A.J. Reiss, Jr. and M. Tonry, eds., *Communities and Crime*. Chicago: University of Chicago Press.

Smith, M.D.
1986   Effects of question format on the reporting of woman abuse. *Victimology* 11:430-438.
1987   The incidence and prevalence of women abuse in Toronto. *Violence and Victims* 2(3):173-187.
1990   Patriarchical ideology and wife beating: A test of a feminist hypothesis. *Violence and Victims* 5(4):257-274.

Smith, M.D., and R.N. Parker
1980   Types of homicide and variation in regional rates. *Social Forces* 59:136-147.

Sonkin, D.J.
1987   *Domestic Violence on Trial: Psychological and Legal Dimensions of Family Violence*. New York: Springer.

Sonkin, D.J., and M. Durphy
1985   *Learning to Live Without Violence: A Handbook for Men*, 2nd re. ed. San Francisco: Volcano Press.

Sonkin, D.J., D. Martin, and L.E. Walker
1985   *The Male Batterer: A Treatment Approach*. New York: Springer

Sorenson, S.B., and C.A. Telles
1991   Self-reports of spouse violence in a Mexican-American and non-Hispanic white population. *Violence and Victims* 6:3-16.

Speckart, G., and M.D. Anglin
1986   Narcotics and crime: A causal modeling approach. *Journal of Quantitative Criminology* 2(1):3-28.

Speiker, G.
1983   What is the linkage between alcohol abuse and violence. Pp.

125-137 in E. Gottheil, K.A. Druley, T.E. Skoloda, and H.M. Waxman, eds., *Alcohol, Drug Abuse and Aggression.* Springfield, Ill.: Charles C. Thomas.

Sprey, J.
1971   On the management of conflict in families. *Journal of Marriage and the Family* 33:722-732.

Stanko, E.A.
1982   Would you believe this woman? In N. Rafter and E.A. Stanko, eds., *Judge, Lawyer, Victim and Thief.* Boston: Northeastern University Press.

Star, B.
1980   Patterns in family violence. *Social Casework Reprint Series* 5-12.

Stark, E., and A. Flitcraft
1983   Social knowledge, social policy, and the abuse of women: The case against patriarchal benevolence. Pp. 330-348 in D. Finkelhor, R.J. Gelles, G.T. Hotaling, and M.A. Straus, eds., *The Dark Side of Families: Current Family Violence Research.* Beverly Hills, Calif.: Sage Publications.

Stark, E., A. Flitcraft, and W. Frazier
1979   Medicine and patriarchical violence: The social construction of a private event. *International Journal of Health Services* 9(3):461-493.

Stark, E., A. Flitcraft, D. Zuckerman, A. Grey, J. Robinson, and W. Frazier
1981   *Wife Abuse in the Medical Setting: An Introduction to Health Personnel.* Monograph Series #7. Washington, D.C.: National Clearinghouse on Domestic Violence.

Stark, R., and J. McEvoy
1970   Middle class violence. *Psychology Today* 4(6):107-112.

Starr, R.H., Jr.
1988   Physical abuse of children. In V.B. van Hasselt, R.L. Morrison, A.S. Bellack, and M. Hersen, eds., *Handbook of Family Violence.* New York: Plenum Press.

Steadman, H.J.
1982   A situational approach to violence. *International Journal of Law and Psychiatry* 5:171-186.

Steinmetz, S.A.
1977   *The Cycle of Violence: Assertive, Aggressive and Abusive Family Interactions.* New York: Praeger.

Stets, J.E., and M.A. Straus
1990   Gender differences in reporting marital violence and its medical and psychological consequences. In M.A. Straus and R.J. Gelles, eds., *Psychical Violence in American Families: Risk Factors and Adaptation to Violence in 8,145 Families.* New Brunswick, N.J.: Transaction Press.

Straus, M.A.
1973 A general systems theory of violence between family members. *Social Science Information* 12:105-125.
1976 Sexual inequality, cultural norms, and wife beating. *Victimology* 1:54-76.
1978 Wife beating: How common and why? *Victimology* 2:443-458.
1979 Measuring family conflict and violence. The Conflict Tactics Scale. *Journal of Marriage and the Family* 41:75-88.
1983 Ordinary violence, child abuse, and wife-beating: What do they have in common and why? In D. Finkelhor, R.J. Gelles, G.T. Hotaling, and M.A. Straus, eds., *The Dark Side of Families: Current Family Violence Research.* Beverly Hills, Calif.: Sage Publications.
1986 Domestic violence and homicide antecedents. *Bulletin of the New York Academy of Medicine* 62:446-465.
1989 Assaults by Wives on Husbands: Implications for Primary Prevention of Marital Violence. Paper presented at the annual meeting of the American Society of Criminology, Reno, Nev., November.
1990a The conflict tactics scales and its critics: An evaluation and new data on validity and reliability. In M.A. Straus and R.J. Gelles, eds., *Physical Violence in American Families: Risk Factors and Adaptation to Violence in 8,145 Families.* New Brunswick, N.J.: Transaction Press.
1990b Injury and frequency of assault and the "representative sample fallacy" in measuring wife beating and child abuse. In M.A. Straus and R.J. Gelles, eds., *Physical Violence in American Families: Risk Factors and Adaptation to Violence in 8,145 Families.* New Brunswick, N.J.: Transaction Press.
Straus, M.A., and R.J. Gelles
1986 Societal change in family violence from 1975 to 1985 as revealed by two national surveys. *Journal of Marriage and the Family* 48:465-479.
Straus, M.A., and R.J. Gelles, eds.
1990 *Physical Violence in American Families: Risk Factors and Adaptations to Violence in 8,145 Families.* New Brunswick, N.J.: Transaction Press.
Straus, M.A., and C. Smith
1990 Violence in Hispanic families in the United States: Incidence rates and structural interpretations. In M.A. Straus and R.J. Gelles, eds., *Physical Violence in American Families: Risk Factors and Adaptation to Violence in 8,145 Families.* New Brunswick, N.J.: Transaction Press.
Straus, M.A., R.J. Gelles, and S.K. Steinmetz
1980 *Behind Closed Doors: Violence in the American Family.* Garden City, N.Y.: Anchor Press, Doubleday.

Sugarman, D.B., and G.T. Hotaling
  1989 Courtship violence: In M.A. Pirog-Good and J.E. Stets, eds., *Violence in Dating Relationships*. New York: Praeger.
Sullivan, J.P., and D.L. Mosher
  1990 Acceptance of guided imagery of marital rape as a function of macho personality. *Violence and Victims* 5(4):275-286.
Sykes, G.M., and D. Matza
  1957 Techniques of neutralization: A theory of delinquency. *American Sociological Review* 22:667-670.
Szinovacz, M.E.
  1983 Using couple data as a methodological tool: The case of marital violence. *Journal of Marriage and the Family* 45:633-644.
Tauchen, G., H. Tauchen, and A.D. Witte
  1986 The Dynamics of Domestic Violence: A Reanalysis of the Minneapolis Experiment. Unpublished manuscript, Police Foundation, Washington, D.C.
Taylor, S.P.
  1983 Alcohol and human physical aggression. Pp. 280-291 in E. Gottheil, K.A. Druley, T.E. Skoloda, and H.M. Waxman, eds., *Alcohol, Drug Abuse and Aggression*. Springfield, Ill.: Charles C. Thomas.
Telch, C.F., and C.U. Lindquist
  1984 Violent vs. non-violent couples: A comparison of patterns. *Psychotherapy* 21:242-248.
Thyfault, R.
  1984 Self-defense: Battered women syndrome on trial. *California Western Law Review* 20:485-510.
Thyfault, R., A. Browne, and L.E. Walker
  1987 When battered women kill: Evaluation and expert testimony techniques. In D.J. Sonkin, ed., *Domestic Violence on Trial: Psychological and Legal Dimensions of Family Violence*. New York: Springer.
Tolman, R.M.
  1989 The development of a measure of the psychological maltreatment of women by their male partners. *Violence and Victims* 4(3):159-178.
Totman, J.
  1978 *The Murderess: A Psychosocial Study of Criminal Homicide*. San Francisco: R. & E. Research Associates.
U.S. Commission on Civil Rights
  1978 *Battered Women: Issues of Public Policy*. Washington, D.C.: U.S. Commission on Civil Rights.
  1982 *Under the Rule of Thumb: Battered Women and the Administration of Justice*. Washington, D.C.: U.S. Commission on Civil Rights.
Waldorf, D.
  1973 *Careers in Dope*. Englewood Cliffs, N.J.: Prentice Hall.

Walker, L.E.
  1979   *The Battered Women.* New York: Harper and Row.
  1984   *The Battered Woman Syndrome.* New York: Springer.
Wardell, L., D.L. Gillespie, and A. Leffler
  1983   Science and violence against wives. In D. Finkelhor, R.J. Gelles,
         G.T. Hotaling, and M.A. Straus, eds., *The Dark Side of Fami-*
         lies: Current Family Violence Research. Beverly Hills, Calif.:
         Sage Publications.
Washburn, C., and I.H. Frieze
  1980   Methodological Issues in Studying Battered Women. Paper pre-
         sented at the first national conference for Family Violence Re-
         searchers, University of New Hampshire, Durham, July.
Weiner, N.A., and M.E. Wolfgang
  1985   The extent and character of violent crime in America, 1969 to
         1982. In L.A. Curtis, ed., *American Violence and Public Policy.*
         New Haven, Conn.: Yale University Press.
Weis, J.G.
  1989   Family violence research methodology and design. In L. Ohlin
         and M. Tonry, eds., *Family Violence*, Vol. 11: *Crime and Jus-*
         tice: An Annual Review of Research. Chicago: Chicago Uni-
         versity Press.
Weisburd, D.L., L. Maher, and L.W. Sherman
  1989   Contrasting Crime-Specific and Crime-General Theories: The
         Case of Hot Spots of Crime. Paper presented at the annual
         meeting of the American Sociological Association, San Fran-
         cisco, August.
Wexler, S.
  1982   Battered women and public policy. In E. Boneparth, ed., *Women,*
         Power and Policy. New York: Pergamon.
White, S.O., and M.A. Straus
  1981   The implications of family violence for rehabilitation strate-
         gies. In S.E. Martin, L. Sechrest, and R. Redner, eds., *New*
         Directions in the Rehabilitation of Criminal Offenders. Wash-
         ington, D.C.: National Academy Press.
Widom, C.S.
  1988   Intergeneration transmission of violence. In N.A. Weiner and
         M.E. Wolfgang, eds., *Violent Crime, Violent Criminals.* Newbury
         Park, Calif.: Sage Publications.
  1989   Child abuse, neglect and violent criminal behavior. *Criminol-*
         ogy 27(2):251-271.
  1990   Implications of biases in sampling techniques for child abuse
         research and policy. In D. Besharov, ed., *Family Violence Re-*
         search and Policy. Lanham, Md.: University Press of America.
Wiersema, B., and C. Loftin
  1994   *Estiamtes of Assault by Inmates from the National Crime Vic-*

timization Survey, 1987. Institute of Criminal Justice & Criminology. College Park, Md.: University of Maryland.

Wilbanks, W.
1983 The female homicide offender in Dade County, Florida. *Criminal Justice Review* 8(2):9-14.

Williams, K.R., and R.L. Flewelling
1988 The social production of criminal homicide: A comparative study of disaggregated rates in American cities. *American Sociological Review* 53(3):421-431.

Williams, K.R., and R. Hawkins
1986 Perceptual research on general deterrence: A critical review. *Law & Society Review* 20:544-572.
1989a The meaning of arrest for wife assault. *Criminology* 27(2):163-181.
1989b Controlling male aggression in intimate relationships. *Law & Society Review* 24(4):591-612.
1992 Wife assault, costs of arrest, and the deterrence process. *Journal of Research and Crime Delinquency* 29:292-310.

Wilson, J.Q.
1977 Foreword. In *Domestic Violence and the Police: Studies in Detroit and Kansas City*. Washington, D.C.: Police Foundation.

Winick, C.
1983 Drinking and disinhibition in popular culture. Pp. 347-373 in R. Room and G. Collins, eds., *Alcohol and Disinhibition: The Nature and Meaning of the Link*. National Institute on Alcohol Abuse and Alcoholism Research Monograph No. 12. Washington, D.C.: U.S. Department of Health and Human Services.

Winkler, I., and I.J. Doherty
1983 Communication styles and marital satisfaction in Israeli and American couples. *Family Process* 22:221-228.

Wolfgang, M.E.
1958 *Patterns in Criminal Homicide*. New York: John Wiley & Sons.
1967 A sociological analysis of criminal homicide. In M.E. Wolfgang, ed., *Studies in Homicide*. New York: Harper and Row.

Wolfgang, M.E., and F. Ferracuti
1967 *The Subculture of Violence: Toward an Integrated Theory of Criminology*. London: Tavistock.

Yllo, K.A.
1983 Sexual equality and violence against wives in American states. *Journal of Comparative Family Studies* 14:67-86.
1988 Political and methodological debates in wife abuse research. In K. Yllo and M. Bograd, eds., *Feminist Perspectives on Wife Abuse*. Beverly Hills, Calif.: Sage Publications.

Yllo, K.A., and M.A. Straus
1984 Patriarchy and violence against wives: The impact of structural

and normative factors. *Journal of International and Comparative Social Welfare* 1(1):16-29.

Zahn, M.A.
1989 Homicide in the twentieth century: Trends, types and causes. In T.R. Gurr, ed., *Violence in America*, Vol. I: *The History of Violence*. Newbury Park, Calif.: Sage Publications.

Zimring, F.E.
1989 Toward a jurisprudence of family violence. In L. Ohlin and M. Tonry, eds., *Family Violence*, Vol. 11: *Crime and Justice: An Annual Review of Research*. Chicago: University of Chicago Press.

Zimring, F.E., S.K. Mukherjee, and B.J. Van Winkle
1983 Intimate violence: A study of intersexual homicide in Chicago. *The University of Chicago Law Review* 50(2):910-930.

Zinberg, N.E.
1984 *Drug, Set, and Setting: The Social Bases of Controlled Drug Use*. New Haven, Conn.: Yale University Press.

Gender and Interpersonal Violence

Candace Kruttschnitt

INTRODUCTION

Are males really more violent than females? Although disagreement on this important question admittedly remains, a number of scholarly works have concluded that gender, perhaps more than any other variable, produces a dramatic and consistent difference in the extent and nature of interpersonal violence. For almost four decades now, men have dominated official reports of violent crime and, regardless of the data source, they appear to engage disproportionately in the most injurious acts of interpersonal violence. Race differences produce some variations among different data sets; gender differences, however, appear and reappear across time and different social contexts in crimes of violence and acts of aggression. From a public policy as well as a theoretical standpoint, this robust association is quite significant. Simply asked, what is it about being female that reduces the likelihood of aggressive or violent behavior? Unfortunately it appears that we know far more about the strength of the association between gender and interpersonal violence than about why it exists. Although numerous scholars have assessed the relationship between gender and crime (e.g., see Widom, 1978; Nagel and Hagan, 1982; Rutter

Candace Kruttschnitt is at the Department of Sociology, University of Minnesota.

and Giller, 1983; Wilson and Herrnstein, 1985), virtually no integrated research reviews focus specifically on acts of violence. Instead the explanations for the relationship between gender and interpersonal violence have remained in disparate intellectual fields and in various theoretical camps, including biological, social psychological, structural, and methodological.

The purpose of this paper is to examine critically the research pertaining to gender and interpersonal violence with an eye toward providing a better understanding of the role of gender in producing different rates and types of interpersonal violence. Every attempt is made to present relevant data from all intellectual traditions.[1] However, as can be seen, the work on violence among males far exceeds the work on violence among females. As a result, readers will find that this review provides a synthesis of the omissions in our knowledge of the relationship between gender and interpersonal violence. We begin by defining the concepts that provide the framework for this analysis.

Definitions and Concepts

The Panel on the Understanding and Control of Violent Behavior limits its consideration of violent *human behavior* to interpersonal violence, which is defined as behavior that "threatens, attempts, or actually inflicts physical harm." This definition of violence is composed of the following three elements: (1) behavior, by one or more persons, that threatens, attempts, or inflicts physical harm (i.e., the harmful act need not be completed to be included in this study); (2) intentional infliction of physical harm (i.e., the definition excludes negligence and recklessness); and (3) one or more persons who are objects of the harmful behavior (i.e., the victims).

The term *sex* is used to refer to genetic sex or the chromosomal makeup of the individual. It is "sex" and not "gender" to which we refer when making the distinction between people who are biologically male or biologically female (Schur, 1984:10). By contrast, the term *gender* refers to the sociological, psychological, and cultural patterns that are used to evaluate and to shape male or female behavior. The evidence suggesting that gender is socially constructed is now well documented (e.g., see Macaulay, 1985; Bender, 1988:15, note 38; Epstein, 1988). However, because gender is imposed on sex by acculturation and socialization, it is not surprising to find that these two concepts are still used interchangeably (cf. Widom, 1984:5). The failure to distinguish sex from gender can have serious implications for research examining behavioral differences between men and women. For example, criminologists frequently refer to sex as one of the most important demographic variables in their research because of the strong association observed between this variable and aggregate arrest rates. Yet a reference to sex differences in arrest statistics implies a biological basis for the disparate rates. Explanations for these differences, however, include socialization and opportunity, as well as biological factors. Similarly, models predicting sex differences in interpersonal violence can be misspecified when they fail to include biological variables; conversely, a gender-based explanation of violence should model exogenous social and cultural variables.

Further confusion arises with the related variables of gender role and gender identity. Gender roles are commonly perceived as a set of behavioral expectations based on an individual's sex in a particular social context, whereas *gender identity* usually refers to an individual's self-conception of being male or female. Each variable can have important and different etiological influences on crime. For example, female gender role socialization might constrain aggression or societal responses to it, whereas a masculine gender identity might encourage it (e.g., see Widom, 1984). However, in the relevant literature we find that (1) "gender/sex roles" often are employed as a generic concept for both social roles and personality traits (Norland and Shover, 1978), and (2) there are both considerable measurement variability (cf. Thornton and James, 1979; Norland et al., 1981; Horwitz and White, 1987) and questionable validity in the underlying constructs of masculinity and femininity (Spence and Sawin, 1985; Gill et al., 1987). Not surprisingly, then, our ability to draw from and build upon previous research pertaining to gender and interpersonal violence is hampered by this lack of conceptual and methodological clarity.

Despite these limitations, this paper attempts to evaluate existing research and to suggest the most promising avenues for future work. The following section presents data on gender and interpersonal violence to address questions such as (1) Are men more violent than women regardless of offense, age, or residence? (2) Do victimization data present a comparable picture? (3) Do we have any evidence to indicate whether the gender gap in violent crime or violent victimizations is converging? (4) How do the violent criminal careers of men and women differ? Then we examine explanations for gender differences in aggression and violence, with particular emphasis on gender role theory and the data relevant to this theory. Attention is also directed to correlates of female violence, and a preliminary set of explanatory hypotheses is offered for the most prominent patterns observed in gender and violent crime. Policy issues concerning the adjudication and sanctioning of violent offenders and sexual assault victims are discussed next. Finally, we conclude with a discussion of the research priorities that may lead to a better understanding of the relationship between gender and interpersonal violence.

DATA

PREVALENCE AND INCIDENCE

Statistical data on gender and interpersonal violence are generally drawn from indicators of violent crime: arrest reports, victimization and self-report surveys, and public health agencies. In this section, we see that certain observations—most notably that females are underrepresented in the most serious/injurious types of violence—are remarkably consistent among all sources of data.

Uniform Crime Reports

Perhaps the best-known data for assessing gender differences in interpersonal violence in the United States are the Uniform Crime Reports (UCR). These reports are collected annually from local law enforcement agencies throughout the country (although there is a higher rate of reporting among urban than rural agencies) by the Federal Bureau of Investigation. UCR data contain information both on offenses known to the police and on arrests. Only the arrest data, however, are broken down by the gender of the offender; these data have a number of well-known limitations: (1) they are limited to offenses that result in arrest; (2) the data vary considerably in the accuracy with which they reflect illegal behavior due to, for example, the misclassification of similar crime events or the nonrecording of a crime (Cressey, 1970; Erickson, 1975; Steffensmeier et al., 1979; Blumstein et al., 1986); (3) as summary statistics, they fail to distinguish multiple offenders from multiple events and include attempted offenses with completed offenses (Steffensmeier and Allan, 1988); and (4) broad offense categories, such as assault, may contain a set of heterogeneous criminal acts (more generally, see Reiss, 1981; Weis, 1986). Despite these problems, scholars argue that for certain purposes (e.g,, when serious offenses are considered), UCR arrest data provide valid indications of the demographic distribution of criminal behavior (Hindelang et al., 1979; Gove et al., 1985).

The following analyses are based on five indices of violent crime for the year 1988: murder/nonnegligent manslaughter, rape, robbery, aggravated assaults, and other assaults. The overall measure of violent crime includes only the four indices used in the violent crime index by the UCR (i.e., it excludes other assaults). To calculate arrest rates, two types of computations were performed on UCR data. These computations were derived from Steffensmeier's extensive work on UCR data and gender differences in arrest rates (see Steffensmeier et al., 1979, 1989; Steffensmeier, 1980, 1982; Steffensmeier and Allan, 1988; Steffensmeier and Streifel, 1989).

First, 1988 arrest data from UCR were combined with census data to compute offense arrest rates that take into account sex distributions in the population.[2] Because few people under the age of 10 commit crimes, the rates are calculated for persons age 10 years and older (or for the population at risk). The formula used to compute the arrest rates is

$$\text{Rate}/100{,}000 = M/P \times N/T \times 100{,}000 \, ,$$

where M = the arrest volume given in the appropriate UCR table, P = the estimated population volume figure from the same UCR table, N = the estimated number of persons who would be in the UCR table if coverage were complete (e.g., total U.S. population, total rural population; this figure is taken from the U.S. census); and T = the estimated number of persons in the target category for whom the arrest figures are given (e.g., females age 10 and over; this figure is from U.S. census data).

Second, to estimate the gender disparity in violent crimes, we calculate the female percentage of arrests (FP/A), controlling for the sex distribution in the target population. The FP/A is calculated as follows

$$\text{FP/A} = \frac{\text{fn}}{\text{fn} + \text{mn}} \times 100$$

where fn = female arrest rate/100,000 for offense (*i*) and year (*j*) and mn = male arrest rate/100,000 for offense (*i*) and year (*j*). The FP/A also facilitates comparing these arrest data with Steffensmeier's earlier longitudinal analyses, ultimately suggesting whether the

TABLE 1 Violent Crime Arrest Rates per 100,000 for Males and Females, and Female Percentage of Arrests to Total Arrest Rates for Violent Crimes, 1988

Type of Crime	Males (101,025,300)[a]	Females (108,223,741)[a]	FP/A
All index violent crimes[b]	1,081.50	161.47	12.99
Murder	15.70	2.04	11.50
Rape	630.73	0.35	1.13
Robbery	111.43	9.67	7.98
Aggravated assault	288.05	41.88	12.69
Other assaults	635.60	107.54	14.47

[a]Numbers in parentheses refer to estimated number of people in the target category (i.e., males and females 10 years of age and older (Bureau of the Census, 1989).

[b]Includes the offenses of murder and nonnegligent manslaughter, forcible rape, robbery, and aggravated assault (U.S. Department of Justice, Federal Bureau of Investigation, 1989).

relative gap in male and female violence has narrowed or widened.

Table 1 presents violent crime arrest rates for males and females for 1988. First, it appears that the male rate of arrest for index violent crimes is about seven times higher than the female rate. Second, although there is some variation in the rates at which men and women are arrested for various types of violent crime, in no case does the female rate exceed, or even approach, one-quarter of the male rate. Not surprisingly, the largest variation appears for the crime of rape and the smallest for other assaults.

Table 2 further disaggregates these data by age. When comparing the same ages and offense categories, the arrest rates of males are substantially higher than those of females. However, if we assume that these data indicate actual rates of offending among males and females, the peak ages of violent activity vary little by gender. For example, in the case of robbery or aggravated and other assaults, the arrest rates for both males and females are highest from the midteens to the late twenties. The only exception to this pattern is murder. Here we find that female involvement seems to continue at a relatively equal, albeit low, rate into the thirties, whereas the male rate drops off in the thirties. The greater tendency for women to engage in intrafamilial homicides

TABLE 2 Violent Crime Arrest Rates per 100,000 for Males and Females (and female percentage of arrests) by Age and Type of Violent Crime, 1988[a]

Sex and Age	Murder	(FP/A)	Rape	(FP/A)	Robbery	(FP/A)	Aggravated Assault	(FP/A)	Other Assaults	(FP/A)
Male[b]										
10-14 (8,514,000)	2.34		16.12		73.55		112.11		315.43	
15-19 (9,278,800)	37.59		60.09		353.86		521.75		1076.24	
20-24 (9,609,100)	39.02		67.32		289.06		620.11		1420.98	
25-29 (10,956,800)	26.24		56.43		194.32		529.06		1240.66	
30-39 (20,378,900)	16.31		37.17		96.57		362.26		796.38	
40+ (42,287,700)	5.27		9.21		11.26		98.90		191.51	
Female[b]										
10-14 (8,092,000)	0.19	(7.51)	0.52	(3.12)	8.22	(10.05)	26.60	(19.18)	120.98	(27.72)
15-19 (8,922,000)	2.90	(7.16)	0.90	(1.47)	25.38	(6.69)	80.70	(13.39)	263.40	(19.66)
20-24 (9,585,400)	4.91	(11.18)	0.68	(1.00)	25.78	(8.19)	94.17	(13.18)	247.65	(14.84)
25-29 (10,917,800)	4.03	(13.31)	0.59	(1.03)	21.98	(10.17)	87.05	(14.13)	201.15	(13.95)
30-39 (20,535,500)	3.15	(16.19)	0.47	(1.25)	10.61	(9.90)	56.19	(13.43)	121.52	(13.24)
40+ (50,171,200)	0.67	(11.28)	0.05	(0.54)	0.83	(6.86)	10.07	(9.24)	21.81	(10.22)

[a]U.S. Department of Justice, Federal Bureau of Investigation (1989).

[b]Numbers in parentheses refer to estimated number of people in the target category (Bureau of the Census, 1989).

(Wolfgang, 1975; Mann, 1988) probably explains why murder rates have a slightly flatter age-related curve for women than men.

A relatively high proportion of the assaults (FP/As for aggravated and other assaults) also occur among the youngest group of females (10-14 years). Possible explanations for this finding encompass age, period, and cohort phenomena.[3] First, because Steffensmeier and Allan's (1988:63) comparable analysis of UCR data for the years 1979-1981 reveals similarly high FP/As for assaults among the youngest age group (13-17 in their analysis), a cohort effect seems unlikely. Second, as to a period effect, one could argue that a gender convergence in crime is occurring due to changes in socialization: women who became parents during the 10-year period following the early stages of the women's movement (in the late 1960s and early 1970s) may have been especially sensitive to the issue of gender equality in the raising and socialization of their children. However, we have little confidence in a period explanation because other studies using various methodologies (Adler, 1975; Smith and Visher, 1980), and spanning a wide range of years, also find a more pronounced narrowing of the gender gap for adolescents than adults. An age effect, combined with social expectations, may be the most plausible explanation (more generally, see Farrington, 1986). These relatively high FP/As for assaults involving young adolescents in both 1979 (Steffensmeier and Allan, 1988) and 1988 may be due to (1) the natural tendency for females at this age to begin spending more time away from home and in the company of peers; (2) the visibility of this offense (Black, 1980:152); and (3) the greater willingness of parents and others to invoke legal authority when the crime involves a female (Hagan et al., 1985).

The final UCR data we present for 1988 involve an analysis of arrest rates for violent crimes by residence (urban and rural) and gender.[4] Here we find that, regardless of gender, arrest rates are higher in urban than in rural areas and that, regardless of residence, the arrest rates of males again far exceed those of females (see Table 3). Notably, however, across most offenses the size of rural/urban differences in FP/A is small or negligible (see also Steffensmeier and Allan, 1988). The observation that residence adds little to our ability to predict proportional female involvement in violent crime may be explained by (1) the basing of arrest statistics on place of arrest rather than place of offender's residence, and (2) the apparent direction of a significant amount of female aggression and violence toward relatives and family members.

TABLE 3 Violent Crime Arrest Rates per 100,000 by Type of Crime and Residence for Males and Females (and female percentage of arrests), 1988[a]

Type of Crime	Males[b]				Females[b]			
	Urban (84,493,000)	Rural (32,152,000)			Urban (91,595,000)	(FP/A)	Rural (32,646,000)	(FP/A)
Murder	17.88	10.93			2.18	(10.87)	1.76	(13.87)
Rape	34.90	21.89			0.39	(1.10)	0.28	(1.26)
Robbery	146.45	37.08			12.56	(7.90)	3.22	(7.99)
Aggravated assault	333.23	191.87			43.30	(12.89)	25.61	(11.77)
Other assaults	750.84	394.17			125.54	(14.32)	68.90	(14.88)

[a]U.S. Department of Justice, Federal Bureau of Investigations (1989).
[b]Numbers in parentheses refer to estimated number of people in the target category (Bureau of the Census, jointly with the U.S. Department of Agriculture, 1989).

National Crime Surveys

Since 1973, the Census Bureau has collected annual data for the National Crime Survey (NCS), using a sample of 60,000 households. The NCS collects data only from victims, age 12 and over, of six crimes, three of which are violent: rape, robbery, and assault (aggravated and simple). Initially, victimization surveys were designed to assess the extent of unreported crime; subsequently, a substantial difference was found in the number of crime victimizations and the number of offenses known to the police (President's Commission on Law Enforcement and Administration of Justice, 1967:21). Methodological differences between the UCR and the NCS in recording crimes may account for some of this discrepancy. For example, when a single robbery incident results in the victimization of more than one person, NCS records information on each victimization, regardless of the number of criminal incidents involved.[5] The UCR, however, records information on offenses (and only the most serious offense if more than one occurs within a given crime event) and arrests, regardless of how many victims are involved. It is also important to remember that victimization surveys rely on the victim's judgment and memory about whether a crime has occurred, and analyses suggest that memory fade may vary with the relational distance between the victim and the offender (Law Enforcement Assistance Administration, 1972:Table 5). Nevertheless, NCS data provide a rich source of complementary crime data. They reveal not only the degree to which violent crime offending and victimization covary within the same gender and age groups, but in examining the perceived characteristics of offenders, they can also help to validate the patterns observed in UCR data.

We begin by presenting victimization rates, for 1987, for the three crimes of violence by gender.[6] Table 4 reveals that, with the exception of rape, males are more likely to be the victims of criminal violence than females. In the case of completed simple assaults with injury, however, the male and female rates are very comparable. Although the proportion of these victimizations that involve domestic violence remains unknown, it seems likely that spouse abuse is an explanatory factor. More generally, gender appears to have little effect on the differences between rates of attempted and completed victimizations: for both men and women, assaults are less likely to be completed than robberies. Finally, it is interesting to note that the rates of attempted and completed rape are virtually the same. It is possible, however, that if knowledge of the victim-offender relationship were available, the data

TABLE 4 Violent Crime Victimization Rates per 1,000 for Males and Females, 1987

Type of Crime	Males (99,959,780)	Females (102,809,700)
All crimes of violence	36.3	21.6
Completed	12.5	8.8
Attempted	23.8	12.8
Rape	0.1[a]	1.3
Completed	0.1[a]	0.6
Attempted	(z)[a,b]	0.7
Robbery	6.6	3.9
Completed	4.0	2.9
Attempted	2.7	0.9
Aggravated assault	11.4	4.4
Completed with injury	3.7	1.3
Attempted with weapon	7.8	3.1
Simple assault	18.1	12.0
Completed with injury	4.8	4.0
Attempted with weapon	13.3	8.0

NOTE: Detail may not add to total shown because of rounding. Numbers in parentheses refer to population in the group.

[a]Estimate is based on about 10 or fewer sample cases.
[b]z = less than 0.05 per 1,000.

SOURCE: U.S. Department of Justice, Bureau of Justice Statistics (1989:Table 3).

would indicate a higher completion rate for rapes involving known offenders (see Russell, 1984:59).

Table 5, which examines gender-age patterns of victimization, reveals that the peak age at which men and women are violent crime victims varies only slightly. Attempted and completed violent crime victimizations peak in the mid- to late teens for men (ages 16-19) and in the early twenties for women. Moreover, rates of completed victimizations are virtually identical for males and females age 25 to 49, and age 65 and over. Thus, regardless of gender, the peak ages for both offending and victimization appear to be from the midteens to the midtwenties (see also Russell, 1984, for comparable self-report data on rape victims and offenders).

TABLE 5 Violent Crime Victimization Rates per 1,000 for Males and Females by Age and Type of Violent Crime, 1987

Gender and Age	Completed Violent Crimes	Attempted Violent Crimes	Rape	Robbery	Aggravated Assault	Simple Assault
Male						
12-15 (6,781,500)	32.8	35.6	0.9[a]	10.4	18.2	39.0
16-19 (7,390,980)	29.7	60.5	0.0[a]	11.9	32.8	45.5
20-24 (9,322,410)	22.8	53.6	0.2[a]	13.0	24.6	38.6
25-34 (21,278,130)	13.6	26.2	0.1[a]	9.4	11.5	18.7
35-49 (22,932,150)	6.0	16.5	0.0[a]	3.6	7.8	11.1
50-64 (15,496,620)	4.7	6.5	0.0[a]	3.4	3.3	4.4
65+ (11,757,990)	2.5	3.0	0.0[a]	1.2[a]	1.4	2.9
Female						
12-15 (6,471,240)	15.6	26.5	1.7[a]	4.0	7.1	29.3
16-19 (7,294,470)	18.0	26.6	4.2	5.9	10.7	23.8
20-24 (9,732,610)	19.2	29.9	2.8	6.8	8.4	31.1
25-34 (21,606,580)	12.6	14.8	2.4	5.8	5.5	13.8
35-49 (23,880,320)	5.5	9.2	0.3[a]	3.1	3.5	7.8
50-64 (17,235,140)	2.3	4.0	0.0[a]	1.6	1.7	2.9
65+ (16,589,340)	2.5	2.9	0.1[a]	2.2	1.2	1.9

[a]Estimate is based on about 10 or fewer sample cases.

SOURCE: U.S. Department of Justice, Bureau of Justice Statistics (1989:Table 5).

Finally, as with the UCR data, we examine violent crime victimization rates by gender and location (metro/central city versus nonmetro). Locality of residence in the NCS data pertains to the place where the person lived at the time of the interview, not to the place where victimization occurred. Table 6 reveals that, regardless of gender and type of violence, victimization rates are higher in metro than nonmetro areas. The victimization rates of women also vary somewhat less by location than those of men, which suggests again that locality/residence has less impact on the frequency with which women are involved in violence (as either victims or offenders) by comparison to men. Further, as can be seen in Table 6, women's violent victimization rates are not always lower than the violent victimization rates for men. In fact, the completed violent crime victimization rate of metro women (13.76) exceeds the comparable rate for nonmetro men (9.66). Although these aggregate violent crime victimization rates for metro women and nonmetro men are significantly influenced by the skewed gender distribution of rape cases, comparable data appear for robbery rates.

A Closer Look at the Data Thus far, the NCS and UCR data on violent crime by gender suggest a considerable degree of parity between victims and offenders. Generally, women are much less likely to be involved in crimes of violence as either offenders or victims than men. The only exceptions to these patterns involve rape victimizations and the interaction of gender and crime location in robbery victimizations. The NCS data, however, can also be utilized to shed light on the validity of UCR data. Because this survey elicits information from crime victims about characteristics of the offender and whether the crime was reported to the police, we can begin to examine (1) the degree to which male dominance in crimes of violence is related to discretionary behavior on the part of police toward female offenders, and (2) whether females underreport victimization experiences as a result of the often-noted relational quality of their aggression.[7]

Table 7 presents data on the perceived sex of the offender from crime victims' reports. These data, again, suggest an overwhelming concentration of male offenders in crimes of violence (85.6% male and 13.7% female). The only offense category in which women even approximate roughly one-fifth of the offender population is simple assaults (males 82.8%, females 16.5%); the FP/A for other assaults in the UCR data was 14.5 percent. Thus, consistent with Hindelang's (1979:147) findings, it appears that

TABLE 6 Violent Crime Victimization Rates per 1,000 for Males and Females by Location and Type of Violent Crime, 1987

Gender and Location	Completed Violent Crimes	Attempted Violent Crimes	Rape	Robbery	Aggravated Assault	Simple Assault
Male						
Metro (26,563,450)	19.13	31.83	0.18[a]	13.10	17.31	20.42
Nonmetro (25,700,120)	9.66	21.03	0.0[a]	2.65	9.81	18.58
Female						
Metro (30,763,070)	13.76	18.47	2.07	7.60	6.74	15.83
Nonmetro (27,332,340)	7.23	11.00	0.83	2.12	4.19	11.18

[a]Estimate is based on about 10 or fewer sample cases.

SOURCE: U.S. Department of Justice, Bureau of Justice Statistics (1989:Table 18).

TABLE 7 Percentage of Single-Offender Victimizations by Type of Crime and Perceived Sex of Offender, 1987

Type of Crime	Perceived Sex of Offender			
	Male	Female	Unknown	Total
Crimes of violence (4,175,130)	85.6	13.7	0.7	100.0
Completed (1,459,690)	85.2	14.0	0.8[a]	100.0
Attempted (2,715,450)	85.8	13.5	0.7	100.0
Rape (131,090)	98.3	0.0[a]	1.7[a]	100.0
Robbery (567,460)	92.7	6.8	0.5[a]	100.0
Completed (355,580)	90.2	9.0	0.8[a]	100.0
Attempted (211,880)	97.0	3.0[a]	0.0[a]	100.0
Aggravated assault (1,090,700)	86.6	12.7	0.7[a]	100.0
Simple assault (2,385,880)	82.8	16.5	0.7	100.0

NOTE: Detail may not add to total shown because of rounding. Number of victimizations shown in parentheses.

[a]Estimate is based on about 10 or fewer cases.

SOURCE: U.S. Department of Justice, Bureau of Justice Statistics (1989:Table 39).

the net gender-linked selection bias through the arrest stage is very small.

Table 8 illustrates the percentage of violent crime victimizations reported to the police by the victim's gender and the victim-offender relationship. First, these data indicate that only about one-half of all violent crimes are reported to the police and that females are slightly more likely than males to report being victimized. Gender-based discrepancies in reporting are particularly notable in the case of robbery (47.5 and 69.6% of the victimizations are reported by men and women, respectively) and simple assault (33.9% of the men report and 47.3% of the women). The greater reporting on the part of female victims of simple assault may be a function of increased recognition and reporting of domestic violence incidents. In the case of robbery, this may be due to differences (perceived or actual) in the seriousness of the event because such factors as extent of physical injury, financial loss, or weapon use are important determinants of crime reporting (Hindelang and Gottfredson, 1976; Gottfredson and Hindelang, 1979). This would also be consistent with our finding that proportionately

TABLE 8 Percentage of Victimizations Reported to the Police by Type of Crime and Victim-Offender Relationship for Male and Female Victims, 1987

Type of Crime	All Victimizations		Stranger Victimizations		Nonstranger Victimizations	
	Male	Female	Male	Female	Male	Female
Crimes of Violence	44.5	54.3	47.8	56.3	38.4	52.7
Completed	52.8	61.3	55.8	68.9	47.9	55.8
Attempted	40.2	49.5	43.8	48.4	32.9	50.4
Rape	58.8[a]	52.8	66.5[a]	53.2	49.1[a]	52.3
Robbery	47.5	69.6	46.8	71.5	51.0	64.1
Completed	58.7	74.4	60.9	78.1	51.4	62.3
Attempted	31.0	54.6	29.3	48.6	49.4[a]	68.5
Aggravated assault	59.4	60.1	60.7	62.5	56.9	58.0
Completed	63.3	57.0	63.8	56.6	62.7	57.1
Attempted	57.6	61.5	59.6	63.8	52.4	58.6
Simple assault	33.9	47.3	38.9	41.9	27.1	49.8
Completed	39.8	53.2	44.6	51.9	33.4	53.5
Attempted	31.8	44.4	36.8	39.5	24.8	47.4

[a]Estimate is based on about 10 or fewer cases.

SOURCE: U.S. Department of Justice, Bureau of Justice Statistics (1989:Table 94).

more robberies are completed with female victims than with male victims (Table 4).

Second, although both men and women show greater willingness to invoke the police when victimized by strangers, this reporting pattern is relatively weak and sometimes variable (cf. Black, 1976:40-48). Perhaps what is most surprising is the lack of variation in women reporting rape to the police based on the victim-offender relationship (cf. Russell, 1984:96). Recent analyses of the characteristics that predict rape reporting suggest that factors that elevate the offense to a higher level of seriousness, or make prosecution easier, may tip the scales in favor of reporting the incident to the police (Lizotte, 1985). In effect, the victim analyzes the strength of her case before deciding whether to report the offense. For example, in addition to the familiarity of the offender (i.e., the more familiar, the less likely the report), the more property a rapist steals and the more serious the physical injury, the more likely it is that the victim will report. Hence with the considerable amount of attention given to the handling of rape cases by criminal justice personnel over the past decade (e.g., see Polk, 1985), it may be that factors other than victim-offender familiarity are influencing a victim's decision to notify the police.

Finally, although NCS data provide information on the gender and the race of violent crime victims, the UCR fails to provide comparable information in arrest data. Because UCR data indicate that a disproportionate amount of violent crime occurs among nonwhites, it is certainly possible that the interaction of gender and race may alter the picture we have of male dominance in crimes of violence. Analysis of other official sources (e.g., health statistics, police files in selected cities) provides an unsystematic but informative examination of the interrelationships among gender, race, and violent offending and victimization.

Race and Gender Virtually all of the research pertaining to the interaction of gender, race, and violent crime focuses on murder. Studies spanning the last decade uniformly suggest that race may be a better predictor of homicide than gender. For example, using homicide data from Detroit police records, Letcher (1979) found that, of the women arrested for murder, black women are more frequently involved in acts of lethal violence, both as victims and as offenders, than are white women. Wilbanks's (1982) analyses of the National Center for Health Statistics data for 1975 confirmed Letcher's finding and further suggested the following rank ordering of homicide victimization rates for the four race-sex groups: nonwhite males, nonwhite females, white males and white females. Mann's (1987) ongoing field research, which involves collecting data from centralized homicide files in the police departments of Chicago, Houston, and Atlanta, also reveals that, of the women arrested for murder, black women are found predominantly in cleared murder cases. Their proportions among total murder arrestees in these cities range from a low of 8.8 percent (Houston, 1979) to a high of 14.2 percent (Atlanta, 1983). The comparable range for white female murders is a low of 1 percent (Chicago, 1983) to a high of 5.2 percent (Atlanta, 1979) (Mann, 1987:177). Finally, in a review of both national and local studies that examine race, gender, and homicide, Riedel (1988a:9-10) finds that (1) the interaction of gender and race, in the case of both homicide offenders and homicide victims, produces the same rank ordering for the four race-sex groups as described by Wilbanks; and (2) the current black female homicide victimization rates are most similar to the rates of white males.

The limited data available on race-gender subgroups pertaining to other crimes of violence generally underscore the patterns observed in studies of homicide. For example, Steffensmeier and Allan (1988) used 1979-1981 statewide statistics, gathered by the Pennsylvania UCR system, to make black-white comparisons in the arrest rates and the FP/As for a full range of offenses. The violent crime (i.e., murder, aggravated and simple assault) arrest rates reveal the same rank ordering by race and gender as previously noted. Offense rates for black females, although closest to those for white males, actually exceed offense rates for both white males and white females. Comparable figures also are reported in NCS data on violent juvenile offending from 1973 through 1981 (Laub and McDermott, 1985). To illustrate more fully these race-gender interactions, Laub and McDermott also computed offending ratios by race and gender subgroups. Regardless of the offense, the lowest ratios appear for white males/black females and the highest for black males/white females. Within racial groups the gender ratio for assaults is reported to be lower for blacks than for whites. Although Laub and McDermott draw attention to this latter finding as a crime-specific pattern, the calculation of gender participation ratios for blacks and whites reveals an identical pattern across a broader range of offenses (e.g., robbery, auto theft, burglary), reflecting greater racial differences in female than male participation (Visher and Roth, 1986:251).

Additional Data Sources

Self-Report Studies Numerous cross-sectional self-report studies have been conducted over the past 30 years, again in an attempt to assess the amount of crime that goes undetected. These data pertain almost uniformly to youthful offenders. Smith and Visher's (1980) meta-analysis of 44 self-report (and some official) studies encompassing the years 1940-1975 treated the magnitude of the association between gender and deviance/crime (gamma) derived from each study as a dependent variable to be explained by the characteristics of the study. By so doing, the gender-crime association appeared to be less for (1) self-report versus official data (a point to which we will return), (2) personal and youth offenses versus violent and property offenses, and (3) nonwhite versus white populations. The relationship was greater for adults and urban samples as opposed to youth and rural samples. Comparable patterns were also uncovered during 1976-1980 by the National Youth Survey. The most pronounced gender differences for both prevalence and incidence rates were for violent offenses (Elliott et al.,

1983); a significantly higher proportion of black than white females reported involvement in violent crimes (Ageton, 1983). Irrespective of age, then, the participation of white females in crime appears to be concentrated in minor acts of deviance rather than serious criminal behavior.

Relational Violence That the magnitude of the gender-violence association may depend on the severity of the behaviors measured is also evident in studies of domestic violence. For example, studies of courtship and marital violence produce rates (per 100 people) that vary from a high of 37 to a low of 1.8 for the husbands/male partners and from a high of 24 to a low of 0.02 for the wives/female partners (Frieze and Browne, 1989:178). Variations in the questions asked of respondents (e.g., whether injuries were sustained, whether the violence was mutual or in self-defense) and difficulties in obtaining accurate recall of these events (especially when they occur frequently and information is elicited from only one party) probably contribute to the wide range of estimates (see also Kurz, 1989). However, what does appear consistently from these studies is that men have higher rates of using the most dangerous and injurious forms of violence (Stark et al., 1979; Berk and Loseke, 1981; Berk et al., 1983; Makepeace, 1983, 1986; Stets and Pirog-Good, 1987; Kratcoski, 1987; Aizenman and Kelley, 1988; Frieze and Browne, 1989).

In a related vein, research on the physical abuse of children frequently reports that mothers are at least as abusive toward their children, if not more so, than fathers (Bennie and Sclare, 1969; Steele and Pollock, 1974; Gil, 1970; Parke and Collmer, 1975; Straus et al., 1980; U.S. Department of Health and Human Services, 1981; Gelles, 1982; Widom, 1987; Gelles and Straus, 1988). Others, however, suggest that sample selection bias (i.e., researchers' and clinicians' focusing only on mothers) and a failure to consider the "time at risk" factor may explain the unusually high rates of female violence in this setting (Pagelow, 1984:187-190). Still others (Gelles, 1979) point out, again, that the most dangerous and potentially injurious acts are performed more by men than by women (for a more complete discussion of the methodological issues involved in analyzing domestic violence data, see Fagan and Browne, in this volume).

Taken together, both official incidence and self-report data paint a very consistent picture of the relationship between gender and interpersonal violence. Women are substantially underrepresented in crimes of violence, most notably when attention is directed to the most serious/injurious acts of violence. Further, although the gender-race interaction produces considerable variation in the rates of serious homicide, less is known about how this interaction affects other types of interpersonal violence. Whether these relationships between gender and violent offending are part of a larger pattern of stability or change remains to be seen.

RATES AND TRENDS

Gender and Violent Offending: 1960-1988

Political and social changes in the lives of women, especially since the rebirth of the women's movement, prompted some scholars to hypothesize that significant increases are occurring, and will continue to occur, in female crime (Adler, 1975; Simon, 1975). In this section we consider whether, since 1960, (1) there has been an increase in women's levels of violent crime in this country, and (2) there has been an increase or decrease in the proportional involvement of females in crimes of violence.

To address these issues, Table 9 presents data from three decades (1960, 1977, 1988) on male and female arrest rates (per 100,000) and the female percentage of total arrests (FP/A) for violent crime.[8] The 1960 and 1977 data are extracted from previous research (Steffensmeier et al., 1979), and the 1988 data appear in Table 1. With regard to the first question, we find a moderate increase from 1960 to 1977 in the rates of female violence, regardless of the specific offense. However, comparable data for males indicate much larger increases across all offenses, suggesting that the relative gender gap has remained stable. Over the next decade (1977-1988), the female murder and robbery rates actually declined, whereas assault rates showed moderate increases. Identical patterns, by offense type, appear for males over the years 1977-1988.

To answer the second question, we examine the female percentage of total arrests (FP/A) for violent crimes from 1960 to 1988. These data replicate some of the same patterns initially identified by Steffensmeier and his colleagues (1979:222). The relative gap between males and females in rates of violent crimes narrowed slightly for robbery and other assaults but widened for homicide; aggravated assaults remain relatively stable over this 28-year period (see also Steffensmeier and Streifel, 1989). Similar analyses of rural and urban violent crime arrest data also produced no significant shifts in the relative gender gap (see Steffensmeier and Jordan, 1978; and Table 3).

TABLE 9 Violent Crime Arrest Rates per 100,000 for Males and Females, and Female Percentage of Arrests to Total Arrest for Violent Crimes: 1960, 1977, and 1988

Type of Crime	1960[a]			1977[a]			1988[b]		
	Males	Females	FP/A	Males	Females	FP/A	Males	Females	FP/A
Murder	11.1	2.2	16.8	18.0	2.9	13.8	15.7	2.0	11.5
Robbery	76.5	3.5	4.4	139.4	10.4	6.9	111.4	9.7	8.0
Aggravated assault	125.7	20.3	13.9	237.2	32.5	12.1	288.0	41.9	12.7
Other assaults	340.2	34.7	9.3	432.6	63.3	13.0	635.6	107.6	14.5

[a]From Steffensmeier et al. (1979:Table 1).
[b]From Table 1, see endnotes.

Finally, we examine whether the involvement of adolescent females in violent crime changed materially over the period in question. Again, by relying on previously published research for our base of comparison, we can determine whether the gender gap in crimes of violence among youth is closing at a faster pace than it is among adults. Specifically, Steffensmeier and Steffensmeier (1980) calculated gender-specific arrest rates on all UCR offense categories (except rape) for the aggregate age group 10 through 17; for comparable ages, our data are disaggregated into two age groupings (10-14 and 15-19); therefore comparisons between our 1988 data and the Steffensmeiers' data should be interpreted cautiously. Only the FP/As for ages 15 to 19 years are used because crime rates tend to be higher among this age group than among 10 to 14 year olds; any decreases in the proportion of adolescent female involvement in violence, then, cannot be attributed to focusing on the least crime-prone group. Examination of the FP/As for 1965, 1977, and 1988 (Table 10) for youth involved in crimes of violence reveals a small narrowing of the gender gap in the case of robbery and other assaults but relatively stable patterns in the case of murder and aggravated assaults. The narrowing of the gender gap for robbery and other assaults, however, largely occurred from 1965 to 1977; from 1977 to 1988 the gender gap widened slightly (see also Ageton, 1983).

Thus, irrespective of age, stability rather than change is reflected in official data on female violent offending. Although rates of female violence show some modest increases, they are far outweighed by the increases in male violence. Not surprisingly,

TABLE 10 Adolescent Female Percentage of Arrests (FP/A) to Total Arrests Rates for Violent Crimes in 1965, 1977, and 1988

Type of Crime	1960[a]	1977[a]	1988[b]
Murder	6.3	8.6	7.2
Robbery	4.6	7.4	6.7
Aggravated assault	13.0	15.4	13.4
Other assaults	16.3	21.3	19.7

[a]From Steffensmeier and Steffensmeier (1980:Table 1), 10-17 year olds.
[b]From Table 2, 15-19 year olds; see endnotes.

then, the absolute gender gap in violent crime (male rate minus female rate) continues to widen (see Steffensmeier et al., 1979; and Table 1). Whether this gender-based pattern of violent crime exists in other societies is difficult to determine. Few scholars have simultaneously addressed cross-cultural and longitudinal trends in female violent crime, in part because of the difficulty of obtaining reliable definitions of types of crimes (see Archer and Gartner, 1984, for an excellent critique of INTERPOL data). Nevertheless, what limited evidence exists suggests that women in both industrialized and nonindustrialized nations continue to play relatively minor roles in violent criminal activities (Adler, 1981; Simon and Baxter, 1989).

Trends in Violent Victimizations

Far less attention has been devoted to gender-specific changes in victimization rates. One recent study, however, utilizing NCS data (on robbery, larceny, and assault) and UCR data (on homicide) found a definite increase in the proportion of female robbery victimizations (rising from 28% in 1973 to 37% in 1982) (Smith, 1987b; see also Bowker, 1981). Changes in the routine lifestyles of women may explain this finding. "Women now may be seen as more accessible and profitable targets than in the past, targets posing less threat for the offender than might confrontations with males" (Smith, 1987b:298). Homicides and assaults, by contrast, are less likely to involve changes in lifestyle because they frequently occur between individuals who are known to one another. Trends in black and white female homicide victimization rates further support this supposition because they have remained relatively constant since 1940 (see Riedel, 1988a:10).

An important qualification to this "lifestyle" explanation of gender differences and changes in violent crime victimization rates can be found in the work of Gartner and her colleagues (1987). Their study is also one of the few longitudinal analyses of victimization rates that employs cross-cultural data. Specifically, using pooled time-series data from 18 industrialized nations for the period 1950-1980 to examine and explain changes in females' risk of homicide victimization, they found that (1) the victimization rates for both males and females increased over the 30-year period in almost every nation; (2) there is a wide range of variation in homicide rates across nations, with the United States having the highest rate, regardless of gender, across the 30 years; and (3) although women's nontraditional activities do increase their risk of victimization, changes in lifestyle are not a sufficient explanation for such an increase. In the context of modern, industrialized societies, it appears that women's risk of victimization increases only when nontraditional activities and lifestyles are matched with traditional patriarchal expectations.

Additional Indicators of Trends in Violent Offending by Gender

Criminal Careers Another way of looking at trends and patterns in violent crime is to focus on the criminal career of the individual violent offender. "A criminal career is the characterization of the longitudinal sequence of crimes committed by an individual offender" (Blumstein et al., 1986:12). Over the last decade, scholars have increasingly moved away from relying on aggregate crime statistics and have started to examine two components of these statistics as key elements in the analysis of a criminal career: participation, the distinction between those who commit crime and those who do not; and frequency, the rate of activity of active offenders (Blumstein et al., 1986:12; see also Blumstein et al., 1988a,b; Weiner, 1989). Analyses of participation and frequency allow one to determine, for example, whether changes in crime statistics are due to a greater proportion of the population initiating criminal activity or merely to changes in the frequency of offending by active criminals. Examination of criminal career data can also answer such important policy issues as age at initiation, escalation and desistance of criminal activity, and causal factors associated with each of these stages of a criminal career.

Unfortunately, the bulk of the data that would allow one to assess such issues as the initiation, specialization, escalation, and termination of violent criminal careers pertains only to males (e.g., see Farrington, 1982; Weiner, 1989). The general tendency to exclude female offenders from longitudinal research on delinquency and antisocial behavior may be due, at least in part, to the greater frequency of violent offending among males. However, even among those studies that contain both males and females in the sample populations, the respondent's gender is often ignored; the researchers simply fail to disaggregate the data by gender (e.g., see Hamparian et al., 1978).

Weiner's (1989) recent analysis of violent career criminals represents an important exception to this pattern. Utilizing research that involved individual data on violent criminal careers from multiple sources (e.g., analyses of arrest histories of an urban birth cohort and self-reports of offending by high school students), Weiner found substantial gender variation in participation, age at initiation, recidivism, and desistance of violent career criminals:

(1) The cumulative violent juvenile participation of females is well below that of males, irrespective of the type of violent crime and irrespective of whether the data are self-reports or official records (Weiner, 1989:49, 56).

(2) Age-specific participation rates for males exhibit a pattern of initial increase over the juvenile years (12-18) followed by a decline after either the more advanced juvenile or the young adult years (19-21).

(3) By contrast, serious violence among females (based on Elliott et al., 1986), which is uniformly below the male rate, declines from the early juvenile years (12-14) through young adulthood (age 21) (Weiner, 1989:63-64).

(4) Age-specific violent career hazard rates (based on Elliott et al., 1986) also indicate that violent female careers appear to both begin and peak earlier than do those of males (Weiner, 1989:102).

(5) Females are at a much lower risk than males of recidivating violently, and females desist from violence at a much greater rate than do males (Weiner, 1989:108-109).

(6) Generally, violent offenses constitute a modest proportion of the total offense accumulation of all offenders in a population; females accumulate an even lower proportion of violent offenses than males, and these offenses tend to be concentrated in the younger age groups (Weiner, 1989:121).

Unfortunately, no systematic attention has been given to gender differences in the various studies of violence specialization or escalation (see also Farrington, 1986).

The National Research Council's Panel on Research on Criminal Careers, which focused primarily on criminal careers that involve robbery, burglary, and aggravated assault, arrived at comparable findings with regard to gender and participation. The most consistent pattern with respect to gender was the extent to which male criminal participation in serious crimes exceeds that of females, regardless of data source, crime type, level of involvement or measure of participation (Blumstein et al., 1986:40). However, that panel's analysis of gender variation in the individual frequencies for active offenders led it to conclude that active female offenders commit crime at rates similar to those of active males (Blumstein et al., 1986:67). By contrast, Weiner (1989:82) finds that, among those who are actively participating in violent crime, the male rate outstrips the female rate. This discrepancy in gender ratios may be, in part, a function of relying on different data sets. The panel's conclusion was based on two studies: Inciardi's (1979) analyses of self-report data from active heroin users and the National Youth Survey (NYS; Elliott et al., 1983). Weiner, focusing only on violent offenders, largely relies on a latter analyses of the NYS data (Elliott et al., 1986), which constrained individual offense rates for "serious violent" youngsters to three violent crimes. Nevertheless, these findings warrant further attention. As the panel suggested, if there is substantially less gender variation in frequency of offending than there is in participation, the large differences found between males and females in aggregate arrest rates may simply be due to differences that arise from gender-based variation in participation rates (Blumstein et al., 1986:67; see also Fagan, 1990). Whether this hypothesis can be generalized to nonwhites and adult violent offenders also warrants further exploration. As we have seen, a simultaneous consideration of gender and race in aggregate homicide data places the rates of black females closer to those of white males than white females. Because race also appears to be a stronger predictor of participation than frequency (Blumstein et al., 1986:72), attention must be directed toward estimating gender differences by race in violent crime participation rates.[9] If the violent crime male/female participation ratio is lower among blacks than whites (see Visher and Roth, 1986:251), we may want to rethink some of the etiological gender-based theories of violent offending.

Gangs Finally, one particular type of criminal career, gang membership, also has received considerable attention in criminological research. Although the bulk of this research has focused on male gang members, one can find selected accounts of the activities of female gang members and, more recently, changes in their roles and status over time.[10]

Prior to 1970, there was little evidence of any substantial changes in the roles or functions of female gang members; they acted primarily as weapon carriers and decoys. The most common form of female gang involvement remained as auxiliaries or branches of male gangs (Thrasher, 1963; Short, 1968; Hanson, 1964; Miller, 1973). Subsequent to 1970, several ethnographic accounts of gangs implied that females were fighting in more arenas than previously and were increasingly employing the weapons that males use. For example, Quicker's (1974) interviews with 13 female Chicana gang members in East Los Angeles revealed that women would fight other female auxiliary gang members, as well as carry weapons for males (cited in Bowker, 1978, and Campbell, 1984). Brown (1977), studying black female gangs in Philadelphia, found that in sexually integrated gangs, females were not relegated to peripheral activities but fought alongside the males in gang warfare. Further, his analysis of an all-female gang (the Holly Ho's) suggested a considerable amount of aggression among the women; the gang was reputed to attack both males and females, and owned weapons that ranged from knives to sawed-off shotguns. Male gang members in Los Angeles also reported some female involvement in violent gang activities; nevertheless, females were excluded from most of the economic criminal activity (Bowker et al., 1980).

A contrasting view of the role and activities of female gang members occurs in concurrent and subsequent studies. A 1975 survey of gang activities in six major U.S. cities suggested that any noted changes in female gang member activities does not alter the general position and role of women in gangs. Specifically, although Miller (1975) documented some reports of increased violence by female gang members, the overall distribution of female participation in gang activities did not differ from the past (cited in Bowker, 1978:145): females still acted as weapon carriers, with the most common form of involvement continuing to be as auxiliaries of male gangs. Campbell (1984), completing an ethnographic study of three nonwhite female gang members in New York City, found little change in female gang members' dependence on male gangs but some change in the internal dynamics of the female gang. According to Campbell (1984:32), although it is still the male gang that paves the way for the female affiliate, a girl's status now depends to a larger extent on her female peers (see also Vigil, 1988). Finally, Fagan (1990), studying predominantly nonwhite youth in three U.S. cities, provides perhaps the most systematic assessment of gender variation in gang and nongang criminal activity. He found that self-reported prevalence rates for violent offenses (i.e., the percentage reporting at least one incident of a felony assault, minor assault, or robbery) were significantly lower for female than for male gang members. However, female gang members' violent crime prevalence rates exceeded the rates of nongang males. The context of the gang itself, or its links to criminal opportunities, then may be a particularly important factor in explaining females' initial participation in violent offending, but there is no evidence that it affects their subsequent frequency of violent offending (Fagan, 1990:12-13).

The data on female gang activity at least suggest the possibility of transition in status and increased violence among women members. However, it is equally probable that these changes represent changes in the attitudes of, and methods used by, researchers studying female offenders as much as they do real qualitative changes in the women's behavior. As Campbell (1984:6) suggests, "It is difficult to separate the true nature of girls' involvement from the particular interpretive stance of the writer (usually male), whose moral and political view most probably reflects the prevailing community standard." Ultimately, answers about changes in female gang activity will depend on the acquisition of longitudinal data from various cities with racially diverse gang populations. In the interim, however, we would do well to concentrate on gender differences both in the etiology of gang participation and in violent criminal careers. The gang appears to be an important source of initiating female violent criminal offending, but at the same time, it remains independent of the development of subsequent rates of offending (cf. Klein and Maxson, 1989; Fagan, 1990). Whether this is due to changes in the nature of gangs themselves or in adolescents' lives in communities where gangs are prominent should be explored.[11]

METHODOLOGICAL ISSUES

The data we have presented suggest that, in most contexts and across various time periods, interpersonal violence is predominantly a male phenomenon. The degree to which these data are valid indicators of the proportional involvement of males and females in criminal violence remains the subject of some controversy.

Citizen Reports of Violent Crime

As we have seen, the primary source of information used in examining gender-related rates of, and trends in, interpersonal violence are police generated arrest statistics that appear annually in the Uniform Crime Reports. Gender differences in officially recorded criminal activity could be biased if citizens fail to notify the police when the offense involves a female or if, once notified, the police are less likely to arrest female suspects. With regard to reporting, there is no evidence of discrimination that would favor female offenders. Hindelang's (1979:151) analysis of NCS data for 1972-1976 reveals that, when the seriousness of the offense is controlled, few differences emerge in the rate of reporting personal crime victimizations by male and female offenders. In fact, for the most serious victimizations, female offender crimes are slightly more likely to be reported to the police than male offender crimes. Further, a simultaneous consideration of offense seriousness and sex of victim uncovered a counterbalancing effect: female victims were less likely to report female than male offenders to the police, whereas male victims reported female offenders more often than they reported male offenders to the police. This reporting pattern may even be sustained when victimizations involving strangers and nonstrangers are considered separately (Hindelang, 1979:152, note 15).

Gender and Arrest Probability

Research on the effects of gender bias in arrest is limited and generally quite poor; traditionally it has involved only observational impressions, a limited number of offenses, and few, if any, statistical controls (Visher, 1983:7-8). Further, although several scholars have speculated that changes in law enforcement practices may account for notable increases in female arrest rates for property offenses (Rans, 1978; Krohn et al., 1983; Steffensmeier and Streifel, 1989), few have focused on violent offenses. Perhaps the best available basis for assessing the effect of gender on arrest probability is Smith and Visher's (1981) analysis of the determinants of police arrest decisions in three metropolitan areas of the United States. Beginning with a probit analysis of the effects of both legal and extralegal variables on the arrest decision, Smith and Visher (1981) found that, all else constant (including offense severity), gender has no significant effect on probability of arrest. Further exploring the possibility that police treat women preferentially, Visher (1983) used the same data set to estimate separate probit models for males and females (the analysis included a t-test for equality of coefficients across equations). Her results indicate that Uniform Crime Reports may overestimate female involvement in property offenses and underestimate the criminality of older white females. Specifically, violent offenses had a greater impact on males, whereas property offenses were more likely to influence arrest probability for female suspects, relative to the suppressed category of public order violations (Visher, 1983:21). Does this suggest that UCR data underestimate female involvement in violence?

The available evidence does not show police discrimination in favor of violent female offenders. First, Visher's rotation of the suppressed offense category revealed that, regardless of gender, the probability of arrest is not substantially affected by whether the offender was suspected of a violent or a property offense. Females and males suspected of property offenses are arrested as often as those suspected of violent offenses. Second, and of greater import, is the homogeneity for offenses included in the analyses: most of the cases recorded in these data as "violent" were domestic assaults or acquaintance fights—not murders, rapes, or robberies. The probability of arrest for men and no arrest for women in such assaults, relative to public order violations, is probably a function of gender-based variations in the severity of the attacks. Lacking analyses for each offense category, with controls for the severity of the crime, such as weapon use and victim injury, we cannot conclude that women are underrepresented in violent crime statistics because of police bias.

A final analysis of this same data set by Smith (1987a) focused only on those cases that involved acts of violence in which the police had contact with both victim and offender ($n = 102$). Smith used a multinomial logit model to predict the odds of separation, mediation, or arrest based on a variety of legal (including injury and weapon use) and nonlegal (including race and gender of the disputing parties) factors. Although the analysis did not include female offenders, the results point to police bias in cases involving female and nonwhite victims. Violence between males or whites was most likely to be resolved by arrest, whereas violence between a male and a female or two nonwhites was most likely to be handled by separation (Smith, 1987a:776). Again, these results do not pertain to a full range of violent crimes or gender combinations of victims and offenders. Nevertheless, they do imply that the accuracy of violent crime data may depend not only on the severity of the criminal acts but also on the victim's attributes (Smith, 1987a:779-780).

A last look at a wider range of violent crimes can be obtained by referring back to Hindelang's (1979) data. Comparing official arrest statistics, disaggregated by gender, and victimization reports of the perceived sex of the offender for the offenses of rape, robbery, and assault (aggravated and simple) revealed comparable findings: by both criteria, males substantially outnumber females. Notably, in the cases of robbery and aggravated assault, Hindelang also found an overrepresentation of females in arrest statistics by comparison to victimization reports.[12]

Implications of Self-Report Data

Gender differences are uniformly smaller in self-report data of delinquency than in official records. Hindelang and his colleagues (1979), however, maintain that the differences are largely due to discrepancies in content and seriousness between the two instruments. Those items in self-report studies that are even roughly comparable to UCR items (e.g., beat up/assault) produce most similar results. More recently, Bridges and Weis (1989), regressing the magnitude of the gender-violence association on design characteristics of 115 studies, found that sources (e.g., official versus self-report data) and domain (types of crime included) do not create major discrepancies in gender-violence research, in part because of the relative accuracy with which violent crime is measured. However, because the correlations based on social aggregates also produced much stronger associations than those based on analyses of individuals, Bridges and Weis (1989:29-30) recommend disaggregating data to obtain the most precise information on the individual characteristics associated with violent offending. As such, an important subsequent step in research pertaining to gender and interpersonal violence may be focusing on those microsocial contexts (e.g., youth gangs, domestic setting) in which violence is prevalent.

Although differences in item content may explain differences in the gender ratio for crime at one point in time, Smith and Visher (1980:698-699) have suggested that other factors may be more important for explaining why self-report data show a greater convergence in the gender gap than official data. Specifically, they suggest either that the gender convergence is limited to only the less serious criminal acts or that official reactions to changes in female crime are occurring at a slower rate than the actual behavior. For several reasons, we feel that the former explanation seems most plausible. First, recall that a closing of the gender gap, regardless of data type, appears to be least evident in the case of violent crimes (Smith and Visher, 1980:696-697). Second, and relatedly, there is strong evidence that self-report measures are most valid when they are applied to the less serious delinquent populations (Hindelang et al., 1981). Third, and finally, analyses of short-term trends in crime and delinquency suggest that rates of discovery of crime by police and arrest rates are both increasing over time (Menard, 1987); we have no evidence that this increased efficiency on the part of the police systematically excludes female offenders (Steffensmeier and Streifel, 1989).

The preceding analysis has put together pieces of relevant information on gender and violence from various articles that speak to the issue of the validity of our measures of crime. It is clear that a more adequate assessment would involve (1) progressively examining the factors that influence victim reporting, police response, and offender accountability solely as they pertain to males and females who commit crimes of violence; and (2) constructing adjustment factors to correct for any gender biases found in these measures. At this point, we can only suggest that the biases existing in official statistics either are nonspecific to gender (in the known underreporting of offenses involving nonstrangers) or, in the case of assaults, have a counterbalancing effect on the probability of males being arrested (male offenders with male victims are more likely to be arrested than male offenders with female victims; Smith, 1987a).[13] The important question before us then is why women are so much less likely than men to be involved in acts of interpersonal violence.

CAUSES AND CORRELATES IN GENDER AND VIOLENCE

EXPLANATIONS FOR GENDER DIFFERENCES IN INTERPERSONAL VIOLENCE

It is now well known that research and policy directed toward female offenders lags far behind that on male offenders (Klein, 1973; Smart, 1976; Datesman and Scarpitti, 1980; Leonard, 1982; Kruttschnitt and Johnson, 1984; Naffine, 1987). Nowhere is this more obvious than in the area of interpersonal violence. Consideration of the substantial gender gap in violent crime has arisen primarily in the context of refuting the hypothesized relationship between the women's movement and changes in female arrest rates for specific property offenses (e.g., see Simon, 1975; Chapman, 1980; Steffensmeier, 1980, 1982). Not surprisingly, sociological and criminological theories offer virtually no explanation for the relative lack of female involvement in crimes of violence (see Siann, 1985; Simon and Baxter, 1989).

Sex Versus Gender: Hormonal Influences or Environmental Factors?

Perhaps the largest body of empirical research relevant to this question comes from the work in experimental psychology on aggression. The relevance of examining gender differences in aggression for criminal violence pertains to both the noted association between aggression in youth and adult criminal violence (Robins,

1966; Farrington, 1978; Magnusson et al., 1983) and the etiological issue of the relative importance of biological or cultural/environmental determinants of violent behavior (Wilson and Herrnstein, 1985:117).

Maccoby and Jacklin (1974, 1980) provided compelling evidence for gender differences in aggression in their review of cross-cultural studies of aggression, studies of subhuman primates, experimental manipulation of sex hormones, and studies of "presocialized" children. These data led them to conclude that males may be biologically predisposed toward aggressive behavior; they did not, however, discount environmental influences. Subsequent reviews and critiques of Maccoby and Jacklin have argued that (1) cross-cultural studies of children (which speak more directly to the etiology of aggression than studies of adults) tend to demonstrate the interplay of social environmental factors in children's behavior (Tieger, 1980:945; White, 1983:6-7); (2) there is a great deal of species-specific variability in the degree of sex differentiation in aggression (Tieger, 1980:945-947; White, 1983:5); (3) the organizing and activating functions of hormones in aggression among humans remains unclear (Tieger, 1980:951; White, 1983:6-7; Siann, 1985:33-36; Widom and Ames, 1988:316-322); and (4) although observational research on aggression among young children provides some support for a biological basis for sex differences, developmental research suggests that parental and environmental factors may be equally important determinants of gender differences in aggression (Tieger, 1980:952-959; White, 1983:8-9). Thus, although there may be some evidence for sex differences in aggression, the most challenging issues appear in the area of understanding how social, situational, or cultural factors ameliorate or aggravate aggressive or violent behavior patterns in males and females (see also Brain in Volume 2).

Developmental Studies of Aggression and Violence in Children

Fagot and her colleagues address some of the questions raised by Maccoby and Jacklin concerning the development of aggression in "presocialized" children. In several studies involving both home and peer play group settings, Fagot observed white children, primarily from intact families, ranging in age from 12 to 48 months. Beginning with the youngest group (12 to 16 months old), Fagot et al. (1985) found no sex differences in aggression (e.g., hit, push, kick, take objects), but they did find that caregivers reacted very differently to the aggression of boys and girls. When girls aggressed, their behavior was ignored 80 percent of the time, whereas aggression by boys was attended to 80 percent of the time. By the time these infants were toddlers, there were marked differences in aggression, with boys being consistently more aggressive than girls. Toddler peer response to the aggression of boys and girls also mimicked that of their caregivers; girls' aggression was ignored more than boys', and boys responded more to the acts of other boys than to the acts of girls. Girls generally showed less gender-based differentiation toward acts of aggression (Fagot and Hagan, 1985). Finally, Fagot and her colleagues (1986) also discovered a significant relationship between the acquisition of gender labels and social behavior. Children who understood the boy-girl distinction (usually acquired by 30 months of age) showed gender-typical differences in aggression, whereas those who did not understand it failed to display such differences. As Fagot et al. (1988:92) conclude, these results suggest that the male's use of aggression is built into the child's construction of his gender schema, whereas aggression is not a part of the girl's gender schema; in fact, the typical female gender schema may include avoidance of the expression of aggression.

Extending this work on the determinants of aggression among males and females to the work that has been done on sibling aggression and generally coercive families, Fagot et al. (1988) attempt to explain the developmental determinants of male aggression against females. Specifically, they argue that three conditions must be met to produce a child who will be a consistent aggressor against females. First, the family must be out of control: the parents lack discipline skills, fail to monitor the child, fail to effectively problem solve, and fail to provide positive role models. Second, the child must have female models on which to practice (mothers or siblings), with no effective punishment of the boy's aggressive behavior toward the female. Third, there must be a system of family values that devalues females, so that they are perceived as appropriate targets of male violence (Fagot et al., 1988:103). Partial support for this model can be found in Felson and Russo's (1988) study of sibling aggression (hitting and slapping) among fourth through seventh graders. Here, no gender differences emerged in levels of aggression among siblings, but differential reinforcement appeared for acts of aggression among boys and girls. Parents were particularly likely to punish boys when they fought with their sisters, and subsequent aggression was more frequent when boys were punished than when some other strategy was used.[14]

Other scholars have focused on the particular contexts in which boys and girls are most likely to aggress. Caplan (1975), for example, argues that (1) the socialization of boys and girls shapes their responses to tests and experimental situations; (2) the need for achievement may be greater for boys and the need for approval greater for girls; and (3) the previous findings of no gender differences, or elevated levels among boys, in aggression can be explained by facets of the study design that elicit these different needs. Caplan's review of the relevant research does reveal covariation between characteristics of the experiment and the presence or absence of gender differences in aggression. Tasks that result in failure experiences (arousing the need for achievement) and those that involve an adult (arousing the need for approval) are more likely to demonstrate that boys are more aggressive than girls; in contrast, success or no-failure experiences and the absence of an adult are conducive to finding no gender differences in aggression. Barrett's (1979) subsequent observational study of 5- to 8-year-old boys and girls at a summer day camp over a six-week period provides comparable results with regard to the effect of an adult's presence. His data also further our understanding of contextual effects by suggesting that the sex of the target, the degree of structure in a setting, and the type of aggression measured affect the magnitude and direction of gender differences in aggression. Specifically, boys appear to be both more physically and more verbally aggressive than girls only when the target is male and the children are engaged in a moderately structured activity (see White, 1983:13).

Finally, numerous studies have identified parental correlates of aggression and antisocial behavior in middle childhood and adolescence. A meta-analysis of longitudinal and cross-sectional research revealed that the most powerful predictors of juvenile conduct problems, including delinquency and aggression, are lack of parental supervision, parental rejection, and low parent-child involvement; to a lesser extent, background variables, such as parents' marital relations and parental criminality, also predict conduct problems (Loeber and Stouthamer-Loeber, 1986). However, two caveats should be noted. First, although it appears that these findings pertain equally to boys and girls, far fewer analyses that relate parental behavior to delinquency and aggression of boys and girls could be found. Second, these findings are based primarily on samples of white youth (Loeber and Stouthamer-Loeber, 1986:316, 321; see also Lewis et al., 1983; VanVoorhis et al., 1988; Farrington, 1989). The importance of disaggregating these data by race and gender can be seen at least preliminarily in studies of the developmental consequences of family violence. Abused and neglected males, and nonwhites, seem to be more likely than their female, and white, counterparts to subsequently engage in violent criminal behavior (Kruttschnitt et al., 1986; Rivera and Widom, 1989; Widom, 1989a).

Thus, although observational studies of aggression in very young children can provide compelling evidence for biologically based sex differences, the developmental perspective suggests that the environment, from birth on, also has a strong influence in shaping the nature, extent, and target of aggression among males and females. We cannot ignore the importance of parental variables, both in the microsocial world of preschoolers and in the emergent social life of adolescents. Regardless of a child's inborn or early acquired disposition, parental behaviors appear to have a strong mediating effect (Reid and Patterson, 1989:116). Clearly, however, we need to expand beyond samples of white youth to explore whether, and how, these socialization experiences reappear among nonwhite families.

Gender Roles, Aggression, and Violence Among Adults

By comparison to the studies of aggression in children, studies of gender differences in adult aggression reveal much smaller and less consistent findings (Frodi et al., 1977; Eagly and Steffen, 1986). The most robust findings suggest that (1) men aggress more than women when they have the opportunity to aggress physically rather than psychologically; and (2) gender differences are larger when women perceive that aggression produces harm to others or anxiety, guilt, or danger for themselves (Eagly and Steffen, 1986). As was true of the studies of gender differences in aggression among children, these results point to the importance of contextual variables in the magnitude of the noted association. However, there are also design factors that speak to the external validity of the study. As Eagly and Steffen (1986:325) point out, the best-known and most popular methods for studying human aggression (laboratory, Buss-paradigm) happen to be the ones that elicit greater aggression in men than women and greater aggression toward men than women. Unfortunately, the most popular subjects for these studies also tend to be white male college students, and the types of aggression observed (delivering electric shocks or honking horns) are not the most common forms found in daily life (Macaulay, 1985). However, if we assume that the variation in the magnitude of gender differences in aggression between children and adults results from social roles that channel and regulate aggression, we would do well to concentrate on those environments in which aggression appears (Eagly and Steffen, 1986:326; Macaulay, 1985).

A number of studies of college students' attitudes toward, and experience with, courtship and marital violence report that men with traditional attitudes toward the role of women are more violent than men with more liberal attitudes (Sigelman et al., 1984; Bernard et al., 1985; Finn 1986). These results concur with both experimental studies (White, 1983) and family violence research that finds higher rates of violence in marriages where husbands make the majority of the decisions as opposed to more egalitarian marriages (Frieze and Browne, 1989:191). The relationship between gender role attitudes and violence is less clear, however, for women. Whereas some field research suggests that women who hold traditional gender role attitudes are more likely to endorse marital violence (Finn, 1986) or less likely to report or act upon being assaulted (Bernard et al., 1985; Walker and Browne, 1985), laboratory studies suggest that traditional females are not always less aggressive than liberal females. A woman's gender role attitudes appear to interact with other factors (e.g., level of provocation, sex of instigator, presence of a supportive observer) in producing levels of aggression (White, 1983:14-15). Some support for the hypothesis that aggression levels among females are mediated by other factors also can be found in the work of Giordano (1978). Using self-reports of criminality from a study of high school students and a group of institutionalized delinquent girls, she found that the more delinquent, aggressive girls were receiving reference group support for their nontraditional behavior (see also Marsh and Paton, 1986). More generally, however, self-report studies either find no association between females' gender role attitudes or gender identity and their reported level of involvement in antisocial and criminally violent behavior (Widom, 1978; Norland et al., 1981; Grasmick et al., 1984) or find that females with the most liberal attitudes are the least likely to be involved in aggressive acts of delinquency (James and Thornton, 1980).

Finally, stemming from the hypothesized relationship between the women's movement and increases in female arrest rates, researchers have endeavored to determine whether trends toward gender equality have affected female involvement in crime. Perhaps stated most strongly by Adler (1975:3), "The movement for full equality has a darker side which has been slighted even by the scientific community . . . . In the same way that women are demanding equal opportunity in the field of legitimate endeavor, a similar number of determined women are forcing their way into the world of major crimes." Initial examination of this hypothesis with UCR violent crime data suggested that female involvement in criminal violence remains unchanged, despite claims of major shifts in women's involvement in all types of crime (Steffensmeier et al., 1979). More sophisticated analyses of this question have involved regressing the FP/A on various indicators of liberation (e.g., percent of women in labor force relative to percent of men, proportion of female college students, fertility rate) for the years 1960-1985. These analyses generally indicate weak support for the liberation hypothesis. Both female labor force participation and the female-to-male ratio of college enrollments were negatively associated with the FP/A for homicide and assault (Steffensmeier and Streifel, 1989; see also Steffensmeier and Allan, 1988). Finally, INTERPOL data, in combination with various measures of female social role participation (e.g., marriage and fertility rate, female labor force participation, percentage of female university students), have also been used to assess this hypothesis. Although the violent crime analyses are limited to homicides, there is no consistent evidence that the equalization of gender roles, which may accompany social and economic development, increases female crime (cf. Hartnagel, 1982; Widom and Stewart, 1986; Steffensmeier et al., 1989). However, as Widom and Stewart (1986) argue, it may be that gender equality or emancipation is a complex construct and that each of its components (social, political, and biological) affects female crime differently.

A comparison of the results of experimental studies of aggression in children and adults suggests that socialization plays a large part in determining gender-related rates and patterns of aggression. However, at this time, we cannot conclude that gender role socialization is a sufficient explanation for the gender gap in violence. On the one hand, if it were, we should observe some convergence in the violent crime rates of men and women who express/engage in nontraditional gender roles. On the other hand, it may be that particular aspects of gender role socialization, such as the repression of aggression in girls or the child rearing functions performed predominantly by mothers, are maintained across generations despite the adoption of nontraditional roles or attitudes. Still others may argue that the fundamental problem lies in the measurement of gender roles. Although there can be no doubt that gender roles can constrain social behavior, research designs influence our observation and understanding of this process. Use of the term, and measurement of the concept, "gender roles" have been less than theoretically precise, encompassing types of activities and attitudes (job preferences/roles, profeminist attitudes), gender identity (masculinity and femininity), and gender orientation (expressive and relational). However, there does not appear to be any consensus as to which of these dimensions is most important or which measure is most valid (e.g., see Norland and Shover, 1978; Spence and Sawin, 1985; Gill et al., 1987; Naffine, 1987).

Structural Explanations for Gender Differences in Violence: Variants on Role Theory

Opportunity Theory and Female Violence In addition to theories involving women's liberation, opportunity theory (Cloward and Ohlin, 1960) has also been invoked to explain changes in female arrest rates. In its most frequent application, it is hypothesized that changes in female labor force participation will create new opportunities for women to commit crimes (e.g. white-collar offenses, embezzlement; see also Steffensmeier, 1980). With regard to violent crime, Simon (1975:2) suggested that as women's employment and educational opportunities expand, their feelings of being victimized and exploited will decrease, and their motivation to kill will become muted. The evidence to support this hypothesis is mixed. Cross-cultural (INTERPOL) data show almost no relationship between women's educational and economic opportunities and female homicide rates (Widom and Stewart, 1986; Simon and Baxter, 1989; Steffensmeier et al., 1989).

However, as we have seen, recent analyses of UCR data do show that decreases in some violent crimes are associated with increased female labor force participation. Steffensmeier and Streifel (1989:24-25) suggest that the latter finding not only supports Simon's original hypothesis but also supplements it in (1) the aspect of family violence theory that points to economic insecurity and financial worry as a proximate cause of domestic violence and (2) the routine activities framework, which would posit that women outside of the home have less opportunity for engaging in violent encounters with children and spouses (see also Steffensmeier and Allan, 1988).

Labeling Theory Changes in the social status of, and opportunities available for, women can affect violent crime rates by affecting the behavior of deviance-processing agents. As previously noted, official measures of crime are a product of the act of defining and responding to behavior as illegal. Viewed this way, the gender gap in violent crime is a function of differential willingness to report and sanction violent females.

Harris (1977) directed attention to social "typescripts," or the everyday assumptions we hold about who does what, including deviance, in society to explain gender-based variations in crime. Specifically, Harris argues that the distribution of these typescripts may provide the single strongest causal account of the empirical differences in male and female criminality. With regard to the underrepresentation of women in violent crime, Harris (1977:12,14) notes that these typescripts are so deeply embedded in society that they impact both motivations for deviance and rates of processing offenders: "It is (still) type-scripted that it is unlikely or 'impossible' for women to attempt assassination, robbery or rape." A comparable set of hypotheses was also developed by Widom (1984). She argued that much of what we know about criminal behavior and psychopathology is influenced by gender role stereotypes because (1) individuals comply with appropriate gender role behavior and (2) expectations about appropriate gender role behavior influence the labeling and diagnosis of deviant acts. She also uses these hypotheses to explain the relatively greater involvement of women in certain types of crimes (prostitution, child abuse, shoplifting) than others (rape, robbery, pedophilia) and the noted associations between certain diagnostic categories and gender role stereotypic behavior (see also Schur, 1984).

As we have seen, it is difficult to confirm empirically that gender role stereotypes provide the motivation for specific kinds of delinquency or crime. However, there is some evidence that violent behavior may be a more common adaptation to stress in males than it is in females. For example, Horwitz and White (1987) found that gender identity was associated with different types and rates of pathology. Among a large sample of adolescents, females displayed the greatest amount of psychological distress whereas males showed more self-reported delinquency (including crimes of violence). Further, over the course of adolescence, masculine gender identity was increasingly associated with high rates of delinquency for males and low rates of psychological distress among both males and females. Widom's (1989a) findings from an analysis of the cycle of violence hypothesis also speak to the question of gender roles and styles of pathology. Specifically, she found that although abused and neglected males had substantially higher arrest rates for violent crimes than a matched group of controls, the same pattern did not appear for females. Instead, abused and neglected females were at increased risk for property, drug, and order offenses. However, it is unclear whether these different developmental patterns are due to an internalization of stereotypes about gender-appropriate behaviors or simply to the difference in types of stress/abuse suffered by males and females.

Research pertaining to the hypothesized influence of gender role stereotypes on the labeling and diagnosis of deviant acts is most pronounced at the latter stages of the criminal justice system and rarely focuses on violent offenders (e.g., see Kruttschnitt and Johnson, 1984; Erez, 1989). However, some evidence concerning changes in police behavior that may affect the probability of female arrests for minor acts of violence can be found in the recent work of Steffensmeier and Streifel (1989). Specifically, Steffensmeier and Streifel found that, for the years 1960-1985, indicators of the formalization of social control/social labeling (i.e., annual changes in police per capita and the percentage of civilians among law enforcement personnel) were significantly associated with female arrests for property offenses and other assaults but not for the more serious violent crimes (aggravated assault and homicide). It should be clear, however, that these data do not provide measures of either police officers' gender role stereotypes or their attitudes toward female offenders; instead they measure changes in police officers' capacity to make arrests (see also Steffensmeier and Allan, 1988, for a similar hypothesis concerning the FP/A for assault among black females).

In summary, the most prominent explanatory variables in current research on gender and interpersonal violence are gender role socialization and, to a lesser extent, gender identity. Gender role socialization is used to account for observed differences in the aggression of infants and toddlers, the incongruent results of gender differences in laboratory studies of aggression in children and adults, and national and cross-cultural data on violent crime among females. However, the data are not always congruent with the hypothesized effects of gender roles on crime. We have little evidence that objective indicators of changes in gender roles (such as the female percentage of the labor force) correlate with changes in levels of interpersonal violence, and we have no evidence that gender role identity or gender role attitudes are associated with violent crime for females. Thus, as a number of feminists argue, we may need to reexamine this explanatory framework and restructure it with both inductive and deductive data.

Rethinking the Connection Between Gender Roles and Crime

Although it is important to acknowledge that there are numerous feminist perspectives in criminology, a dominant theme emerging from them is that the study of crime has been a male phenomenon (Daly and Chesney-Lind, 1988; Simpson, 1989). As a result, it is argued, explanations for female crime are really explanations of male criminality (Klein, 1973; Smart, 1976; Leonard, 1982; Naffine, 1987). Role theory was acknowledged as one of the first theories that explained female criminality in other than psychological or biological terms, and that addressed the significance of such factors as differential socialization, differential opportunity, and differential social reaction in understanding female crime (Smart, 1976:66). However, despite its contributions, role theory is criticized both for failing to take account of the historical and political derivation of gender roles (Smart, 1976; Leonard, 1982) and for employing the culturally variable and empirically unreliable concepts of masculinity and femininity (Carlen, 1985; Naffine, 1987). Further, its clear application to questions such as, Why are women less likely than men to be involved in crime? and What explains gender differences in rates of arrest and types of criminal activity? places it squarely in what is termed the "gender ratio" paradigm.

Daly and Chesney-Lind (1988:515-516) argue that theories of gender and crime can be built in several ways. The most common approaches focus on either the generalizability problem or the gender ratio problem. The former concerns the degree to which theories of men's crime apply to women, and the latter focuses on what explains gender differences in rates and types of criminal activity. Work on the gender ratio problem, they believe, is dominated by male scholars who rely on statistical evidence and elements of existing theory to develop new theoretical formulations that, in reality, are only variations of old theories of male criminality (e.g, social control and conflict theory as recently applied to the issue of gender and delinquency by Hagan et al., 1987). More generally, a number of feminist scholars believe that a more fruitful approach to answering questions about both inter- and intragender variability in crime is to give equal weight to different methodological approaches to studying crime. Our understanding of the causes of crime among both men and women could be improved by emphasizing qualitative, historical, and subjectivist approaches in addition to the dominant, quantitative, research paradigm (Daly and Chesney-Lind, 1988; Simpson, 1989; for similar arguments pertaining to research in other fields, see Macaulay,

1985; Harding, 1986). Such approaches might provide more accurate portrayals of how women become involved in crime, what keeps them involved, and what factors influence their desistance. None of these scholars have formulated their own theory to explain the role of gender in crime or in violent crime; nevertheless, their work is significant in pointing out how the reliance on one type of methodology or style of work can limit our understanding of whether, and how, the processes that lead to violence differ for men and women and, within gender, for whites and nonwhites (Simpson, 1989).

Correlates of Interpersonal Violence

Research on the demographic and social correlates of violent crime suggests considerable gender variation. However, the quantity of the research is limited and the quality is varied (e.g, based on institutional populations, uneven coverage of all types of violent crime and, within crime categories, of the demographic correlates). The largest body of data comes from studies of homicide. As previously noted, these data indicate that black women are more often involved in homicides (as both victims and offenders) than white men or women; regardless of gender, this offense appears to be primarily intraracial. However, although the data on gender and race also suggest that women's homicides are more often intersexual and intrafamilial than men's (Benedek, 1982; Mann, 1987; Riedel, 1988a), there is additional evidence that black women tend to kill friends, acquaintances, and other females more often than do their white counterparts. Women appear to be infrequently involved in felony homicides (Mann, 1987:182).

It is much more difficult to obtain a portrait of women involved in other types of serious violent crime. Analysis of NCS data, as well as probation and prison data, pertaining to females involved in assaultive offenses reaffirms at least one of the patterns found in homicide data: the victims of these women are frequently known to or involved with them (Ward et al., 1969; Kruttschnitt, 1985a), especially when the women are acting as lone offenders (Young, 1979). Parisi (1982) examined NCS data and PROMIS (Prosecutor Information System) data from Washington, D.C. for 1974 and 1975 and found that, overall, females were more likely to commit crimes alone, rather than with an accomplice, and were less likely to use lethal weapons than males. Unfortunately, however, she did not specify the types of offenses included in these data. The study by Ward and his colleagues

(1969) of female inmates in California indicated that women often commit robberies with a partner, and only infrequently with a weapon, but act alone in the commission of assaults and homicides where lethal force is much more likely to occur. With regard to robbery, some comparable findings appeared in a recent study of 33 female robbers incarcerated in Florida: only one-third of these women committed their offense alone, but most used a firearm (Fortune et al., 1980).

Certainly more exploration is needed about the patterns and correlates of female violence. Further analyses might address some of the following omissions in our knowledge of violent female offenders: (1) Do the race and gender patterns observed for homicide (i.e., intraracial and, generally, intersexual) reoccur for robbery and assault? (2) If a woman is more likely to commit a robbery (as opposed to homicide or assault) with an accomplice, what is her relationship to the accomplice? (3) Are violent women offenders more or less likely than their male counterparts to have a substance abuse problem or to use drugs or alcohol before committing a crime, or does substance use vary with the type of crime (e.g., is it more likely to occur in domestic assaults and relational homicides than in robberies)? (4) Do female career criminals specialize in certain types of offending? (5) Do the women who commit felony homicides and aggravated assaults against strangers present a very different social and demographic profile from those who commit domestic homicides and nonstranger or relational assaults?

Because a sizable proportion of women's violence appears in encounters with nonstrangers (Ward et al., 1969; Mann, 1987; Riedel, 1988a), special attention should be directed toward whether, and how, women who engage in relational violence differ from those who direct their violence toward a stranger. As Fagan and Wexler (1987:7) point out, incorporating family violence into the study of criminal violence may enhance the explanatory power of existing theory derived from the separate disciplines. Mann's (1988) analysis of women who kill in domestic and nondomestic encounters in six U.S. cities provides one significant attempt to bridge this gap. Although many of her findings confirm previous research (e.g, homicides committed by women are generally intersexual, intraracial, and intrafamilial, and offenders are usually older members of low-income minority groups), others suggest that this type of violence may not be so much a product of self-defense or a violent intimate relationship as it is a continuation of a violent background. Women involved in domestic homicides (58.3%) were just as likely to premeditate their crimes as women involved in nondomestic homicides (58%). Further, the domestic homicide offenders who claimed self-defense had more prior arrests than the nondomestic offenders claiming self-defense, and there was little difference in violent offense histories between the two groups (30% of the domestic homicide offenders and 37.5 percent of the nondomestic homicide offenders). As is true of men, then, it may be that women who are extremely violent in the home are also the ones who are more likely to be violent outside the home; women's choice of victims may also not be as static as it is commonly believed to be (Fagan and Wexler, 1987:12; Hotaling et al., 1989).

IMPLICATIONS FOR A THEORY OF GENDER AND INTERPERSONAL VIOLENCE

We are now at a point where it is possible to offer some speculative propositions about gender and interpersonal violence. Three predominant patterns emerge from the data we have presented: (1) female participation in crimes of violence is significantly lower than that of males; (2) race may represent an important variation in the gender-violent crime paradigm since black females have higher rates of homicide, and possibly other violent crimes, than white males; and (3) by comparison to male violence, the target of female violence is more often relational. Because a good theory both parsimoniously explains known facts and accurately generates predictions, we begin our explanatory model with these three factors of participation, racial variation, and target. We then integrate psychological, social, and situational/contextual variables to suggest the following preliminary hypotheses.

First, from infancy forward, aggression in boys appears to be attended to, and reinforced, more than it is in girls. Although most boys gradually learn to repress their aggression, physical aggression is always in the male's background as a gender-acceptable behavior; girls typically drop aggression from their behavioral repertoire at a very early age (Fagot et al., 1988). Second, contributing to this initial difference in the place of aggression according to gender schema is the role of parenting in middle childhood and adolescence. A lack of supervision and parental involvement appears to predict antisocial and violent behavior among both boys and girls (Loeber and Stouthamer-Loeber, 1986). However, poor parenting may be especially detrimental for boys both because of their known propensity for being more vulnerable than girls to stressful life events (Hetherington, 1981; Rutter, 1982; Eme, 1984) and because of the traditional pattern of gender role socialization in which the activities of boys are often monitored less carefully than those of girls (Hagan et al., 1987). Further, because there is also evidence that parental involvement and supervision vary by race as well as gender, with white girls being the most protected group (Matsueda and Heimer, 1987; Jensen and Thompson, 1990), we should expect to see higher rates of violence among nonwhite females than among white females. Finally, for the relatively few girls who do engage in violence, their greater propensity to select relational targets may be due to a combination of childhood exposure to family violence and specific contextual stressors such as current victimization, isolation, and economic stress (e.g., see Widom, 1987). Because it is now well known that prior exposure to family violence is not a sufficient explanation for engaging in subsequent familial violence (Widom, 1989b) and that the presence of a number of stressful events increases the probability of subsequent violence (Kruttschnitt et al., 1987), it seems most likely that women who engage in relational violence are those who are also currently experiencing family-related stressors.

In sketching these propositions, we do not mean to exclude other social and cultural factors (e.g., criminal opportunities, community norms toward crime and violence) that may either reinforce or counterbalance existing developmental patterns (e.g., see Fagan and Wexler, 1987; Fagot et al., 1988). In fact, our ability to extend a theory of gender and interpersonal violence into a broader explanation of the major variations in gender and crime will probably require the inclusion of these variables. Again, gender role socialization may be a necessary, but not sufficient, explanatory variable for both the absolute gender gap in crime and the greater concentration of females in selected, "gender-appropriate" offense categories. However, to explain the relative narrowing of the gender gap in larceny, fraud, and forgery (and perhaps robbery), we need to look more closely at the role of other social and cultural factors.

Steffensmeier and Streifel (1989:22) suggest, for example, that larger and more bureaucratized police forces result in greater diligence in counting and pursuing minor, instead of only serious, offenders. Because women commit relatively more minor than serious offenses, these larger and more formalized police departments have had a greater effect on female levels of reported crime. It is also possible, as they suggest (Steffensmeier and Streifel, 1989:23,35-36), that the growth of consumer products, illicit drug use, and female economic marginality has created more opportunities and more motivation for female involvement in crime (see also Fagan, 1990).

Drug use may be particularly important in explaining observed increases in female property offenses. The use of addictive drugs, such as cocaine and heroin, appears to be at least as prevalent, if not more so, among female as among male arrestees (Wish and Gropper, 1990:371). Further, although the association between drug use and crime is strongest for high-frequency drug users regardless of their gender, the criminal activities in which these users engage, is not gender neutral. Females who use drugs frequently are less likely than their male counterparts to engage in predatory crimes; instead, they resort to prostitution, shoplifting, and other covert, nonviolent, crimes at high rates (Chaiken and Chaiken, 1990:212-213). Increasing rates of female drug addiction then could well be contributing to the rise in female property crimes (see also Anglin et al., 1987). Relatedly, the rise in female-headed households and the attending increases in poverty (Center for the Study of Social Policy, 1986) may motivate more women to commit property crimes, but the evidence for this association has yet to be established. Multivariate analyses of the effect of female economic marginality on property crime are rare and do not provide particularly strong support for this hypothesis (cf. Chapman, 1980; Steffensmeier, 1980; Giordano et al., 1981; and Steffensmeier and Streifel, 1989). More generally, however, an assessment of the full range of individual and situational conditions (e.g., frequency of drug use, peer group influences, and expanded criminal opportunities) that could impact the levels of female property crime, including economic marginality, has yet to be undertaken.

Thus, at this time, we know too little about the factors that elicit and sustain female crime and about the range, or degree of specialization, of women's criminality to offer more than this speculative explanation. At the very least, however, the data we have reviewed do suggest that any theory that fails to consider past and current differences in socialization and opportunities for women and men will be incomplete (see also Heidensohn, 1985).

POLICY

Research on patterns and trends in violent offending by females has generally proceeded as if it had no relevance to sanctions and sentencing. Deterrence research, for example, virtually ignores potential gender variations in analyzing both the deterrent influence of threats of criminal sanctions and the effectiveness of the criminal justice system's activities in controlling crime rates (e.g., see Cook, 1980; Simpson, 1989:620-621). Although in large part this omission can be attributed to the infrequent involvement of women in violent crime, two important questions remain: do gender-based differences in criminal court processing exist and, if so, are they related to subsequent levels of female involvement in crimes of violence? In this section we are particularly concerned with the ways in which the processing of women through the criminal justice system could either aggravate or mitigate their subsequent involvement in acts of interpersonal violence.[15] We review what little literature there is on sanctioning of both male and female violent offenders; what, if any, conclusions can be drawn; and what questions remain. We then suggest additional areas of inquiry that could affect criminal justice policy pertaining to interpersonal violence.

GENDER VARIATIONS IN THE TREATMENT OF VIOLENT OFFENDERS
BY THE CRIMINAL JUSTICE SYSTEM

Juvenile Court Decisions

The vast majority of both quantitative and qualitative analyses of gender variations in the treatment of juveniles addresses the issue of differential selection and processing of male and female status offenders (see Chesney-Lind, 1973, 1974, 1977, 1988; Boisvert and Wells, 1980; Shelden, 1981). Among the few studies that include a broader array of juvenile offenders, no clear association among gender, offense type, and severity of disposition emerges. The relationships among these variables appear to vary by study and stage of criminal court processing. For example, in deciding who will be formally adjudicated in juvenile court, Cohen and Kluegal (1979a) find that violent offenders, regardless of gender, are less likely to be treated informally than juveniles charged with other types of offenses. However, in the case of pretrial detention, violent female offenders are treated more leniently than their male counterparts (Cohen and Kluegal, 1979b). Similar results were reported for the decision to incarcerate by Staples (1984). Nevertheless, the contrary conclusion—that females are treated more *severely* than males in these latter two stages of criminal justice processing—was supported by evidence from a different jurisdiction (Feld, 1989).

One study suggests that, once the decision to incarcerate has been made, violent females are much less likely than violent males to be sent to a correctional school. Lewis and her colleagues (1981) compared the psychiatric symptoms, violent behaviors, and medical histories of an entire one-year sample of adolescents from the same community who were sent either to the correctional school or to the only state hospital adolescent psychiatric unit serving the area. They found that although the degree of violence and psychiatric symptomatology were not associated with placement, gender was. Aggressive behaviors in adolescent boys were treated as the deliberate acts of healthy youngsters whereas the same acts were considered as psychologically aberrant when performed by girls (Lewis et al., 1981:518). Certainly, replicating this study in other jurisdictions and following these youngsters forward to obtain criminal career data would provide much-needed information on the consequences of mental health sanctions, as opposed to penal sanctions, for youthful violent offenders, as well as the potential interactions among gender, treatment mode, and recidivism.

Adult Criminal Court Decisions

As with juveniles, few analyses of the effects of gender on adult criminal justice processing decisions focus on violent crime. Accordingly, the following review relies heavily on studies including felony offenses and either controlling for or analyzing offense severity in interaction with the defendant's gender.[16]

Information on the relationship between gender and various presentencing adjudicatory decisions (e.g., the decision to prosecute, pretrial release, charge bargaining, and severity of final conviction) is both sparse and inconsistent. Women may actually be treated more severely than men in the decision to prosecute and plea negotiations (Figueira-McDonough, 1985; Ghali and Chesney-Lind, 1986) but less severely in the pretrial release and final conviction decisions (Stryker et al., 1983; Farrell and Swigert, 1986; Wilbanks, 1986).

However, analyses of sentence severity, the most studied aspect of adjudication, repeatedly find that women are less likely to be recipients of prison sentences, and receive shorter prison sentences when incarcerated, than men (Frazier and Bock, 1982; Curran, 1983; Zingraff and Thomson, 1985; Spohn and Welch, 1987). Additionally, although attention has been directed to the interaction of race and gender in sentencing outcomes, there are too few studies—and the outcomes of these studies are too disparate—to draw any firm conclusions (see Daly, 1989b).

The noted gender differences in sentence severity can be explained in two ways. One explanation pertains to the methodological variations and omissions in this research. For example, does either a failure to consider qualitative differences in the violence of men and women, or a failure to model the outcome of prior deviance processing decisions, produce leniency toward females (Kruttschnitt and Green, 1984; Zatz and Hagan, 1985; Miethe, 1987)? The other explanation pertains to the gender role attitudes and stereotypes of the judiciary, as encompassed by the chivalry and paternalism theses (see Nagel and Hagan, 1982, for a review of these theories; and Kritzer and Uhlman, 1977; Gruhl et al., 1981; Kruttschnitt, 1985b, for analyses of the effects of the gender of deviance-processing agents). Most recently, the paternalism thesis has been extended/reformulated to include a specific discussion of the way in which family status interacts with gender to produce leniency for female offenders (Daly, 1987, 1989a,b). Daly's (1989a:15) analysis provides some evidence that family ties have a stronger mitigating effect on the sanctions accorded women, regardless of offense severity, than men (see also Kruttschnitt, 1984). For our purposes, however, the important question is whether the apparent leniency extended to female offenders subsequently affects their probability of recidivating.

The Sentenced Violent Offender: Probation, Prison, and Parole

Probation If women are more likely to be given probation than men, are they also more likely to complete probation successfully? Norland and Mann (1984), in perhaps the only study focusing on this question, examined rates of probation violations for both men and women. The authors found that men were charged with committing new crimes while on probation in much greater proportion than women. New charges for women were disproportionately for technical violations of probation. In fact, probation officers regarded these women as troublesome not because of their criminality but because they made time-consuming demands that tended to be organizationally disruptive.

Prison Over the past decade the issue of inmate violence and victimization in institutions for adult males has dominated the field of penology. The vast majority of research on female inmates, however, focuses on (1) female patterns of adaptation to prison life, including the role of homosexuality and the development of pseudofamilies in this process; (2) the effects of incarceration on mothers and their children; and (3) historical accounts of the development of women's prisons (see Kruttschnitt and Krmpotich, 1990). Despite evidence of violence and degradation in women's institutions, empirical research documenting this phenomenon is scarce. What little we do know suggests that both the extent and the nature of aggression in women's prison facilities differ from the aggression and violence found in men's prison facilities. Although women may be punished and put "on report" more frequently than men for offenses against prison discipline (Dobash et al., 1986; Mandaraka-Sheppard, 1986), their proportional involvement in prison violence appears to be considerably lower than men's. There is little evidence of either predatory sexual behavior or collective violence in women's prisons (Bowker, 1980; Kruttschnitt and Krmpotich, 1990).

The correlates of inmate violence also vary significantly by gender. Whereas a minority racial status, a conviction for violent offenses, a lengthy current sentence, or a previous history of incarceration is each associated with a higher rate of violence in male correctional facilities (Carroll, 1974; Ellis et al., 1974; Bennett, 1976; Sylvester et al., 1977; Bowker, 1980; Irwin, 1980), none of these variables seems to be associated with prison violence among females. Instead, age and family composition (both family of origin and procreative family) appear to be the most significant correlates of female prison violence. The most aggressive women are young, single, and childless and, more often than not, were raised in a traditional two-parent household (Mandaraka-Sheppard, 1986; Kruttschnitt and Krmpotich, 1990).

These conclusions about female inmate aggression should be treated cautiously. They are based largely on data obtained from only two studies, one conducted in the United States (Kruttschnitt and Krmpotich, 1990) and the other in Great Britain (Mandarka-Sheppard, 1986). Nevertheless, the significant gender variations that emerge from them suggest that this area of research may improve our understanding of the processes that affect rates and trends of interpersonal violence by men and women. By replicating and extending these studies in other correctional facilities for women, questions such as the following, relevant to both theory and policy, could be addressed: (1) Has violence among female inmates increased over time? (2) Do institutional characteristics predict rates of inmate violence, regardless of gender (e.g., cf. Ekland-Olson, 1986; Mandaraka-Sheppard, 1986)? (3) Upon release, do violent inmates' rates of offending vary by gender? (4) Do the effects of violent prison victimization differ by gender?

Parole Finally, we examine whether men and women released from prison on parole have different success rates. Unfortunately, there appears to be little information on gender variation in the parole performance of violent offenders. However, in one study of female parolees, violent offenders (assaultive women) were no more likely to violate parole than women convicted of other offenses (Spencer and Berocochea, 1972). Among the few studies that compare male and female parolees, regardless of the offense of conviction, there is evidence that women have a greater probability of parole success than men: women are less likely than men to be returned to prison either for technical violations or for new major convictions (Moseley and Gerould, 1975; Mowbray, 1982). Women with drug histories, however, may be an important exception to this pattern (Moseley and Gerould, 1975; Simon, 1979; Mowbray, 1982).

We began by asking whether violent female offenders are treated differently from their male counterparts in the criminal justice system and, if so, whether this affects their probability of engaging in subsequent violence. The extant research offers no definitive answer to this question. Although the available data suggest that, at least in the sentencing phase, women receive preferential treatment, there is no evidence that this leniency amplifies their violence. Both during and after periods of incarceration, women exhibit less violence and subsequent criminality than men. Is it because, relative to gender socialization and informal social control, criminal justice interventions have little influence on behavior? As Heidensohn (1985:198) suggests, women are the one segment of society whose policing has already been "privatized," even though public means of control are still employed. Or is it simply that our knowledge of the careers of violent female offenders is so limited that we are unable at this time to detect the influence of sanctions on women's behavior?

Although the leniency extended to women has been attributed primarily to their family status/ties, the interaction between gender and violent offense type, with family status being controlled for, needs to be assessed more carefully (cf. Bernstein et al., 1979). Certainly, a systematic examination of race and gender variations in these outcomes is warranted. The general omission of race in these analyses is surprising, given that at least half of all incarcerated women are black and that the social locations of and pressures for criminal involvement may differ for black women as opposed to women of other cultures or races (Lewis, 1981; Young, 1986; Daly, 1989b).

Variations in the Treatment of Victims of Interpersonal Violence

Up to this point, the analyses of gender and interpersonal violence largely exclude the crime of rape. Because of the virtual dominance of male offenders, rape is not a useful offense for studying gender variations in violent offending, victimization, and adjudication. However, when we turn to the questions of whether and how the criminal justice system's treatment of violent crime victims impacts subsequent violence, rape—and more recently domestic violence (see Fagan and Browne, in this volume)—take center stage. Concern over the level of female violent crime victimizations has drawn increasing attention to the ways in which official treatment of female assault victims may encourage subsequent victimizations (e.g., see Brownmiller, 1975; Dobash and Dobash, 1979; Klein, 1982; Russell, 1984). Specifically, the diminution of rape victims, or of their criminal cases, may result in lowering the perceived costs of committing a rape. Although child sexual abuse cases are also relevant to our discussion, at this time, too few cases proceed to the point of prosecution to make a systematic assessment possible (Stewart, 1985). Thus, the following discussion focuses on adult victims of sexual assaults/rape.[17]

Sexual Assault Victims

Reporting Simply stated, women are generally reluctant to report sexual assaults to the police. Factors that appear to affect the likelihood of reporting include peer support, a woman's conviction that a rape has occurred, and the evidentiary strength of the case. For example, Holmstrom and Burgess's (1978) study of 94 rape victims admitted to a city hospital revealed that only 23 percent of these women reported the rape on their own initiative; 10 percent of the cases were reported by a stranger; and in 38 percent a police report resulted from friends and family members prompting the victim to report the crime (see also Feldman-Summers and Ashworth, 1981). Empirical analyses of NCS data also suggest that evidentiary variables influence reporting decisions: a greater amount of property stolen, serious injury, an unknown offender, and a married victim all increased the likelihood that a rape will be reported to the police (Lizotte, 1985). A study of women in rape crisis centers (admittedly not highly representative of the population) produced comparable results (Williams, 1984).

Finally, Russell's (1984) interviews with 930 randomly selected adult females in San Francisco showed that black victims and offenses involving black offenders were most likely to be reported. However, because the race of the offender was confounded with the relational distance between the victim and the offender (i.e., black rapists were overrepresented among stranger rapists), this latter finding pertaining to the offender's race must be treated with caution.

Police Processing Just as there is a significant amount of self-selection in the willingness of victims to invoke legal action in sexual assault cases, so also is there selection bias from the responses of the police to these victims. LaFree (1989) analyzed 904 sexual assault cases that occurred in 1970, 1973, and 1975 in Indianapolis, focusing on the participation of police in arrest, charge seriousness, and felony screening decisions (which were strongly influenced by the detectives). The arrest decision was significantly influenced by such evidentiary concerns as suspect identification, victim willingness to testify, prompt reporting, and presence of a weapon. The probability of arrest also increased when the offense involved an acquaintance, rather than a stranger. LaFree (1989:78) suggests that this may be due, as in domestic assaults, to the use of arrest by the police to protect the victim from further attack. Finally, consistent with feminist arguments, arrest was less likely when the victim engaged in "nonconformist" behaviors (e.g., hitchhiking, using alcohol at the time of the offense, willingly going with the suspect).

The same evidentiary factors (weapon, reporting promptness, and victim testimony) also predicted the more serious charges. Additionally, if (1) the offense included sexual penetration, (2) the victim was both white and older, and (3) the suspect was black, the case resulted in more serious charges. The best predictors of the decision to file a case as a felony were charge seriousness, the presence of multiple offenders, and victims over 18 years of age. This latter finding was attributed to the increased likelihood that incidents involving younger suspects included characteristics that usually make the case less serious to the detectives (e.g., "date rapes"; LaFree, 1989:79).

As in the reporting of sexual assaults, these data indicate that there is no easy answer to the question of whether sexual assault cases are affected more by the behavior of the victim or by the behavior of the offender. Subsequent analysis of the processing of these cases through the court system, however, sheds further light on this issue and speaks directly to the role of victim credibility in the processing of sexual assault cases in criminal court (e.g., see Randall and Rose, 1981).

Criminal Court Processing Although few systematic analyses of the court processing of rape cases exist, the available data implicate victim characteristics and behaviors in both pretrial and final case dispositions. PROMIS data from the District of Columbia, for example, revealed that in forcible sex cases, victims who know the offender and who abuse alcohol are more likely to have their cases dropped by prosecutors at the initial screening (Williams, 1976). LaFree (1989:91-113) subsequently determined that once charges have been filed, legally relevant factors (e.g., weapon use, type, and seriousness of offense; victim's willingness to testify and to identify the suspect) and victim credibility both influence court decisions. Specifically, victims who exhibited "nonconforming" behaviors (e.g., drinking in a bar unescorted), who failed to report the assault promptly to the police, and who were black were less likely to obtain guilty verdicts or convictions of guilt (by trial or plea). It is important to note that these cases with black victims refer primarily to intraracial offenses because there were too few white offenders with black victims to be included in the analyses.

Feminist concerns about the selectivity with which rape cases are handled by the criminal justice system and the treatment accorded victims seem to be at least partially justified (cf. Myers and LaFree, 1982). The data suggest that both the legal seriousness of the case and factors pertaining to the victim's credibility/reputation influence a victim's willingness to report being assaulted, police response, and criminal prosecution of the case. It may not be surprising, then, that over the past two decades we have seen a concerted effort by feminists to change state laws that contribute to low conviction rates in rape cases.

Changes in Legal Procedures in Rape Cases Statutory changes in the processing of rape cases aim at reducing the role of victim attributes/credibility and increasing conviction rates. These include redefining rape in a broader offense category, relaxing proof requirements, and restricting testimony concerning the complainant's sexual history (Gates, 1978; Polk, 1985). Evaluations of the effects of these statutory reforms on prosecution and conviction rates are, however, rare.

Some states, such as Michigan and Minnesota, placed rape in the broader category of assaults. California, on the other hand, adopted a multifaceted approach that included (1) providing enhancements for the use of weapons or violence, (2) including a rape shield law (to constrain the use of prior sexual history in proving consent), (3) establishing gender-neutral language in defining rape, and (4) removing the spousal exception in cases of rape (Polk, 1985:193).

Polk (1985) examined California's Bureau of Criminal Statistics data, for 1977-1982, to determine whether these statutory changes affected the processing (i.e., arrests, the filing of felony complaints, felony convictions, superior convictions, and state institutional sentences) of rape cases relative to other predatory crimes. The changes he found were not specific to rape and were limited to the tail end of the criminal justice system. There was no evidence that police were more likely to clear a reported incidence of rape with an arrest, and although prosecutors showed some tendency to file more rape cases as felonies, the felony conviction rates for rapes did not systematically increase over the years. Even at the sentencing level, the increase in incarceration rates was not unique to rape cases but instead appeared to be part of California's general shift toward increased penalties for all serious felonies. An early analysis of legal reform in the state of Washington also showed a "tail end" effect that was consistent with the penal philosophy of "treating" rather than incarcerating those convicted of sexual assaults (Loh, 1980).

Caringella-MacDonald (1985) examined similar data for Michigan five years after the enactment of the model Michigan rape law. She found that sexual assault cases were more likely to be authorized for prosecution than nonsexual assault cases, but it is unclear whether this is an artifact of offense severity. The nonsexual assault cases included simple as well as aggravated assaults and case characteristics were not controlled. Further, among the cases authorized for prosecution, victim credibility problems (e.g., inconsistent statements, implausible accounts) were noted in a significantly higher proportion of the criminal sexual assaults, perhaps because of the absence of other strong case characteristics (corroborative evidence, presence of weapon, stranger assailant; see also Reskin and Visher, 1986). At subsequent stages of processing, Caringella-MacDonald uncovered no significant differences in the proportion of cases terminated with conviction or plea bargained. However, criminal sexual assaults were reduced to a greater extent than other assaults. The objective of treating criminal sexual assaults like nonsexual assaults did not then appear to have been fully realized in Michigan.

Indiana's attempts to improve rape conviction rates and lessen the importance of victim characteristics also seem somewhat unsuccessful. LaFree (1989) gathered extensive data (e.g., on victim, defendant, courtroom characteristics and testimony, interviews with jurors, and questionnaires from judges) from 38 trials three years after the passage of the Indiana rape shield law. Additionally, he developed operational definitions of traditional and nontraditional victim behavior; the latter included (1) alcohol or drug use in general and at the time of the incident, (2) extramarital sexual activity, (3) having illegitimate children, and (4) having a reputation as a "partyer."

First, LaFree (1989:203) found that the rape shield law was invoked in only one-third of the trials observed, but that in virtually all of these trials the women had allegedly engaged in nontraditional behavior (LaFree, 1989:203). Because the point of this law was to ensure that information about the victim's nontraditional behavior was not introduced in the courtroom and courtroom observers coded only the evidence of nontraditional behavior that was presented in the court while the jury was present, the rape shield law appeared to be totally ineffective.

Second, LaFree (1989:201-208) also examined the interrelationships among the victim's behavior, defense strategy, and verdict.[18] This analysis revealed that allegations of nontraditional behavior were always made when the issue was whether the victim consented to the sexual act but never when it was the defendant's *diminished responsibility*. Further, those cases that used the consent defense were least likely to result in a guilty verdict, whereas those that employed diminished responsibility were most likely to obtain the guilty verdict.

Third, and finally, LaFree (1989:208-233) also analyzed what factors influenced jurors' perceptions of the defendant's guilt. The victim's behavior was important only when consent and no-sex defenses were mounted, and in these cases, it was more important than measures of physical evidence and seriousness of offense. Women who engaged in extramarital sex, used alcohol and drugs regularly, knew the assailant, or were black were "blamed" for the offense. Notably, LaFree's (1989:220) interviews with jurors led him to conclude that this latter finding is due to the stereotypes that white middle-class jurors hold about black women, such as "they are more likely to consent to sex or they are more sexually experienced and hence less harmed by the assault."

Legal reforms aimed at increasing conviction rates and reducing the role of victim attributes in the processing of sexual assault cases have been, at best, only partially successful. Despite the passage of rape shield laws in more than 45 states and the elimination of corroboration of the victim's testimony as a prerequisite for conviction in most states, the victim's credibility remains a central issue in the processing of sexual assault cases. Attending to the victim's behavior can be understood, in part, when relevant evidentiary concerns (e.g., weapon use, injury, eyewitness) are missing from a case, but as we have seen, the victim's behavior can be weighted more heavily than the legal seriousness of the cases when a no-consent or no-sex defense is mounted. An important policy question arises here that should be considered a priority for future research: Do attorneys select their mode of defense based on the victim's credibility, or does the defense selected dictate whether the victim's behavior will be raised as an issue? An additional and related priority for future research pertains to the role of the victim's race in the processing of sexual assaults. The clear message from LaFree's (1989) findings is that only sexual assaults involving white victims are considered seriously by the criminal justice system. We need to determine whether the victim's race has a similar effect in other jurisdictions and in other violent crimes; recall that at least one empirical analysis of police responses to assaults revealed that the probability of arrest was least likely when the assault involved nonwhites.

Admittedly, our knowledge of the criminal court processing of sexual assault cases is limited to specific jurisdictions and time periods. Perhaps evaluation data from a broader array of states, agencies dealing with victims of sexual assaults (hospitals, social agencies, crisis center), and postlegislative reform years, may reveal cause for a more optimistic outlook. Popular and scientific interest in rape victims has generated a considerable amount of change in the reporting rates, treatment, and even some aspects of processing offenders. At this time, however, it appears that we are not doing enough to raise the ante for the perpetrators of sexual assault.

PRIORITIES FOR FUTURE RESEARCH

Almost every review of women and crime ends with a litany of topics for future research. This has been useful because it has generated considerably more information on, for example, patterns and trends in female offending and factors that influence the processing of female offenders. It has not, however, generated much interest in violent female offending or, more generally, the problem of explaining the gender gap in crimes of violence. As such, the plan for future research begins by suggesting that if we want to advance our understanding of the relationship between gender and crime we cannot exclude violent offending. We will not significantly change our knowledge about the etiology and careers of violent female offenders by continuing to study violent male offenders with the excuse that the smaller sample sizes of seriously violent females make firm conclusions more difficult.

THE CONTEXT OF VIOLENCE

It may be that there are specific contexts in which women are as violent as men. Hints of this potential phenomenon appear in several areas of the literature that we have reviewed. For example, the data on domestic violence suggest that for the less serious types of interpersonal violence, female rates may equal male rates. Fagan's (1990) research on self-reported violence among gang and nongang members also suggests that participation rates of female gang members exceeded those of nongang males. Even laboratory studies of gender differences in aggression among adults conclude that contextual factors, such as the presence of supportive observers, the level of provocation, and the level/nature of the aggression (e.g., verbal versus physical retaliation), influence the magnitude of the gender ratio. In the aggregate, then, although women do appear to be less violent than men, it may be that in specific supportive contexts where violence is encouraged or viewed as appropriate, women's levels of violence equal those of men. A closer contextual analysis may also reveal more variation in the targets of female violence than is frequently assumed. For example, the homicide data gathered by Mann (1987) suggested that black women tend to kill friends and acquaintances (including other females) more often than white women. Thus, as recently suggested by both Bridges and Weis (1989) and a number of feminist criminologists, in order to create a more valid profile of the gender/violence paradigm, we need to disaggregate the data and examine both the nature and the extent of violence in different contexts.

GENDER, RACE, AND VIOLENT OFFENDING

Certainly, the racial variations we observe in the gender ratio for homicides and, more generally, in self-report studies provide one of the most important avenues for future research. We need to determine whether the narrower gender gap for blacks, by comparison to whites, applies to all types of interpersonal violence (e.g., see Visher and Roth, 1986:251) and to both participation rates and frequency of offending. These data may lead to a more informed approach to biological and sociological explanations for gender and interpersonal violence. With regard to biology, for example, we might expect that less attention would be focused on hormonal antecedents of violence and more attention would be directed toward prenatal and peri- or postnatal antecedents (e.g., see Shanok and Lewis, 1981). With regard to the latter, a greater emphasis might be directed to understanding the contribution of race, independent of social class and other familial or social constraints. A limited number of studies that control for social class report black-white differences in serious crime (Rutter and Giller, 1983:154-155; Visher and Roth, 1986:257). However, as Rutter and Giller (1983:154-155) point out, these data are inadequate for determining whether this race difference is explicable in terms of family circumstances, living conditions, or area of residence.

With the exception of gang research, virtually all of our knowledge about the relationships among gender, race, and crime come from aggregate data that dichotomize race into white and black, or white and "nonwhite." In the first instance, all other ethnic groups are ignored; in the second, all other ethnic groups are assumed to be equal (Simpson, 1989:618). Criminologists are only beginning to explore the relevance of etiological theory for crime among blacks; their preliminary work suggests that although the mechanisms that produce crime may be racially invariant (e.g., differential association, gender- and class-linked mechanisms of social control, poor parenting), the structural and cultural contexts (e.g., presence of, and opportunities for involvement in, illegal markets; underlying norms and values) in which these etiological factors emerge are not (e.g, see Matsueda and Heimer, 1987). Future research may suggest that these larger structural and cultural variables are indispensable for etiological theories pertaining to violence among men and women of different ethnic origins.

Gender and Other Types of Pathology

A large body of research has accumulated on the relationship between gender role and pathology. For our purposes the most important aspect of this research is whether men and women develop different styles of, or responses to, distress. The Dohrenwends (1976), for example, suggest that each sex has a distinct style of expressing mental disorder: for males, this involves acting-out behaviors such as personality disorders, drug and alcohol problems; for females, it entails internalization, with symptoms of depression, anxiety, and other neuroses. Although there is some controversy over whether drug, alcohol, and antisocial behaviors stem from different causal factors than disorders involving subjective distress (Gove, 1978), it could well be, as Horwitz and White (1987:159) argue, that some underlying variable such as gender identity or gender role socialization leads men and women to express pathology in fundamentally different ways. Another important avenue for future inquiry, then, is to explore whether women are less likely to engage in violence than men but more likely to exhibit other forms of psychological distress. We envision this research tackling the large bodies of data on vulnerable populations: abused, neglected, and economically deprived children, as well as children of alcoholic and divorced parents. It would also be important to consider the effects of gender roles themselves on the diagnosis and labeling of these populations. As Lewis and her colleagues (1981) found, among boys and girls with the same violent history and symptomatology, girls were more likely to be sent to a state hospital and boys to a correctional school. Thus, gender may be important not only in the etiology of specific kinds of pathology but also in the responses to pathology.

Gender and Victimology

Finally, we also want to direct attention to the role of victim attributes in the processing of violent crimes. Both Smith (1987a) and LaFree (1989) found that cases involving female or nonwhite victims were treated less seriously by the police and the courts. Although these data pertain to only two types of violent crimes—assault and rape—they suggest that we need to examine more carefully whether victim attributes influence responses to all types of interpersonal violence. Our ability to deter violence, and to assist those who provide services to victims, will depend on whether we can apply sanctions for violence without regard to the victim's race or gender.

CONCLUSION

A thorough knowledge of the relationship between gender and interpersonal violence is imperative for implementing new policies and interventions that may curb the incidence of this phenomenon. We hope that this paper will assist in that endeavor, as much perhaps by the acknowledgment of what remains to be uncovered by future research as by what the current data reveal.

NOTES

1   Because an excellent assessment of strictly biological contributions to female crime, including violence, was recently completed (see Widom and Ames, 1988), this topic is largely excluded from this review.

2   The Census Bureau data for 1988 (Projections of the Population of the United States by Age, Sex and Race, Series P-25) include the military in all estimates of the population by age and sex. They also allow one to delete all military or only overseas military from these estimates. Based on the fact that few members of the military live in barracks and that crimes committed by military personnel living off base would appear in UCR statistics (personal communication with Dr. Albert J. Reiss), we excluded only the overseas military from our estimates of the U.S. population by age and gender (Tables 1 and 2).

3   Age effects refer to changes that occur with age; for example, aging produces the onset of puberty. Period effects refer to influences specific to a given time period (e.g., one of high unemployment). A cohort is a group of people who all experience the same event (most commonly birth) within the same time interval (Farrington, 1990:5-6).

4   The UCR and the Census Bureau do not provide exactly comparable classifications of urban and rural areas. The UCR calculates gender by residence for three categories of residence: (1) central cities, which includes central cities and suburban cities with populations of 50,000 or more; (2) suburban areas/counties, which includes cities with fewer than 50,000 inhabitants, in addition to counties within the Metropolitan Statistical Area; and (3) rural counties. The Bureau of the Census (1989), Current Population Reports (series P-20) classifies the population in urbanized areas

(with a population of 50,000 or more) or rural areas, which contain all other farm and nonfarm areas. The key question is whether we should include suburban UCR data in our calculation of arrest rates by gender and residence. First, we calculated the rates by eliminating suburban UCR data and including only central cities and rural data; second, we recalculated the data, combining the UCR suburban data with the UCR rural data to obtain the urban/rural distinction used. By the second method, the rural arrest rates for both men and women increased; the increase in the rate for men was more substantial, ranging from +0.46 in the case of murder to +32.90 in the case of other assaults. None of the patterns we initially observed changed, nor was there any significant change in the FP/As. We believe that this second method is the most accurate, given the Census Bureau's dichotomous classification of urbanized areas (50,000 or more people) and rural areas (i.e., all other farm and nonfarm).

Finally, it should also be noted that all ages were included in these calculations (as opposed to age 10 and over in Tables 1 and 2) because the census data pertaining to urban/rural population breakdowns only provide information on all ages or age 15 and older, whereas the UCR data provide residence by gender for all ages or age 18 and older.

5   Incident figures are given in NCS data but they are used to describe the setting and circumstances in which crimes occurred (e.g., time and place of occurrence, number of victims and offenders, and use of weapons). Unfortunately, these data are not broken down by the gender of the victim(s) involved in the incident or the perceived gender of the offender.

6   Because we relied on 1988 UCR data, we hoped to obtain 1988 NCS data. However, the most recent NCS data available to us were from 1987. Tables 4 through 8 are thus based on 1987 data.

7   It should be noted that even NCS data are affected by the relationship between the victim and the offender. There is evidence from reverse record checks that victimizations between persons known to each other are less likely than stranger victimizations to be mentioned to survey interviewers (Gottfredson and Hindelang, 1979:7, note 5).

8   Table 9 includes only individual violent offenses because Steffensmeier at al. (1979:221) included negligent manslaughter and other assaults in their "all violent crime index." It should also be noted that in Steffensmeier's early publications he refers to the percentage that the female rate contributes to the male rate

and female rate for each offense (%FC) rather than the female percentage of arrests (FP/A). An inspection of the formulas used to calculated both %FC and FP/A reveals, however, that they are identical.

9   Although criminologists are increasingly drawing attention to race and gender variations in crime and delinquency (Visher and Roth, 1986; Shannon, 1988; Jensen and Thompson, 1990), few have focused specifically on violent crime. Individual studies of homicide, of course, remain the exception (Riedel, 1988b).

10   Aggregate statistics on gang membership are a relatively recent phenomenon. In the 1970s, police departments in major cities began setting up gang intelligence units. Miller (1975) attempted to estimate the size of the gang problem for a government report. He suggested that female gangs were no more than one-tenth of male gangs and that only six were autonomous female gangs. More recently, Campbell (1984) suggested that in New York City, 10 percent of the gang members are female. These statistics should be treated with caution; changes in the methods of recording gang membership and extrapolating from known gang members to the actual size of the gang population could make the estimates highly unstable (more generally see, Klein and Maxson, 1989).

11   Another aspect of a criminal career that warrants further attention is terroristic activities. The evidence on the changing role of women in terrorism is scant and mixed. Some authors argue that the involvement of women in terrorist activities will continue and intensify, moving away from support functions to full-scale terrorist operations (Corrado, 1980; Mann, 1984); others suggest that data from both 1974 and 1980 indicate that there are still significant gender differences in the reasons for becoming involved in terrorist activities and the roles men and women play (Weinberg and Eubank, 1987).

12   It is also interesting to note that Hindelang (1979) examined the estimated percentages of offenders reported by victims to have been female for the years 1972-1976 and for the offenses of rape, robbery, and aggravated and simple assault. His findings reveal a relatively stable pattern of female violent offending across this five-year time span. Moveover, comparing Hindelang's data to the data we present in Table 7 suggests even further stability over the last decade. Although his data were calculated on the basis of incidents, rather than victimizations (to facilitate the comparison he made between UCR and NCS data), the reported percentage of female offender crimes is relatively similar:

	1976	1987
Rape	1%	0%
Robbery	4%	7%
Aggravated Assault	8%	13%
Simple Assault	14%	16%

13   This second hypothesis holds only if we assume that a violent crime victim has an equal probability of being male or female. This should be true for Smith's (1987a) data because a large proportion of the cases involved domestic disputes.

14   Because a key variable in the study of coercive family processes is parental discipline, it is unfortunate that Felson and Russo (1988) did not specify the mode of punishment used by parents when they intervened in sibling fights.

15   Unfortunately, space limitations preclude examining the equally important issue of the ways in which noncriminal justice system agencies affect violence by and against women. Relevant reviews of this literature (e.g., the role of counseling centers and crisis intervention) can be found in the paper by Fagan and Browne in this volume.

16   The data on gender effects in criminal court processing decisions up to 1981 suggest that women charged with the more serious offenses are treated no differently from comparable men (Nagel and Hagan, 1982:136). This review begins with data published subsequent to 1981, not only because Nagel and Hagan reviewed publications prior to that date but also because the later analyses are generally more methodologically sophisticated (i.e., appropriate analytic techniques and controls are used).

17   As Chappell (1989:77) recently reported, social scientists studying sexual assaults rarely distinguish "sexual assault" from rape. Sexual assaults (e.g., rape, incest, and molestation) cover a broader range of illegal behavior than rape, and more recently, the legislative move to distinguish degrees of criminal assaultive sexual acts has served to further recognize varying types of sexual violence by their seriousness, the amount of coercion used, the injury inflicted, and the age of the victim. Unfortunately, the studies reviewed here provided no definitional uniformity. Some authors use the terms rape and sexual assault interchangeably whereas others refer only to the latter but fail to distinguish the types of assaults included in their data.

18   LaFree (1989:205) summarizes the types of prosecutorial and defense strategies used in rape cases as follows. To convict a defendant of a forcible sex offense, the state's burden is to show that (1) a sexual act occurred or was attempted, (2) the victim did

not consent but submitted under force or imminent threat of force, and (3) the person charged is the perpetrator (i.e., correct *identification*). For acquittal, the defense must successfully counter at least one of these elements or acknowledge the assault but show that because of intoxication or insanity the offender has *diminished responsibility* for his act.

REFERENCES

Adler, F.
1975 *Sisters in Crime.* New York: McGraw-Hill.
1981 *The Incidence of Female Criminality in the Contemporary World.* New York: New York University Press.
Ageton, S.
1983 The dynamics of female delinquency, 1976-1980. *Criminology* 21(4):555-584.
Aizenman, M., and G. Kelley
1988 The incidence of violence and acquaintance rape in dating relationships among college men and women. *Journal of College Student Development* 29(4):305-311.
Anglin, D., Y. Hser, and W. McGlothin
1987 Sex differences in addict careers. *American Journal of Drug and Alcohol Abuse* 13:59-71.
Archer, D., and R. Gartner
1984 *Violence and Crime in Cross-National Perspective.* New Haven, Conn.: Yale University Press.
Barrett, D.E.
1979 A naturalistic study of sex differences in children's aggression. *Merrill-Palmer Quarterly* 25:193-207.
Bender, L.
1988 A lawyer's primer on feminist theory and tort. *Journal of Legal Education* 38(1 & 2):3-36.
Benedek, E.P.
1982 Women and homicides. Pp. 150-164 in B.L. Canto, J. Bruhns, and A.H. Kutscher, eds., *The Human Side of Homicide.* New York: Columbia University Press.
Bennett, L.A.
1976 The study of violence in California prisons: A review with policy implications. Pp. 149-168 in A.K. Cohen, G.F. Cole, and R.G. Bailey, eds., *Prison Violence.* Lexington, Mass.: Lexington Books.
Bennie, A.B., and A.B. Sclare
1969 The battered child syndrome. *American Journal of Psychiatry* 125(Jan.):975-979.
Berk, S.F., and D. Loseke
1981 "Handling" family violence: Situational determinants of police

arrest in domestic disturbances. *Law & Society Review* 15(2):317-346.

Berk, R., S.F. Berk, D. Loseke, and D. Rauma
1983   Mutual combat and other family violence myths. Pp. 197-212 in D. Finkelhor, R.J. Gelles, G.T. Hotaling, and M.A. Straus, eds., *The Dark Side of Families: Current Family Violence Research*. Beverly Hills, Calif.: Sage Publications.

Bernard, J.L., S.L. Bernard, and M.L. Bernard
1985   Courtship violence and sex-typing. *Family Relations: Journal of Applied Family and Child Studies* 34(4):573-576.

Bernstein, I.N., J. Cardascia, and C.E. Ross
1979   Defendant's sex and criminal court decisions. Pp. 329-354 in R. Alvarez, K.G. Lutterman et al., eds., *Discrimination in Organizations*. San Francisco: Jossey-Bass.

Black, D.
1976   *The Behavior of Law*. New York: Academic Press.
1980   *The Manners and Customs of the Police*. New York: Academic Press.

Blumstein, A., J. Cohen, J.A. Roth, and C.A. Visher, eds.
1986   *Criminal Careers and "Career Criminals"*, Vol. 1. Panel on Research on Criminal Careers, Committee on Research on Law Enforcement and the Administration of Justice, National Research Council. Washington, D.C.: National Academy Press.

Blumstein, A., J. Cohen, and D.P. Farrington
1988a   Criminal career research: Its value for criminology. *Criminology* 26(1):1-35.
1988b   Longitudinal and criminal career research: Further clarifications. *Criminology* 26(1):57-74.

Boisvert, M.J., and R. Wells
1980   Toward a rational policy on status offenders. *Social Work* 25(3):230-234.

Bowker, L.H.
1978   Gangs and prostitutes: Two case studies of female crime. Pp. 143-169 in L.H. Bowker, ed., *Women, Crime and the Criminal Justice System*. Lexington, Mass.: Lexington Books.
1980   *Prison Victimization*. New York: Elsevier.
1981   Women as victims: An examination of the results of LEAA's National Crime Survey Program. Pp. 158-179 in L.H. Bowker, ed., *Women and Crime in America*. New York: Macmillan.

Bowker, L.H., H.S. Gross, and M.W. Klein
1980   Female participation in delinquent gang activities. *Adolescence* 15:509-515.

Bridges, G.S., and J.G. Weis
1989   Measuring violent behavior. Pp. 14-34 in N.A. Weiner and M.E. Wolfgang, eds., *Violent Crime, Violent Criminals*. Newbury Park, Calif.: Sage Publications.

Brown, W.K.
1977 Black female gangs in Philadelphia. *International Journal of Offender Therapy and Comparative Criminology* 21(3):221-228.
Brownmiller, S.
1975 *Against Our Will: Men, Women and Rape*. New York: Simon and Schuster.
Bureau of the Census
1989 *Projections of the Population of the United States, by Age, Sex and Race: 1988 to 2080*. Current Population Reports, Series P-25, No. 1018. Washington, D.C.: U.S. Department of Commerce.
Bureau of the Census (jointly with the Department of Agriculture)
1989 *Rural and Rural Farm Population: 1988*. Current Population Reports, Series P-20, NO. 439. Washington, D.C.: U.S. Department of Commerce.
Campbell, A.
1984 *The Girls in the Gang*. Oxford, England: Basil Blackwell.
Caplan, P.J.
1975 Sex differences in antisocial behavior: Does research methodology produce or abolish them? *Human Development* 18:444-460.
Caringella-MacDonald, S.
1985 The comparability in sexual and nonsexual assault case treatment: Did statute change meet the objective? *Crime and Delinquency* 31(2):206-222.
Carlen, P.
1985 *Criminal Women*. Cambridge: Polity Press.
Carroll, L.
1974 *Hacks, Blacks, and Cons: Race Relations in a Maximum Security Prison*. Lexington, Mass.: D.C. Heath and Company.
Center for the Study of Social Policy
1986 The "flip-side" of black families headed by women: The economic status of black men. Pp. 232-238 in R. Staples, ed., *The Black Family: Essays and Studies*. Belmont, Calif.: Wadsworth.
Chaiken, J.M., and M.R. Chaiken
1990 Drugs and predatory crime. Pp. 203-239 in M. Tonry and J.Q. Wilson, eds., *Drugs and Crime*. Chicago: University of Chicago Press.
Chapman, J.R.
1980 *Economic Realities and the Female Offender*. Lexington, Mass.: Lexington Books.
Chappell, D.
1989 Sexual criminal violence. Pp. 68-108 in N.A. Weiner and M.E. Wolfgang, eds., *Pathways to Criminal Violence*. Newbury Park, Calif.: Sage Publications.

Chesney-Lind, M.
1973 Judicial enforcement of the female sex role: The family court and the female delinquent. *Issues in Criminology* 8(Fall):51-70.
1974 Juvenile delinquency: The sexualization of female crime. *Psychology Today* 7:43-46.
1977 Judicial paternalism and the female status offender. *Crime and Delinquency* 23(2):121-130.
1988 Girls in jail. *Crime and Delinquency* 34:150-168.
Cloward, R.A., and L.E. Ohlin
1960 *Delinquency and Opportunity. A Theory of Delinquent Gangs.* New York: Free Press.
Cohen, L.E., and J.R. Kluegal
1979a Selecting delinquents for adjudication. *Journal of Research in Crime and Delinquency* 16:143-163.
1979b The detention decision: A study of the impact of social characteristics and legal factors in two metropolitan courts. *Social Forces* 58(1):146-161.
Cook, P.J.
1980 Research in criminal deterrence: Laying the groundwork for the second decade. Pp. 211-268 in N. Morris and M. Tonry, eds., *Crime and Justice, An Annual Review of Research*, Vol. 2. Chicago: University of Chicago Press.
Corrado, R.R.
1980 Female terrorists: Competing perspectives. Pp. 37-50 in C.T. Griffiths and M. Nance, eds., *The Female Offender*. Selected Papers from an International Symposium, Vancouver, Canada. Simon Fraser University: Criminology Research Centre.
Cressey, D.
1970 Measuring crime rates. Pp. 55-59 in A.L. Guenther, ed., *Criminal Behavior and Social Systems*. Chicago: Rand McNally.
Curran, D.A.
1983 Judicial discretion and defendent's sex. *Criminology* 21(1):41-58.
Daly, K.
1987 Discrimination in the criminal courts: Family, gender, and the problem of equal treatment. *Social Forces* 66(1):152-175.
1989a Rethinking judicial paternalism: Gender, work-family relations, and sentencing. *Gender and Society* 3(1):9-36.
1989b Neither conflict nor labeling nor paternalism will suffice: Intersections of race, ethnicity, gender and family in criminal court decisions. *Crime and Delinquency* 35(1):136-168.
Daly, K., and M. Chesney-Lind
1988 Feminism and criminology. *Justice Quarterly* 5(4):497-535.
Datesman, S.K., and F.R. Scarpitti
1980 The extent and nature of female crime. Pp. 3-64 in S.K. Datesman and F.R. Scarpitti, eds., *Women, Crime, and Justice*. New York: Oxford University Press.

Dobash, R.E., and R. Dobash
1979 *Violence Against Wives: A Case Against the Patriarchy.* New York: Free Press.
Dobash, R.P., R. Emerson, and S. Gutteridge
1986 *The Imprisonment of Women.* Totowa, N.J.: Basil & Blackwell.
Dohrenwend, B.P., and B.S. Dohrenwend
1976 Sex differences in psychiatric disorders. *American Journal of Sociology* 81:1447-1454.
Eagly, A., and V.J. Steffen
1986 Gender and aggressive behavior: A meta-analytic review of the social psychological literature. *Psychological Bulletin* 100:309-330.
Ekland-Olson, S.
1986 Crowding, social control and prison violence: Evidence from the post-Ruiz years in Texas. *Law & Society Review* 20(3):389-421.
Elliott, D., S. Ageton., D. Huizinga, B. Knowles, and R. Canter
1983 *The Prevalence and Incidence of Delinquent Behavior: 1976-1980.* National Youth Survey, Report No. 26. Boulder, Colo.: Behavioral Research Institute.
Elliott, D.S., D. Huizinga, and B. Morse
1986 Self-reported violent offending: A descriptive analysis of juvenile violent offenders and their offending careers. *Journal of Interpersonal Violence* 1:472-514.
Ellis, D., H.G. Grasmick, and B. Gilman
1974 Violence in prisons: A sociological analysis. *American Journal of Sociology* 80:16-43.
Eme, R.
1984 Sex roles, sex differences and child psychopathology. Pp. 279-316 in C.S. Widom, eds., *Sex Roles and Psychopathology.* New York: Plenum.
Epstein, C.F.
1988 *Deceptive Distinctions: Sex, Gender and the Social Order.* New Haven, Conn.: Yale University Press.
Erez, E.
1989 Gender rehabilitation and probation decisions. *Criminology* 27(2):307-327.
Erickson, M.L.
1975 Delinquency in a birth cohort: A new direction in criminological research? *Journal of Criminal Law and Criminology* 66:362-367.
Fagan, J.
1990 Social processes of delinquency and drug use among urban gangs. In C.R. Huff, ed., *Gangs in America.* Newbury Park, Calif.: Sage Publications.
Fagan, J., and S. Wexler
1987 Crime at home and crime in the streets: The relationship be-

tween family and stranger violence. *Violence and Victims* 2(1):5-23.

Fagot, B.I., and R. Hagan
  1985 Aggression in toddlers: Responses to the assertive acts of boys and girls. *Sex Roles* 12:341-351.

Fagot, B.I., R. Hagan, M.B. Leinbach, and S. Kronsberg
  1985 Differential reactions to assertive and communicative acts of toddler boys and girls. *Child Development* 56:1499-1505.

Fagot, B.I., M.D. Leinbach, and R. Hagan
  1986 Gender labeling and adoption of gender role behaviors. *Developmental Psychology* 22:440-443.

Fagot, B.I., R. Loeber, and J.B. Reid
  1988 Developmental determinants of male-to-female aggression. Pp. 91-105 in G.W. Russell, ed., *Violence in Intimate Relationships.* New York: PMA Publishing Corp.

Farrell, R.A., and V.L. Swigert
  1986 Adjudication in homicide: An interpretative analysis of the effects of defendant and victim social characteristics. *Journal of Research in Crime and Delinquency* 23(4):349-369.

Farrington, D.P.
  1978 The family background of aggressive youths. Pp. 73-93 in L.A. Hersov, M. Berger, and D. Shaffer, eds., *Aggression and Antisocial Behavior in Childhood and Adolescence.* Oxford: Pergamon.
  1982 Longitudinal analyses of criminal violence. Pp. 171-201 in M.E. Wolfgang and N.A. Weiner, eds., *Criminal Violence.* Beverly Hills, Calif.: Sage Publications.
  1986 Age and crime. Pp. 189-250 in M. Tonry and N. Morris, eds., *Crime and Justice*, Vol. 7. Chicago: University of Chicago Press.
  1989 Early predictors of adolescent aggression and adult violence. *Violence and Victims* 4(2):79-100.
  1990 Age, period, cohort, and offending. Pp. 51-75 in D.M. Gottfredson and R.V. Clarke, eds., *Policy and Theory in Criminal Justice: Contributions in Honour of Leslie T. Wilkins.* Aldershot, England: Avebury.

Feld, B.C.
  1989 The right to counsel in juvenile court: An empirical study of when lawyers appear and the difference they make. *Journal of Criminal Law and Criminology* 79(4):1185-1346.

Feldman-Summers, S., and C.D. Ashworth
  1981 Factors related to intentions to report a rape. *Journal of Social Issues* 37:53-70.

Felson, R.B., and N. Russo
  1988 Parental punishment and sibling aggression. *Social Psychology Quarterly* 51(1):11-18.

Figueira-McDonough, J.
  1985 Gender differences in informal processing: A look at charge

bargaining and sentence reduction in Washington D.C. *Journal of Research in Crime and Delinquency* 22(2):101-133.

Finn, J.
1986   The relationship between sex role attitudes and attitudes supporting marital violence. *Sex Roles* 14(5-6):235-244.

Fortune, E.P., M. Vega, and I.J. Silverman
1980   A study of female robbers in a southern correctional institution. *Journal of Criminal Justice* 8:324.

Frazier, C.E., and E.W. Bock
1982   Effects of court officials on sentence severity. *Criminology* 20(2):257-272.

Frieze, I.H., and A. Browne
1989   Violence in marriage. Pp. 163-218 in L. Ohlin and M. Tonry, eds., *Family Violence*. Chicago: University of Chicago Press.

Frodi, A., J. Macaulay, and P.R. Thome
1977   Are women always less aggressive than men? A review of the experimental literature. *Psychological Bulletin* 84:634-660.

Gartner, R., K. Baker, and F.C. Pampel
1987   The Sex Differential in Homicide Victimization. Paper presented at a meeting of the American Society of Criminology, Montreal, Canada.

Gates, M.
1978   Victims of rape and wife abuse. Pp. 176-201 in W.L. Hepperle and L. Crites, eds., *Women in the Courts*. Williamsburg, Va.: National Center for State Courts.

Gelles, R.J.
1979   *Family Violence*. Beverly Hills, Calif.: Sage Publications.
1982   Domestic criminal violence. Pp. 201-235 in M.E. Wolfgang and N.A. Weiner, eds., *Criminal Violence*. Beverly Hills, Calif.: Sage Publications.

Gelles, R.J., and M.A. Straus
1988   *Intimate Violence*. New York: Touchstone.

Ghali, M.A., and M. Chesney-Lind
1986   Sex bias and the criminal justice system: An empirical investigation. *Sociology and Social Research* 70(2):164-171.

Gil, D.
1970   *Violence Against Children: Physical Child Abuse in the United States*. Cambridge, Mass.: Harvard University Press.

Gill, S., J. Stockard, M. Johnson, and S. Williams
1987   Measuring gender differences: The expressive dimension and critique of androgyny scales. *Sex Roles* 17(7-8):375-400.

Gilligan, C.
1982   *In a Different Voice: Psychological Theory and Women's Development*. Cambridge, Mass.: Harvard University Press.

Giordano, P.
1978   Research note: Girls, guys and gangs: The changing social

context of female delinquency. *Journal of Criminal Law and Criminology* 69(1):126-132.

Giordano, P., S. Kerbel, and S. Dudley
1981 The economics of female criminality: An analysis of police blotters, 1890-1976. Pp. 65-82 in L. Bowker, ed., *Women and Crime in America*. New York: Macmillan.

Gottfredson, M., and M. Hindelang
1979 A study of the behavior of law. *American Sociological Review* 44:3-18.

Gove, W.R.
1978 Sex differences in mental illness among adult men and women. *Social Science and Medicine* 12B:187-198.

Gove, W.R., M. Hughes, and M. Geerken
1985 Are Uniform Crime Reports a valid indicator of the index crimes? An affirmative answer with minor qualifications. *Criminology* 23:451-501.

Grasmick, H.G., N.J. Finley, and D.L. Glaser
1984 Labor force participation, sex-role attitudes and female crime. *Social Science Quarterly* 65(3):703-718.

Gruhl, J., C. Spohn, and S. Welch
1981 Women as policymakers: The case of trial judges. *American Journal of Political Science* 25(2):308-322.

Hagan, J., A.R. Gillis, and J. Simpson
1985 The class structure of gender and delinquency: Toward a power-control theory of common delinquent behavior. *American Journal of Sociology* 90(6):1151-1178.

Hagan, J., J. Simpson, and A.R. Gillis
1987 Class in the household: A power-control theory of gender and delinquency. *American Journal of Sociology* 92(4):788-816.

Hamparian, D.M., R. Schuster, S. Dinitz, and J.P. Conrad
1978 *The Violent Few: A Study of Dangerous Juvenile Offenders.* Lexington, Mass.: Lexington.

Hanson, K.
1964 *Rebels in the Streets: The Story of New York's Girl Gangs.* New York: Prentice Hall.

Harding, S.
1986 *The Science Question in Feminism.* Ithaca, N.Y.: Cornell University Press.

Harris, A.
1977 Sex and theories of deviance. *American Sociology Review* 42:3-16.

Hartnagel, T.F.
1982 Modernization, female social roles and female crime: A cross-national investigation. *Sociological Quarterly* 23(4):477-490.

Heidensohn, F.M.
1985 *Women and Crime.* New York: New York University Press.

Hetherington, E.M.
    1981 Children and divorce. Pp. 33-58 in R. Henderson, ed., *Parent-Child Interaction: Theory, Research and Prospect*. New York: Academic Press.
Hindelang, M.J.
    1979 Sex differences in criminal activity. *Social Problems* 27(2):143-156.
Hindelang, M., and M. Gottfredson
    1976 The victim's decision not to invoke the criminal process. Pp. 57-78 in W. McDonald, ed., *The Victim and the Criminal Justice System*. Beverly Hills, Calif.: Sage Publications.
Hindelang, M.J., T. Hirschi, and J.G. Weis
    1979 Correlates of delinquency: The illusion of discrepancy between self-report and official measures. *American Sociological Review* 44:995-1014.
    1981 *Measuring Delinquency*. Beverly Hills., Calif.: Sage Publications.
Holmstrom, L.L., and A.W. Burgess
    1978 *The Victim of Rape: Institutional Reactions*. New York: Wiley-Interscience.
Horwitz, A.V., and H.R. White
    1987 Gender role orientations and styles of pathology among adolescents. *Journal of Health and Social Behavior* 28(2):158-170.
Hotaling, G.T., M.A. Straus, and A.J. Lincoln
    1989 Intrafamily violence, and crime and violence outside the family. Pp. 315-375 in L. Ohlin and M. Tonry, eds., *Family Violence*. Chicago: University of Chicago Press.
Inciardi, J.A.
    1979 Heroin use and street crime. *Crime and Delinquency* 25:335-346.
Irwin, J.
    1980 *Prisons in Turmoil*. Boston: Little Brown & Co.
James, J., and W. Thornton
    1980 Women's liberation and the female delinquent. *Journal of Research in Crime and Delinquency* 17(2):230-244.
Jensen, G.F., and K. Thompson
    1990 What's class got to do with it? A further examination of power-control theory. *American Journal of Sociology* 95(4):1009-1023.
Klein, D.
    1973 The etiology of female crime: A review of the literature. *Crime and Social Justice: Issues in Criminology* (Fall):3-30.
    1982 Violence against women: Some considerations regarding its cause and eliminations. Pp. 203-222 in B.R. Price and N.J. Sokologg, eds., *The Criminal Justice System and Women*. New York: Clark Boardman Co.
Klein, M.W., and C.L. Maxson
    1989 Street gang violence. Pp. 198-234 in N.A. Weiner and M.E.

Wolfgang, eds., *Violent Crime, Violent Criminals*. Newbury Park, Calif.: Sage Publications.

Kratcoski, P.C.
1987 Families who kill. *Marriage and Family Review* 12(1-2):47-70.

Kritzer, H.M., and T.M. Uhlman
1977 Sisterhood in the courtroom: Sex of judge and defendant in criminal case disposition. *Social Science Journal* 14(2):77-78.

Krohn, M.D., J.P. Curry, and S. Nelson-Kilger
1983 Is chivalry dead: An analysis of changes in police dispositions of males and females. *Criminology* 21:417-437.

Kruttschnitt, C.
1984 Sex and criminal court dispositions: The unresolved controversy. *Journal of Research in Crime and Delinquency* 21(3):213-232.
1985a "Female crimes" or legal labels? The effect of deviance processing agents on our understanding of female criminality. Pp. 76-94 in I.L. Moyer, ed., *The Changing Roles of Women in the Criminal Justice System*. Prospect Heights, Ill.: Waveland.
1985b Legal outcomes and legal agents. Adding another dimension to the sex-sentencing controversy. *Law and Human Behavior* 9(3):287-303.

Kruttschnitt, C., and D. Green
1984 The sex-sanctioning issue: Is it history? *American Sociology Review* 21:213-232.

Kruttschnitt, C., and C. Johnson
1984 Sentencing recommendations and women offenders: The biopsychological model and the treatment of female offenders. *Law and Inequality* 2(1):97-120.

Kruttschnitt, C., and S. Krmpotich
1990 Aggressive behavior among female inmates: An exploratory study. *Justice Quarterly* 7(2):371-389.

Kruttschnitt, C., L. Heath, and D. Ward
1986 Family violence, television viewing habits, and other adolescent experiences related to violent criminal behavior. *Criminology* 24:235-267.

Kruttschnitt, C., D. Ward, and M. Sheble
1987 Abuse-resistant youth: Some factors that may inhibit violent criminal behavior. *Social Forces* 66(2):501-519.

Kurz, D.
1989 Social science perspectives on wife abuse: Current debates and future directions. *Gender and Society* 3(4):489-505.

LaFree, G.D.
1989 *Rape and Criminal Justice. The Social Construction of Sexual Assault*. Belmont, Calif.: Wadsworth.

Laub, J.H., and M.J. McDermott
1985 An analysis of serious crime by young black women. *Criminology* 23(1):81-99.

Law Enforcement Assistance Administration
1972   San Jose Methods Test of Known Crime Victims.   Statistics
       Technical Report No. 1, National Institute of Law Enforcement
       and Criminal Justice, Statistics Division, U.S. Department of
       Justice, Washington, D.C.
Leonard, E.G.
1982   *Women, Crime and Society.* New York: Longmans.
Letcher, M.
1979   Black women and homicide. In H.M. Rose, ed., *Lethal Aspects
       of Urban Violence.* Lexington, Mass.: D.C. Heath.
Lewis, D.K.
1981   Black women offenders and criminal justice: Some theoretical
       considerations. Pp. 89-105 in M.Q. Warren, ed., *Comparing
       Female and Male Offenders.* Research Progress Series in Crimi-
       nology, Vol. 21. Beverly Hills, Calif.: Sage Publications.
Lewis, D.O., S.S. Shanok, R.J. Cohen, M. Kligfeld, and G. Frisone
1981   Race bias in the diagnosis and disposition of violent adoles-
       cents. *Annual Progress in Child Psychiatry and Child Devel-
       opment* 14:508-520.
Lewis, D.O., S.S. Shanok, M. Grant, and E. Rita
1983   Homicidally aggressive young children: Neuropsychiatric and
       experiential correlates. *American Journal of Psychiatry* 140(2):148-
       153.
Lizotte, A.J.
1985   The uniqueness of rape: Reporting assaultive violence to the
       police. *Crime and Delinquency* 31(2):169-190.
Loeber, R., and M. Stouthamer-Loeber
1986   Family factors as correlates and predictors of juvenile conduct
       problems and delinquency. Pp. 219-339 in M. Tonry and N.
       Morris, eds., *Crime and Justice*, Vol. 7. Chicago: University of
       Chicago Press.
Loh, W.D.
1980   The impact of common law reform and rape statutes on pros-
       ecution: An empirical study. *Washington Law Review* 55:543-
       652.
Macaulay, J.
1985   Adding gender to aggression research: Incremental or revolu-
       tionary change? Pp. 191-224 in V.E. O'Leary, R.K. Unger and
       B.S. Wallston, eds., *Women, Gender and Social Psychology.*
       Hillsdale, N.J.: Lawrence Erlbaum.
Maccoby, E.E., and C.N. Jacklin
1974   *The Psychology of Sex Differences.* Stanford, Calif.: Stanford
       University Press.
1980   Sex differences in aggression: A rejoinder and reprise. *Child
       Development* 51:964-980.
Magnusson, D., H. Stottin, and A. Duner
1983   Aggression and criminality in a longitudinal perspective. Pp.

277-301 in K.T. Van Dusen and S.A. Mednick, eds., *Antecedents of Aggression and Antisocial Behavior.* Boston: Kluwer-Nijhoff.

Makepeace, J.M.
1983 Life events stress and courtship violence. *Family Relations: Journal of Applied Family and Child Studies* 32(1):101-109.
1986 Gender differences in courtship violence victimization. *Family Relations: Journal of Applied Family and Child Studies* 35(3):383-388.

Mandaraka-Sheppard, A.
1986 *The Dynamics of Aggression in Women's Prisons in England.* Brookfield, Vt.: Gower.

Mann, C.R.
1984 *Female Crime and Delinquency.* Huntsville: University of Alabama Press.
1987 Black women who kill. Pp. 157-186 in R.L. Hampton, ed., *Violence in the Black Family.* Lexington, Mass.: Lexington Books.
1988 Getting even? Women who kill in domestic encounters. *Justice Quarterly* 5(1):33-51.

Marsh, P., and R. Paton
1986 Gender, social class and conceptual schemes of aggression. Pp. 59-86 in A. Campbell and J. Gibbs, eds., *Violent Transactions. The Limits of Personality.* New York: Basil Blackwell.

Matsueda, R.L., and K. Heimer
1987 Race, family structure and delinquency: A test of differential association and social control theories. *American Sociological Review* 52:826-846.

Menard, S.
1987 Short-term trends in crime and delinquency: A comparison of UCR, NCS and self-report data. *Justice Quarterly* 4(3):455-474.

Miethe, T.D.
1987 Stereotypical conceptions and criminal processing: The case of the victim-offender relationship. *Justice Quarterly* 4(4):571-593.

Miller, W.B.
1973 The Molls. *Society* 11:32-35.
1975 *Violence by Youth Gangs and Youth Groups as a Crime Problem in Major American Cities.* Washington, D.C.: U.S. Government Printing Office.

Moseley, W.H., and M.H. Gerould
1975 Sex and parole: A comparison of male and female parolees. *Journal of Criminal Justice* 3:47-57.

Mowbray, E.J.
1982 Parole Prediction and Gender. Paper presented at the annual meeting of the American Society of Criminology, Toronto, Canada.

Myers, M.A., and G.D. LaFree
1982 The uniqueness of sexual assault: A comparison with other

crimes. *Journal of Criminal Law and Criminology* 73:1282-1305.

Naffine, N.
1987 *Female Crime: The Construction of Women in Criminology.* Sydney, Australia: Allen and Unwin.

Nagel, I.H., and J. Hagan
1982 Gender and crime: Offense patterns and criminal court sanctions. Pp. 91-144 in N. Morris and M. Tonry, eds., *Crime and Justice*, Vol. 4. Chicago: University of Chicago Press.

Norland, S., and P.J. Mann
1984 Being troublesome—Women on probation. *Criminal Justice and Behavior* 11(1):115-135.

Norland, S., and N. Shover
1978 Gender roles and female criminality. *Criminology* 15:87-104.

Norland, S., R.C. Wessel, and N. Shover
1981 Masculinity and delinquency. *Criminology* 19(3):421-433.

Pagelow, M.D.
1984 *Family Violence.* New York: Praeger.

Parisi, N.
1982 Exploring female crime patterns. Pp. 111-129 in N.H. Rafter and E.A. Stanko, eds., *Judge, Lawyer, Victim, Thief.* Boston, Mass.: Northeastern University Press.

Parke, R.D., and C.W. Collmer
1975 Child abuse: An interdisciplinary analysis. Pp. 1-102 in M. Hetherington, ed., *Review of Child Development Research*, Vol. 5. Chicago: University of Chicago Press.

Polk, K.
1985 Rape reform and criminal justice processing. *Crime and Delinquency* 31(2):191-205

President's Commission on Law Enforcement and Administration of Justice
1967 *The Challenge of Crime in a Free Society.* Washington, D.C.: U.S. Government Printing Office.

Quicker, J.C.
1974 The Chicana Gang: A Preliminary Description. Paper presented at the annual meeting of the Pacific Sociological Association, San Jose, Calif.

Randall, S.C., and V.M. Rose
1981 Barriers to becoming a "successful" rape victim. Pp. 336-354 in L.H. Bowker, ed., *Women and Crime in America.* New York: Macmillan.

Rans, L.
1978 Women's crime: Much ado about . . . .? *Federal Probation* 42:45-49.

Reid, J.B., and G.R. Patterson
1989 The development of antisocial behavior patterns in childhood and adolescence. *European Journal of Personality* 3:107-119.

Reiss, A.J.
  1981 Problems in developing statistical indicators of crime. Presentation for the XXXI Cours International de Criminologie, Connaître la Criminalité: Le Dernier État de la Question, Aix-en-Provence, December 7-11.
Reskin, B.F., and C.A. Visher
  1986 The impact of evidence and extralegal factors in jurors' decisions. *Law & Society Review* 20:423-438.
Riedel, M.
  1988a Black Women and Homicide: Rates, Patterns, and Perspectives. Paper presented at the annual meeting of the American Society of Criminology.
  1988b Murder, Race and Gender: A Test of Hagan's Hypotheses. Paper presented at the annual meeting of the American Society of Criminology, Chicago, Ill.
Rivera, B., and C.S. Widom
  1989 Childhood Victimization and Violent Offending. Unpublished paper. Departments of Criminal Justice and Psychology, Indiana University.
Robins, L.N.
  1966 *Deviant Children Grow Up: A Sociological and Psychiatric Study of Sociopathic Personality.* Baltimore, Md.: Williams and Wilkins.
Russell, D.E.H.
  1984 *Sexual Exploitation. Rape, Child Sexual Abuse and Workplace Harassment.* Beverly Hills, Calif.: Sage Publications.
Rutter, M.
  1982 Epidemiological-longitudinal approaches to the study of development. Pp. 105-144 in W.A. Collins, ed., *The Concept of Development: Minnesota Symposia on Child Psychology*, Vol. 15. Hillsdale, N.J.: Lawrence Erlbaum.
Rutter, M., and H. Giller
  1983 *Juvenile Delinquency. Trends and Perspectives* New York: The Guilford Press.
Schur, E.M.
  1984 *Labeling Women Deviant: Gender, Stigma and Social Control.* New York: Random.
Shannon, L.W.
  1988 *Criminal Career Continuity. Its Social Context.* New York: Human Sciences Press.
Shanok, S.S., and D.O. Lewis
  1981 Medical histories of female delinquents. *Archives of General Psychiatry* 38:211-213.
Shelden, R.G.
  1981 Sex discrimination in the juvenile justice system: Memphis, Tennessee, 1900-1917. Pp. 55-72 in M.Q. Warren, ed., *Compar-*

ing Female and Male Offenders. Beverly Hills, Calif.: Sage Publications.

Short, J.F., Jr.
  1968 *Gang Delinquency and Delinquent Subcultures.* New York: Harper & Row.

Siann, G.
  1985 *Accounting of Aggression: Perspectives on Aggression and Violence.* Winchester, Mass.: Allen and Unwin.

Sigelman, C.K., C.J. Berry, and K.A. Wiles
  1984 Violence in college students' dating relationships. *Journal of Applied Social Psychology* 14(6):530-548.

Simon, R.J.
  1975 *Women and Crime.* Lexington, Mass.: D.C. Heath.
  1979 The parole system: How women fare. Pp. 380-385 in F. Adler and R.J. Simon, eds., *The Criminology of Deviant Women.* Boston: Houghton Mifflin.

Simon, R.J., and S. Baxter
  1989 Gender and violent crime. Pp. 171-197 in N.A. Weiner and M.E. Wolfgang, eds., *Violent Crime, Violent Criminals.* Newbury Park, Calif.: Sage Publications.

Simpson, S.S.
  1989 Feminist theory, crime and justice. *Criminology* 27(4):605-632.

Smart, C.
  1976 *Women, Crime and Criminology.* London: Routledge & Kegan Paul.

Smith, D.A.
  1987a Police response to interpersonal violence: Defining the parameters of legal control. *Social Forces* 65(3):767-782.

Smith, D.A., and C.A. Visher
  1980 Sex and involvement in deviance/crime: A quantitative review of the empirical literature. *American Sociological Review* 45(4):691-701.
  1981 Street-level justice: Situational determinants of police arrest decisions. *Social Problems* 29(2):167-177.

Smith, D.M.
  1987b Changes in the victimization of women: Is there a "new female victim"? *Journal of Research in Crime and Delinquency* 24(4):291-301.

Spence, J.T., and L.L. Sawin
  1985 Images of masculinity and femininity: A reconceptualization. Pp. 35-66 in V.E. O'Leary, R.K. Unger and B.S. Wallston, eds., *Women, Gender and Social Psychology.* Hillsdale, N.J.: Lawrence Erlbaum.

Spencer, C., and J.E. Berocochea
  1972 Recidivism Among Women Parolees: A Long Term Survey. Report No. 47, California Research Division, Department of Corrections.

Spohn, C., and S. Welch
  1987 The effect of prior record in sentencing research: An examination of the assumption that any measure is adequate. *Justice Quarterly* 4(2):287-302.
Staples, W.G.
  1984 Toward a structural perspective on gender bias in the juvenile court. *Sociological Perspectives* 27(3):349-367.
Stark, E., A. Flitcraft, and W. Frazier
  1979 Medicine and patriarchal violence: The social construction of a "private" event. *International Journal of Health Services* 98:461-491.
Steele, B.F., and C.A. Pollock
  1974 A psychiatric study of parents who abuse infants and small children. Pp. 89-134 in R.E. Helfer and C.H. Kempe, eds., *The Battered Child*, 2nd ed. Chicago: University of Chicago Press.
Steffensmeir, D.J.
  1980 Sex differences in patterns of adult crimes, 1965-77: A review and assessment. *Social Forces* 58(4):1080-1108.
  1982 Trends in female crime. It's still a man's world. Pp. 117-129 in R.R. Price and N.J. Solkoloff, eds., *The Criminal Justice System and Women*. New York: Clark Boardman Co.
Steffensmeier, D.J., and E.A. Allan
  1988 Sex disparities in arrests by residence, race and age: An assessment of the gender convergence/crime hypothesis. *Justice Quarterly* 5(1):53-80.
Steffensmeier, D.J., and C. Jordan
  1978 Changing patterns of female crime in rural America, 1962-1975. *Rural Sociology* 43(1):87-102.
Steffensmeier, D.J., and R.H. Steffensmeier
  1980 Trends in female delinquency. *Criminology* 18(1):62-85.
Steffensmeier, D.J., and C. Streifel
  1989 Women's Status and the Female Share of Offending, 1960-1985: A Time Series Analyses of Sex Differences in Person and Property Crime Involvement. Unpublished paper, Department of Sociology, Pennsylvania State University.
Steffensmeier, D.J., R.H. Steffensmeier, and A. Rosenthal
  1979 Trends in female violence, 1960-1977. *Sociological Focus* 12(3):217-227.
Steffensmeier, D.J., E.A. Allan, and C. Streifel
  1989 Development and female crime: A cross-national test of alternative explanations. *Social Forces* 68(1):262-283.
Stets, J.E., and M.A. Pirog-Good
  1987 Violence in dating relationships. *Social Psychology Quarterly* 50(3):237-246.
Stewart, J.K.
  1985 Prosecution of child sexual abuse: Innovations in practice. *National*

Institute of Justice. Research in Brief. Washington, D.C.: U.S. Department of Justice.

Straus, M.A., R.J. Gelles, and S.K. Steinmetz
  1980 *Behind Closed Doors: Violence in the American Family.* New York: Doubleday/Anchor.

Stryker, R., I.H. Nagel, and J. Hagan
  1983 Methodological issues in criminal court research: Pretrial release decisions for federal defendants. *Sociological Methods and Research* 11(4):469-500.

Sylvester, S., J. Reed, and D. Nelson
  1977 *Prison Homicide.* New York: Spectrum.

Thornton, W.E., and J. James
  1979 Masculinity and delinquency revisited. *British Journal of Criminology* 19(3):225-241.

Thrasher, F.M.
  1963 *The Gang.* Chicago: University of Chicago Press.

Tieger, T.
  1980 On the biological basis of sex differences in aggression. *Child Development* 51:943-963.

U.S. Department of Health and Human Services
  1981 *National Study of the Incidence and Severity of Child Abuse and Neglect.* Washington, D.C.: U.S. Department of Health and Human Services.

U.S. Department of Justice, Bureau of Justice Statistics
  1989 *Criminal Victimization in the United States, 1987.* A National Crime Survey Report, NCJ-115524. Washington, D.C.: U.S. Department of Justice.

U.S. Department of Justice, Federal Bureau of Investigation
  1989 *Uniform Crime Reports for the United States, 1988.* Washington, D.C.: U.S. Department of Justice.

VanVoorhis, P., F.T. Cullen, R.A. Mathers, and C.C. Garner
  1988 The impact of family structure and quality on delinquency: A comparative assessment of structural and functional factors. *Criminology* 26(2):235-261.

Vigil, J.D.
  1988 *Barrio Gangs.* Austin: University of Texas Press.

Visher, C.A.
  1983 Gender, police arrest decisions and notions of chivalry. *Criminology* 21(1):5-28.

Visher, C.A., and J.A. Roth
  1986 Participation in criminal careers. Appendix A. Pp. 211-291 in A. Blumstein, J. Cohen, J.A. Roth, and C.A. Visher, eds., *Criminal Careers and "Career Criminals"*, Vol. 1. Washington, D.C.: National Academy Press.

Walker, L.E., and A. Browne
  1985 Gender and victimization by intimates. Special issue: Concep-

tualizing gender in personality theory and research. *Journal of Personality* 53(2):179-195.

Ward, D.A., M. Jackson, and R.E. Ward
1969 Crimes of violence by women. Pp. 843-909 in D.J. Mulvihill and M.M. Tumin, eds., *Crimes of Violence*, Vol. 13. Washington, D.C.: U.S. Government Printing Office.

Weinberg, L., and W.L. Eubank
1987 Italian women terrorists. *Terrorism* 9(3):241-262.

Weiner, N.A.
1989 Violent criminal careers and "violent career criminals." Pp. 35-138 in N.A. Weiner and M.E. Wolfgang, eds., *Violent Crime, Violent Criminals*. Newbury Park, Calif.: Sage Publications.

Weis, J.G.
1986 Issues in the measurement of criminal careers. Pp. 1-51 in A. Blumstein, J. Cohen, J.A. Roth and C.A. Visher, eds., *Criminal Careers and "Career Criminals"*, Vol. 2. Washington, D.C.: National Academy Press.

White, J.W.
1983 Sex and gender issues in aggression research. Pp. 1-26 in R.G. Geen and E.I. Donnerstein, eds., *Aggression: Theoretical and Empirical Reviews*. Vol. 2. *Issues in Research*. New York: Academic Press.

Widom, C.S.
1978 Toward an understanding of female criminality. Pp. 245-308 in A. Mafier, ed., *Progress in Experimental Personality Research*, Vol. 8. New York: Academic Press.
1984 Sex roles, criminality and psychopathology. Pp. 183-217 in C.S. Widom, ed., *Sex Roles and Psychopathology*. New York: Plenum.
1987 Family Violence and Infanticide. Paper presented at the Pennsylvania State University Conference on Perspectives on Postpartum Depression and Criminal Responsibility.
1989a Child abuse, neglect and violent criminal behavior. *Criminology* 27:251-271.
1989b The intergenerational transmission of violence. Pp. 137-201 in N.A. Weiner and M.E. Wolfgang, eds., *Pathways to Criminal Violence*. Newbury Park, Calif.: Sage Publications.

Widom, C.S., and A. Ames
1988 Biology and female crime. Pp. 308-331 in T.E. Moffitt and S.A. Medinick, eds., *Biological Contributions to Crime Causation*. Dordrecht: Martinus Nijhoff.

Widom, C.S., and A.J. Stewart
1986 Female criminality and the status of women. *International Annals of Criminology* 24:137-162.

Wilbanks, W.
1982 Murdered women and women who murder: A critique of the literature. Pp. 151-180 in N.H. Rafter and E.A. Sanko, eds.,

Judge, Lawyer, Victim, Thief: Women, Gender Roles and Criminal Justice. Boston: Northeastern University Press.

1986 Are female felons treated more leniently by the criminal justice system. *Justice Quarterly* 3(4):517-529.

Williams, K.M.

1976 The effects of victim characteristics on the disposition of violent crimes. Pp. 177-213 in W.F. McDonald, ed., *Criminal Justice and the Victim.* Beverly Hills, Calif.: Sage Publications.

Williams, L.S.

1984 The classic rape: When do victims report? *Social Problems* 31(4):459-467.

Wilson, J.Q., and R.J. Herrnstein

1985 *Crime and Human Nature.* New York: Simon and Schuster.

Wish, E.D., and B.A. Gropper

1990 Drug testing by the criminal justice system: Methods, research and applications. Pp. 321-391 in M. Tonry and J.Q. Wilson, eds., *Drugs and Crime.* Chicago: University of Chicago Press.

Wolfgang, M.E.

1975 *Patterns in Criminal Homicide.* Montclair, N.J.: Patterson Smith.

Young, V.D.

1979 Victims of female offenders. Pp. 72-87 in W.H. Parsonage, ed., *Perspectives on Victimology.* Beverly Hills, Calif.: Sage Publications.

1986 Gender expectations and their impact on black female offender and victims. *Justice Quarterly* 3(2):305-327.

Zatz, M.J., and J. Hagan

1985 Crime, time and punishment: An exploration of selection bias in sentencing research. *Journal of Quantitative Criminology* 1(1):103-126.

Zingraff, M.T., and R.J. Thomson

1985 Differential sentencing of women and men in the U.S.A. *International Journal of the Sociology of Law* 12:401-413.

Alcohol, Drugs of Abuse, Aggression, and Violence

*Klaus A. Miczek, Joseph F. DeBold, Margaret Haney,
Jennifer Tidey, Jeffrey Vivian, and Elise M. Weerts*

The alcohol-drug abuse-violence nexus presents itself in several distinctly different facets: alcohol and other drugs of abuse may act on brain mechanisms that cause a high-risk individual to engage in aggressive and violent behavior. Individuals with costly heroin or cocaine habits may commit violent crimes in order to secure the resources for further drug purchases. Narcotic drug dealers, but not alcohol vendors, practice their trade in a violent manner. Alcohol, narcotics, hallucinogens, and psychomotor stimulants differ substantially from each other and in the way that they are related to different kinds of violent and aggressive behavior. Generalizations about the linkage of alcohol, drugs of abuse, and violence are complicated by the many direct and indirect levels of interaction (e.g., Goldstein 1985); these range from (1) drugs activating aggression-specific brain mechanisms, through (2) drugs acting as licensure for violent and aggressive behavior, as well as (3) drugs as commodities in an illegal distribution system that relies upon violent enforcement tactics, to (4) violent behavior representing one of the means by which a drug habit is maintained. The persistently overwhelming alcohol-violence link as well as

Klaus Miczek, Joseph DeBold, Margaret Haney, Jennifer Tidey, Jeffrey Vivian, and Elise Weerts are at the Department of Psychology, Tufts University.

the recent outbreaks of "crack" cocaine and "ice" methamphetamine epidemics in the United States provide dramatic examples of serious and complex public health problems that need to be dissected in a careful and comprehensive manner.

Systematic evidence for alcohol and other drugs of abuse acting on aggression-specific brain mechanisms stems mainly from studies in animals, although a few neuroendocrine and other neurochemical and neurophysiologic measures have been obtained in humans. Data from studies in animals represent the primary means to investigate experimentally the proximal and distal causes of aggressive behavior, whereas studies in humans most often attempt to infer causative relationships mainly by correlating the incidence of violent and aggressive behavior with past alcohol intake or abuse of other drugs.

It is the objective of the present discussion to consider, integrate, and highlight accounts of empirical data that relate alcohol, opiates, amphetamines, cocaine, cannabis, and other hallucinogens to aggressive and violent behavior, with a particular emphasis on the pharmacologic determinants and potential biologic mechanisms. The major methodological features and the key results of the empirical studies are detailed in tables that appear at the end of this paper. The information is organized so that (1) for each drug class, tables for the data on aggression and violence in animals and in humans are separated; (2) the data on human violence are organized according to how they were collected by separating those that stem from criminal statistics, public health records, psychological evaluations, and experimental manipulations; and (3) drug effects on different types of aggressive and violent behavior in animals are grouped according to the aggression- and violence-provoking conditions.

ANIMAL MODELS OF AGGRESSION AND VIOLENCE

During the past two decades the focus of research on animal aggression has been ethological investigations of adaptive forms of aggressive behavior (e.g., Archer, 1988; Huntingford and Turner, 1987; see also Table 1). Defense of a territory, rival fighting among mature males during the formation and maintenance of a group, defense of the young by a female, and antipredator defense are examples of these types of aggressive, defensive, and submissive behavior patterns, oftentimes referred to as agonistic behavior (Scott, 1966). Sociobiologic analysis portrays these behavior patterns as having evolved as part of reproductive strategies ultimately serving the transmission of genetic information to the next generation (Wilson, 1975). The damaging and injurious consequences of adaptive agonistic behavior exclude—at least transiently—competing individuals from access to important resources. Strikingly, even in the absence of physical injury, among the most severe consequences of being exposed to aggression or the threat of aggression is the prevention of reproductive behavior. One such example is the so-called psychological castrate monkey who maintains group membership but resides at the periphery, with subordinate access to protected sleeping places, nutritious and palatable foods, grooming interactions, and rest periods. However, the focus on aggressive behavior as it serves an adaptive function in reproductive strategies complicates the extrapolation to violent behavior as it is defined at the human level. How human violence and animal aggression are related in their biologic roots remains to be specified; excessively aggressive behavior may represent an extreme on a continuum with adaptive aggressive behavior patterns. Alternatively, however, adaptive and maladaptive aggressive behavior patterns may differ fundamentally in their functions and causes.

Particularly during the 1960s, in a different research tradition, experimental preparations were developed that focused on aversive environmental manipulations to engender certain elements of defensive and aggressive behavior in otherwise placid, domesticated laboratory animals. These so-called animal models of aggression relied on prolonged isolated housing or crowding; exposure to noxious, painful electric shock pulses; omission of scheduled rewards; or restricted access to limited food supplies, as the major environmental manipulations (Malick, 1979; Valzelli et al., 1967; Sheard, 1981; Blanchard and Blanchard, 1984; Kelly, 1974; Looney and Cohen, 1982). The behavioral end point resulting from such experimental setups rarely extended beyond defensive postures and bites that were difficult to interpret in terms of the ethology of the animal. Such preparations have been questioned in terms of their validity for modeling human aggressive and violent behavior. Similarly, human aggression research under controlled laboratory conditions has employed aversive environmental manipulations that entail the administration of electric shocks, noxious noise, or loss of prize money to a fictitious opponent (e.g., Taylor, 1967; Cherek and Steinberg, 1987). Again, this type of experimental aggression research highlights the dilemma of attempting to model the essential features of "real-world" violence under controlled laboratory conditions without risking the potential harm and injury that are characteristic of violence.

A third approach used to investigate aggressive behavior in animals under laboratory conditions relies on physiologic and pharmacologic manipulations. Histopathological findings of brain tumors in violent patients (e.g., Mark and Ervin, 1970) prompted the development of experimental procedures that ablate and destroy tissue in the septal forebrain, medial hypothalamus, or certain mesencephalic regions of laboratory rats and other animals. Such experimental manipulations may result in rage-like defensive postures and biting, often called rage, hyperreactivity, or hyperdefensiveness (e.g., Brady and Nauta, 1953; Albert and Walsh, 1982, 1984). Alternatively, electrical stimulation of discrete subcortical regions can evoke predatory attack, as well as aggressive and defensive responses in certain animal species (see Delgado, 1963; Flynn et al., 1979; Kruk et al., 1979; Mirsky and Siegel, in Volume 2). Treatment with near-toxic amphetamine doses and other catecholaminergic agonist drugs may result in bizarre, rage-like responses in otherwise placid laboratory animals (Chance, 1946; Randrup and Munkvad, 1969; Maj et al., 1980). Similarly, aggressive and defensive behavioral elements are induced by exposure to very high doses of hallucinogens and during withdrawal from opiates (e.g., Sbordone et al., 1981; Gianutsos and Lal, 1978). It is noteworthy that mescaline-, amphetamine- and morphine-withdrawal-induced aggressive responses in rats, in conjunction with exposure to electric foot shock, are proposed as "pathological" aggression. The inappropriate context, the unusually fragmented behavioral response patterns, and the limitation to domesticated laboratory rodents render aggressive and defensive reactions that are induced by lesions, electrical brain stimulation, drugs, and toxins problematic in their interpretation. Often these laboratory phenomena are termed bizarre and ambiguous.

This brief introduction to and critique of the methodological and conceptual frameworks for studies of animal aggression will guide the subsequent discussion of research findings. It also highlights how a consideration of different kinds of human violence and animal aggression spans a range of environmental determinants, social contexts, functions, causative mechanisms, and consequences in general physiology and, particularly, in the central nervous system (CNS). Even a rudimentary understanding of the evolutionary origins of violent behavior in humans and its underlying brain mechanisms needs to begin with an appreciation of the range of agonistic behavior patterns subserving important survival functions in various animal species. There is no direct evidence, however, that demonstrates homology between the neural circuitry and physiologic activity that mediate aggressive behaviors in animals and those responsible for human violence. As a matter of fact, as reviewed repeatedly (see also Brain, and Mirsky and Siegel, in Volume 2), one major conclusion from work with cats and rats is that discrete neural circuits underlie each type of aggressive, defensive, and submissive behavior, and that the concept of a single neural center or command unit for aggressive behavior, as it has been studied in invertebrates, may not be simply extrapolated to complex mammalian nervous functions.

Concluding Statement

The evolutionary origins of aggressive and violent behavior need to be investigated by systematic comparisons of animals belonging to different species in order to delineate functional and neurobiologic common developments. The current animal models of aggression focus mostly on adaptive forms of agonistic behavior during social conflict. In order to relate experimental preparations in animals to issues of human violence, harmful and injurious forms of aggressive behavior must be considered. Similarly, there is a need to define how experimental laboratory measures of irritable, hostile, and aggressive human behavior relate to violence outside the laboratory context. However, such considerations prompt ethical demands about reducing harm and risk to animal and human research subjects.

ALCOHOL, AGGRESSION, AND VIOLENCE

The strong statistical association between alcohol and engaging in a violent or aggressive act or being the target of violent behavior prompts the identification of possible causal relationships. Conventional wisdom attributes disinhibiting effects to alcohol that release aggressive impulses from their cortical inhibition. Yet, the experimental evidence from studies in animals as well as in humans provides a complex pattern of results at the level of the cellular site of action, physiological system, whole organism, social setting, and culture that requires detailed examination.

In fact, alcohol's effects on a given individual's aggressive and violent behavior do not follow simply a monotonic pharmacologic dose-effect relationship; this is evident from three decades of research with various animal species and humans under many conditions. Whether or not alcohol, in a range of doses ingested orally, causes a certain individual to act aggressively more frequently or even to engage in "out-of-character" violent behavior depends on a host of interacting pharmacologic, endocrinologic, neurobiologic, genetic, situational, environmental, social, and cultural determinants.

PHARMACOLOGIC DETERMINANTS

Experimental studies in animals and humans demonstrate that the effects of acutely given alcohol engender a biphasic dose-effect curve on a range of aggressive and competitive behaviors. Low acute alcohol doses increase, and high doses decrease, threat and attack behavior in fish, mice, rats, cats, dogs, primates, college students, and other paid experimental subjects (see Tables 2A and 3). This dose-dependent increase and decrease in aggressive behavior are seen in virtually all experimental models of animal aggression. The biphasic pattern of alcohol dose dependence characterizes many behavioral, endocrinologic, and other physiologic actions of this drug (Pohorecky, 1977). However, Tables 2A and 3 also summarize reports that do not detect a reliable aggression-enhancing effect of low alcohol doses under a range of experimental conditions. During more than two decades of laboratory research in humans, the aggression-heightening effects with acutely consumed drinks containing 0.6, 0.8, 0.9, or 2.5 ml/kg of 50 percent alcohol (vodka) or 0.8-1.25 ml/kg of ethanol have been repeatedly confirmed. For example, Cherek et al. (1984, 1985) documented extensive alcohol dose-effect determinations on human aggressive behavior in an experimental competition task, showing large aggression-heightening effects in a dose range from 0.5 to 1.25 ml/kg of 50 percent alcohol. Outside of the controlled laboratory situation, no comparable alcohol dose determinations for violence-heightening effects are available.

One critical issue in the analysis of alcohol dose-effect relationships pertains to the use of group statistics. Population samples in virtually all animal species are composed of individuals that show clear-cut aggression-enhancing effects and those that show a reduction in aggressive behavior in the same range of alcohol doses. Individual differences in the aggression-enhancing effects of alcohol are not adequately detected by the use of pooled data and statistical averages. The source of the individual differences in sensitivity to the proaggressive effects of alcohol may eventually be traced to genetic and neurobiologic determinants, current and past social experiences, and other situational variables.

Alcohol is a short-acting drug whose early phases of action are associated most often with motor-activating, arousing, euphoric effects that contrast with the dysphoric and depressive effects during the later phases of its action (e.g., Babor et al., 1983). Experimental studies on acute alcohol doses and aggressive behavior have focused on the early activating phase of drug action (i.e., 15-30 minutes after administration), limiting their relevance to the problem of increased violent and aggressive behavior in later phases of alcohol action.

Detailed ethological analyses of a range of behavioral elements and signals during social confrontations begin to identify how the effects of alcohol qualitatively change as a function of increasing dose in mice, rats, and monkeys (Krsiak, 1975, 1976; Miczek and Barry, 1977; Miczek and O'Donnell, 1980; Yoshimura and Ogawa, 1983; Miczek, 1985; Winslow and Miczek, 1985, 1988; Blanchard et al., 1987c). Whereas very low alcohol doses (0.1-0.6 grams (g) per kilogram) increase elements of threat and attack under appropriate conditions, a two- to threefold increment in alcohol dose (1.2-1.6 g/kg) decreases the initiation of aggressive acts and postures, and a further twofold increase in alcohol dose leads to sedation.

Chronic alcohol administration, at intoxicating levels, and aggressive behavior have been investigated in a few methodologically diverse studies in mice, rats, and rhesus monkeys (Table 2B). There are several demonstrations of unusual and intense forms of aggressive behavior in stressed animals when given alcohol chronically (e.g., Tramill et al., 1980, 1983; Pucilowski et al., 1987). For example, recently Peterson and Pohorecky (1989) reported that three daily alcohol administrations caused resident rats to attack and wound intruders more severely by targeting their bites at unusual sites of the opponent. This shift in aggressive behavior appears to indicate a disruption of species-specific ritualized patterns of fighting and an exaggeration to more intense and injurious forms of attack. The evidence on chronic alcohol effects in primates is limited to a few studies that show increased play fighting in juveniles, self-biting in isolation-reared rhesus monkeys, and aggressive displays in pigtail macaques (Chamove and Harlow, 1970; Cressman and Cadell, 1971; Kamback, 1973). Although most relevant to the human situation, the evidence from chronic alcohol studies under controlled laboratory conditions is still preliminary.

The effects of alcohol abuse on human aggression and violence have to be inferred from statistics involving individuals who were at various stages of intoxication at the time of the aggressive or violent activity (see Table 3). Violent crimes such as murder, rape, and assaults are prevalent in alcohol-abusing individuals that are diagnosed as alcoholic, as well as those that do not fulfill psychiatric criteria of alcoholism. Alcohol abuse was found to be consistently and highly represented among convicted rapists (50%, Shupe, 1954; 53%, McCaldon, 1967; 35%/57%, Rada 1975, and Rada et al., 1978; 72%, Johnson et al., 1978; 65%, Barnard et al., 1979); incestuous offenders (49%, Virkkunen, 1974b; 50%, Browning and Boatman, 1977); wife abusers and individuals committing other types of family violence (40%, Gayford, 1979; 15-20%, Eberle, 1982; 83%, Livingston, 1986); individuals with a history of injurious violent acts (29%, Schuckit and Russell, 1984), particularly at home (48-56%, Kroll et al., 1985); imprisoned murderers (36%, Wilentz and Brady, 1961; 10%, Scott, 1968; 57%, Grunberg et al., 1978; 56%/83%, Bloom, 1980; 56%, Lindqvist, 1986); adolescents convicted of homicides (61%, Tinklenberg and Ochberg, 1981), and convicted felons (33%, Guze et al., 1968; 57%, Mayfield, 1976), although there are also occasional reports indicating no overrepresentations of alcoholics, as for example, among Swedish female criminal offenders (e.g., Medhus, 1975). These overwhelming statistics stem mainly from studies in Scandinavia, the United Kingdom, Australia, Canada, and various localities in the United States, indicating wide generality. The marked correlations between alcoholism and various types of violent acts do not permit, however, any clear insight into the pharmacologic conditions of alcohol exposure that are necessary or sufficient for these violence-promoting effects. Based on verbal recall by convicted felons, Collins and Schlenger (1988) indicated that those who were drinking just before the offense were 1.74 times more likely to be in prison for a violent crime than those who said that they were not drinking. Of course, these and similar types of data based on verbal report are tainted by the amnesic effects of alcohol intoxication. Blood alcohol levels in excess of 0.06 percent were found in nearly half of the convicted murderers at the time of the arrest (Lindqvist, 1986). Unfortunately, blood alcohol levels, if determined at all, frequently refer to values only after considerable time has elapsed since the violent act was performed.

A critically limiting issue in studies on alcohol with animals is the way in which the drug is administered. Whereas oral self-administration is the rule in humans, animal studies most often rely on alcohol administration by the experimenter or on forced drinking. Voluntary intake of alcohol at intoxicating doses has been achieved only in selected experimental preparations in animals (e.g., Samson et al., 1989; Crowley and Andrews, 1987), but these methodologies have not been applied to the issue of alcohol's effects on aggressive behavior. There is also some indication that distilled beverages are more effective than beer in enhancing aggressive tendencies in laboratory competitive task in humans (Pihl et al., 1984a,b).

ENDOCRINOLOGIC INFLUENCES

The frequent statistical association between sexual violence and alcohol in humans (see Table 2) may suggest an alcohol effect that targets endocrine processes. Alcohol's action on androgens and its trophic hormones was postulated to mediate its effects on aggression (e.g., Mendelson and Mello, 1974; Mendelson et al., 1978). As a matter of fact, acute alcohol doses generally decrease testosterone in blood and higher doses also impair the gonadotropic hormones from the pituitary, such as luteinizing hormone (LH) and follicle-stimulating hormone (FSH) in animals and in humans (Van Thiel et al., 1988). The decrease in testosterone in blood is primarily due to alcohol's action on the testes and the liver, rather than on the neuroendocrine events governing testosterone synthesis. That the action of alcohol outside the brain is relevant to the aggression- and violence-increasing effects of this substance is unlikely.

Direct experimental investigations of alcohol-androgen interactive effects on aggression were conducted in mice, rats, and squirrel monkeys (DeBold and Miczek, 1985; Winslow and Miczek, 1988; Winslow et al., 1988; Lisciotto et al., 1990; see Table 2A). In individuals with experimentally or naturally elevated blood testosterone levels, acute low alcohol doses increase aggressive behavior toward a drug-free opponent. This alcohol-testosterone interaction appears to depend on the actions of testosterone on targets in brain rather than on peripheral sites of action.

Males and females differ as to whether or not they engage in violent and aggressive behavior after alcohol (see Table 3). However, this difference is chiefly a statistical phenomenon due to social or environmental factors, rather than to endocrine differences. Men and women students differ in their expectations about the aggression-heightening effects of alcohol and about male versus female targets of aggression under the influence of alcohol

(Crawford, 1984; Gustafson, 1986b,c). Epidemiologic data find male and female victims of homicides and suicides associated with alcohol abuse in comparable proportions, although males are much more frequently represented than females (Rydelius, 1988; Schuckit et al., 1978). No experimental data exist on human violent behavior that directly compare males and females while under the influence of alcohol.

NEUROBIOLOGIC MECHANISMS

At least a dozen mechanisms have been proposed and continue to be investigated for alcohol's action on the central nervous system (Anggard, 1988; Koob and Bloom, 1988; Myers, 1989), ranging from fluidization of neuronal membranes to relatively specific actions on receptors that are associated with gamma-aminobutyric acid (GABA), serotonin (5-HT), catecholamines, peptides, and steroids. Alcohol's violence- or aggression-heightening effects have not been linked firmly to a specific mechanism, although several proposals deserve attention.

The relationship between high incidences of violent and aggressive behavior in alcoholics and some aspects of brain serotonin metabolism or serotonin receptor regulation has been investigated (Table 3; e.g., Linnoila et al., 1983; Virkkunen et al., 1989a,b). This correlational research finds some evidence for a link between low cerebrospinal fluid (CSF) levels of 5-HIAA (5-hydroxyindoleacetic acid) and poor impulse control found in some violent alcohol abusers (see also discussion of 5-HT in Miczek, Haney, et al., in Volume 2).

Recently, some of alcohol's behavioral and neurochemical effects were linked with the action on the GABA-A receptor complex in brain (e.g., Suzdak et al., 1986; Lister and Nutt, 1988). Pharmacologic blockade of the benzodiazepine sites on the GABA-A receptor complex has already proven to be effective in antagonizing some of alcohol's neurochemical (e.g., Harris et al., 1988; Mehta and Ticku, 1988) and behavioral effects in animals (e.g., Lister, 1988a,b; Koob et al., 1989). Preliminary data demonstrate that antagonists at the benzodiazepine-GABA-A receptor complex block the aggression-heightening effects of alcohol in rats and monkeys (e.g., Weerts et al., 1993). At present, these experimental substances have not been explored in humans for their effects on alcohol-enhanced violence or aggression.

In a small subgroup of individuals having committed a violent crime or antisocial act, a challenge dose of alcohol produces an abnormal electroencephalogram (EEG), suggesting temporal lobe damage that is aggravated by the drug (Marinacci and von Hagen, 1972). Individuals with underlying neurologic disturbances may represent a small proportion of the total number of alcohol-related violent acts. More recently, a study of EEG and event-related potentials (ERPs) in alcoholics found that the P300 component of ERPs was reduced in amplitude in alcoholics with a history of violence but not in alcoholics in general (Branchey et al., 1988). These studies suggest that there may be some physiologic differences between those few alcohol abusers that become violent and those that never experience any proaggressive effects of alcohol.

GENETICS AND PERSONALITY FACTORS

There are consistent demonstrations of a genetic component of alcohol abuse based on several series of studies in Scandinavia and in the United States (e.g., Goodwin, 1973). In parallel, antisocial personality has also been found to have a strong genetic component, and these two disorders frequently co-occur (see Table 3; also Schubert et al., 1988). The question as to whether or not there is a common genetic basis for antisocial personality disorder and alcoholism remains a source of controversy, with some claiming independence (e.g., Cadoret et al., 1985) and others linkage, at least in some alcoholics (e.g., Cloninger et al., 1989). In a recent sample of 32 identical twins from the United States, the heritability of alcohol abuse was very small and somewhat higher for antisocial personality (Grove et al., 1990). However, due to the small nonclinical sample size, no firm conclusions on the "permissive" role of the genetic influence on the gene-environment interaction are possible as yet. It is most astounding that no systematic investigations into the genetic influence on the alcohol-aggression link have been performed in animal preparations; promising starting points for such studies are animals that are selectively bred for high-preference for alcohol or for high levels of aggressive behavior.

The evidence on personality factors of alcoholics differentiates several "alcoholic personalities" (see Table 3). Most significantly, a subpopulation of alcoholics may be identified as sociopathic via several personality testing instruments (e.g., O'Leary et al., 1978; Yates et al., 1987), and conversely, individuals that are diagnosed with antisocial personality disorder frequently abuse alcohol as well as other drugs. It is these latter individuals that are more likely to be violent than alcohol abusers with other personality subtypes. There is evidence that they may also form a specific genetic subtype (Cloninger, 1987).

ENVIRONMENTAL DETERMINANTS

The most significant environmental factors in determining the direction and magnitude of alcohol's effects on aggressive and violent behavior are the past and current social conditions ("set" and "setting"). Situational, social, and personal characteristics prior to alcohol consumption contribute significantly to the aggression-promoting effects of alcohol in barroom environments, in addition to the type and amount of alcoholic beverage (e.g., Boyatzis, 1975; Graham et al., 1980).

An important question in this field is whether alcohol increases aggression and violence because of pharmacologic actions or because the drinker expects an increase in aggression as part of the effects of alcohol. In laboratory experiments, it has been demonstrated that subjects believe that a drunk will behave more aggressively (Gustafson, 1986b,c). Some researchers have reported that subjects will behave aggressively in the laboratory if they think they have consumed alcohol independent of their actual blood-alcohol content (BAC) (e.g., Lang et al., 1975; Rohsenow and Bachorowski, 1984), but others find that the pharmacologic effects of alcohol on aggression are stronger than any expectancy effects (e.g., George and Marlatt, 1986; Pihl and Zacchia, 1986).

The behavioral history of aggressive and violent behavior is a critical determinant in whether or not alcohol will increase these types of behavior, as demonstrated in studies with animals (e.g., Pettijohn, 1979; Miczek and Barry, 1977) and also with humans (e.g., Rydelius, 1988). In a longitudinal Finnish sample, 20-year-old violent male offenders were more likely to have been more aggressive at age 8; aggressiveness at age 8 also predicted heavy drinking by age 20 (Pulkkinen, 1983). Alcohol more than doubled the rate of attack and threat behavior by mice, rats, and monkeys that had previously exhibited these behaviors during social confrontations, whereas alcohol did not induce aggressive behavior in individuals who had displayed primarily submissive and defensive behavior during previous confrontations (Blanchard et al., 1987b; Winslow and Miczek, 1985; DeBold and Miczek, 1985). The interaction between the predisposition to antisocial personality and alcoholism on the one hand, and early life history with family and peers on the other, needs to be investigated systematically to specify the respective contributions of these factors.

Research findings from the animal and human literature on alcohol, however, differ in that violent acts by alcohol-intoxicated humans preferentially target family members and friends, but animals direct their injurious aggressive acts toward unfamiliar opponents and less intensely toward their kin.

Alcohol in the victim or target of aggressive and violent behavior has been documented both in animals and in humans (Tables 2A and 3). Acutely or chronically alcohol-treated mice, rats, or monkeys provoke more frequent attacks and threats by an alcohol-free opponent (e.g., Miczek et al., 1984; Peterson and Pohorecky, 1989; Blanchard et al., 1987c). Correlational statistics in humans identify alcoholics as risking injury, often fatally, in violent interactions more often than nonalcoholics (Table 3; especially Wolfgang and Strohm, 1956; Virkkunen, 1974a; Abel et al., 1985). However, these statistics cannot assess the contribution by the alcoholics to the escalating interaction that eventually led to their being victims.

In a variety of countries, such as Australia, Finland, Sweden, South Africa, Canada, and the United States, an association between alcohol and violence has been noted. The major source of cultural differences in the prevalence of this association is usually attributed to nonbiologic factors. For example, the high rate of violent deaths and alcohol abuse in native Americans has been interpreted as part of a strategy to cope with acculturation (e.g., Westermeyer and Brantner, 1972; Seltzer, 1980). MacAndrew and Edgerton's (1969) accounts of alcohol effects in South and North American tribal societies emphasized social learning as the main source for the varied impact of imbibing alcoholic beverages on aggressive and violent behavior. Drinking parties transform the Abipone from nonargumentative and calm social intercourse into combative individuals, but cause the head-hunting Yurunas to withdraw socially. A simple disinhibition model is an inadequate explanation for these diametrically opposed effects of alcohol on social and aggressive behavior as reported in anthropological studies.

CONCLUDING STATEMENT

Alcohol stands out as the drug that is most consistently and seriously linked to many types of aggressive and violent behavior. Systematic experimental studies have identified (1) the early phase after a low acute alcohol dose as a condition that increases the probability of many types of social interactions, including aggressive and competitive behaviors; and (2) the high alcohol dose intoxication as the condition most likely to be linked to many different kinds of violent activities. Individuals differ markedly in their propensity to become intoxicated with alcoholic beverages and to subsequently engage in violence, and group statistics describe the alcohol-violence link poorly. The sources of these individual differences may be sought in genetic, developmental, social, and environmental factors. Genetic linkage between antisocial personality, possibly diagnosed with the aid of certain electrophysiologic measures, and alcoholism remains to be firmly established. At present, the neurobiologic mechanisms of alcohol action remain to be identified for a range of physiologic and behavioral functions, although the actions on brain serotonin and the benzodiazepine-GABA-A receptor complex may become especially relevant to alcohol's effect on aggressive and violent behavior. Similarly, the actions of alcohol on neuroendocrine events that control testosterone and adrenal hormones are a promising lead for elucidating the mechanisms of alcohol's aggression-heightening effects. Among the environmental determinants of alcohol's effects on violence that are of paramount significance rank social expectations and cultural habits, as well as behavioral history in situations of social conflict. Impaired appraisal of consequences, inappropriate sending and receiving of socially significant signals, and disrupted patterns of social interactions are characteristic of alcohol intoxication that contribute to the violence-promoting effects. A particularly consistent observation is the high prevalence of alcohol in victims and targets of aggression and violence. In contrast to heroin or cocaine, alcohol's link to violence is not a characteristic of the economic distribution network for this substance.

OPIATES, AGGRESSION, AND VIOLENCE

In confirmation of experiences originating with the ancient opium culture, the earliest studies in experimental animal psychopharmacology began to show that acute administration of opiates reduces aggressive behavior. Morphine and similar drugs decrease different kinds and elements of aggressive behavior in fish, mice, rats, cats, and squirrel monkeys (see Table 4A). For example, drug- and brain stimulation-induced rage reactions, defensive biting in response to pain, and attack and threat behavior by territorial males and by lactating females are suppressed by opiates. However, this antiaggressive effect is part of the opiate sedative, tranquilizing effects in both animals and humans.

Single opiate doses also decrease human hostility as, for example, reviewed by Sutker and Archer (1984; see Table 5). The reported feeling of well-being, and oftentimes euphoria, in humans under the influence of opiates is one of the key causes for the high abuse potential of this class of drugs.

Under conditions of chronic heroin use, the direct effects of drug administration on mood significantly change. The euphorigenic effects of opiates are often replaced with feelings of confusion, hostility, and suspicion (Mirin and Meyer, 1979). In animals, chronic methadone does not increase aggressive behavior, but continues to decrease social intercourse (see Table 4A).

A special focus of studies on opiates and animal aggression for the past 25 years has been the prolonged increase in irritability, defensive responses and aggressive acts during withdrawal from chronic exposure to opiates (e.g., Gianutsos and Lal, 1976, 1978; Miczek, 1987). Table 4B summarizes studies showing that under a range of pharmacologic parameters, withdrawal from chronic opiates leads to the display of aggressive and defensive acts and postures in pairs of mice, hamsters, and rats that extends in time beyond the physiologic withdrawal syndrome (Martin et al., 1963; Vivian and Miczek, 1991; Tidey and Miczek, 1992). The exact nature of the aggressive and defensive acts during opiate withdrawal varies as a function of the animal species, with attack bites being more common in pairs of mice and hamsters, and defensive postures and vocalizations being characteristic of rats (e.g., Lal, 1975a,b; Kantak and Miczek, 1986). Rhesus monkeys continuously shift from aggressive threat displays to exaggerated signs of submission when withdrawn from chronic morphine injections (Kreiskott, 1966).

Experimentally, opiate withdrawal may be precipitated if an opiate receptor antagonist such as naloxone is administered or if opiate administrations are suddenly discontinued. The effects of the opiate antagonists naloxone or naltrexone in opiate-naive animals are small and inconsistent. If given at high doses, opiate antagonists may increase certain types of defensive reactions (e.g., Fanselow et al., 1980; Rodgers, 1982; Tazi et al., 1983; Puglisi-Allegra and Olivierio, 1981), but may decrease offensive attack behavior in male mice, rats, and squirrel monkeys (e.g., Olivier and van Dalen, 1982; Benton, 1984; Winslow and Miczek, 1988).

The neurochemical mechanisms of aggression during opiate

withdrawal involve several neurotransmitters and neuromodulators. Disturbances in opioid receptors, as for example during narcotic addiction, may be responsible for altered affect and communication during social interactions. During the past decade, a critically significant role for endogenous opioid peptides and their receptors in social behavior became apparent, particularly in affective responses associated with conflict situations (e.g., Panksepp, 1981; Miczek et al., 1991b). For example, distress signals in infant rodents and juvenile primates, as well as feline defensive reactions, are potently attenuated by certain opioid peptides (e.g., Benton and Brain, 1988; Kalin and Shelton, 1989; Shaikh et al., 1990). By extrapolation, it may be expected that communicative signal systems during social conflict situations in several mammalian species, including humans, require intact endogenous opioid systems.

Many studies have focused on brain dopamine and norepinephrine and their receptors in mediating behavioral symptoms of opiate withdrawal (e.g., Lal, 1975b; Redmond and Krystal, 1984). Pharmacologic activation of brain dopamine receptors potentiates aggressive and defensive acts during opiate withdrawal, whereas blockade of dopamine synthesis or receptors reduces these behaviors (Gianutsos et al., 1974; Puri and Lal, 1973; Kantak and Miczek, 1988). Of particular clinical interest is the proposed application of clonidine, an α_2-adrenergic receptor agonist, in the management of opiate withdrawal, possibly including the aggression-precipitating components (e.g., Fielding et al., 1978; Redmond and Krystal, 1984; Gold et al., 1981). At present, the neurobiologic mechanisms for the physiologic and behavioral phenomena during opiate withdrawal in humans can only be extrapolated from studies in rodents and primates.

Chronic methadone in the management of withdrawal from narcotic addiction given under controlled conditions in a hospital setting did not result in significant changes in hostility. Although withdrawal from methadone was associated with increased tension and anxiety, levels of hostility remained unchanged (Woody et al., 1983). Narcotic addicts self-administering heroin under controlled conditions reported increased feelings of hostility when they unknowingly received an opiate antagonist. However, hostility measures did not change when addicts were aware of the antagonist administration (Mirin and Meyer, 1979).

Opiate administration and withdrawal are accompanied by marked gonadal and adrenal hormone fluctuations. Plasma testosterone and cortisol are suppressed during acute and chronic opiate administration, while prolactin levels are elevated (Ellingboe et al.,

1979; Mirin and Meyer, 1979). During opiate withdrawal, cortisol levels exceed those of controls, while testosterone levels remain suppressed for up to three weeks (Woody et al., 1983). These data do not preclude or strongly support a hormonal role in the altered mood and behavior during phases of opiate administration and withdrawal.

Both men and women show a large increase in criminal activity during periods of narcotic addiction (Johnson et al., 1985; Anglin and Hser, 1987). The most important association between violence and narcotic addiction comes from the socioeconomic context of supporting a relatively expensive drug habit. Heroin addicts commit mainly property crimes and are less likely to be arrested for violent crimes compared to nonaddicted convicts (McGlothin, 1979). Violent crimes that are committed by heroin addicts usually occur in the course of property crimes and in interaction with drug dealers (Gossop and Roy, 1977; Simonds and Kashani, 1979b). In fact, drug sales and crime are more strongly related than drug use and crime (Chaiken and Chaiken, 1990). In the illicit drug business, violence or the threat of violence appears to be the primary means of maintaining order (Johnson et al., 1985).

Not all heroin addicts commit crime, in fact the majority do not. Only those individuals who already commit crimes at a high rate show a systematic increase in criminal activity with increasing drug use (Chaiken and Chaiken, 1990). It is difficult to break the circularity between sociopathy and narcotic addiction, since the latter often contributes to the definition of the former (see Table 5). High-frequency drug use often starts in adolescence, as does high-frequency criminal activity, but the onset of sociopathic behavior largely predates drug use (e.g., Hewett and Martin, 1980; Sutker and Archer, 1984). Although drug addiction enhanced certain types of criminal activity, the majority of both male and female heroin addicts had committed crime prior to their initiation to drugs (Anglin and Hser, 1987; Anglin and Speckart, 1988).

CONCLUDING STATEMENT

Neither animal nor human data suggest a direct, pharmacologic association between violence and acute or chronic opiate administration. Violence in the context of narcotic addiction is foremost instrumental in securing the resources to maintain the drug habit and in interacting with drug dealers. Although measures of hostility and anger are increased in addicts seeking methadone treatment, these feelings usually do not lead to aggressive or violent acts. Rather, the tendency to commit violent crimes correlates with preaddiction rates of criminal activity. Experimental studies in animals point to the phase of withdrawal from chronic opiates as the most vulnerable period to be provoked to heightened levels of aggressive behavior. Although humans undergoing opiate withdrawal may experience increased feelings of anger, there is no evidence suggesting that they are more likely to become violent as a result.

AMPHETAMINES, AGGRESSION, AND VIOLENCE

Weckamine, originally synthesized in 1887, received their name for their arousing, antifatigue, endurance-enhancing effects, which may contribute to their effects on aggressive and violent behavior. The major types of amphetamines that relate to the topic of violence and aggression include *dextro-* and *levo*-amphetamine as well as *d*-methamphetamine. Recently, several ring-substituted methamphetamines have become of substantial health concern due to their potential neurotoxic effects; these "designer" drugs include MDA ("eve") and MDMA ("ecstasy"). However, there is as yet no evidence that these later two compounds are linked to any heightened aggressive or violent behavior. This fact is remarkable because MDMA and MDA exert severe and long-lasting cytotoxic actions on serotonin-containing neurons, particularly in primates (Ricaurte et al., 1985). "Ice" is methamphetamine in smokable form, first produced in 1893 in Japan, that leads to a "high" for 8-24 hours. The American Council for Drug Education reported late in 1989 that ice has become a widespread problem in Hawaii, causing aggressive behavior, hallucinations, paranoia, and fatal kidney failure.

PHARMACOLOGIC DETERMINANTS

The most significant pharmacologic determinants of the amphetamine-aggression/violence link are the *dose*, the *route of administration*, and the *chronicity* of exposure to the drug. It is useful to differentiate several important pharmacologic conditions and phases: (1) the aggression-enhancing effects of an acute low amphetamine dose, usually a single bolus dose; (2) the homicidal tendencies during dose escalations and bingeing, often as part of amphetamine-induced paranoid psychosis; and (3) the disruptive and disorganizing effects of intermediate amphetamine doses on social, sexual, and agonistic interactions.

At acute low doses, amphetamines may increase various aggressive and defensive behaviors in several animal species, as well as competitive aggressive behavior in humans. Table 6 summarizes studies in fish, pigeons, mice, rats, cats, and monkeys that demonstrate how acutely given low amphetamine doses increase threat and attack behavior directed toward a territorial intruder or rival opponent, defensive-aggressive responses in reaction to pain, brain stimulation-evoked killing responses, and defensive reactions. Similarly, in experimental laboratory studies with human subjects, acute low doses of d-amphetamine increase aggressive and competitive behavior (Table 7; Cherek et al., 1986, 1989). Clear demonstrations of aggression-enhancing effects of low amphetamine doses come from studies in animals undergoing withdrawal from opiates (e.g., Lal et al., 1971; Kantak and Miczek, 1988) and from studies in animals that are habituated to aggression-provoking conditions (Winslow and Miczek, 1983).

Under many experimental conditions and in most animal species, amphetamines, however, do not increase offensive-aggressive behavior, but with increasing dose, defensive and flight reactions are enhanced and organized sequences of pursuit, threat, attack, and dominance displays are disrupted (see Table 6; e.g., Miczek et al., 1989). This disorganizing effect of high amphetamine doses extends to a range of social interactions from copulatory to maternal, play, and agonistic behavior. Correspondingly, human amphetamine users are rated to display less impulse control (Milkman and Frosch, 1980). Very high, near-toxic amphetamine doses induce in otherwise placid laboratory rodents, biting reactions and exaggerated defensive postures that deviate from the expected behavioral repertoire (e.g., Chance, 1946; Randrup and Munkvad, 1969).

Long-term amphetamine administration in animals, as well as long-term use in humans, result in dramatic changes in social behavior. Under experimental conditions, sensitization as well as tolerance develop to prominent behavioral effects of amphetamine, depending on the interval between consecutive amphetamine administrations (e.g., Segal et al., 1980). Discrete daily injections with methamphetamine or d-amphetamine decrease attack and threat behavior in mice, while continuous exposure to amphetamine initially results in social withdrawal and eventually in heightened threat and defensive reactions, as well as in violent fighting (e.g., Bovet-Nitti and Messeri, 1975; Richardson et al., 1972; O'Donnell and Miczek, 1980; Ellison et al., 1978). These progressive amphetamine-induced changes in the quality and nature of social interactions in animals may be mimicked nonpharmacologically by restricting the environmental resources of the social group (Sorensen, 1987; Sorensen and Randrup, 1986). Continuously worsening social withdrawal also became evident in macaque monkeys or marmosets that were treated chronically with amphetamine (Garver et al., 1975; Schlemmer et al., 1976; Ridley et al., 1979). It is tempting to interpret the socially disruptive chronic amphetamine effects in rodents and monkeys as analogous to the suspicious and paranoid reactions of human amphetamine users (e.g., Schiørring, 1977).

In humans, numerous psychiatric evaluations of chronic amphetamine abusers and police records during the past three decades point repeatedly to individuals in whom chronic stimulant use engenders paranoid and psychotic behavior, which in turn is accompanied by violent behavior (see Table 7). Probably no other report is more frequently cited than Ellinwood's (1971) account of 13 male and female cases in whom chronic amphetamine use or high acute amphetamine doses induced paranoia that was directly linked to their homicidal activity. In fact, several clinical observations do find that aggressiveness and hostility, culminating in physical assaults and homicides, are secondary to the psychotic paranoid state produced by intravenous use of high amphetamine doses, often chronically (see Table 7; e.g., Rickman et al., 1961; Angrist and Gershon, 1969; Siomopoulos, 1981; Rawlin, 1968).

Although there is little disagreement as to the seriousness and intensity of violence during amphetamine psychosis, opinions differ substantially as to the actual frequency of these phenomena (see Table 7). The lowest reported proportions refer to 12 chronic amphetamine abusers out of 130 patients displaying episodic violent behavior (Bach-y-Rita et al., 1971), and 1 out of 50 juvenile delinquents committing an assault under the influence of amphetamine (Tinklenberg and Woodrow, 1974); a frequently mentioned proportion in the psychiatric literature is around 60 percent of each sample (see Table 7: 62%, Angrist and Gershon, 1969; 60%, Simonds and Kashani, 1979a,b). Recently, a substantially higher statistic was reported from San Diego county in 1987 where methamphetamine and cocaine were associated with one-third of all homicides for that year (Bailey and Shaw, 1989). To place these statistics into perspective, it is worth remembering that the many therapeutic applications of amphetamines in eating and sleep disorders do not mention increased aggressive, hostile, or violent behavior as problems (e.g., Leventhal and Brodie, 1981; Allen et al., 1975). Moreover, amphetamines and similarly acting drugs actually reduce aggressive behavior in youngsters who had been diagnosed as hyperkinetic, autistic, explosive, unsocialized, or emotionally disturbed (Conners, 1972; Winsberg et al., 1972; Arnold et al., 1973; Maletzky, 1974).

BEHAVIORAL DETERMINANTS

The nature of the behavioral change that is brought about by amphetamine differs fundamentally according to the individual's prior history of amphetamine self-administration and aggressive behavior, as well as the environmental context, even under closely similar pharmacologic conditions. Clinical experiences, experimental evidence and drug abusers concur in highlighting the euphorigenic effects of amphetamines (e.g., Laties, 1961; Griffiths et al., 1977). Some amphetamine abusers also attribute anxiogenic effects to the drug (Smith and Davis, 1977). In terms of social behavior, withdrawal from social contact after chronic amphetamine exposure contrasts with the increased frequency of socializing after an acute amphetamine dose (e.g., Schiørring, 1977; Griffiths et al., 1977; Higgins and Stitzer, 1988). The assaultive and violent behavior represents yet a further facet in the behavioral profile of high-dose amphetamine action that appears limited to predisposed individuals. At present, neither prospective nor retrospective evidence from long-term studies in human amphetamine abusers or in experimental models in animals informs on the critical factors that predispose to violent behavior under the influence of amphetamine.

Amphetamine differentially alters offensive attack and threat behavior versus defensive and flight behavior in several animal species (see Table 6; Chance and Silverman, 1964; Hoffmeister and Wuttke, 1969; Miczek, 1974; Krsiak, 1975; Ellison et al., 1978; Sieber et al., 1982). At higher amphetamine doses, defensive and flight reactions are mainly enhanced, whereas attack sequences are disrupted. At present, it is not possible to specify an amphetamine dose-dependent behavioral profile for different types of human aggressive and violent behavior. When sufficient amphetamine has been administered to produce paranoia and psychosis, the probability of violent behavior appears to increase in 10-60 percent of the individuals (e.g., Allen et al., 1975; Sheard, 1977a). Lower amphetamine doses may increase a range of social behaviors such as speaking or competing (Stitzer et al., 1978; Cherek et al., 1989) but do not specifically increase violent behavior.

The past and present success in social confrontations defines the social status or rank of an individual within a group that in turn determines how amphetamines influence individual levels of aggressive behavior. Experimental evidence from studies with laboratory rodents and primates shows that amphetamines may increase submissive displays and flight reactions in macaque monkeys that are very high or very low ranking in their groups, and may increase aggressive behavior in certain dominant animals (e.g., Schlemmer and Davis, 1981; Haber et al., 1981; Miczek and Gold, 1983; Smith and Byrd, 1984; Krsiak, 1975). The only possible parallel in humans may be found in retrospective psychiatric evaluations that find increased likelihood of violent episodes after amphetamine in individuals who had a history of unusual social behavior (Rubin, 1972; Black and Heald, 1975; Brook et al., 1976). It will be important to specify the constraints imposed on an individual by past and current social interactions as potential determinants of whether or not amphetamine will increase the likelihood of engendering violent outbursts.

NEUROBIOLOGIC MECHANISMS

The specific neurochemical mechanisms of action for amphetamine's effects on aggressive and violent behavior remain to be identified. Amphetamine acts as a sympathomimetic amine; one of its major actions in the brain is the release of dopamine from nerve endings in the striatum leading indirectly to dopamine receptor activation (e.g., Kuczenski, 1983). Many features of endogenous and amphetamine psychosis are successfully managed by antipsychotics that block the D_2 subtype of dopamine receptors (e.g., Seeman, 1987). In laboratory rodents, the so-called amphetamine rage response and opiate-withdrawal aggression, as well as other stimulant-induced motor stereotypies, depend on an intact nigrostriatal dopamine system (Randrup and Munkvad, 1969; Lal et al., 1971; Hasselager et al., 1972; Rolinski, 1973, 1977; Kantak and Miczek, 1988). However, the socially disruptive effects of amphetamine have not been reversed by dopamine receptor blocking drugs (e.g., Schiørring, 1977; Miczek and Yoshimura, 1982; Poli and Palermo-Neto, 1986). The current evidence indicates that indirect dopamine receptor activation by amphetamine or, alternatively, the blockade of these receptors by certain antipsychotics potently modulates aggressive or violent behavior, however, not in a selective fashion.

CONCLUDING STATEMENT

The most serious link of amphetamine to violence refers to those individuals who, after intravenous amphetamine, most often chronically, develop a paranoid psychotic state and commit violent acts. Most psychiatric reports and police records do not support Ellinwood's stern conclusion from 1971 that "even hippies have noted the dangerous aspects of amphetamine abuse in their slogan 'Speed Kills.' Reports of law enforcement personnel, psychiatrists, and drug abusers themselves indicate that amphetamines, more than any other group of drugs, may be related specifically to aggressive behavior." The prevalence of violence by individuals who experience amphetamine paranoid psychosis may be less than 10 percent in general population samples and as high as two-thirds among individuals who showed evidence of psychopathology prior to amphetamine use. Low acute amphetamine doses may increase various positive and negative social behaviors; higher doses often lead to disorganizing effects on social interactions and severe social withdrawal. At present, the neurobiologic mechanisms for the range of amphetamine effects on aggressive and social behavior remain unknown, rendering the development of a rationale pharmacologic treatment uncertain.

COCAINE, AGGRESSION, AND VIOLENCE

The crack-cocaine epidemic during the past decade in the United States has dramatically transformed the customs and traditions surrounding this drug in previous decades and centuries. Violence during the interactions between crack-cocaine dealers and users has attracted considerable media attention, and it is this aspect that has been the focus of several recent and ongoing epidemiologic research efforts.

Psychiatric examinations of chronic and recreational cocaine users during the 1970s emphasized the drug's potential to alter brain functions that are conducive to violent behavior (see Table 8; e.g., Post, 1975; Siegel, 1977; Fink and Hyatt, 1978; Egan and Robinson, 1979; Grinspoon and Bakalar, 1979). Similar to the sequence of events in chronic amphetamine users, violent or aggressive behavior is viewed as secondary to the occasional paranoia and psychosis that are triggered by chronic cocaine use. Notably, one account found no difference in the frequency of violent acts committed by institutionalized cocaine users and those committed by inpatients who did not use this drug (Swett, 1985).

Pharmacologic studies in laboratory animals have attempted to characterize the dosage and environmental conditions under which cocaine may increase aggressive and defensive behavior (see Table 9). Acute but not chronic cocaine increases defensive bites and postures in mice, rats, and monkeys after isolated housing, crowding, or exposure to painful stimuli (e.g., Brunaud and Siou, 1959; Miczek and O'Donnell, 1978; Emley and Hutchinson, 1983). By contrast, aggressive behavior in confrontations with a rival or in territorial defense is disrupted by cocaine, similar to amphetamine's effects (e.g., Miczek, 1979b; Miczek and Yoshimura, 1982; Kantak, 1989). Significantly, chronic treatment with cocaine did not result in increased aggressive behavior in several animal species (e.g., Moore and Thompson, 1978; Kantak, 1989).

The recent increase in cocaine's association with violence appears to be dissociated from the direct neurobiologic and pharmacologic characteristics of this drug. Several recent studies support an association between cocaine use and violent crime in which this violence appears to result mainly from interactions with cocaine-crack dealers who practice their trade in a violent manner. For example, one account reports that the percentage of homicide victims with detectable cocaine rose from 1 to 18 percent in four years (Lowry et al., 1988); in San Diego county in 1987, cocaine was involved in one-fifth of homicides (Bailey and Shaw, 1989). Although 91 percent of a sample of adolescent drug-using criminals in inner city Miami reported frequently using cocaine or crack, the majority of offenses committed by this group was related to the drug business (59.9%) or represented property crimes (25.5%). However, the potential for violence among these individuals is ominous: 88.4 percent of this sample reported that they carry weapons most or all of the time (Inciardi, 1989). Furthermore, although crack users may not be extraordinarily violent among drug users, crack dealers are reported to engage in a wider range of violent acts than either heroin or marihuana dealers, and this violence is not limited to the drug-selling context (Fagan and Chin, 1989, 1991).

CONCLUDING STATEMENT

A small literature on pharmacologic and psychiatric evidence for cocaine's effects on aggression and violence points to psychopathologic individuals who may develop the propensity to engage in violent acts. However, the far more significant problem is the violence associated with the supplying, dealing, and securing cocaine-crack as documented by ongoing epidemiologic studies.

HALLUCINOGENS, AGGRESSION, AND VIOLENCE

Hallucinogens comprise substances that are of disputed or limited medicinal value, but are mainly of ceremonial, recreational, and social significance. Their molecular diversity conveys varied effects and mechanisms of action, prompting separate discussions for each type of hallucinogen.

Cannabis

Cannabis is one of the few psychoactive drugs acting on the CNS that does not contain a nitrogen in its molecule, with a poorly understood mechanism of action (Pertwee, 1985). It is used ubiquitously throughout the world, mostly in social settings, and in various forms (e.g., marihuana, hashish, bang). The violence-provoking image of cannabis was shaped by anecdotes such as Marco Polo's tale of the cannabis-intoxicated arabic assassins that gave rise to the name hashish, and by U.S. government-sponsored propaganda movies (e.g., *Reefer Madness*). However, all major reviews of the literature on cannabis and human aggression and violence during the past two decades conclude that cannabis has no effect on or actually decreases various indices of aggression (e.g., Casto, 1970; Abel, 1977; Tinklenberg, 1974; Cherek and Steinberg, 1987; Miczek, 1987).

As summarized in Table 10A, acute administration of cannabis extracts or the psychoactive ingredient Δ^9-tetrahydrocannabinol (THC) decreases attack and threat behavior by isolated mice; by resident fish, rats, squirrel monkeys, and baboons; by pigeons or rats when provoked by omission of scheduled reinforcement, or by brain-stimulated cats (e.g., Dubinsky et al., 1973; Miczek, 1978; Frischknecht, 1984; Sieber, 1982). However, the antiaggressive effects of THC or cannabis extracts are often seen only at sedative doses (e.g., Olivier et al., 1984).

A further prominent effect of cannabis extracts or THC in social confrontations in animals entails the increase in submissive and flight reactions. Detailed ethological analyses document that acutely given THC promotes submissive and flight responses in those animals that are targets of social or aggressive behavior (e.g., Siegel and Poole, 1969; Frischknecht et al., 1984; Cutler et al., 1975; Olivier et al., 1984; see also Table 10A).

Evidence on the effects of acutely given or self-administered cannabis on aggression in humans comes from crime and health statistics, personality evaluations, and experimental studies (see Table 11). For example, in laboratory studies, marihuana or THC decreased all measures of hostility in a staged social setting, and in punitive actions against a fictitious competitor (e.g., Taylor et al., 1976; Salzman et al., 1976).

Of more significance are the findings on chronic cannabis, aggression, and violence. As reviewed previously (e.g., Krsiak, 1974; Abel, 1975; Frischknecht, 1984; Miczek, 1987), animal studies on pain-induced defensive reactions; isolation-induced, territorial, and dominance-related aggressive behavior; and frustration-provoked aggression show enduring decreases in aggression in most species over the course of chronic administration of cannabis extracts or THC (Table 10B, e.g., Cherek et al., 1980; Miczek, 1979a). Most studies on chronic THC in rats, mice, and hamsters find no evidence for tolerance to the drug's antiaggressive effects (see Table 10B).

Anecdotal reports and case studies of humans, ranging from GIs in Vietnam or naval criminal offenders to hemp abusers in India or Brazilian psychiatric patients, concur that there is no consistent relationship between long-term cannabis use and violent behavior (e.g., Chopra et al., 1942; Bromberg and Rodgers, 1946; Moraes Andrade, 1964; Colbach, 1971). In contrast to some questionnaire data and ratings of college students that suggest higher values for aggression, anger, and hostility, experimental indices of human aggression actually reveal decreases in hostility and aggression (see Table 11, especially Burdsal et al., 1973, versus Babor et al., 1978a,b; Salzman et al., 1976). Psychopathologic illness and cannabis use interact in a complex way, each possibly aggravating the other (e.g., Halikas et al., 1972; Bernhardson and Gunne, 1972; Stefanis et al., 1976a,b; Weller and Halikas, 1985).

The most persuasive large-scale studies in incarcerated adolescent delinquents show that marihuana was the drug least likely to be implicated in serious sexual or assaultive crimes (Tinklenberg and Woodrow, 1974; Tinklenberg et al., 1974a,b, 1976). Correspondingly, experienced long-term cannabis users expect other users to be less violent than nonusers, which in fact is borne out by the low rate of commission of violent acts in cannabis users (e.g., Soueif, 1971; see Table 11).

Concurrent exposure to certain stresses and chronic cannabis administration may be particularly significant in the emergence of certain unusual forms of aggressive behavior, as noted repeatedly in reviews of the animal as well as human literature (Carlini, 1972; Krsiak, 1974; Carlini et al., 1976; Abel, 1975, 1977; Cherek and Steinberg, 1987). When otherwise placid animals are exposed to such experimental stressors as REM (rapid eye movement) sleep deprivation, food deprivation, repeated and prolonged exposure to electric shock pulses, or neurotoxin treatment, chronic high-dose THC or cannabis extract injections and occasionally single administrations may induce self-mutilating responses, indiscriminate biting, intense bizarre defensive reactions, and killing behavior (e.g., Carlini and Masur, 1970; Carlini et al., 1972; Fujiwara et al., 1984; see Table 10B). So-called psychosocial stress due to crowding may also potentiate hyperirritability in rhesus monkeys treated chronically with THC (Sassenrath and Chapman, 1976), although similarly treated baboons do not show any alteration in social interactions (Levett et al., 1977). The significance of stress-cannabis interactions is mainly limited to experimental laboratory situations with rodents. At present, it remains unclear whether or not these reports are relevant to disturbed affect, impaired impulse control, and triggered psychopathologies including violent reactions in humans.

Concluding Statement

The majority of the evidence in experimental studies with animals and humans, as well as most data from chronic users, emphasizes that cannabis preparations (e.g., marihuana, hashish) or THC decrease aggressive and violent behavior. Due to its relatively widespread access, lower cost, and characteristic pattern of use, socioeconomic causes of violence in cannabis dealing and procuring are less significant than they are with cocaine or heroin.

LSD

With the discovery of selectively acting serotonin receptor drugs, it has become possible to link the hallucinogenic effects of LSD to the actions of this drug on brain 5-HT$_2$ receptors (e.g., Cunningham and Appel, 1987; Green, 1985; Freedman, 1986). By contrast, LSD's psychotomimetic effects, as well as its specific effects on social, aggressive, defensive, and violent behavior, have not been identified in terms of their mechanisms of action.

Evidence of the effect of LSD on aggression in animals stems primarily from the 1960s and 1970s. As summarized in Table 12 (section A), low acute doses of LSD (less than 100 micrograms (μg) per kilogram exaggerate defensive and timid reactions in mice and in rats, particularly when these responses are prompted by aversive, noxious stimuli (e.g., Brunaud and Siou, 1959; Krsiak, 1975; Sheard et al., 1977; Sbordone et al., 1979). Stumptail macaque monkeys display more frequent submissive gestures when given the hallucinogen 5-methoxy-N,N-methyltryptamine (Schlemmer and Davis, 1981). Aggressive displays may be enhanced when fish or rats are given a very low LSD dose (1-4 μg/kg), although most studies on attack and threats by isolated mice found systematic dose-dependent decreases after LSD administration (e.g., Abramson and Evans, 1954; Silverman, 1966; Krsiak, 1979; Rewerski et al., 1971; Siegel and Poole, 1969; see Table 12). It has been suggested that LSD treatment causes animals to become hypersensitive to social and environmental stimuli (Siegel, 1971). Similar to LSD, mescaline decreases or has no effect on aggressiveness in isolation- and drug-induced or dominance-related paradigms, but increases defensive reactions in procedures involving shock (see Table 12, section B). There have been very few reports of chronic LSD or mescaline administration and animal aggression.

Reviewers of the human literature agree that LSD use is infrequently associated with violence (e.g., Szara, 1967; Hollister, 1984; see Table 13). Anecdotal and case studies emphasize the rarity of LSD violence and associate violent reactions with individuals who are borderline personalities (e.g., Barter and Reite, 1969; Duncan, 1974). If psychopathology predates drug usage, LSD exacerbates these disturbances, including violent outbursts (e.g., Smart and Jones, 1970; Fink et al., 1966). At present, LSD use is not epidemic and no new information has become available to evaluate the significance of the LSD-violence link.

Concluding Statement

LSD is not of significance in the present violence discussion. The older literature suggests that certain psychopathological individuals who begin using LSD may engage in violent acts; however, this phenomenon is rare.

PHENCYCLIDINE (PCP)

PCP was introduced as synthetic surgical anesthetic in 1956, was withdrawn from human use because it induced psychotic reactions in a significant number of patients, and then reappeared from illicit sources as a street drug (e.g., "angel dust," "peace pill," "rocket fuel") in the mid-1960s. Repetitive, prolonged, and unusual acts of violence by individuals intoxicated with PCP have attracted considerable attention in the media (e.g., Siegel, 1980).

In the limited studies with animals, acutely administered PCP has been found to have unpredictable effects on aggressive behavior. Some studies find PCP to disrupt aggressive and defensive behavior engendered by painful stimuli, isolated housing, or territorial defense (see Table 12, section C). However, in other samples, PCP may increase some aspects of aggressive behavior in mice, rats, and squirrel monkeys (e.g., Burkhalter and Balster, 1979; Musty and Consroe, 1982; Emley and Hutson, 1983; Russell et al., 1984; Wilmot et al., 1987). In selected individuals, acute PCP has dose-dependent biphasic effects, with low doses increasing and high doses decreasing aggressive behavior (Miczek and Haney, in press). Notably, PCP-treated mice and stumptail macaque monkeys become the targets of more frequent aggressive behavior by drug-free opponents or group members, presumably due to inappropriate social signals, provocative actions, and hyperactivity (e.g., Tyler and Miczek, 1982; Schlemmer and Davis, 1983). In view of the use pattern in humans, it is surprising that no studies on chronic PCP and aggressive behavior in animals have been conducted.

In humans, PCP is usually part of polydrug use, including alcohol; therefore it is difficult to dissect the PCP-specific effects, especially those on aggressive and violent behavior (e.g., Hollister, 1984; Brecher et al., 1988). No experimental studies on PCP and human violence or aggression have been conducted. As summarized in Table 13, clinical reports from emergency rooms or psychiatric hospital settings indicate a prevalence of PCP psychosis and analgesia, and it is in this context that PCP-associated violence appears most often. Reports from different localities in the United States over the past two decades refer to cases of chronic PCP-induced psychosis that also include agitation, physical assaults, self-directed injuries, and homicidal activities due to poor judgment, panic reactions, and imagined frustrations (e.g., Fauman and Fauman, 1979; Yesavage and Zarcone, 1990; Convit et al., 1988; see Table 13). Overall these cases are relatively infrequent, but stand out by their bizarre and repulsive, stereotyped, repetitive nature.

Physical or pharmacologic restraint of PCP-agitated individuals is difficult to manage clinically. Since the neurobiologic action of PCP is only beginning to be identified with the characterization of specific neural receptor sites, clinically useful agents interacting with PCP receptors will become available soon. Until that time, clinicians resort to antipsychotic drugs in order to manage PCP psychosis (see especially Smith and Wesson, 1980, and reviews in Table 13).

Concluding Statement

"Phencyclidine is not a magical drug. It does not magically produce violent, assaultive, or criminal behavior" (Siegel, 1978). Generally, personality predispositions and a history of violent behavior appear to determine whether or not PCP intoxication leads to violence. PCP violence is a relatively rare phenomenon, although it stands out by its highly unusual form and intensity, and it depends on the social and personal background of the individual.

SUMMARY

Drugs produce some of their effects on violent and aggressive behavior via action on the central nervous system. This action, however, can modify neural functions in a very intricate way and at multiple levels that ultimately target aggression-specific brain mechanisms. Alcohol and drugs of abuse do not engender violent behavior in every individual, and many imbibe alcoholic beverages or self-administer drugs without becoming violent. The impact of genetic predispositions to be susceptible to dependence-producing drugs such as alcohol, heroin, or cocaine and to act violently has, as of yet, not been delineated in terms of specific neural mechanisms. Similarly, the modulating influences of learning, social modeling, or parental physical abuse on the neural substrate for drug action and for aggressive behavior and impulse control have not been specified. Since these critical connections remain ill understood, it is not possible at present to propose specific modes of intervention at the neurobiologic level.

Alcohol is the drug that is most prevalent in individuals committing violence and those who are victims of violence. This association applies to various types of violent behavior and aggressive tendencies. Experimental studies have repeatedly demonstrated that alcohol causes an increase in aggressive behavior, in both animals and humans. Despite its apparent limitations, laboratory research represents the primary avenue to delineate the causative relationship among alcohol, aggression, and violence.

Alcohol's action on the brain mechanisms for aggressive behavior is modulated by genetic predispositions, learned expectations, social restraints, and cultural habits. Recent progress in understanding the actions of alcohol on brain serotonin and GABA systems may eventually offer diagnostic tools for individuals at risk and therapeutic options for intervention.

The violence associated with cocaine-crack is substantially different in nature and context from the aggression-enhancing effects of alcohol. Violent behavior under the influence of amphetamines, cocaine, LSD, and PCP is rare in the general population, but is considerably more likely in those individuals whose psychopathology predates the drug use. Significantly, most of the violence associated with cocaine and narcotic drugs results from the business of supplying, dealing, and acquiring these substances, not from the direct neurobiologic actions of these drugs.

We need to identify those individuals in whom either alcohol, opiates, cocaine, amphetamines, PCP, LSD, or other hallucinogens promote violent and aggressive behavior by attending to the precise pharmacologic conditions at the time of the violent act; the individual's physiologic conditions; the genetic, developmental, and social background; and the prevailing social conditions. Clearly, alcohol and other drugs of abuse differ markedly from each other in terms of pharmacology and neurobiologic mechanisms, dependence liability, legal and social restraints, expectations, and cultural traditions; no general and unifying principle applies to all of these substances. It should not be surprising that the conditions that promote violence in individuals under the influence of alcohol cannot be simply extrapolated to cocaine-crack or to narcotic drugs. Rational intervention strategies need to be based on an adequate understanding of the specific circumstances, individuals, and pharmacologic conditions that are implicated in any specific type of violent act.

REFERENCES

Abel, E.L.
    1972 Changes in personality response ratings induced by smoking marihuana. *British Journal of Addiction* 67:221-223.
    1975 Cannabis and aggression in animals. *Behavioral Biology* 14:1-20.
    1977 The relationship between cannabis and violence: A review. *Psychological Bulletin* 84:193-211.

Abel, E.L., and P. Zeidenberg
  1985 Age, alcohol and violent death: A postmortem study. *Journal of Studies on Alcohol* 46:228-231.
Abel, E.L., E.L. Strasburger, and P. Zeidenberg
  1985 Seasonal, monthly, and day-of-week trends in homicide as affected by alcohol and race. *Alcoholism: Clinical and Experimental Research* 9:281-283.
Abramson, H.A., and L.T. Evans
  1954 Lysergic acid diethylamide (LSD 25). II. Psychobiological effects on the Siamese fighting fish. *Science* 120:990-991.
Albert, D.J., and M.L. Walsh
  1982 The inhibitory modulation of agonistic behavior in the rat brain: A review. *Neuroscience and Biobehavioral Reviews* 6:125-143.
  1984 Neural systems and the inhibitory modulation of agonistic behavior: A comparison of mammalian species. *Neuroscience and Biobehavioral Reviews* 8:5-24.
Al Hazmi, M., and P.F. Brain
  1984 Effects of age, habituation and alcohol administration on tube restraint-induced attack by Swiss mice (abstract). *Aggressive Behavior* 10:145.
Allen, J.R., and L.J. West
  1968 Flight from violence: Hippies and the green rebellion. *American Journal of Psychiatry* 125:120-126.
Allen, R.P., D. Safer, and L. Covi
  1975 Effects of psychostimulants on aggression. *Journal of Nervous and Mental Disease* 160:138-145.
Alves, C.N., and E.A. Carlini
  1973 Effects of acute and chronic administration of *Cannabis sativa* extract on the mouse-killing behavior of rats. *Life Sciences* 13:75-85.
Alves, C.N., A.C. Goyos, and E.A. Carlini
  1973 Aggressiveness induced by marihuana and other psychotropic drugs in REM sleep deprived rats. *Pharmacology Biochemistry and Behavior* 1:183-189.
Anderson, A.C.
  1982 Environmental factors and aggressive behavior. *Journal of Clinical Psychiatry* 43:283.
Anggard, E.
  1988 Ethanol, phosphoinositides, and transmembrane signalling—Towards a unifying mechanism of action. Pp. 50-59 in M. Lader, ed., *The Psychopharmacology of Addiction* (British Association for Psychopharmacology Monograph No. 10). Oxford: Oxford University Press.
Anglin, M.D., and Y.-I. Hser
  1987 Addicted women and crime. *Criminology* 25:359-397.

Anglin, M.D., and G. Speckart
  1988 Narcotic use and crime: A multisample, multimethod analysis. *Criminology* 26:197-233.
Angrist, B.M., and S. Gershon
  1969 Amphetamine abuse in New York City—1966-1968. *Seminars in Psychiatry* 1:195-207.
  1976 Clinical effects of amphetamine and L-DOPA on sexuality and aggression. *Comprehensive Psychiatry* 17:715-722.
Apfeldorf, M., and P.J. Hunley
  1976 Exclusion of subjects with F scores at or above 16 in MMPI research on alcoholism. *Journal of Clinical Psychology* 32:498-500.
Archer, J.
  1988 *The Behavioural Biology of Aggression.* Cambridge: Cambridge University Press.
Arnold, L.E., V. Kirilcuk, S.A. Corson, and E.O. Corson
  1973 Levoamphetamine and dextroamphetamine: Differential effect on aggression and hyperkinesis in children and dogs. *American Journal of Psychiatry* 130:165-170.
Atkinson, J.H.
  1982 Managing the violent patient in the general hospital. *Postgraduate Medicine* 71:193-201.
Avis, H.H., and H.V.S. Peeke
  1975 Differentiation by morphine of two types of aggressive behavior in the convict cichlid (*Cichlasoma nigrofasciatum*). *Psychopharmacologia* 43:287-288.
  1979 Morphine withdrawal induced behavior in the Syrian hamster (*Mesocricetus auratus*). *Pharmacology Biochemistry and Behavior* 11:11-15.
Babor, T.F., J.H. Mendelson, D. Gallant, and J.C. Kuehnle
  1978a Interpersonal behavior in group discussion during marijuana intoxication. *International Journal of the Addictions* 13:89-102.
Babor, T.F., J.H. Mendelson, B. Uhly, and J.C. Kuelnle
  1978b Social effects of marijuana use in a recreational setting. *International Journal of the Addictions* 13:947-959.
Babor, T.F., S. Berglas, J.H. Mendelson, J. Ellingboe, and K. Miller
  1983 Alcohol, affect, and the disinhibition of verbal behavior. *Psychopharmacology* 80:53-60.
Bach-y-Rita, G., J.R. Lion, C.E. Climent, and F.R. Ervin
  1971 Episodic dyscontrol: A study of 130 violent patients. *American Journal of Psychiatry* 127:1473-1478.
Bailey, D.N.
  1979 Clinical findings and concentrations in biological fluids after nonfatal intoxication. *American Journal of Clinical Pathology* 72:795-799.
Bailey, D.N., and R.F. Shaw
  1989 Cocaine and methamphetamine-related deaths in San Diego County

(1987): Homicides and accidental overdoses. *Journal of Forensic Sciences* 34:407-422.

Bailey, D.S., K.E. Leonard, J.W. Cranston, and S.P. Taylor
1983 Effects of alcohol and self-awareness on human physical aggression. *Personality and Social Psychology Bulletin* 9:289-295.

Baker, A.A.
1970 Hospital admissions due to lysergic-acid diethylamide. *Lancet* 714-715.

Baldwin, J.J., and D.L. Randolph
1982 The effects of a provocation on aggression for three types of alcohol users. *Journal of Clinical Psychology* 38:439-444.

Ball, J.C., L. Rosen, J.A. Flueck, and D.N. Nurco
1983 Lifetime criminality of heroin addicts. Pp. 26-40 in E. Gottheil, K.A. Druley, T.E. Skolada, and H.M. Waxman, eds., *Alcohol, Drug Abuse and Aggression.* Springfield, Ill.: Charles C. Thomas.

Bammer, G., and B. Eichelman
1983 Ethanol effects on shock-induced fighting and muricide by rats. *Aggressive Behavior* 9:175-181.

Barnard, G.W., C. Holzer, and H. Vera
1979 A comparison of alcoholics and non-alcoholics charged with rape. *Bulletin of the American Academy of Psychiatry and the Law* 7:432-440.

Barr, G.A., K.E. Moyer, and J.L. Gibbons
1976 Effects of imipramine, *d*-amphetamine, and tripelennamine on mouse and frog killing by the rat. *Physiology and Behavior* 16:267-269.

Barr, G.A., J.L. Gibbons, and W.H. Bridger
1977 Inhibition of rat predatory aggression by acute and chronic *d*- and *l*-amphetamine. *Brain Research* 124:565-570.

Barter, J.T., and M. Reite
1969 Crime and LSD: The insanity plea. *American Journal of Psychiatry* 126:113-119.

Baxter, B.L.
1964 The effect of chlordiazepoxide on the hissing response elicited via hypothalamic stimulation. *Life Sciences* 3:531-537.
1968 The effect of selected drugs on the "emotional" behavior elicited via hypothalamic stimulation. *International Journal of Neuropharmacology* 7:47-54.

Beachy, G.M., D.M. Petersen, and F.S. Pearson
1979 Adolescent drug use and delinquency: A research note. *Journal of Psychedelic Drugs* 11:313-316.

Beatty, W.W., K.B. Costello, and S.L. Berry
1984 Suppression of play fighting by amphetamine: Effects of catecholamine antagonists, agonists and synthesis inhibitors. *Pharmacology Biochemistry and Behavior* 20:747-755.

Beezley, D.A., A.B. Gantner, D.S. Bailey, and S.P. Taylor
   1987   Amphetamines and human physical aggression. *Journal of Research in Personality* 21:52-60.
Bennett, R.M., A.H. Buss, and J.A. Carpenter
   1969   Alcohol and human physical aggression. *Quarterly Journal of Studies on Alcohol* 30:870-876.
Benton, D.
   1984   The long-term effects of naloxone, dibutyryl cyclic CMP, and chlorpromazine on aggression in mice monitored by an automated device. *Aggressive Behavior* 10:79-89.
Benton, D., and P.F. Brain
   1988   The role of opioid mechanisms in social interaction and attachment. Pp. 217-235 in R.J. Rodgers and S.J. Cooper, eds., *Endorphins, Opiates and Behavioural Processes*. Chichester, England: John Wiley & Sons.
Benton, D., and R. Smoothy
   1984   The relationship between blood alcohol levels and aggression in mice. *Physiology and Behavior* 33:757-760.
Benton, D., R. Smoothy, and P.F. Brain
   1985   Comparisons of the influence of morphine sulphate, morphine-3-glucuronide and tifluadom on social encounters in mice. *Physiology and Behavior* 35:689-693.
Berglund, M.
   1984a Mortality in alcoholics related to clinical state at first admission: A study of 537 deaths. *Acta Psychiatrica Scandinavica* 70:407-416.
   1984b Suicide in alcoholism. *Archives of General Psychiatry* 41:888-891.
Bernhardson, G., and L.-M. Gunne
   1972   Forty-six cases of psychosis in cannabis abusers. *International Journal of the Addictions* 7:9-16.
Bertilson, H.S., J.D. Mead, M.K. Morgret, and H.A. Dengerimk
   1977   Measurement of mouse squeals for 23 hours as evidence of long-term effects of alcohol on aggression in pairs of mice. *Psychological Reports* 41:247-250.
Berzins, J.I., W.F. Ross, and G.E. English
   1974   Subgroups among opiate addicts: A typological investigation. *Journal of Abnormal Psychology* 83:65-73.
Black, F.W., and A. Heald
   1975   MMPI characteristics of alcohol and illicit drug-abusers enrolled in a rehabilitation program. *Journal of Clinical Psychology* 31:572-575.
Blanchard, D.C., and R.J. Blanchard
   1984   Inadequacy of pain-aggression hypothesis revealed in naturalistic settings. *Aggressive Behavior* 10:33-46.
Blanchard, R.J., J.K. Flannelly, K. Hori, and D.C. Blanchard
   1987a Ethanol effects on female aggression vary with opponent size

and time within session. *Pharmacology Biochemistry and Behavior* 27:645-648.

Blanchard, R.J., K. Hori, D.C. Blanchard, and J. Hall
1987b Ethanol effects on aggression of rats selected for different levels of aggressiveness. *Pharmacology Biochemistry and Behavior* 27:641-644.

Blanchard, R.J., K. Hori, K. Flannelly, and D.C. Blanchard
1987c The effects of ethanol on the offense and defensive behaviors of male and female rats during group formation. *Pharmacology Biochemistry and Behavior* 26:61-64.

Blanchard, R.J., K. Hori, P. Tom, and D.C. Blanchard
1987d Social structure and ethanol consumption in the laboratory rat. *Pharmacology Biochemistry and Behavior* 28:437-442.

Bloom, J.D.
1980 Forensic psychiatric evaluation of Alaska native homicide offenders. *International Journal of Law and Psychiatry* 3:163-171.

Bohman, M.
1978 Some genetic aspects of alcoholism and criminality. *Archives of General Psychiatry* 35:269-276.
1983 Alcoholism and crime: Studies of adoptees. *Substance and Alcohol Actions/Misuse* 4:137-147.

Bond, A., and M. Lader
1986 The relationship between induced behavioural aggression and mood after the consumption of two doses of alcohol. *British Journal of Addiction* 81:65-75.

Borgen, L.A., J.H. Khalsa, W.T. King, and W.M. Davis
1970 Strain differences in morphine-withdrawal-induced aggression in rats. *Psychonomic Science* 21:35-36.

Boshka, S.C., H.M. Weisman, and D.H. Thor
1966 A technique for inducing aggression in rats utilizing morphine withdrawal. *Psychological Record* 16:541-543.

Boulougouris, J.C., A. Liakos, and C. Stefanis
1976 Social traits of heavy hashish users and matched controls. Pp. 17-23 in R.L. Dornbush, A.M. Freedman, and M. Fink, eds., *Chronic Cannabis Use.* (Annals of the New York Academy of Sciences, Vol. 282.) New York: New York Academy of Sciences.

Bovet-Nitti, F., and P. Messeri
1975 Central stimulating agents and population growth in mice. *Life Sciences* 16:1393-1402.

Boyatzis, R.E.
1975 The predisposition toward alcohol-related interpersonal aggression in men. *Journal of Studies on Alcohol* 36:1196-1326.

Bradford, J.M.W., and D. McLean
1984 Sexual offenders, violence and testosterone. *Canadian Journal of Psychiatry* 29:335-343.

Brady, J.V., and W.J.H. Nauta
  1953   Subcortical mechanisms in emotional behavior: Affective changes following septal forebrain lesion in the albino rat. *Journal of Comparative and Physiological Psychology* 46:339-346.
Brain, P.F.
  1986   *Alcohol and Aggression.* London: Croom Helm.
Branchey, L., M. Branchey, S. Shaw, and C.S. Lieber
  1984   Depression, suicide, and aggression in alcoholics and their relationship to plasma amino acids. *Psychiatry Research* 12:219-226.
Branchey, M.H., L. Buydens-Branchey, and C.S. Lieber
  1988   P3 in alcoholics with disordered regulation of aggression. *Psychiatry Research* 25:49-58.
Braud, W.G., and J.E. Weibel
  1969   Acquired stimulus control of drug-induced changes in aggressive display in *Betta splendens.* *Journal of the Experimental Analysis of Behavior* 12:773-777.
Brecher, M., B.W. Wang, H. Wong, and J.P. Morgan
  1988   Phencyclidine and violence: Clinical and legal issues. *Journal of Clinical Psychopharmacology* 8:397-401.
Brickman, H.R.
  1968   The psychedelic "hipscene": Return of the death instinct. *American Journal of Psychiatry* 125:78-84.
Brill, H.
  1969   Drugs and aggression. *Medical Counterpoint* 33.
Bromberg, W., and T.C. Rodgers
  1946   Marihuana and aggressive crime. *American Journal of Psychiatry* 102:825-827.
Brook, R., B. Szandorowska, and P.C. Whitehead
  1976   Psychosocial dysfunctions as precursors to amphetamine abuse among adolescents. *Addictive Diseases: An International Journal* 2:465-478.
Brower, K.J., F.C. Blow, and T.P. Beresford
  1988   Forms of cocaine and psychiatric symptoms. *Lancet* 1(8575):50.
Browning, D.H., and B. Boatman
  1977   Incest: Children at risk. *American Journal of Psychiatry* 134:69-72.
Brunaud, M., and G. Siou
  1959   Action de substances psychotropes, chez le rat, sur un etat d'agressivite provoquee. Pp. 282-286 in P.B. Bradley, P. Deniker, and C. Radouco-Thomas, eds., *Neuro-Psychopharmacology.* Amsterdam: Elsevier.
Burdsal, C., G. Greenberg, and R. Timpe
  1973   The relationship of marihuana usage to personality and motivational factors. *Journal of Psychology* 85:45-51.

Burkhalter, J.E., and R.L. Balster
  1979   The effects of phencyclidine on isolation-induced aggression in mice. *Psychological Reports* 45:571-576.
Busch, K.A., and S.H. Schnoll
  1985   Cocaine-review of current literature and interface with the law. *Behavioral Sciences and the Law* 3:283-298.
Bushman, B.J., and H.M. Cooper
  1990   Effects of alcohol on human aggression: An integrative research review. *Psychological Bulletin* 107:341-354.
Butts, S.V., and F.C. Shontz
  1970   Invitation of punishment by excessive drinkers in treatment. *Journal of Consulting and Clinical Psychology* 34:216-220.
Cadoret, R.J., T.W. O'Gorman, E. Troughton, and E. Heywood
  1985   Alcoholism and antisocial personality. *Archives of General Psychiatry* 42:161-167.
Cameron, J.S., P.G. Specht, and G.R. Wendt
  1965   Effects of amphetamines on moods, emotions, and motivations. *Journal of Psychology* 61:93-121.
Campion, J., J.M. Cravens, A. Rotholc, H.C. Weinstein, F. Covan, and M. Alpert
  1985   A study of 15 matricidal men. *American Journal of Psychiatry* 142:312-317.
Carder, B., and J. Olson
  1972   Marihuana and shock induced aggression in rats. *Physiology and Behavior* 8:599-602.
Carder, B., and R. Sbordone
  1975   Mescaline treated rats attack immobile targets. *Pharmacology Biochemistry and Behavior* 3:923-925.
Carey, J.T., and J. Mandel
  1969   The Bay Area "speed scene." *Journal of Psychedelic Drugs* 2:189-209.
Carlini, E.A.
  1968   Tolerance to chronic administration of *Cannabis sativa* (marihuana) in rats. *Pharmacology* 1:135-142.
  1972   Acute and chronic behavioral effects of *Cannabis sativa*. *Pharmacology and the Future of Man* 1:31-43.
  1974   *Cannabis sativa* and aggressive behavior in laboratory animals. *Archivos de Investigacion Medica* 5:161-172.
  1977   Further studies of the aggressive behavior induced by Δ^9-tetrahydrocannabinol in REM sleep-deprived rats. *Psychopharmacology* 53:135-145.
Carlini, E.A., and C. Gonzales
  1972   Aggressive behavior induced by marihuana compounds and amphetamine in rats previously made dependent on morphine. *Experientia* 28:542-544.
Carlini, E.A., and C.J. Lindsey
  1975   Pharmacological manipulations of brain catecholamines and the

aggressive behavior induced by marihuana in REM-sleep-deprived rats. *Aggressive Behavior* 1:81-99.

Carlini, E.A., and J. Masur
1969 Development of aggressive behavior in rats by chronic administration of *Cannabis sativa* (marihuana). *Life Sciences* 8:607-620.
1970 Development of fighting behavior in starved rats by chronic administration of (–)Δ⁹-trans-tetrahydrocannabinol and cannabis extracts. *Communications in Behavioral Biology* 5:57-61.

Carlini, E.A., A. Hamaoui, and R.M.W. Marzt
1972 Factors influencing the aggressiveness elicited by marihuana in food-deprived rats. *British Journal of Pharmacology* 44:794-804.

Carlini, E.A., C.J. Lindsey, and S. Tufik
1976 Environmental and drug interference with effects of marihuana. *Annals of the New York Academy of Sciences* 281:229-242.

Carlini, E.A., C.J. Lindsey, and S. Tufik
1977 Cannabis, catecholamines, rapid eye movement sleep and aggressive behavior. *British Journal of Pharmacology* 61:371-379.

Caster, D.U., and O.A. Parsons
1977 Relationship of depression, sociopathy, and locus of control to treatment outcome in alcoholics. *Journal of Consulting and Clinical Psychology* 45:751-756.

Casto, D.M., III
1970 Marijuana and the assassins—An etymological investigation. *International Journal of the Addictions* 5:747-755.

Chaiken, J.M., and M.R. Chaiken
1990 Drugs and predatory crime. Pp. 203-239 in M. Tonry and J.Q. Wilson, eds., *Drugs and Crime* (*Crime and Justice: A Review of the Literature*, Vol. 13). Chicago: University of Chicago.

Chamove, A.S., and H.F. Harlow
1970 Exaggeration of self-aggression following alcohol ingestion in rhesus monkeys. *Journal of Abnormal Psychology* 75:207-209.

Chance, M.R.A.
1946 A peculiar form of social behavior induced in mice by amphetamine. *Behaviour* 1:60-70.

Chance, M.R.A., and A.P. Silverman
1964 The structure of social behaviour and drug action. Pp. 65-79 in H. Steinberg and A.V.S. de Reuck, eds., *Animal Behaviour and Drug Action*. London: Churchill.

Chance, M.R.A., J.H. Mackintosh, and A.K. Dixon
1973 The effects of ethyl alcohol on social encounters between mice. *Journal of Alcoholism* 8:90-93.

Charpentier, J.
1969 Analysis and measurement of aggressive behaviour in mice. Pp. 86-100 in S. Garattini and E.B. Sigg, eds., *Aggressive Behaviour*. Amsterdam: Excerpta Medica Foundation.

Cheek, F.E., and C.M. Holstein
  1971 Lysergic acid diethylamide tartrate (LSD-25) dosage levels, group differences, and social interaction. *Journal of Nervous and Mental Disease* 153:133-147.
Cherek, D.R., and J.L. Steinberg
  1987 Effects of drugs on human aggressive behavior. Pp. 239-290 in G.D. Burrows and J.S. Werry, eds., *Advances in Human Psychopharmacology.* Greenwich, Conn.: JAI Press.
Cherek, D.R., T. Thompson, and G.T. Heistad
  1972 Effects of Δ^1-tetrahydrocannabinol and food deprivation level on responding maintained by the opportunity to attack. *Physiology and Behavior* 9:795-800.
Cherek, D.R., T. Thompson, and T. Kelly
  1980 Chronic Δ^9-tetrahydrocannabinol administration and schedule-induced aggression. *Pharmacology Biochemistry and Behavior* 12:305-309.
Cherek, D.R., J.L. Steinberg, and R.V. Vines
  1984 Low doses of alcohol affect human aggressive responses. *Biological Psychiatry* 19:263-267.
Cherek, D.R., J.L. Steinberg, and B.R. Manno
  1985 Effects of alcohol on human aggressive behavior. *Journal of Studies on Alcohol* 46:321-328.
Cherek, D.R., J.L. Steinberg, T.H. Kelly, and D.E. Robinson
  1986 Effects of *d*-amphetamine on human aggressive behavior. *Psychopharmacology* 88:381-386.
Cherek, D.R., R. Spiga, and J.L. Steinberg
  1989 Effects of secobarbital on human aggressive and non-aggressive responding. *Drug and Alcohol Dependence* 24:21-29.
Choi, S.Y.
  1975 Death in young alcoholics. *Journal of Studies on Alcohol* 36:1224-1229.
Chopra, G.S., and B.S. Jandu
  1976 Psychoclinical effects of long-term marijuana use in 275 Indian chronic users: A comparative assessment of effects in Indian and USA users. Pp. 95-108 in R.L. Dornbush, A.M. Freedman, and M. Fink, eds., *Chronic Cannabis Use* (Annals of the New York Academy of Sciences, Vol. 282). New York: New York Academy of Sciences.
Chopra, R.M., G.S. Chopra, and I.C. Chopra
  1942 *Cannabis sativa* in relation to mental disease and crime in India. *Indian Journal of Medical Research* 30:155-171.
Cleary, J., J. Herakovic, and A. Poling
  1981 Effects of phencyclidine on shock-induced aggression in rats. *Pharmacology Biochemistry and Behavior* 15:813-818.
Climent, C.E., F.R. Ervin, and H. Ervin
  1972 Historical data in the evaluation of violent subjects. *Archives of General Psychiatry* 27:621-624.

Cloninger, C.R.
1987 Neurogenetic adaptive mechanisms in alcoholism. *Science* 236:410-416.
Cloninger, C.R., and S.B. Guze
1975 Hysteria and parental psychiatric illness. *Psychological Medicine* 5:27-31.
Cloninger, C.R., K.O. Christiansen, T. Reich, and I.I. Gottesman
1978 Implications of sex differences in the prevalences of antisocial personality, alcoholism, and criminality for familial transmission. *Archives of General Psychiatry* 35:941-951.
Cloninger, C.R., S. Sigvardsson, S.B. Gilligan, A.-L. Von Knorring, T. Reich, and M. Bohman
1989 Genetic heterogeneity and the classification of alcoholism. Pp. 3-16 in E. Gordis, B. Tabakoff, and M. Linnoila, eds., *Alcohol Research from Bench to Bedside*. Binghamton, N.Y.: Haworth Press.
Cockett, R., and V. Marks
1969 Amphetamine taking among young offenders. *British Journal of Psychiatry* 115:1203-1204.
Coid, J.
1979 Mania a potu: A critical review of pathological intoxication. *Psychological Medicine* 9:709-719.
Coid, J.
1986a Alcohol, rape and sexual assault. Pp. 161-183 in P.F. Brain, ed., *Alcohol and Aggression*. London: Croom Helm.
1986b Socio-cultural factors in alcohol-related sexual assault. Pp. 184-211 in P.F. Brain, ed., *Alcohol and Aggression*. London: Croom Helm.
Colbach, E.
1971 Marijuana use by GIs in Viet Nam. *American Journal of Psychiatry* 128:96-99.
Collins, J.J., and W.E. Schlenger
1988 Acute and chronic effects of alcohol use on violence. *Journal of Studies on Alcohol* 49:516-521.
Collins, J.J., W.E. Schlenger, and B.K. Jordan
1988 Antisocial personality and substance abuse disorders. *Bulletin of the American Academy of Psychiatry and the Law* 16:187-198.
Collins, R.J., J.R. Weeks, M.M. Cooper, P.I. Good, and R.R. Russell
1984 Prediction of abuse liability of drugs using IV self-administration by rats. *Psychopharmacology* 82:6-13.
Combs-Orme, T., J.R. Taylor, E.B. Scott, and S.J. Holmes
1983 Violent deaths among alcoholics: A descriptive study. *Journal of Studies on Alcohol* 44:938-949.
Concool, B., H. Smith, and B. Stimmel
1979 Mortality rates of persons entering methadone maintenance: A

seven-year study. *American Journal of Drug and Alcohol Abuse* 6:345-353.

Conley, J.J.
1981 An MMPI typology of male alcoholics: Admission, discharge and outcome comparisons. *Journal of Personality Assessment* 45:33-39.

Conners, C.K.
1972 Symposium: Behavior modifications by drugs. II. Psychological effects of stimulant drugs in children with minimal brain dysfunction. *Pediatrics* 49:702-708.

Consolo, S., S. Garattini, R. Ghielmetti, and L. Valzelli
1965a Concentrations of amphetamine in the brain in normal or aggressive mice. *Journal of Pharmacy and Pharmacology* 17:666.

Consolo, S., S. Garattini, and L. Valzelli
1965b Amphetamine toxicity in aggressive mice. *Journal of Pharmacy and Pharmacology* 17:53-54.

Convit, A., Z.C. Nemes, and J. Volavka
1988 History of phencyclidine use and repeated assaults in newly admitted young schizophrenic men. *American Journal of Psychiatry* 145:1176.

Cook, L., and E. Wiedley
1960 Effects of a series of psychopharmacological agents on isolation induced attack behavior in mice. *Federation Proceedings* 19:22.

Cooper, A.J.
1988 A clinical study of violence in patients referred on a Form I to a general hospital psychiatric unit. *Canadian Journal of Psychiatry* 33:711-715.

Corenblum, B.
1983 Reactions to alcohol-related marital violence: Effects of one's own abuse experience and alcohol problems on causal attributions. *Journal of Studies on Alcohol* 44:665-674.

Costello, R.M., and S.L. Schneider
1974 Mortality in an alcoholic cohort. *International Journal of the Addictions* 9:355-363.

Crabtree, J.M., and K.E. Moyer
1972 Sex differences in fighting and defense induced in rats by shock and *d*-amphetamine during morphine abstinence. *Physiology and Behavior* 11:337-343.

Crawford, A.
1984 Alcohol and expectancy—II. Perceived sex differences in the role of alcohol as a source of aggression. *Alcohol and Alcoholism* 19:71-75.

Cressman, R.J., and T.E. Cadell
1971 Drinking and the social behavior of rhesus monkeys. *Quarterly Journal of Studies on Alcohol* 32:764-774.

Crompton, M.R.
  1985 Alcohol and violent accidental and suicidal death. *Medicine, Science and the Law* 25:59-62.
Crowley, T.J.
  1972 Dose-dependent facilitation or suppression of rat fighting by methamphetamine, phenobarbital, or imipramine. *Psychoharmacologia* 27:213-222.
Crowley, T.J., and A.E. Andrews
  1987 Alcoholic-like drinking in simian social groups. *Psychopharmacology* 92:196-205.
Crowley, T.J., A.J. Stynes, M. Hydinger, and I.C. Kaufman
  1974 Ethanol, methamphetamine, pentobarbital, morphine, and monkey social behavior. *Archives of General Psychiatry* 31:829-838.
Crowley, T.J., M. Hydinger, A.J. Stynes, and A. Feiger
  1975 Monkey motor stimulation and altered social behavior during chronic methadone administration. *Psychopharmacologia* 43:135-144.
Cunningham, K.A., and J.B. Appel
  1987 Neuropharmacological reassessment of the discriminative stimulus properties of *d*-lysergic acid diethylamide (LSD). *Psychopharmacology* 91:67-73.
Cutler, M.G.
  1976 Changes in the social behaviour of laboratory mice during administration and on withdrawal from non-ataxic doses of ethyl alcohol. *Neuropharmacology* 15:495-498.
Cutler, M.G., J.H. Mackintosh, and M.R.A. Chance
  1975 Effects of the environment on the behavioural response of mice to non-ataxic doses of ethyl alcohol. *Neuropharmacology* 14:841-846.
DaVanzo, J.P., M. Daugherty, R. Ruckart, and L. Kang
  1966 Pharmacological and biochemical studies in isolation-induced fighting mice. *Psychopharmacologia* 9:210-219.
Davis, W.M., and J.H. Khalsa
  1971 Some determinants of aggressive behavior induced by morphine withdrawal. *Psychonomic Science* 24:13-15.
Deardorff, C.M., F.T. Melges, C.N. Hout, and D.J. Savage
  1975 Situations related to drinking alcohol. *Journal of Studies on Alcohol* 36:1184-1195.
DeBold, J.F., and K.A. Miczek
  1985 Testosterone modulates the effects of ethanol on male mouse aggression. *Psychopharmacology* 86:286-290.
Delgado, J.M.R.
  1963 Cerebral heterostimulation in a monkey colony. *Science* 141:161-163.

Dembo, R., L. Williams, A. Getreu, L. Genung, J. Schmeidler, E. Berry, E.D. Wish, and L. LaVoie
  1991 A longitudinal study of the relationships among marijuana/hashish use, cocaine use and delinquency in a cohort of high-risk youths. *Journal of Drug Issues* 21:271-312.
Dermen, K.H., and W.H. George
  1988 Alcohol expectancy and the relationship between drinking and physical aggression. *Journal of Psychology* 123:153-161.
Derrick, E.H.
  1967 A survey of the mortality caused by alcohol. *Medical Journal of Australia* 914-919.
De Souza, H., and J. Palermo Neto
  1978 Effects of anti-acetylcholine drugs on aggressive behaviour induced by *Cannabis sativa* in REM sleep-deprived rats. *Journal of Pharmacy and Pharmacology* 30:591-592.
DeWeese, J.
  1977 Schedule-induced biting under fixed-interval schedules of food or electric-shock presentation. *Journal of the Experimental Analysis of Behavior* 27:419-431.
Dewey, W.L.
  1986 Cannabinoid pharmacology. *Pharmacological Reviews* 38:151-178.
Dole, V.P., W. Robinson, J. Orraca, E. Towns, P. Searcy, and E. Caine
  1969 Methadone treatment of randomly selected criminal addicts. *New England Journal of Medicine* 280:1372-1375.
Domino, E.F., P. Rennick, and J. Pearl
  1974 Dose-effect relations of marijuana smoking on various physiological parameters in experienced male users. Observations on limits of self-titration of intake. *Clinical Pharmacology and Therapeutics* 15:514-520.
Dorr, M., and H. Steinberg
  1976 Effects of Δ^9-tetrahydrocannabinol on social behavior in mice. *Psychopharmacology* 47:87-91.
Dotson, L.E., L.S. Robertson, and B. Tuchfeld
  1975 Plasma alcohol, smoking, hormone concentrations and self-reported aggression: A study in a social-drinking situation. *Journal of Studies on Alcohol* 36:578-586.
Downs, W.R., B.A. Miller, and D.M. Gondoli
  1987 Childhood experiences of parental physical violence for alcoholic women as compared with a randomly selected household sample of women. *Violence and Victims* 2:225-240.
Dubinsky, B., R.C. Robichaud, and M.E. Goldberg
  1973 Effects of (−)Δ^9-trans-tetrahydrocannabinol and its selectivity in several models of aggressive behavior. *Pharmacology* 9:204-216.

Duncan, J.W.
  1974 Persisting psychotic states in adolescent drug users. *Child Psychiatry and Human Development* 5:51-62.
Eberle, P.A.
  1982 Alcohol abusers and non-users: A discriminant analysis of differences between two subgroups of batterers. *Journal of Health and Social Behavior* 23:260-271.
Edwards, A.E., M.H. Bloom, and S. Cohen
  1969 The psychedelics: Love or hostility potion? *Psychological Reports* 24:843-846.
Egan, D.J., and D.O. Robinson
  1979 Cocaine: Magical drug or menace? *International Journal of the Addictions* 14:231-241.
Eisenberg, L., R. Lachman, P.A. Molling, A. Lockner, J.D. Mizelle, and C.K. Conners
  1963 A psychopharmacologic experiment in a training school for delinquent boys: Methods, problems, findings. *American Journal of Orthopsychiatry* 33:431-447.
Eison, M.S., W.J. Wilson, and G. Ellison
  1978 A refillable systen for continuous amphetamine administration: Effects upon social behavior in rat colonies. *Communications in Psychopharmacology* 2:151-157.
Ellingboe, J., S.M. Mirin, R.E. Meyer, and J.H. Mendelson
  1979 Effect of opiates on neuroendocrine function plasma cortisol, growth hormone, and thyrotropin. Pp. 151-175 in R.E. Meyer and S.M. Mirin, eds., *The Heroin Stimulus*. New York: Plenum Medical Book Co.
Ellinwood, E.H.
  1971 Assault and homicide associated with amphetamine abuse. *American Journal of Psychiatry* 127:90-95.
  1979 Amphetamines/anorectics. Pp. 221-231 in R.L. Dupont, A. Goldstein, and J. O'Donnell, eds., *Handbook on Drug Abuse*. Washington, D.C.: National Institute on Drug Abuse.
Elliott, F.A.
  1987 Neuroanatomy and neurology of aggression. *Psychiatric Annals* 17:385-388.
Elliott, M.L., and R.J. Sbordone
  1982 Drug-induced ataxia in opponents elicits "pathological" fighting in undrugged rats exposed to footshock. *Pharmacology Biochemistry and Behavior* 16:63-66.
Elliott-Harper, C.A., and D.W. Harper
  1981 Alcoholism and the forensic-psychiatric patient: A comparative study. *Canadian Journal of Psychiatry* 26:108-109.
Ellison, G., M.S. Eison, H.S. Huberman, and F. Daniel
  1978 Long-term changes in dopaminergic innervation of caudate nucleus

after continuous amphetamine administration. *Science* 201:276-278.

Ellison, G., F. Daniel, and R. Zoraster
  1979   Delayed increases in alcohol consumption occur in rat colonies but not in isolated rats after injections of monoamine neurotoxins. *Experimental Neurology* 65:608-615.

Ellman, G.L., M.J. Herz, and H.V.S. Peeke
  1972   Ethanol in a cichlid fish: Blood levels and aggressive behavior. *Proceedings of the Western Pharmacological Society* 15:92-95.

Ely, D., J.P. Henry, and C.J. Jarosz
  1975   Effects of marihuana (Δ^9-THC) on behavior patterns and social roles in colonies of CBA mice. *Behavioral Biology* 13:263-276.

Emley, G.S., and R.R. Hutchinson
  1972   Basis of behavioral influence of chlorpromazine. *Life Sciences* 11:43-47.
  1983   Unique influences of ten drugs upon post-shock biting attack and pre-shock manual responding. *Pharmacology Biochemistry and Behavior* 19:5-12.

Enos, W.F., and J.C. Beyer
  1980   Prostatic acid phosphatase, aspermia, and alcoholism in rape cases. *Journal of Forensic Sciences* 25:353-356.

Evans, C.M.
  1980   Alcohol, violence and aggression. *British Journal on Alcohol and Alcoholism* 15:104-117.
  1986   Alcohol and violence: Problems relating to methodology, statistics and causation. Pp. 138-160 in P.F. Brain, ed., *Alcohol and Aggression*. London: Croom Helm.

Evans, L.T., and H.A. Abramson
  1958   Lysergic acid diethylamide (LSD-25): XXV. Effect on social order of newts, *Triturus V. viridescens*. *Journal of Psychology* 45:153-169.

Everill, B., and M.S. Berry
  1987   Effects of ethanol on aggression in three inbred strains of mice. *Physiology and Behavior* 39:45-51.

Ewart, F.G., and M.G. Cutler
  1979   Effects of ethyl alcohol on development and social behavior in the offspring of laboratory mice. *Psychopharmacology* 62:247-251.

Fagan, J.A.
  1990a Intoxication and aggression. Pp. 241-320 in J.Q. Wilson and M. Tonry, eds., *Drugs and Crime (Crime and Justice: An Annual Review of Research*, Vol. 13). Chicago: University of Chicago Press.
  1990b Violence as regulation and social control in the distribution of crack. Pp. 8-43 in M. De La Rosa, E.Y. Lambert, and B. Gropper, eds., *Drugs and Violence: Causes, Correlates, and Consequences.*

NIDA Research Monograph Series, Vol. 103. Rockville, Md.: National Institute on Drug Abuse.

Fagan, J.A., and K.L. Chin
1989 Initiation into crack and powdered cocaine: A tale of two epidemics. *Contemporary Drug Problems* 16:579-618.
1990 *Violence as Regulation and Social Control in the Distribution of Crack.* NIDA Research Monograph No. 103. Rockville, Md.: National Institute on Drug Abuse.
1991 Social processes of initiation into crack cocaine. *Journal of Drug Issues* 21:313-331.

Fagan, R.W., O.W. Barnett, and J.B. Patton
1988 Reasons for alcohol use in maritally violent men. *American Journal of Drug and Alcohol Abuse* 14:371-392.

Fanselow, M.S., R.A. Sigmundi, and R.C. Bolles
1980 Naloxone pretreatment enhances shock-elicited aggression. *Physiological Psychology* 8:369-371.

Fauman, B.J., and M.A. Fauman
1982 Phencyclidine abuse and crime: A psychiatric perspective. *Bulletin of the American Academy of Psychiatry and the Law* 10:171-176.

Fauman, B., G. Aldinger, M. Fauman, and P. Rosen
1976 Psychiatric sequelae of phencyclidine abuse. *Clinical Toxicology* 9:529-538.

Fauman, M.A., and B.J. Fauman
1977 The differential diagnosis of organic based psychiatric disturbance in the emergency department. *Journal of the American College of Emergency Physicians* 6:315-323.
1979 Violence associated with phencyclidine abuse. *American Journal of Psychiatry* 136:1584-1586.
1980a Chronic phencyclidine (PCP) abuse: A psychiatric perspective. *Journal of Psychedelic Drugs* 12:307-315.
1980b Chronic phencyclidine (PCP) abuse: A psychiatric perspective. Part 1: General aspects and violence. *Psychopharmacology Bulletin* 16:70-72.

Ferguson, J., and W. Dement
1969 The behavioral effects of amphetamine on REM deprived rats. *Journal of Psychiatric Research* 7:111-118.

Fico, T.A., and C. Vanderwende
1988 Phencyclidine during pregnancy: Fetal brain levels and neurobehavioral effects. *Neurotoxicology and Teratology* 10:349-354.

Fielding, S., J. Wikler, M. Hynes, M. Szewczak, W.J. Novick, and H. Lal
1978 A comparison of clonidine with morphine for antinociceptive and antiwithdrawal actions. *Journal of Pharmacology and Experimental Therapeutics* 207:899-905.

Filibeck, U., S. Cabib, C. Castellano, and S. Puglisi-Allegra
1988 Chronic cocaine enhances defensive behaviour in the laboratory

mouse: Involvement of D₂ dopamine receptors. *Psychopharmacology* 96:437-441.

Fink, L., and M.P. Hyatt
1978   Drug use and criminal behavior. *Journal of Drug Education* 8:139-149.

Fink, M., J. Simeon, W. Haque, and T. Itil
1966   Prolonged adverse reactions to LSD in psychotic subjects. *Archives of General Psychiatry* 15:450-454.

Fisher, G., and A. Steckler
1974   Psychological effects, personality and behavioral changes attributed to marihuana use. *International Journal of the Addictions* 9:101-126.

Fitzpatrick, J.P.
1974   Drugs, alcohol, and violent crime. *Addictive Diseases* 1:353-367.

Flynn, J.P., D. Smith, K. Coleman, and C.A. Opsahl
1979   Anatomical pathways for attack behavior in cats. Pp. 301-315 in M. von Cranach, K. Foppa, W. Lepenies, and D. Ploog, eds., *Human Ethology. Claims and Limits of a New Discipline.* Cambridge: Cambridge University Press.

Fog, R., A. Randrup, and H. Pakkenberg
1970   Lesions in corpus striatum and cortex of rat brains and the effect on pharmacologically induced stereotyped, aggressive and cataleptic. *Psychopharmacologia* 18:346-356.

Fossier, A.E.
1931   The marihuana menace. *New Orleans Medical and Surgical Journal* 44:247-252.

Foster, H.M., and N. Narasimhachari
1986   Phencyclidine in CSF and serum: A case of attempted filicide by a mother without a history of substance abuse. *Journal of Clinical Psychiatry* 47:428-429.

Freedman, D.X.
1986   Hallucinogenic drug research—If so, so what? (symposium summary and commentary). *Pharmacology Biochemistry and Behavior* 24:407-415.

Frischknecht, H.R.
1984   Effects of cannabis drugs on social behaviour of laboratory rodents. *Progress in Neurobiology* 22:39-58.

Frischknecht, H.R., B. Siegfried, M. Schiller, and P.G. Waser
1984   Hashish extract impairs learning of submissive behaviour in mice. Pp. 303-309 in D.J. Harvey, ed., *Marihuana '84. Proceeding of the Oxford Symposium on Cannabis.* Oxford: IRL Press Limited.

Fujiwara, M., and S. Ueki
1978   Muricide induced by single injection of Δ⁹-tetrahydrocannabinol. *Physiology and Behavior* 21:581-585.
1979   The course of aggressive behavior induced by a single injection

of Δ^9-tetrahydrocannabinol and its characteristics. *Physiology and Behavior* 22:535-539.

Fujiwara, M., N. Ibii, Y. Kataoka, and S. Ueki
  1980 Effects of psychotropic drugs on Δ^9-tetrahydrocannabinol-induced long-lasting muricide. *Psychopharmacology* 68:7-13.

Fujiwara, M., Y. Kataoka, Y. Hori, and S. Ueki
  1984 Irritable aggression induced by Δ^9-tetrahydrocannabinol in rats pretreated with 6-hydroxydopamine. *Pharmacology Biochemistry and Behavior* 20:457-462.

Galizio, M., R.L. Woodard, and J. Keith
  1985 Effects of ethanol and naltrexone on aggressive display in the Siamese fighting fish, *Betta splendens*. *Alcohol* 2:637-640.

Gambill, J.D., E. Kornetsky, and L. Valzelli
  1976 Effects of chronic *d*-amphetamine on social behavior of the rat: Implications for an animal model of paranoid schizophrenia. *Psychopharmacology* 50:215-223.

Garattini, S.
  1965 Effects of a cannabis extract on gross behaviour. Pp. 70-94 in G.E.W. Wolstenholme and J. Knight, eds., *Hashish: Its Chemistry and Pharmacology*. London: J. and A. Churchill, Ltd.

Gardikas, C.G.
  1950 Hashish and crime. *Enkephalos* 2:201-211.

Garver, D.L., R.F. Schlemmer Jr., J.W. Maas, and J.M. Davis
  1975 A schizophreniform behavioral psychosis mediated by dopamine. *American Journal of Psychiatry* 132:33-38.

Gay, P.E., R.C. Leaf, and F.B. Arble
  1975 Inhibitory effects of pre- and posttest drugs on mouse-killing by rats. *Pharmacology Biochemistry and Behavior* 3:33-45.

Gayford, J.J.
  1979 Battered wives. *British Journal of Hospital Medicine* 22:496-503.

Gellert, V.F., and S.B. Sparber
  1979 Effects of morphine withdrawal on food competition hierarchies and fighting behavior in rats. *Psychopharmacology* 60:165-172.

George, W.H., and G.A. Marlatt
  1986 The effects of alcohol and anger on interest in violence, erotica, and deviance. *Journal of Abnormal Psychology* 95:150-158.

Gianutsos, G., and H. Lal
  1976 Drug-induced aggression. Pp. 198-220 in W. Essman and L. Valzelli, eds., *Current Developments in Psychopharmacology*. New York: Plenum Press.

  1978 Narcotic analgesics and aggression. Pp. 114-138 in L. Valzelli, T. Ban, F.A. Freyhan, and P. Pichot, eds., *Modern Problems of Pharmopsychiatry: Psychopharmacology of Aggression*. New York: S. Karger.

Gianutsos, G., M.D. Hynes, S.K. Puri, R.B. Drawbaugh, and H. Lal
    1974   Effect of apomorphine and nigrostriatal lesions on aggression
            and striatal dopamine turnover during morphine withdrawal:
            Evidence for dopaminergic supersensitivity in protracted absti-
            nence. *Psychopharmacologia* 34:37-44.
Gianutsos, G., M.D. Hynes, R.B. Drawbaugh, and H. Lal
    1975   Paradoxical absence of aggression during naloxone-precipitated
            morphine withdrawal. *Psychopharmacologia* 43:43-46.
Gianutsos, G., M.D. Hynes, and H. Lal
    1976   Enhancement of morphine-withdrawal and apomorphine-induced
            aggression by clonidine. *Psychopharmacology Communications*
            2:165-171.
Giono-Barber, P., M. Paris, G. Bertuletti, and H. Giono-Barber
    1974   Cannabis effects on dominance behavior in the Cynocephale
            monkey. *Journal of Pharmacology* 5:591-602.
Gold, M.S., A.L.C. Pottash, I. Extein, and A. Stoll
    1981   Clinical utility of clonidine in opiate withdrawal. Pp. 95-100 in
            L.S. Harris, ed., *Problems of Drug Dependence*. NIDA Research
            Monograph Series, Vol. 34. Rockville, Md.: National Institute
            on Drug Abuse.
Goldstein, P.J.
    1985   The drugs-violence nexus: A tripartite conceptual framework.
            Journal of Drug Issues 15:493-506.
Gonzalez, S.C., V.K.R. Matsudo, and E.A. Carlini
    1971   Effects of marihuana compounds on the fighting behavior of
            Siamese fighting fish (*Betta splendens*). *Pharmacology* 6:186-
            190.
Goodwin, D.W.
    1973   Alcohol in suicide and homicide. *Quarterly Journal of Studies
            on Alcohol* 34:144-156.
Gorney, B.
    1989   Domestic violence and chemical dependency: Dual problems,
            dual interventions. *Journal of Psychoactive Drugs* 21:229-238.
Gossop, M., and A. Roy
    1977   Hostility, crime and drug dependence. *British Journal of Psy-
            chiatry* 130:272-278.
Graham, K.
    1980   Theories of intoxicated aggression. *Canadian Journal of Behavioural
            Science* 12:141-158.
Graham, K., L. La Rocque, R. Yetman, T.J. Ross, and E. Guistra
    1980   Aggression and barroom environments. *Journal of Studies on
            Alcohol* 41:277-292.
Grande, T.P., A.W. Wolf, D.S.P. Schubert, M.B. Patterson, and K. Brocco
    1984   Associations among alcoholism, drug abuse, and antisocial per-
            sonality: A review of literature. *Psychological Reports* 55:455-
            474.

Green, R.A.
    1985   *Neuropharmacology of Serotonin.* New York: Oxford University Press.
Greenberg, S.W.
    1976   The relationship between crime and amphetamine abuse: An empirical review of the literature. *Contemporary Drug Problems* 5:101-130.
Greene, M.H., R.L. DuPont, and R.M. Rubenstein
    1973   Amphetamines in the District of Columbia. *Archives of General Psychiatry* 29:773-776.
Griffiths, R.R., M. Stitzer, K. Corker, G. Bigelow, and I. Liebson
    1977   Drug-produced changes in human social behavior: Facilitation by *d*-amphetamine. *Pharmacology Biochemistry and Behavior* 7:365-372.
Grinspoon, L., and J.B. Bakalar
    1979   Cocaine. Pp. 241-247 in R.L. Dupont, A. Goldstein, and J. O'Donnell, eds., *Handbook on Drug Abuse.* Washington, D.C.: National Institute on Drug Abuse.
Grove, W.M., E.D. Eckert, L. Heston, T.J. Bouchard, N. Segal, and D.T. Lykken
    1990   Heritability of substance abuse and antisocial behavior: A study of monozygotic twins reared apart. *Biological Psychiatry* 27:1293-1304.
Grunberg, F., B.I. Klinger, and B.R. Grumet
    1978   Homicide and community-based psychiatry. *Journal of Nervous and Mental Disease* 166:868-874.
Gunn, J.
    1972   Epileptic prisoners and their drinking problems. *Epilepsia* 13:489-497.
Gustafson, R.
    1984   Alcohol, frustration, and direct physical aggression: A methodological point of view. *Psychological Reports* 55:959-966.
    1985a   Frustration as an important determinant of alcohol-related aggression. *Psychological Reports* 57:3-14.
    1985b   Alcohol and aggression: Pharmacological versus expectancy effects. *Psychological Reports* 57:955-966.
    1986a   Threat as a determinant of alcohol-related aggression. *Psychological Reports* 58:287-297.
    1986b   A possible confounding variable in different versions of the "aggression machine" when used in research on alcohol. *Psychological Reports* 58:303-308.
    1986c   Alcohol, aggression and the validity of experimental paradigms with women. *Psychological Reports* 59:51-56.
    1987   Alcohol and aggression: A test of an indirect measure of aggression. *Psychological Reports* 60:1241-1242.
    1988a   Beer intoxication and physical aggression in males. *Drug and Alcohol Dependence* 21:237-242.

1988b Effects of beer and wine on male aggression as measured by a paper-and-pen test. *Psychological Reports* 62:795-798.

1990 Wine and male physical aggression. *Journal of Drug Issues* 20:75-86.

Guze, S.B., E.D. Wolfgram, J.K. McKinney, and D.P. Cantwell

1968 Delinquency, social maladjustment, and crime: The role of alcoholism. *Diseases of the Nervous System* 29:238-243.

Haber, S., P.R. Barchas, and J.D. Barchas

1977 Effects of amphetamine on social behaviors of rhesus macaques: An animal model of paranoia. Pp. 107-115 in I. Hanin and E. Usdin, eds., *Animal Models in Psychiatry and Neurology*. New York: Pergamon Press.

1981 A primate analogue of amphetamine-induced behaviors in humans. *Biological Psychiatry* 16:181-195.

Hadfield, M.G.

1982 Cocaine: Peak time of action on isolation-induced fighting. *Neuropharmacology* 21:711-713.

Hadfield, M.G., E.A. Nugent, and D.E. Mott

1982 Cocaine increases isolation-induced fighting in mice. *Pharmacology Biochemistry and Behavior* 16:359-360.

Haertzen, C.A., W.R. Martin, B.B. Hewett, and V. Sandquist

1978 Measurement of psychopathy as a state. *Journal of Psychology* 100:201-214.

Halikas, J.A., and J.D. Rimmer

1974 Predictors of multiple drug abuse. *Archives of General Psychiatry* 31:414-418.

Halikas, J.A., D.W. Goodwin, and S.B. Guze

1972 Marihuana use and psychiatric illness. *Archives of General Psychiatry* 27:162-165.

Haney, M., and K.A. Miczek

1989 Morphine effects on maternal aggression, pup care and analgesia in mice. *Psychopharmacology* 98:68-74.

Haney, M., K. Noda, R. Kream, and K.A. Miczek

1990 Regional serotonin and dopamine activity: Sensitivity to amphetamine and aggressive behavior in mice. *Aggressive Behavior* 16:259-270.

Hanks, S.E., and C.P. Rosenbaum

1977 Battered women: A study of women who live with violent alcohol-abusing men. *American Journal of Orthopsychiatry* 47:291-306.

Haramis, S.L., and E.E. Wagner

1980 Differentiation between acting-out and non-acting-out alcoholics with the Rorschach and Hand test. *Journal of Clinical Psychology* 36:791-797.

Harris, R.A., A.M. Allan, L.C. Daniell, and C. Nixon

1988 Antagonism of ethanol and pentobarbital actions by benzodiazepine inverse agonists: Neurochemical studies. *Journal of Pharmacology and Experimental Therapeutics* 247:1012-1017.

Hart Hansen, J.P., and O. Bjarnason
1974 Homicide in Iceland 1946-1970. *Forensic Science* 4:107-117.

Hasselager, E., Z. Rolinski, and A. Randrup
1972 Specific antagonism by dopamine inhibitors of items of amphetamine induced aggressive behaviour. *Psychopharmacologia* 24:485-495.

Haver, B.
1986 Female alcoholics. *Acta Psychiatrica Scandinavica* 74:597-604.

Heather, N.
1981 Relationships between delinquency and drunkenness among Scottish young offenders. *British Journal on Alcohol and Alcoholism* 16:50-61.

Hechtman, L., G. Weiss, and T. Perlman
1984 Hyperactives as young adults: Past and current substance abuse and antisocial behavior. *American Journal of Orthopsychiatry* 54:415-425.

Heilig, S.M., J. Diller, and F.L. Nelson
1982 A study of 44 PCP-related deaths. *International Journal of the Addictions* 17:1175-1184.

Heller, M.S., and S.M. Ehrlich
1984 Actuarial variables in 9,600 violent and non-violent offenders referred to a court psychiatric clinic. *American Journal of Social Psychiatry* 4:30-36.

Helzer, J.E., and T.R. Pryzbeck
1988 The co-occurrence of alcoholism with other psychiatric disorders in the general population and its impact on treatment. *Journal of Studies on Alcoholism* 49:219-224.

Hemmi, T.
1969 How we handled the problem of drug abuse in Japan. Pp. 147-153 in F. Sjogvist and M. Tottie, eds., *Abuse of Central Stimulants.* Stockholm: Almquist and Wiksell.

Henderson, M.
1986 An empirical typology of violent incidents reported by prison inmates with convictions for violence. *Aggressive Behavior* 12:21-32.

Henn, F.A., M. Herjanic, and R.H. Vanderpearl
1976 Forensic psychiatry: Profiles of two types of sex offenders. *American Journal of Psychiatry* 133:694-696.

Herzog, M.A., and A.S. Wilson
1978 Personality characteristics of the female alcoholic. *Journal of Clinical Psychology* 34:1002-1004.

Hewett, B.B., and W.R. Martin
1980 Psychometric comparisons of sociopathic and psychopathological behaviors of alcoholics and drug abusers versus a low drug

use control population. *International Journal of the Addictions* 15:77-105.

Higgins, S.T., and M.L. Stitzer
1988 Time allocation in a concurrent schedule of social interaction and monetary reinforcement: Effects of *d*-amphetamine. *Pharmacology Biochemistry and Behavior* 31:227-231.

Hine, B., M.B. Wallach, and S. Gershon
1975 Involvement of biogenic amines in drug-induced aggressive pecking in chicks. *Psychopharmacologia* 43:215-221.

Hodge, G.K., and L.L. Butcher
1975 Catecholamine correlates of isolation-induced aggression in mice. *European Journal of Pharmacology* 31:81-93.

Hoffmeister, F., and W. Wuttke
1969 On the actions of psychotropic drugs on the attack- and aggressive-defensive behaviour of mice and cats. Pp. 273-280 in S. Garattini and E.B. Sigg, eds., *Aggressive Behavior*. Amsterdam: Excerpta Medica Foundation.

Holcomb, W.R., and N.A. Adams
1985 Personality mechanisms of alcohol-related violence. *Journal of Clinical Psychology* 41:714-722.

Holcomb, W.R., and W.P. Anderson
1983 Alcohol and multiple drug abuse in accused murderers. *Psychological Reports* 52:159-164.

Hollister, L.E.
1984 Effects of hallucinogens in humans. Pp. 19-33 in B.L. Jacobs, ed., *Hallucinogens: Neurochemical, Behavioral, and Clinical Perspectives*. New York: Raven Press.

Honer, W.G., G. Gewirtz, and M. Turey
1987 Psychosis and violence in cocaine smokers. *Lancet* 451.

Hore, B.D.
1988 Alcohol and crime. *Alcohol and Alcoholism* 23:435-439.

Horovitz, Z.P., P.W. Ragozzino, and R.C. Leaf
1965 Selective block of rat mouse-killing by antidepressants. *Life Sciences* 4:1909-1912.

Horovitz, Z.P., J.J. Piala, J.P. High, J.C. Burke, and R.C. Leaf
1966 Effects of drugs on the mouse-killing (muricide) test and its relationship to amygdaloid function. *International Journal of Neuropharmacology* 5:405-411.

Huntingford, F.A., and A.K. Turner
1987 *Animal Conflict*. New York: Chapman and Hall.

Hutchinson, R.R., G.S. Emley, and N.A. Krasnegor
1976 The selective effects of acute and chronic cocaine administration on aggressive behavior. *Psychopharmacology Bulletin* 12:42-43.
1977 The effects of cocaine on the aggressive behavior of mice, pigeons and squirrel monkeys. Pp. 457-480 in E.H. Ellinwood, Jr.,

and M.M. Kilbey, eds., *Cocaine and Other Stimulants*. New York: Plenum Press.

Inciardi, J.A.
1989   The crack/violence connection within a population of hard-core adolescent offenders. In *Drugs and Violence*. NIDA Research Monograph Series. Rockville, Md.: National Institute on Drug Abuse.

Ingle, D.
1973   Reduction of habituation of prey-catching activity by alcohol intoxication in the frog. *Behavioral Biology* 8:123-129.

Irwin, S., R. Kinohi, M. Van Sloten, and M.P. Workman
1971   Drug effects on distress-evoked behavior in mice: Methodology and drug class comparisons. *Psychopharmacologia* 20:172-185.

Jacobsson, L.
1985   Acts of violence in a traditional Ethiopian society in transition. Acta *Psychiatrica Scandinavica* 71:601-607.

Jaffe, J.H., T.F. Babor, and D.H. Fishbein
1988   Alcoholics, aggression and antisocial personality. *Journal of Studies on Alcohol* 1988:211-218.

James, I.P.
1974   Blood alcohol levels following successful suicide. *Quarterly Journal of Studies on Alcohol* 35:23-29.

Janssen, P.A.J., A.H. Jageneau, and J.E. Niemegeers
1960   Effects of various drugs on isolation-induced fighting behavior of male mice. *Journal of Pharmacology and Experimental Therapeutics* 129:471-475.

Janssen, P.A.J., C.J.E. Niemegeers, and F.J. Verbruggen
1962   A propos d'une methode d'investigation de substances susceptibles de modifier le comportement agressif inne du rat blanc vis-a-vis de la souris blanche. *Psychopharmacologia* 3:114-123.

Jarvis, M.F., M. Krieger, G. Cohen, and G.C. Wagner
1985   The effects of phencyclidine and chlordiazepoxide on target biting of confined male mice. *Aggressive Behavior* 11:201-205.

Jeavons, C.M., and S.P. Taylor
1985   The control of alcohol-related aggression: Redirecting the inebriate's attention to socially appropriate conduct. *Aggressive Behavior* 11:93-101.

Jenkins, R.L.
1968   The varieties of children's behavioral problems and family dynamics. *American Journal of Psychiatry* 124:1440-1445.

John, H.W.
1978   Rape and alcohol abuse: Is there a connection? *Alcohol Health and Research World* 6:34-37.

Johnson, B.D., P.J. Goldstein, E. Preble, J. Schmeidler, D.S. Lipton, B. Spunt, and T. Miller
1985   Victimized victimizers. Pp. 173-180 in B.D. Johnson, P.J. Goldstein, E. Preble, J. Schmeidler, D.S. Lipton, B. Spunt, and T. Miller,

eds., *Taking Care of Business*. Lexington, Mass.: Lexington Books.

Johnson, S.D., L. Gibson, and R. Linden
1978 Alcohol and rape in Winnipeg, 1966-1975. *Journal of Studies on Alcohol* 39:1887-1894.

Jones, B.C., D.L. Clark, P.F. Consroe, and H.J. Smith
1974 Effects of (-)Δ^9-*trans*-tetrahydrocannabinol on social behavior of squirrel monkey dyads in water competition situations. *Psychopharmacologia* 37:37-43.

Kalant, O.J.
1972 Report of the Indian Hemp Drugs Commission, 1893-94: A critical review. *International Journal of the Addictions* 7:77-96.

Kalin, N.H., and S.E. Shelton
1989 Defensive behavior in infant rhesus monkeys: Environmental cues and neurochemical regulation. *Science* 243:1718-1721.

Kamback, M.C.
1973 The hippocampus and motivation: A re-examination. *Journal of General Psychology* 89:313-324.

Kantak, K.M.
1989 Magnesium alters the potency of cocaine and haloperidol on mouse aggression. *Psychopharmacology* 99:181-188.

Kantak, K.M., and K.A. Miczek
1986 Aggression during morphine withdrawal: Effects of method of withdrawal, fighting experience and social role. *Psychopharmacology* 90:451-456.
1988 Social, motor, and autonomic signs of morphine withdrawal: Differential sensitivities to catecholaminergic drugs in mice. *Psychopharmacology* 96:468-476.

Karczmar, A.G., and C.L. Scudder
1967 Behavioral responses to drugs and brain catecholamine levels in mice of different strains and genera. *Federation Proceedings* 26(4):1186-1191.

Karli, P.
1958 Action de l'amphetamine et de la chlorpromazine sur l'agressivite interspecifique rat-souris. *Comptes Rendus de Societé de Biologie* 152:1796-1798.
1959 Recherches pharmacologiques sur le comportment d'agression rat-souris. *Comptes Rendus de Societé de Biologie* 153:497-498.

Karniol, I.G., and E.A. Carlini
1973 Pharmacological interaction between cannabidiol and Δ^9-tetrahydrocannabinol. *Psychopharmacologia* 33:53-70.

Kaufman Kantor, G., and M.A. Straus
1987 The "drunken bum" theory of wife beating. *Social Problems* 34:213-230.

Keller, D.E., and D.S. Poster
  1970 Effects of psychoactive drugs on stereotyped aggressive behavior of *Betta splendens. American Zoologist* 10:288.
Kellett, P.
  1966 Attempted suicide in Durban: A general hospital study. *South Africa Medical Journal* 40:90-95.
Kelly, D.D.
  1974 The experimental imperative: Laboratory analyses of aggressive behaviors. Pp. 21-41 in S.H. Frazier, ed., *Aggression*. Baltimore: Williams and Wilkins.
Kelly, T.H., D.R. Cherek, J.L. Steinberg, and D. Robinson
  1988 Effects of provocation and alcohol on human aggressive behavior. *Drug and Alcohol Dependence* 21:105-112.
Kelly, T.H., D.R. Cherek, and J.L. Steinberg
  1989 Concurrent reinforcement and alcohol: Interactive effects on human aggressive behavior. *Journal of Studies on Alcohol* 50:399-405.
Khajawall, A.M., T.B. Erickson, and G.M. Simpson
  1982 Chronic phencyclidine abuse and physical assault. *American Journal of Psychiatry* 139:1604-1606.
Khantzian, E.J.
  1974 Opiate addiction: A critique of theory and some implications for treatment. *American Journal of Psychotherapy* 28:59-70.
Kido, R., K. Hirose, K.-I. Yamamoto, and A. Matsushita
  1967 Effects of some drugs on aggressive behaviour and the electrical activity of the limbic system. Pp. 365-387 in W.R. Adley and P. Tokizane, eds., *Progress in Brain Research*. Amsterdam: Elsevier.
Kilbey, M.M., G.E. Fritchie, D.M. McLendon, and K.M. Johnson
  1972 Attack behavior in mice inhibited by Δ^9-tetrahydrocannabinol. *Nature* 238:463-465.
Kilbey, M.M., J.W. Moore, and M. Hall
  1973a Δ^9-Tetrahydrocannabinol induced inhibition of predatory aggression in the rat. *Psychopharmacologia* (Berlin) 31:157-166.
Kilbey, M.M., J.W. Moore Jr, and R.T. Harris
  1973b Effects of Δ^9-tetrahydrocannabinol on appetitive and aggressive-rewarded maze performance in the rat. *Physiological Psychology* 1:174-176.
Kilbey, M.M., K.M. Johnson, and D.M. McLendon
  1977 Time course of Δ^9-tetrahydrocannabinol inhibition of predatory aggression. *Pharmacology Biochemistry and Behavior* 7:117-120.
King, L.J., G.E. Murphy, L.N. Robins, and H. Darvish
  1969 Alcohol abuse: A crucial factor in the social problems of Negro men. *American Journal of Psychiatry* 125:1682-1690.

Kinsley, C.H., and R.S. Bridges
    1986 Opiate involvement in postpartum aggression in rats. *Pharmacology Biochemistry and Behavior* 25:1007-1011.
Klapper, J.A., M.A. McColloch, F.R. Sidell, and E. Arsenal
    1972 The effects on personality of reactivity to 1,2-dimethylheptyl tetrahydrocannabinol. *Archives of General Psychiatry* 26:483-485.
Klepfisz, A., and J. Racy
    1973 Homicide and LSD. *Journal of the American Medical Association* 223:429-430.
Knudsen, K.
    1967 Homicide after treatment with lysergic acid diethylamide. *Acta Psychiatrica Scandinavica* 40:389-395.
Kocur, J., A. Jurkowski, and J. Kedziora
    1977 The influence of haloperidol and propranolol on behavior and biochemical changes in the brain of mice treated with LSD. *Polish Journal of Pharmacology and Pharmacy* 29:281-288.
Kofoed, L., and J. MacMillan
    1986 Alcoholism and antisocial personality. *Journal of Nervous and Mental Disease* 174:332-335.
Koob, G.F., and F.E. Bloom
    1988 Cellular and molecular mechanisms of drug dependence. *Science* 242:715-723.
Koob, G.F., L. Percy, and K.T. Britton
    1989 The effects of Ro 15-4513 on the behavioral actions of ethanol in an operant reaction time task and a conflict test. *Pharmacology Biochemistry and Behavior* 31:757-760.
Kostowski, W.
    1966 A note on the effects of some psychotropic drugs on the aggressive behavior in the ant, *Formica rufa*. *Journal of Pharmacy and Pharmacology* 18:747-749.
Kostowski, W., and B. Tarchalska
    1972 The effects of some drugs affecting brain 5-HT on the aggressive behaviour and spontaneous electrical activity of the central nervous system of the ant, *Formica rufa*. *Brain Research* 38:143-149.
Kostowski, W., W. Rewerski, and T. Piechocki
    1972 The effects of some hallucinogens on aggressiveness of mice and rats. *Pharmacology* 7:259-263.
Kovach, J.K.
    1967 Maternal behavior in the domestic cock under the influence of alcohol. *Science* 15:835-837.
Kramer, J.C.
    1969 Introduction to amphetamine abuse. *Journal of Psychedelic Drugs* 2:1-16.

Kratcoski, P.C.
   1985   Youth violence directed toward significant others. *Journal of Adolescence* 8:145-157.
   1988   Families who kill. *Marriage and Family Review* 12:47-70.
Kreiskott, H.
   1966   Das Entzugssyndrom morphinsüchtiger Rhesusaffen—Modell einer pharmakogenen Psychose? *Arzneimittel-Forschung* (Drug Research) 16:219-220.
Kreutzer, J.S., H.G. Schneider, and C.R. Myatt
   1984   Alcohol, aggression and assertiveness in men: Dosage and expectancy effects. *Journal of Studies on Alcohol* 45:275-278.
Kroll, P.D., D.F. Stock, and M.E. James
   1985   The behavior of adult alcoholic men abused as children. *Journal of Nervous and Mental Disease* 173:689-693.
Krsiak, M.
   1974   Behavioral changes and aggressivity evoked by drugs in mice. *Research Communications in Chemical Pathology and Pharmacology* 7:237-257.
   1975   Timid singly-housed mice: Their value in prediction of psychotropic activity of drugs. *British Journal of Pharmacology* 55:141-150.
   1976   Effect of ethanol on aggression and timidity in mice. *Psychopharmacology* 51:75-80.
   1979   Effects of drugs on behaviour of aggressive mice. *British Journal of Pharmacology* 65:525-533.
Krsiak, M., and M. Borgesova
   1973   Effect of alcohol on behaviour of pairs of rats. *Psychopharmacologia* 32:201-209.
Krsiak, M., M. Borgesova, and O. Kadlecova
   1971   LSD-accentuated individual type of social behaviour in mice. *Activitas Nervosa Superior* 13:211-212.
Krstic, S.K., K. Stefanovic-Denic, and D.B. Beleslin
   1982   Effect of morphine and morphine-like drugs on carbachol-induced fighting in cats. *Pharmacology Biochemistry and Behavior* 17:371-373.
Kruk, M.R., A.M. van der Poel, and T.P. de Vos-Frerichs
   1979   The induction of aggressive behaviour by electrical stimulation in the hypothalamus of male rats. *Behaviour* 70:292-321.
Kuczenski, R.
   1983   Biochemical actions of amphetamine and other stimulants. Pp. 31-61 in I. Creese, ed., *Stimulants: Neurochemical, Behavioral, and Clinical Perspectives.* New York: Raven Press.
Kulkarni, A.S., and N.P. Plotnikoff
   1978   Effects of central stimulants on aggressive behavior. Pp. 69-81 in L. Valzelli, ed., *Psychopharmacology of Aggression. Modern Problems of Pharmacopsychiatry.* Basel, Switzerland: Karger.

Kurtines, W., R. Hogan, and D. Weiss
1975 Personality dynamics of heroin use. *Journal of Abnormal Psychology* 84:87-89.

Lagerspetz, K.M.J., and K. Ekqvist
1978 Failure to induce aggression in inhibited and in genetically non-aggressive mice through injections of ethyl alcohol. *Aggressive Behavior* 4:105-113.

Lal, H.
1975a Morphine-withdrawal aggression. Pp. 149-171 in S. Ehrenpreis and E.A. Neidel, eds., *Methods in Narcotic Research*. New York: Marcel Dekker.
1975b Narcotic dependence, narcotic action and dopamine receptors. *Life Sciences* 17:483-496.

Lal, H., and S.K. Puri
1971 Morphine-withdrawal aggression: Role of dopaminergic stimulation. Pp. 301-310 in J.M. Singh, L. Miller and H. Lal, eds., *Drug Addiction: Experimental Pharmacology*. Mount Kisco, N.Y.: Futura Publishing.

Lal, H., J. O'Brien, and S.K. Puri
1971 Morphine-withdrawal aggression: Sensitization by amphetamines. *Psychopharmacologia* 22:217-223.

Lal, H., G. Gianutsos, and S.K. Puri
1975 A comparison of narcotic analgesics with neuroleptics on behavioral measures of dopaminergic activity. *Life Sciences* 17:29-32.

Lang, A.R., D.J. Goeckner, V.J. Adesso, and G.A. Marlatt
1975 Effects of alcohol on aggression in male social drinkers. *Journal of Abnormal Psychology* 84:508-518.

Langevin, R., M. Ben-Aron, G. Wortzman, R. Dickey, and L. Handy
1987 Brain damage, diagnosis, and substance abuse among violent offenders. *Behavioral Sciences and the Law* 5:77-94.

Laties, V.G.
1961 Modification of affect, social behavior and performance by sleep deprivation and drugs. *Journal of Psychiatric Research* 1:12-25.

Le Douarec, J.C., and L. Broussy
1969 Dissociation of the aggressive behaviour in mice produced by certain drugs. Pp. 281-295 in S. Garattini and E.B. Sigg, eds., *Aggressive Behavior*. Amsterdam: Excerpta Medica Foundation.

Le Roux, L.C., and L.S. Smith
1964 Violent deaths and alcoholic intoxication. *Journal of Forensic Medicine* 11:131-147.

Leichner, P.P., D.S. Janowsky, and A.E. Reid
1976 Intravenous methylphenidate as a diagnostic and psychotherapeutic instrument in adult psychiatry. *Canadian Psychiatric Association Journal* 21:489-496.

Leonard, K.E.
  1984 Alcohol consumption and escalatory aggression in intoxicated and sober dyads. *Journal of Studies on Alcohol* 45:75-80.
Leonard, K.E., E.J. Bromet, D.K. Parkinson, N.L. Day, and C.M. Ryan
  1985 Patterns of alcohol use and physically aggressive behavior in men. *Journal of Studies on Alcohol* 46:279-282.
Lester, D.
  1980 Alcohol and suicide and homicide. *Journal of Studies on Alcohol* 41:1220-1223.
  1989 Alcohol consumption and rates of personal violence (suicide and homicide). *Activitas Nervosa Superior* 31:248-251.
Leventhal, B.L., and H.K.H. Brodie
  1981 The pharmacology of violence. Pp. 85-106 in D.A. Hamburg and M.B. Trudeau, eds., *Biobehavioral Aspects of Aggression.* New York: Alan R. Liss.
Levett, A., G.S. Saayman, and F. Ames
  1977 The effects of *Cannabis sativa* on the behavior of adult female chacma baboons (*Papio ursinus*) in captivity. *Psychopharmacology* 53:79-81.
Levine, S.V., D.D. Lloyd, and W.H. Longdon
  1972 The speed user: Social and psychological factors in amphetamine abuse. *Canadian Psychiatric Association Journal* 17:229-241.
Lewis, C.E., J. Rice, N. Andreasen, P. Clayton, and J. Endicott
  1985a Alcoholism in antisocial and nonantisocial men with unipolar major depression. *Journal of Affective Disorders* 9:253-263.
Lewis, C.E., L. Robins, and J. Rice
  1985b Association of alcoholism with antisocial personality in urban men. *Journal of Nervous and Mental Disease* 173:166-174.
Lindman, R., P. Jarvinen, and J. Vidjeskog
  1987 Verbal interactions of aggressively and nonaggressively predisposed males in a drinking situation. *Aggressive Behavior* 13:187-196.
Lindquist, C.U.
  1986 Battered women as coalcoholics: Treatment implications and case study. *Psychotherapy* 23:622-628.
Lindqvist, P.
  1986 Criminal homicide in northern Sweden 1970-1981: Alcohol intoxication, alcohol abuse and mental disease. *International Journal of Law and Psychiatry* 8:19-37.
Linnoila, M., M. Virkkunen, M. Scheinin, A. Nuutila, R. Rimon, and F.K. Goodwin
  1983 Low cerebrospinal fluid 5-hydroxyindoleacetic acid concentration differentiates impulsive from nonimpulsive violent behavior. *Life Sciences* 33:2609-2614.

Linnoila, M., J. De Jong, and M. Virkkunen
  1989 Family history of alcoholism in violent offenders and impulsive fire setters. *Archives of General Psychiatry* 46:613-616.
Lisciotto, C.A., J.F. DeBold, and K.A. Miczek
  1990 Sexual differentiation and the effects of alcohol on aggressive behavior in mice. *Pharmacology Biochemistry and Behavior* 35:357-362.
Lister, R.G.
  1988a Partial reversal of ethanol-induced reductions in exploration by two benzodiazepine antagonists (flumazenil and ZK 93426). *Brain Research* Bulletin 21:765-770.
  1988b Antagonism of the behavioral effects of ethanol, sodium pentobarbital and Ro 15-4513 by the imidazodiazepine Ro 15-3505. *Neuroscience Research Communications* 2:85-92.
Lister, R.G., and L.A. Hilakivi
  1988 The effects of novelty, isolation, light and ethanol on the social behavior of mice. *Psychopharmacology* 96:181-187.
Lister, R.G., and D.J. Nutt
  1988 Alcohol antagonists—The continuing quest. *Alcoholism: Clinical and Experimental Research* 12:566-569.
Livingston, L.R.
  1986 Measuring domestic violence in an alcoholic population. *Journal of Sociology and Social Welfare* 13:934-953.
Løberg, T.
  1983 Belligerence in alcohol dependence. *Scandinavian Journal of Psychology* 24:285-292.
Loev, B., P.E. Bender, F. Dowalo, E. Macko, and P.J. Fowler
  1973 Cannabinoids. Structure-activity studies related to 1,2-dimethylheptyl derivatives. *Journal of Medicinal Chemistry* 16:1200-1206.
Looney, T.A., and P.S. Cohen
  1982 Aggression induced by intermittent positive reinforcement. *Biobehavioral Reviews* 6:15-37.
Lowry, P.W., S.E. Hassig, R.A. Gunn, and J.B. Mathison
  1988 Homicide victims in New Orleans: Recent trends. *American Journal of Epidemiology* 128:1130-1136.
Luisada, P.V.
  1978 The phencyclidine psychosis: Phenomenology and treatment. Pp. 241-253 in R.C. Petersen and R.C. Stillman, eds., *Phencyclidine (PCP) Abuse: An Appraisal*. NIDA Research Monograph Series, Vol. 21. Rockville, Md.: National Institute on Drug Abuse.
Luthra, Y.K., H. Rosenkrantz, I.A. Heyman, and M.C. Braude
  1975 Differential neurochemistry and temporal pattern in rats treated orally with Δ^9-tetrahydrocannabinol for periods up to six months. *Toxicology and Applied Pharmacology* 32:418-431.

MacAndrew, C., and R.B. Edgerton
  1969 *Drunken Comportment: A Social Explanation.* Chicago: Aldine.
MacDonnell, M.F., and M. Ehmer
  1969 Some effects of ethanol on aggressive behavior in cats. *Quarterly Journal of Studies on Alcohol* 30:312-319.
MacDonnell, M.F., L. Fessock, and S.H. Brown
  1971 Ethanol and the neural substrate for affective defense in the cat. Quarterly *Journal of Studies on Alcohol* 32:406-419.
Maeda, H., T. Sato, and S. Maki
  1985 Effects of dopamine agonists on hypothalamic defensive attack in cats. *Physiology and Behavior* 35:89-92.
Maj, J., E. Mogilnicka, and A. Kordecka-Magiera
  1980 Effects of chronic administration of antidepressant drugs on aggressive behavior induced by clonidine in mice. *Pharmacology Biochemistry and Behavior* 13:153-154.
Maletzky, B.M.
  1974 *d*-Amphetamine and delinquency: Hyperkinesis persisting? *Diseases of the Nervous System* 35:543-547.
  1976 The diagnosis of pathological intoxication. *Journal of Studies on Alcohol* 37:1215-1228.
Malick, J.B.
  1975 Differential effects of *d*- and *l*-amphetamine on mouse-killing behavior in rats. *Pharmacology Biochemistry and Behavior* 3:697-699.
  1976 Pharmacological antagonism of mouse-killing behavior in the olfactory bulb lesion-induced killer rat. *Aggressive Behavior* 2:123-130.
  1979 The pharmacology of isolation-induced aggressive behavior in mice. Pp. 1-27 in W.B. Essman and L. Valzelli, eds., *Current Developments in Psychopharmacology.* New York: SP Medical and Scientific Books.
Malmquist, C.P.
  1971 Premonitory signs of homicidal aggression in juveniles. *American Journal of Psychiatry* 128:461-465.
Manning, F.J., and T.F. Elsmore
  1972 Shock-elicited fighting and Δ^9-tetrahydrocannabinol. *Psychopharmacologia* 25:218-228.
Marek, Z., J. Widacki, and T. Hanausek
  1974 Alcohol as a victimogenic factor of robberies. *Forensic Science* 4:119-123.
Marinacci, A.A., and K.O. von Hagen
  1972 Alcohol and temporal lobe dysfunction: Some of its psychomotor equivalents. *Behavioral Neuropsychiatry* 3:2-11.
Marini, J.L., J.K. Walters, and M.H. Sheard
  1979 Effects of *d*- and *l*-amphetamine on hypothalamically-elicited movement and attack in the cat. *Agressologie* 20:155-160.

Mark, V.H., and F.R. Ervin
  1970 *Violence and the Brain.* New York: Harper and Row.
Martin, R.L., C.R. Cloninger, and S.B. Guze
  1979 The evaluation of diagnostic concordance in follow-up studies: II. A blind, prospective follow-up of female criminals. *Journal of Psychiatric Research* 15:107-125.
Martin, S.P., E.O. Smith, and L.D. Byrd
  1990 Effects of dominance rank on *d*-amphetamine-induced increases in aggression. *Pharmacology Biochemistry and Behavior* 37:493-496.
Martin, W.R., A. Wikler, C.G. Eades, and F.T. Pescor
  1963 Tolerance to and physical dependence on morphine in rats. *Psychopharmacologia* 4:247-260.
Masur, J., R.M.W. Martz, D. Bieniek, and F. Korte
  1971 Influence of (−)Δ⁹-*trans*-tetrahydrocannabinol and mescaline on the behavior of rats submitted to food competition situations. *Psychopharmacologia* 22:187-194.
Masur, J., I.G. Karniol, and J.P. Neto
  1972 *Cannabis sativa* induces "winning" behaviour in previously "loser" rats. *Journal of Pharmacy and Pharmacology* 24:262.
Matte, A.C.
  1975 Effects of hashish on isolation induced aggression in wild mice. *Psychopharmacologia* 45:125-128.
Mayfield, D.
  1976 Alcoholism, alcohol, intoxication and assaultive behavior. *Diseases of the Nervous System* 37:288-291.
McCaldon, R.J.
  1967 Rape. *Canadian Journal of Criminology and Corrections* 9:37-59.
McCarron, M.M., B.W. Schulze, G.A. Thompson, M.C. Conder, and W.A. Goetz
  1981 Acute phencyclidine intoxication: Clinical patterns, complications, and treatment. *Annals of Emergency Medicine* 10:290-297.
McCarty, R.C., and G.H. Whitesides
  1976 Effects of D- and L-amphetamine on the predatory behavior of southern grasshopper mice, *Onychomys torridus. Aggressive Behavior* 2:99-105.
McCord, J.
  1981 Alcoholism and criminality. *Journal of Studies on Alcohol* 42:739-748.
McDonald, A.L., and N.W. Heimstra
  1964 Modification of aggressive behavior of green sunfish with *dextro*-lysergic acid diethylamide. *Journal of Psychology* 57:19-23.
McDonough, J.H., Jr, F.J. Manning, and T.F. Elsmore
  1972 Reduction of predatory aggression of rats following administration of Δ⁹-tetrahydrocannabinol. *Life Sciences* 11:103-111.

McGlothlin, W.H.
  1979 Drugs and crime. Pp. 357-364 in R.I. Dupont, A. Goldstein, and
        J. O'Donnell, eds., *Handbook on Drug Abuse*. Washington, D.C.:
        U.S. Government Printing Office.
Means, L.W., C.W. Medlin, R.D. Russ, J.L. Higgins, and S.L. Gray
  1984 Shock-induced aggression is not affected by prenatal exposure
        to ethanol. *IRCS Medical Science* 12:177.
Medhus, A.
  1975 Criminality among female alcoholics. *Scandinavian Journal of
        Social Medicine* 3:45-49.
Mehta, A.K., and M.K. Ticku
  1988 Ethanol potentiation of GABAergic transmission in cultured spinal
        cord neurons involves γ-aminobutyric acid$_A$-gated chloride channels.
        Journal of Pharmacology and Experimental Therapeutics 246:558-
        564.
Meinecke, R.O., and A. Cherkin
  1972 Failure of ethanol or pentobarbital to suppress fighting in the
        pit gamecock (*Gallus gallus*). *Psychopharmacologia* 25:189-194.
Melander, B.
  1960 Psychopharmacodynamic effects of diethylpropion. *Acta
        Pharmacologia et Toxicologica* 17:182-190.
Mendelson, J.H., and N.K. Mello
  1974 Alcohol, aggression and androgens. Pp. 225-247 in S.H. Frazier,
        ed., *Aggression*. Baltimore: Williams and Wilkins.
Mendelson, J.H., N.K. Mello, and J. Ellingboe
  1978 Effects of alcohol on pituitary-gonadal hormones, sexual func-
        tion, and aggression in human males. Pp. 1677-1692 in M.A.
        Lipton, A. DiMascio, and K.F. Killam, eds., *Psychopharmacol-
        ogy: A Generation of Progress*. New York: Raven Press.
Mendelson, J.H., P.E. Dietz, and J. Ellingboe
  1982 Postmortem plasma luteinizing hormone levels and antemortem
        violence. *Pharmacology Biochemistry and Behavior* 17:171-173.
Miczek, K.A.
  1974 Intraspecies aggression in rats: Effects of *d*-amphetamine and
        chlordiazepoxide. *Psychopharmacologia* 39:275-301.
  1976 Does THC induce aggression? Suppression and induction of
        aggressive reactions by chronic and acute Δ^9-tetrahydrocannab-
        inol treatment in laboratory rats. Pp. 499-514 in M. Braude and
        S. Szara, eds., *Pharmacology of Marihuana*. New York: Raven
        Press.
  1977a A behavioral analysis of aggressive behaviors induced and modulated
        by Δ^9-tetrahydrocannabinol, pilocarpine, *d*-amphetamine and L-
        DOPA. *Activitas Nervosa Superior* 19:224-225.
  1977b Effects of L-DOPA, *d*-amphetamine and cocaine on intruder evoked
        aggression in rats and mice. *Progress in Neuro-Psychopharma-
        cology* 1:272-277.

1978 Δ⁹-Tetrahydrocannabinol: Antiaggressive effects in mice, rats, and squirrel monkeys. *Science* 199:1459-1461.

1979a Chronic Δ⁹-tetrahydrocannabinol in rats: Effect on social interactions, mouse killing, motor activity, consummatory behavior, and body temperature. *Psychopharmacology* 60:137-146.

1979b A new test for aggression in rats without aversive stimulation: Differential effects of *d*-amphetamine and cocaine. *Psychopharmacology* 60:253-259.

1985 Alcohol and aggressive behavior in rats: Interaction with benzodiazepines. *Society for Neuroscience Abstracts* 11:1290.

1987 The psychopharmacology of aggression. Pp. 183-328 in L.L. Iversen, S.D. Iversen and S.H. Snyder, eds., *New Directions in Behavioral Pharmacology* (*Handbook of Psychopharmacology*, Vol. 19). New York: Plenum.

Miczek, K.A., and H. Barry III
1974 Δ⁹-Tetrahydrocannabinol and aggressive behavior in rats. *Behavioral Biology* 11:261-267.

1976 Pharmacology of sex and aggression. Pp. 176-257 in S.D. Glick and J. Goldfarb, eds., *Behavioral Pharmacology*. Saint Louis, Mo.: C.V. Mosby.

1977 Effects of alcohol on attack and defensive-submissive reactions in rats. *Psychopharmacology* 52:231-237.

Miczek, K.A., and J.F. DeBold
1983 Hormone-drug interactions and their influence on aggressive behavior. Pp. 313-347 in B.B. Svare, ed., *Hormones and Aggressive Behavior*. New York: Plenum Press.

Miczek, K.A., and L.H. Gold
1983 *d*-Amphetamine in squirrel monkeys of different social status: Effects on social and agonistic behavior, locomotion, and stereotypies. *Psychopharmacology* 81:183-190.

Miczek, K.A., and M. Haney
1994 Psychomotor stimulant effects of *d*-amphetamine, MDMA and PCP: Aggressive and schedule-controlled behavior in mice. *Psychopharmacology* (in press).

Miczek, K.A., and M. Krsiak
1978 Intruder-evoked aggression in isolated and nonisolated mice: Effects of psychomotor stimulants and L-DOPA. *Psychopharmacology* 57:47-55.

1979 Drug effects on agonistic behavior. Pp. 87-162 in T. Thompson and P.B. Dews, eds., *Advances in Behavioral Pharmacology*. New York: Academic Press.

1980 Alcohol and chlordiazepoxide increase suppressed aggression in mice. *Psychopharmacology* 69:39-44.

Micazek, K.A., and J.M. O'Donnell
1978 Intruder-evoked aggression in isolated and nonisolated mice: Effects

of psychomotor stimulants and *l*-dopa. *Psychopharmacology* 57:47-55

1980 Alcohol and chlordiazepoxide increase suppressed aggression in mice. *Psychopharmacology* 69:39-44.

Miczek, K.A., and M.L. Thompson
1983 Drugs of abuse and aggression: An ethopharmacological analysis. Pp. 164-188 in E. Gottheil, K.A. Druley, T.E. Skoloda, and H.M. Waxman, eds., *Alcohol, Drug Abuse and Aggression.* Springfield, Ill.: Charles C. Thomas.

Miczek, K.A., and J.W. Tidey
1989 Amphetamines: Aggressive and social behavior. Pp. 68-100 in K. Asghar and E. DeSouza, eds., *Pharmacology and Toxicology of Amphetamine and Related Designer Drugs.* NIDA Research Monograph Series, Vol. 94. Rockville, Md.: National Institute on Drug Abuse.

Miczek, K.A., and J.T. Winslow
1987 Psychopharmacological research on aggressive behavior. Pp. 27-113 in A.J. Greenshaw and C.T. Dourish, eds., *Experimental Psychopharmacology.* Clifton, N.J.: Humana Press.

Miczek, K.A., and H. Yoshimura
1982 Disruption of primate social behavior by *d*-amphetamine and cocaine: Differential antagonism by antipsychotics. *Psychopharmacology* 76:163-171.

Miczek, K.A., J. Woolley, S. Schlisserman, and H. Yoshimura
1981 Analysis of amphetamine effects on agonistic and affiliative behavior in squirrel monkeys (*Saimiri sciureus*). *Pharmacology Biochemistry and Behavior* 14(supp. 1):103-107.

Miczek, K.A., J.T. Winslow, and J.F. DeBold
1984 Heightened aggressive behavior by animals interacting with alcohol-treated conspecifics: Studies with mice, rats and squirrel monkeys. *Pharmacology Biochemistry and Behavior* 20:349-353.

Miczek, K.A., M. Haney, J. Tidey, T. Vatne, E. Weerts, and J.F. DeBold
1989 Temporal and sequential patterns of agonistic behavior: Effects of alcohol, anxiolytics and psychomotor stimulants. *Psychopharmacology* 97:149-151.

Miczek, K.A., M.L. Thompson, and W. Tornatzky
1991a Subordinate animals: Behavioral and physiological adaptations and opioid tolerance. Pp. 323-357 in M.R. Brown, G.F. Koob, and C. Rivier, eds., *Stress: Neurobiology and Neuroendocrinology.* New York: Marcel Dekker.

Miczek, K.A., W. Tornatzky, and J. Vivian
1991b Ethology and neuropharmacology: Rodent ultrasounds. Pp. 409-427 in B. Olivier, J. Mos, and J.L. Slangen, eds., *Animal Models in Psychopharmacology (Advances in Pharmacological Sciences).* Basel, Switzerland: Birkhäuser Verlag.

Miczek, K.A., E.M. Weerts, W. Tornatzky, J.F. DeBold, and T.M. Vatne
In   Alcohol and "bursts" of aggressive behavior: Ethological analy-
press   sis of individual differences in rats. *Psychopharmacology.*
Milkman, H., and W. Frosch
1980   Theory of drug use. *National Institute of Drug Abuse Research
        Monograph Series* 30:38-45.
Miller, B.A., W.R. Downs, D.M. Gondoli, and A. Keil
1987   The role of childhood sexual abuse in the development of alco-
        holism in women. *Violence and Victims* 2:157-172.
Miller, B.A., W.R. Downs, and D.M. Gondoli
1989a   Delinquency, childhood violence, and the development of alco-
        holism in women. *Crime and Delinquency* 35:94-108.
1989b   Spousal violence among alcoholic women as compared to a ran-
        dom household sample of women. *Journal of Studies on Alco-
        hol* 50:533-540.
Miller, R.E., J.M. Levine, and I.A. Mirsky
1973   Effects of psychoactive drugs on nonverbal communication and
        group social behavior of monkeys. *Journal of Personality and
        Social Psychology* 28:396-405.
Mills, M.A., and P. Brawley
1972   The psychopharmacology of *Cannabis sativa*: A review. *Agents
        and Actions* 2:201-213.
Milman, D.H.
1969   The role of marihuana in patterns of drug abuse by adolescents.
        Journal of Pediatrics 74:283-290.
Mio, J.S., G. Nanjundappa, D.E. Werleur, and M.D. De Rios
1986   Drug abuse and the adolescent sex offender: A preliminary
        analysis. *Journal of Psychoactive Drugs* 18:65-72.
Mirin, S.M., and R.E. Meyer
1979   Psychopathology and mood during heroin use. Pp. 93-118 in
        R.E. Meyer and S.E. Mirin, eds., *The Heroin Stimulus: Implica-
        tions for a Theory of Addiction.* New York: Plenum Medical
        Book Co.
Molina, V.A., S. Gobaille, and P. Mandel
1985   Effects of ethanol withdrawal on muricidal behavior. *Aggres-
        sive Behavior* 11:235-243.
Molina, V., L. Ciesielsski, S. Gobaille, and P. Mandel
1986   Effects of the potentiation of the GABAergic neurotransmission
        in the olfactory bulbs on mouse-killing behavior. *Pharmacol-
        ogy Biochemistry and Behavior* 24:657-664.
Monforte, J.R., and W.U. Spitz
1975   Narcotic abuse among homicide victims in Detroit. *Journal of
        Forensic Sciences* 20:186-190.
Moore, J.
1990   Gangs, drugs, and violence. Pp 160-176 in M. De La Rosa, E.Y.
        Lambert, and B. Gropper, eds., *Drugs and Violence: Causes,
        Correlates, and Consequences.* NIDA Research Monograph Se-

ries, Vol. 103. Rockville, Md.: National Institute on Drug Abuse.

Moore, M.S., and D.M. Thompson
1978 Acute and chronic effects of cocaine on extinction-induced aggression. *Journal of the Experimental Analysis of Behavior* 29:309-318.

Moraes Andrade, O.
1964 The criminogenic action of cannabis (marihuana) and narcotics. *Bulletin on Narcotics* 16:23-28.

Mos, J., and B. Olivier
1988 Differential effects of selected psychoactive drugs on dominant and subordinate male rats housed in a colony. *Neuroscience Research Communications* 2:29-36.

Mosher, D.L., and M. Sirkin
1984 Measuring a macho personality constellation. *Journal of Research in Personality* 18:150-163.

Muehlenhard, C.L., and M.A. Linton
1987 Date rape and sexual aggression in dating situations: Incidence and risk factors. *Journal of Counseling Psychology* 34:186-196.

Munkvad, I.
1975 The mechanism of action of psychopharmacological agents on behavior. *Acta Pharmacologica et Toxicologica* 36:20-30.

Munro, A.D.
1986 The effects of apomorphine, d-amphetamine and chlorpromazine on the aggressiveness of isolated *Æquidens pulcher* (Teleostei, Cichlidæ). *Psychopharmacology* 88:124-128.

Murdoch, D., and R.O. Pihl
1985 Alcohol and aggression in a group interaction. *Addictive Behaviors* 10:97-101.

Murdoch, D.D., R.O. Pihl, and D. Ross
1988 The influence of dose, beverage type, and sex of interactor on female bar patrons' verbal aggression. *International Journal of the Addictions* 23:953-966.

Musty, R.E., and P.F. Consroe
1982 Phencyclidine produces aggressive behavior in rapid eye movement sleep-deprived rats. *Life Sciences* 30:1733-1738.

Musty, R.E., C.L. Lindsey, and E.A. Carlini
1976 6-Hydroxydopamine and the aggressive behavior induced by marihuana in REM sleep-deprived rats. *Psychopharmacology* 48:175-179.

Myers, R.D.
1989 Isoquinolines, ß-carbolines and alcohol drinking: Involvement of opioid and dopaminergic mechanisms. *Experientia* 45:436-443.

Myers, T.
1982 Alcohol and violent crime re-examined: Self-reports from two

sub-groups of Scottish male prisoners. *British Journal of Addiction* 77:399-413.

1986   An analysis of context and alcohol consumption in a group of criminal events. *Alcohol and Alcoholism* 21:389-395.

Myerscough, R., and S. Taylor
1985   The effects of marijuana on human physical aggression. *Journal of Personality and Social Psychology* 49:1541-1546.

Nadelmann, E.A.
1989   Drug prohibition in the United States: Costs, consequences, and alternatives. *Science* 245:939-947.

Nelson, P.B.
1967   The effects of alcohol upon frustrative non-reward produced aggression. *Quarterly Journal of Studies of Alcohol* 31:221-279.

Noguchi, T.T., and G.R. Nakamura
1978   Phencyclidine-related deaths in Los Angeles County, 1976. *Journal of Forensic Sciences* 23:503-507.

Norton, R.N., and M.Y. Morgan
1989a The role of alcohol in mortality and morbidity from interpersonal violence. *Alcohol and Alcoholism* 24:565-576.

1989b Improving information on the role of alcohol in interpersonal violence in Great Britain. *Alcohol and Alcoholism* 24:577-589.

Nurco, D.N., J.W. Shaffer, J.C. Ball, T.W. Kinlock, and J. Langrod
1986   A comparison by ethnic group and city of the criminal activities of narcotic addicts. *Journal of Nervous and Mental Disease* 174:112.

O'Donnell, J.M., and K.A. Miczek
1980   No tolerance to antiaggressive effect of *d*-amphetamine in mice. *Psychopharmacology* 68:191-196.

Öjesjö, L.
1983   Alcohol, drugs, and forensic psychiatry. *Psychiatric Clinics of North America* 6:733-749.

O'Leary, M.R., E.F. Chaney, L.S. Brown, and M.A. Schuckit
1978   The use of the Goldberg indices with alcoholics: A cautionary note. *Journal of Clinical Psychology* 34:988-990.

Olivier, B., and D. van Dalen
1982   Social behaviour in rats and mice: An ethologically based model for differentiating psychoactive drugs. *Aggressive Behavior* 8:163-168.

Olivier, B., H. van Aken, I. Jaarsma, R. van Oorshot, T. Zethof, and D. Bradford
1984   Behavioural effects of psychoactive drugs on agonistic behaviour of male territorial rats (resident-intruder model). Pp. 137-156 in K.A. Miczek, M.R. Kruk, and B. Olivier, eds., *Ethopharmacological Aggression Research*. New York: Alan R. Liss.

Palermo Neto, J., and E.A. Carlini
1972   Aggressive behaviour elicited in rats by *Cannabis sativa*: Ef-

fects of *p*-chlorophenylalanine and DOPA. *European Journal of Pharmacology* 17:215-220.

Palermo Neto, J., and F.V. Carvalho
1973   The effects of chronic cannabis treatment on the aggressive behavior and brain 5-hydroxytryptamine levels of rats with different temperaments. *Psychopharmacologia* 32:383-392.

Palermo Neto, J., J.F. Nunes, and F.V. Carvalho
1975   The effects of chronic cannabis treatment upon brain 5-hydroxytryptamine, plasma corticosterone and aggressive behavior in female rats with different hormonal status. *Psychopharmacologia* 42:195-200.

Palmstierna, T., and B. Wistedt
1988   Prevalence of risk factors for aggressive behavior: Characteristics of an involuntarily admitted population. *Acta Psychiatrica Scandanavica* 78:227-229.

Panksepp, J.
1971   Drugs and stimulus-bound attack. *Physiology and Behavior* 6:317-320.
1981   Brain opioids—A neurochemical substrate for narcotic and social dependence. Pp. 149-175 in S.J. Cooper, ed., *Theory in Psychopharmacology.* London: Academic Press.

Panksepp, J., R. Meeker, and N.J. Bean
1980   The neurochemical control of crying. *Pharmacology Biochemistry and Behavior* 12:437-443.

Pascale, R., M. Hurd, and L.H. Primavera
1980   The effects of chronic marijuana use. *Journal of Social Psychology* 110:273-83.

Paton, W.D.M.
1975   Pharmacology of marijuana. *Annual Review of Pharmacology* 15:191-220.

Paul, D.M.
1975   Drugs and aggression. *Medicine, Science and the Law* 15:16-21.

Peeke, H.V.S., and M.H. Figler
1981   Modulation of aggressive behavior in fish by alcohol and congeners. *Pharmacology Biochemistry and Behavior* 14(supp. 1):79-84.

Peeke, H.V.S., G.E. Ellman, and M.J. Herz
1973   Dose dependent alcohol effects on the aggressive behavior of the conflict cichlid (*Cichlasoma nigrofaciatum*). *Behavioral Biology* 8:115-122.

Peeke, H.V.S., S.C. Peeke, H.H. Avis, and G. Ellman
1975   Alcohol, habituation and the patterning of aggressive responses in a cichlid fish. *Pharmacology Biochemistry and Behavior* 3:1031-1036.

Pernanen, K.
1976   Alcohol and crimes of violence. Pp. 351-444 in B. Kissin and H.

Begleiter, eds., *Social Aspects of Alcoholism*. New York: Plenum Press.

Persky, H., C.P. O'Brien, E. Fine, W.J. Howard, M.A. Khan, and R.W. Beck
  1977 The effect of alcohol and smoking on testosterone function and aggression in chronic alcoholics. *American Journal of Psychiatry* 134:621-625.

Pertwee, R.G.
  1985 Cannabis. Pp. 364-391 in D.G. Grahame-Smith, ed., *Psychopharmacology:* Vol. 2. *Preclinical Psychopharmacology*. Amsterdam: Elsevier.

Petersen, R.C.
  1980 Phencyclidine: A NIDA perspective. *Journal of Psychedelic Drugs* 12:205-209.

Peterson, J.T., and L.A. Pohorecky
  1989 Effect of chronic ethanol administration on intermale aggression in rats. *Aggressive Behavior* 15:201-215.

Peterson, J.T., L.A. Pohorecky, and M.W. Hamm
  1988 Neuroendocrine and b-adrenoceptor response to chronic ethanol and aggression in rats. *Pharmacology Biochemistry and Behavior* 34:247-253.

Petersson, B.
  1988 Analysis of the role of alcohol in mortality, particularly sudden unwitnessed death, in middle-aged men in Malmo, Sweden. *Alcohol and Alcoholism* 23:259-263.

Petrich, J.
  1976 Rate of psychiatric morbidity in a metropolitan county jail population. *American Journal of Psychiatry* 133:1439-1444.

Pettijohn, T.F.
  1979 The effects of alcohol on agonistic behavior in the Telomian dog. *Psychopharmacology* 60:295-301.

Pihl, R.O., and C. Zacchia
  1986 Alcohol and aggression: A test of the affect-arousal hypothesis. *Aggressive Behavior* 12:367-375.

Pihl, R.O., A. Zeichner, R. Niaura, K. Nagy, and C. Zacchia
  1981 Attribution and alcohol-mediated aggression. *Journal of Abnormal Psychology* 90:468-475.

Pihl, R.O., M. Smith, and B. Farrell
  1984a Individual characteristics of aggressive beer and distilled beverage drinkers. *International Journal of the Addictions* 19:689-696.

Pihl, R.O., M. Smith, and B. Farrell
  1984b Alcohol and aggression in men: A comparison of brewed and distilled beverages. *Journal of Studies on Alcohol* 45:278-282.

Plonsky, M., and P.R. Freeman
  1982 The effects of methadone on the social behavior and activity of the rat. *Pharmacology Biochemistry and Behavior* 16:569-571.

Pohorecky, L.A.
 1977   Biphasic action of ethanol. *Biobehavioral Reviews* 1:231-240.
Poli, A., and J. Palermo-Neto
 1986   Effects of *d,l*-propranolol and haloperidol on aggressive behavior induced in mice by isolation and isolation plus amphetamine treatment. *Brazilian Journal of Medical and Biological Research* 19:411-417.
Pollock, V.E., J. Briere, L. Schnieder, J. Knop, S.A. Mednick, and D.W. Goodwin
 1990   Childhood antecedents of antisocial behavior: Parental alcoholism and physical abusiveness. *American Journal of Psychiatry* 147:1290-1293.
Poshivalov, V.P.
 1974   Pharmacological analysis of aggressive behaviour of mice induced by isolation. *Journal of the Higher Nervous Activity* 24:1079-1081.
 1980   The integrity of the social hierarchy in mice following administration of psychotropic drugs. *British Journal of Pharmacology* 70:367-373.
 1981   Pharmaco-ethological analysis of social behaviour of isolated mice. *Pharmacology Biochemistry and Behavior* 14(supp. 1):53-59.
 1982   Ethological analysis of neuropeptides and psychotropic drugs: Effects on intraspecies aggression and sociability of isolated mice. *Aggressive Behavior* 8:355-369.
Posner, I., W.M. Miley, and N.J. Mazzagatti
 1976   Effects of *d*-amphetamine and pilocarpine on the mouse-killing response of hungry and satiated rats. *Physiological Psychology* 4:457-460.
Post, R.M.
 1975   Cocaine psychoses: A continuum model. *American Journal of Psychiatry* 132:225-231.
Powell, D.A., K. Walters, S. Duncan, and J.R. Holley
 1973   The effects of chlorpromazine and *d*-amphetamine upon shock-elicited aggression. *Psychopharmacologia* 30:303-314.
Pradhan, S.N.
 1984   Phencyclidine (PCP): Some human studies. *Neuroscience and Biobehavioral Reviews* 8:493-501.
Pradhan, S.N., B. Ghosh, C.S. Aulakh, and A.K. Bhattacharyya
 1980   Effects of Δ^9-tetrahydrocannabinol on foot shock-induced aggression in rats. *Communications in Psychopharmacology* 4:27-34.
Pucilowski, O., E. Trzaslowska, and W. Kostowski
 1987   Differential effects of chronic ethanol on apomorphine-induced locomotion, climbing and aggression in rats. *Drug and Alcohol Dependence* 20:163-170.

Puglisi-Allegra, S., and A. Oliverio
  1981   Naloxone potentiates shock-induced aggressive behavior in mice. *Pharmacology Biochemistry and Behavior* 15:513-514.
  1977   A technique for the measurement of aggressive behavior in mice S. *Behavior Research Methods and Instrumentation* 9:503-504.
Pulkkinen, L.
  1983   Youthful smoking and drinking in a longitudinal perspective. *Journal of Youth and Adolescence* 12:253-283.
Puri, S.K., and H. Lal
  1973   Effect of dopaminergic stimulation or blockade on morphine-withdrawal aggression. *Psychopharmacology* 32:113-120.
  1974   Reduced threshold to pain induced aggression specifically related to morphine dependence. *Psychopharmacology* 35:237-241.
Rada, R.T.
  1975   Alcoholism and forcible rape. *American Journal of Psychiatry* 132:444-446.
Rada, R.T., R. Kellner, D.R. Laws, and W.W. Winslow
  1978   Drinking, alcoholism, and the mentally disordered sex offender. *Bulletin of the American Academy of Psychiatry and the Law* 6:296-300.
Rada, R.T., D.R. Laws, R. Kellner, L. Stivastava, and G. Peake
  1983   Plasma androgens in violent and nonviolent sex offenders. *Bulletin of the American Academy of Psychiatry and the Law* 11:149-158.
Randrup, A., and I. Munkvad
  1969   Pharmacological studies on the brain mechanisms underlying two forms of behavioral excitation: Stereotyped hyperactivity and "rage." Pp. 928-938 in E. Tobach, ed., *Experimental Approaches to the Study of Emotional Behavior.* (Annals of the New York Academy of Sciences, Vol. 159.) New York: New York Academy of Sciences.
Rawlin, J.W.
  1968   Street level abusage of amphetamines. Pp. 51-65 in J.R. Russo, ed., *Amphetamine Abuse.* Springfield, Ill.: Charles C. Thomas.
Rawson, R.A., F.S. Tennant, P.H. McCann, and M.A. McCann
  1982   Characteristics of 68 chronic phencyclidine abusers who sought treatment. Pp. 483-487 in L.S. Harris, ed., *Problems of Drug Dependence 1981.* NIDA Research Monograph Series, Vol. 41. Rockville, Md.: National Institute on Drug Abuse.
Raynes, A.E., and R.S. Ryback
  1970   Effect of alcohol and congeners on aggressive response in *Betta splendens. Quarterly Journal of Studies on Alcohol* 5:130-135.
Raynes, A., R. Ryback, and D. Ingle
  1968   The effect of alcohol on aggression in *Betta splendens. Communications in Behavioral Biology* 2:141-146.

Razdan, R.K., B.Z. Terris, H.G. Pars, N.P. Plotnikoff, P.W. Dodge, A.T. Dren, J. Kyncl, and P. Somani
  1976a Drugs derived from cannabinoids. 2. Basic esters of nitrogen and carbocyclic analogs. *Journal of Medicinal Chemistry* 19:454-461.
Razdan, R.K., B.Z. Terris, G.R. Handrick, H.C. Dalzell, H.G. Pars, J.F. Howes, N.P. Plotnikoff, P. Dodge, A. Dren, J. Kyncl, L. Shoer, and W.R. Thompson
  1976b Drugs derived from cannabinoids. 3. Sulfur analogs, thiopyranobenzopyrans and thienobenzopyrans. *Journal of Medicinal Chemistry* 19:549-551.
Razdan, R.K., G.R. Handrick, H.C. Dalzell, J.F. Howes, M. Winn, N.P. Plotnikoff, P.W. Dodge, and A.T. Dren
  1976c Drugs derived from cannabinoids. 4. Effect of alkyl substitution in sulfur and carbocyclic analogs. *Journal of Medicinal Chemistry* 19:551-553.
Redmond, D.E., and J.H. Krystal
  1984 Multiple mechanisms of withdrawal from opioid drugs. *Annual Review of Neuroscience* 7:443-478.
Reich, P., and R.B. Hepps
  1972 Homicide during a psychosis induced by LSD. *Journal of the American Medical Association* 219:869-871.
Renson, G.J., J.E. Adams, and J.R. Tinklenberg
  1978 Buss-Durkee assessment and validation with violent versus nonviolent chronic alcohol abusers. *Journal of Consulting and Clinical Psychology* 46:360-361.
Rewerski, W., W. Kostowski, T. Piechocki, and M. Rylski
  1971 The effects of some hallucinogens on aggressiveness of mice and rats. *Pharmacology* 5:314-320.
Rewerski, W.J., T. Piechocki, and M. Rylski
  1973 Effects of hallucinogens on aggressiveness and thermoregulation in mice. Pp. 432-436 in E. Schonbaum and P. Lomax, eds., *The Pharmacology of Thermoregulation*. New York: Karger.
Ricaurte, G., G. Bryan, L. Strauss, L. Seiden, and C. Schuster
  1985 Hallucinogenic amphetamine selectively destroys brain serotonin nerve terminals. *Science* 229:986-988.
Richardson, D., A.G. Karczmar, and C.L. Schudder
  1972 Intergeneric behavioral differences among methamphetamine treated mice. *Psychopharmacologia* 25:347-375.
Rickman, E.E., E.Y. Williams, and R.K. Brown
  1961 Acute toxic psychiatric reactions related to amphetamine medication. *Medical Annals of the District of Columbia* 30:209-212.
Riddick, L., and J.L. Luke
  1978 Alcohol-associated deaths in the District of Columbia—A postmortem study. *Journal of Forensic Sciences* 23:493-502.

Ridley, R.M., H.F. Baker, and P.R. Scraggs
  1979 The time course of the behavioral effects of amphetamine and their reversal by haloperidol in a primate species. *Biological Psychiatry* 14:753-765.
Ripley, H.S.
  1973 Suicidal behavior in Edinburgh and Seattle. *American Journal of Psychiatry* 130:995-1000.
Roberts, A.R.
  1987 Psychosocial characteristics of batterers: A study of 234 men charged with domestic violence offenses. *Journal of Family Violence* 2:81-93.
Roberts, S.S.
  1990 Murder, mayhem, and other joys of youth. *Journal of National Institute of Health Research* 2:67-72.
Robins, E., K.A. Gentry, R.A. Munoz, and S. Marten
  1977 A contrast of the three more common illnesses with the ten less common in a study and 18-month follow-up of 314 psychiatric emergency room patients. *Archives of General Psychiatry* 34:285-291.
Robins, L.N.
  1978 Sturdy childhood predictors of adult antisocial behaviour: Replications from longitudinal studies. *Psychological Medicine* 8:611-622.
Rodgers, R.J.
  1982 Differential effects of naloxone and diprenorphine on defensive behavior in rats. *Neuropharmacology* 21:1291-1294.
Rohsenow, D.J., and J. Bachorowski
  1984 Effects of alcohol and expectancies on verbal aggression in men and women. *Journal of Abnormal Psychology* 93:418-432.
Rolinski, Z.
  1973 Analysis of aggressiveness-stereotypy complex induced in mice by amphetamine or nialamide and L-DOPA. *Polish Journal of Pharmacology and Pharmacy* 25:551-558.
  1977 The role of serotonergic and cholinergic systems in the aggression-stereotypy complex produced by amphetamine in mice. *Polish Journal of Pharmacology and Pharmacy* 29:591-602.
Rosenbaum, A., and S.K. Hoge
  1989 Head injury and marital aggression. *American Journal of Psychiatry* 146:1048-1051.
Rosenbaum, A., and K.D. O'Leary
  1981 Marital violence: Characteristics of abusive couples. *Journal of Consulting and Clinical Psychology* 49:63-71.
Rosenkrantz, H., and M.C. Braude
  1974 Acute, subacute and 23-day chronic marihuana inhalation toxicities in the rat. *Toxicology and Applied Pharmacology* 28:428-441.

Roslund, B., and C.A. Larson
  1976 Mentally disturbed violent offenders in Sweden. *Neuropsychobiology* 2:221-232.
  1979 Crimes of violence and alcohol abuse in Sweden. *International Journal of the Addictions* 14:1103-1115.
Roy, A., M. Virkkunen, S. Guthrie, R. Poland, and M. Linnoila
  1986 Monoamines, glucose metabolism, suicidal and aggressive behavior. *Psychopharmacology Bulletin* 22:661.
Rubin, B.
  1972 Prediction of dangerousness in mentally ill criminals. *Archives of General Psychiatry* 27:397-407.
Russell, J.W., G. Singer, and G. Bowman
  1983 Effects of interactions between amphetamine and food deprivation on covariation of muricide, consummatory behaviour and activity. *Pharmacology Biochemistry and Behavior* 18:917-926.
Russell, J.W., B.D. Greenberg, and D.S. Segal
  1984 The effects of phencyclidine on spontaneous aggressive behavior in the rat. *Biological Psychiatry* 19:195-202.
Ruusunen, S., G. Johansson, A. Huhtala, H. Niskanen, and T. Pääkkänen
  1975 Ethyl alcohol and defence behaviour in the cat. *Medical Biology* 53:475-480.
Rydelius, P.A.
  1988 The development of antisocial behaviour and sudden violent death. *Acta Psychiatrica Scandinavica* 77:398-403.
Salama, A.I., and M.E. Goldberg
  1970 Neurochemical effects of imipramine and amphetamine in aggressive mouse-killing (muricidal) rats. *Biochemical Pharmacology* 19:2023-2032.
Salzman, C., B.A. Van Der Kolk, and R.I. Shader
  1976 Marijuana and hostility in a small-group setting. *American Journal of Psychiatry* 133:1029-1033.
Samson, H.H., G.A. Tolliver, L. Lumeng, and T.K. Li
  1989 Ethanol reinforcement in the alcohol nonpreferring rat: Initiation using behavioral techniques without food restriction. *Alcoholism: Clinical and Experimental Research* 13:378-385.
Santos, M., M.R.P. Sampaio, N.S. Fernandez, and E.A. Carlini
  1966 Effects of Cannabis sativa (marihuana) on fighting behavior of mice. *Psychopharmacologia* 8:437-444.
Sassenrath, E.N., and L.F. Chapman
  1976 Primate social behavior as a method of analysis of drug action: Studies with THC in monkeys. *Federation Proceedings* 35:2238-2244.
Saxena, A., B.K. Bhattacharya, and B. Mukerji
  1962 Behavioural studies in fish with mescaline, LSD, and thiopropazate and their interactions with serotonin and DOPA. *Archives of International Pharmacodynamics* 140:327-335.

Sbordone, R.J., and B. Carder
  1974 Mescaline and shock induced aggression in rats. *Pharmacology Biochemistry and Behavior* 2:777-782.
Sbordone, R.J., J.A. Wingard, M.L. Elliott, and J. Jervey
  1978 Mescaline produces pathological aggression in rats regardless of age or strain. *Pharmacology Biochemistry and Behavior* 8:543-546.
Sbordone, R.J., J.A. Wingard, D.A. Gorelick, and M.L. Elliott
  1979 Severe aggression in rats induced by mescaline but not other hallucinogens. *Psychopharmacology* 66:275-280.
Sbordone, R.J., D.A. Gorelick, and M.L. Elliott
  1981 An ethological analysis of drug-induced pathological aggression. Pp. 369-385 in P.F. Brain and D. Benton, eds., *Multidisciplinary Approaches to Aggression Research*. Amsterdam: Elsevier/North Holland Biomedical.
Schiørring, E.
  1977 Changes in individual and social behavior induced by amphetamine related compounds in monkeys and man. Pp. 481-522 in E.H. Ellinwood and M.M. Kilbey, eds., *Cocaine and Other Stimulants*. New York: Plenum Press.
  1981 Psychopathology induced by "speed drugs." *Pharmacology Biochemistry and Behavior* 14(supp. 1):109-122.
Schlemmer, R.F., and J.M. Davis
  1981 Evidence for dopamine mediation of submissive gestures in the stumptail macaque monkey. *Pharmacology Biochemistry and Behavior* 14(supp. 1):95-102.
  1983 A comparison of three psychomimetic-induced models of psychosis in non-human primate social colonies. Pp. 33-78 in K.A. Miczek, ed., *Ethopharmacology: Primate Models of Neuro-psychiatric Disorders*. New York: Alan R. Liss.
Schlemmer, R.F., N. Narasimhachari, V.D. Thompson, and J.M. Davis
  1977 The effect of a hallucinogen, 5-methoxy-N, N-dimethyltryptamine, on primate social behavior. *Communications in Psychopharmacology* 1:105-118.
Schlemmer, R.F. Jr., R.C. Casper, F.K. Siemsen, D.L. Garver, and J.M. Davis
  1976 Behavioral changes in a juvenile primate social colony with chronic administration of *d*-amphetamine. *Psychopharmacology Communications* 2:49-59.
Schneider, C.
  1968 Behavioural effects of some morphine antagonists and hallucinogens in the rat. *Nature* 220:586-587.
Schrold, J., and R.F. Squires
  1971 Behavioural effects of *d*-amphetamine in young chicks treated with *p*-Cl-phenylalanine. *Psychopharmacologia* 20:85-90.
Schubert, D.S.P., A.W. Wolf, M.B. Patterson, T.P. Grande, and L. Pendleton
  1988 A statistical evaluation of the literature regarding the associa-

tions among alcoholism, drug abuse, and antisocial personality disorder. *International Journal of the Addictions* 23:797-808.

Schuckit, M.A., and E.R. Morrissey
1979   Psychiatric problems in women admitted to an alcoholic detoxification center. *American Journal of Psychiatry* 136:611-617.

Schuckit, M.A., and J.W. Russell
1984   An evaluation of primary alcoholics with histories of violence. Journal of *Clinical Psychiatry* 45:3-6.

Schuckit, M.A., E.R. Morrissey, and M.R. O'Leary
1978   Alcohol problems in elderly men and women. *Addictive Diseases* 3:405-416.

Schuerger, J.M., and N. Reigle
1988   Personality and biographic data that characterize men who abuse their wives. *Journal of Clinical Psychology* 44:75-81.

Scott, J.P.
1966   Agonistic behavior of mice and rats: A review. *American Zoologist* 6:683-701.

Scott, J.P., C. Lee, and J.E. Ho
1971   Effects of fighting, genotype, and amphetamine sulfate on body temperature of mice. *Journal of Comparative and Physiological Psychology* 76:349-352.

Scott, P.D.
1968   Offenders, drunkenness and murder. *British Journal of Addiction to Alcohol and Other Drugs* 63:221-226.

Seeman, P.
1987   Dopamine receptors and the dopamine hypothesis of schizophrenia. *Synapse* 1:133-152.

Segal, D.S., S.B. Weinberger, J. Cahill, and S.J. McCunney
1980   Multiple daily amphetamine administration: Behavioral and neuro-chemical alterations. *Science* 207:904-906.

Seltzer, A.
1980   Acculturation and mental disorder in the Inuit. *Canadian Journal of Psychiatry* 25:173-181.

Selzer, M.L.
1967   The personality of the alcoholic as an impediment to psychotherapy. *Psychiatric Quarterly* 41:38-45.
1971   The Michigan Alcoholism Screening Test: The quest for a new diagnostic instrument. *American Journal of Psychiatry* 127:1653-1658.

Sethi, B.B., J.K. Trivedi, P. Kumar, A. Gulati, A.K. Agarwal, and N. Sethi
1986   Antianxiety effect of cannabis: Involvement of central benzodiazepine receptors. *Biological Psychiatry* 21:3-10.

Shaffer, J.W., D.N. Nurco, J.C. Ball, T.W. Kinlock, K.R. Duszynski, and J. Langrod
1987   The relationship of preaddiction characteristics to the types and

amounts of crime committed by narcotic addicts. *International Journal of the Addictions* 22:153-165.

Shaikh, M.B., M. Dalsass, and A. Siegel
1990 Opioidergic mechanisms mediating aggressive behavior in the cat. *Aggressive Behavior* 16:191-206.

Shapiro, R.J.
1982 Alcohol and family violence. Pp. 69-89 in L.R. Barnhill, ed., *Clinical Approaches to Family Violence*. Rockville, Md.: Aspen Systems Corp.

Sheard, M.H.
1967 The effects of amphetamine on attack behavior in the cat. *Brain Research* 5:330-338.
1977a The role of drugs in precipitating or inhibiting human aggression. *Psychopharmacology Bulletin* 13:23-25.
1977b Animal models of aggressive behavior. Pp. 247-257 in I. Hanin and E. Usdin, eds., *Animal Models in Psychiatry and Neurology*. Oxford: Pergamon Press.
1981 Shock-induced fighting (SIF): Psychopharmacological studies. *Aggressive Behavior* 7:41-49.
1983 Psychopharmacology of aggression. Pp. 188-201 in H. Hippius and G. Winokur, eds., *Clinical Psychopharmacology*. Amsterdam: Excerpta Medica.

Sheard, M.H., and M. Davis
1976 *p*-Chloramphetamine: Short and long term effects upon shock-elicited aggression. *European Journal of Pharmacology* 40:295-302.

Sheard, M.H., D.I. Astrachan, and M. Davis
1977 The effect of *d*-lysergic acid diethylamide (LSD) upon shock-elicited fighting in rats. *Life Sciences* 20:427-430.

Sheppard, C., E. Ricca, J. Fracchia, and S. Merliss
1975 Need conflicts of suburban narcotic abusers who apply to a county methadone maintenance program. *Journal of Clinical Psychology* 31:140-145.

Shintomi, K.
1975 Effects of psychotropic drugs on methamphetamine-induced behavioral excitation in grouped mice. *European Journal of Pharmacology* 31:195-206.

Shupe, L.M.
1954 Alcohol and crime. A study of the urine alcohol concentration found in 882 persons arrested during or immediately after the commission of a felony. *Journal of Criminal Law, Criminology and Police Science* 44:661-664.

Sieber, B.
1982 Influence of hashish extract on the social behavior of encountering male baboons (*Papio c. anubis*). *Pharmacology Biochemistry and Behavior* 17:209-216.

Sieber, B., H.-R. Frischknecht, and P.G. Waser

1980a Behavioral effects of hashish in mice. I. Social interactions and nest-building behavior of males. *Psychopharmacology* 70:149-154.

1980b Behavioral effects of hashish in mice. III. Social interactions between two residents and an intruder male. *Psychopharmacology* 70:273-278.

1981 Behavioral effects of hashish in mice. IV. Social dominance, food dominance, and sexual behavior within a group of males. *Psychopharmacology* 73:142-146.

1982 Behavioural effects of hashish in mice in comparison with psychoactive drugs. *General Pharmacology* 13:315-320.

Siegel, R.K.

1971 Studies of hallucinogens in fish, birds, mice and men: The behavior of "psychedelic" populations. Pp. 311-318 in O. Vinar, Z. Votava, and P.B. Bradley, eds., *Advances in Neuro-psychopharmacology*. London: Czechoslovak Medical Press.

1973 An ethologic search for self-administration of hallucinogens. *International Journal of the Addictions* 8:373-393.

1977 Cocaine: Recreational use and intoxication. Pp. 119-136 in R.C. Petersen and R.C. Stillmas, eds., *Cocaine: 1977*. NIDA Research Monograph Series, Vol. 13. Rockville, Md.: National Institute on Drug Abuse.

1978 Phencyclidine, criminal behavior, and the defense of diminished capacity. Pp. 272-288 in R.C. Peterson and R.C. Stillman, eds., *Phencyclidine (PCP) Abuse: An Appraisal*. NIDA Research Monograph Series, Vol. 21. Rockville, Md.: National Institute on Drug Abuse.

1980 PCP and violent crime: The people vs. peace. *Journal of Psychedelic Drugs* 12:317-330.

Siegel, R.K., and J. Poole

1969 Psychedelic-induced social behavior in mice: A preliminary report. *Psychological Reports* 25:704-706.

Siegel, R.K., J.M. Brewster, and M.E. Jarvik

1974 An observational study of hallucinogen-induced behavior in unrestrained *Macaca mulatta*. *Psychopharmacologia* (Berlin) 40:211-223.

Siegel, R.K., J.M. Brewster, C.A. Johnson, and M.E. Jarvik

1976 The effects of hallucinogens on blind monkeys. *International Pharmacopsychiatry* 11:150-156.

Silverman, A.P.

1966 Barbiturates, lysergic acid diethylamide, and the social behaviour of laboratory rats. *Psychopharmacologia* 10:155-171.

Simon, W.E.

1974 Psychological needs, academic achievement and marijuana consumption. *Journal of Clinical Psychology* 30:496-498.

Simonds, J.F., and J. Kashani
  1979a Phencyclidine use in delinquent males committed to a training school. *Adolescence* 14:721-725.
  1979b Drug abuse and criminal behavior in delinquent boys committed to a training school. *American Journal of Psychiatry* 136:1444-1448.
Siomopoulos, V.
  1979 Drug involvement in crimes committed by mentally ill offenders. *Psychological Reports* 45:875-879.
  1981 Violence: The ugly face of amphetamine abuse. *Illinois Medical Journal* 159:375-377.
Smart, R.G., and D. Jones
  1970 Illicit LSD users: Their personality characteristics and psychopathology. *Journal of Abnormal Psychology* 75:286-292.
Smith, D.E., and D.R. Wesson
  1980 PCP abuse: Diagnostic and psychopharmacological treatment approaches. *Journal of Psychedelic Drugs* 12:293-299.
Smith, E.O., and L.D. Byrd
  1984 Contrasting effects of *d*-amphetamine on affiliation and aggression in monkeys. *Pharmacology Biochemistry and Behavior* 20:255-260.
Smith, R.C., and D. Crim
  1969 The world of the Haight Ashbury speed freak. *Journal of Psychedelic Drugs* 2:172-188.
Smith, R.C., and J.M. Davis
  1977 Comparative effects of *d*-amphetamine, *l*-amphetamine, and methylphenidate on mood in man. *Psychopharmacology* 53:1-12.
Smoothy, R., and M.S. Berry
  1983 Effects of ethanol on behavior of aggressive mice from two different strains: A comparison of simple and complex behavioral assessments. *Pharmacology Biochemistry and Behavior* 19:645-653.
  1984 Effects of ethanol on murine aggression assessed by biting of an inanimate target. *Psychopharmacology* 83:268-271.
Smoothy, R., N.J. Bowden, and M.S. Berry
  1982 Ethanol and social behaviour in naive Swiss mice. *Aggressive Behavior* 8:204-207.
Smoothy, R., M.S. Berry, and P.F. Brain
  1983 Acute influences of ethanol on murine social aggression: Effects of dose, strain and fighting experience (abstract). *Aggressive Behavior* 9:119-120.
Smoothy, R., P.F. Brain, M.S. Berry, and M. Haug
  1986 Effects of ethanol on social behaviour directed towards male intruders by lactating Swiss mice. *Alcohol and Alcoholism* 21:241-245.

Sobell, L.C., and M.B. Sobell
1975 Drunkenness, a "special circumstance" in crimes of violence: Sometimes. *International Journal of the Addictions* 10:869-882.

Solursh, L.P.
1975 Psychoactive drugs, crime and violence. *Psychological Reports* 37:1177-1178.

Sorensen, G.
1987 Stereotyped behaviour, hyperaggressiveness and "tyrannic" hierarchy induced in bank voles (*Clethrionomys glareolus*) by a restricted cage milieu. *Progress in Neuro-Psychopharmacology and Biological Psychiatry* 11:9-21.

Sorensen, G., and A. Randrup
1986 Possible protective value of severe psychopathology against lethal effects of an unfavourable milieu. *Stress Medicine* 2:103-105.

Sorrells, J.M.
1979 Kids who kill. *Crime and Delinquency* 25:312-321.

Soueif, M.I.
1971 The use of cannabis in Egypt: A behavioural study. *Bulletin on Narcotics* 23:17-21.

Spencer, D.J.
1970 Cannabis induced psychosis. *British Journal of Addiction* 65:369-372.
1971 Cannabis-induced psychosis. *International Journal of the Addictions* 6:323-326.

Stefanis, C., A. Liakos, J. Boulougouris, and M. Fink
1976a Chronic hashish use and mental disorder. *American Journal of Psychiatry* 133:225-227.

Stefanis, C., A. Liakos, and J.C. Boulougouris
1976b Incidence of mental illness in hashish users and controls. Pp. 58-63 in R.L. Dornbush, A.M. Freedman, and M. Fink, eds., *Chronic Cannabis Use.* (Annals of the New York Academy of Sciences, Vol. 282.) New York: New York Academy of Sciences.

Stefanis, C., A. Liakos, J.C. Boulougouris, R.L. Dornbush, and C. Ballas
1976c Experimental observations of a 3-day hashish abstinence period and reintroduction of use. Pp. 113-120 in R.L. Dornbush, A.M. Freedman, and M. Fink, eds., *Chronic Cannabis Use.* (Annals of the New York Academy of Sciences, Vol. 282.) New York: New York Academy of Science.

Stille, G., H. Ackermann, E. Eichenberger, and H. Lauener
1963 Vergleichende pharmakologische Untersuchung eines neuen zentralen Stimulans, 1-*p*-tolyl-1-oxo-2-pyrro-lidino-*n*-pentan-HCl. *Arzneimittel-Forschung* (Drug Research) 13:871-877.

Stitzer, M.L., R.R. Griffiths, and I. Liebson
  1978 Effects of *d*-amphetamine on speaking in isolated humans. *Pharmacology Biochemistry and Behavior* 9:57-63.
Stolerman, I.P., C.A. Johnson, P. Bunker, and M.P. Jarvik
  1975 Weight loss and shock-elicited aggression as indices of morphine abstinence in rats. *Psychopharmacologia* 45:157-161.
Stoner, S.B.
  1988 Undergraduate marijuana use and anger. *Journal of Psychology* 122:343-347.
Sutker, P.B., and R.P. Archer
  1984 Opiate abuse and dependence disorders. Pp. 585-621 in H.E. Adams and P.B. Sutker, eds., *Comprehensive Handbook of Psychopathology.* New York: Plenum.
Suzdak, P.D., R.D. Schwartz, P. Skolnick, and S.M. Paul
  1986 Ethanol stimulates γ-aminobutyric acid receptor-mediated chloride transport in rat brain synaptoneurosomes. *Proceedings of the National Academy of Sciences* 83:4071-4075.
Swett, C., Jr.
  1985 History of street drug use: Relationship to diagnosis and violent behavior among admissions to a prison hospital. *Journal of Prison and Jail Health* 5:94-101.
Szara, S.
  1967 The hallucinogenic drugs—Curse or blessing? *American Journal of Psychiatry* 123:1513-1517.
Szymusik, A.
  1972 Studies on the psychopathology of murderers. *Polish Medical Journal* 11:752-757.
Takahashi, R.N., and I.G. Karniol
  1975 Pharmacological interaction between cannabinol and Δ^9-tetrahydrocannabinol. *Psychopharmacologia* 41:277-284.
Tamerin, J.S., and J.H. Mendelson
  1969 The psychodynamics of chronic inebriation: Observations of alcoholics during the process of drinking in an experimental group setting. *American Journal of Psychiatry* 125:886-899.
Tamimie, H.S.
  1968 Response of chicks to alcohol treated females. *Poultry Science* 47:1634-1635.
Tardiff, K., and A. Sweillam
  1980 Assault, suicide, and mental illness. *Archives of General Psychiatry* 37:164-169.
Taylor, S.P.
  1967 Aggressive behavior and physiological arousal as a function of provocation and the tendency to inhibit aggression. *Journal of Personality* 35:297-310.
  1983 Alcohol and human aggression. Pp. 280-291 in E. Gottheil, K.A. Druley, T.E. Skoloda, and H.M. Waxman, eds., *Alcohol,*

Drug Abuse and Aggression. Springfield, Ill.: Charles C. Thomas.

Taylor, S.P., and C.B. Gammon
1975 Effects of type and dose of alcohol on human physical aggression. *Journal of Personality and Social Psychology* 32:169-175.
1976 Aggressive behavior of intoxicated subjects: The effect of third-party intervention. *Journal of Studies on Alcohol* 37:917-930.

Taylor, S.P., and J.D. Sears
1988 The effects of alcohol and persuasive social pressure on human physical aggression. *Aggressive Behavior* 14:237-243.

Taylor, S.P., C.B. Gammon, and D.R. Capasso
1976 Aggression as a function of the interaction of alcohol and threat. *Journal of Personality and Social Psychology* 34:938-941.

Taylor, S.P., G.T. Schmutte, and K.E. Leonard, Jr.
1977 Physical aggression as a function of alcohol and frustration. *Bulletin of the Psychonomic Society* 9:217-218.

Tazi, A., R. Dantzer, P. Mormede, and M. Le Moal
1983 Effects of post-trial administration of naloxone and ß-endorphin on shock-induced fighting in rats. *Behavioral and Neural Biology* 39:192-202.

Telch, C.F., and C.U. Lindquist
1984 Violent versus nonviolent couples: A comparison of patterns. *Psychotherapy* 21:242-248.

ten Ham, M., and Y. de Jong
1975 Absence of interaction between Δ^9-tetrahydrocannabinol and cannabidiol (CBD) in aggression, muscle control and body temperature experiments in mice. *Psychopharmacologia* 41:169-174.

ten Ham, M., and J. van Noordwijk
1973 Lack of tolerance to the effect of two tetrahydrocannabinols on aggressiveness. *Psychopharmacologia* 29:171-176.

Thompson, G.R., M.M. Mason, H. Rosenkrantz, and M.C. Braude
1973 Chronic oral toxicity of cannabinoids in rats. *Toxicology and Applied Pharmacology* 25:373-390.

Thor, D.H.
1971 Amphetamine induced fighting during morphine withdrawal. *Journal of General Psychology* 84:245-250.

Thor, D.H., and B.G. Teel
1968 Fighting of rats during post-morphine withdrawal: Effect of prewithdrawal dosage. *American Journal of Psychology* 81:439-442.

Thor, D.H., M.H. Weisman, and S.C. Boshka
1967 Chemical suppression of fighting in the Siamese fighting fish. *Psychonomic Science* 9:161-162.

Thor, D.H., D.L. Hoats, and C.J. Thor
1970 Morphine induced fighting and prior social experience. *Psychonomic Science* 18:137-139.

Tidey, J.W., and K.A. Miczek
  1992 Morphine withdrawal aggression: Modification with D1 and D2 receptor agonists. *Psychopharmacology* 108:177-184.
Tinklenberg, J.R.
  1973 Alcohol and violence. Pp. 195-210 in P.G. Bourne and R. Fox, eds., *Alcoholism: Progress in Research and Treatment.* New York: Academic Press.
  1974 Marijuana and human aggression. Pp. 339-357 in L.L. Miller and W.G. Drew, eds., *Marijuana: Current Research.* New York: Academic Press.
Tinklenberg, J.R., and P. Murphy
  1972 Marihuana and crime: A survey report. *Journal of Psychedelic Drugs* 5:183-191.
Tinklenberg, J.R., and F.M. Ochberg
  1981 Patterns of adolescent violence: A California sample. Pp. 121-140 in D.A. Hamburg and M.B. Trudeau, eds., *Biobehavioral Aspects of Aggression.* New York: Alan R. Liss.
Tinklenberg, J.R., and R.C. Stillman
  1970 Drug use and violence. Pp. 327-365 in D.N. Daniels, M.F. Gilula, and F.M. Ochberg, eds., *Violence and the Struggle for Existence.* Boston: Little, Brown and Company.
Tinklenberg, J.R., and K.M. Woodrow
  1974 Drug use among youthful assaultive and sexual offenders. *Aggression* 52:209-224.
Tinklenberg, J.R., B.S. Kopell, W.T. Roth, and C.F. Darley
  1974a Drugs, delinquency, and aggression. *Psychopharmacology Bulletin* 10:62-63.
Tinklenberg, J.R., P.L. Murphy, P. Murphy, C.F. Darley, W.T. Roth, and B.S. Kopell
  1974b Drug involvement in criminal assaults by adolescents. *Archives of General Psychiatry* 30:685-689.
Tinklenberg, J.R., W.T. Roth, B.S. Kopell, and P. Murphy
  1976 Cannabis and alcohol effects in assaultiveness in adolescent delinquents. Pp. 85-94 in R.L. Dornbush, A.M. Freedman and M. Fink, eds., *Chronic Cannabis Use.* (Annals of the New York Academy of Sciences, Vol 282.) New York: New York Academy of Sciences.
Tinklenberg, J.R., P. Murphy, P.L. Murphy, and A. Pfefferbaum
  1981 Drugs and criminal assaults by adolescents: A replication study. Journal of *Psychoactive Drugs* 13:277-287.
Tomim, B., and A.G. Glenn
  1968 Psychotherapy with drug abusers in a male admitting service. *Psychiatric Quarterly* 42:144-155.
Tramill, J.L., P.E. Turner, D.A. Sisemore, and S.F. Davis
  1980 Hungry, drunk, and not real mad: The effects of alcohol injections on aggressive responding. *Bulletin of the Psychonomic Society* 15:339-341.

Tramill, J.L., A.L. Wesley, and S.F. Davis
  1981 The effects of chronic ethanol challenges on aggressive respond-
        ing in rats maintained on a semideprivation diet. *Bulletin of
        the Psychonomic Society* 17:51-52.
Tramill, J.L., K. Gustavson, M.S. Weaver, S.A. Moore, and S.F. Davis
  1983 Shock-elicited aggression as a function of acute and chronic
        ethanol challenges. *Journal of General Psychology* 109:53-58.
Tuason, V.B.
  1971 The psychiatrist and the violent patient. *Diseases of the Ner-
        vous System* 32:764-768.
Tyler, C.B., and K.A. Miczek
  1982 Effects of phencyclidine on aggressive behavior in mice. *Phar-
        macology Biochemistry and Behavior* 17:503-510.
Tyler, C.B., R.F. Schlemmer, Jr., N. Narasimhachari, and J.M. Davis
  1978 Behavioral changes induced by 2,5-dimethoxy 4-methyl-amphet-
        amine (DOM, STP) in primate dyads. *Communications in Psy-
        chopharmacology* 2:337-342.
Ueki, S., S. Murimoto, and N. Ogawa
  1972 Effects of psychotropic drugs on emotional behavior in rats with
        limbic lesions, with special reference to olfactory bulb abla-
        tions. *Folia Psychiatrica Neurologica Japonica* 26:246-255.
Uyeno, E.T.
  1966a Effects of *d*-lysergic acid diethylamide and 2-bromo-lysergic acid
        diethylamide on dominance behavior in the rat. *International
        Journal of Neuropharmacology* 5:317-322.
  1966b Inhibition of isolation-induced attack behavior of mice by drugs.
        Journal of Pharmaceutical Sciences 55:215-216.
  1967a Lysergic acid diethylamide and dominance behavior of the squirrel
        monkey. *Archives Internationales de Pharmacodynamie et de
        Therapie* 169:66-69.
  1967b Lysergic acid diethylamide and sexual dominance behavior of
        the male rat. *International Journal of Neuropsychiatry* 3:188-
        190.
  1972 Effects of 2,5-dimethoxy-4-methylamphetamine on the behav-
        ior of rats on competition for food. *International Pharmaco-
        psychiatry* 7:244-248.
  1976 Effects of Δ^9-tetrahydrocannabinol and 2,5-dimethoxy-4-methyl-
        amphetamine on rat sexual dominance behavior. *Proceedings
        of the Western Pharmacology Society* 19:369-372.
Uyeno, E.
  1978 Effects of psychodysleptics on aggressive behavior of animals.
        Pp. 103-113 in L. Valzelli, T. Ban, F.A. Freyhan and P. Pichot,
        eds., *Modern Problems of Pharmacopsychiatry: Psychopharma-
        cology of Aggression*. New York: S. Karger.
Uyeno, E.T., and W.M. Benson
  1965 Effects of lysergic acid diethylamide on attack behaviour of male
        albino mice. *Psychopharmacologia* 7:20-26.

Valzelli, L.
   1967   Drugs and aggressiveness. *Advances in Pharmacology* 5:79-108.
Valzelli, L., and S. Bernasconi
   1971   Differential activity of some psychotropic drugs as a function of emotional levels in animals. *Psychopharmacologia* 20:91-96.
Valzelli, L., E. Giacalone, and S. Garattini
   1967   Pharmacological control of aggressive behavior in mice. *European Journal of Pharmacology* 2:144-146.
Van Hasselt, V.B., R.L. Morrison, and A.S. Bellack
   1985   Alcohol use in wife abusers and their spouses. *Addictive Behaviors* 10:127-135.
Van Thiel, D.H., J.S. Gavaler, and R.E. Tarter
   1988   The effects of alcohol on sexual behavior and function. Pp. 478-498 in J.M.A. Sitsen, ed., *Handbook of Sexology*, Vol.6: *The Pharmacology of Endocrinology and Sexual Function*. Amsterdam: Elsevier Science Publishers.
Van Valkenburg, C., M. Lowry, G. Winokur, and R. Cadoret
   1977   Depression spectrum disease versus pure depressive disease: Clinical, personality, and course differences. *Journal of Nervous and Mental Disease* 165:341-347.
Van Valkenburg, C., H.S. Akiskal, and V. Puzantian
   1983   Depression spectrum disease or character spectrum disorder? A clinical study of major depressives with familial alcoholism or sociopathy. *Comprehensive Psychiatry* 24:589-595.
Virkkunen, M.
   1974a Alcohol as a factor precipitating aggression and conflict behaviour leading to homicide. *British Journal of Addiction* 69:149-154.
   1974b Incest offences and alcoholism. *Medicine, Science, and the Law* 14:124-128.
   1979   Alcoholism and antisocial personality. *Acta Psychiatrica Scandinavica* 59:493-501.
   1983   Serum cholesterol levels in homicidal offenders: A low cholesterol level is connected with a habitually violent tendency under the influence of alcohol. *Neuropsychobiology* 10:65-69.
Virkkunen, M., and E. Kallio
   1987   Low blood glucose nadir in the glucose test and homicidal spouse abuse. *Aggressive Behavior* 13:59-66.
Virkkunen, M., J. De Jong, J. Barko, F.K. Goodwin, and M. Linnoila
   1989a Relationship of psychobiological variables to recidivism in violent offenders and impulsive fire setters. *Archives of General Psychiatry* 46:600-603.
Virkkunen, M., J. De Jong, J. Bartko, and M. Linnoila
   1989b Psychobiological concomitants of history of suicide attempts among violent offenders and impulsive fire setters. *Archives of General Psychiatry* 46:604-606.

Vivian, J.A., and K.A. Miczek
  1991 Ultrasounds during morphine withdrawal in rats. *Psychopharmacology* 104:187-193.
Votava, Z.
  1969 Aggressive behavior evoked by LSD-25 in rats pretreated with reserpine. Pp. 236-237 in S. Garattini and E.B. Sigg, eds., *Aggressive Behaviour*. Amsterdam: Excerpta Medica Foundation.
Walaszek, E.J., and L.G. Abood
  1956 Effect of tranquilizing drugs on fighting response of Siamese fighting fish. *Science* 124:440-441.
Walker, D.L., and E.H. Gregory
  1985 Differential effect of alcohol on aggressive behavior in dominant and subordinate hamsters. *Psychological Reports* 56:275-282.
Waller, J.A., and E.B. Whorton
  1973 Unintentional shootings, highway crashes and acts of violence—A behavior paradigm. *Accident Analysis and Prevention* 5:351-356.
Walters, J.K., M.H. Sheard, and M. Davis
  1978 Effects of *N,N*-dimethyltryptamine (DMT) and 5-methoxy-*N,N*-dimethyltryptamine (5-MeODMT) on shock elicited fighting in rats. *Pharmacology Biochemistry and Behavior* 9:87-90.
Weerts, E.M., W. Tornatzky, and K.A. Miczek
  1993 Prevention of the proaggressive effects of alcohol by benzodiazepine receptor antagonists in rats and in squirrel monkeys. *Psychopharmacology* 111:144-152.
Weiss, N.S.
  1976 Recent trends in violent deaths among young adults in the United States. *American Journal of Epidemiology* 103:416-422.
Weitz, M.K.
  1974 Effects of ethanol on shock-elicited fighting behavior in rats. Quarterly *Journal of Studies on Alcohol* 35:953-958.
Welch, B.L., and A.S. Welch
  1969 Aggression and the biogenic amine neurohumors. Pp. 188-202 in S. Garattini and E.B. Sigg, eds., *Aggressive Behavior*. Amsterdam: Excerpta Medica Foundation.
Weller, R.A., and J.A. Halikas
  1985 Marijuana use and psychiatric illness: A follow-up study. *American Journal of Psychiatry* 142:848-850.
Westermeyer, J., and J. Brantner
  1972 Violent death and alcohol use among the Chippewa in Minnesota. *Minnesota Medicine* 55:749-752.
White, H.R., R.J. Pandina, and R.L. LaGrange
  1987 Longitudinal predictors of serious substance use and delinquency. *Criminology* 25:715-737.

Whitelock, P.R., J.E. Overall, and J.H. Patrick
   1971   Personality patterns and alcohol abuse in a state hospital popu-
          lation. *Journal of Abnormal Psychology* 78:9-16.
Whitters, A.C., R.J. Cadoret, and M.K. McCalley-Whitters
   1987   Further evidence for heterogeneity in antisocial alcoholics. *Com-
          prehensive Psychiatry* 28:513-519.
Wikler, A.
   1944   Studies on the action of morphine on the central nervous sys-
          tem of cat. *Journal of Pharmacology and Experimental Thera-
          peutics* 80:176-187.
Wilentz, W.C., and J.P. Brady
   1961   The alcohol factor in violent deaths. *American Practitioner
          Digest Treatment* 12:829-835.
Williams, J.S., and B.K. Singh
   1986   Alcohol use and antisocial experiences. *Advances in Alcohol
          and Substance Abuse* 6:65-75.
Williams, J.S., B.K. Singh, and J.H. McGrath III
   1985   Victims of firearms assaults: An empirical explanation. *Victimology*
          9:492-499.
Williams, L.N.
   1969   LSD and manslaughter. *Lancet* 9:332.
Williams, R.L., K.U. Gutsch, R. Kazelskis, J.P. Verstegen, and J. Scanlon
   1980   An investigation of relationships between level of alcohol use
          impairment and personality characteristics. *Addictive Behav-
          iors* 5:107-112.
Williams, T.A., G. Calhoun, and R.L. Ackoff
   1982   Stress, alcoholism, and personality. *Human Relations* 35:491-
          510.
Wilmot, C.A., C. Vanderwende, and M.T. Spoerlein
   1987   The effects of phencyclidine on fighting in differentially housed
          mice. *Pharmacology Biochemistry and Behavior* 28:341-346.
Wilson, E.O.
   1975   *Sociobiology.* Cambridge: Belknap Press.
Winn, M., D. Arendsen, P. Dodge, A. Dren, D. Dunnigan, R. Hallas, K.
Hwang, J. Kyncl, Y.H. Lee, N. Plotnikoff, P. Young, and H. Zaugg
   1976   Drugs derived from cannabinoids. 5. $\Delta^{6a,10a}$-Tetrahydrocannab-
          inol and heterocyclic analogs containing aromatic side chains.
          Journal of Medicinal Chemistry 19:461-471.
Winsberg, B.G., I. Bialer, S. Kupietz, and J. Tobias
   1972   Effects of imipramine and dextroamphetamine on behavior of
          neuropsychiatrically impaired children. *American Journal of
          Psychiatry* 128:1425-1431.
Winslow, J.T., and K.A. Miczek
   1983   Habituation of aggression in mice: Pharmacological evidence of
          catecholaminergic and serotonergic mediation. *Psychopharma-
          cology* 81:286-291.
   1985   Social status as determinant of alcohol effects on aggressive

behavior in squirrel monkeys (*Saimiri sciureus*). *Psychopharmacology* 85:167-172.

1988　Androgen dependency of alcohol effects on aggressive behavior: A seasonal rhythm in high-ranking squirrel monkeys. *Psychopharmacology* 95:92-98.

Winslow, J.T., J. Ellingboe, and K.A. Miczek
1988　Effects of alcohol on aggressive behavior in squirrel monkeys: Influence of testosterone and social context. *Psychopharmacology* 95:356-363.

Wolf, A.S.
1984　Alcohol and violence in the Alaskan native: A follow-up and theoretical considerations. *Alcoholism Treatment Quarterly* 1:133-138.

Wolfgang, M.E., and R.B. Strohm
1956　The relationship between alcohol and criminal homicide. *Quarterly Journal of Studies on Alcohol* 17:411-425.

Woodruff, R.A., S.B. Guze, and P.J. Clayton
1971　The medical and psychiatric implications of antisocial personality (sociopathy). *Diseases of the Nervous System* 32:712-714.

Woodruff, R.A. Jr, S.B. Guze, P.J. Clayton, and D. Carr
1973　Alcoholism and depression. *Archives of General Psychiatry* 28:97-100.

Woods, J.
1977　Behavioral effects of cocaine in animals. Pp. 63-95 in R.C. Petersen and R.C. Stillman, eds., *Cocaine 1977*. NIDA Research Monograph Series, Vol. 13. Rockville, Md.: National Institute on Drug Abuse.

Woody, G.E., H. Persky, A.T. McLellan, C.P. O'Brien, and I. Arndt
1983　Psychoendocrine correlates of hostility and anxiety in addicts. Pp. 227-244 in E. Gottheil, K.A. Druley, T.E. Skoloda and H.M. Waxman, eds., Alcohol, *Drug Abuse and Aggression*. Springfield, Ill.: Charles C. Thomas.

Wormith, J.S., J.M.W. Bradford, A. Pawlak, M. Borzecki, and A. Zohar
1988　The assessment of deviant sexual arousal as a function of intelligence, instructional set and alcohol ingestion. *Canadian Journal of Psychiatry* 33:800-808.

Wright, H.H.
1980　Violence and PCP abuse. *American Journal of Psychiatry* 137:752-753.

Wurmser, L.
1974　Psychoanalytic considerations of the etiology of compulsive drug use. *Journal of the American Medical Association* 22:820-843.

Yanai, J., and B.E. Ginsburg
1976　Long-term effects of early ethanol on predatory behavior in inbred mice. *Physiological Psychology* 4:409-411.

1977　Long-term reduction of male agonistic behavior in mice following early exposure to ethanol. *Psychopharmacology* 52:31-34.

Yanai, J., B.E. Ginsburg, and B. Vinopal
1976   Comparison of early effects of ethanol on agonistic behavior in inbred strains of mice. *Behavioral Genetics* 6:122-123.

Yates, W.R., W. Meller, and E.P. Troughton
1987   Behavioral complications of alcoholism. *A.F.P.* 35:171-175.

Yates, W.R., F. Petty, and K. Brown
1988   Alcoholism in males with antisocial personality disorder. *International Journal of the Addictions* 23:999-1010.

Yen, H.C.Y., M.H. Katz, and S. Krop
1970   Effects of various drugs on 3,4-dihydroxyphenylalanine (DL-DOPA)-induced excitation (aggressive behavior) in mice. *Toxicology and Applied Pharmacology* 17:597-604.

Yesavage, J.A., and V. Zarcone
1990   History of drug abuse and dangerous behavior in inpatient schizophrenics. *Journal of Clinical Psychiatry* 13:3-5.

Yoshimura, H., and K.A. Miczek
1983   Separate neural sites for *d*-amphetamine suppression of mouse killing and feeding behavior in rats. *Aggressive Behavior* 9:353-363.

Yoshimura, H., and N. Ogawa
1983   Pharmaco-ethological analysis of agonistic behavior between resident and intruder mice: Effects of ethyl alcohol. *Folia Pharmacologica Japonica* 81:135-141.

Yoshimura, H., M. Fujiwara, and S. Ueki
1974   Biochemical correlates in mouse-killing behavior of the rat: Brain acetylcholine and acetylcholinesterase after administration of Δ^9-tetrahydrocannabinol. *Brain Research* 81:567-570.

Zagrodzka, J., and T. Jurkowski
1988   Changes in the aggressive behavior of cats treated with amphetamine. *International Journal of Neuroscience* 41:287-296.

Zeichner, A., and R.O. Pihl
1978   Effects of alcohol and behavior contingencies on human aggression. *Journal of Abnormal Psychology* 88:153-160.
1980   Effects of alcohol and instigator intent on human aggression. *Journal of Studies on Alcohol* 41:265-276.

Zeichner, A., R.O. Pihl, R. Niaura, and C. Zacchia
1982   Attentional processes in alcohol-mediated aggression. *Journal of Studies on Alcohol* 43:714-74.

Zeichner, A., R.O. Pihl, R. Niaura, and C. Zachia
1982   Attentional processes in alcohol-mediated aggression. *Journal of Studies on Alcohol* 43:714-724.

TABLE 1 Major Experimental Models of Aggression in Laboratory Animals

Model and Species	Procedure	Behavioral Topography	Biological Function
A. Aversive environmental manipulations			
Isolation-induced aggression, mostly in mice	Isolated housing before confrontation with another isolate or group-housed animal	Complete agonistic behavior pattern: isolates attack, threaten, pursue opponent	Territorial defense or compulsive, abnormal, pathological behavior
Pain-elicited or shock-induced aggression, mostly in rats, also in monkeys	Pairs of animals are exposed to pulses of electric shock delivered through grid floor or to the tail	Defensive reactions, including upright postures, bites toward face of opponent, audible vocalizations; bites toward inanimate targets	Some similarity to reaction toward predator or toward large opponent
Aggression due to omission of reward, mostly in pigeons, also in monkeys	Conditioning history; schedule-controlled operant behavior; omitted or infrequent reinforcement	Attack bites or pecks, threat displays towards suitable object or conspecific	Competition for resources such as food, sex, protected niches (?)
B. Brain manipulations			
Brain lesion-induced aggression, mostly in rats, also in cats	Destruction of neural tissue, and subsequent social or environmental challenges	Defensive reactions, biting	Neurological disease
Brain stimulation-induced aggression, mostly in cats, also in rats	Electrical excitation of tissue in diencephalon and mesencephalon, also in other limbic or cerebellar areas	(1) Defensive reactions accompanied by autonomic arousal	Defense against attacker
		(2) Predatory attack and killing	Predation
C. Ethological situations			
Aggression by resident toward intruder, in most species and in both sexes	Confrontation with an unfamiliar adult member of the species	Full repertoire of agonistic behavior (attack and threat vs. defense, submission, and flight)	Territorial or group defense (?); rivalry among males and among females
Female aggression, mostly in maternal rodents	Lactating female, in the presence of litter, confronting an intruder male	Species-specific repertoire of attack and threat behavior toward intruder	Defense of young, competition for resources and territory

469

Dominance-related aggression, mostly in monkeys, mice, and rats	Formation or maintenance of a social group	Species-specific repertoire of signals (displays, sounds, odors) between group members of different social rank; low level and intensity of agonism	Social cohesion and dispersion

D. Killing

Muricide, mostly in rats, cats	Presence of prey, food deprivation	Stalking, seizing, killing, sometimes consuming prey	Food source; "killer instinct"

Source: Adapted from Miczek and DeBold (1983).

470

Table 2A: Effects of acute alcohol on aggression in animals

References	Methods and Procedures	Results and Conclusions
Isolation-induced aggression		
Chamove and Harlow, 1970	Self-directed aggression in rhesus monkeys self administering ethanol	Biting and slapping increased proportional to the amount of ethanol consumed until sedation was observed; High doses reduced self mutilative behavior.
Chance et al. 1973 Krsiak, 1976 Yoshimura and Ogawa, 1983 Lister and Hilakivi, 1988	Single-housed male mice confront group-housed intruder in home cage	A low ETOH dose (0.4-0.5 g/kg, i.p.) increased compound measure of "aggression"; Higher ETOH doses produced sedation and reduced aggression.
Lagerspetz and Ekqvist 1978 Smoothy et al. 1982 Smoothy and Berry 1983	Single-housed male mice confronted group-housed intruder in home cage	ETOH (1-12 g/kg, i.p) decreased aggression and produced sedation.
Smoothy et al., 1983	Aggression in pairs of isolated male mice	ETOH (0.5-2.0 g/kg) dose dependently reduced time spent in agonistic behaviors and increased flight/defensive behaviors.
Benton and Smoothy, 1984	Aggression in pairs of ETOH-treated male mice	ETOH (0.5-2.0 g/kg) reduced aggressive behavior in resident-intruder confrontations.
Pain-induced Aggression and Defense		
Irwin et al. 1971	Electric foot shock in pairs of male mice	ETOH (1-4.8 g/kg, i.p., p.o.) decreased defensive attacks.
Weitz 1974 Tramill et al. 1980, 1983 Bammer and Eichelman 1983	Electric foot shock in pairs of male rats	A low ETOH dose (0.6 g/kg, i.p.; 1.97 g/kg/day, i.p.) increased defensive aggression; Higher ETOH doses decreased it.
Al Hazmi and Brain, 1984 Smoothy and Berry 1984	Restraint-induced attack in single-housed mice	ETOH (0.125-2.0 g/kg) dose dependently reduced target biting; 1.0 g/kg increased latency to first bite.

Defensive Aggression Induced by Electrical Brain Stimulation

Reference	Model	Findings
MacDonnell et al., 1971	Electrical brain stimulation in corticomedial or basomedial portion of the amygdala in female cats faced with an untreated stimulus cat	Low dose ETOH (0.37 g/kg) reduced the latency of "hissing" at the stimulus cat, whereas a higher dose (1.5 g/kg) prolonged hissing latencies.
Ruusunen et al., 1975	Electrical brain stimulation in cats	ETOH (1.5 g/kg) reduced defensive behaviors, where as lower doses (0.25-1.0 g/kg) did not alter behavior significantly.

Aggression by Resident toward Intruder

Reference	Model	Findings
Ellman et al., 1972	Resident cichlid fish confronted intruder protected inside clear tube	0.18% ETOH in aquarium water increased aggressive displays and bites, whereas 0.34% ETOH reduced these behaviors.
Peeke et al., 1973 Peeke et al., 1975 Peeke and Figler, 1981	Resident cichlid fish confronted intruder protected inside clear tube	0.15-0.18% ETOH increased attacks and reduced the duration of threats, whereas 0.30-0.33% prolonged threats and reduced attacks.
Raynes et al., 1968 Raynes and Ryback, 1970 Galizio et al., 1985	Aggressive displays of Siamese fighting fish directed at mirror image	Low dose ETOH 0.25-29% increased aggressive displays; Higher doses (0.50%-0.75%) reduced displays.
Krsiak and Borgesova, 1973	Interactions between pairs of familiar male rats	ETOH (1.2-3.0 g/kg) reduced aggressive interactions.
Bertilson et al., 1977	Territorial aggression in pairs of male mice	ETOH (10-30%) dose dependently reduced aggression-prompted squeals, presumably by the targets of attack bites.
Miczek and O'Donnell, 1980	Resident male mice confront group-housed intruder in neutral and home cages	In the neutral environment, low doses of ETOH (0.1-0.5 g/kg, p.o.) increased attack and threat behaviors whereas higher doses reduced these behaviors.
DeBold and Miczek, 1985	Confrontations between castrated, testosterone treated residents vs. intact intruder mice	ETOH (3.0 g/kg) reduced aggression in intact males, whereas animals treated with a high dose of testosterone showed altered ETOH response; Specifically, 1.0-1.7 g/kg increased attacks and threats and a higher dose (5.6 g/kg) was required to suppress aggression.

Reference	Paradigm	Results
Blanchard et al., 1987b	Resident male rats grouped according to baseline aggressive levels confront male intruder	ETOH (0.3-0.6 g/kg) increased frequency and duration of attack and threat postures in low to moderately aggressive animals, but not in highly aggressive animals; High dose (1.2 g/kg) ETOH reduced aggression in all animals.
Everill and Berry, 1987	Resident male mice of C57, DBA and BALB strains confronted group-housed intruders	ETOH (1.0 g/kg, i.p.) reduced aggression in isolated DBA mice, and increased defensive flight behavior in C57 and BALB mice; A low dose (0.5 g/kg) did not alter aggression in any strain.
Mos and Olivier, 1988	Group-housed (2 male, 2 female) resident rats confronted with naive male intruder	ETOH (2.0 mg/kg) reduced aggression in the dominant animal; Low doses (0.5-1.0 g/kg) did not enhance aggression.
Lisciotto et al., 1990	Confrontations between neonatally gonadectomized and androgenized residents and intact intruder mice	ETOH (1.0 g/kg) increased attacks in sham-gonadectomized males, with no suppression at 3.0 g/kg; Androgenized females and neonatally gonadectomized males only showed a suppression of aggression at 3.0 g/kg ETOH.
Miczek et al., in press	Confrontations between socially housed resident male rats vs. naive single-housed intruder male rats	ETOH (0.1-1.0 g/kg) increased aggressive threats and attack bites in a subgroup of animals while suppressing these behaviors in other animals; high doses (1.7-3.0 g/kg) supressed aggression in all animals. Sequential analysis indicated that once initiated, the attack sequence was preserved regardless of dose. In animals that showed enhanced aggression, low doses increased time spent in and number of elements within aggressive "bursts". Pro-aggressive effects of ETOH suggested to prevent termination of an aggressive sequence rather than alteration in initiation of these behaviors.

Female Aggression

Smoothy et al., 1986	Confrontations between singly-housed lactating female resident and group-housed male intruders	ETOH (0.5-2.0 g/kg) did not alter the duration of time spent in aggression except, at the highest dose, duration of aggression decreased.

473

Reference	Behavior	Effect
Blanchard et al., 1987a	Resident female rats confronted male intruders of different sizes	ETOH (0.3 g/kg) increased attacks by female residents towards male intruders; Smaller intruders were attacked more often than larger opponents.

Dominance-related Aggression

Reference	Behavior	Effect
Crowley et al., 1974	Aggression in group-housed pig-tailed macaques	ETOH (0.5-2.0 g/kg) did not alter aggressive behaviors, but 2.0 g/kg increased "playful" (non-injurious) fighting.
Miczek and Barry, 1977	Aggression by male rats during food competition	A low dose (0.5 g/kg) ETOH increased aggressive behavior in dominant rats but not in subordinate male rats.
Pettijohn, 1979	Aggressive displays in male and female Telomian dogs competing for food	ETOH (0.8 g/kg) increased the frequency of attacks in subordinate dogs but reduced attacks in higher ranking dogs; 1.6 g/kg ETOH reduced attacks in all dogs.
Miczek et al., 1984 Winslow and Miczek, 1985 Winslow and Miczek, 1988	Aggression in squirrel monkeys toward group members of both sexes	Low doses of ethanol (0.1-0.3 g/kg, p.o.) increased aggressive threats by dominant males, whereas higher doses (0.6-1.0 g/kg) reduced them; Subordinate males treated with higher doses of ETOH received more threats from untreated group members.
Walker and Gregory, 1985	Aggression in pairs of male hamsters	Dominant males treated with ETOH (2.0 g/kg) reduced incidence of fighting, whereas when subordinates were treated with the same dose, fighting remained at control levels.
Blanchard et al., 1987c	Aggression in male and female during group formation in rats	Female rats were attacked more frequently than males by males treated with ETOH (0.3-1.2 g/kg).
Winslow et al., 1988	Aggression in testosterone-treated male squirrel monkeys towards group members of both sexes	Low doses (0.1-0.3 g/kg) ETOH increased aggressive displays in testosterone-treated dominant males, but not in subordinate males.

Killing

Reference	Behavior	Effect
MacDonnell and Ehmer, 1969	"Quiet biting" attack elicited by electrical brain stimulation of hypothalamus in cats	ETOH (0.37-1.5 g/kg) dose dependently increased latency to attack, but increased force of biting.

Ingle, 1973

Attacks in frogs presented with simulated prey or dummy "worm"

Frogs placed in ETOH (400 mg/100 ml for 2-2.5 hrs) consistently struck at moving dummy "worms" whereas control frogs habituated to the test.

TABLE 2B Effects of Chronic Alcohol on Aggression in Animals

References	Methods and Procedures	Results and Conclusions
Pain-induced Aggression and Defense		
Tramill et al., 1980	ETOH (0.25-0.75 ml/100 g of 30%/15 days) in restrained, food deprived male rats exposed to electrical foot shock	Low to moderate dose ETOH (0.25-0.5 ml/100 g of 30%) increased target biting, whereas a higher dose (0.75 ml/100 g of 30% ETOH) reduced the biting response.
Tramill et al., 1983	Chronic (15 days) and acute ETOH-treated (0.25 ml/100 g of 30%, i.p.) restrained male rats exposed to electrical foot shock	Chronic ETOH treated rats had higher rates of target biting than acute ETOH treated or control rats.
Means et al., 1984	Male offspring of female rats treated with ETOH (14.08 g/kg/day) throughout pregnancy exposed to electrical foot shock as adults; Both animals treated	Prenatal exposure to ETOH did not alter aggressive behavior when tested as adults.
Aggression Induced by Omission of Reward		
Nelson, 1967	Pairs of male rats trained to traverse runway on a 50% or 100% reinforcement schedule treated with ETOH (1.2 g/kg/day for 30 days) and confronted another subject at the goal box	ETOH-treated animals showed less aggression compared to dextrose-treated animals; when treatment groups were reversed, ETOH reduced aggression in highly aggressive dextrose-treated animals.
Drug-Induced Aggression		
Pucilowski et al., 1987	20% ETOH administered for 3 weeks in pairs of male rats treated with apomorphine (10.0 mg/kg)	ETOH increased aggressive postures and vocalizations, but did not alter attacks.
Aggression by Resident Towards Intruder		
Cutler et al., 1975	5% ETOH administered for 10 days in male mice housed in compartments of same cage of group-housed	ETOH given before establishment of territory resulted in the alcohol treated mouse expanding its territory to the entire area; No effect was seen if ETOH was given after the territories were established.

Reference	Method	Results
Cutler, 1976	Interactions in a neutral cage between ETOH-treated (8% for 3 weeks) and untreated group-housed mice	Defensive and flight behaviors were increased following cessation of alcohol administration.
Yanai and Ginsberg, 1976	Conspecific directed aggression in male offspring of C57 and DBA mice fed ETOH (10%) from 28 days of age through pregnancy and/or 14 days post parturition	DBA and C57 offspring had longer latencies to attack and a reduction in fighting; Time spent fighting was reduced by ETOH postnatal exposure and by both prenatal and postnatal exposure.
Ewart and Cutler, 1979	Conspecific directed aggression in offspring of CFW mice fed ETOH (5%) through pregnancy and 3 weeks post parturition	Frequency and duration of social interactions were reduced and defensive/flight behaviors were increased by prenatal and postnatal ETOH exposure.
Peterson et al., 1988 Peterson and Pohorecky, 1989	24 hour observations of confrontations between untreated resident male rats with ETOH-treated intruders (1.0-2.0 g/kg 3 x day), and ETOH-treated residents (1.0-1.5 g/kg 3 x day) with untreated intruders; All animals were implanted with gastric and jugular catheters	ETOH-treated intruders received more threats and displayed an increase in defensive freezing in the first 20 minutes of testing. Blood corticosterone and epinephrine of ETOH-treated intruders were increased (338% and 129%, respectively) 20 minutes into the test and remained elevated (98% and 107%) 24 hours into the test; ETOH-treated residents wounded untreated intruders more severely and shifted point of attack from upper back to lower back and hind quarters. Blood norepinephrine levels were increased in residents (216%) and remained elevated 24 hours into testing.

Female Aggression

Tamimie, 1968	5-10 ml/kg of 33 % ETOH administered 2 x day and once nightly in White rock hens	More chicks were killed, stamped, and pecked by water treated hens than hens treated with ETOH.

Dominance-Related Aggression

Cressman and Cadell, 1971	Social interactions in juvenile rhesus monkeys during self administration of ETOH (2-7%) for 21 days	Mauling, biting and wrestling play behaviors increased in proportion to amount of ETOH consumed and time course of the drug.
Meinecke and Cherkin, 1972	Pairs of pit gamecocks treated with 10-30 ml/kg of 33% ETOH	ETOH did not alter attack latencies or fighting.

477

| Ellison et al., 1979 | Control and monoamine neurotoxin-treated (6-OHDA) group-housed and isolated male rats treated with ETOH (10% for 25 days) | Group-housed rats showed a delayed preference for ETOH concurrent with increased fighting and deterioration of the dominance hierarchy; Isolated rats did not show this effect. |
| Blanchard et al., 1987d | Group-housed male and female rats self administered 8% ETOH | ETOH reduced "composite" of aggression by dominant males; Subordinate males consumed more alcohol than dominants, and females consumed more than males. |

Killing

Kovach, 1967	9 ml/kg of 33% ETOH administered for 5 days in domestic cocks	ETOH treated cocks sheltered and defended chicks, whereas control cocks attacked and actively killed chicks.
Yanai et al., 1976 Yanai and Ginsburg, 1977	Predatory aggression in offspring of C57 and DBA mice fed ETOH (10 %) from 28 days of age through pregnancy and/or parturition	DBA offspring with postnatal exposure to ETOH showed a 58% reduction in predation.
Molina et al., 1985	Isolated male rats treated with ETOH (11.5 g/kg/day for 1 mo.); tested with a mouse one day after ETOH withdrawal	One day of withdrawal from ETOH increased the percentage of rats displaying mouse killing behavior.

478

Table 3 Effects of Alcohol on Aggression and Violence in Humans

References	Methods and Procedures	Results and Conclusions
Criminal Violence		
Shupe, 1954	Urine analysis for ethanol in 42 men arrested for rape in Ohio.	50% of rapists had ethanol in urine at time of arrest.
Wolfgang and Strohm, 1956	Review of Philadelphia police homicide records 1948-52.	Alcohol was involved in 64% of 588 homicides, 44% of the time in both victim and offender.
McCaldon, 1967	Psychiatric interviews and MMPI of 30 prisoners convicted of rape.	10% of rapists reported they were drunk, 53% were drinking at the time and for 6% the primary diagnosis was alcoholic.
Scott, 1968	Psychiatric interviews with 50 male murderers from British prisons.	10% of the murderers were alcoholics, 22% were intoxicated during crime.
Guze et al., 1968	Psychiatric interviews of 260 first degree relatives of convicted felons.	The authors found a high proportion of the male relatives of convicted felons were alcoholic (33%) and that 53% of these alcoholic relatives had histories of excessive fighting and 21% had a felony conviction of their own. This compared to 6% in nonalcoholic relatives.
Jenkins, 1968	Analysis of records of 1500 children examined at Institute for Juvenile Research, Chicago.	The fathers of children whose records showed stealing (215) were more likely to be classified as alcoholic than those of overanxious or hostile, disobedient children.
Selzer, 1971	Validation of Michigan Alcoholism Screening Test (MAST) with driving under the influence and drunk and disorderly arrestees.	Over 50% of DUI and D and D arrestees scored in the alcoholic range on the MAST.
Tuason, 1971	Interview of 30 mental patients selected for a history of assault or harmful acts of violence.	40% of the violent patients were chronic alcoholics and 20% were problem drinkers.

479

Study	Method	Findings
Gunn, 1972	Interviews and medical records of prisoners in the UK, comparing 155 epileptic and control prisoners.	Both groups were similar in the incidence of alcoholism (15-17%) and violence, although alcoholics more often had a history of arrests for violent crimes.
Szymusik, 1972	Psychiatric interviews with 50 male deliberate murderers from Polish prison.	60% had history of "heavy" drinking, 12% were intoxicated during crime.
Waller and Whorton, 1973	Analysis of the DMV driving records of 62 people who "unintentionally" shot someone in Vermont in 1967 compared to the records of controls.	21% of the shooters had records of arrests involving alcohol compared to 5% of drivers not involved in shootings.
Hart-Hansen and Bjarnason, 1974	Review of records on all 21 homicides occurring in Iceland 1946-70.	In 77% of incidents the murderer was under the influence of alcohol, 7 of the victims were also.
Tinklenberg et al., 1974	Interviews with 50 physically assaultive and 80 nonassaultive adolescent offenders at California Youth Authority and review of medical and police records.	Alcohol or secobarbital were being used at the time of offense in 64% of the assaults, however the nonassaultive group used more drugs.
Virkkunen, 1974a	Autopsy and court records for 116 homicides in Helsinki 1963-68.	Alcohol was present in victim or murderer in 79% of cases, generally in both. Alcohol was particularly associated with homicides preceded by an altercation.
Virkkunen, 1974b	Analysis of case histories of 45 men examined at the Psychiatric Clinic of Helsinki University (1945-72) who had committed incest.	49% were alcoholic and of the alcoholics 77% had committed previous crimes and 88% were reported to have exhibited violence in the home.
Medhus, 1975	Follow-up of 71 female alcoholics who had undergone compulsory treatment by the Temperance Board in Malmo, Sweden, 1961-68.	38 probands committed 88 criminal offences through 1970. However, there was no higher rate of violent crime in these individuals than committed by Swedish women in general.
Rada, 1975	Analysis of autobiographies written by 77 convicted rapists as part of their treatment at Atascadero State Hospital in California.	35% of rapists were alcoholic and 50% were drinking at the time of commission (43% drunk).
Sobell and Sobell, 1975	Public opinion poll of 50 randomly selected Orange County, California respondents (29% refusal rate).	Respondents felt that the alcoholic who commits a violent crime while drunk should receive a more severe penalty than a non-alcoholic in the same circumstance.

Solursh, 1975	Analysis of 19 criminal cases seen in a private psychiatric practice.	Significant quantities of alcohol were reported in association with 6 of the 7 homicides in this sample.
Henn et al., 1976	Review of mental health records for 67 rapists.	In 4.3% the primary psychiatric diagnosis was drug or alcohol abuse, but it was the predominant secondary diagnosis.
Mayfield, 1976	Interviews with 307 new prisoners convicted of violent crime in North Carolina.	57% were drinking at the time and 36% were problem drinkers. Only 17% of the victims were strangers.
Petrich, 1976	Interviews of 96 felons given psychiatric referrals in Seattle jail.	26% of men and 30% of women prisoners were diagnosed as alcoholic.
Roslund and Larson, 1979	Psychiatric examination of 16 mentally disturbed men who had committed violent crimes in Sweden.	In 9 of the 16 alcoholism or habitual heavy drinking was part of the diagnosis and all but one was intoxicated during the crime. The authors suggest that alcohol weakened self-control and triggered violence.
Browning and Boatman, 1977	Analysis of case histories of 14 incest victims seen at the Child Psychiatry Clinic of University of Oregon.	50% of the fathers or uncles involved were alcoholics and many were described as prone to violence.
Hanks and Rosenbaum, 1977	Interviews with 22 repeatedly battered women and their alcohol-abusing male partners during counseling.	Identifies 3 clusters of family backgrounds differing in terms of parental style toward these women as children.
Grunberg et al., 1978	Analysis of court records of all convicted murderers (48) in Albany County, NY 1963-75.	Alcohol was involved in the crime 54% of the time.
Johnson et al., 1978	Review of Police files of 217 rapes in Winnipeg 1966-75.	Alcohol was involved in 72% of rapes (only the victim in 9%, only the offender in 24%).
Rada et al., 1978	Questionnaires given to 382 sex offenders, including 122 rapists.	57% of rapists were drinking at the time of rape and 48% were alcoholics. Similar data for child molesters, exhibitionists and incest offenders.
Sorrells, 1979	29 male juvenile offenders (murder) diagnosed as anxious or depressed with some being hostile and explosive.	1/4 of the homicides were committed when the assailant was intoxicated.

481

Reference	Method	Findings
Barnard et al., 1979	Psychiatric interviews with 88 men arrested for rape.	65% had been drinking, 34% heavily, at the time of the rape. 27% were alcoholics and for the alcoholics the victim was usually an acquaintance or relative.
Martin et al., 1979	Interviews of 66 female felons from Missouri State Board of Probation 1969 and follow-up of 42, 5 years later.	47% diagnosed as alcoholic in 1969, 33% in 1974. Higher rates than the normal female population.
Bloom, 1980	Psychiatric interviews of 30 native and 27 non-native Alaskans on trial for murder.	83% of the native Alaskans and 56% of non-native subjects had been drinking just before the homicide.
Enos and Beyer, 1980	Case studies of rapes by alcoholics who were infertile due to the alcoholism.	Chronic alcohol abuse can cause aspermia.
Lester, 1980	Comparison of data on alcohol consumption and homicide and suicide rates in US 1940-73.	Suicide, but not murder, rates were highest in states with highest per capita alcohol consumption.
Tardiff and Sweillam, 1980	Psychiatric records of 5233 male and 4132 female patients in Long Island, NY mental hospitals.	21% of patients had histories of assaults or suicide attempts, but there was less alcohol abuse in these patients than in the non-violent patients.
Elliot-Harper and Harper, 1981	Gave a modified MAST to 16 criminal psychiatric patients, 16 psychiatry patients, 16 alcoholic patients and 16 surgical patients.	Both psychiatric groups showed more alcohol related problems than the medical patients but fewer than the alcoholics in for detoxification.
Heather, 1981	Questionnaire to 200 young (16-21) Scottish offenders.	63% had committed their crime under the influence of alcohol, however, the number of violent crimes was not different between drunk and sober offenders.
Rosenbaum and O'Leary, 1981	Level of physical abuse, marital adjustment and alcoholism of spouse assessed in 52 abused wives and 20 control women in NY.	Alcoholism was most common in husbands of physically abused wives, less common in non-violent, maritally discordant couples and least common in control couples.
Tinklenberg and Ochberg, 1981	Police records of and interviews with 95 male adolescents convicted of homicide or assault with a deadly weapon.	Alcohol alone or in combination with other drugs was involved in 61% of the crimes.

Eberle, 1982	Interviews with 390 battered women in Denver and Discriminate Analysis of violence and alcohol abuse by the batterer in 4 episodes.	Alcohol abuse by the batterer predicted more severe injuries to woman and more likely abuse of children. In addition alcohol abuse by the batterer was frequently associated with the victim's use of alcohol.
Myers, 1982	Analysis of self report, police records, reports from wives or cohabitants, and victims for 50 violent Scottish prisoners and 50 control prisoners.	Violent offenders were more likely to have consumed alcohol at the time of the offence than non-violent offenders.
Bohman, 1983	Follow-up of all illegitimate births in Stockholm 1930-49 and later adopted. Correlational analysis of alcohol abuse, arrests, occupation and socio-economic status with biological and adoptive parents.	Found genetic as well as environmental factors in alcohol abuse and criminality. When alcohol abuse and criminality co-occurred the crime was often repetitive and violent.
Corenblum, 1983	A.A. members, assigning responsibility to fictional abusing and abused spouses that were intoxicated or sober; Self report of histories.	Subjects who abused their spouses when intoxicated were not likely to do so when sober. Subjects assigned blame to fictional characters in relation to their situation (i.e. victims assigned blame to victims).
Holcomb and Anderson, 1983	Analysis of pretrial evaluations of 110 men charged with 1° murder (police reports, histories, medical records).	24% of the offenders were drinking at the time the offense occurred; correlations for history of alcohol abuse.
Rada et al., 1983	44 subjects were selected from a pool of 150 child molesters and rapists from a program for the treatment of mentally disordered offenders in California. Criteria for inclusion in the study were that the offender acted alone, that the offense was either brutally violent or non-violent, and that victims were over 18 for rapists or under 13 for child molestors.	55% of rapists (total n=18) and 46% of child molesters (total n=26) were intoxicated at the time the offense occurred. Violent rapists and child molesters were more likely to be intoxicated at the time of the offense than their non-violent counterparts
Bradford and McLean, 1984	Psychiatric interviews of 50 men charged with sex offenses, 20 of whom inflicted serious physical injury.	A high level of violence was correlated with a history of alcohol abuse and dependency. There was no relationship with testosterone level.

483

Hechtman et al., 1984	10 year psychiatric follow up of 75 hyperactive subjects (90% male) originally referred to Montreal Children's Hospital and 44 from local schools.	More hyperactives described as alcohol abusers and had a period of heavy drinking. Aggression was described as a problem in 55% of hyperactives vs 31% of controls and 47% vs 32% had been in court (types of offences not different and authors do not relate crime to alcohol use).
Heller and Ehrlich, 1984	Analysis of pre-sentence psychiatric reports randomly selected from 9600 done in 1966-83 in Philadelphia. Includes 431 non-violent offenders, 779 violent offenders and 315 violent recidivists.	Alcohol abuse and having alcohol-related prior convictions were more common among violent offenders and violent recidivists.
Roberts, 1987	Analysis of legal records on 234 men charged with battering wife (or cohabitant) in Indianapolis 1984-1985.	60% of the battered women reported that the abuser was under the influence of alcohol at the time and 21.8% used both alcohol and drugs.
Schuckit and Russell, 1984	Psychiatric interviews and background analysis of 275 male primary alcoholics in treatment at San Diego V.A.	29% of primary alcoholics had a violent history, including having used weapons in fights and inflicting injuries requiring medical attention.
Telch and Lindquist, 1984	Questionnaires to 19 violent couples (wife battering), 24 nonviolent but in counseling couples and 24 matched happy couples.	Significantly more drinking problems in couples with wife abuse.
Abel and Zeidenberg, 1985 Abel et al., 1985	Analysis of violent deaths and BAC from medical examiners files over a ten year period.	Alcohol (10-100 mg/dl or greater) was involved in all major categories of violent death ranging from homicides to traffic accidents.
Campion et al., 1985	15 case studies of men admitted to Bellevue who murdered their mothers.	4 of 15 had histories of alcohol abuse.
Kratcoski, 1985	Questionnaire on experience with violence (among other items) was given to 305 youths (75% male) in high school or a juvenile justice center.	Violence against parents was highest (43%) in families characterized as having a low integration level. The authors mention that the case records for these youths frequently include accounts of alcohol and drug abuse.

484

Kroll et al., 1985	Compared histories of 31 alcoholics severely physically abused as children with 21 age-matched nonabused alcoholics all from Ann Arbor V.A.	83% of the abuse was by alcoholic fathers and the abused alcoholic was about 10x more likely to have been involved in adult domestic violence (56% vs 6%), property destruction (48% vs 3%), legal difficulties (48% vs 0) and suicide attempts (23% vs 3%).
Leonard et al., 1985	Self report and family interview for 484 blue-collar men.	No direct correlation for alcohol consumption and fighting, but physical marital conflict was correlated with alcohol misuse or dependence (DSM III).
Van Hasselt et al., 1985	Questionnaires, including MAST, given to 26 couples referred because of wife abuse, 26 maritally discordant but non-violent couples and 15 happy couples.	Husbands that physically abused their wives had higher MAST scores (17.0 vs 3.5 & 4.6). No increase in problem drinking by the wives.
Haver, 1986	Follow-up interviews of 44 Norwegian women treated for alcoholism 3-10 years in past.	Current alcohol consumption correlated with history of sexual abuse by mother ($r = 0.42$).
Henderson, 1986	Interviews of 44 English inmates of a maximum security prison (about 50% murderers).	Found 8 different types of violent circumstances, alcohol most frequently involved in domestic violence at night and in fights outside of pubs.
Lindqvist, 1986	Sweden 1970-80 and corresponding court records of homicides.	30 of 64 murderers were intoxicated (BAC > 0.06%) and 56% were alcoholics. 47% of victims were intoxicated.
Lindqvist, 1986	Counseling of battered women to deal with abusive, alcoholic partner, illustrative case study.	Intervention's focus is on support for the woman and getting the alcoholic's social network to encourage treatment for alcoholism.
Livingston, 1986	107 adults (90% male) receiving residential treatment for alcoholism and substance abuse given two psychological tests (MAST and CTS-Form N) to assess alcoholism and behavior in family conflicts.	83% of alcoholics had been violent in past relationships (55% in the past year) compared to 28% of nonalcoholics. Family violence by alcoholics was also more frequent and more intensely violent.
Myers, 1986	Interviews of 50 men in Scottish prison for violent crime and 50 men imprisoned for non-violent offences.	92% of the violent offenders reported consuming alcohol just prior to the offence as compared to 72% of controls.

485

Reference	Method	Findings
Langevin et al., 1987	As a test for possible brain damage, 21 accused murderers, 21 men accused of assault and 16 controls were administered a battery neuro-psychological tests and EEG.	Differences in measures of neurological impairment approached significance ($p < .10$) with killers and assaulters showing more pathology than controls. 22% of killers and 23% of assaulters also drank daily vs. 8% of controls, and violent subjects more often scored in alcoholic range on MAST. However, there was no correlation between alcohol abuse and impairment.
Muehlenhard and Linton, 1987	Questionnaires to 341 female and 294 male hetero-sexual undergraduates.	15% of women and 7% of men had been involved in date rape. Heavy alcohol use (in self and partner) was reported to be more common on dates with sexual aggression.
White et al., 1987	Longitudinal data from interviews of 441 male and 441 female adolescents tested when they were 12, 15, or 18 years old and again 3 years later when they were 15, 18, or 21 years old	52% of problem drinkers and 42% of the heavy drinkers of alcohol were also classified as delinquents or heavy delinquents (committed any offense >3 times in last 3 years).
Collins and Schlenger, 1988	Analysis of court records of and interviews with 1149 male felons in NC prisons. Multiple regression of demographic and criminal history with drinking and offense.	Those who reported drinking just before the offense were 1.74 times more likely to be in prison for a violent crime than those who said that they were not drinking, but alcoholism was not predictive of offense type.
Fagan et al., 1988	Compared the quantity and frequency of drinking in maritally violent men (44) with married violent criminals (33) and control groups. Also administered a questionnaire on reasons for drinking.	Maritally violent men were most likely to drink at lunch, after work or alone. They also were the most likely to agree with the statement that they drank to forget. Drinking seen more as a consequence than a cause of marital violence.
Miller et al., 1989a, b	Interviews of 45 alcoholic women and 40 non-alcoholic women. Statistical analysis of conflict between the women and their spouse.	More of the alcoholic women had experienced verbal abuse and violence from their spouse (53% vs. 13%). Relationship to alcohol abuse in spouse was borderline ($p < 0.06$).
Rosenbaum and Hoge, 1989	Medical evaluation of 31 men referred for marital violence.	61% had histories of head trauma and most of these also abused alcohol, more frequently than those without trauma.

486

Reference	Method	Findings
Pollock et al., 1990	Interviews and bio-medical evaluations of 131 sons of alcoholic fathers chosen from Danish registry and 70 controls. Both groups were 18 - 21 yrs old.	18% reported being violently abused by alcoholic fathers vs. 11% of controls, but sons of alcoholic fathers were not any more likely to engage in violent or antisocial acts. However, those that had been beaten as children were more likely to report that they had hit someone in a fight.
Dembo et al., 1991	Self-reported drug use, urinalysis test results and self-reported delinquency examined as possible predictors of delinquency in 201 incarcerated males and females; mean age 16 years	Self-reported use of alcohol consistently predicted drug sales offenses, index offenses, crimes against persons and total delinquency at follow-up.

Health Statistics

Reference	Method	Findings
Wilentz and Brady, 1961	Review of New Jersey Medical Examiner records 1933-59.	In 31% of suicides, 36% of murders, and 49% of traffic deaths alcohol intoxication was a factor.
Le Roux and Smith, 1964	Review of autopsies and court records in 1739 deaths in South Africa.	22% had died violent deaths (traffic or homicide) and alcohol was associated with 64% of the victims.
Kellett, 1966	Interviews of 71 patient admitted for suicide attempts over a 3 month period in Durban, South Africa.	Alcohol abuse played a significant role in 33.8% of suicide attempts.
Derrick, 1967	Records and recollections of the pathologist to the coroner of Queensland.	In 1965 250 deaths in Australia due to alcoholism, 1541 traffic deaths probably related to alcohol, 547 deaths from cirrhosis of the liver and 27 deaths from alcoholic psychosis. Concludes that alcohol is probably the sixth most common cause of death in Australia.
King et al., 1969	Random sample interviews of 223 black men 31-35 born in St. Louis.	62% had some history of heavy drinking, including 17% who had medical or social problems directly attributable to alcohol since age 25. The heavy drinkers were more likely to have been arrested for crimes against property and violence than the "never heavy" drinkers.
Climent et al., 1972	Interviews of 80 emergency room patients, half of whom presented with a history of violence.	The violent patients were more often heavy drinkers and more frequently had alcoholic parents.

Reference	Description	Findings
Westermeyer and Brantner, 1972	Review of Minneapolis autopsy data of deaths of Chippewa people 1965-67.	25.8% of Chippewa deaths were violent vs 5.3% among general population. In the majority of these violent deaths BAC was elevated.
Ripley, 1973	Interviews of 121 patients admitted to hospital in Seattle after suicide attempts 1957-1958 and 100 similar patients in Edinburgh, Scotland in 1970. Also analysis of Coroner's records of 114 suicide deaths in Seattle and 91 in Edinburgh for the same time periods.	43% of suicide attempters in Seattle and 28% in Edinburgh were problem drinkers and 36% and 25% respectively were drinking at the time of the attempt. 68% of suicide deaths in Seattle and 45% in Edinburgh had alcoholic problems.
Costello and Schneider, 1974	Follow-up of 400 admissions to an alcohol rehabilitation facility.	The alcoholics had a high death rate with violent deaths, particularly in the first few years after identification of problem, excessively over-represented.
James, 1974	Autopsy results on 107 suicides in Australia 1961-62.	48% of males and 18% of female suicides had BAC > 0.05 and 7% had been under psychiatric care for alcoholism.
Marek et al., 1974	Review of 1970 robbery reports in Krakow, Poland.	69% of the victims were intoxicated.
Choi, 1975	Follow-up of 863 patients seen in Alcoholism Clinic in St. Louis 7/69-6/72.	By 7/72 45 of these alcoholics had died: 24% by homicide and 4% suicides (all men) and average age of 42.
Weiss, 1976	Statistical analysis of violent death rates 1960-73 from National Center for Health Statistics.	Correlates increase in violent deaths with increase in per capita alcohol consumption.
Riddick and Luke, 1978	604 autopsies in Washington DC (8/74-2/75) of un-natural deaths and sudden death in those under 45.	176 had BAC > 0.03: 48% of homicides, 27% of suicides, 46% of traffic accident deaths. In many of those with out BAC there was autopsy evidence of alcohol abuse (e.g. cirrhosis).
Robins et al., 1977	18-month follow-up interviews of 299 patients from a psychiatric emergency room.	A third were alcoholics, none had committed homicide or suicide.
Bohman, 1978	Review of Swedish records of 2324 adoptees and their biological parents.	Good evidence for a genetic predisposition for alcohol abuse but not criminality.
Robins, 1978	Interviews and records of three different samples of men to collect information on childhood and adult behaviors.	Childhood (before 15) alcohol abuse is correlated with later adult antisocial behaviors.

488

Reference	Method	Findings
Schuckit et al., 1978	Interviews of 186 men admitted to Seattle V.A. 9/75-6/76 and 191 women admitted to Seattle Detox Center.	10% of male and 34% of female alcoholics attempted suicide and 18% of male and 6% of female alcoholics had been arrested for felonies at least once in their lives.
McCord, 1981	Follow-up interviews of 224 men who had been part of the Cambridge-Somerville Youth Project 1936-45.	40 were both criminals and alcoholics, 30 were alcoholic only and 34 were criminals but not alcoholic. The personal characteristics of alcoholic criminals were closer to non-alcoholic criminals than to non-criminal alcoholics.
Mendelson et al., 1982	Measured plasma LH at autopsy of 28 men killed while being violent or as victims.	LH levels were higher in the violent group than the nonviolent or controls. Suicides had higher LH if they also were positive for alcohol.
Combs-Orme et al., 1983	Follow-up of 1289 alcoholics 6-9 years after treatment.	22% had died and of these 3.5% were suicides, 3.2% were homicides.
Linnoila et al., 1983	Measured CSF levels of norepinephrine, catechol metabolites and 5-HIAA in 36 alcohol abusers arrested for murder or attempted murder.	The impulsive offenders (non-premediated), those with explosive or antisocial personalities, had lower 5-HIAA levels than the other offenders.
Pulkkinen, 1983	Longitudinal interview study of 196 Finnish boys and 173 girls starting in second grade and 135 followed until age 20.	Aggressiveness in boys at age 8 significantly predicted heavy drinking at age 20, it also predicted more violent offences and criminality.
Berglund, 1984a, b	Follow-up of 1312 alcoholics admitted to University Hospital in Lund 1949-1969. Mean age = 42 and mean follow-up was 18 years.	537 had died -- 2.5 times the expected number. Suicide and violent death contributed 51% of the excess mortality.
Branchey et al., 1984	Interviews and blood chemistry of 43 alcoholic patients, 7 of whom had history of assault-and 3 had attempted suicide.	Only alcoholic patients with a past history of violence had significantly higher levels of tyrosine and phenylalanine and lower tryptophan, suggesting altered serotonin turn-over.
Crompton, 1985	Analysis of autopsy data on 406 English suicides 1970-80.	61% of suicides had BAC > 0.1.
Jacobsson, 1985	Analysis of a physician's records on 316 assault victims seen in western Ethiopia 1962.	In 20% of cases the victim had been drinking and in 36% the assailant.

Reference	Method	Findings
Williams et al., 1985	Statistical analysis of survey data collected by the National Opinion Research Center in urban areas of the US 1973-1980 ($\underline{n}$ = 6419).	29.9% responded that they had been threatened with a gun or shot at. Alcohol use was a weak descriminative predictor of being a victim of gun abuse.
Williams and Singh, 1986	Statistical analysis of survey data collected by the National Opinion Research Center in 1980 and 1984 of urban areas of the US (n = 2045).	Alcohol abusers were more likely to have been shot, beaten, arrested, or have aggressive attitudes than moderate drinkers or abstainers.
Virkkunen and Kallio, 1987	Glucose tolerance tests on 60 male prisoners who had killed or attempted to kill their wife or female companion.	The lowest glucose levels were seen in those with a history of violence under the influence of alcohol.
Branchey et al., 1988	Recorded EEG and event-related potentials in 51 alcoholic men during a tone discrimination task.	The alcoholics that had histories of violent crime had smallest P3 amplitude in their ERPs. No differences in P3 latencies.
Dermen and George, 1988	Questionnaires to 114 male undergraduates.	Relationship between drinking habits and frequency of fist fights was strongest amongst those who expected alcohol to increase aggression.
Helzer and Pryzbeck, 1988	Statistical analysis of alcoholism and psychological disorders from the Epidemiological Catchment Area study (1984, $\underline{n}$ = 20000, randomly selected urban dwellers).	13% had diagnosis of alcohol abuse/dependence and these people were 3 times more likely to also be diagnosed as antisocial personality.
Kratcoski, 1988	Review of Cuyahoga County, Ohio coroner's records on 1775 cases of homicide in which the assailant was known, 1970-83.	Only 21% were killed by a stranger. Of those killed by a family member 40.3% had alcohol in their blood and 23.6% were legally drunk. For those killed by an acquaintance the figures were 50.8% and 29% and by a stranger 34.9% and 16.5%.
Petersson, 1988	Investigation of 347 deaths of men approximately 50 years of age participating in a preventative medicine program and control men in Sweden.	151/347 deaths were alcohol related. 75% of the sudden unwitnessed deaths were of men registered with the Department of Alcohol Diseases.
Rydelius, 1988	Statistical analysis of violent death rates 1967-85 of cohort of 832 boys and 224 girls admitted to Swedish reform schools in 1967 (does not separate alcohol from "drug" use).	47/110 male and 7/22 female deaths had an alcohol and/or drug abuse-related factor.

Lester, 1989	Statistical analysis of suicide and homicide rates, per capita alcohol consumption in US 1980, and social variables (e.g. income, population density, unemployment rate, etc.).	Suicide, but not murder, rates were highest in states with highest per capita alcohol consumption, however alcohol consumption was highest in states with less social integration (e.g., highest divorce rates).
Linnoila et al., 1989 Virkkunen et al., 1989b	Interviews and biochemical measurements in 54 alcohol abusers arrested for assault or arson.	The offenders with an alcoholic father had lower CSF 5-HIAA than those with a nonalcoholic father. Suicide attempters also had lower 5-HIAA. The authors liken these violent alcohol abusers to Cloninger's Type II alcoholics.

Personality Evaluations of Aggression

Selzer, 1967	An essay illustrated with two psychiatric case studies.	Describes the "alcoholic personality" as dependent, hostile, egocentric, and self-destructive.
Tomim and Glenn, 1968	Review of psychiatric admissions at Brooklyn State Hospital 4/67-9/67.	Of 446 patients diagnosed with psychopathic personalities 58 were alcoholics.
Whitelock et al., 1971	136 male psychiatric patients given MMPI and an alcohol abuse questionnaire.	Found subtypes of alcohol abusers based on MMPI scores. Moderate abusers' patterns were dominated by Pd (hostile psychopathic) while those with higher abuse scores had MMPI patterns dominated by D and Pt components (neurotic depressive).
Woodruff et al., 1971	Interviews with 35 sociopaths (a history of fighting was one criterion in the diagnosis).	60% of these patients were alcoholics.
Woodruff et al., 1973	Psychiatric interviews of 29 alcoholics, 139 depressives and 29 with alcoholism and unipolar depression.	Those men and women with both alcoholism and depression were the most antisocial and had more of a history of violence.
Cloninger and Guze, 1975	Psychiatric interviews of parents of 66 female felons.	55% of the fathers were alcoholic or sociopathic and in 76% of the families one parent had either alcoholism, sociopathy or hysteria. Sociopathy in fathers was predictive of hysteria in the daughter.

491

Reference	Description	Findings
Deardorff et al., 1975	Power Orientation Semantic Differential and the Situations for Drinking questionnaires given to 253 problem drinkers, including 8 men with a history of violence.	Violent drinkers scored highest on the personal power scales, suggesting they drink in order to feel a sense of power.
Apfeldorf and Hunley, 1976	MMPI given to 233 residents at W. Va. V.A.	The F scale (considered to reflect overt hostility) distinguished problem drinkers (highest F) from alcoholics from controls.
Caster and Parsons, 1977	Personality inventories on 78 alcoholic veterans in a therapeutic program and 27 controls.	Alcoholics that failed to complete the program and recidivists scored highest on depression and sociopathy.
Van Valkenburg et al., 1977, 1983	Interviews of patients diagnosed as clinically depressed.	A subtype (Depression Spectrum Disorder) of depression includes patients more likely to be problem drinkers and show antisocial behavior. These patients were also more likely to have a parent that is/was alcoholic or have an antisocial personality.
Cloninger et al., 1978	Statistical analysis of alcoholism in male and female relatives of alcoholics.	Although alcoholism is more frequent in men than women, male and female alcoholics have equal numbers of alcoholic relatives. The correlation is stronger for men ($r = .53$ vs .18) suggesting non-familial variables are more important in women.
Herzog and Wilson, 1978	Personal Reaction Inventory administered to female alcoholic inpatients and controls in Wisconsin.	Assertive antisocial behavior was higher in alcoholic women and predicted drinking behavior.
O'Leary et al., 1978	MMPI administered to male alcoholic inpatients in Seattle V.A.	48 out of 173 had sociopathic profiles.
Renson et al., 1978	26 male outpatients at a clinic for alcohol abuse and violent behavior were administered Buss-Durkee inventory self-rating true/false items to yield a total hostility score.	Violent alcohol abusers have higher hostility ratings than nonviolent abusers, scoring higher on scales measuring assault, irritability, verbal hostility and resentment.

Schuckit and Morrissey, 1979	Interview of 293 women admitted to Seattle detoxification center in 4/76-9/76.	53% of patients were primary alcoholics (the initial disorder), however primary antisocial personality patients (14%) were also secondary alcoholics. These patients actually drank the most, had the most legal problems and attempted suicide most often.
Virkkunen, 1979	Interviews of 50 adult male criminals referred for psychiatric exams in Helsinki 1975-77 and 50 juvenile delinquent prisoners all of whom were alcoholic and had antisocial personality. They were compared to 42 alcoholic prisoners without ASP.	The offenders with antisocial personality were more likely to have committed violent crimes under the influence of alcohol than those without antisocial personality (84% vs 40%).
Haramis and Wagner, 1980	60 alcoholic patients of Ashtabula County Council on Alcoholism and Drug Abuse, half with background of violent crime, given Rorschach and Hand Tests.	The alcoholics with the aggressive, criminal record scored higher on hostility, impulsivity, immaturity, lack of control, and had poor judgement. More than one "alcoholic personality".
Williams et al., 1980	166 undergraduates, in- and out-patients and staff of mental health center given Personality Research Form and Alcohol Use Inventory.	Aggression was the personality variable most highly correlated with the extent of alcohol use.
Conley, 1981	MMPI given to 337 male alcoholics at admission to Hazelden Foundation, to 265 of those at discharge and a 12-month follow-up interview to 228.	Half of the admissions could be classified into 4 groups: neurotic (high D), classic (high D, Pd and Pt), psychopathic (high Pd and Ma), and psychotic (high Sc, Pa, Pt and Ma). All but the psychopathic type showed foreshortening of the profile at discharge (they were also the youngest).
Williams et al., 1982	Questionnaires given to alcoholics in treatment and controls.	44% of alcoholics (8% controls) were using alcohol as their preferred way of coping with stress. 9% of alcoholics (1% controls) preferred starting a fight as a coping strategy.
Løberg, 1983	Interview, MMPI and neuropsychological assessments of 110 hospitalized alcoholics in Norway. Divided into passive (28), moderately belligerent (65), and highly belligerent (17 recent fighting while drinking).	The high belligerence group was earlier in onset of alcohol abuse and had more pronounced neuropsychological deficits and a more pathologically deviate personality.

Reference	Method	Findings
Mosher and Sirkin, 1984	Administered "hypermasculinity" inventory and alcohol use survey to 135 male undergraduates.	Significant positive correlation (0.28) between alcohol abuse and the macho constellation, also with viewing violence as manly and danger as exciting.
Cadoret et al., 1985	Statistical analysis of 127 male and 87 female adoptees in Iowa selected by the researchers for antisocial or alcoholic family backgrounds. The adoptees were interviewed at an average age of 25.	Although antisocial personality and alcohol abuse were frequently associated the genetic determinants appear separate. However, the authors feel their sample is too small and young to look for the two different types of alcoholism as suggested by Cloninger.
Collins et al., 1988	Self report, medical and school records in black men rated by three psychiatrists.	Individuals with antisocial personality had a higher rate of alcoholism; drinking within the family, low education and increased irritability also were related.
Holcomb and Adams, 1985	Compared MMPIs from 41 men who committed murder while intoxicated, 48 sober murderers, 130 men admitted to a detox unit (no crime) and 40 acute psychiatric admissions with no alcoholic history.	Men who committed murder while intoxicated were less aware of psychological problems (high L scores). Sober murderers were more psychopathic (high P_D) and less interpersonally sensitive (low M_F).
Lewis et al., 1985a	Self report in unipolar depressive men rated by skilled observer using PHDD and SADS, and RDC by a family member.	Depressed men with antisocial personality have a higher incidence of alcoholism, more family disruption, and a lower socioeconomic status than depressive men without antisocial personality.
Lewis et al., 1985b	Reanalysis of King et al. 1969 interview data on urban black males.	About half were diagnosed as antisocial and those men had higher rates of alcohol abuse. Antisocial alcoholics had more alcohol related problems.
Downs et al., 1987 Miller et al., 1987	Retrospective interviews of 45 alcoholic women and 40 nonalcoholic women. Statistical analysis of conflict between the women as children and their parents, and incidence of sexual abuse.	More of the alcoholic women had experienced conflict with and violence from their fathers, but they were not different from the controls in conflict with mother. More of the alcoholic women had been sexually abused (rarely by a relative).

494

Whitters et al., 1987	DIS/DSM-III interviews of 41 alcohol abusers with antisocial personality disorder.	Two clusters varying in concurrent level of depression, those with more depressive symptoms also had more symptoms of other psychopathologies as well.
Yates et al., 1987	Review of records of 274 patients treated at the Univ. of Iowa Chemical Dependency Center.	Twice as many alcoholics with antisocial personality had attempted suicide or were classified as violent as non-ASP alcoholics.
Collins et al., 1988	DIS/DSM-III interviews of 1149 convicted felons in North Carolina prison system.	28% of the felons met the criteria for antisocial personality disorder, of those 71% were alcoholic/abusers (compared to 40% of non-ASP). Those with alcohol problems also had more ASP symptoms.
Cooper, 1988	Analysis of records on 34 subjects involuntarily admitted to a psychiatric ward in Canada, 1984-85.	Assaultive behavior was one of the characteristics in 29%, and 35% were alcoholic along with other psychopathology; frequently antisocial personality disorder.
Jaffe et al., 1988	Behavior of 77 hospitalized, alcoholic patients, grouped by levels of childhood aggression and antisocial personality were rated while drinking and while sober.	Alcoholics report more anger and aggression when drinking than when sober without any relationship to presence of antisocial personality; Patients with high levels of childhood aggression showed a greater effect.
Palmstierna and Wistedt, 1988	Psychiatric analysis of 105 patients involuntarily admitted to a Swedish psychiatric clinic 10/85-4/86.	24 patients had history of alcohol abuse and 41 were physically violent (does not specify overlap or correlation between these two descriptors).
Schuerger and Reigle, 1988	Psychological assessment of 246 men (follow-up on 32) being treated for wife abuse in Ohio. Various personality and violence inventories used and alcoholism quantified with MAST.	69% of group considered alcoholic based on MAST score and report a positive correlation (.24-.33) between MAST and degree of violence.
Yates et al., 1988	DSM-III interviews of 260 male alcoholics at Iowa V.A.	24% met criteria for antisocial personality disorder. ASP alcoholics had begun drinking earlier in life, drank more and had more alcohol related problems, including violence while intoxicated, than non-ASP alcoholics.

Study	Methodology	Findings
Cloninger et al., 1989	Review of data on alcoholism in 1775 people born 1930-42 in Stockholm and their biological and adoptive parents and personality data from 286 hospitalized alcoholics in St. Louis.	Concludes there are two, partly over-lapping, subtypes of alcoholism. Type 1 is characterized by passive-dependent personality traits and has a larger environmental component. Type 2 is characterized by antisocial personality traits and has a larger genetic component.
Grove et al., 1990	32 monozygotic twins who had been separated shortly after birth and raised apart were interviewed separately as adults.	12 individuals met criteria for alcohol abuse but these were distributed among 10 pairs for a concordance rate of 33% and a minimal heritability for this characteristic. They report a somewhat higher heritability estimate for ASP. Cautions that this small, non-clinical sample may not be optimal for detecting genetic contribution.

Experimental Measures of Aggression

Study	Methodology	Findings
Bennett et al., 1969	16 male undergraduates given 0, 0.33, 0.67 and 1ml/kg ethanol in orange juice on separate days and given opportunity to select shock intensity administered to a confederate of the experimenter in a fake learning paradigm.	No statistically significant effect of alcohol on aggression under these test conditions.
Tamerin and Mendelson, 1969	4 male alcoholics from an inpatient hospital were observed and interviewed during a regime consisting of 2 weeks without alcohol. Then they were given alcohol (0.5 to 2.0 ml/kg of 86 proof bourbon) 4 times per day for 3 weeks, then 21 days of free access drinking and finally, 10 day withdrawal.	Euphoria was observed during the initial phase of intoxication. Depression and anxiety and feelings of guilt increased with intoxication. Increases in verbalization and aggressive interactions were also observed.
Butts and Shontz, 1970	20 alcoholic men were paired with either their wives or unfamiliar women. Subjects participated in a lab learning paradigm. Alcoholics received shocks chosen by the partner if his responses were too slow (passive invitation of shock) or if he admitted a mistake (invitation of punishment).	Alcoholic subjects received more shocks from partners than controls, and had less of a tendency to admit mistakes when it led to aversive stimuli.
Marinacci and Von Hagen, 1972	EEG testing of 800 patients accused of violent crime or antisocial acts, results illustrated with 13 case histories.	In 13% of total 2 oz alcohol induced abnormal EEG, suggests there is a small subpopulation with temporal lobe damage aggravated by alcohol.

Reference	Method	Findings
Boyatzis, 1975	149 adult male volunteers attended staged parties. Each party had either distilled spirits, beer or soft drinks available. During the parties they were videotaped and filled out personality, mood checklists and TAT.	Measures of aggression were highest with distilled spirits. Heavy drinkers showed the most verbal aggression toward other "party" attendees. Those subjects also scored lowest on social integration.
Dotson et al., 1975	Administered Buss-Durkee Hostility Inventory and measured plasma testosterone before the beginning of a staged party. Alcoholic and soft drinks were freely available for 3 hrs. A second blood sample was taken at the end.	No correlation with pre-party testosterone or hydrocortisone levels or of pre-party levels and aggression. However, post-party BAC was correlated with aggression rating ($r = .23$) and change in testosterone ($r = .26$). Testosterone decreased with low to moderate BAC and increased with high BAC.
Lang et al., 1975	96 male undergraduates drank 1.3 ml/kg ethanol in tonic or placebo and were informed or misinformed about alcohol content. Then tested for "aggression" with modified Buss shock apparatus (willingness to administer high shock intensities to confederate).	If they thought they had received alcohol, independent of BAC, they delivered greater shock intensities (expectancy effect).
Taylor and Gammon, 1975	40 male undergraduates consumed 0.83 or 2.48 ml/kg of 100 proof bourbon or vodka in ginger ale. Tested in a reaction time competition with shock to the loser. The subject chose the level of shock to administer to the "opponent". Over trials the shock from the "opponent" was increased (provocation).	The mean shock intensity settings were higher with the higher dose of alcohol and increased with provocation. There was a trend for a greater effect with vodka. Although there was no control in this experiment, the authors state that the low dose of alcohol reduced aggression below normal.
Maletzky, 1976	22 patients with a history of violence under the influence were observed while receiving 25% ethanol i.v. 200 cc/hr.	41% showed inappropriate rage, 18% had a psychotic reaction and 9% showed a mixture of these responses. Response generally occurred at a high BAC.
Taylor et al., 1976	40 male undergraduates consumed 1.25 g/kg ethanol in ginger ale or control. Tested in a reaction time competition with shock to the loser. The subject chose the level of shock to administer to the "opponent". For half the subjects it was made clear that the opponent would only use the least intense shock ("no-threat").	In the "no-threat" condition alcohol had no effect on aggression (shock given to the opponent) but alcohol doubled the average shock setting when there was some degree of threat.

Taylor and Gammon, 1976	40 male undergraduates consumed 1.25 g/kg ethanol in ginger ale or control. Tested in a reaction time competition similar to Taylor et al. 1976 but no threat manipulation. An observer was present and for half of the subjects he provided verbal pressure re the subjects' performance.	Alcohol increased the intensity of shock the subject was willing to administer and the subject evaluated the opponent in less favorable terms. An observer that commented on performance moderated these effects.
Persky et al., 1977	40 alcoholic volunteers were admitted to Clinical Research Center PGH. Subjects abstained from alcohol and tobacco for 1 week, then were assigned to groups: 1, unlimited alcohol and cigarettes; 2, unlimited alcohol; 3, unlimited cigarettes; or 4, continued abstinence for a week. Psychological state assessed and testosterone measured.	Plasma testosterone decreased with unlimited alcohol access. Although these alcoholics had high levels of hostility and aggression as assessed by psychological tests, alcohol availability did not affect this. Cigarettes did not have any significant effects.
Taylor et al., 1977	40 male undergraduates consumed 1.25 g/kg ethanol in ginger ale or control and were tested in a reaction time competition with an artificial opponent. Frustration was produced in the subjects with an insoluble puzzle.	Alcohol increased the intensity of shock the subject was willing to administer but there was no effect of frustration on shock intensity or interaction with alcohol.
Mendelson et al., 1978	8 alcoholic men and 16 controls had hormone levels measured before, during and after bourbon (ad lib).	Testosterone levels were reduced during alcohol in both alcoholics and controls; without an initial suppression of LH. Authors suggest LH may be important in alcohol's effects on aggression.
Graham et al., 1980	Direct observations (633 hr) of social interactions and aggressive behavior in 185 Vancouver bars.	The frequency of verbal and physical aggression varied across bars. The "aggressive bars" had a reputation for violence and were generally in poor areas.
Zeichner and Pihl, 1978	72 men drank 1.25 ml/kg ethanol in orange juice, placebo, or nothing and then were tested with a modified Buss shock machine. During the test subjects heard aversive tones, half thought there was malicious intent.	Subjects that received alcohol were most aggressive (highest and longest shocks) independent of intent manipulation.
Pihl et al., 1981	48 men trained on a modified Buss task (see Zeichner and Pihl, 1978) then drank 1.25 ml/kg ethanol or placebo and informed or misinformed about alcohol content.	Alcohol increased aggression independent of expectancy, but placebo subjects also were more aggressive if they thought they had received alcohol.

Reference	Methods	Results
Baldwin and Randolph, 1982	Southern Mississippi undergraduates were divided on the basis of Alcohol Use Inventory into 308 light drinkers, 30 moderate drinkers and 30 abstainers. In the laboratory students received either a negative or a positive evaluation from a confederate and were then asked to rate the confederate with checklists.	Provocation (negative evaluation) produced higher hostility-aggression scores on the ratings. Moderate drinkers scored higher on these scales than light drinkers with abstainers intermediate.
Zeichner et al., 1982	72 men were trained on modified Buss task and drank 1.25 ml/kg ethanol or placebo. While in the task half recorded the level of pain they thought the confederate was receiving (forced attention).	Alcohol increased aggression but there was no effect of forcing the subject to attend to the consequences of his actions.
Bailey et al., 1983	Frustration-induced aggression measured with a modified version of Buss' aggression machine. 40 undergraduate males received either 0.83 or 2.48 ml/kg of 50% ethanol. Half of the subjects competed in the presence of a mirror and video camera (self aware).	Non-self-aware subjects administered higher shocks; alcohol increased the shock settings, but there was no interaction for awareness and dose.
Virkkunen, 1983	Psychiatric interviews of and fasting serum cholesterol measurements in 280 Finnish male murderers.	173 had a history of violence under the influence of alcohol and 73 of these had an antisocial personality. These 173 had lower mean cholesterol levels than those without this history.
Crawford, 1984	50 male and 50 female Scottish undergraduates asked to describe typical situations in which aggression is shown by (a) males and (b) females.	Alcohol was commonly seen as part of the cause of aggression in males by 60% of men and 36% of women but less commonly viewed as a source of female aggression (20% of men and 4% of women.
Gustafson, 1984	Frustration (failure to receive a monetary reward) induced aggression measured with Buss' aggression machine in 8 male undergraduates given brandy in orange juice (0, 0.33, 0.66 or 1.0 ml ethanol/kg). Subjects thought they were using shock to help shape learning in an unseen confederate.	No effect of either alcohol or frustration on shock administered in this paradigm perhaps because the subjects took the "teacher" role very seriously.
Kreutzer et al., 1984	54 male undergraduates given beer (0, 0.5 or 1.0 ml/kg alcohol) and tested verbal reaction to hypothetical situation and gave variety of psychological tests.	Hostility was increased by alcohol and profanity was increased with the high dose.

499

Study	Method	Findings
Leonard, 1984	30 pairs of male undergraduates given 0.96 g/kg ethanol or control and tested in intoxicated, sober or mixed dyads on Taylor competition paradigm.	Intoxicated dyads administered the highest shock level to each other and escalated the level over trials.
Rohsenow and Bachorowski, 1984	Male and female undergraduates drank tonic ± ethanol (informed or misinformed about the contents of the drink) and then received a negative evaluation of their personality by a confederate and were given a chance to retaliate.	Men told they were drinking alcohol had decreased verbal aggression. In women the lower dose of alcohol (0.75 ml/kg) increased aggression but at 1.1 ml/kg same result as with men. Authors emphasize expectancy effect.
Pihl et al., 1984a	60 male "social drinkers" given MMPI, at a subsequent session given ethanol in orange juice, beer or control drinks and aggression measured with a Buss artificial shock paradigm.	Both ethanol and beer resulted in BAC = 0.7. The beer subjects that gave the highest shocks were also highest on family problems; the aggressive ethanol subjects scored high on social maladjustment.
Pihl et al., 1984b	Frustration-induced aggression measured with the Buss aggression machine in 64 male paid social drinkers.	Aggression was higher in subjects that drank or believed they had consumed distilled spirits than in subjects that drank beer or believed that they had drank beer (BAC = 0.7 in both); no differences between alcohol and placebo.
Wolf, 1984	15 Alaskan Native men that had committed murder while drunk were given the same amount of alcohol in the lab as they had when the crime was committed.	As BAC passed 150 mg % a "blackout" was recreated; EEG slowed to 3-7 Hz and each verbalized about one past salient event.
Gustafson, 1985a	Frustration-induced aggression measured with Buss' aggression machine in 30 male military recruits given brandy in orange juice (0, .33, or .6 ml/kg ethanol). Subjects thought they were using shock as feedback for incorrect performance in a vigilance task.	The 0.6 ml/kg dose of alcohol (BAC = 0.05%) increased mean shock intensity given during the frustration trials.
Gustafson, 1985b	The role of expectancy was tested in 48 male undergraduates and soldiers. Subjects consumed 0.8 ml/kg ethanol in tonic or control and were either informed or misinformed about alcoholic content. Expectancy was manipulated with film and readings on the link between alcohol and violence.	Shock intensity and duration were greatest in subjects that received alcohol independent of expectancy factors. The author does not rule out that expectancy can have important effects.

Reference	Description	Findings
Jeavons and Taylor, 1985; Taylor et al., 1976	Frustration-induced aggression measured with a modified version of Buss' aggression machine in male undergraduates given vodka (45 ml of 100 proof/40 lbs bw) in ginger ale with peppermint oil or ginger ale and peppermint oil with 1/20 of an ounce of vodka as control.	Intoxicated subjects initiated higher levels of attack than sober subjects in "threatening situation"; intoxicated subjects that competed against a non-threatening opponent did not show similar effects.
Murdoch and Pihl, 1985	44 men drank 1.25 ml/kg ethanol or placebo and were informed or misinformed about alcohol level. They were then observed while interacting with either an obnoxious confederate or a friendly confederate.	There was little aggression in the social inter-actions, but the alcohol group showed the most.
Bond and Lader, 1986	45 adult paid male and female subjects drank 0, 0.25 or 0.75 g/kg alcohol in tonic. They completed a variety of scales and then "competed" in a Taylor reaction time task.	The subjects which received the highest dose of alcohol were consistently more aggressive (higher settings) on the competition task, however, they rated themselves as less aggressive.
George and Marlatt, 1986	Male undergraduates drank tonic $\pm$ ethanol (informed or misinformed about the alcoholic content) and then were allowed ad lib exposure to violent, erotic, violent-erotic and neutral slides. Later assessed aggression and sexual arousal with a questionnaire.	Alcohol expectancy more than BAC increased viewing of violent-erotic slides and sexual arousal but there was no effect of alcohol or expectancy on verbal aggression.
Gustafson, 1986a	Threat (being told the stooge was likely to use a high shock on them) -induced aggression measured with Buss' "shock-machine" in 40 male undergraduates and soldiers given vodka in orange juice (0 or 0.80 ml ethanol/kg). Subjects could vary the level of shock they thought they were using as a signal of incorrect performance in a vigilance task.	Alcohol (BAC = 0.065%) increased shock intensity and duration even in the absence of any instigation (e.g. frustration). Threat inhibited the increase.
Gustafson, 1986b, c	48 sober male and 48 sober female undergraduates had the Taylor version of the Buss' "shock machine" explained to them. Half of each sex were told the opponent was drunk. Aggression assessed by asking the subjects what shock intensity they thought the opponent would give them and what shock they would administer to the opponent.	Males expected "drunk" opponents to be more aggressive and retaliated by giving higher shocks to drunks. Females also expected drunk opponents to be more aggressive but unlike men did not choose a more aggressive response.

Pihl and Zacchia, 1986	48 men were asked to imagine positive and negative moods then drank 1.25 ml/kg ethanol, placebo or nothing and were tested in a modified Buss shock machine paradigm.	Alcohol but not placebo (expectancy) increased aggression. This was not altered by mood. Authors argue for a direct drug effect.
Gustafson, 1987	Aggression indirectly assessed in 28 male undergraduates. They drank 0.8 ml ethanol/kg in orange juice (or control) and then watched a violent movie. Afterwards they wrote TAT stories and filled out semantic differential scales.	The alcohol group had a less negative reaction to the violent movie.
Lindman et al., 1987	Compared 25 male undergraduates selected to be aggressively or non-aggressively predisposed. They were tested in groups of 4 (2 aggressive and 2 not), allowed alcohol ad lib and measured mood, social interactions, BAC and salivary testosterone.	The aggressive subjects had higher testosterone but both groups had similar BACs. The aggressive subjects were more dominant in social interactions and showed more verbal aggression, but alcohol did not change these behaviors.
Gustafson, 1988b	Aggression assessed in 40 male undergraduates. They drank beer, non-alcoholic beer, wine or non-alcoholic wine and later completed a personality inventory and had blood alcohol determined.	Neither beer or wine (0.8 ml/kg, BAC = 0.05%) altered responses on aggression scale.
Gustafson, 1988a	Frustration induced aggression measured with Buss' aggression machine in beer drinking male undergraduates.	Beer (0.8 ml alcohol/kg bw) did not alter aggression.
Kelly et al., 1988, 1989	4 and 6 male volunteers tested in the Cherek free-operant procedure (money reward for button presses with option to subtract money from another subject instead) given 0, .125, .25, .5 and .75 g/kg ethanol.	0.75 g/kg ethanol increased aggressive responding (money subtraction), lower doses (0.25 and 0.5 g/kg) had less effect. The effect of the higher doses was greatest when the work load was increased (FR 500 schedules).
Murdoch et al., 1988	39 female bar patrons drinking only beer or only distilled liquor while in all female groups filled out questionnaire. Verbal aggression was assessed according to the subjects answers to four questions. No control group.	Verbal aggression in subjects with high estimated BAC (> 0.05) was not significantly different from subjects with low estimated BAC. Both groups became more aggressive with repeated questioning; the high BAC group became aggressive sooner, but the low BAC group was most aggressive on the last question.

Reference	Description	Findings
Taylor and Sears, 1988	18 male undergraduates drank ± 2.5 ml/kg ethanol in ginger ale and then were tested in a reaction time competition similar to Taylor et al., 1976. Assessed the effect of a pressure from a confederate to administer high shock intensities.	Alcohol resulted in the subjects being more compliant to pressure from the experimenter's confederate and these subjects were willing to give potentially injurious shocks to the "opponent."
Wormith et al., 1988	23 male patients from Sexual Behaviors Clinic in Ottawa (all had been charged or convicted of sex offences) listened to 2 min. audiotapes depicting rape, consensual sex and nonsexual assault encounters and had penile circumference measured in response to tapes. Tested ± alcohol (BAC = 0.08%).	Alcohol reduced sexual arousal in nonrapist sex offenders but rapists were equally or more aroused with intoxication.
Gustafson, 1990	20 male undergraduates consumed either wine (0.8 ml alcohol/kg bw) or non-alcoholic wine and provocation induced aggression was measured with Buss' aggression machine.	Wine (BAC = .0455) did not increase shock intensity or duration, unlike ethanol but similar to the lack of effect of beer (Gustafson, 1988a) suggesting different expectancies about effects.
Literature Reviews		
Goodwin, 1973	Literature review of alcohol in suicide and homicide (58 refs).	Homicide is associated more with drinking than with alcoholism but alcoholism is a common diagnosis of suicides.
Tinklenberg, 1973	Literature review on alcohol-violence relationships (77 refs).	Concludes that although other factors are important, excessive alcohol increases the probability of violence.
Fitzpatrick, 1974	Review of link between drugs and crime (29 references, primarily other reviews).	States that the most abundant evidence for a link between a drug and crime is with alcohol.
Pernanen, 1976	Critical literature review on the link between alcohol abuse and violent crime (218 refs).	Although alcohol may predispose an individual to violence, there are many other non-pharmacological factors which bias the statistical data on this relationship.
John, 1978	Literature review, 19 references.	Frequent association between alcohol in the offender and commission of rape, but the causal relationships are unclear.

503

Coid, 1979	Literature review of "pathological intoxication" in which consumption of alcohol is followed by senseless violence (52 refs).	This review argues that no explanation of the etiology of "pathological intoxication" has any clear experimental support. The author questions the psychological and legal usefulness of the term.
Gayford, 1979	Literature review on battered wives (44 refs).	40% of cases of violence only occurred when husband was drunk and 10-20% of the women went through a phase of heavy drinking, but many other factors to be considered.
Evans, 1980, 1986	Critical literature reviews on the methodological and statistical problems in the literature associating alcohol and violent crime.	Cautions that the published correlations may be misleading and that causal interpretations are premature.
Graham, 1980	Review of the major theories on the role of alcohol in aggression (94 refs).	Groups theories on alcohol-aggression interaction into 4 types: direct-causation; indirect; indirect conditional upon motive; and predisposition/situational. The conclusion is that the theories all have merit, as well as problems, and that they are not mutually exclusive.
Seltzer, 1980	Literature review on psychosocial strain in Eskimos (39 refs), illustrated with 2 case histories.	The author concludes that alcohol abuse and violence are both coping strategies to alleviate the stress of acculturation.
Anderson, 1982	Literature review (87 refs) on the environmental influence on aggression	Suggests alcohol increases aggressive feelings and behavior. Some studies showed that subjects that were provoked but were unable to express anger, consumed more alcohol than non-angered counterparts.
Shapiro, 1982	Literature review (41 refs) and a few case studies.	Reviews the alcohol and violence relationship focussing on violence against the family and the role of the family therapist in treatment.
Öjesjö, 1983	Critical literature review (76 refs) on the associations between alcohol and other drugs with crime.	Concludes that alcohol has an ill-defined role in violent crime but that it is one of many factors.

504

Reference	Description	Findings
Taylor, 1983	Literature review (29 refs) on experimental studies on the associations between alcohol and human physical aggression	Concludes that neither pharmacological effects nor cues in the drinking situation can independently explain enhanced aggressive behavior following alcohol consumption. Suggests an interactive role of instigative cues and neuropharmacological mechanisms
Grande et al., 1984 Schubert et al., 1988	Literature reviews and meta-analysis of studies.	Approximately 80% of the reviewed studies find a positive association between alcoholism and anti-social personality.
Kaufman Kantor and Straus, 1987	Literature review (93 refs) and telephone interviews with couples in 5159 households.	Linear relationship between drinking index and wife battering (19% of binge drinkers were batterers), but best correlation was between approval of violence and actual battering.
Brain, 1986	Edited volume on alcohol and aggression which contains 8 chapters on the topic from many points of view.	The most relevant chapters are cited separately in this table.
Coid, 1986 a	Critical literature review (61 refs) on the association between alcohol and sexual assault.	Cautions against considering alcohol as a single important factor in rape.
Coid, 1986 b	Literature review (62 refs) on many of the socio-cultural factors in alcohol-related aggression and some of the different responses to alcohol in different societies.	Discusses the role of cultural attitudes toward alcohol and drinking on shaping the likelihood of aggressive behavior following alcohol consumption. However, this does not rule out direct pharmacological effects as well.
Roy et al., 1986	Literature review of research on biochemical correlates of alcohol-violence relationship (67 refs).	Stresses the correlation of impulsive violence with low CSF 5-HIAA and with reactive hypoglycemia.
Kofoed and MacMillan, 1986	Literature review on the association of alcoholism and antisocial personality (28 refs).	The authors suggest that the association between alcoholism and antisocial personality can be explained by sociobiology.
Elliot, 1987	Review of 27 references on assesment and treatment of aggressive disorders	Concludes that in lower doses, alcohol interfers with inhibitory mechanisms to "disinhibit" aggressive behaviors. Individuals with poor impulse control are particularly susceptable.

505

Cloninger, 1987	Literature review on possible biological bases of clinical subgroups of alcoholism (93 refs).	Reviews the evidence for specific subtype of alcoholism (Type 2) with violence during drinking, a genetic background of alcohol abuse and perhaps different neurochemical responses to alcohol.
Hore, 1988	Critical review (44 refs) of the relationship between crime and alcohol.	Concludes the nature of the link between alcohol and crime is complex.
Norton and Morgan, 1989a, b	Literature reviews and meta-analysis on role of alcohol in violent crime in Great Britain (41 & 45 refs).	Alcohol was seen to greatly increase the risk of being involved in acts of violence, but there are also many acts of violence with no alcohol involvement. Also makes suggestions on how to improve the gathering of alcohol-violence information.
Van Thiel et al., 1988	Literature review on alcohol effects on testosterone and sexual behavior, including sex offenses (72 refs).	Separates alcohol's deleterious effects on testosterone and sexual functioning from its pro-aggressive effects.
Gorney, 1989	Review (54 refs) of the co-occurrence of domestic violence and abuse of alcohol and other drugs.	Concludes that effective therapy must treat both the violence and the substance abuse. Nature of the link between alcohol and crime is complex.
Bushman and Cooper, 1990	Literature review (81 refs) and meta-analysis of 30 experimental studies on alcohol induced aggression.	The meta-analysis indicates that alcohol can cause an increase in aggressive behavior in the laboratory, but that this is not a purely pharmacological effect.
Fagan, 1990a	Review (271 refs) of theories and research on the influence of alcohol and other drugs on aggression.	Makes the point that intoxication does not consistently lead to aggression and that other mediating internal and external factors are important. Concludes with a model of how these various factors may interact.

506

TABLE 4A Effects of Opiate Administration on Aggression in Animals

References	Methods and Procedures	Results and Conclusions
Isolation-induced Aggression		
Janssen et al., 1960 Cook and Wiedley, 1960 DaVanzo et al., 1966 Poshivalov, 1974, 1982	Male mice confronted a group-housed male intruder.	Morphine, methadone, codeine and fentanyl decreased attack behavior, primarily at doses that also suppressed motor behavior.
Pain-induced Aggression and Defense		
Irwin et al., 1971	Footshock in groups of female mice	Methadone (3, 6 ml/kg p.o.) decreased the duration of defensive and aggressive behavior at doses that also decreased motor activity.
Lal et al., 1975a	Footshock in pairs of male rats	Morphine (5.0, 10.0 mg/kg) decreased the frequency of fighting
Emley and Hutchinson, 1983	Tail shock-induced target biting in individually-housed male and female squirrel monkeys	A low dose of morphine (1.25 mg/kg s.c.) increased target biting, while higher doses (2.5-20 mg/kg s.c.) decreased target biting.
Brain lesion-induced aggression		
Wikler, 1944	Sham rage in individually-housed cats following removal of cortical and subcortical tissue	Morphine (2-5 mg/kg i.v.) decreased the motor components of sham rage, at doses that decreased the righting reflex.
Defensive Aggression induced by brain stimulation		
Kido et al., 1967	Sham rage induced by electrical stimulation of the posterior hypothalamus in cats	Morphine (5 mg/kg i.v.) increased the threshold to induce sham rage.
Drug-induced aggression		
Yen et al., 1970	DOPA-induced target biting in male mice	Morphine decreased target biting (ED_{50}= 5.2 mg/kg i.p.).
Lal et al., 1975a	Apomorphine and d-amphetamine-induced fighting in groups of mice. Sex unspecified	Morphine (20.0 mg/kg) decreased the frequency of attack biting.

Krstic et al., 1982	Carbachol-induced fighting in groups of 4-6 male and female cats	Morphine (.2-1.0 mg i.c.v.) decreased the duration of aggressive responses at doses that altered locomotor activity. Methadone (.2-1.0 mg i.c.v.) did not affect aggression levels.

Aggression by Resident toward Intruder

Walaszek and Abood, 1956 Braud and Weibel, 1969	Male Siamese fighting fish confronting a male conspecific	Morphine (40 μg/ml) slightly increased attack and threat behavior.
Avis and Peeke, 1975	Male convict cichlids confronting a male conspecific	Morphine (5 mg/l, 10 mg/l) decreased aggressive gill display frequency.
Sieber et al., 1982 Benton et al., 1985	Male and female mice confronting a male conspecific	Morphine (1.0, 2.5, 20 mg/kg) did not significantly alter aggressive behavior.

Female Aggression

Panksepp et al., 1980	Lactating mice confronting a male conspecific	Morphine (1.0 mg/kg) decreased aggressive behavior.
Haney and Miczek, 1989	Lactating mice confronting a female conspecific	Morphine (6.0, 10.0 mg/kg i.p.) decreased aggressive behavior at doses that did not alter locomotor activity.
Plonsky and Freeman, 1982	Pairs of female rats were administered methadone daily and tested in a neutral arena for 6 consecutive days	Acute methadone (2.5, 4.0 mg/kg s.c.) decreased the duration of social behaviors, including aggressive grooming at doses that also suppressed locomotor activity. With chronic methadone, social behavior but not locomotion continued to be suppressed.
Kinsley and Bridges, 1986	Lactating rats confronting a male conspecific	Morphine (5 mg/kg s.c.) decreased the proportion of rats that attacked.

Dominance-related Aggression

Crowley et al., 1975	Established colony of 1 male and 4 female pigtail macaques: Each simultaneously administered morphine	Neither acute (.05-.20 mg/kg i.m.) or chronic (15-30 mg/kg p.o.) morphine significantly altered dominance or submission related aggressive behaviors.

Killing

Janssen et al., 1962

Muricide by isolated male rats

Morphine (10-80 mg/kg s.c.) decreased muricide at doses that also suppressed motor behavior.

TABLE 4B Effects of Withdrawal from Chronic Opiate Administration on Aggression in Animals

References	Methods and Procedures	Results and Conclusions
Kreiskott, 1966	Observation of singly-housed rhesus monkeys	Withdrawal from chronic morphine was associated with alternating threat and defensive behavior toward a human observer.
Pain-induced aggression		
Crabtree and Moyer, 1972 Puri and Lal, 1974 Lal, 1975a Stolerman et al., 1975	Footshock in pairs of male and female rats. Morphine was administered in incremental doses 2-3 times daily (i.p.) for a minimum of 6 days. Terminal doses ranged from 80-405 mg/kg.	Withdrawal from chronic morphine enhanced sensitivity to shock-induced fighting; d-amphetamine (2 mg/kg) potentiated aggressive responding in male-male pairings and defensive responding in male-female pairings; female-female pairings were not associated with high levels of aggressive or defensive behavior.
Aggression by a resident toward an intruder		
Kantak and Miczek, 1986, 1988	Male mice confronting a group-housed male conspecific. Morphine pellets (75 mg s.c.) were implanted for 4-5 days. Behavioral testing occurred 48 hrs following pellet removal	Aggression in morphine-dependent residents and intruders is increased following withdrawal. Naloxone (1 mg/kg) did not increase agonistic behavior in morphine dependent mice. Sensitivity to the aggression-enhancing effect of dopaminergic agonists increases during morphine withdrawal, while sensitivity to the aggression-inhibiting effects of dopaminergic antagonists declines.
Female Aggression		
Avis and Peeke, 1979	Female hamsters housed in groups of 4. Morphine pellets (75 or 150 mg s.c.) were implanted for 1, 2 or 3 days	Naloxone administration (.5-4.0 mg/kg) following chronic morphine increased aggressive and defensive behaviors; this effect was potentiated by d-amphetamine (2 mg/kg).

Reference	Procedure	Findings
Davis and Khalsa, 1971	Female rats housed in groups of 4 or 6. Morphine was administered in incremental doses (15-400 mg/kg/day i.p.) for 15 days. Behavior was observed over a 6 day period following the last morphine administration	Withdrawal from chronic morphine was not associated with heightened aggressive behavior.

Dominance-related Aggression

Reference	Procedure	Findings
Thor et al., 1970 Thor, 1971	Singly-housed male rats were administered morphine in incremental doses (10-600 mg/kg/day) for 5 days. Following the last morphine injection, treated subjects were housed in groups of 6. Vocalizations were continuously recorded and used as indices of aggression	Withdrawal from chronic morphine was associated with increased vocalizations; this effect was potentiated by d-amphetamine (200 mg/ml p.o.). The number of vocalizations was positively associated with the amount of morphine received during chronic administration.
Avis and Peeke, 1979	Hamsters housed in groups of 4. Morphine pellets (75 or 150 mg s.c.) were implanted for 1, 2 or 3 days	Naloxone administration (.5-4.0 mg/kg) following chronic morphine increased aggressive and defensive behaviors; this effect was potentiated by d-amphetamine (2 mg/kg).
Boshka et al., 1966 Thor and Teel, 1968 Borgen et al., 1970 Davis and Khalsa, 1971 Lal and Puri, 1971 Lal et al., 1971 Puri and Lal, 1973,1974 Lal, 1975a Gianutsos et al., 1975 Gianutsos et al., 1976	Rats housed in groups of 4-6. Morphine was administered in incremental doses (10-405 mg/kg/day i.p.) for 9-15 days. Administration of additional psychoactive drugs occurred 4-72 hours after the last morphine injection. Behavior was observed over a 6 day period	Withdrawal from chronic morphine increases the frequency of aggressive and defensive attack; this effect is potentiated by catecholaminergic agonists. Naloxone (4, 8 mg/kg did not precipitate aggression in morphine dependent rats, but nalorphine (2 mg/kg) did.
Carlini and Gonzales, 1972	Pair-housed rats. Morphine was administered in incremental doses (12-768 mg/kg/day i.p.) for 16 days. Behavioral observation occurred 24, 48 and 72 hours following the last morphine injection	THC (5 mg/kg) or d-amphetamine (2 mg/kg) 48 or 72 hours into withdrawal increased the duration of aggressive behavior.

Reference	Procedure	Results
Gellert and Sparber, 1979	Food-deprived rats competing for food reinforcement. Morphine was administered in incremental doses (25-100 mg/kg i.p.) 2 times/day for 9 days	Withdrawal from chronic morphine disrupted dominance-submissive hierarchies and increased the duration of aggressive behavior.
Crowley et al., 1975	Dominance-related aggression in group-housed male pigtail macaques. Methadone (15-30 mg/kg p.o.) was administered for 10 weeks	Frequency of aggressive acts did not change during withdrawal from chronic methadone.

TABLE 5 Effects of Opiates on Aggression in Humans

References	Methods and Procedures	Results and Conclusions
Experimental Studies of Aggression		
Woody et al., 1983	Male opiate addicts were administered: Hopkins Symptom Checklist, Beck Depression Inventory and Profile of Mood States both during methadone treatment and following detoxification. Hospital staff served as controls	Measures of anger in hostile and non-hostile opiate addicts were not significantly different from controls during chronic methodone or following withdrawal.
Mirin and Meyer, 1979	Heroin was self-administered (i.v.) in a research ward setting, with and without the concurrent administration of opiate antagonists. Male opiate addicts were administered the Current and Past Psychopathology Scales, Brief Psychiatric Rating Scale and were evaluated by staff for levels of physical and verbal aggression prior to and during heroin self-administration, as well as during heroin-blockade	Acute heroin administration is associated with euphoria and tension release. Continuous self-administration increases feelings of suspicion, belligerence and hostility. Pharmacological blockade of heroin increased anger in double-blind but not in non-blind conditions.
Crime		
Dole et al.,1969	1500 incarcerated heroin addicts were given the opportunity to volunteer for methadone treatment 10 days before release	Prisoners who sought methadone treatment were less likely to be re-incarcerated than prisoners that did not seek treatment.
Greene et al., 1973	Criminal records, urine analysis and interview data were measured in 2,133 arrestees	Arrestees with heroin or methadone present in the urine committed a higher proportion of non-violent:violent crime, compared to arrestees with negative urine results.
Gossop and Roy, 1977	25 male narcotic addicts and 15 non-narcotic drug users undergoing drug rehabilitation were interviewed and administered the Hostility and Direction of Hostility Questionnaire	Narcotic addicts were more likely to have been convicted of violent crime than non-narcotic addicts.

Study	Method	Findings
McGlothin, 1979	Reviewed four studies comparing arrest records in narcotic addicts and non-drug users	Narcotic addicts had a higher proportion of property crime arrests and a lower proportion of violent crime arrests than non-addicted drug controls.
Simonds and Kashani, 1979b	Interview of incarcerated male juveniles	Delinquents reporting a history of heroin use were more likely to commit crimes against people (robbery, murder, rape) than crimes against property alone (vandalism, burglary, auto theft).
Tinklenberg et al., 1981	Compilation of police, laboratory, social worker and interview data compared in 293 incarcerated male juveniles	Relative incidence of narcotic abuse was comparable in juveniles classified as physically assaultive, sexually assaultive and non-assaultive. Heroin intoxication during the criminal act was infrequent.
Ball et al., 1983	243 male narcotic addicts randomly selected from a population of 4,069 addicts with police records were interviewed; validity of self-reports was compared to official records	12.4% of total arrests involved violent crimes.
Heller and Ehrlich, 1984	1,525 defendants undergoing court-ordered psychiatric evaluations were classified as non-violent, violent (1 violent conviction) or violent recidivists (more than 1 violent conviction); 245 demographic, socioeconomic and clinical variables were compared in the 3 groups	Non-violent offenders has a higher incidence of heroin abuse than violent offenders.
Nurco et al., 1986 Shaffer et al., 1987	Interview of 100 black, 100 white and 50 hispanic male heroin addicts undergoing out-patient methadone treatment	Self-report data indicate both violent and non-violent criminal activity increase during periods of active addiction. The rate of violent crime in heroin addicts is correlated with pre-addiction rates of criminal activity and precocious drug experimentation.

Anglin and Hser, 1987 Anglin and Speckart, 1988	Examined criminal activity before, during and after narcotic addiction and methadone maintenance in 671 males and 238 women attending methadone treatment centers	Property crime and drug dealing are significantly higher during periods of elevated narcotic use (pre- and post-methadone treatment). Rate of violent crime was low and did not vary as a function of narcotic use. Deviant behavior pre-dated narcotics initiation in the majority of subjects.

Personality Assessments and Aggression

Sheppard et al., 1975	51 male, 6 female active heroin addicts seeking out-patient methadone treatment were interviewed and administered the Edwards Personal Preference Schedule and the Standard Progressive Matrices	Heroin addicts did not exceed *a priori* criteria of high aggressivity.
Berzins et al., 1974	1500 MMPI scores from male and female opiate addicts seeking drug rehabilitation	Multivariate clustering delineated 2 personality profiles: Type 1 (33%) had elevated levels of personal and social maladjustment. Type 2 (7%) scored above-average in personal and social competence. 60% of the addicts remained unclustered. Profile types did not differ as a function of sex or treatment motivation.
Khantzian, 1974 Wurmser, 1974	Psychoanalytic interpretation of opiate addiction based on personal observation of addicts undergoing methadone treatment	Theorize individuals with aggressive impulses become addicted to opiates to relieve dysphoria associated with rage and aggression. Methadone treatment decreases reported feelings of rage in heroin addicts undergoing psychotherapy.
Kurtines et al., 1975	59 male heroin addicts undergoing drug rehabilitation were administered the California Psychological Inventory. Scores were compared to male marijuana users, psychiatric patients, incarcerated delinquents and police officers	Heroin addicts scored significantly lower on levels of responsibility and socialization. Measures of interpersonal effectiveness and neurosis were comparable to other males, suggesting addicts have sociopathic as opposed to psychiatric difficulties.

Hewett and Martin, 1980	Incarcerated narcotic addicts, reformed alcoholics and controls with no drug or alcohol abuse history were administered the Personal History Questionnaire	Narcotic addict prisoners were more sociopathic than alcoholics and controls. The severity of adult sociopathy was inversely proportional to the age drug use was initiated. Both alcoholics and narcotic abusers were sociopathic pre-dating substance abuse.
Sutker and Archer, 1984	Reviewed literature on opiate abuse and psychopathology	MMPI indicators of sociopathy are consistently elevated in addicts across varied assessment conditions. Sociopathy appears to pre-date addiction.
Health Statistics		
Monforte and Spitz, 1975	207 homicide victims were analyzed for the presence of narcotic and non-narcotic drugs.	11.3% of victims had morphine in their system at the time of death. 30.9% had needle tracks.
Concool et al., 1979	Reviewed deaths in 1,156 persons who had enrolled in a methadone program	37.8% of the 45 deaths occurring either during or after methadone treatment were due to violence.

Table 6 Effects of Amphetamines on Aggression in Animals

References	Methods and Procedures	Results and Conclusions
Isolation-induced aggression		
Melander, 1960	Male mice, individually-housed, tested in pairs for latency to attack for up to 120 minutes after drug administration	10 mg/kg d-amphetamine increased activity and caused disorientation thereby decreasing aggressiveness.
DaVanzo et al., 1966	Male mice, individually-housed, tested in pairs	ED50 for inhibition of aggression was $\geq$ 3 mg/kg i.p.
Valzelli et al., 1967	Male mice, individually-housed, tested in groups of three; rating scale	5 mg/kg amphetamine did not inhibit aggressive behavior.
Charpentier, 1969	Male mice, individually-housed, tested in pairs; rating scale	2 mg/kg i.p. amphetamine decreased latency to attack and increased fighting duration.
Le Douarec and Broussy, 1969	Male and female mice, individually-housed, tested in pairs in resident/intruder paradigm; rating scale	d-Amphetamine did not affect aggressiveness at low doses (0.5 and 2 mg/kg i.p.), inhibited aggressiveness at higher doses (4 mg/kg i.p.).
Welch and Welch, 1969	Male mice, individually-housed, tested in pairs in a clean cage; measured frequency of attack	Fighting was enhanced by a low amphetamine dose (2.0 mg/kg) and suppressed by a high dose (6.0 mg/kg).
Scott et al., 1971	Male mice, individually-housed, tested in pairs	10 mg/kg i.p. dl-amphetamine decreased fighting in C57BL/6 but not BALB/c, possibly due to hyperthermia
Hodge and Butcher, 1975	Male mice, individually-housed, tested in pairs; measured latency, frequency and duration of fighting	d-Amphetamine increased frequency of fighting at low doses (1.0-4.0 mg/kg i.p.) and decreased fighting at high (8.0 mg/kg) doses.
Krsiak, 1979	Male mice (n=404), individually-housed, confronted a group-housed male intruder; measured frequencies of motor, social, and aggressive acts	0.25-1.0 mg/kg amphetamine decreased threats and attacks without affecting locomotor behavior.

| Poshivalov, 1981 | Male mice, individually-housed, tested with a group-housed male mouse | 0.5-3 mg/kg i.p. amphetamine decreased aggressive behavior in both normal mice and mice pre-treated with the dopamine-hydroxylase inhibitor FD-008 (100 mg/kg). |
| Poli and Palermo-Neto, 1986 | Male mice, individually-housed, tested in groups of 15-20; measured latency, frequency, and duration of attack behavior | 6 mg/kg i.p. *d*-amphetamine decreased attack frequency and duration, increased latency to attack; haloperidol (0.5, 1 mg/kg) further decreased aggressiveness; stereotypy may mask amphetamine effects on aggressiveness. |

Aggression induced by crowded housing

| Bovet-Nitti and Messeri, 1975 | Measured population growth of densely housed mice (26 populations of 13-15 mice each); chronic administration | Amphetamine (0.25 g/kg in food, approximately 40 mg/kg/day) resulted in violent fighting (male-male and cannibalism of newborns) and a decrease in population. |

Pain-induced aggression and defense

Stille et al., 1963 Kostowski, 1966 Hoffmeister and Wuttke, 1969 Irwin et al., 1971	Male mice, tested in pairs while exposed to electric foot shock	Amphetamine (0.1 mg/kg i.p.) increased aggressive behavior. Methamphetamine (0.3, 0.5 mg/kg p.o.) increased defensive-aggressive behavior.
Emley and Hutchinson, 1972, 1983 Hutchinson et al., 1977	Male and female squirrel monkeys, individually-housed, electric tail shock, bit inanimate object	Amphetamine increased biting responses at doses of 0.125-1.0 mg/kg s.c. and decreased biting at 2.0 mg/kg.
Crowley, 1972	Male rats, individually-housed, tested in pairs while exposed to electric foot shock	Methamphetamine increased fighting time at low (0.25-1.0 mg/kg i.p.) doses and decreased fighting at higher (4.0 mg/kg) doses.
Powell et al., 1973	Male and female rats, pair-housed, exposed to electric shock through grid floor or subdermally	*d*-Amphetamine (0.2-5 mg/kg s.c.) had little or no effect on footshock-elicited aggression; when shock was administered subdermally, 1.0 mg/kg increased threat and attack and 3.0 mg/kg decreased aggression.

Reference	Description	Results
Crowley et al., 1974	Male rats, individually-housed, tested in pairs while exposed to electric foot shock; chronic administration	d-Methamphetamine (5 mg/kg-20 mg/kg/day in drinking water for 35 days) suppressed fighting; rats withdrawn from d-methamphetamine 24 hours prior to tests fought more than methamphetamine-treated but less than controls.
Sheard and Davis, 1976	Male rats, tested in pairs while exposed to electric foot shock	p-Chloroamphetamine (1.5, 2.5, and 5 mg/kg) initially depressed, and later enhanced aggression; the initial inhibition of aggression may be due to changes in pain threshold; 5-HT depletion is associated with increased aggression.
DeWeese, 1977	Male squirrel monkeys, individually-housed, aggression measured as bites to an inanimate object, intermittent shock and food reinforcement schedule	0.01-1 mg/kg d-amphetamine increased lever responding at low doses and decreased responding at higher doses while rate of biting only decreased.

Defensive aggression induced by brain stimulation

Reference	Description	Results
Panksepp, 1971	Male rats, electrical stimulation of hypothalamus, measured latency to attack mice	2 mg/kg methamphetamine increased affective attack and slightly decreased quiet-biting attack.
Sheard, 1967	Male and female cats, electrical stimulation of lateral hypothalamus and reticular formation, measured latency to attack rats	Amphetamine (5 and 10 mg/5 ml water, i.p.) facilitated attack behavior.
Baxter, 1968	Cats, electrical stimulation of hypothalamus, measured hissing behavior	1-4 mg/kg i.p. dl-amphetamine did not significantly inhibit hissing.
Marini et al., 1979	Male and female cats, electrical stimulation of medial and lateral hypothalamus, measured latency to attack an anethetized rat	Low doses of amphetamine (0.125-0.5 mg/kg i.p.) facilitated attack, higher doses (1.0-1.5 mg/kg) inhibited attack.
Maeda et al., 1985	Cats, electrical stimulation of left medial hypothalamic area, measured directed attack and hissing	0.5-3 mg/kg i.p. methamphetamine dose-dependently lowered the thresholds for defensive attack responses, these effects were almost identical to those of apomorphine (1 mg/kg i.p.) suggesting that this effect is dopamine-mediated.

Drug-induced aggression

Chance, 1946 Randrup and Munkvad, 1969 Hasselager et al., 1972 Rolinski, 1973, 1977	Male mice, group-housed	High doses of amphetamine (>10 mg/kg) increased biting and defensive-aggressive postures; these effects were antagonized with neuroleptic drug treatment, implicating a dopaminergic mechanism.
Consolo et al., 1965a,b	Male mice, housed in groups or individually, tested in groups	Both individually- and group-housed aggressive mice were more sensitive to the toxic effects of amphetamine than normal controls.
Shintomi, 1975	Male mice, densely-confined; measured the effects of various drugs on methamphetamine-induced aggression; rating scale	5 mg/kg s.c. methamphetamine resulted in hyperactivity, fighting behavior, and increased vocalizations; fighting behavior was inhibited with dopamine antagonist or benzodiazepine administration.
Kantak and Miczek, 1988 Tidey and Miczek, 1992	Male mice confronted a group-housed male intruder	d-Amphetamine (0.1-2.5 mg/kg i.p.) increased aggressive behavior in morphine-withdrawn mice and decreased aggressive behavior in normal mice. Morphine-withdrawn mice exhibited higher levels of aggressive behavior after d-amphetamine (0.1-10 mg/kg) administration than normal controls.
Schrold and Squires, 1971	5 day-old chicks, pre-treated with p-Cl-phenylalanine (150 mg/kg i.p. 5 times per day for 3 days), tested in groups of 4	p-Cl-phenylalanine lowered brain 5-HT and 5-HIAA concentrations to approximately 30%; in these animals, d-amphetamine (6, 10 mg/kg i.p.) induced strong aggressive pecking to other chicks.
Hine et al., 1975	218 pairs of male and female chicks, group-housed observed in pairs (both treated); measured frequency of pecks for 4 hours	d-Amphetamine (3, 6 mg/kg i.p.) increased pecking, higher doses (9, 12 mg/kg) decreased pecking; imipramine administration did not affect amphetamine-induced pecking; haloperidol (10 mg/kg) selectively blocked amphetamine-induced pecking.
Fog et al., 1970	Individually-housed male rats with striatal lesions; tested in pairs	Striatal lesions suppress amphetamine (10 mg/kg)-induced stereotypy without affecting "rage" reactions.

Reference	Paradigm	Results
Lal et al., 1971 Puri and Lal, 1973	Male rats, group-housed during morphine withdrawal, measured attack biting and defensive rearing	*d*-Amphetamine (2, 4, and 8 mg/kg i.p.) increased attack bites, defensive rearing, and vocalizations 72 hours into morphine withdrawal; this is attributed to stimulation of "sensitized" dopamine receptors.
Thor, 1971	Male rats, group-housed during morphine withdrawal, measured attack frequency and vocalizations	Increased ingestion of *d*-amphetamine (approximately 5 and 20 mg/kg in drinking water) was correlated with increased intensity of fighting and vocalizations.
Eison et al., 1978 Ellison et al., 1978	Male rats, housed in social colonies for 75 days; implanted with amphetamine pellets or a refillable subcutaneous amphetamine delivery system; tested in groups; chronic administration	After 4-5 days of continuous amphetamine administration, rats which received amphetamine exhibited more aggressive behaviors than controls.

Aggression induced by REM sleep deprivation

Ferguson and Dement, 1969	125 male and female rats, housed on water-surrounded pedestals; tested in groups, measured duration of aggressive bouts	0.25-23 mg/kg i.p. *d*-amphetamine caused substantial stereotyped aggressive behavior in REM-deprived rats; neither REM deprivation nor amphetamine administration alone produced these effects.

Aggression by resident toward intruder

Miczek, 1977a,b, 1979b Miczek and O'Donnell, 1978 O'Donnell and Miczek, 1980	Male mice and rats confronted a group-housed male intruder; resident drug treated	*d*-Amphetamine increased aggression at low doses in rats only and decreased aggression at higher doses in both mice and rats
Winslow and Miczek, 1983	Male mice confronted a group-housed male intruder in 10 consecutive tests; resident drug treated	*d*-Amphetamine (0.1-5.0 mg/kg) increased low levels of aggressive behavior induced by repeated confrontations.
Kantak and Miczek, 1988 Tidey and Miczek, 1992	Male mice confronted a group-housed male intruder; resident drug treated	*d*-Amphetamine (0.1-2.5 mg/kg i.p.) increased aggressive behavior in morphine-withdrawn mice and decreased aggressive behavior in normal mice. Morphine-withdrawn mice exhibited higher levels of aggressive behavior after *d*-amphetamine (0.1-10 mg/kg) administration than normal controls.

Reference		
Haney et al., 1990	Male mice, housed individually or pair-housed (with or without fighting experience) confronted group-housed intruders; resident drug treated	0.1, 1.0 mg/kg *d*-amphetamine (i.p.) enhanced aggression and 10 mg/kg *d*-amphetamine suppressed aggression in isolated and inexperienced pair-housed mice. All doses suppressed aggression in experienced pair-housed mice.
Silverman, 1966	Male rats, individually housed; resident drug treated	1-5 mg/kg *dl*-amphetamine (i.p.) reduced aggressive behavior.

Female and juvenile aggression

Karczmar and Scudder, 1967 Richardson et al., 1972	6 genera and several strains of mice living in a large colony were evaluated (checklist) for motor, social, and maternal aggressive behavior	Methamphetamine (7 mg/kg) decreased aggression in all strains; methamphetamine seems to increase stereotypic and motor activity while decreasing goal-directed behavior.
Beatty et al., 1984	Male juvenile rats, individually-housed, tested in pairs, both treated, repeated testing	*d*-Amphetamine (0.05, 0.1 mg/kg i.p.) decreased play-fighting; this was not antagonized by haloperidol, clonidine, chlorpromazine, phenoxybenzamine or *α*-methyltyrosine.

Dominance-related aggression

Keller and Poster, 1970	Male fish, individually-housed, paired with a like-treated male	*d*-Amphetamine (1.0, 2.0 mg % tank water) and *dl*-amphetamine (1.0 mg % tank water) decreased both mobility and aggressive behavior.
Munro, 1986	Fish, individually-housed, measured aggressive activity toward mirrors and models of conspecifics	Immersion in *d*-amphetamine (20-200 mg/101 tank water) did not affect aggressive responses; intracranial injection of *d*-amphetamine (10 and 20 µg/fish) significantly decreased aggressive displays and frequency of bites.
Gambill et al., 1976	Male rats, housed and tested in a social colony; rated for the presence or absence of aggressive and other behaviors; chronic administration	High doses of *d*-amphetamine inhibited the initiation of aggression in dominant rats; *d*-amphetamine induced hypervigilance and defensive behavior in subordinate rats.
Hoffmeister and Wuttke, 1969	Male cats confronted male conspecifics; rating scale	Methamphetamine (1-4 mg/kg p.o.) enhanced defensive-aggressive behavior but decreased attack behavior.

Reference	Findings
Miller et al., 1973	Male rhesus monkeys, conditioned to avoid electric shock by detecting and interpreting the facial signals of a paired monkey (cooperative conditioning); their dominance and social behaviors were later tested.	Amphetamine (0.25 mg/kg i.m.) slightly facilitated cooperative conditioning and social behaviors while reducing aggression.
Crowley et al., 1974	Male macaque monkeys, living in a social group	d-Methamphetamine (.0625-.25 mg/kg i.m.) decreased dominance behaviors such as pursuits, bites, and attacks; administration of 2 mg/kg to one monkey engendered aggressive behavior toward that subject from others in the group.
Garver et al., 1975	Male stumptail macaques, living in social colonies, chronic administration	d-Amphetamine (2 mg/kg administered via nasogastric tubing every 12 hours for 3-20 days) initially increased and later reduced the initiation of social activity and threats; haloperidol (0.57 mg/kg) "normalized" social behavior.
Haber et al., 1977, 1981	Rhesus monkeys, housed in social groups; chronic administration	Amphetamine (0.1-1.0 mg/kg i.m. for 3 weeks) significantly increased aggressive behavior by dominant monkeys and submissive behavior by subordinate monkeys.
Miczek et al., 1981 Miczek and Yoshimura, 1982	Male squirrel monkeys, housed in social groups	d-Amphetamine (0.5, 1 mg/kg p.o. three times over 24 hours) decreased social and aggressive behaviors and increased agonistic behavior by non-drugged animals to the amphetamine-treated monkey.
Schlemmer and Davis, 1981	Male and female stumptail macaques, housed in social groups; chronic administration	d-Amphetamine (3.2 mg/kg/day for 12 days) increased submissive gesturing in dominant-ranking females without increasing aggressive behaviors directed toward that monkey; the effects of amphetamine were very similar to those of apomorphine (1 mg/kg/day for 12 days).
Miczek and Gold, 1983	Male squirrel monkeys, housed in social groups, measured social behavior to others in group	d-Amphetamine (0.1, 0.3 mg/kg) decreased aggressive behavior initiated by dominant monkeys, higher doses (0.6, 1.0 mg/kg) caused dominant monkeys to receive aggression from others.

Winslow and Miczek, 1988	Male and female squirrel monkeys, housed in social groups; Male mice, tested with group-housed male intruders	d-Amphetamine (0.1-0.6 mg/kg i.m. in monkeys, 10 mg/kg i.p. in mice) decreased aggressive behavior; naltrexone enhanced the suppression of aggressive behavior by d-amphetamine.
Martin et al., 1990	2 adult male stumptail macaques, housed in social groups of males and females; social rank was disrupted to study within-subjects effects	d-Amphetamine (0.01-0.3 mg/kg, i.m.) increased aggressive behavior overall; a rise in dominance resulted in decreased sensitivity to the effects of amphetamine, and a decrease in dominance position resulted in increased sensitivity to amphetamine's effects.

Killing

McCarty and Whitesides, 1976	Male and female mice, pair-housed, tested for predatory behavior toward crickets	Both d- and l-amphetamine (1, 10 mg/kg i.p.) dose-dependently decreased predatory behavior.
Karli, 1958 Horovitz et al., 1965, 1966 Salama and Goldberg, 1970 Malick, 1975, 1976 Gay et al., 1975 Barr et al., 1976	Male and female rats, individually housed, selected for muricidal behavior, acute administration	Amphetamine (0.125-15 mg/kg) dose-dependently inhibited muricidal behavior.
Panksepp, 1971	Male rats, electrical stimulation of hypothalamus, measured latency to attack mice	2 mg/kg methamphetamine increased affective attack and slightly decreased quiet-biting attack.
Fujiwara et al., 1980	Measured inhibition of THC-induced muricide in 8 singly-housed male rats	Methamphetamine (1-2 mg/kg) dose-dependently suppressed muricidal behavior while increasing motor activity.
Posner et al., 1976	Male rats, individually-housed, selected for muricidal behavior; one group food-deprived	d-Amphetamine (2 mg/kg s.c.) inhibited muricide in satiated rats but not in food-deprived rats.
Barr et al., 1977	36 male rats, individually-housed, selected for muricidal behavior; chronic administration	Inhibition of muricidal behavior was decreased by d-amphetamine (2.4 mg/kg twice daily for 8 days) but not by l-amphetamine (3.1 mg/kg twice daily for 8 days).
Russell et al., 1983	200 male rats, individually-housed, food-deprived	d-Amphetamine (0.5-3 mg/kg) dose-dependently inhibited muricide.

Reference	Method	Findings
Yoshimura and Miczek, 1983	113 male rats, individually-housed, selected for muricidal behavior, feeding restricted and implanted with cannulae to 6 brain sites	d-Amphetamine (10-30 µg) injected to the lateral ventricles, lateral hypothalamus or central amygdala abolished muricidal behavior while injections to the substantia nigra, ventral caudate or nucleus accumbens were ineffective.
Sheard, 1967	Male and female cats, electrical stimulation of lateral hypothalamus and reticular formation, measured latency to attack rats	Amphetamine (5 and 10 mg/5 ml water, i.p.) facilitated attack behavior.
Marini et al., 1979	Male and female cats, electrical stimulation of medial and lateral hypothalamus, measured latency to attack an anethesized rat	Low doses of amphetamine (0.125-0.5 mg/kg i.p.) facilitated attack, higher doses (1.0-1.5 mg/kg) inhibited attack.
Zagrodzka and Jurkowski, 1988	Male cats, measured attack behavior toward mice	Amphetamine (1.5 mg/kg, i.m.) suppressed mouse-killing behavior and offensive behavior toward other cats.

Literature Reviews

Reference	Method	Findings
Munkvad, 1975	Review of 34 articles spanning 1959-1975 concerning drug-elicited aggression	d-Amphetamine (15 mg/kg) induces aggressive behavior in mice tested in groups of 4; in monkeys, amphetamine administration reduces social activities; in humans, amphetamines can produce aggressive behavior and stereotypy; these effects of amphetamine administration can be antagonized by DA receptor antagonists.
Gianutsos and Lal, 1976	Review of 112 articles spanning 1948-1976 concerning drug-elicited aggression	d- or l-amphetamine alone, combined with l-DOPA, and during morphine-withdrawal increases defensive rearing, biting, and vocalizations; evidence is strong for the involvement of DA in aggression.
Kulkarni and Plotnikoff, 1978	Review of 101 articles spanning 1965-1975 concerning the effects of stimulants on muricidal, isolation-induced, shock-induced, lesion-induced, stimulant-induced and spontaneous aggression	While small doses of amphetamine may enhance aggression in certain models, the effects of amphetamines on aggressive behavior are predominantly inhibitory; amphetamine can potentiate aggression elicited by other drugs.

| Looney and Cohen, 1982 | Comparative review of aggression induced by the omission of reward in pigeons, rats, monkeys, and humans | While most drugs reduce aggression at doses which do not affect operant responding, d-amphetamine has been found to both increase and decrease aggression. |
| Miczek, 1987
Miczek and Winslow, 1987
Miczek and Tidey, 1989 | Review of over 1500 articles concerning the psychopharmacology of aggression in humans and other animals | At intermediate and higher doses, amphetamine decreases isolation- and extinction-induced aggression while increasing motor activity; single low doses may increase isolation-induced aggression; amphetamine more consistently increases pain-induced aggression; the primary effect of amphetamines is to disorganize patterns of social and aggressive behavior. |

TABLE 7 Effects of Amphetamines on Aggression in humans

References	Methods and Procedures	Results and Conclusions
Criminal Violence		
Eisenberg et al., 1963	Ratings of 15 male institutionalized juvenile delinquents by peers, teachers, and supervisors	Symptoms of disturbed behavior improved with all doses of amphetamine (5-40 mg/day).
Cockett and Marks, 1969	Psychological evaluation of 82 juvenile delinquents (HDHQ and Form C of 16 PF personality tests) in London	Amphetamine users had significantly higher hostility scores, were more self-critical, introverted, and guilt-prone.
Hemmi, 1969	Interviews with male prisoners	28% were amphetamine users; these prisoners were more likely to have committed violent crimes.
Rubin, 1972	Literature review and anecdotal report of aggression in mentally ill criminals	While amphetamine abuse has been implicated in violent behavior, this relationship is probably not causal; a predisposing personality is likely necessary; drugs (including amphetamines) may act as "releasers" in predisposed persons.
Tinklenberg and Woodrow, 1974	Interviews of 152 male juvenile delinquents incarcerated in a moderate security facility in California	Amphetamines were involved in only 2% of offenses; subjects who had used amphetamines expressed opinions that these drugs do not affect aggressiveness.
Paul, 1975	Anecdotal account of acts of aggression perpetrated under the influence of amphetamines and other drugs	Suggested that amphetamines alone or combined with alcohol contribute considerably to aggressive behavior by releasing inhibitions.
Fink and Hyatt, 1978	Anecdotal overview of the association between crime and drug use	Suggested that although reports of ties between criminal behavior and amphetamine use are increasing, no definite association has been established.
Simonds and Kashani, 1979b	Interviews of 109 male juvenile delinquents institutionalized in Missouri, using DSM III criteria	60% of delinquents who committed crimes against persons were amphetamine users.

527

Siomopoulos, 1979	Psychiatric evaluation of 451 males referred to a psychiatric institute after being found unfit to stand trial in Cook county, Illinois; interviews were primarily concerned with drug use within 24 hours of a crime being committed	64% of the subjects had a history of drug abuse; 11% of the sample used drugs during the 24 hours preceding the criminal act; significantly more crimes were committed under the influence of amphetamines and amphetamine-like substances than with heroin, LSD, marihuana, or PCP; these crimes included murder, attempted murder, and unlawful use of a weapon.
Swett, 1985	214 male inpatients from a maximum security ward for the criminally insane	Many were poly-drug users; amphetamines were used by 23% of the sample; subjects who had used amphetamines were not more likely to commit violent acts than subjects who had not used amphetamines.
Mio et al., 1986	7 juvenile sex offenders completed questionnaires concerning their drug history, family history, and history of crime	4 of the 7 had used amphetamines among other drugs, all of these subjects reported that amphetamines and other drugs were used by family members; relationship between drug use and criminal behavior is correlative only.
Health Statistics		
Scott, 1968	Anecdotal report of incidence of alcohol and drug abuse by 50 murderers in Great Britian	In 4 cases, amphetamine use may have played a part in the perpetration of the murder.
Carey and Mandel, 1969	Anecdotal reports from drug agents of 30 incidents of violence	Suggested that violent acts by amphetamine users are not usually premeditated; the violence is unpredictable and sparked by paranoia.
Greene et al., 1973	A survey of drug use in 2133 people incarcerated in the District of Columbia; a separate study reported on a sample of 144 incarcerated subjects surveyed for their history of amphetamine use; charges against the subjects were classified into violent and nonviolent categories	81.8% of the subjects who tested positive for amphetamine at the time of arrest (urine test) also tested positive for an opiate (heroin or methadone); in this population, the incidence of violent crime was lower in the drug abuse group than in the non-abuser group and amphetamine abusers were no more likely to have committed a violent crime than non-amphetamine abusers.

Bailey and Shaw, 1989	A retrospective report of methamphetamine- and cocaine-related deaths in San Diego county in 1987	Methamphetamine was involved in 23 homicides, 1/8 of homicides in San Diego county for that year. Methamphetamine combined with cocaine was involved in 4 homicides.

Personality Evaluations

Rickman et al., 1961	18 case studies of male and female chronic amphetamine users	Long-term amphetamine usage is accompanied by suspiciousness and aggressiveness.
Rawlin, 1968	Anecdotal account of the contemporary street use of amphetamines	Amphetamine use can lead to paranoid hallucinations resulting in attacks on bystanders, friends, or policemen.
Angrist and Gershon, 1969	Psychiatric reports of aggressive behavior in 60 male and female patients hospitalized for amphetamine use	62% of these patients had police records for offenses ranging from vandalism to attempted murder, however this relationship is more likely correlative than causal; paranoid behavior was present in 50% and was occasionally accompanied by violent behavior.
Smith and Crim, 1969	Anecdotal description of the lifestyle of the typical chronic amphetamine abuser in the Haight-Ashbury community	Paranoid amphetamine abusers are highly prone to erratic and violent behavior; most often this comes in the context of drug procurement.
Bach-y-Rita et al., 1971	Psychiatric evaluation of 130 patients displaying episodic violent behavior	12 of the 130 patients were chronic amphetamine users.
Ellinwood, 1971	13 case studies of male and female acute and chronic amphetamine users	Amphetamine-induced paranoia directly results in homicidal behavior.
Levine et al., 1972	Structured interview of 218 male and female young, middle class amphetamine users regarding health, drug history, family history	A high percentage of the subjects were depressed, with >80% showing psychiatric symptomatology; most engaged in multiple drug use; poor family and social histories appear to pre-date amphetamine use.

529

Black and Heald, 1975	MMPI evaluations of 40 male alcoholics and 50 male drug abusers from a military rehabilitation program; 72% of this group were amphetamine or other stimulant abusers	The drug-abuser sample showed a greater incidence of psychopathic, general personality maladjustment and significant emotional dysfunction than the alcoholic sample; a causal relationship between these illnesses and drug abuse could not be inferred.
Angrist and Gershon, 1976	Psychiatric evaluation of 9 chronic abusers after the administration of large doses of amphetamine	Violent behavior, associated with episodes of psychotic and/or paranoid behavior, was observed; however its incidence is infrequent.
Brook et al., 1976	Psychiatric evaluation (MMPI, WAIS, parent questionnaire, school records) of 117 residents of a drug treatment center in London, all chronic amphetamine abusers	Subjects scored consistently higher than controls on schizophrenic, psychopathic deviate, depression and other scales; drug use is probably a manifestation of underlying problems and not a cause.
Schiørring, 1977, 1981	Inverviews with 50 Swedish and Danish stimulant abusers in drug treatment programs	Amphetamine use leads to stereotyped motor and social activity, social withdrawal, paranoia, and hallucinations.
Siomopoulos, 1981	8 case studies of male acute and chronic amphetamine users	Amphetamine-induced emotional lability and paranoia lead to criminal and homicidal behavior.
Atkinson, 1982	Anecdotal reports of violent behavior in hospitalized patients	Stimulants such as cocaine, amphetamines and methylphenidate can produce violence-prone paranoid or manic states.

Experimental Studies on Aggression

Laties, 1961	16 male subjects, sleep deprived and non-sleep deprived, completed questionnaires and were tested in groups for cooperative behavior	Sleep-deprivation slightly increased hostility and significantly decreased social initiation and task involvement; amphetamine (10 mg) and secobarbital (100 mg) increased friendliness, social initiation and task involvement.
Cameron et al., 1965	Questionnaires completed by 239 male and female college students before and 2 hours after amphetamine administration	d-Amphetamine (5 mg) and d,l-amphetamine (10 mg) increased positive mood and socialization and decreased negative mood.

Study	Description	Findings
Leichner et al., 1976	30 male and female psychiatric inpatients (diagnosed as schizophrenic, depressive, alcoholic or antisocial) were rated for sociability following methylphenidate administration	Methylphenidate (0.5 mg/kg i.v.) increased talkativeness in every group except antisocial subjects; methylphenidate also increased psychotic symptomatology in schizophrenics.
Griffiths et al., 1977 Higgins and Stitzer, 1988	3 male subjects with a history of amphetamine use were rated for social behavior, 11 normal volunteers were rated for behavior during dyadic verbal interactions; 4 male and female subjects, tested in same-sex pairs, were able to either socialize or perform a task for monetary reinforcement	*d*-Amphetamine (5-30 mg) increased socializing.
Smith and Davis, 1977	16 normal male and female subjects completed mood scales (POMS) after ingestion of amphetamine	Amphetamine (10 or 20 mg) increased both euphoria and anxiety.
Milkman and Frosch, 1980	10 male amphetamine users were administered 30 mg amphetamine, rated for sexual and aggressive drive states; with control group	Amphetamine users display less control over impulses and drives; aggressive behavior is more often verbal than physical.
Cherek et al. 1986, 1989	8 male subjects pushed buttons to earn points exchangeable for money; a second button allowed them to aggress toward (subtract points from) confederate "opponents"	Amphetamine increased aggressive responding at low and moderate doses (5, 10 mg/70 kg) and decreased aggressive responding at the highest (20 mg/70 kg) dose.
Beezley et al., 1987	30 male subjects competed with confederate "opponents" in a reaction time task; subjects were able to vary the intensity of shock delivered to opponents	No relationship between *d*-amphetamine dose (2.5, 5 or 10 mg) and aggressive responding was found.

Literature Reviews

Study	Description	Findings
Kramer, 1969	Review of 28 articles spanning 1939-1968 which address problems of amphetamine abuse	Amphetamines predispose users to violent behavior by producing suspiciousness, hyperactivity and mood lability.
Allen et al., 1975	Review of 54 articles spanning 1937-1974 concerning the relation between psychostimulant drugs and aggression	Amphetamine use does not lead to aggressive behavior except when the dose and pattern of usage induce a state of paranoid psychosis.

Reference		
Fitzpatrick, 1974	Discussion of the relationship of drug use or abuse to violent or nonviolent crime	Amphetamine users are no more likely to commit crimes of violence than non-drug users.
Greenberg, 1976	Review of 75 articles spanning 1952-1975 on the relationship between amphetamine abuse and crime	A causal connection between amphetamine use and criminal behavior cannot be inferred from present studies; amphetamine use is not particularly tied to violence, this connection involves more variables.
Sheard, 1977a, 1983	Two reviews (1977: 14 references spanning 1939-1975, 1983: 60 references spanning 1956-1981) of literature linking drug use and aggression	While amphetamine use does not lead to aggression except when psychosis is induced, amphetamine use indirectly increases the potential for violence by causing reckless hyperactive and impulsive behavior.
Ellinwood, 1979	Review of 113 articles from 1967 to 1979 on the behavioral effects of amphetamines	Chronic amphetamine psychosis is marked by paranoia and hallucinations.
Cherek and Steinberg, 1987	Review of 191 articles spanning 1937-1986 on the effects of drugs on aggressive behavior	Amphetamine use could predispose individuals toward violence due to its stimulant and paranoia-inducing effects; d-amphetamine treatment often reduces aggression in hyperactive children and may be effective in treating aggressive adult patients.
Miczek, 1987	A review of over 1500 articles concerning the psychopharmacology of aggressive behavior in humans and other species	Evidence that amphetamine use leads to aggressive behavior is split; when aggression occurs it is most likely secondary to the psychotic paranoia induced by high doses administered intravenously.
Miczek and Tidey, 1989	A literature review of over 150 articles investigating the link between amphetamines and aggressive and social behavior	While amphetamines may induce dose-dependent biphasic effects on aggression in experimental studies, the main overall effect of amphetamines is to disrupt social and aggressive behavior patterns.

TABLE 8 Effects of Cocaine on Aggression in Animals

References	Methods and Procedures	Results and Conclusions
Isolation-induced aggression		
Hadfield, 1982 Hadfield et al., 1982	Male mice, individually housed, tested in groups of 4 identically treated animals under high-density crowding	Cocaine (10, 35 mg/kg i.p.) dose dependently increased fight duration; this increase peaks at 30 minutes after injection and may be due to general stimulatory effects.
Miczek and O'Donnell, 1978	Male mice, housed individually or pair-housed with a female, tested with a group-housed "intruder"	Cocaine (0.125-8 mg/kg i.p.) selectively decreased aggressive behavior; isolated mice were less sensitive to the aggression-reducing effects of cocaine than non-isolated mice.
Pain-induced aggression and defense		
Brunaud and Siou, 1959	15 male rats, tested in pairs while receiving electric foot shock	Cocaine (5-50 mg/kg) increased the display of aggressive postures.
Emley and Hutchinson, 1983	23 male and female squirrel monkeys bit a rubber hose in response to electric tail shock	Cocaine (0.3-10 mg/kg s.c.) dose-dependently increased biting and lever pressing responses; higher doses (20, 30 mg/kg) decreased both response types.
Aggression due to the omission of reward		
Hutchinson et al., 1976	Acute and chronic effects of cocaine measured using shock-induced aggression and extinction-induced aggression paradigms in squirrel monkeys, mice and pigeons	Acute and chronic cocaine generally decreases aggressive behavior relative to nonaggressive activity.
Moore and Thompson, 1978	2 male pigeons pecked on a response key for food reinforcement; aggression elicited during extinction was measured by pecks to a mirror; acute and chronic administration	Acute cocaine (.01-17 mg/kg i.m.) decreased aggressive behavior at doses which did not affect key responding. Chronic cocaine (1-13.3 mg/kg/day for 150-160 days total) resulted in partial tolerance to food-reinforced but not aggressive responding.

533

Drug-induced aggression

Reference	Subjects	Findings
Kantak and Miczek, 1988	Male mice, pair-housed with a female, confronted a group-housed male intruder	0.05-10 mg/kg cocaine increased attack bites and threats in morphine-withdrawn but not control mice.

Aggression by resident toward intruder

Reference	Subjects	Findings
Miczek, 1977b; Miczek and O'Donnell, 1978	Male mice, singly housed or pair-housed with a female, confronted a group-housed male intruder	Cocaine (0.125-8 mg/kg i.p.) selectively decreased aggressive behavior; isolated mice were less sensitive to the aggression-reducing effects of cocaine than non-isolated mice.
Miczek, 1979b	10 male rats, pair-housed with a female, confronted a male intruder in the home cage	Low doses of cocaine (0.5, 2 mg/kg) did not affect aggressive behavior; higher doses (8, 32 mg/kg) significantly and selectively decreased attack and threat behavior.
O'Donnell and Miczek, 1980	30 male mice, pair-housed with a female, confronted an intruder in the home cage; tested with cocaine while being treated chronically with amphetamine or saline	Cocaine (2-16 mg/kg) dose-dependently decreased attack frequency in both amphetamine- and saline-maintained animals.
Kantak, 1989	123 male mice, pair-housed with females and tested with a male intruder in the home cage; acute and chronic	Acute cocaine (.125-20 mg/kg i.p.) increased attacks and threats at low doses and decreased aggressive behavior at high doses. Chronic cocaine (.5 mg/kg i.p. daily for 15 days) significantly decreased aggressive behavior. Dietary magnesium altered the effects of cocaine.

Dominance-related aggression

Reference	Subjects	Findings
Miczek and Yoshimura, 1982	Male squirrel monkeys, housed in social groups	Cocaine (10 mg/kg p.o., 3 times over 24 hours) decreased all social and aggressive behavior; these effects were unchanged by administration of antipsychotic drugs.
Filibeck et al., 1988	40 group-housed male mice were treated chronically with cocaine (20 mg/kg, twice per day for 10 days), were administered a challenge dose and tested with an untreated intruder	Cocaine (20 mg/kg) caused an increase in defensive upright and escape in chronically-treated animals.

Literature Reviews

Woods, 1977	Review of the behavioral effects of cocaine (116 articles, 1932-1977)	Cocaine can both increase and decrease aggression elicited by environmental events in pigeons, rodents, and squirrel monkeys.

TABLE 9: Effects of Cocaine on Aggression in Humans

References	Methods and Procedures	Results and Conclusions
Criminal Violence		
Fink and Hyatt, 1978	Anecdotal report of the association between criminal behavior and drug use	Suggested that while relationship beteeen cocaine use and criminal behavior is unknown, the pharmacologic effects of cocaine suggest a potential for drug-induced violence.
Inciardi, 1989	Interviews of 611 males and females adolescent drug using criminals in inner city Miami	91% used some form of cocaine or crack 3 or more times per week; 14.9% reported having committed assault and 59.1% reported having participated in robbery during the 12 months preceding the interview.
Moore, 1990	Interviews of males and females who have been gang members in East Los Angeles	No significant relationship was found between gang member involvement in cocaine sales and violence; crack dealing may involve violence but firm evidence is lacking.
Roberts, 1990	Discussion of the evolutionary and social roots of violence	Gang-related violence throughout the United States is increasing, as is the involvement of gangs in the drug trade. Author cites reports that 83% of arrested men in New York City in 1986 had traces of cocaine in their urine.
Dembo et al., 1991	201 incarcerated males and females in a Florida prison, mean age 16 years; self report of drug use, delinquency; urinalysis; interviews and urine samples took place within 48 hours of admission; longitudinal study	Self-reported cocaine use did not significantly predict delinquency; self-reported drug use, positive urinalysis test and delinquency predicted cocaine use at follow-up.
Health Statistics		
Swett, 1985	214 male inpatients from a maximum security ward for the criminally insanc; drug use history related to violent behavior	Many were poly-drug users and cocaine was used by 22% of the sample. Subjects who had used cocaine were not more likely to commit violent acts than subjects who had not used cocaine.

536

Reference	Study	Findings
Honer et al., 1987	Evaluation of 52 male and 28 female cocaine and crack users admitted to an emergency room in 1985 and 1986	Crack users exhibited significantly more psychotic symptoms and threats or acts of violence than freebase, intravenous, or intranasal cocaine users; this may be due to route of administration (hence rate of absorption), dose or frequency of use, or differences in socioeconomic background or personality.
Brower et al., 1988	Reports of 100 admissions to a psychiatric emergency room	Method of ingestion (intranasal, intravenous, smoking) did not significantly affect violent behavior. Violent cocaine users ingested more cocaine in the month before interview than non-violent cocaine users.
Lowry et al., 1988	Reports of 694 criminal homicide victims killed in New Orleans during 4 years	Cocaine was among the 3 most commonly abused drugs by black victims; percentage of victims with detectable cocaine increased from 1 to 18% in the years tested.
Bailey and Shaw, 1989	Report of methamphetamine- and cocaine-related deaths in San Diego county in 1987	Cocaine was involved in 39 homicides, this constituted 1/5 of homicides in San Diego county for that year. Cocaine combined with methamphetamine was involved in 4 homicides.
Fagan and Chin, 1989	Analysis of 3,403 crack arrests and 3,424 cocaine arrests from New York City	Violence was not a factor in arrests for either cocaine or crack; felony violence was charged in fewer than 4% of either crack or cocaine arrests.

Personality Evaluations

Reference	Study	Findings
Siegel, 1977	Physical and psychological examination, including MMPI, administered to 85 male recreational cocaine users; no control group	Along with stimulant and euphoric effects, subjects reported occasional negative effects such as hyperexcitability, irritability, anxiety, restlessness and paranoia.
Atkinson, 1982	Anecdotal reports of violent behavior in hospitalized patients	Stimulants such as cocaine, amphetamines and methylphenidate can produce violence-prone paranoid or manic states.

Fagan and Chin, 1990, 1991	Interviews of 559 male and female drug users in northern Manhattan	While crack users more often reported feelings of depression and paranoia, crack users did not differ from other drug users in violent behavior. Crack sellers are more violent than marihuana or heroin sellers, and their violence is not confined to the drug selling context.

Literature Reviews

Post, 1975 Egan and Robinson, 1979	Review of articles concerning the physiological and psychological safety of cocaine	Cocaine can induce a psychotic state, characterized by hallucinations, delusions of persecution, and the potential for violent behavior.
Grinspoon and Bakalar, 1979	Review of the acute and chronic physical and behavioral effects of cocaine use	Cocaine can produce irritability and paranoia, may cause physical aggression and crime but there is no evidence of any consistent association.
Busch and Schnoll, 1985	Review of criminal violence, health statistics, and psychiatric evaluations	In some cases, either acute or chronic cocaine use may be associated with violent behavior resulting from paranoia or loss of impulse control, however, the literature is too premature to draw conclusions.
Nadelman, 1989	Discussion of the costs and consequences of drug prohibition in the United States	Evidence does not yet support the depiction of crack cocaine as a drug which unleashes aggressive tendencies.

TABLE 10A Effects of Acute Cannabis on Aggression in Animals

References	Methods and Procedures	Results and Conclusions
Isolation-induced Aggression		
Garattini, 1965 Santos et al., 1966 Dubinsky et al., 1973 ten Ham and de Jong, 1975 Dorr and Steinberg, 1976 Miczek, 1978	Male Swiss and T.O. mice; resident or intruder drug treated	0.125-1.0 mg/kg i.p. THC had no effect on attack frequency. 2.5-400 mg/kg THC dose dependently decreased attacks and sideways threat, increased crouch and upright behaviors; maximal effects 1-2 hr after administration, not due to behavioral depression. Higher doses had a general depressant effect.
Kilbey et al., 1972	Learning of maze rewarded with an opportunity to attack a conspecific in male Balb/cJ mice	0.6-2.5 mg/kg i.v. THC dose dependently decreased attacks and attack latency.
Matte, 1975	Male wild mice; both subjects drug treated; aggression score comprised of motor activity, attack latency and fight duration	Prefight: 20 mg/kg i.p. hashish increased tail rattling and irritability. Dyadic interactions: hashish had no effect on total fighting time, decreased the latency to attack and increased aggression scores.
Frischknecht et al., 1984	Learning of submissive behaviors in male C3H mice	1-10 mg/kg p.o. THC dose dependently decreased submissive behaviors (defensive upright, sideways and immobility).
Pain-induced aggression and defense		
Carder and Olson, 1972	Footshock to pairs of male Sprague-Dawley rats; both subjects drug treated	0.5 mg/kg i.p. THC increased the number of attacks in one or both animals and induced more fighting at higher shock intensities.
Manning and Elsmore, 1972	Footshock to pairs of male Walter Reed albino rats; both subjects drug treated	0.064-6.400 mg/kg i.p. THC had no effect on percentage of fights elicited, regardless of vehicle or time after administration.

Reference	Method	Results
Dubinsky et al., 1973	(1) Footshock to male albino mice or Long-Evans rats (2) Reactions to prodding with an inanimate object in restrained bilaterally septal lesioned male Long-Evans rats rated with 0-3 scoring system	(1) THC dose dependently decreased fighting duration 1-3 hr after administration; ED50 (mice): 22 mg/kg i.p., ED50 (rats): 14.9 mg/kg. Antiaggressive effects might be due to sedation. (2) 10-40 mg/kg i.p. THC dose dependently increased excitable and aggressive behavior 1 hr after administration.
Loev et al., 1973 Razdan et al., 1976a,b,c Winn et al., 1976	Footshock to pairs of male albino BALB/cJ mice; responsiveness to prodding with an inanimate object in rhesus monkeys	Various carbocyclic and sulfur analogues (with and without alkyl substitution), esters of nitrogen of cannabinoids predominantly increased aggression. Heterocyclic analogues containing aromatic side chains predominantly decreased aggression.
Fujiwara and Ueki, 1979	Female Wistar rats 22 hr food deprived for 30 days followed by 70 days ad lib; responsiveness to prodding with inanimate object	Prior to 6 mg/kg i.p. THC, rats did not attack the inanimate object. 1 hr after administration, attack behavior approached 100% and showed no signs of decrease. Attack behavior was abolished when animals were group housed.
Pradhan et al., 1980	Footshock to male Wistar rats; 3 point aggression scale	5-25 mg/kg i.p. THC dose dependently decreased attack scores at 40 min and increased attack scores at 120 min after administration.
Sethi et al., 1986	Footshock to male and female albino mice; both subjects drug treated	100 mg/kg p.o. cannabis had no effect on the frequency of fighting.

Aggression due to omission of reward

Reference	Method	Results
Masur et al., 1971 Masur et al., 1972	Food competition between pairs of male and female Wistar rats; dominant or subordinate drug treated	2.5-10 mg/kg i.p. cannabis extract dose dependently increased "winning" behavior.
Cherek et al., 1972	Aggression toward restrained conspecific due to intermittent reinforcement schedule in pigeons	0.125-1.0 mg/kg i.m. THC decreased attack responses.
Jones et al., 1974	Water competition between pairs of male squirrel monkeys; dominant and/or subordinate drug treated	0.25 mg/kg p.o. THC increased competition and 1 mg/kg decreased competition without changing the frequency of fighting.
Uyeno, 1976	Competition for female in estrus between pairs of male Wistar rats; one subject drug treated	0.25-1.0 mg/kg i.p. THC dose dependently decreased dominance; maximal effects after 2 hr

Reference	Paradigm	Findings
Giono-Barber et al., 1974	Food competition between pairs of Cynocephalus monkeys; dominant drug treated	30-100 mg/kg (in food supply) cannabis dose dependently decreased dominance.
Miczek and Barry, 1974	Food competition in male albino Sprague-Dawley rats; dominant or subordinate drug treated	1-4 mg/kg i.p. THC decreased defensive-submissive behaviors of subordinate animals, attacks and threats of dominant animals.

Defensive aggression induced by brain stimulation

Dubinsky et al., 1973	Hissing response of male mongrel cats elicited with hypothalamic stimulation	5-20 mg/kg i.p. THC elevated the hiss threshold due to sedation.

Drug-induced aggression

Carlini and Gonzalez, 1972	Pairs of male Wistar rats undergoing morphine withdrawal	48 and 72 hr after morphine abstinence, 5 mg/kg i.p. THC and 10 mg/kg marihuana extract produced aggressive behavior appearing 30 min after administration.
Fujiwara et al., 1984	Social behavior among groups of bilaterally 6OHDA lesioned (i.c.v.) male Wistar rats	6 mg/kg i.p. THC produced fighting and marked hyperirritability from 10-100 days after lesioning.

Aggression induced by REM sleep deprivation

Alves et al., 1973 Karniol and Carlini, 1973 Carlini and Lindsey, 1975 Takahashi and Karniol, 1975 Musty et al., 1976 Carlini, 1977 Carlini et al., 1977 DeSouza and Palermo Neto, 1978	Pairs of male and female Wistar 96 hr REM sleep-deprived rats; various DA and NE pre-and post-treatments	1.25-20.0 mg/kg i.p. Δ^9-THC (and various cannabis extracts) dose dependently increased elements of fighting, decreased submissive behavior. This was potentiated with 250 μg pretreatment of 6OHDA. THC or REM sleep deprivation alone did not produce aggressive behavior. THC induced aggression by altering the DA/NE balance.

Aggression by resident toward intruder

Siegel and Poole, 1969	Novel mice ("strangers") introduced to group housed male CF1 mice	2-10 mg/kg i.p. THC and 50-100 mg/kg i.p. Cannabis sativa extract reduced aggression and group aggregation. Stranger males treated with THC or cannabis were hypersensitive to auditory and tactile stimuli and aggregated in small groups apart from the rest of the mice.

Reference	Subjects	Findings
Miczek, 1977a Miczek, 1978 Sieber et al., 1982	Male Swiss or C3H/HeJ mice, Sprague-Dawley rats or male squirrel monkeys; resident or intruder drug treated	THC dose dependently decreased resident and intruder elements of aggressive behavior (mice: 20 mg/kg p.o., rats: 0.125-1.0 mg/kg i.p., monkeys: 0.25-2.0 mg/kg p.o.). THC treated intruder mice displayed increased submissive behaviors and THC had no effect on rat or monkey submissive behaviors.
Sieber et al., 1980a,b	Dominant-subordinate interactions with and without an intruder between male C3H/HeJ mice; dominant and/or subordinate drug treated	20 mg/kg p.o. THC produced sedation, decreased aggression and had inconsistent effects on submissive behaviors. THC had no effect on the dominant-subordinate relationship.
Olivier et al., 1984	Resident-intruder interactions between male Wistar or Wezob rats; resident drug treated	At doses below 1.0 mg/kg i.p., THC produced minimal effects on aggression; at 1.0 mg/kg i.p. THC decreased aggression moderately (40%) while markedly increasing inactivity (175%).
Dominance-related aggression		
Siegel and Poole, 1969	Social behavior in groups of male CF1 mice; novel mice ("strangers") introduced to group housed mice	2-10 mg/kg i.p. THC and 50-100 mg/kg i.p. Cannabis sativa extract reduced aggression and group aggregation.
Cutler et al., 1975	Pairs of male CFW mice; one subject drug treated	4-50 mg/kg i.p. cannabis dose dependently increased flight behavior without altering aggression.
Ely et al., 1975	Social behavior among groups of male and female CBA mice; dominant or subordinate drug treated	0.5 mg/kg i.v. THC decreased aggressive behavior by dominant without altering hierarchy while 2, 20 mg/kg decreased aggressive behavior and dominance permanently when a rival was present. 20 mg/kg had no effect on aggressive behavior of the subordinate.
Sassenrath and Chapman, 1976	Social settings in groups of monkeys	0.6-2.4 mg/kg (in food supply) THC generally reduced aggressive interactions.
Sieber, 1982	Dyadic observation of male baboons (Papio c. anubis)	40 mg/kg (in food supply) THC decreased threats and attacks.

542

Killing

McDonough et al., 1972	Turtle (*Pseudomys ornata*) killing behavior in male albino Walter Reed rats	6.4 mg/kg i.p. THC decreased attacks by approximately 50% relative to control for the first 2 hr after administration. Control attack behavior returned by 4 hr.
Alves and Carlini, 1973	Muricidal behavior in male Wistar rats	20 mg/kg i.p. cannabis extract decreased muricidal behavior.
Dubinsky et al., 1973	Muricidal behavior in male Long-Evans rats; rat killing behavior elicited by hypothalamic stimulation in male mongrel cats	Rats: 2.5-10 mg/kg i.p. THC dose dependently decreased muricidal behavior; ED50: 4.9 mg/kg. Cats: 5-20 mg/kg i.p. THC increased attack latency. Antiaggressive effect was not due to behavioral depression.
Kilbey et al., 1973a,b Kilbey et al., 1977	Frog killing behavior in female Holtzman and male Long-Evans rats with and without 23 hr food deprivation	0.25-2.5 mg/kg i.v. THC dose dependently decreased attack latency and kills in females and food deprived males with maximal effect 30 min after administration; increased whole brain 5HT levels were associated with inhibition of aggression.
Yoshimura et al., 1974 Fujiwara and Ueki, 1978 Fujiwara and Ueki, 1979 Fujiwara et al., 1980	Muricidal behavior in male and female Wistar King-A rats 24 hr food deprived up to 30 days followed by 70 days ad lib	Prior to THC, rats did not display muricidal behavior; 2-16 mg/kg i.p. THC dose dependently induced muricide 1 hr after administration in 60-70% of the rats and stabilized at 50% over the following 100 days. No differences in ACh, AChE levels between muricidal and non-muricidal rats. Group housing decreased muricide.

Literature Reviews

Siegel, 1971 Siegel, 1973	Review of over 65 articles between 1943 and 1973 on hallucinogens and behavior	Cannabis induces hypersensitivity and decreases social interactions.
Carlini, 1972 Carlini et al., 1972 Carlini, 1974 Paton, 1975	Review of over 265 animal and human articles between 1942 and 1975 on the acute and chronic administration of cannabis	Cannabis decreases spontaneous and isolation-induced aggression in *Betta splendens* and mice and does not decrease fighting in the electric shock paradigm.

543

Reference	Description	Findings
Mills and Brawley, 1972	Review of 92 animal and human articles between 1944 and 1972 on the psychopharmacology of cannabis	Reduced aggression accompanies hypoactivity, increased aggression accompanies food deprived and food competitive animals. This aggression is more pronounced in the female.
Krsiak, 1974	Review of 193 articles between 1948 and 1974 on the acute and chronic administration of drugs and aggression	Low doses of cannabis increase electric shock-elicited aggression and muricide.
Abel, 1975	Review of 90 articles between 1934 and 1975 on the acute and chronic administration of cannabis and animal aggression	Cannabis decreases aggression due to suppression of locomotor activity and motivation. Cannabis increases aggression in stressed (cold environment, REM sleep deprivation, foot shock) animals.
Carlini et al., 1976	Review of 80 articles between 1964 and 1976 on the environmental effects on acute and chronic administration of marihuana	High doses of marihuana induce hyperexcitability and aggressiveness in rats stressed by cold environment, food- and REM sleep-deprivation and morphine withdrawal through sensitized dopaminergic systems.
Miczek and Barry, 1976 Miczek and Krsiak, 1979 Miczek and Thompson, 1983 Miczek, 1987	Review of over 1500 animal and human articles between 1920 and 1987 on the pharmacology of aggression	Cannabis reduces aggression in isolation, pain, schedule controlled, brain stimulation and predatory paradigms; attack and threat behavior is decreased at low doses (0.25-4.0 mg/kg) in mice, rats, squirrel monkeys and rhesus monkeys. Higher doses (>10 mg/kg) reduce defensive and submissive behaviors. Cannabis increases aggression in REM sleep deprived rats.
Frischknecht, 1984	Review of 139 articles between 1963 and 1984 on the acute and chronic administration of cannabis and social behavior in rodents	Cannabis reduces aggression in isolated males and territorial residents, higher doses cause sedation.
Dewey, 1986	Review of 300 human and animal articles between 1929 and 1986 on cannabis pharmacology	Generally, cannabinoids induce aggressiveness in laboratory animals and potentiate aggressiveness in laboratory animals induced by other modalities such as foot-shock, hunger, sleep deprivation.

TABLE 10B Effects of Chronic Cannabis on Aggression in Animals

References	Methods and Procedures	Results and Conclusions
Isolation-induced Aggression		
Carlini, 1968	28 day administration to male mice; resident drug treated	20 mg/kg i.p. cannabis extract decreased fighting duration until day 4; subsequently, there were no differences between treated and untreated rats.
ten Ham and van Noordwijk, 1973	30 day administration to male Swiss-Webster mice; both animals drug treated	50 mg/kg i.p. Δ^8-THC, 5 mg/kg i.p. Δ^9-THC decreased fighting which showed no signs of tolerance.
Pain-induced aggression and defense		
Carder and Olson, 1972	Footshocks to pairs of male Sprague-Dawley rats; 14 day administration; both subjects drug treated	0.12-0.5 mg/kg THC increased and 1.0-2.0 mg/kg THC reduced defensive aggression on test day 1. On day 7 and 14, 0.12-2.0 mg/kg THC decreased aggression.
Pradhan et al., 1980	Footshocks to pairs of male Wistar rats; 19 day administration; 3 point aggression scale	20 mg/kg THC decreased aggression 40 min after administration and produced minimal to moderate increases 120 min after administration.
Sethi et al., 1986	Footshocks to pairs of male and female albino mice; 28 day administration; both subjects drug treated	100 mg/kg p.o. cannabis increased the frequency of fighting.
Aggression due to omission of reward		
Cherek et al., 1980	40 day administration and aggression toward restrained conspecific due to intermittent reinforcement schedule in pigeons	0.5, 1.0 mg/kg i.m. THC markedly decreased aggressive behavior and showed no signs of tolerance.
Giono-Barber et al., 1974	35 day administration and food competition between pairs of Cynocephalus monkeys; dominant drug treated	Initially, 100 mg/kg (in food supply) cannabis was depressive with a loss of dominance; after 7 days, increased aggressiveness was present and showed no signs of tolerance.

Drug-induced aggression

Citation	Description
Carlini and Masur, 1969 Carlini and Masur, 1970 Carlini et al., 1972 Palermo Neto and Carlini, 1972	18-30 day administration to pairs of male and female Wistar rats with and without footshock; PCPA and DOPA pretreatment	Doses up to 10 mg/kg i.p. THC produced no effect on "spontaneous" aggressive behavior in male and female rats. 10-20 mg/kg increased irritability and spontaneous and shock-induced aggression in both sexes appearing within 2-18 days in 22 hr food deprived rats. This was potentiated with a cold environment (14° C), 40 mg/kg i.p. DOPA and/or 300 mg/kg i.p. PCPA.
Palermo Neto and Carvalho, 1973	30 day administration to pair-housed male Wistar rats separated into two "emotional" groups (HIGH, LOW)	Highly emotional animals were more susceptible to cannabis-induced (0.39 mg/kg i.p./day) aggression than less emotional animals. Whole brain 5HT levels decreased to 50% of control in aggressive highly emotional animals, mainly in cerebral hemispheres, midbrain and hypothalamus.
Palermo Neto et al., 1975	25 day administration to ovariectomized female Wistar rats; both subjects drug treated	After 6-7 days, 20 mg/kg i.p. cannabis produced irritability and hyperactivity. Aggressive behavior appeared after 8 days in estrogen-treated rats and after 14 days in subjects without estrogen. Estrus reduced aggression due to chronic cannabis administration.

Aggression by resident toward intruder

Citation	Description
Sieber et al., 1980a,b	Dominant-subordinate interactions with and without an intruder between male C3H/HeJ mice; 4 administrations; dominant and/or subordinate drug treated	Tolerance developed to the sedating and antiaggressive effects of 20 mg/kg p.o. THC after 4 administrations. Effects on submissive behaviors were inconsistent.

Dominance-related aggression

Citation	Description
Gonzalez et al., 1971	9 administrations to pairs of male adult Siamese fighting fish (*Betta splendens*)	0.5 µg/mL THC and 1.0 µg/mL (in aquarium water) cannabis extract decreased fighting episodes, produced mild signs of depression and no escape response. After 9 exposures, THC treated fish regained control levels of aggression.

546

ten Ham and van Noordwijk, 1973	30 day administration to male Chinese hamsters; both animals drug treated	50 mg/kg i.p. Δ^8-THC abolished and 5 mg/kg i.p. Δ^9-THC decreased fighting which showed no signs of tolerance.
Rosenkrantz and Braude, 1974	26 day administration to male and female Fischer rats	Inhalation of 0.7–4.2 mg/kg marihuana dose dependently increased aggression after 15-19 days. Fighting occured 1-2 hr after administration and lasted for 2-10 min; aggression was more pronounced in high dosed females.
Cutler et al., 1975	14 day administration followed by 7 day abstinence to pairs of male CFW mice; dominant or subordinate drug treated	23 mg/kg (in food supply) cannabis increased flight behaviors and had no effect on aggressive behaviors of dominants; abstinence increased aggression. Cannabis administration and abstinence had no effect on aggressive or timid behaviors of subordinates.
Luthra et al., 1975 Thompson et al., 1973	4-6 month administration to male and female Fischer rats	Initially, cannabinoids produced sedation; fighting developed within 2-3 weeks, was greater in males than in females and more marked at 10 mg/kg p.o. Δ^9-THC than at 50 mg/kg. Tolerance might develop to proaggressive effects. Proaggressive potencies were: Δ^9-THC > Δ^8-THC > marihuana extract.
Sassenrath and Chapman, 1976	15 month administration to groups of monkeys	Initially, 2.4 mg/kg (in food supply) THC reduced aggression, after 2 months, hyperirritability, increased aggressiveness was evidenced which was potentiated by psychosocial stress (e.g., crowding).
Levett et al., 1977	14 day administration to pairs of female Chachma baboons (*Papio ursinus*)	Daily administration of 33 g (in food supply) cannabis did not effect aggressive interactions.
Miczek, 1977a Miczek, 1979a	60 day administration to pairs of male Sprague-Dawley, Long-Evans, Wistar and Fischer rats	10-50 mg/kg THC did not produce aggressive behavior regardless of route of administration (i.p. or p.o.), rat strain or vehicle.
Sieber et al., 1981	3 day administration to groups of male C3H/HeJ mice; dominant and subordinate animals drug treated	20 mg/kg p.o. THC weakened dominant position in social, food and sexual interactions which recovered after 2-3 days except with drug treated dominants in the food interaction test.

Killing

Reference	Description	Findings
Ueki et al., 1972	Muricidal behavior in female King A Wistar rats; 30 day administration; 22 hr food deprived	6 mg/kg i.p. THC induced muricide on the 17th day of administration and showed no signs of tolerance even after the drug was withdrawn; muricide was potentiated in individually housed and food deprived rats.
Alves and Carlini, 1973	Muricidal behavior in "killer" and "non-killer" male Wistar rats; 4 day administration to killer rats, 50 day administration to non-killer rats with or without 22 hr food deprivation	20 mg/kg i.p. cannabis extract decreased muricidal behavior and showed no sign of tolerance in killer rats; after 10 days of administration of 20 mg/kg, non-killer rats displayed muricide which was potentiated with food deprivation.
Miczek, 1976 Miczek, 1977a Miczek, 1979a	Muricidal behavior in single and pair housed male Sprague-Dawley, Long-Evans and Fischer rats over a 60 day period	THC (2-50 mg/kg i.p.) dose dependently increased the proportion of rats displaying muricide; maximal effects with 10, 20 mg/kg and after 5-6 weeks of treatment. Increased motor behavior and housing conditions had no effect on muricide induced by THC.

Literature Reviews

Reference	Description	Findings
Carlini, 1972 Carlini et al., 1972 Carlini, 1974 Krsiak, 1974 Paton, 1975 Carlini et al., 1976 Frischknecht, 1984	Review of over 300 animal and human articles between 1942 and 1984 on the acute and chronic administration of cannabis	Cannabis induces aggressive behavior on "stressed" (food- and REM sleep-deprived, cold environment, morphine withdrawn) animals, mainly due to changes to catecholamine systems.
Abel, 1975	Review of 90 articles between 1934 and 1975 on the acute and chronic administration of cannabis and animal aggression	Cannabis increases "irritability" while decreasing inter-male aggression.
Miczek and Barry, 1976 Miczek and Krsiak, 1979 Miczek and Thompson, 1983 Miczek, 1987	Review of over 1500 animal and human articles between 1920 and 1987 on the pharmacology of aggression	Cannabis reduces attack and threat behavior in mice, hamsters, rats and monkeys.

548

TABLE 11 Effects of Cannabis on Aggression in Humans

References	Methods and Procedures	Results and Conclusions
Criminal violence		
Fossier, 1931	Anecdotal account of cannabis violence	Acute and chronic cannabis increased criminality and violence.
Bromberg and Rodgers, 1946	Criminality and psychiatric classification of 8280 male Naval criminal offenders from 1943 to 1945	No relationship between marihuana use and aggressive crime. 8240 nonusers of marihuana more likely to commit aggressive crimes than 40 (0.0048%) users. Users more likely to have asocial personality or schizophrenia.
Gardikas, 1950	Criminality of 379 Greek cannabis users from 1919 to 1950; no control	Acute and chronic cannabis increased violent crimes (possession of firearms, threats and assaults).
Moraes Andrade, 1964	120 cannabis users committed to a Brazilian psychiatric hospital from 1951 to 1960	No relationship between cannabis use and criminality.
Malmquist, 1971	Psychiatric evaluation of 17 male and 3 female juveniles (age: 13 to 18 years) charged with murder in Minnesota	Events prior to homicide included drug use, behavioral and emotional changes. Drug use occurred in two ways: sporadic use of amphetamines and psychotomimetics with or without marihuana, barbiturates and tranquilizers to "contain" impulses and affects.
Soueif, 1971	Criminality of 553 hashish users and 458 hashish nonusers from 1967 to 1968 in Egyptian prisons; questionnaire to 850 hashish users and 839 hashish nonusers	Except for hashish related offenses, 5.7% of the users versus 13.5% of the nonusers had criminal records. 6% of users thought criminal action more likely in users than nonusers whereas 56% of the nonusers thought criminal action more likely in users than nonusers.
Tinklenberg et al., 1974 Tinklenberg et al., 1976 Tinklenberg et al., 1981	Structured interview, police and clinical records of over 350 male adolescents imprisoned between 1971 and 1977 in northern California	Only 6% of the drug-related assaults involved cannabis. Cannabis is the single drug most likely to decrease the possibility of violence. Cannabis use was not a positive predictor of assaultive crime.

549

Reference	Description	Findings
Dembo et al., 1991	Self report of drug use, delinquency, psychiatric evaluation and urinalysis of 201 male and female adolescent (mean age: 16 years) detainees in Florida	Use of marijuana is not significantly associated with delinquency.
Health statistics		
Chopra et al., 1942	Psychiatric, medical diagnosis of 1500 cases of acute and chronic hemp drug abuse in India. Subjects were male and female, 15+ years of age	Excessive use of hemp in healthy and susceptible individuals decreased the probability of violent behavior and premeditated and spontaneous crime. "Delusional and hallucinatory insanity" occurred in 12.5% of the inviduals within which homicidal acts were not uncommon.
Allen and West, 1968	Anecdotal account of the "Green Rebellion" of 1967-68 in Haight-Ashbury	Marihuana was crucial in the "hippie" rebellion and these individuals show decreased aggressiveness and competitiveness.
Brickman, 1968	Interpretation of psychedelic experiences due to marihuana in terms of Freudian death instinct	Psychedelic experience caused "the symbolic rebirth and a development of a new self which, affirming death, no longer needs to externalize destructiveness."
Spencer, 1970 Spencer, 1971	12 marihuana induced psychoses; chronic users, male and under 25 years of age admitted to Bahama hospital	Psychosis included aggressive behavior (property damage) and psychomotor hyperactivity; 3 of 12 patients effectively treated with up to 9 mg/day haloperidol, 4 others treated with ECT.
Colbach, 1971	15 case studies of marihuana use by GIs in Vietnam	Up to 70% of the GIs had tried marihuana; there was no relationship between marihuana use and violence or disciplinary problems.
Bernhardson and Gunne, 1972	46 chronic cannabis users treated for psychosis in Sweden, 1966-1970	52% of the patients experienced psychotic episodes lasting 1-5 weeks (episodic) of which 63% were violent and aggressive. Marihuana use aggravated but did not precede psychoses in 64% of the chronic patients.
Beachy et al., 1979	Structured interviews and school records of 600 male and female high school students in Atlanta; delinquency and aggression indices	Marihuana users scored higher on self-reported deliquency and aggression than nonusers.

550

Personality evaluations

Reference	Method	Findings
Edwards et al., 1969	Psychiatric inventory administered to 60 male and female "heavy" psychedelic users (more than 50 experiences including marihuana) and nonusers	Polydrug use was common. Drug experienced subjects were more hostile than controls (Comrey test); hostility was not related to drug usage.
Milman, 1969	Psychiatric inventory administered to 9 male and 2 female adolescents (age: 10-18 years) with preexisting personality disorders	Polydrug use was common. Passive personality evidenced in all males. Violence, hostility was not related to drug usage.
Halikas et al., 1972 Halikas and Rimmer, 1974 Weller and Halikas, 1985	Structured interview, personality inventory (Feighner diagnostic evaluation) of over 150 male and female users and nonusers in St. Louis; follow-up interview 6-7 years later	12% of the users received a diagnosis of sociopathy compared to none of the nonusers; psychiatric illness precipitated marihuana use. At follow-up, antisocial personality more prevalent in users than nonusers (21 vs 2%).
Burdsal et al., 1973	Personality inventories (16 PF, MAT) and marihuana use questionnaire of 104 male and female Kansas undergraduate students	Four personality and motivational patterns were related to marihuana use: (1) antisocial norm group, (2) frustrated upper-middle class group, (3) hostile rebel group, and (4) follower group.
Fisher and Steckler, 1974	Marihuana use and personality trait questionnaire of 530 male and female trial (1-3 times in life), past (current nonusers), occasional (less than once per week), regular (1-6 times per week) and daily users in southern California	Cannabis decreased anger in all drug use groups; trial users reported more negative side effects than other groups.
Simon, 1974	EPPS assessment and marihuana use questionnaire of 88 male and female northeast United States undergraduate students	Marihuana users (1-2x/week) scored higher on aggression, autonomy, change, and lower on achievement and order indices than nonusers.
Chopra and Jandu, 1976	Structured interview, personality and mood assessment of 292 American and European male and female chronic cannabis users and "hippies" in India	Cannabis use might have precipitated later psychiatric disorders and/or aggravated preexisiting psychiatric problems.

Reference	Method	Findings
Stefanis et al., 1976a,b Boulougouris et al., 1976	Psychiatric (DSM2) and neurologic examinations of 47 long-term hashish users (5 g/day for 23 years) compared with 40 matched controls	Hahish users 2-3x more likely to have had psychopathology (including antisocial personality) and psychiatric treatment than nonusers. Except for hashish related offenses, hashish users (65%) more likely to have criminal record than nonusers (26%). There were no signs of organic abnormalities in either group.
Stoner, 1988	Anger expression scale and marihuana use questionnaire administered to 497 male and female Midwestern US undergraduates	Increased marihuana use associated with higher anger out (AO) index and increased aggressive behavior.

Experimental studies of aggression

Reference	Method	Findings
Abel, 1972	Personality inventory (PRF) administered to 22 male and female (ages: 21-30 years) users and nonusers prior to and after inhalation of 1 marihuana cigarette	Marihuana decreased feelings of exhibitionism; user preferred being inconspicuous and withdrawn. Marihuana stabilized autonomy and dominance.
Klapper et al., 1972	Administration of MMPI prior to various synthetic THC compounds in 40 male Army personnel (ages: 18-29 years); subsequent administration of NF, SC, PB and Army general intelligence (GT) tests	10-60 μg/kg p.o., 1-10 μg/kg i.m. and 1.5-2.8 μg/kg THC produced greater decreases in cognitive functioning in "sensitive" than in "resistant" individuals who were more intelligent, adventurous, hostile and aggressive.
Domino et al., 1974	Clyde Mood test administered to thirty 21-33 year old experienced male marihuana users prior to and after inhalation of 0, 0.5% and 2.9% THC	THC had no effect on index of aggression.
Babor et al., 1978a,b	Social behavior in 4 person groups comprised of 12 moderate (11.4 cigarettes/month) and 14 heavy marihuana (42.9 cigarettes/month) users (males, 21-27 years of age) during 21-31 day controlled access to 1 g, 2.1% THC in a hospital setting	Marihuana intoxication decreased social interaction, increased isolation and coaction in moderate users. Social behaviors of heavy users were unaffected. There was no evidence for aggression or violence.
Salzman et al, 1976	Hostility assessment (BDHI, SCL-90) of 60 experienced male marihuana users prior to and after 2.2% THC or placebo; 3 person groups (double blind, placebo control)	After a frustrating stimulus, marihuana decreased all measures of hostility (placebos show an increase). Marihuana increased negative verbal behavior relative to controls.

552

Stefanis et al., 1976c	Self-rating (anxiety, fatigue, irritability) scales administered concurrently with cannabis withdrawal and reintroduction to 16 long-term (24 years) male cannabis users (mean age: 40.8 years) in a hospital setting; double-blind, placebo control	Termination of 125-190 mg (inhaled) per day of Δ^9-THC produced no effect on indices of depression, anxiety, restlessness and irritability.
Pascale et al., 1980	Rotter Incomplete Sentences, MMPI and a delayed gratification task administered to 18 male and female Caucasian marihuana users and nonusers between 15 and 19 years of age	Marihuana users (8-13 cigarettes/week) and nonusers did not differ on indices of aggression or reaction to frustration.
Myerscough and Taylor, 1985	30 male undergraduates in reaction time task in competition with fictitious opponent	0.1 mg/kg THC did not facilitate aggressive behavior.

Literature Reviews

Brill, 1969 Tinklenberg and Stillman, 1970 Kalant, 1972 Tinklenberg and Murphy, 1972 Tinklenberg, 1974 Abel, 1977 Sbordone et al., 1981 Sheard, 1983 Cherek and Steinberg, 1987 Miczek, 1987	Review of over 1500 articles between 1893 and 1987 on drug use and violence	Marihuana inhibits assaultive behavior and is associated only infrequently with violence. Circumstances which increase the likelihood of violence are: idiosyncratic reactions in susceptible people, high concentration of THC.
Casto, 1970	Entymological investigation of marihuana and the "Assassins"	A causal relationship between marihuana use and violence is not supported with the legend of the Assassins.

553

TABLE 12 Effects of Hallucinogenic Drugs on Aggression in Animals

References	Methods and Procedures	Results and Conclusions
A. LSD		
Isolation-induced Aggression		
Uyeno and Benson, 1965 Uyeno, 1966b Valzelli et al., 1967 Valzelli and Bernasconi, 1971	Male Swiss albino mice, resident drug treated; 5 point aggression scale	0.1-1.6 mg/kg i.p. LSD 25 dose dependently decreased the number of animals attacking.
Rewerski et al., 1971 Rewerski et al., 1973	Male Swiss albino mice; interaction with 2 conspecifics; 5 point aggression scale	50, 500 µg/kg i.p. LSD 25 strongly inhibited aggression in mice isolated for 14 days and was less effective in 28 day isolates. 250 µg/kg had no effect on aggression in 14 and 28 day isolates.
Krsiak et al., 1971 Krsiak, 1975 Krsiak, 1979	Male Swiss albino mice; aggressive (33% of all subjects) or timid (39%) subject drug treated	0.01 mg/kg p.o. LSD potentiated aggressiveness in aggressive mice. In timid mice, 0.01 and 1 mg/kg increased escaping and both alert and defensive upright postures.
Kocur et al., 1977	Male albino Swiss mice; resident drug treated	0.6 mg/kg i.p. decreased aggressiveness.
Pain-induced aggression and defense		
Brunaud and Siou, 1959	Footshocks to pairs of male rats; both subjects drug treated	25-100 µg/kg LSD 25 increased defensive postures.
Kostowski, 1966	Footshocks to pairs of mice; both subjects drug treated	0.1 mg/kg i.p. LSD increased the percentage of fighting pairs 1-2.5 hr after administration.
Sheard et al., 1977b	Footshocks to pairs of male albino Sprague-Dawley rats; both subjects drug treated	20-160 µg/kg i.p. LSD dose dependently increased the percentage of animals fighting with increasing intensity of shock; 640 µg/kg had no effect on fighting.
Sbordone et al., 1979	Footshocks to pairs of male Sprague-Dawley rats; both subjects drug treated	25-400 µg/kg i.p. LSD had no effect on any measure of aggression.

554

Reference	Paradigm	Results
Elliott and Sbordone, 1982	Footshocks to pairs of male Sprague-Dawley rats; one subject drug treated	20, 100 µg/kg i.p. LSD increased "boxing" of undrugged rat toward drugged opponent. Drug treated animal more likely to be aggressed upon if ataxic, submissive or displaying locomotor activity.

Aggression due to omission of reward

Reference	Paradigm	Results
Uyeno, 1966a	Food competition between pairs of male Wistar rats; one subject drug treated	0.001-0.016 mg/kg i.p. LSD 25 dose dependently decreased attack behavior; maximal effects at 15 min
Uyeno, 1967a	Escape from water competition between pairs of female squirrel monkeys	0.032-0.128 mg/kg i.p. LSD dose dependently decreased "dominance" behavior.
Uyeno, 1967b	Competition for estrous female between pairs of male Wistar rats; one subject drug treated	0.008-0.032 mg/kg i.p. LSD 25 dose dependently decreased "dominance" behavior; maximal effects at 15 min

Defensive aggression induced by brain stimulation

Reference	Paradigm	Results
Baxter, 1964	Hissing response of cats elicited with electrical stimulation of the hypothalamus	Toxic doses (1.0-3.0 mg/kg i.p.) of LSD 25 did not change the minimal current necessary to elicit hissing.

Drug-induced aggression

Reference	Paradigm	Results
Schneider, 1968	Pairs of male weanling Wistar rats	Toxic dose (5 mg/kg s.c) of LSD produced fighting similar to that observed for 2.5 mg/kg s.c. apomorphine but with less intensity.
Votava, 1969	Female albino rats singly or repeatedly treated with reserpine (5 mg/kg i.p. in toto)	Toxic dose (1 mg/kg i.p) of LSD 25 produced aggressive behavior after a single reserpine treatment; LSD after repeated reserpine treatment had no effect on aggressive behavior.
Carlini and Masur, 1970	30 day administration of 10 mg/kg i.p. THC to produce aggression in pairs of 22 hr food deprived and footshocked female Wistar rats; both subjects drug treated	0.2 mg/kg i.p. LSD abolished attacks, fighting postures and bites induced by THC regimen.
Siegel et al., 1974; Siegel et al., 1976	Threat and aggressive behavior of solitary rhesus monkeys	50, 100 µg/kg i.m. LSD did not increase threat behavior.

Aggression induced by REM sleep deprivation

Reference	Subjects	Results
Alves et al., 1973 Carlini, 1977	Pairs of male 96 hr REM sleep-deprived Wistar rats; both subjects drug treated	0.02-0.1 mg/kg i.p. LSD 25 did not induce aggression.

Dominance-related aggression

Reference	Subjects	Results
Abramson and Evans, 1954	Groups of male and female, adult and juvenile Siamese fighting fish (*Betta splendens*)	0-50 µg/mL LSD 25 dose dependently decreased attack frequency, duration and counterattack frequency by producing a stuporous state.
Evans and Abramson, 1958	Groups of male and female, adult and juvenile newts (*Trituru V. Viridescens*); subordinate drug treated	0.1 mg (in aquarium water) LSD 25 increased aggressive behavior of subordinate newts.
Saxena et al., 1962	Male *Colisa lalia* fish	0.1-0.3 µg i.m. LSD decreased or completely abolished fighting for approx. 24 hr.
McDonald and Heimstra, 1964	Green sunfish (*Lepomis cyanellus*) in groups of 4; drug treated subordinate	Toxic dose (2.0 mg/kg i.p.) of LSD 25 increased the frequency of attacks by the subordinate.
Silverman, 1966	Male Agouti rats; resident drug treated	1, 4 µg/kg i.p. LSD dose dependently increased biting and flight behavior.
Siegel and Poole, 1969	Social behavior in groups of 40-50 male CF1 mice	2-30 µg/kg (in water supply) LSD reduced aggression and group aggregation.

Aggression by resident toward intruder

Reference	Subjects	Results
Siegel and Poole, 1969	Introduction of novel mice ("strangers") to groups of 40-50 male CF1 mice	Stranger mice were hypersensitive to auditory and tactile stimulation and aggregated in small groups after administration of 2-30 µg/kg (in water supply) LSD.

Killing

Reference	Subjects	Results
Karli, 1959	Muricidal behavior in male Albino rats	1 mg/kg i.p. LSD 25 had no effect on muricidal behavior.
Kostowski, 1966 Kostowski and Tarchalska, 1972	Beetle attacked by groups of 10 ants (*Formica rufa*)	0.025-0.1 µg/mg (in food) LSD decreased "aggressiveness" after 2-3 hr and increased "aggressiveness" after 18-24 hr.

Citation	Study	Findings
Rewerski et al., 1971 Valzelli and Bernasconi, 1971	Muricidal behavior in male Wistar rats	5-500 µg/kg i.p. LSD 25 had no effect on muricidal behavior.

Literature Reviews

Citation	Study	Findings
Valzelli, 1967	Review of 223 articles between 1916 and 1967 on drugs and aggression	LSD induces aggression in experimentally naive animals but has an inhibitory effect on isolation-induced aggression.
Siegel, 1971 Siegel, 1973	Review of over 65 articles between 1943 and 1973 on hallucinogens and behavior	LSD induces hypersensitivity and decreases social interactions.
Krsiak, 1974	Review of 193 articles between 1948 and 1974 on drugs and aggression	In mice, doses below 0.1 mg/kg increase electric shock-elicited and isolation-induced aggression. Higher doses do not change or decrease the level of aggression. In nonaggressive isolated mice, LSD does not induce aggressiveness. In isolated rats, 0.001-0.004 mg/kg i.p. LSD increases aggressiveness but is probably due to nonspecific effects.
Miczek and Barry, 1976 Miczek and Krsiak, 1979 Miczek and Thompson, 1983 Miczek, 1987	Review of over 1500 animal and human articles between 1920 and 1987 on the pharmacology of aggression	Aggressive behavior is not reliably altered with LSD in foot shock, isolation-induced, competitive, social behavior and predatory paradigms.
Sheard, 1977b	Review of 119 articles between 1928 and 1977 on animal models of aggressive behavior	20-160 µg/kg LSD enhances electric shock-elicited fighting in rats, higher doses have no effect.
Uyeno, 1978	Review of 32 articles between 1956 and 1978 on hallucinogens and aggressive behavior	Majority of investigators report LSD decreases aggression in mice and rhesus monkeys; reports of increases uninterpretable due to small sample size or lack of statistical test.
Sbordone et al., 1981	Review of 73 human and animal articles between 1939 and 1981 on drug-induced aggression; electric shock-elicited paradigm highlighted with animals	When both animals are drug treated, low doses of LSD have no effect on aggression; at high doses LSD decreases aggression. When one animal is drug treated, low and high doses of LSD fail to elicit biting.

557

B. Mescaline

Isolation-induced Aggression

Reference	Method	Results
Uyeno, 1966b	Male Swiss-Webster mice; resident drug treated	1-30 mg/kg i.p. mescaline dose dependently decreased the number of animals attacking; maximal effects 15-30 min after administration
Valzelli et al., 1967	Male Swiss albino mice; resident drug treated; 5 point aggression scale	5 mg/kg i.p. mescaline had no effect on aggressive behavior.
Rewerski et al., 1971 Rewerski et al., 1973	Male Swiss albino mice; aggression test with 2 conspecifics; 5 point aggression scale	10 mg/kg i.p. mescaline strongly inhibited aggression in mice isolated for 14 days and was less effective in 28 day isolates. 50 mg/kg abolished aggression in 14 and 28 day isolates.

Pain-induced aggression and defense

Reference	Method	Results
Brunaud and Siou, 1959	Footshocks to pairs of male rats; both subjects drug treated	50-500 mg/kg mescaline increased defensive postures.
Sbordone and Carder, 1974 Carder and Sbordone, 1975 Sbordone et al., 1978 Sbordone et al., 1979 Elliott and Sbordone, 1982	Footshocks to pairs of male Wistar, Long-Evans and Sprague-Dawley rats; one or both subjects drug treated	Regardless of age or strain, 10, 50 mg/kg i.p. mescaline dose dependently increased duration of fighting bouts which did not change with repeated administration. High doses of mescaline induced aggression in untreated animals due to catatonia.

Aggression due to omission of reward

Reference	Method	Results
Masur et al., 1971	Food competition between pairs of male and female Wistar rats; dominant or subordinate drug treated	5 mg/kg i.p. mescaline increased "winning" behavior.

Drug-induced aggression

Reference	Method	Results
Carlini and Masur, 1970	30 day administration of 10 mg/kg i.p. THC to produce aggression in pairs of 22 hr food deprived and footshocked female Wistar rats	40 mg/kg i.p. mescaline abolished attacks, fighting postures and bites.

Aggression induced by REM sleep deprivation

Reference	Method	Results
Alves et al., 1973	Pairs of female 96 hr REM sleep-deprived Wistar rats; both subjects drug treated	80 mg/kg i.p. mescaline did not induce aggressiveness.

Dominance-related aggression

Reference	Design	Result
Saxena et al., 1962	Acute and chronic (18 day) administration to male *Colisa lalia* fish	0.1-0.3 µg i.m. mescaline dose dependently decreased fighting for up to 24 hr; there were no signs of tolerance to antiaggressive effects during repeated administration of 3 µg.
Poshivalov, 1980	Acute and chronic (14 day) administration to groups of male CC57W mice; dominant drug treated	In acute and chronic studies, 30 mg/kg i.p. mescaline decreased aggression in dominant animals.

Killing

Reference	Design	Result
Karli, 1959 Rewerski et al., 1971	Muricidal behavior in male albino, Wistar rats	10, 100 mg/kg i.p. mescaline produced no effect on muricidal behavior.

Literature Reviews

Reference	Design	Result
Valzelli, 1967	Review of 223 articles between 1916 and 1967 on drugs and aggression	Mescaline induces aggression in experimentally naive animals but has an inhibitory effect on isolation-induced aggression.
Miczek and Barry, 1976	Review of over 500 articles between 1932 and 1976 on the pharmacology of sex and aggression	Aggressive behavior is not reliably altered with mescaline in foot shock, isolation-induced, competitive, social behavior and predatory paradigms.
Uyeno, 1978	Review of 32 articles between 1956 and 1978 on hallucinogens and aggressive behavior	Mescaline decreases or has no effect on aggressiveness in isolated mice, predatory rats and cats. Mescaline increases aggressiveness in rats in the shock paradigm.
Sbordone et al., 1981	Review of 73 human and animal articles between 1939 and 1981 on drug-induced aggression; electric shock-elicited paradigm highlighted with animals	When both animals are drug treated, mescaline increases aggressive behavior. 50 mg/kg i.p. treatment of one animal increases biting from the untreated animal and is correlated with ataxic movements from the treated animal. Aggression in the shock-elicited paradigm is produced by an incoordination of social signals normally effective in reducing aggression.

C. Phencyclidine (PCP)

Isolation-induced Aggression

Reference	Subject/Procedure	Results
Rewerski et al., 1971 Rewerski et al., 1973	Male albino Swiss mice; aggression test with 2 conspecifics; 5 point aggression scale	1 mg/kg i.p. PCP abolished aggression in mice isolated for 14 days and was less effective in 28 day isolates. 5 mg/kg increased aggression in 14 and 28 day isolates.
Wilmot et al., 1987	Male CF-1 mice; resident drug treated	1.25-5.0 mg/kg i.p. PCP dose dependently decreased the number of animals fighting after 21 days isolation. In animals that fought (55-82%), 1.25, 2.5 mg/kg increased fight duration.
Burkhalter and Balster, 1979	Male albino ICR mice; resident drug treated	1.0 mg/kg i.p. PCP increased attack bites and the number of animals that fought, 3.0 mg/kg produced no effect on aggression.
Fico and Vanderwende, 1988	Male CF-1 mice offspring of dam administered 20 mg/kg s.c. PCP prenatally	PCP produced no effect on the percentage of mice fighting, ontogeny or intensity of aggressive behavior.
Miczek and Haney, (in press)	Male albino Swiss-Webster mice; resident drug treated	0.1, 0.3 mg/kg i.p. PCP produced increased and 6, 10 mg/kg decreased aggressive behavior.

Pain-induced aggression and defense

Reference	Subject/Procedure	Results
Cleary et al., 1981	Exp. 1: Footshocks to pairs of male Sprague-Dawley rats; both subjects drug treated. Exp. 2: Footshocks and reaction to inanimate bite target in 3 restrained male Wistar rats	0.5-2.0 mg/kg i.p. PCP dose dependently decreased mutual upright and bites in dyads and biting toward inanimate object.
Emley and Hutchinson, 1983	Exp.1: Footshocks and reaction to inanimate bite target in restrained male squirrel monkeys. Exp. 2: Same procedure without shock delivery	Exp. 1: 0.01-0.4 mg/kg s.c. PCP increased biting in first administration and decreased biting in second. Exp. 2: 0.01-0.4 mg/kg had no effect on biting.
Jarvis et al., 1985	Footshocks and reaction to inanimate bite target in restrained male Swiss mice	1-8 mg/kg i.p. PCP dose dependently decreased biting.

Aggression induced by REM sleep deprivation

Musty and Consroe, 1982	Male Sprague-Dawley 72 hr REM sleep-deprived and nonsleep-deprived rats; both subjects drug treated	0.025-0.2 mg/kg i.p. PCP modestly increased aggressive postures and attacks in rats not deprived of sleep. 0.025-0.2 mg/kg increased aggression in sleep-deprived rats with maximal effects at 0.05 mg/kg.

Aggression by resident toward intruder

Tyler and Miczek, 1982	Male albino Swiss-Webster mice; resident or intruder drug treated	3-10 mg/kg i.p. PCP dose dependently decreased aggressive behavior in resident mice while increasing motor behavior. 3-10 mg/kg increased attacks toward PCP treated intruders.

Dominance-related aggression

Miller et al., 1973	Groups of male rhesus monkeys	0.25 mg/kg i.m. PCP increased aggressive displays by untreated toward drug treated animals.
Russell et al., 1984	Pairs of male Wistar rats; one subject drug treated	0.25 mg/kg s.c. PCP increased attack behavior by drug treated animals; 1.0 mg/kg decreased attack behavior by drug treated animal and increased attack behavior of saline treated animal. PCP alters responses to social signals which prevent attack behavior.

Killing

Rewerski et al., 1971	Muricidal behavior in male Wistar rats	5 mg/kg i.p. PCP non-significantly decreased muricidal behavior and increased the number of non-reacting animals.
Musty and Consroe, 1982	Muricidal behavior in male 72 hr REM sleep-deprived and nonsleep-deprived Sprague-Dawley rats	0.025-0.2 mg/kg i.p. PCP produced no effect on muricide in rats not deprived of sleep. 0.025-0.2 mg/kg increased muricide in sleep-deprived rats with maximal effects at 0.05 mg/kg.

Literature Reviews

Krsiak, 1974	Review of 193 articles between 1948 and 1974 on drugs and aggression	5 mg/kg i.p. PCP increases aggression in isolated mice but only with animals which have a low baseline level of aggression.

561

Reference	Method	Results
Miczek and Barry, 1976; Miczek and Krsiak, 1979; Miczek and Thompson, 1983; Miczek, 1987	Review of over 1500 animal and human articles between 1920 and 1987 on the pharmacology of aggression	Increases in aggression due to PCP are inconsistent; increases in aggression toward PCP treated subjects is a robust finding. PCP alters sending and receiving of communicative signals important in social and aggressive interactions.
Uyeno, 1978	Review of 32 articles between 1956 and 1978 on hallucinogens and aggressive behavior	PCP decreases or has no effect on isolation-induced, predatory and spontaneous aggression.

D. Other Hallucinogens

Isolation-induced Aggression

Reference	Method	Results
Uyeno, 1966b	Psilocybin or BOL-148 administered to male Swiss-Webster mice; resident drug treated	1-8 mg/kg i.p. psilocybin dose dependently decreased the number of animals attacking; maximal effects 30 min after administration. 0.5-2.0 mg/kg i.p. BOL-148 dose dependently decreased the number of animals attacking; maximal effects 30 min after administration
Valzelli et al., 1967; Valzelli and Bernasconi, 1971	Hybogaine or yohimbine administered to male Swiss albino mice; resident drug treated; 5 point aggression scale	20 mg/kg i.p. ibogaine decreased aggressive behavior; 10 mg/kg i.p. yohimbine abolished aggression for 6 hr.
Kostowski et al., 1972	Psilocybin, JB-336, ibogaine or bufotenine administered to male Swiss albino mice; resident drug treated	10 mg/kg i.p. psilocybin, 5 mg/kg i.p. JB-336, 10 mg/kg i.p. ibogaine and 10 mg/kg i.p. bufotenine decreased aggressiveness.
Rewerski et al., 1973	JB-336 administered to male Swiss albino mice; aggression test with 2 conspecifics; 5 point aggression scale	5 mg/kg i.p. JB-336 strongly inhibited aggressiveness in mice isolated for 14 days and had no effect in 28 day isolates.

Pain-induced aggression and defense

Reference	Method	Results
Walters et al., 1978	Footshocks to pairs of male albino Sprague-Dawley rats; both subjects treated with DMT or 5MeODMT	4-8 mg/kg DMT and 2.0 mg/kg 5MeODMT dose dependently decreased the percentage of animals fighting.
Sbordone et al., 1979	Footshocks to pairs of male Sprague-Dawley rats; both subjects treated with psilocin, DMT, DMPEA	0.4-10 mg/kg i.p. psilocin, 0.4-10 mg/kg i.p. DMT and 8-200 mg/kg i.p. DMPEA decreased the number of fights and duration of fighting.

562

Aggression due to omission of reward

Reference	Description	Effects
Uyeno, 1966a	Food competition between pairs of male Wistar rats; one subject drug treated with BOL-148	0.4-1.0 mg/kg i.p. BOL-148 dose dependently decreased attack behavior; maximal effects after 45 min
Uyeno, 1972	Food competition between pairs of male Wistar rats; one subject drug treated with DOM	0.4-1.2 mg/kg i.p. DOM dose dependently decreased attack behavior and "dominance"; maximal effects after 30-45 min
Uyeno, 1976	Competition for female in estrus between pairs of male Wistar rats; one subject drug treated with DOM	0.25-1.0 mg/kg i.p. DOM dose dependently decreased "dominance"; maximal effects after 45 min

Drug-induced aggression

Reference	Description	Effects
Siegel et al., 1974 Siegel et al., 1976	Solitary rhesus monkeys treated with DMT or BOL-148	0.5-4.0 mg/kg i.m. DMT, 100 µg/kg i.m. BOL-148 modestly decreased threat behavior.

Aggression by resident toward intruder

Reference	Description	Effects
Siegel and Poole, 1969	Introduction of novel mice ("strangers") to groups of male CF1 mice; bufotenine administered to both group housed and intruder subjects	5-30 mg/kg (in water supply) bufotenine decreased aggression and group aggregation. Bufotenine treated strangers were hypersensitive to auditory and tactile stimulation and aggregated in small groups.

Dominance-related aggression

Reference	Description	Effects
Thor et al., 1967	Male Siamese fighting fish (_Betta splendens_) treated with diethylamine	1, 2 mg/cc (in aquarium water) diethylamine abolished fighting in pairs of fish for 40 and 48 hr, respectively.
Siegel and Poole, 1969	Social interaction within groups of male CF1 mice treated with bufotenine	5-30 mg/kg (in water supply) bufotenine decreased aggression and group aggregation.

563

Reference	Description	Findings
Schlemmer et al., 1977 Schlemmer and Davis, 1981	Colonies of female Stumptail macaques treated with acute and chronic (12 day) 5MeODMT	Acute: 5-250 µg/kg i.m. 5MeODMT dose dependently decreased normal affiliative and increased submissive behaviors. Chronic: Daily administration of 250 µg/kg 5MeODMT increased submissive gestures displayed by the treated animal without increasing aggressive gestures by untreated animals; there were no signs of tolerance.
Tyler et al., 1978	Pairs of female Stumptail macaques treated with acute and chronic (5 day) DOM; one subject drug treated	0.17 mg/kg i.m. DOM decreased social and submissive behaviors with modest signs of tolerance after 5 days.

Killing

Reference	Description	Findings
Valzelli and Bernasconi, 1971	Muricidal behavior by male Wistar rats treated with yohimbine; 3 point aggression scale	10 mg/kg i.p. yohimbine abolished muricide for 1.5 hr and decreased "friendly" in favor of "indifferent" behavior for 4 hr.
Kostowski et al., 1972	Muricidal behavior by male Wistar rats treated with psilocybin, JB-336, ibogaine or bufotenine	10 mg/kg i.p. psilocybin, 5, 10 mg/kg i.p. JB-336, 10 mg/kg i.p bufotenine decreased the number of kills. 10 mg/kg i.p. ibogaine had no effect on muricidal behavior.
Molina et al., 1986	Muricidal behavior by olfactory bulbectomized or nonlesioned male Wistar rats treated with 5MeODMT	1, 1.5 mg/kg i.p. 5MeODMT dose dependently decreased muricidal behavior in lesioned and nonlesioned animals; maximal effects 15 min after administration

Literature Reviews

Reference	Description	Findings
Siegel, 1971 Siegel, 1973	Review of over 65 articles between 1943 and 1973 on hallucinogens and behavior	Bufotenine induces hypersensitivity and decreases social interactions.
Miczek and Barry, 1976	Review of over 500 articles between 1932 to 1976 on the pharmacology of sex and aggression	Aggressive behavior is decreased with psilocybin in isolation-induced, competitive, social behavior and predatory paradigms.

Sheard, 1977b	Review of 119 articles between 1928 and 1977 on animal models of aggressive behavior	DMT has a weak and inconsistent excitatory effect on electric shock-elicited fighting between 0.125-1 mg/kg; 4 and 8 mg/kg DMT decrease aggression. 5MeODMT has no effect on electric shock-elicited fighting at low doses, and depressant effects at high doses (range: 0.12-8.0 mg/kg).
Uyeno, 1978	Review of 32 articles between 1956 and 1978 on hallucinogens and aggressive behavior	Bufotenine, DOM, ibogaine, JB-336 and psilocybin have no effect or decrease aggression in isolation-induced, predatory and competition paradigms.
Sbordone et al., 1981	Review of 73 human and animal articles between 1939 and 1981 on drug-induced aggression; electric shock-elicited paradigm highlighted with animals	When both animals are drug treated, low doses of psilocin, DMT and DMPEA have no effect on aggression; at high doses these hallucinogens decrease aggression.

TABLE 13 Effects of Hallucinogenic Drugs on Aggression in Humans

References	Methods and Procedures	Results and Conclusions
A. LSD		
Criminal violence		
Knudsen, 1967	Case study of a 25 year old female who committed homicide after 5 LSD treatments (50 ng LSD)/treatment for depression, anxiety) in Norway	LSD diminished some behavioral control, including aggressive impulses.
Barter and Reite, 1969	Case studies of 3 LSD induced homicide	Homicide associated with LSD use was rare, perhaps due to a disorganization of purposeful conduct.
Williams, 1969	Case study of a 37 year old male who committed homicide in the U.K.	Subject experienced "bad trip" and had amnesia for the homicide.
Baker, 1970	Case studies of 67 LSD related hospital admissions in the U.K. between 1966 and 1967	5 categories of LSD effects: acute psychotic reaction (39%) including assaultiveness, suicidal (3%), aggressive (4%), LSD specific effects uncertain due to multidrug use (39%) and other (13%).
Reich and Hepps, 1972	Case study of a 22 year old male, long term LSD user who committed homicide in Massachusetts	200 μg (normal dose) LSD produced persecutory delusions ("bad trip").
Klepfisz and Racy, 1973	Case study of a 22 year old male, long term LSD user who committed homicide in New York	Physical assault occurred within 12 hours of LSD ingestion, homicide within 48 hours. Subject was psychotic during homicide and for the 6 previous months. Not known if LSD exaggerated the psychosis or caused it.
Duncan, 1974	Case studies of 4 male incarcerated adolescent schizophrenics	All 4 patients had ingested LSD and were assaultive. LSD induced psychoses in 2 patients and exaggerated existing psychoses in others.

566

Health statistics

Reference	Study	Findings
Allen and West, 1968	Interpretation of the "Green Rebellion" of 1967-68 in Haight-Ashbury	LSD was crucial in the "hippie" rebellion; these individuals showed decreased aggressiveness and competitiveness.
Brickman, 1968	Interpretation of psychedelic experiences due to LSD and mescaline in terms of Freudian death instinct	Psychedelic experience caused "the symbolic rebirth and development of a new self which, affirming death, no longer needs to externalize destructiveness."

Personality evaluations

Reference	Study	Findings
Edwards et al., 1969	Psychiatric evaluation of 60 male and female heavy psychedelic users (LSD, DMT, STP) and nonusers	Polydrug use common; drug experienced subjects were more hostile than controls (Comrey test); hostility was not related to drug usage.
Smart and Jones, 1970	Psychiatric evaluation of 100 male and female LSD users and 46 non user controls (age: 15-37 years) in Canada	LSD users showed more psychological disturbances and scored higher on MMPI scales Hy, Ma, Pd, Sc, Mf (males only) than nonusers; psychopathology predated drug use.

Experimental studies of aggression

Reference	Study	Findings
Fink et al., 1966	Repeated administration of LSD (0.5-10.0 µg/kg) to 65 long-term psychotic patients	Adverse reactions including hostility and irritability occurred in only 2% of the patients and were not dose related.
Cheek and Holstein, 1971	Social behavior measured among 16 male reformatory inmates after LSD administration	25, 50 µg p.o. LSD increased and 200 µg decreased social interaction. Hostility increased among behaviorally aggressive reformatory patients; positive and negative behaviors were increased in schizophrenics.

Literature Reviews

Reference	Study	Findings
Szara, 1967 Brill, 1969 Sbordone et al., 1981 Sheard, 1983 Hollister, 1984 Miczek, 1987	Review of over 1500 human and animal articles between 1920 and 1987 on the pharmacology of drugs and aggression	LSD use is rarely associated with violence. Effects are dependent on the psychopathology and expectations of the subject and the environmental surroundings. Exaggeration of psychoses will result if given to psychotic, borderline psychotic and not informed normally functioning subjects.

567

B. Phencyclidine (PCP)

Criminal violence

Reference	Study	Findings
Fauman et al., 1976 Fauman and Fauman, 1977 Fauman and Fauman, 1979 Fauman and Fauman, 1980a,b Fauman and Fauman, 1982	Psychiatric classification of PCP violence via interview; case studies	Acute administration of PCP produced psychosis in a small fraction of users and was related to pathologic personality; polydrug use was common. Chronic PCP use was associated with violence.
Noguchi and Nakamura, 1978	Study of 16 PCP related deaths in Los Angeles County in 1976	PCP use might be related to psychosis, homicide and accidental death.
Simonds and Kashani, 1979a	Structured interview and review of juvenile files of 109 delinquent males (mean age: 16 years) in Missouri	8% of the subjects used PCP and were polydrug users. Of these, 22% reported fighting or hostile feelings while using PCP.
Siegel, 1980	Study of 51 PCP related violent crimes in males and females in California between 1977 and 1979	PCP might produce abrupt spontaneous changes in personality functioning resulting in violent acts. PCP users had polydrug history, were assaultive and combative. Verbal or physical fighting reported during PCP intoxication in 50% of Supreme Court cases.
Foster and Narasimhachari, 1986	30 year old female with no history of substance abuse who attempted homicide	Flu-like illness followed by confusion and delusion preceded attempted homicide. Patient recovered with 2 mg/day haloperidol and urine acidification.
Brecher et al., 1988	Review of 350 published reports on PCP use in humans from 1966 to 1986	Polydrug use common in PCP users; reports of violence due to PCP exaggerated (only 0.8% of the reports demonstrated PCP use and violence). Clinical and forensic assumptions about PCP and violence were not warranted.

Health statistics

Reference	Study	Findings
Luisada, 1978	11 male exclusive PCP users admitted to a Washington DC hospital from 1973 to 1974	PCP psychosis was nearly indistinguishable from schizophrenia and might last for weeks. Violent behavior was more likely to occur in the first 5 days.

568

Reference	Description	Findings
Bailey, 1979	Relationship between plasma and urine PCP concentrations and physical symptoms of PCP intoxication in 22 California patients	Combativeness-agitation present in 64% of the patients; there was no correlation between plasma PCP levels and behavior.
Smith and Wesson, 1980	Diagnosis and treatment of PCP intoxication in San Francisco	PCP and violent reactions were exaggerated. Acute PCP toxicity included combativeness (usually low doses), catatonia, convulsions, and coma; treatable with diazepam, chlorpromazine. PCP toxic psychosis included agitation and usually occurred with chronic users; treatable with haloperidol. PCP-precipitated psychotic episode included agitation and was treated with haloperidol, chlorpromazine.
McCarron et al., 1981	1000 case studies of acute PCP intoxication in males and females in Los Angeles	High doses of PCP produced "acute brain syndrome" (24.8%), toxic psychosis (16.6%), catatonic syndrome (11.7%) and coma (10.6%). Low doses produced lethargy and bizarre behavior including violence and agitation which lasted for a few hours.
Heilig et al., 1982	Psychiatric assessment of 44 1977-78 male and female Los Angeles County PCP related deaths	PCP users had a history of physical fighting and polydrug use. There was considerable psychosocial maladjustment evidenced.
Personality evaluations		
Wright, 1980	Interview of 10 schizophrenics and frequency of PCP use	Violent behavior and PCP use was indicated in 6/10 schizophrenic patients (3 chronic and 3 first time users). Chronic users best described by Fauman and Fauman Type 2 classification.
Khajawall et al., 1982	Comparison of PCP or heroin rehabilitation in California hospital setting with 325 chronic users	No difference between PCP and heroin patients on measures of aggression; PCP users demonstrated low levels of overt aggression. There was no correlation between urine PCP levels and aggression.
Rawson et al., 1982	68 male and female (age: 14-38 years) chronic PCP users seeking detoxification in Los Angeles County hospital between 1979 and 1980	More than 30% of the patients report increased anger and violent behavior while using PCP.

Convit et al., 1988 Yesavage and Zarcone, 1990	Psychiatric evaluation of 85 male schizophrenics in California hospital; 79 male schizophrenics in New York hospital; follow up 6 months after release	Polydrug use common, PCP use strongly related to assaults during hospital stay and 6 month follow up.
Literature Reviews		
Siegel, 1978 Petersen, 1980 Sbordone et al., 1981 Hollister, 1984 Pradhan, 1984 Cherek and Steinberg, 1987 Miczek, 1987	Review of over 1500 human and animal articles between 1920 and 1987 on the pharmacology of aggression	Incidence of violent behavior with PCP intoxication is very rare. Polydrug use common; personality predispositions and history of violent behavior is important in determining PCP effects. Acute: Low doses can induce aggression during psychotic episodes. Chronic PCP use may lead to aggressive outbursts due to real or imagined frustrations, poor judgement and panic reactions.

570

Index